Sex and the Nazi Soldier

Series Editors: Victoria M. Basham and Sarah Bulmer

The Critical Military Studies series welcomes original thinking on the ways in which military power works within different societies and geopolitical arenas.

Militaries are central to the production and dissemination of force globally, but the enduring legacies of military intervention are increasingly apparent at the societal and personal/bodily levels as well, demonstrating that violence and war-making function on multiple scales. At the same time, the notion that violence is an appropriate response to wider social and political problems transcends militaries: from private security, to seemingly 'non-military' settings such as fitness training and schooling, the legitimisation and normalisation of authoritarianism and military power occurs in various sites. This series seeks original, high-quality manuscripts and edited volumes that engage with such questions of how militaries, militarism and militarisation assemble and disassemble worlds touched and shaped by violence in these multiple ways. It will showcase innovative and interdisciplinary work that engages critically with the operation and effects of military power and provokes original questions for researchers and students alike.

Titles in the *Advances in Critical Military Studies* series include:

Published:

Resisting Militarism: Direct Action and the Politics of Subversion
Chris Rossdale

Making War on Bodies: Militarisation, Aesthetics and Embodiment in International Politics
Catherine Baker

Disordered Violence: Gendered Neo-Orientalism and Terrorism
Caron Gentry

Sex and the Nazi Soldier: Violent, Commercial and Consensual Encounters during the War in the Soviet Union, 1941–45
Regina Mühlhäuser (translated by Jessica Spengler)

The Military-Peace Complex: Gender and Materiality in Afghanistan
Hannah Partis-Jennings

Forthcoming:

Inhabiting No-Man's-Land: Army Wives, Gender and Militarisation
Alexandra Hyde

Sex and the Nazi Soldier

Violent, Commercial and Consensual Encounters During the War in the Soviet Union, 1941–45

REGINA MÜHLHÄUSER

Translated by Jessica Spengler

EDINBURGH
University Press

Edinburgh University Press is one of the leading university presses in the UK. We publish academic books and journals in our selected subject areas across the humanities and social sciences, combining cutting-edge scholarship with high editorial and production values to produce academic works of lasting importance. For more information visit our website: edinburghuniversitypress.com

© Regina Mühlhäuser, 2010, 2022
English translation © Jessica Spengler, revised and extended edition, 2021, 2022

Originally published in German as: Eroberungen. Sexuelle Gewalttaten und intime Beziehungen deutscher Soldaten in der Sowjetunion 1941–1945

© 2010 by Hamburger Edition HIS Verlagsges. mbH, Hamburg, Germany
This translation from German is published by arrangement with Hamburger Edition.

Edinburgh University Press Ltd
The Tun – Holyrood Road, 12(2f) Jackson's Entry, Edinburgh EH8 8PJ

First published in hardback by Edinburgh University Press 2010

Typeset in 10.5/13 ITC Giovanni Std by
Servis Filmsetting Ltd, Stockport, Cheshire

A CIP record for this book is available from the British Library

ISBN 978 1 4744 5907 5 (hardback)
ISBN 978 1 4744 5908 2 (paperback)
ISBN 978 1 4744 5909 9 (webready PDF)
ISBN 978 1 4744 5910 5 (epub)

The right of Regina Mühlhäuser to be identified as the author of this work has been asserted in accordance with the Copyright, Designs and Patents Act 1988, and the Copyright and Related Rights Regulations 2003 (SI No. 2498).

The translation of this work was funded by Geisteswissenschaften International – Translation Funding for Work in the Humanities and Social Sciences from Germany, a joint initiative of the Fritz Thyssen Foundation, the German Federal Foreign Office, the collecting society VG WORT and the Börsenverein des Deutschen Buchhandels (German Publishers & Booksellers Association).

CONTENTS

List of Figures	vii
Acknowledgements	x
Abbreviations	xii
Map: Eastern Europe before World War II	xiv

1. **Introduction: War, Violence, Sexuality**   1
   Points of Departure   2
   Sources on Sexual Encounters   10

Private Photographs by Wehrmacht Soldiers, Part 1   19

2. **Sexual Violence**   27
   Forms and Functions of Sexual Violence   31
   Situations   34
   Negotiations in the Military   84

3. **Sexual Transactions**   117
   Occasional Sexual Bartering   120
   Professional Prostitution   123
   Persecution of Women 'Suspected of Prostitution'   125
   Disciplining Wehrmacht Soldiers   129
   Appeals to SS Men   144
   Wehrmacht Brothels   149

4. **Consensual Relations**   192
   The Men's Desire for Normality   195

The Women's Desire for New Experiences	200
Regulation by the Wehrmacht	206
SS Directives	211
Negotiations Regarding Marriage Applications	215
Rhetoric of Defeat	230

Private Photographs by Wehrmacht Soldiers, Part 2 — 245

5. **Occupation Children** — 253
   - Population Policy Strategies — 255
   - Control Measures — 261

6. **Concluding Remarks: Gender, Sexuality and Violence in the War and Post-War Period** — 304

7. **Epilogue: What Can We Learn from the Nazi Case?** — 316
   - Racist 'Pollution Taboos' — 317
   - Conflicting Military Interests — 322
   - Sexual Violence and Sexuality — 325
   - Soldiers' Corporeality — 328
   - Sexual Violence as a Weapon — 330

Bibliography — 337
Index — 384

LIST OF FIGURES

Map: Eastern Europe before World War II. © Peter Palm, Berlin	xiv
1 Gisbert Witte, bundle of photographs, photo 227, private collection of Margret Witte-Ebel, Lüneburg	19
2 Gisbert Witte, bundle of photographs, photo 290, private collection of Margret Witte-Ebel, Lüneburg	20
3 Herbert Achenbach, bundle of photographs, slide 100, private collection of Christiane Feuerhake, Leer	20
4 Hans Mayer, album, page 25, Spielhahnjäger Museum, Bad Tölz	21
5 Hans-Georg Schulz, album II, page 13, private collection of Schwarz/Dippold	21
6 Walter Gerloff, album III, page 11, private collection of Achim Gerloff, Hamburg	21
7 Georg Möller, album, page 19, private collection of Peter Möller, Varel	21
8 Gisbert Witte, bundle of photographs, photo 317, private collection of Margret Witte-Ebel, Lüneburg	22
9 Jürgen W., diary, page 113, Archives of the Hamburg Institute for Social Research	22
10 Willi Rose, bundle of photographs, private collection of Thomas Eller, Berlin	23
11 Georg Möller, album, page 25, private collection of Peter Möller, Varel	24
12 Anonymous album, page 43, ('Album Heer 622'), Auris Media Verlag	24
13 Anonymous album, page 4, ('Album Heer 429'), Auris Media Verlag	24

14	Karl-Heinz Müller, album, page 11, private collection of Dr Wolfgang Müller, Hatten	25
15	Anonymous album, page 44, ('Album Heer 622'), Auris Media Verlag	25
16	Heinrich Hindersmann, bundle of photographs, photo 137, private collection of Horst Hindersmann, Dörpen	26
17	Dr Karl Dieter Zoller, album, page 16, private collection of Archiv Zoller, Rastede	26
18	Anonymous album, page 8, ('Album Heer 429'), Auris Media Verlag	62
19	Heinrich Kleemeyer, album, page 15, private collection of Mike Voigt, Syke	245
20	Johannes Gravemeyer, bundle of photographs, booklet 1, photo 20, private collection of Archiv Gravemeyer, Wittmund	246
21	Karl Hellbusch, bundle of photographs, photo 3, private collection of Karl Gerd Hellbusch, Oldenburg	246
22	Heribert Osburg, album, page 13, private collection of Rita Stüwe, Buchholz	247
23	Heinrich Hindersmann, bundle of photographs, photo 4, private collection of Horst Hindersmann, Dörpen	247
24	Heinrich Kleemeyer, album, page 22, private collection of Mike Voigt, Syke	248
25	Gisbert Witte, bundle of photographs, photo 87, private collection of Margret Witte-Ebel, Lüneburg	248
26	Heinrich Hindersmann, bundle of photographs, photo 187, private collection of Horst Hindersmann, Dörpen	249
27	Hermann Jaspers, album, page 19, private collection	249
28	Willi Rose, bundle of photographs, private collection of Thomas Eller, Berlin	249
29	Helmut Severin, album, page 30, private collection of Gabriele Schröter, Westoverledingen, Ulrike Severin, Cologne	250
30	Hans-Georg Schulz, album II, page 7, private collection of Schwarz/Dippold	250
31	Willi Rose, bundle of photographs, private collection of Thomas Eller, Berlin	250
32	Gisbert Witte, bundle of photographs, photo 168, private collection of Margret Witte-Ebel, Lüneburg	251
33	Heinrich Kleemeyer, album, page 17, private collection of Mike Voigt, Syke	251
34	Heinrich Hindersmann, bundle of photographs, photo 178, private collection of Horst Hindersmann, Dörpen	251

35	Heinrich Hindersmann, bundle of photographs, photo 179, private collection of Horst Hindersmann, Dörpen	252
36	Willi Rose, bundle of photographs, private collection of Thomas Eller, Berlin	252
37	Anonymous album, page 10, ('Album Heer 372'), Auris Media Verlag	313

ACKNOWLEDGEMENTS

The study at hand is a revised version of my doctoral dissertation, which was accepted in March 2008 by the Faculty of Arts and Humanities of the University of Cologne. My research project received financial support from the Hamburg Foundation for the Advancement of Research and Culture and the German Historical Institute in Washington, DC.

The initial impetus for this project can be traced back to discussions in the Working Group on War and Gender at the Hamburg Institute for Social Research (HIS). My special thanks here go to Gaby Zipfel, who inspired and encouraged me from the start, and who supported me throughout the project – right up to its publication as a book – with 'criticism, black coffee and cigarettes' (Ella Fitzgerald).

I would like to thank Gudrun Schwarz for her heartfelt support, in particular at the beginning of this project, as well as my spiritual doctoral supervisor, Birthe Kundrus, for her stimulating conversations and constructive criticism; it was for formal reasons alone that she was unable to review the work as a referee. Margit Szöllösi-Janze agreed to step in here after the concept was already fairly advanced. Many thanks go to her for the openness and sensitivity she brought to our discussions and to the manuscript. I owe my deep gratitude to my second referee, Norbert Finzsch, who stood by my side even during my master's dissertation. He believed in this topic from the start and provided me with many critical suggestions and personal support over the years. I would additionally like to thank Hanjo Berressem, Jost Dülffer, Hans-Peter Ullmann and Barbara Potthast, who opened up new perspectives for me with their thoughtful questions. Special thanks go to Bernd Greiner, Jan Philipp Reemtsma and Michael Wildt for their many suggestions, constructive criticism and support.

Over the years, I had the opportunity to present the initial results of this study in various seminars and to discuss my theses, which were often not yet fully formed. For their willingness to engage in such discussions, I thank all of my colleagues in the research group on the Theory and History of Violence at the HIS (led by Bernd Greiner), the doctoral seminar at the HIS (led by Birthe Kundrus and Michael Wildt), the research colloquium at the University of Bremen (led by Inge Marszolek), the postdoc platform of the University of Cologne (led by Jost Dülffer, Margit Szöllösi-Janze and Hans-Peter Ullmann), the research colloquium at the German Historical Institute in Washington, DC (led by Dirk Schumann) and the Working Group on War and Gender at the HIS.

Many friends and colleagues contemplated the issues addressed by this book over the years, scrutinised my work and provided intellectual and material support while I was writing. For their critical reading, discussions, and literature and source material suggestions, as well as their forbearance, I would like to thank Christine Achinger, Petra Bopp, Andreas Ehresmann, Michael Esch, Insa Eschebach, Monika Flaschka, Carsten Gericke, Anna Hajkova, Nina Hälker, Elizabeth Heineman, Christiane Hess, Michaela Hampf, Dagmar Herzog, Amy Holmes, Janina Jentz, Olaf Kistenmacher, Claudia Lenz, Susann Lewerenz, Elissa Mailänder Koslov, Astrid Kusser, Andreas Meyer, Torsten Michaelsen, Jutta Mühlenberg, Therese Roth, Martin Schäfer, Mark Schumacher, Ingwer Schwensen, Harriet Scharnberg, Robert Sommer, Andreas Strippel, Gerhard Wolf and the PoMo. The people closest to me made it possible for me to pursue this project to the end, despite all hurdles.

Last but not least, I owe thanks to the archivists who helped me hunt down source materials over the years: at the German Federal Archives in Berlin-Lichterfelde, the Military Archives in Freiburg im Breisgau, the National Archives and Records Administration and the United States Holocaust Memorial Museum in Washington, DC and the HIS. The HIS offered the ideal framework, both personally and intellectually, for completing and revising my manuscript. Special thanks are due to the staff of the library and the archive, who were always prepared to offer suggestions, patiently answered my questions, and tolerated the fact that I monopolised the library rooms for nights on end. Andrea Böltken, Paula Bradish, Birgit Otte, Jürgen Determann, Hannes Sieg and Wilfried Gandras made it possible for me to turn my academic work into a book. Thank you very much!

Hamburg, 16 December 2009

ABBREVIATIONS

A.K.	Armeekorps (Army Corps)
AOK	Armeeoberkommando (Army Command)
ICC	International Criminal Court
KdS	Kommandeur der Sicherheitspolizei und des SD (Commander of the Security Police and Security Service)
Korück	Kommandant rückwärtiges Armeegebiet (Commander Rear Army Area)
KSSVO	Kriegssonderstrafrechtsverordnung (Special Wartime Penal Code)
Lw.	Luftwaffe (German Air Force)
NKVD	People's Commissariat for Internal Affairs of the USSR (Secret Police)
NSDAP	Nationalsozialistische Deutsche Arbeiterpartei (Nazi Party)
NSV	Nationalsozialistische Volkswohlfahrt (National Socialist People's Welfare)
OK	Oberkommando (High Command)
OKH	Oberkommando des Heeres (Army High Command)
OKW	Oberkommando der Wehrmacht (Wehrmacht High Command)
O.Qu.	Oberquartiermeister (Senior Quartermaster)
Qu.	Quartiermeister (Quartermaster)
RF-SS	Reichsführer-SS (SS Reich Leader)
RKF	Reichskommissar für die Festigung deutschen Volkstums (Reich Commissioner for the Consolidation of the Ethnic German Nation)

RKO	Reichskommissar/Reichskommissariat Ostland (Reich Commissioner/Reich Commissariat for Ostland)
RKU	Reichskommissar/Reichskommissariat Ukraine (Reich Commissioner/Reich Commissariat for Ukraine)
RMbO	Reichsminister/Reichsministerium für die besetzten Ostgebiete (Reich Minister/Reich Ministry for the Occupied Eastern Territories)
RSHA	Reichssicherheitshauptamt (Reich Security Main Office)
RuSHA	Rasse- und Siedlungshauptamt (Race and Settlement Main Office)
SA	Sturmabteilung (Storm Troopers)
SD	Sicherheitsdienst der SS (Security Service of the SS)
SS	Schutzstaffel (Protection Squad)
St.Qu.	Stellvertretender Quartiermeister (Deputy Quartermaster)
WiStab Ost	Wirtschaftsstab Ost (Economic Staff East)
W.San.	Wehrmachtssanitätsdienst (Wehrmacht Medical Service)
ZStD.	Zentralstelle im Lande Nordrhein-Westfalen für die Bearbeitung von nationalsozialistischen Massenverbrechen bei der Staatsanwaltschaft Dortmund (Central Office in North Rhine-Westphalia of the Dortmund Public Prosecutor for Prosecuting Nazi Mass Crimes)

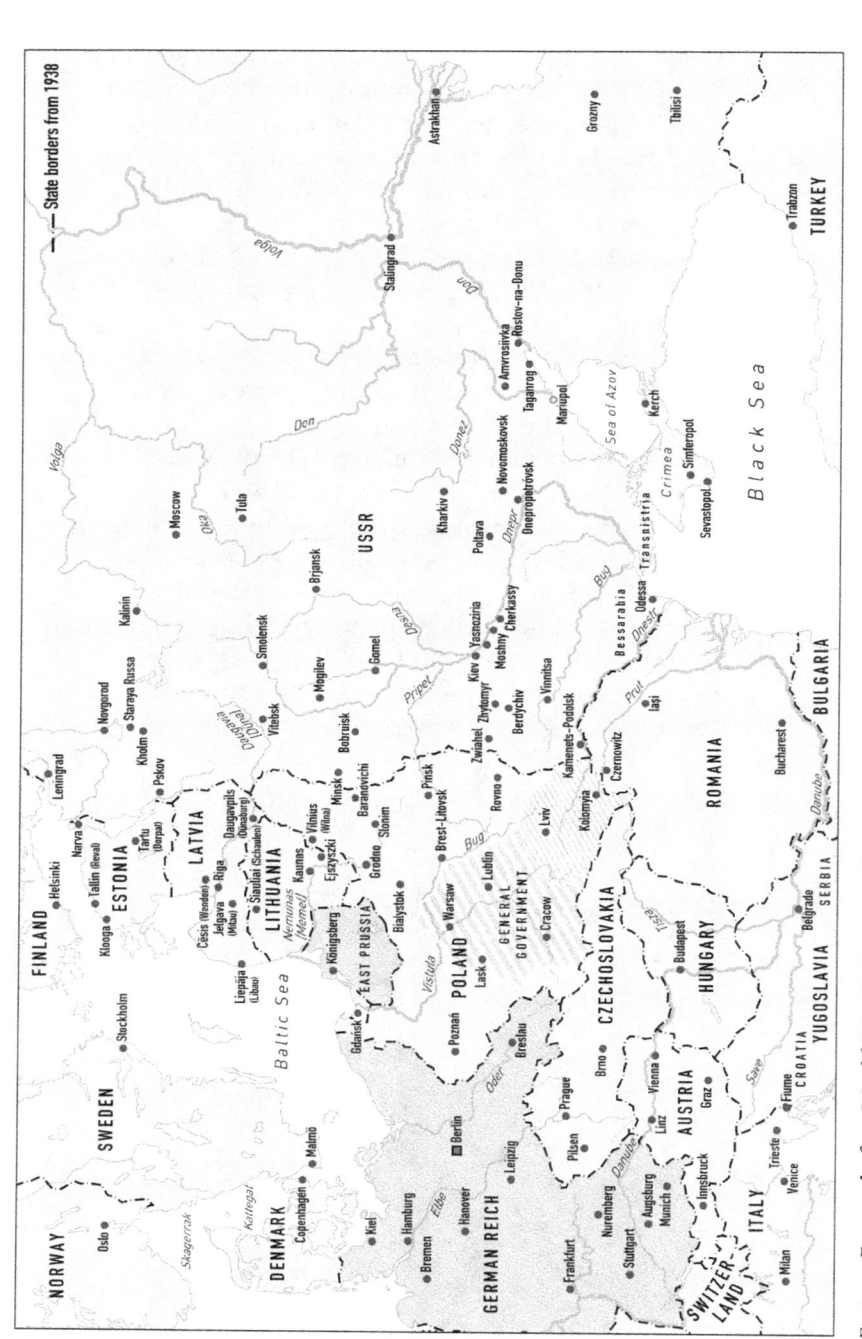

Eastern Europe before World War II. © Peter Palm, Berlin

CHAPTER 1

Introduction: War, Violence, Sexuality

Otto Pauls was stationed in the Soviet Union as a young man. In an interview with the documentary filmmaker Hartmut Kaminski, he says that many a German soldier had 'a girl' in every town: 'There's no way the soldiers behaved like pigs, raped women. I never saw anything like that. We didn't have to. The Ukraine welcomed us with open arms.'[1]

Pauls generally acknowledges the crimes of the German army (*Wehrmacht*). It is all the more notable, therefore, that he describes the contact with local women as merely a harmless side aspect beyond the actual deeds of war. This reflects a widespread notion, which persists to this day, that the military conquest of a territory almost automatically goes hand in hand with the sexual conquest of local women.[2] In this book, I want to explore the reality behind such romanticising narratives of conquest. What forms of sexual encounters – violent and non-violent, consensual and non-consensual, commercial and non-commercial – occurred during the war, the occupation and the genocide in the Soviet Union? How can we grasp the ways in which these practices were connected to the perpetration and experience of extreme, cruel and deadly violence? And how did the military commands of the Wehrmacht and SS handle sexual encounters, including sexual violence; did they punish, tacitly tolerate and/or support and incite their soldiers' behaviour?

The sources in this book also challenge us to think about sexuality and violence in war and armed conflict in more general terms.[3] Recently, Western scholarship on sexual violence has tended to focus on Arab and African countries, thereby obscuring the occurrence of this form of violence in other regions, in particular in the Western world.[4] Looking at the German military during World War II can counter this trend and support long-standing feminist efforts to understand the pervasiveness as well as the variations of this form of violence throughout history and to the present day. Furthermore, this case study shows how sexual encounters in their many forms can become an intrinsic part of warfare and military operations and that the sexuality of soldiers is a central problem for military policy.

Points of Departure

It seems as trivial as it is true to say that the conduct of the German men towards the local population in the Soviet Union was shaped by their respective bodily and sexual experiences, self-perceptions and norms. Young men, in particular, anticipated that the war years – spent away from the traditional monitoring mechanisms in their families and communities, from norms and moral restraints – would be a time of excitement, pleasure and new experiences. Many hoped that the war would offer opportunities for sexual escapades; many longed for interpersonal contact and intimacy. Both aspects applied to the first phase of the war, when the men often still viewed the murderous campaign as an adventure, as well as to later periods, when the German military was forced to retreat and the soldiers' fear and desperation grew.

'National Socialism presented to the world a seamless front of dominant masculinity', observes Raewyn Connell, 'hard, decisive, armed, modern, organized'. But the everyday reality behind this public face was much more ambivalent.[5] The Wehrmacht was a conscript army fielding seventeen million 'citizen-soldiers', of whom approximately ten million served at the Eastern Front. They came from different social strata; they were Catholic, Protestant or atheist; and their political beliefs ranged from apolitical through socialist, liberal, social democratic and conservative to fanatically National Socialist.[6] In comparison, the SS (*Schutzstaffel*) comprised recruits whose level of prior ideological indoctrination was much higher, and who harboured a self-image as an elite and illustrious Nazi organisation. Still, these men came from very different backgrounds as well. The SS consisted primarily of volunteers but from 1943 onwards recruited members by coercion, too.[7] It should also be noted that it was a comparably small organisation. The active units of the Waffen-SS never comprised more than about 370,000 men, just over 4 per cent of the size of the Wehrmacht at the Eastern Front. From 1941, both the Wehrmacht and Waffen-SS increasingly attracted foreign volunteers.[8]

These diverse men naturally had different ideas about masculinity and being a soldier.[9] The experiences they had differed – not only with regard to the varying circumstances at the military front, in the occupied territories and in the killing fields, but also depending on their role in the army or SS, their particular assignment and their socio-cultural background. Nevertheless, most of the men seem to have had one thing in common: they saw themselves as distinct from civilian society.

Experiencing a particular independence from the world at home is, in fact, something that soldiers have described throughout history and to the present day.[10] This soldierly perception suggests a clear division between front and home. Such a division, however, does not coincide with the experiences of civilian men, women and children when whole societies are involved in waging war.[11] As Kevin McSorley observes, the precarity that characterises life in war does not only affect soldiers:

> The reality of war is not just politics by any other means but politics incarnate, politics written on and experienced through the thinking and feeling bodies of men and women. From steeled combatants to abject victims, from the grieving relative to the exhausted aid worker, war occupies innumerable bodies in a multitude of ways, profoundly shaping lives and ways of being human.[12]

When entire societies are militarised, everybody is affected.[13] Still, soldiers come to see their experiences as being fundamentally different. This seems to be connected to a specific set of knowledge and experiences in the masculinist society of the military, including sensory impressions, emotions, cognitive and imaginary frameworks. John Hockey's work on soldiers' sensory experiences can help us explore one part of this gap between their life during military operations and at home. In order to survive, he argues, British infantrymen learn the practice of 'moving, seeing, hearing, touching and smelling in a particular occupational fashion'. In time, these new skills no longer take the form of extrinsic rules, but instead become part of the corporeality of the men, of their subconscious repertoire of (re)acting.[14] Even after returning home, soldiers thus experience, sense, feel and understand the world in a different way.

What becomes clear is how central the embodied practices, somatic impressions, emotions and affects are when it comes to understanding what soldiers actually do in war. And one crucial element of the soldiers' corporeal experiences is sexuality – sexual norms, expectations and imaginations, affects, feelings and practices. This is also a subject of male bonding, of including and excluding men and boys in the masculinist society of the military. In Germany, youth culture had been inscribed with an 'ostentatious virility' (Thomas Kühne) since the 1920s, which was expressed in group penis comparisons, masturbation and proof of orgasm. Those at the bottom of the hierarchy in such groups thus often experienced psychological and physical violence.[15] In the Wehrmacht, the 'trials' of war – drills, the use of violence, the danger of death – went hand in hand with rituals of masculinity such as excessive alcohol consumption and visiting brothels.[16] This also included exchanging pornographic pictures, making snappy remarks and boasting about drinking sprees and (past or present) sexual experiences.[17] For many of the younger men, whose conscription into the Wehrmacht was the first time they had left their childhood home, such events represented an initiation into the world of men and thus an important moment in which to prove themselves to their comrades.

The men in the Wehrmacht cooperated closely with the SS, the police, and the civilian occupation authorities in what resulted in the mass murder of Jewish men and women and other horrendous crimes that characterised the war of annihilation in the Soviet Union.[18] The question of how and why 'ordinary men' (Christopher Browning) adapted to this situation of extreme violence so quickly, leaving moral considerations and civilian norms behind and acting in ways that had been unthinkable to them before the war, is a subject of ongoing research and debate.[19] What the sources in this book show is that sexuality was part of the story.

Taking my cue from Gaby Zipfel, I want to emphasise that it is necessary not only to examine sexual violence in the narrower sense, but to ask more generally about sexual perceptions, sensations and desires in times of extreme violence.[20] In *Sexuality and Nazism: The Doubly Unspeakable*, Elizabeth Heineman questions the functions and effects of sex for SS members, policemen and soldiers on the Eastern Front. She cites Browning's description of the ways that 'alcohol first helped men of the shooting squads to commit atrocities, then dulled memories of the shootings, making it possible to work another day', and continues: 'Could sex also have served to release tension – a release necessary to the continuing functioning of the genocide?'[21] In other words, do sexual encounters help soldiers and the perpetrators of genocide commit violence? This study does not attempt answer this question, but it provides a material base that can support this debate – not merely with regard to the historical example of the war of annihilation, but in thinking about war and genocide in general.

Contemporary and post-war eyewitness accounts as well as official military documents indicate that sexual violence against women and girls was a widespread reality during the war and the genocide in the Soviet Union and included coerced disrobement, genital beatings, genital mutilation, sexual torture, sexual assault, sexual blackmail, rape with the penis, rape with fingers or objects, gang rape, and sexual enslavement. In addition, German soldiers visited secret prostitutes and official military brothels, they coerced women into sexual bartering and engaged in relations with women who traded sex for protection, food or other scarce goods. In some cases, German men were involved in consensual liaisons, which led at times, especially in Estonia and Latvia, to applications for marriage permits. Recently, sexual encounters between men have also become a subject of research, including sexual violence against boys and men as well as homosexual contacts.[22] Furthermore, some cases have been discussed in which female concentration camp guards committed acts of sexual violence against female as well as male prisoners.[23] The study at hand only addresses these latter situations in passing.[24]

In order to grasp the entire spectrum of sexual contacts between two or more people, I suggest using the term 'sexual encounters', which emphasises the various moments of collision – between men and women, between power and powerlessness, between different cultures and positions. As we will see in the course of this book, the boundaries between consensual and forced, between non-violent and violent sexual encounters are fluid. 'Consensual', for example, did not mean that these encounters were based on an equal footing. Rather, such encounters were largely asymmetrical and often developed due to fears, specific needs and pragmatic choices. In a situation in which women were on their own and faced a variety of material hardships and the threat of death (for themselves, their children and their families), sexual contacts with German men could become an option to ensure survival and, sometimes, to flee the harsh reality of war for a moment of pleasure – in a grey zone between subjection, autonomy and desire.[25]

Taking a closer look at the scope of such encounters, it becomes clear that the soldiers' actions were certainly not, as Otto Pauls would have it, situated beside or beyond the actual situation of war and violence. On the contrary, all encounters between German men and local women – be they violent or non-violent, consensual or non-consensual, commercial or non-commercial – were based on and shaped by the conditions and experiences of the war, the occupation and the genocide. Moreover, the perpetration and experience of violence was frequently connected to sexual affects (such as arousal or disinhibition), emotions (such as pain or pleasure) and practices (such as gendered cruelty or rape).

In their interviews with state army soldiers from the Democratic Republic of Congo (DRC), Maria Eriksson Baaz and Maria Stern observe that the men distinguish between what they call 'lust rapes' and 'evil rapes'. In their self-conception, some soldiers rape women and girls because of sexual need. To them this is an understandable or even natural requirement of male biology, for which there is no other 'outlet' in times of war. They do not consider these rapes to be cruel, their aim being sexual satisfaction. Even though they acknowledge them to be wrong, they justify them by conjuring up their miserable and frustrating situation as combatants. 'Evil rapes', by contrast, are presented as a result of anger and frustration, they are often carried out not with the penis but with some object, and their aim is said to be the annihilation rather than appropriation of women. The victims of 'evil rapes' are frequently severely injured or killed.[26] Ruth Seifert has pointed out that the explanations these DRC soldiers give are strikingly similar to narratives from other scenarios of armed conflict. Soviet soldiers in Berlin in 1945, for example, produced 'what amounts to a discourse of recreational rape and – probably even more often – of rape out of anger and wrath as revenge for the crimes of the Wehrmacht'. In the 1990s, Serbian fighters, too, legitimised their actions, including acts of sexual violence, by referring to their anger, frustration and fear. In all cases, Seifert concludes, 'the perpetrators of extreme violence [. . .] attributed the atrocities they committed to the "insanity of war" and the "loss of normalcy and decency"'.[27]

This construction of war as a 'state of emergency' (*Ausnahmezustand*) can also be found in narratives by German WWII veterans, and it generates the idea that war in its many forms is a natural phenomenon with no prehistory and no posthistory. This does not reflect, however, the overlapping and mutual influence of pre-war, war and post-war dynamics that we can usually observe in armed conflicts. It may appear easier to confront sexual violence if we view it as something abnormal that only happens in a state of emergency. Yet, as Elizabeth D. Heineman observes,

> wartime sexual violence shares a great deal with sexual violence in civilian settings, from the context of institutionalized male privilege, through consequences such as the denial of reproductive autonomy, to situational detail like the public nature of gang rape. (Heinemann, *Sexual Violence in Conflict Zones*, p. 3.)

Expanding our analysis to include the practices of sexual violence in civilian life might thus help us understand what actually happens in times of armed conflict. We can assume that no man really knows in advance what actually awaits him in war, how he will experience it and in which ways he will (re)act (this is obviously true for female soldiers, too, but here I will concentrate on men). Still, soldiers have assumptions and expectations generated by the social cultural setting from which they come, as well as the social environment in which they operate. Only if we take this into account can we understand why sexual violence can become such a readily available option for action (*Handlungsoption*) for men in military settings.

The soldiers interviewed by Baaz and Stern do not interpret any of the rapes committed by their troops to be political or a direct aspect of a military strategy as such.[28] This corresponds with a widely held view that acts of sexual violence are opportunistic acts carried out by individual soldiers that have little to do with the actual military operations. Indeed, we must assume that most of the soldiers who commit sexual violence do not have strategic considerations in mind. This does not mean, however, that these rapes cannot become part of a commander's calculations. As a general rule, military commanders expect (or at least suspect) that some of their men will commit sexual violence. It is thus (implicitly or explicitly) a part of their knowledge. As long as they do not strictly reprimand their men and take active measures against this form of violence, they are tacitly accepting and condoning their men's behaviour and, what is more, they are exploiting it for their own interests (which range from generating cohesion and loyalty within the troops to harming the enemy).

In order to grasp this tacit acceptance that we find in many armies, it is necessary to carefully examine the communication between an army command, officers, small units and ordinary recruits. As I will show in the course of this book, the Wehrmacht High Command (*Oberkommando der Wehrmacht*, OKW), Army High Command (*Oberkommando des Heeres*, OKH) and Personal Staff Reichsführer-SS (*Persönlicher Stab Reichsführer-SS*, RF-SS) knew about the sexual encounters of their men and took both a positive and negative view of the effects these had on the health of the troops, the morale of the soldiers and the cohesion of the units. The leaders of the Wehrmacht as well as the SS were concerned with how soldiers' sexual activities could be beneficial or detrimental to their warfare, and they attempted to keep their men under control. While commanders seldom seem to have ordered the perpetration of sexual violence (as in cases when subordinates were asked to procure women), they assumed that their men would act in certain ways and they took the effects into account. Indeed, the Wehrmacht regarded male sexuality as something that could and should be productively incited, as can be seen in the large-scale organisation of Wehrmacht brothels, for example. To use Foucault's terminology, Nazi sexual politics were not solely repressive; in fact, they facilitated and produced various forms of sexual practices.

The sexual preconceptions, norms and habits from pre-war times that were part of the soldiers' self-perception were largely shared by the victims and bystanders. They were, however, markedly different for men and women.[29] Indeed, it will become apparent in the course of this book that the perspective of the men distinctly differed from that of the women (what this means for male victims of sexual violence has yet to be explored). Researchers have recently started to discuss how to grasp the harm suffered by the victims of sexual violence beyond potential physical injury, the harm to the social subjectivity of persons. 'An integral part of the harm is', writes Kirsten Campbell, 'to reduce persons to social identities defined by the violence of the perpetrator, and in particular to their sex', for example a 'Slavic' or a Jewish woman. Moreover, this violence can then destroy the person's membership in her social community.[30] It has also become clear that acts of sexual violence in war and crisis zones can cause lasting damage and destruction to the entire fabric of the victims' society. Commercial sex and consensual relationships between occupying soldiers and local women also have short- and long-term consequences for the individuals and their communities. In this book, I only touch on the effects that such encounters had on women and girls, as well as their respective societies in the countries of the former Soviet Union. Nonetheless, these questions are addressed through the documented eyewitness accounts. While I try to explore the victims' and perpetrators' sexuality in parallel, the focus of this book is the German troops – the individual men, as well as the military leaderships and the civil occupation authorities.

Pregnancy was one of the issues some women and girls had to contend with after sexual encounters with German soldiers. As we will see, some women opted for an abortion while others gave birth. In general, these children of local women and an occupying soldier are referred to as *Besatzungskinder* (occupation children). This term encompasses children who were sired by rape during a war or occupation as well as the children of romantic relationships. Such children can be found in nearly all wars and in many countries. Depending on one's perspective of the war and occupation, they are also known as 'liberation children', 'war children', 'soldiers' children' or 'collaboration children'.[31]

At the end of 1942, the German authorities turned their attention to the children born of sexual encounters between German men and local women 'in the East'.[32] Just how many children there were remained uncertain until the end of the war, but the people involved had no doubt that the number was substantial. The potential value of these children for the German *'Volksgemeinschaft'* ('people's community')[33] was debatable, however. The last chapter of this book will trace how the military and civilian occupying authorities dealt with this issue. What role was played by considerations about race and ethnic affiliation? And what kind of future did the authorities imagine for the *'Soldatenkinder'* (soldiers' children)?

When the first version of this book was published in Germany in 2010, the weekly magazine *Der Spiegel* concluded that 'the final myth of the clean Wehrmacht is destroyed'.[34] Indeed, for a long time, rape seemed to be the only form of violence not perpetrated by Wehrmacht soldiers, SS members and policemen. While the atrocities that German men committed during the war and genocide in the Soviet Union were subject to extensive research, it was widely assumed that German men who were devoted to Nazi ideology had exercised 'racially aware' self-restraint, and that Wehrmacht soldiers, SS men and policemen who did violate the racial laws were harshly punished. Often, such claims were made in order to illustrate the depths of Nazi racism.[35]

What we have to ask ourselves is how the myth of the sexually abstinent German man could be held up for such a long time. The sources presented in this book testify to the fact that Nazi sexual violence was never completely concealed. They shed light on the question of who spoke about it (or remained actively silent), when and in which ways. But such sources have only recently become a subject of in-depth historical research and are only seldom discussed in the larger public. Why is this the case? Why were scholars so ready to believe that the Nazi laws against 'race defilement' led German men at the front and in the occupied territories to behave in a coherent, self-controlled and sexually abstinent way?[36] Which societal narratives and developments did this ignorance feed?

This study does not aim to provide an exhaustive account of the sexual encounters or military regulatory measures that would apply to all territories equally. This would require detailed and local studies that are beyond the scope of this book. Instead, I am interested in two things. First, by bringing together and presenting very different types of sources, I want to illustrate the complexity of the phenomenon with its reciprocal effects. This is why I have decided to look at the entire spectrum of sexual encounters, from sexual violence and sexual trade to consensual relationships and the resulting children. Second, I am interested in the decoding and theoretical interpretation of the source material in view of Foucault's insight that bodily perceptions, sexual ideas and practices are not something given, fixed and biologically invariable, but instead represent a form of power/knowledge that must be continually reproduced and re-established.[37] Jürgen Martschukat and Olaf Stieglitz follow Foucault in interpreting sexuality as the 'engine and effect of conflicts within a socio-cultural web of power'.[38] What did this look like against the backdrop of the war of annihilation in the former Soviet Union?

Sources on Sexual Encounters

As awareness of sexual violence has grown, scholars have begun to recognise, record and explore its practices, experiences and effects, not only after the end of a war but also in ongoing conflicts. Over the past three decades, numerous empirical cases have been documented and studied. While new possibilities for data collection and documentation allow novel and more detailed insights, a number of methodological and epistemological problems have also arisen.[39]

A substantial amount of data on sexual violence is collected by US and Western European scholars, fact-finding missions in the context of NGO work, investigations by states or international organisations or the collection of evidence for proceedings at international or internationalised tribunals. The approach of the researchers and investigators – the information they look for or the way they ask questions – is subject to certain logics and expectations that correspond to how they perceive and interpret a given conflict.[40] Moreover, witnesses sometimes try to present their stories in such a way that they correspond to what the researchers and investigators would like to hear (or to be more precise: to what witnesses *think* they would like to hear).[41]

The way the data is interpreted and presented is also shaped by particular interests and demands for action. As Ngwarsungu Chiwengo has pointed out with regard to the Democratic Republic of Congo (DRC), there are no clear objectives regarding the composition of fact-finding papers, NGO reports or media productions. The majority of representations of sexual violence in the DRC are aimed at a Western audience and informed by Africanist stereotypes (often long-standing colonial understandings). The actual harm and suffering of the victims, and in particular of women and girls, is distorted, obfuscated and silenced.[42] Nevertheless, this kind of material is often used uncritically and provides the basis for far-reaching assumptions and quantifications as well as prevention measures and policies.[43]

What becomes clear is that records of sexual violence are not neutral data. This is true for sexual encounters in times of armed conflict in general. The information conveyed – in written material as well as oral accounts – is shaped by time-dependent assumptions about gender, power, sexuality and violence in a particular cultural and socio-political setting at a given time. Researchers must attempt to decode such assumptions in order to understand the forms, meanings and functions of sexual violence and, more broadly, sexuality in times of violent conflict. While knowledge of the time-dependent, socio-political and cultural context is generally necessary to understand records about war and armed conflict, exploring sexuality and violence seems to pose a particular challenge. Scholarship indicates that the relationship between violence and sexuality both presumes and provokes ideas, images, emotions and affects in a way other subject matters do not.[44] Whoever speaks or writes about sexual encounters in times of violent conflict makes certain assumptions.

To grasp the complexity of sexual encounters in violent conflict thus requires an interdisciplinary and comparative approach as well as critical self-reflection on the part of the researcher.[45] Finding out what becomes visible at which point in time (and what does not) is an indispensable part of the interpretation of the object under investigation. Which interests – and whose interests – underlie mentions of sexual encounters in different times and places? What kinds of assumptions do the speakers make? And which ideational underpinnings about war, power, violence, gender and sexuality inform these assumptions?

To identify silences as well as exaggerations in the historical record and detect who does what to whom, it is necessary to explore how gendered and sexual behaviour is understood at a given time. The construction of gender identities through social institutions (family, school, military), the social positioning of the sexes (material, legal and sexual autonomy), the regulation of sexual practices (the institution of marriage, the system of prostitution, welfare measures), legal procedures, demographic implications, the way emotions and affects are expressed – these are key aspects for understanding how individuals experience sexual violence and what the individual and societal effects and consequences of this form of violence are.

When I began my research in the late 1990s on sexuality and violence during the German war of annihilation, I asked some male colleagues for advice. While they did not doubt for a second that sexual violence had been pervasive, they saw no need to study it. They were also convinced I would not find any sources. In hindsight, I think their reaction reveals that the perpetration of sexual violence appeared so self-evident that it was not worth exploring. In fact, the sources that researchers have uncovered since then were not previously unknown material. The scholars who had reviewed them before simply had not been aware that this was a subject for investigation, so they did not recognise the hints, questions and silences in the historical record. Since then, however, a growing body of research has revealed a large variety of sources, including literary works and visual material.

The materials used for this book can be roughly divided into four groups: (1) contemporary letters, diaries and photographs, as well as later memoirs and oral testimonies of German men who were stationed in the Soviet Union as members of the Wehrmacht or SS; (2) archival documents of the Wehrmacht, the SS and police leaders and the civilian occupation authorities in the 'occupied Eastern territories'; (3) testimonies, memoirs, and oral history recollections of people who were persecuted on 'racial' or political grounds during the German war of annihilation in the Soviet Union; and (4) accounts of the local population, whose position could shift over the course of the years between collaboration, biding time and resistance.

In the past decades, feminist scholars have critically discussed source material and methodologies in dealing with National Socialism and the Holocaust. My approach relies on their insights regarding experience, language, textuality and representation.[46] Working with ego sources such as letters, diaries, memoirs or interview narratives poses a particular challenge. On the one hand, these are sources of factual information. This does not merely mean 'hard facts', such as dates or details of concrete events (these must, in fact, always be approached with caution due to the conditions and interests that shape the narratives, as well as the incompleteness of the memory). Instead, ego sources provide a material basis that can give us information about the occurrence of events, behaviours and practices of the people (soldiers as well as civilians) and their opportunities for sexual encounters.[47]

On the other hand, ego documents are also a central source for gaining insights into the contemporaries' experiences, perceptions, interpretations and patterns of action. Analysing them involves looking not only at what the narrators say but also how they say it and situate themselves within it. Soldiers' letters, for example, do not convey unfiltered impressions but instead use traditional cultural interpretive models to glorify, trivialise or conceal the events of the war. They reflect the soldiers' subjectively created constructs of meaning and identity.[48] The same applies to the diaries, which generally convey the impressions of soldiers with a middle-class background or of officers (soldiers who had received less formal education usually did not keep or leave behind such records).[49]

In post-war narratives such as testimonies, memoirs and oral history interviews, contemporaries give their memories a form and a meaning that is determined by their present situation in life. The present-day perspective shapes their view of the past and the ways in which they make sense of it. They (consciously or unconsciously) select which experiences to relate and how to present them. By considering the constructed nature of a narrative as text, we can gain an insight into the value systems, norms and mentalities at a given time.[50]

While ego sources provide multifaceted insights into the thoughts and perceptions of the contemporaries, blatant references to sexuality and sexual violence are rare. Sexuality was (and is) something they might have thought about, but they generally did not write or speak about it in public.

Stories of women who reveal that they themselves were raped are particularly rare. Most such experiences described by women are related as secondhand accounts. For example, a woman might recount how her neighbour was raped, sometimes in a way that leaves the interviewer wondering if the narrator herself was that neighbour. Women who do give accounts of sexual attacks they experienced personally often emphasise that they were able to avoid the actual execution of rape – by pretending to have a contagious disease, for example, or reminding the perpetrators about the Nazi race laws.

Overall, the sources clearly reveal that the women in the countries of the former Soviet Union who experienced sexual encounters with German soldiers during the war faced a high risk if they talked about it – regardless of whether they voluntarily entered into an intimate relationship with a German or whether they were victims of sexual violence. For example, in some reports of the *Narodnyy Komissariat Vnutrennikh Del* (NKVD; the Soviet People's Commissariat for Internal Affairs), in which members of the Soviet secret police complained about locals collaborating with the occupiers, a particular emphasis was placed on fraternisation between young women and German officers and infantrymen.[51]

Even women who experienced sexual violence found themselves confronted with the insinuation that they had voluntarily gotten involved with the Germans. Former field nurse Tatiana Polikarpovna Nanieva was captured by the Germans in 1942 as a member of the Red Army and imprisoned in a camp in southern Poland. During her imprisonment, she witnessed a number of brutal rapes by the German guards. When the camp was liberated by the Red Army in January 1945, two Soviet officers approached her and accused her of being a 'whore' who had sexually amused herself in the camp.[52] By reducing her from a comrade-in-arms to a woman who had 'live[d] it up', the men symbolically denied her any participation in the victory of this battle. In a bizarre turnaround, she seemed to be culpable for what she had witnessed and experienced, and she was suddenly under pressure to justify herself.

The atmosphere of shame and suspicion fostered by such accusations and distortions created an additional burden on the women who had already been humiliated by the sexual violence itself. We can assume that, for many women who had been raped, there was no space for them to reveal their violation, much less to publicly defend themselves against the injustice done to them. Many probably decided to suppress what had happened to them not least in order to restore their sense of everyday normality. This likely also means that numerous women have not even come close to processing their experiences of sexual violence.[53]

German men also largely silenced stories regarding sexual encounters. Generally, these men were reluctant to admit their behaviour to outsiders and, indeed, anticipated that the revelation of their brutal experiences and criminal deeds would fundamentally alter the way they were viewed and treated in civilian life, particularly by women. Dagmar Herzog has furthermore suggested that men sometimes also remained silent about sexual activity – be it forced or consensual, violent or non-violent – because they were shocked when they realised that extreme violence could be connected to sexual excitement and the disappearance of inhibitions, an experience that had been unthinkable in their prior civilian life.[54] If the subject was broached at all, the men would recount usually innocent flirts or the sexual experiences of their comrades.

In records from military and civilian authorities or judicial and penal institutions, sexual encounters, including sexual violence, were only mentioned when they were regarded as harmful to military or political aims (for example, in reports concerned with sexually transmitted diseases, the soldiers' lack of military discipline or the need to maintain the men's fighting spirit). Another challenge regarding documentation, therefore, is that we know much less about the sexual encounters (including violent ones) that the Wehrmacht and SS did not view as a risk to their missions.[55]

Although acts of sexual violence were largely glossed over, rumours as well as generalised and sensationalised stories circulated in a wide range of media. Fictional depictions of the sexual enslavement of Jewish women by Nazi men were disseminated in Jewish communities in the

US, Palestine and later Israel.[56] Stories such as the *Martyrdom of the 93 Maidens* or Ka-Tzetnik's *House of Dolls* emerged in particular societal and political constellations and served a number of functions at a time when there was not much knowledge and understanding of the Holocaust in non-European Jewish communities. They affirmed the perpetrators' depravity, generated empathy for the victims, and created outrage. During the war, the stories were politicised to appeal for intervention on behalf of women and children.[57] Furthermore, Pascale R. Bos argues, a sexual violence narrative made the extreme genocidal violence of the Holocaust more comprehensible, particularly overseas: 'Without an adequate analogy to convey the horror, this violence was instead imagined in the form of rape or sexual enslavement, both of which were crimes for which there was historic familiarity, thus making the inconceivable conceivable'.[58] While such accounts are clearly fictional, we still struggle to get a better picture of how pervasive sexual violence against Jewish women actually was.[59]

What becomes clear is that the historians' traditional methodological tool kit is inadequate when it comes to exploring sexual encounters in war and armed conflict. Finding, interpreting and representing sources on this subject pose a challenge. Researchers who work with this kind of material must aim at reading between the lines and identifying hints, gaps and silences in the historical record. At the same time, they must interrogate the references and meanings of generalised stories and stereotypical narratives. In both cases, they have to decode spoken and unspoken cultural assumptions about violence, gender and sexuality.

Notes

1. Kaminski, *Liebe im Vernichtungskrieg*, documentary film.
2. Seifert, 'War and Rape', p. 58; Lauretis, 'The Violence of Rhetoric', p. 45. Narratives of territorial conquest as a love story have been explored primarily in the context of colonial history to date; see Zantop, *Colonial Fantasies*, pp. 43ff.
3. Recent research has started to explore what is sexual about sexual violence, e.g. Zipfel, 'What is Sexual about Sexual Violence?'; Eriksson Baaz and Stern, 'Curious Erasures'; Boesten, 'Of Exceptions'.
4. For a reflection on the state of the art of the debate see, for example, Zipfel, Mühlhäuser and Campbell (eds), *In Plain Sight*; *Revisiting Methods*; Heineman (ed.), *Sexual Violence*. For a comprehensive collection of research literature see 'Selected Bibliography "Sexual Violence in Armed Conflict"', <http://www.warandgender.net/bibliography> (last accessed 8 March 2020). Cf. also Gabriel, 'The Literature Database'; Schwensen, 'Sexuelle Gewalt in kriegerischen Konflikten'; Mühlhäuser and Schwensen, 'Sexuelle Gewalt in Kriegen'.

5. Connell, 'Maculinity and Nazism', p. 38. See also Diehl, *Macht – Mythos – Utopie*.
6. Hartmann, 'Verbrecherischer Krieg'; Römer, *Kameraden*.
7. Schulte, Lieb and Wegner, *Waffen-SS*; Klausch, *Antifaschisten in SS-Uniform*.
8. Müller, *The Unknown Eastern Front*.
9. I am basing my argument here on the concept of 'hegemonic masculinty' developed by Raewyn Connell, who proposes that there is a dominant notion of ideal masculinity that exists alongside many others that are 'marginalised'. They all ultimately benefit from the power and advantages of the socially dominant model (Connell, *Masculinities*). For a discussion of this concept, cf. Martschukat and Stieglitz, *'Es ist ein Junge!'*, pp. 55ff.
10. See, e.g., Bulmer and Jackson, '"You do not live in my skin"', p. 29.
11. Hageman and Schüler-Springorum (eds), *Home/Front*.
12. McSorley, 'War and the Body', p. 1; cit. in Zipfel, 'What Do Bodies Tell?', p. 189.
13. See, e.g., Enloe, *Maneuvers*. Victoria Basham shows how Western liberal democracies prepare their populations for war and the perpetration of extreme violence (Basham, 'Liberal Militarism').
14. Hockey, '"Switch On"', pp. 481, 490. See also Hockey, 'No More Heroes'; Higate, '"Switching On" for cash'; McSorley, 'War and the Body'.
15. Kühne, *Kameradschaft*, p. 127; Kühne, *The Rise and Fall of Comradeship*, pp. 117f. Cf. also Bruns, *Politik des Eros*, pp. 391ff.
16. Kühne, *Kameradschaft*, pp. 121, 128, 141, 162f.; Buchmann, *Österreicher*, pp. 161f.
17. Cf. e.g. Fritz, *Frontsoldaten*, pp. 77ff.; Jürgen W., *Tagebuch in Russland*, HIS-Arch, NS-O 22, Box 4. Regarding photographs of women that were often remarkably similar to the pin-ups in American magazines, cf. e.g. Rutz, *Signal*, pp. 319ff.
18. See, e.g., Pohl, *Herrschaft der Wehrmacht*; Hamburger Institut für Sozialforschung (ed.), *Vernichtungskrieg*.
19. See, e.g., Bartov, *The Eastern Front*; Browning, *Ordinary Men*; Paul, *Die Täter*; Schneider, 'Täter ohne Eigenschaften'; Welzer, *Täter*; Wildt, *An Uncompromising Generation*; Reemtsma, *Trust and Violence*.
20. Zipfel, 'What Do Bodies Tell?'
21. Heineman, 'Sexuality and Nazism', p. 64.
22. E.g., Glowacka, 'Sexual Violence Against Boys And Men'; Herzog, 'Sexual Violence Against Men'; Friedman, *Speaking the Unspeakable*; Mühlhäuser, 'Sex, Race, Violence, "Volksgemeinschaft"', pp. 468–73; Beorn, 'Bodily Conquest'; Röger, *Kriegsbeziehungen*, p. 189–90. Soldiers in the Soviet Union also engaged in homosexual and autoerotic practices; see, e.g., Snyder, *Sex Crimes*, pp. 103ff.; Giles, 'Denial of Homosexuality'; Fout, 'Homosexuelle in der NS-Zeit'; Dörner, 'Heimtückische Nachrede'; Steinkamp, *Devianz-Problematik in der Wehrmacht*, pp. 302ff., 234ff.; Steinkamp, 'Ungewöhnliche Todesfälle'.
23. Mailänder, quoted in Bergoffen, Bos, Bourke et al., 'Gaps and Traps', pp. xxxiff.; Sjoberg, *Women as Wartime Rapists*.
24. It also does not examine the sexual encounters between German men and female German Wehrmacht and SS auxiliaries or German women who were

stationed in the Soviet Union in connection with the Reich Labour Service (*Reichsarbeitsdienst*).
25. The spectrum of sexual encounters during WWII has recently been explored in two special issues of the *Journal of the History of Sexuality*, 26(3), 2017, and *German History*, 28(3), 2020. Regarding women's agency, the following articles are particularly helpful: Usborne, 'Female Sexual Desire'; Gusarov, 'Sexual Barter and Jewish Women's Efforts to Save Their Lives'; Fauroux, 'Shared Intimacies'; Hajkova, 'Queer Desire'.
26. Eriksson Baaz and Stern, 'Why Do Soldiers Rape?'
27. Seifert, 'Vicissitudes of Gender', p. 268.
28. Eriksson Baaz and Stern, 'Why Do Soldiers Rape?'
29. I have explored these in more detail in the German version of this book, pp. 30–58.
30. Campbell, 'The Gender of Justice?', pp. 237ff.
31. Recently, the situation and rights of such children have become the object of historical, psychological and legal studies. Cf. generally Carpenter, 'Gender, ethnicity and children's human rights', pp. 24ff. Regarding children in the former Yugoslavia, cf. e.g. Nikolić-Ristanović, *Women, Violence and War*, pp. 68ff. Regarding the children of US Army soldiers and Vietnamese women, cf. e.g. Yarborough, *Surviving Twice*. Regarding the children of US Army soldiers and Philippine women, cf. Rhodes, 'Amerasians in the Philippines'.
32. Regarding the Nazi use of the term 'East', see Harvey, *Women and the Nazi East*, pp. 119ff.
33. For the debate surrounding the meanings of this term, see Wildt, 'Volksgemeinschaft'.
34. Jan Friedmann, 'Zweiter Weltkrieg. Die Mär von den keuschen Deutschen', *Der Spiegel*, 22 March 2010, pp. 39–40.
35. Heineman, 'Sexuality and Nazism', p. 60.
36. In the introduction to *Beyond the Racial State*, Pendas, Roseman and Wetzell discuss how clear-cut ideas about Nazi racial policy and practice often turn out to be an obstacle rather than an aid to understanding the historical reality. See also Mühlhäuser, 'Understanding Sexual Violence during the Holocaust'.
37. Foucault, *The History of Sexuality*, pp. 127ff. Regarding the paradigm shift from an old 'history of sexuality' in the sense of a 'history of morality' to a discursive history of sexuality, see Finzsch, 'Geschichte der Sexualität', pp. 201f.
38. Martschukat and Stieglitz, 'Es ist ein Junge!', p. 178.
39. Boesten, 'Revisiting methodologies'; Campbell, 'The Gender of Justice?'
40. Mibenge, *Sex and International Tribunals*; Combs, *Fact-Finding without Facts*.
41. Utas, 'Victimicy, Girlfriending, Soldiering'.
42. Chiwengo, 'When Wounds and Corpses Fail to Speak'; Chiwengo, 'Bestialisation, Dehumanisation and Counter-Interstitial Voices'.
43. Engle Merry, *Seductions of Quantification*.
44. Heineman, 'Sexuality and Nazism'. See also the workshop 'Traps and Gaps: The Politics of Generating Knowledge', organised by the International Research Group

'Sexual Violence in Armed Conflict' (SVAC), The Hague, 16–18 June 2016, <https://warandgender.net/workshops/2016-traps-and-gaps/> (last accessed 8 March 2020).
45. Zipfel, Mühlhäuser and Campbell (eds), *In Plain Sight*.
46. See, e.g., Jureit, *Erinnerungsmuster*, vol. 1; Bos, 'Women and the Holocaust', pp. 29–33; Eschebach, '"Ich bin unschuldig"'.
47. Latzel, *Deutsche Soldaten*, p. 27; Wette, 'Militärgeschichte von unten', p. 20.
48. Latzel, *Deutsche Soldaten*, pp. 33f., 129ff.
49. Niethammer, 'Heimat und Front', p. 163. Analysing diaries provides unusually deep insights into the thoughts and actions of their authors, as demonstrated by Lieb, 'Täter aus Überzeugung?', pp. 523ff.
50. Bos, 'Women and the Holocaust', p. 31. For different disciplinary approaches to oral history narratives, cf. Jureit, *Erinnerungsmuster*, vol 1.
51. Burds, 'Sexual Violence in Europe', p. 40.
52. Quoted in Rees, *Their Darkest Hour*, p. 104.
53. Sinnreich, 'The Rape of Jewish Women', p. 108.
54. Herzog, *Sex After Fascism*.
55. Regarding the value of interrogation records as a source, cf. Angrick, *Besatzungspolitik und Massenmord*, pp. 16, 26ff.; Eschebach, '"Ich bin unschuldig"', pp. 65ff.
56. E.g. Baumel and Schacter, 'Ninety-three'; Bartov, 'Kitsch and Sadism'; Horowitz, 'The Gender'; and Seidman, 'The Last Will'.
57. Bos, 'Sexual Violence in Ka-Tzetnik's House of Dolls', p. 112.
58. Ibid.
59. Waxman, 'An Exceptional Genocide?'; Mühlhäuser, 'Understanding Sexual Violence During the Holocaust'.

Private Photographs by Wehrmacht Soldiers, Part 1

Selection and research by Petra Bopp

The scenes photographed by soldiers document how these men – most of whom were still very young – viewed themselves and others. They capture the men engaged in everyday tasks such as cutting each other's hair, bathing in fountains or rivers, delousing their clothing, trading with locals and preparing meals together.

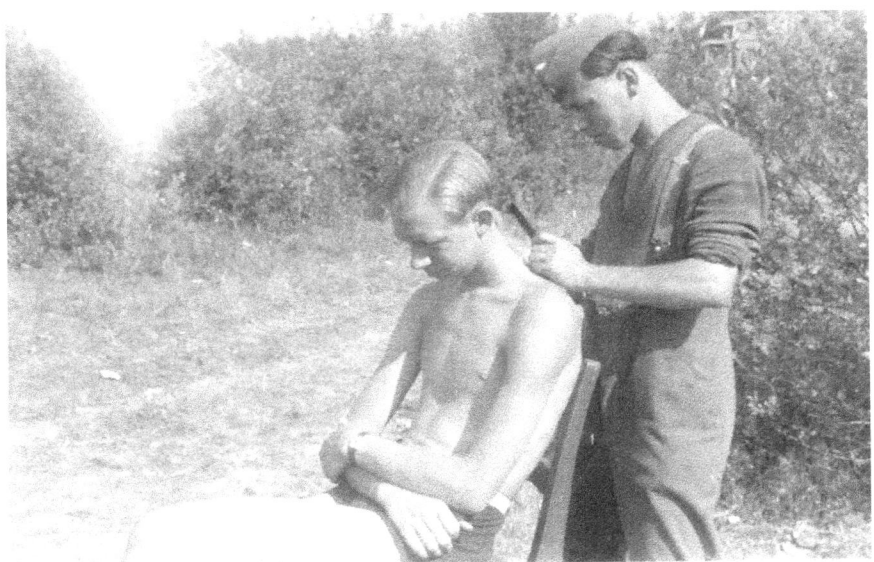

Fig. 1 Gisbert Witte, bundle of photographs, Soviet Union, near Moscow, 1941

Fig. 2 Gisbert Witte, bundle of photographs, Soviet Union, near Moscow, 1941

Fig. 3 Herbert Achenbach, bundle of photographs, Ukraine, between 1941 and 1943

Fig. 4 Hans Mayer, album, 'Under the shower', Ukraine, 1941–2

Fig. 5 Hans-Georg Schulz, album II, Soviet Union, 1942

Fig. 6 Walter Gerloff, album III, Ukraine, 1941

Fig. 7 Georg Möller, album, 'Delousing', Ukraine, between 1941 and 1944

Some pictures reveal that the soldiers carried out their everyday activities in the immediate vicinity of local women.

Fig. 8 Gisbert Witte, bundle of photographs, Soviet Union, 1941

Fig. 9 Jürgen W., diary, 'Lively bartering takes place at our position: kerchiefs from Zelwa for geese, eggs and honey', Soviet Union, 1941

Fig. 10 Willi Rose, bundle of photographs, 'Dealing in eggs: from Donets to Don', Ukraine, 1942

Fig. 11 Georg Möller, album, 'Breaking flax', Ukraine, 1941–2

Fig. 12 Anonymous album, 'Bantering with a village beauty', Sea of Asov, Soviet Union, 1942

Fig. 13 Anonymous album, Soviet Union, undated

Fig. 14 Karl-Heinz Müller, album, Soviet Union, undated

Fig. 15 Anonymous album, 'Bathing beauties,' Sea of Asov, Soviet Union, 1942

Fig. 16 Heinrich Hindersmann, bundle of photographs, 'Sunday afternoon', Soviet Union, 1941

Fig. 17 Dr Karl Dieter Zoller, album, 'Panjinkas dancing', Soviet Union, 1942–3

CHAPTER 2

Sexual Violence

Willi Peter Reese was born in 1921. He wanted to be a writer, and when he was drafted into the Wehrmacht, he recorded his experiences as a soldier with the *Heeresgruppe Mitte* (Army Group Centre) in a war diary he intended to publish later. Reese died during the Wehrmacht's rearguard action in Belarus at the end of June 1944, and his diary, along with letters and other writings, were given to his mother. Nearly 60 years after Reese's death, *Stern* journalist Stephan Schmitz used this material to produce a book entitled *Mir selber seltsam fremd*, published in English as *A Stranger to Myself*. In one passage, the young Reese describes a break taken by his unit near Gomel[1] (Belarus) while they were fleeing from the Red Army in September 1943:

> We sang over claret and liqueurs, vodka and rum, plunged into intoxication like doomed men, talked drunkenly about sex and science, [. . .] talked about our lovelornness and homesickness, started laughing again, and went on drinking, whooped and skipped over the rails, danced in the cars, and fired into the air, made a Russian woman prisoner dance naked for us, greased her tits with boot polish, got her as drunk as we were, and sobered up only when we reached Gomel after five days.[2]

The frenzy of intoxication that Reese depicts here involves, almost as a matter of course, the sexual humiliation of a 'Russian woman prisoner'. Her degradation is slotted seamlessly into the description of the drinking binge with which the 'doomed men' sought to forget their feelings of fear, forlornness and homesickness. Thomas Kühne has shown that communal alcohol consumption in Wehrmacht units strengthened and regenerated the soldiers' sense of comradeship, and that sexual experiences could quickly become material for 'adventure stories' to be recounted later.[3] In the situation described here, the act of sexual violence – which follows discussions of 'sex' and 'lovelornness', along with laughter, whooping and dancing – is the culmination of the soldiers' revelry. Reese did not deem it necessary to explain the presence of the Russian woman, either before or after this scene. When was she captured? Had she been held by Reese's unit for a long time? And why had she been targeted by the Germans in the first place? This gap in the narrative reduces the woman entirely to her role as an object of amusement for the soldiers in Reese's account. The men probably did not even view her humiliation as an act of sexual violence – in keeping with the notion prevalent both then and now that sexual violence is 'a natural if forced act between a man and a woman that is not really injurious as long as extreme violence is not used'.[4]

Notably, there was much less ambiguity surrounding the sexually violent offences described on the basis of eyewitness reports and published by Vyacheslav M. Molotov, the People's Commissioner for Foreign Affairs of the USSR, on 7 January 1942. Four years later, Molotov's report was produced as Exhibit Number USSR-51 and used as evidence in the first Nuremberg trial:

> In the village Semenovskoe, in the region of Kalinin, the Germans bound with twine the arms of Olga Tikhonova, the twenty-five-year-old wife of a Red Army man and mother of three children, who was in the last stage of pregnancy, and raped her. After violating her, the Germans cut her throat, stabbed her through both breasts and sadistically bored them out. [. . .]
>
> Women and young girls are vilely outraged in all the occupied areas.
>
> In the Ukrainian village of Borodayevka, in the Dniepropetrovsk region, the fascists violated every one of the women and girls.
>
> In the village of Berezovka, in the region of Smolensk, drunken German soldiers assaulted and carried off all the women and girls between the ages of sixteen and thirty.
>
> In the city of Smolensk, the German Command opened a brothel for officers in one of the hotels into which hundreds of women and girls were driven; they were mercilessly dragged down the street by their arms and hair. [. . .]
>
> In the city of Lvov, thirty-two women working in a garment factory were first violated and then murdered by German storm troopers. Drunken German soldiers dragged the girls and young women of Lvov into Kesciuszko Park, where they savagely raped them. An old priest, V. I. Pomaznew, who, cross in hand, tried to prevent these outrages, was beaten up by the fascists. They

tore off his cassock, singed his beard and bayonetted him to death. Near the town of Borissov in Bielorussia, seventy-five women and girls attempting to flee at the approach of the German troops, fell into their hands. The Germans first raped and then savagely murdered thirty-six of their number. By order of a German officer named Hummer, the soldiers marched L. I. Melchukova, a sixteen-year-old girl, into the forest, where they raped her. A little later some other women who had also been dragged into the forest saw some boards near the trees and the dying Melchukova nailed to the boards. The Germans had cut off her breasts in the presence of these women, among whom were V. I. Alperenko and V. H. Bereznikova.[5]

The excerpts from Reese's war diary and Molotov's report hint at the range of acts of sexual violence committed by German troops in the occupied territories of the Soviet Union. In Molotov's depiction, the violent and criminal character of sexual violence appears unequivocally clear above all because the acts he describes were accompanied by extreme, often deadly, violence. Admittedly, no verifiable conclusions about exactly what happened in the region can be drawn from Molotov's list of offences. He does not identify his informants, his descriptions are fragmentary and imprecise and the tone suggests that the text was produced for propaganda purposes.[6] Nevertheless, no one present in the Nuremberg courtroom expressed doubts about the document's fundamental assertion that acts of sexual violence by German men in Eastern Europe and Russia were not isolated incidents. In fact, sexual violence – including rape, sexual torture, genital mutilation and forced sterilisation – was repeatedly discussed at other points during the trial and by the investigation committees, as well as in subsequent post-war proceedings.[7] Such practices were regarded as 'heinous, but not enough on their own to warrant formal prosecution'.[8] Molotov's report thus seems to have served primarily to highlight the special cruelty and perversion of the perpetrators and emphasise their breach of civilisation.

The perpetrators, in turn, cited cases of sexual violence as a way of demonstrating that they had explicitly not overstepped the bounds of 'decency'. Field Marshal Erich von Manstein, former Commander-in-Chief of Army Group South, who testified as a witness, mentioned the sentencing of two men from his corps in an attempt to prove that the Wehrmacht had been made up of 'decent soldiers'. He said the two soldiers had been sentenced to death right at the start of the Russian campaign for having violated the moral code – as individuals – by raping and then murdering an old woman.[9] Hermann Göring, former Chief Justice and Commander-in-Chief of the German Air Force, who was indicted at the first Nuremberg trial, also claimed that he had not tolerated any incidents of *'Notzucht'* (rape). He defended himself by contending that he would 'absolutely and gladly take responsibility for even the most serious things', but that rape had always 'particularly contradicted [his] sense of justice'.[10]

Regardless of whether the punishments mentioned were actually meted out,[11] it is noteworthy that both defendants, without being asked, brought up their handling of cases of sexual violence against women as evidence of their personal decency and that of the Wehrmacht. It is clear here that sexual violence could become a symbolic interface between a sense of honour and a loss of honour. As I will show in this chapter, while rape was certainly viewed as a demonstration of masculinity and, by extension, of male honour within the male community of the military *(Männerbund)*, men who committed rape could also quickly be branded as 'deviant' criminals who had acted on their own and 'dishonoured' the army, particularly after Germany's defeat.

However, this revaluation of rape did not result in more detailed enquiries before the Nuremberg tribunal into the cases of sexual violence that had been documented during the taking of evidence. Although it would have been possible, according to the law of the time, to charge and sentence defendants for rape and other forms of sexual violence,[12] none of the witnesses were questioned about the subject in any detail.[13] One could argue that this was because the focus of the court was on crimes of aggression. Looking at other post-war trials, however, it becomes clear that there was generally little interest in sanctioning this form of violence against women. As Michael Gilad (Goldman), a prosecutor's assistant in the Eichmann trial and himself a Holocaust survivor, remembers: 'We did not think about it. [The marginalisation of women's stories] was unintentional. We were simply unaware of that'.[14]

At the International Military Tribunal for the Far East (IMTFE), held in Tokyo between April 1946 and November 1948, the public prosecutor's office did actually prosecute rape as a war crime under the Hague Convention (1907) and the Geneva Convention (1929). During the collection of evidence, witnesses were heard who testified to mass rapes during the Japanese conquest of the Chinese city of Nanking. In its judgment, the court concluded that '[a]pproximately 20,000 cases of rape occurred within the city during the first months of occupation'.[15] Ultimately, several defendants were found guilty of war crimes – including rape. But again, no female victims were heard as witnesses. Furthermore, there was a notable silence surrounding the systematic sexual enslavement of women and girls for Japanese soldiers in the so-called 'comfort stations'.[16]

This form of organised rape was only prosecuted in the trials in the former Dutch colony of Indonesia. The tribunal in Batavia (now Jakarta) in 1946 sentenced a Japanese bar owner for forcing thirty-five Dutch women to engage in prostitution in his establishment under threat of imprisonment if they refused.[17] And in Makassar, nine Japanese soldiers were sentenced to death in 1947 for crimes against humanity and war crimes after being charged with forcing women to undress, exposing them to public view, and raping a Dutch woman.[18] However, these were exceptional cases shaped by power-political considerations. In the former, the victims were Caucasian, and the latter case was connected to an affront to the American national flag by the Japanese. Only these two cases relating to thirty-six of the approximately 100 to 200 white Dutch women who had been victimised were tried, even though several thousand Indonesian women were also victims of wartime rape and sexual enslavement in the 'comfort stations' of the Japanese Army[19] – an indication that the trials were not intended primarily to punish sexual violence against women, but rather to pursue national interests.[20] Indeed, even though Allied military investigators had collected substantial information about the sexual enslavement of women in 'comfort stations' for the Japanese army, they did not regard it 'as a war crime and a case that seriously violated international law'.[21] In fact, soldiers of the Allied forces also committed sexual violence and visited brothels.[22]

Overall, there was neither a clear assessment of the criminal nature of sexual violence nor a real understanding and acknowledgment of the harm the individual victims had suffered – in either Asia or Europe. On the contrary, we can observe broad agreement amongst the military, the general public, politicians and legislators alike that sexual violence was still viewed in the mid-twentieth century as an honour crime and almost natural by-product of war, or a mere opportunistic transgression by individual men.[23]

Forms and Functions of Sexual Violence

In the 1970s, feminists began to explore the pervasiveness of sexual violence more systematically – in times of war and peace.[24] While the women's liberation movement interpreted sexual violence primarily as a mechanism of patriarchal power and hierarchical gender relations, African-American feminists insisted on the influence of racist ideologies and politics.[25] Another socio-critical intervention drew attention to the economic aspects of the gendered division of labour, sexual autonomy and violence.[26] At the same time, the anti-Vietnam War protests and the international peace movement focused on sexual violence as part of the military conditioning of soldiers in warfare against enemy civilians.[27]

With the growing debate about human rights after 1989, this new awareness also found its way into international policy and law. During the wars in the former Yugoslavia, as well as the genocide against the Tutsis and the war in Rwanda and its neighbouring states, the perpetration of sexual violence became central to understanding these conflicts while they were still raging. Non-governmental organisations (NGOs) began devoting resources to supporting the victims of sexual violence and their rights. In the United Nations (UN) system, Special Rapporteurs compiled reports from different theatres of war. Since 1999, the UN Security Council has passed a series of resolutions condemning sexual violence in armed conflict and identifying its widespread or strategic use as a threat to international peace and security. With the jurisprudence of the International Criminal Tribunal for the Former Yugoslavia (ICTY, 1993–2017), the International Criminal Tribunal for Rwanda (ICTR, 1995–2015), and the statute of the permanent International Criminal Court (ICC, 2002) as well as other *ad hoc* and mixed tribunals, sexual violence was reasserted as a war crime and established as an act of genocide and a crime against humanity, with prosecutions depending on the specific circumstances of each case.[28] Intensive feminist lobbying contributed to these developments, and findings from feminist research were incorporated into this new legislation.[29] The key insights here were that acts of sexual violence committed against women are not merely a matter of honour but rather violent crimes which are just as serious as other crimes, and that they are not merely 'personally motivated' or 'opportunistic' but can become an intrinsic part of military operations.[30]

This new emphasis on sexual violence as an element of belligerent action made it possible to grasp and convey the societal relevance of this form of violence in times of armed conflict. At the same time, however, the phenomenon itself was isolated, as it came to seem as if such acts were limited to warfare against an enemy collective and detached from everyday gendered practices of sexual violence. To date, sexual violence is largely understood to be – to use a phrase from Doris Buss – the 'product of elite-orchestrated, ethnically inflected violence', where men from one nationality or ethnic community systematically target women from another, subjecting them to sexual violence in order to harm the enemy collective.[31] As Rhonda Copelon has pointed out, however, this conceptualisation carries the risk of downplaying the pervasiveness of wartime sexual violence once again. It seems that only when rape is viewed as an exceptionally abhorrent act and a vehicle for war and genocide is it recognised as a crime and a grave breach of international criminal law. Sexual violence is less visible, even obscured, and appears less severe if it is not identified as part of a widespread and systematic or orchestrated attack against an (ethnic, political, national or religious) enemy.[32]

A narrow focus on widespread and/or systematic sexual violence against an enemy collective furthermore runs the risk of misrepresenting the actual occurrence of this form of violence. Firstly, the focus is directed away from the question of who does what to whom, when and why. Secondly, acts that are not explicitly directed against the women of the enemy are obfuscated. Thirdly, it conceals the fact that sexual violence that is not widespread can nevertheless be a systematic part of warfare. As Michelle Jarvis and Kate Vigneswaran argue in their evaluation of the ICTY:

> A single act of rape or a limited number of rapes can very well form part of a pattern of violent crime, for example, to persecute a population and cause people to flee. In a fact pattern often reflected in ICTY cases, forces sweeping through a village might go from one house to the next, mistreating the inhabitants in a variety of ways. Some might be killed, others beaten, and some might be raped. At the same time, property is looted, houses are burned and the remaining inhabitants are expelled. In a scenario like this, the number of rapes might be small, with no evidence that they were officially ordered. However, viewed in proper context, they are as integral to the expulsion campaign as all of the other violent and persecutory acts. We are unlikely to consider that a small number of beatings or murders committed in such circumstances did not form part of the criminal campaign.[33]

Such insights from current cases are very helpful when trying to understand the perpetration of sexual violence in historical scenarios. They demonstrate how important it is to fathom the conditions of individual cases in order to understand the meanings and impact of sexual violence on the whole.

The sources I will introduce in the following indicate that the fact pattern described by Jarvis and Vigneswaran can also be found during the war of annihilation in the Soviet Union. While not all soldiers and SS men perpetrated sexual violence, it was clear and uncontested among all of them that such violence would occur and nothing could be done about it. Although we can never know how much sexual violence was perpetrated, the overall picture reveals that this form of violence was an intrinsic part of the German *'Ostfeldzug'* (Eastern campaign).

In the following I describe the various forms this violence could take in the context of the war, the occupation and the genocide in the Soviet Union. Who did what to whom when sexual violence occurred? How can we understand the actions of the perpetrators? And what were the functions and effects of sexual violence, both in itself and when coupled with other forms of violence? Following these questions, I then explore the internal views of the German military. How did the military leadership of the Wehrmacht and SS handle acts of sexual violence? How was this form of violence communicated within the military hierarchy? And did the Wehrmacht and/or SS make use of sexual violence as a weapon of war?[34]

Situations

Any study of the history of sexual violence during World War II must inevitably rely on accounts shaped by mid-twentieth-century conceptions and subjective experiences of heterosexual violence, as well as by gender-specific attributions of guilt and shame. Overall, the historical sources provide few reliable details. Today it is generally not possible to prove whether the situations in question actually took place as described. For example, we must take into account that victims and eyewitnesses may conceal some details that seem too intimate while embellishing others to emphasise the particular cruelty of the perpetrators (the subtext being that the victims were at the mercy of the German men and any countermeasures were beyond the realm of possibility). One of my main aims is thus to document how this subject was broached, which aspects were brought forward (or silenced) by whom at what point in time and which interests were at stake.

Considering such problems, the following deliberations are concerned less with individual narratives, which are presented merely as examples, and more with the abundance and ensemble of sources. For every existing account, there are others that describe similar acts of sexual violence. When taken as a whole, the gender-specific aspects of the narrative styles – of the perpetrators, victims and witnesses – also become clear. Since this work aims to illuminate the approach to sexual violence in the 'occupied Eastern territories' in general, accounts from different regions are juxtaposed here; the specific events in each location are only broadly outlined.

Conquest

On 22 June 1941, German troops invaded the Soviet Union. They advanced rapidly, and cities such as Vilnius[35] and Kaunas[36] (Lithuania), Bialystok[37] and Minsk[38] (Belarus), and Riga[39] (Latvia) were captured within a matter of days. Many of the photographs taken by German soldiers in the first weeks of the occupation show local people, particularly women, welcoming the strangers with friendliness and curiosity.[40] These pictures were not at all staged; they reflected the mood of a large majority of the people in the annexed western territories of the Soviet Union, who had a cautious but distinctly positive attitude towards the Germans, whom they viewed as 'liberators from the Bolshevists'.[41] However, this attitude often changed within a few weeks or months, when the local populations realised that the Germans had their own plans for occupation, exploitation and persecution, as we will see in Chapter 4.

Antisemitism was widespread, particularly since large swathes of society associated Jews with the hated communist system.[42] The Jewish population thus faced persecution and violence right from the start. Naum Epelfeld was thirteen years old when the German army invaded Berdychev (Ukraine) on 5 July 1941. Fleeing from air-raids, he and his family found shelter in the cellar of a nearby hospital. 'Everybody sensed that some horrible events were approaching', he remembered after the end of the war:

> The night fell. The power went down. We sat in darkness, close to one another, and spoke in whispers. Suddenly we heard some people breaking into the hospital building. We heard abrupt commands in a foreign language. I remember the sound of shattered glass and automatic guns shooting. It became clear what had just happened.
>
> The Germans took Berdychev. Some time later two soldiers entered the basement where we stayed. They lit their way with torches and kept saying something, but we couldn't understand them. Then they started walking among people sitting on the floor and shining torches into their faces. Then they stopped near a girl and a woman, and ordered them to follow. They took them into an empty office and raped them. The girl's name was Gusta; she was our neighbour's daughter. Gusta Glozman was fourteen or fifteen years old. Soon she would be killed, together with her parents.
>
> Thus the occupation began for me. It was the most horrible stage in my life.[43]

Epelfeld describes a situation directly after the invasion of the city. The Germans felt entitled to take over Berdychev and capture everything they found, including women and girls – a symbol of victorious trespassing. In many wars, the 'sexual conquest' of the enemy women appears to be a reward for and booty after the military success. Ruth Seifert has pointed out that, in the sweep of history, it has been an unwritten rule of war that the victor is allowed to commit violence against women in the brief, deregulated periods immediately following combat.[44] These crimes are officially prohibited by the military authorities under threat of severe punishment, but in reality they tend to be prosecuted rarely (and only then when they jeopardise the military operation) and are instead generally covered up, kept secret and denied.

In the case described here, however, the occurrence of sexual violence might appear somewhat surprising, since not only was the rape of Jewish women prohibited by the military laws against sexual assault, Nazi racial ideology also denoted sexual intercourse between men who were considered 'Aryan' and women who were classified as Jewish to be *'Rassenschande'* (race defilement) and a crime.[45] For the divisions on the front lines – which were the first to advance into new territories, where they often only stayed for a few days – it was not always possible to determine whether the women they encountered were Jewish.[46] As soon as the major fighting was over, however, the Wehrmacht would install a military administration, which registered the population – an activity that also entailed recording and identifying the Jewish inhabitants.[47] But even after this, Jewish women and girls (and sometimes boys and men) continued to be raped.

While the 1935 Nazi 'Law for the Protection of German Blood and German Honour' was formally not in effect in the military operation zones outside of the borders of the Reich, its regulations were integrated in military policies and laws. In an order issued in April 1944, Reichsführer-SS Heinrich Himmler reminded his men that 'any sexual liaison with women and girls of a different race' was strictly prohibited.[48] In the Wehrmacht, too, antisemitic propaganda and legislation, particularly the 'race defilement' prohibition, were a core element of the soldiers' political education.[49] Additionally, in June 1942 the OKH published a leaflet with rules of conduct for German soldiers, according to which 'sexual intercourse with Jewish women violates the Race Law and will result in legal punishment'.[50]

As we will see in the course of this chapter, however, the command authorities of the Wehrmacht and SS had little interest in pursuing and prosecuting men who committed 'race defilement' in the occupied Eastern territories. In addition, non-German collaborators, some of whom worked as guards in labour, concentration and extermination camps in the Nazi 'East', often had little knowledge of the German 'Blood Protection Law', as it was commonly called, and the German leadership displayed little interest in disciplining their behaviour.[51] Moreover, acts of sexual violence that did not involve genital intercourse were generally not considered 'race defilement'.

In this atmosphere of high tolerance and tacit acceptance of 'race defilement', the men in the small units of the Wehrmacht and SS could develop a perception of themselves and their mission that led them to believe they were entitled to 'have' Jewish women and girls. We know from the account of a former Wehrmacht soldier, for example, that men sometimes took the opportunity in the confusing first days of a city's occupation to break into private houses and rape women and girls, including Jews. Parents or neighbours who tried to come to the women's aid ran the risk of being murdered immediately, just like the rape victims.[52]

In fact, the soldiers did not necessarily view rape as 'race defilement'. A case from Poland illustrates this point. When Wehrmacht soldier Frank Rothe and two of his comrades were accused of raping twenty-one-year-old Hinda Kaufmann in front of her family while the apartments and houses of the Jewish population in Busko (Poland) were being searched at the end of 1939, Rothe was questioned by the 682nd Field Police Section. During the interrogation, he conceded:

> The Nuremberg laws are known to me. I nevertheless attempted to have sex with her because at the moment I did not think that this act was punishable. We also did not think this act was punishable because we forced her to have sex with us at pistol-point.[53]

Rothe argued that the rape was part of the attack against the Jews and thus part of the military operation rather than a violation of the law. In fact, the 'race defilement' cases that were tried in civil courts within the Reich and described in newspapers primarily involved consensual encounters. It is thus plausible that some soldiers might have acted on the assumption that the 'Blood Protection Law' was mainly applicable in cases where a gentile had developed an affectionate relationship with a Jew.[54]

Alexander Rossino argues that the fact that the German military police investigated Rothe's case at all is evidence that the Wehrmacht was still 'guided by racial concerns' at the beginning of the Eastern campaign in Poland 1939.[55] By the time the Wehrmacht invaded the Soviet Union two years later, however, such cases were no longer pursued.

Rothe's line of reasoning that rape was violence and not sex suggests that German men might have felt entitled to rape Jewish women and girls during the war of annihilation not only despite the German 'Blood Protection Law' but because of it. This law contributed to establishing the Jews as predators who deceived, ruined and, ultimately, destroyed the 'Aryan people' through the most intimate, sexual means. Did these laws, as Steven T. Katz has argued, thus also fuel and facilitate a mindset of antisemitic hatred and revenge fantasies in which men like Rothe believed they were allowed to act the way they did?[56] As we will see in the course of this chapter, different sources indicate that German soldiers, SS members and policemen sometimes singled out Jewish women and girls in particular.

Accounts of women who describe their own experiences of sexual violence in detail are rare. I therefore want to quote two examples here in full, even though the events depicted took place in Poland in 1939–40, long before the German invasion of the Soviet Union. Barbara Stimler was thirteen years old when her family fled from Aleksandrów Kujawski (Poland) in the autumn of 1939. In a 1997 interview, she recalls how they took shelter with another Jewish family, the Kronzilbers, in Kutno and tried to live quietly and avoid the Germans. But one night in February 1940, some uniformed Germans knocked on the door. Thinking that they had come for the men, her father and Mr Kronzilber fled the house. When Mrs Kronzilber opened the door, the Germans went right up to the room where Stimler's family was staying:

> My mother said to me: 'Run'. I'm in the nightdress without shoes, in the snow, I'm running. [. . .] But they got hold of my mother, on the street, and they started beating her. And she said to me that they tried . . . they told her to call me. But she didn't want me to come back. But when I heard what they were doing to my mother, and my mother was screaming from pain, twisting her hands and beating her, so I came back. I came back. They took me to the kitchen, they tore my nightie off me. And the stuff I had pinned on, some money and some jewelry, it was all on the floor, and I could see they were not bothering to take anything, they just bothered about something else. They told me to go on the bed. I am not going to tell you what they were doing . . . They didn't rape me.[57]

Stimler's depiction suggests that the German men knew that they were entering a Jewish house and were not interested in plundering material goods, but came directly up to their family room to attack her and her mother. Stimler describes the situation in some detail, but does not relate any specifics about the act, other than 'they didn't rape me'. It is possible that she makes this remark to stress that she had not been 'dishonoured'. However, elsewhere in the interview she openly relates that she was raped by two Polish men at the end of the war. This suggests that her emphasis in this case – 'they didn't rape me' – instead expresses her understanding of what happened, namely, that no sexual intercourse took place. Only relatively recently has the definition of rape been reconceptualised and broadened in a number of national jurisdictions to encompass forced penetration of the vulva, vagina, anus and mouth with the penis, fingers or objects.[58] This interpretation was not conceivable at the time. It thus remains unclear what kind of violence and torture Stimler experienced. Towards the end of the interview, however, she comes back to the story and emphasises that this experience was of a sexual nature and affected her for her entire life, particularly in her relationship with her husband: 'I think this all comes to a certain point: That my sex life was not a sex life.'

Other witnesses, too, report that German soldiers would sexually torture young Jewish women in particular, verbally reproaching them for the fact that intimate contact with them was forbidden, or that they would kill Jewish women with the remark that they were 'too beautiful'.[59] An especially detailed account is provided by Sala Pawlowicz, who published her memoirs in 1964 under the title of *I Will Survive*. Sala Pawlowicz was fifteen years old when the Germans occupied Łask (Poland).[60] Right from the start of the military occupation, she and other young people were forced to work for the Germans. One day she noticed that the policeman who guarded her group – a so-called *Volksdeutscher* or 'ethnic German' – was watching her. He finally asked her if she was Jewish, and she said yes. That same evening, as she waited at the police station to be given permission to go home, the guard spoke to her again:

> 'You! You with the red hair!' he shouted, pointing at me.
> 'Come up here – the rest of you trash get out of here before you make me throw up! Move!' I started to leave with them. '*You!* Damn you, get *up* here!' Somehow, I turned and climbed the steps. 'Scum!' He slapped me across the back with his riding crop and pushed me into the room. Several other Germans were talking together. The officer left me in the middle of the room and spoke with them for a minute. They laughed and pointed obscenely at me. I could not hear what they were saying; my head whirled. I had seen one or two of the girls they had assaulted. It sickened me inside and I tried not to think about what might happen to me.

> The young Polish-German came back and walked up and down in front of me.
> 'All right, you, strip those off!' I stared at him. 'Take off your clothes!' My face felt hot and prickly. With leaden fingers I slowly unbuttoned my blouse and then my hands dropped of their own weight.
> 'What? You still deaf? Off! Off! That's not off, dear, that's only unbuttoned!' I removed the blouse and dropped it at my feet. He looked at me for several seconds. 'What's the matter? You're not ashamed, are you? You're nothing special, but I like you! Come on, come on! Proceed!' I was incapable of moving. 'Then–I will do–it–for–you!' he shouted and ripped my skirt and slip from me. 'That's a start! Now let's have the rest!' and he tore my underwear off. I blinked and staggered back, covering myself.
> 'Stand up!' He grabbed me and wrenched me upright. 'Let's have a look!' He slapped me in the face. 'There, now . . . very pretty . . . very pretty, don't you think so?' He turned to the others and they nodded and laughed.
> The room started spinning, faster and faster. I felt his hands on me and then I was in a small office and the German had a long heavy whip in his hand.
> 'You don't know how to obey . . . I'll show you. But I can't have you, scum, because you're Jewish and filthy. What a shame!' He swung the whip across my breasts. 'Here's what you can have for being a dirty Jew – instead of me – this!' He lashed the whip again and again and I fainted.[61]

Pawlowicz's memoir is based on several interviews conducted with her by NPR journalist Kevin Klose over a two-year period at the beginning of the 1960s. One has to assume it is no coincidence that the most outspoken and detailed memoir on sexual violence was written by a man. Still, the book was published with Pawlowicz's approval. At any rate, the cited passage indicates that we have to ask if the criminal offence of 'race defilement' induced particular forms of sexual violence, that is, if sexual or sexualised acts that did not involve genital intercourse were purposefully directed against Jewish women because the perpetrators were not allowed to 'really have' them. Indeed, acts that did not involve genital intercourse and were thus outside of the sphere of reproduction – such as enforced disrobement, sexual humiliation, sexual torture, rape with fingers and hands, rape with non-bodily objects – were likely to be interpreted as acts that did not violate the German 'Blood Protection Laws'.

Sala Pawlowicz's description suggests that her tormentor wanted to punish her precisely because he desired her, but it ran counter to his convictions to have sexual intercourse with her, a 'racially alien' ('*artfremde*') Jew. He took her into his office in front of the other Germans and even exchanged obscene remarks with them, clearly counting on them to go along with him. Pawlowicz's account of her torture revolves primarily around the riding crop in the hand of her tormentor. Other Jewish and non-Jewish witnesses, as well as former soldiers, have also reported that German men used whips, and sometimes guns or canes, to torture naked or half-naked women.[62] The practice of hitting women on their breasts and genitals was apparently a common method of intimidation and torture.[63]

Soldiers sometimes also used guns or canes to touch men between the legs or hit their genitals.[64] In connection with this, Antjie Krog quotes the political scientist Sheila Meintjes, who proposes that sexual torture serves different purposes depending on the gender of the victim. Meintjes says that while the sexual torture of men leads to 'sexual passivity' and is meant to destroy physical strength and political power, the goal of the sexual torture of women is the 'activation' of female sexuality; the perpetrators thus emphatically assign women to a social position in which they are available as sexual objects.[65]

Many accounts reveal that local collaborators with the Nazis as well as foreign volunteers in the Wehrmacht and SS also committed acts of sexual violence against women, including Jewish women, sometimes alone and sometimes together with Germans. For example, Jewish women and girls who were taken to the prison in Lviv (Ukraine) after the city was occupied were forced by Ukrainian policemen to undress in front of the Germans and then have their photographs taken while half-naked.[66] In their study *The 'Final Solution' in Riga*, Andrej Angrick and Peter Klein provide accounts of the rape of women by officers from the Arajs Kommando, a Latvian auxiliary unit of the German Security Police (*Sicherheitspolizei*). The Jewish survivor Ella Medalje, who was interrogated and humiliated in the headquarters of the Arajs Kommando in the summer of 1941, described these events to a Hamburg court in the 1970s. She said she had gotten off relatively lightly, which she attributed to the fact that one of the guards thought she was a gentile. Other women suffered a worse fate:

> One evening, when we were already on the floor of our bivouac, the door opened and two Thunder Cross men with flashlights entered. They shined their light in the face of each woman and looked her over. Then they ordered the women who had been sought out to follow them, one after the other. After some time, a woman would come back in a horrible emotional state, and the Thunder Cross men would take another woman with them. In this way, they took six to seven women upstairs, where the office of their superior

was located [. . .] The next day, these six to seven women were put on a truck that was located in the courtyard and driven off somewhere. I can only assume that they were shot.[67]

Women (especially Jewish women) who were captured in the first days of the occupation and taken to police prisons were sometimes raped in the presence or in earshot of their fellow prisoners.[68] Even when they were brought to another location, as in the case described above, their fellow prisoners knew or suspected what had happened to them. In addition to the specific humiliation that the victims could feel in this situation, there was a concern that people outside the prison might find out about the rape as well. The knowledge of what had happened could also produce a sense of shame amongst the women's fellow prisoners, along with fears that they might be next. Rape thus functioned as a direct threat, as a symbol of power and as a means of non-verbal communication between the occupiers and the occupied.[69]

In imprisonment situations in particular, gang rapes could also occur. Witness statements about this are notably rare.[70] This, however, does not necessarily mean that gang rape itself was especially rare. Ultimately, we do not know how rare or frequent such practices were. Joshua Goldstein has shown that the pressure to conform plays a large role in gang rapes, and committing such deeds often strengthens the feeling of loyalty within a unit. He argues that collective perpetratorship often leads the individual to feel no sense of responsibility whatsoever. Miranda Alison, by contrast, has proposed that the bond between the men involved actually arises from their awareness of *shared* responsibility.[71]

Research has additionally suggested that gang rapes in wartime are often carried out following a hierarchical order. The highest-ranking officer is the first to perform the violent act (often in private in another room). His subordinates grant him respect and wait their turn. As Ruth Seifert and Rolf Pohl interpret it, this is a way for the men to reaffirm their bond and reinforce the reliability of the military hierarchy in the life-threatening situation of war, in which the men are heavily dependent on one another. With a 'mixture of lust and a desire for destruction', they join together, one after the other, and thus mutually affirm their masculinity and sexual virility.[72] We must assume that men in this kind of situation feel a high level of pressure to perform and comply. Some sources indicate that men who refused to participate were ridiculed and excluded by comrades and colleagues.[73]

The propaganda book *Comrade Genia*, published in London in late 1941, describes this aspect of group action in detail. In this book, Genia

Demianova, a Russian schoolteacher, recounts her sexual enslavement from a first-person perspective. It is not possible for me to judge whether this woman actually existed or the deeds described were based on the experiences of a real person. I mention the story here nonetheless to show that such descriptions of sexual violence appeared so normal and self-evident that they could easily be exploited for propaganda purposes. The book describes Genia Demianova's arrest on 5 August 1941 in Pskov[74] (Russia) and interrogation in a school building, her previous place of work which had become the German headquarters. After a failed escape attempt, the commanding officer tortures her with a whip and brutally rapes her. Afterwards he boasts of his sexual conquest:

> There is a roar of cheering, the clinking of many glasses. The serjeant is standing in the open doorway:
> 'The wild cat is tamed,' he is saying. 'Boys, she was a virgin. What do you say to that?'
> Another burst of cheering then he closes the door. But I am not left alone for long. The others came in. Ten, a hundred, a thousand. Perhaps the whole German army, one after another. They flung themselves upon me digging into my wounds while they defiled me. [. . .] Then everything passed. The Germans kept coming, spitting obscene words towards me, guffawing as they tortured me. I saw them, but felt no pain. I was in a trance, I just guessed what was happening to me, but did not know for certain.[75]

An important factor here is that, prior to the rape, the victim was a 'virgin', a state associated with purity and innocence in Russia and many other countries during World War II.[76] A woman who was raped lost the cultural ascription of innocence and was considered to be spiritually and morally compromised. In the eyes of society, therefore, her honour was just as violated as that of the male collective that was incapable of protecting her.[77] The virginity of rape victims played a significant role not only in propaganda but also in witness testimonies. The narrators used the aspect of virginity to highlight the innocence of the victims while simultaneously emphasising the inhumanity of the perpetrators. The rape of sexually 'untouched' women thus had high symbolic value. The prevalence of this motif, however, does not necessarily mean that acts of sexual violence against young girls were especially frequent. Instead, it indicates that this narrative was (and still is) authorised in the dominant interpretation of history and therefore communicable, unlike others.[78]

Research has yet to be conducted into whether or to what extent German members of the Wehrmacht and SS thought about their responsibility for acts of sexual violence. But the ego documents of former soldiers suggest that they did not necessarily view rape as an act of violence. In some accounts, the 'conquest' of women is described in a humorous and occasionally salacious tone as something that took place beyond the actual acts of war. For example, on 7 October 1941, *Generalmajor* Jürgen W., an artilleryman with the 20th Infantry Division, wrote in his diary about his unit's military success in the Navlya[79] region (Russia):

> The btl. [battalion] charges left past the forest around midday in the direction of Saltanovka, where the Russians are thought to have scarpered. We soon follow suit, take up position close to the location in a basic southerly direction; we're supposed to comb through the kilometres-long village before we advance further. According to the local residents, there were still around twenty tanks and over 1,000 men here early this morning. If we had stumbled into that! Gentlemen! The village is purged and in a spirited attack, á la military training ground, the 6th Cp. [Company] proceeds, takes 120 prisoners and ample spoils. A caravan with 'little ladies' for the brave Russians is also captured, though the occupants have been slightly damaged by M.G. fire; but then, why do they go to war? 'Tasty girls' the *Landser* say when they come back.[80]

Jürgen W.'s account reveals a certain degree of pride as well as relief about the good timing and swift, professional execution of the operation. He skates around the violence that must have occurred when the village was 'purged', saying only that the attack was 'spirited'. The single unusual factor he mentions are the female 'spoils', and he implies that these women were prostitutes in the retinue of the Red Army. It is not possible to prove whether this corresponds to historical reality or whether the women he dismisses as 'little ladies' were actually female soldiers or nurses in the Red Army. In any case, his rhetorical question – 'why do they go to war?' – makes it clear that he views military operations as a purely male preserve.

It apparently goes without saying for Jürgen W. that the *Landser* (common soldiers) would be allowed to take possession of the 'women of the enemy'. He does not go into any detail on where the soldiers have actually returned from when they 'come back'. It is in keeping with this that Jürgen W. portrays the women as goods, 'slightly damaged' but 'tasty'. The idea that the soldiers were due a reward as compensation for the hardships and deprivations of the war runs through Jürgen W.'s entire diary. Week after week he writes of 'tasty' food and 'fine' luxuries such as real coffee, red wine and champagne (probably seized during looting raids), and he tries to justify why he and his men have earned all of these things.[81] Women, as is clear from his choice of words in the diary entry above, fall into the same category in his view.

Jürgen W.'s depiction also hints at the negotiation of sexual violence within the military hierarchy. Scholars of military sociology such as John Hockey have explored how social cohesion helps determine the effectiveness of military operations. Indeed, the survival of soldiers largely depends upon trust and teamwork.[82] Creating and maintaining cohesion is thus one of the army leadership's most important tasks. Guy Siebold distinguishes between primary group cohesion (peer and leader bonding) and secondary group cohesion (organisational and institutional bonding):

> Peer or horizontal bonding is among members at the same military hierarchical level (e.g. squad or group members). Leader or vertical bonding is between those at different levels (e.g. between squad or group members and their leaders). Peer and leader bonding within a small group (e.g. a platoon) together compose primary group cohesion.[83]

Conforming to this pattern, Wehrmacht training aimed to produce officers who were adept at creating conditions in which their men could bond with each other while remaining loyal to their superiors. For men like *Generalmajor* Jürgen W., granting subordinates the 'liberty' of sexual violence was useful in negotiating this balance.

The photo collection accompanying Jürgen W.'s 'Diary in Russia' also hints at sexual violence. One photograph shows the corpse of a woman, judging by the shape of the legs and upper torso. Her legs are bare, slightly bent and spread, her long stockings twisted around her feet. The photographer took the picture at an angle from above while standing over her; the body takes up the bottom third of the photograph. Although Jürgen W. meticulously labelled nearly all of the pictures in his collection, there is no text on the back of this photo. Only the location and date have been noted in pencil: '30 June 1941, near Jeziornico'.[84] Motifs such as this were photographed by soldiers during the entire 'Eastern campaign', not just in the first days of the war and not just in particular regions. Although it involves taking a detour from the military conquest phase, a general discussion of these photographs is called for at this point. The question here is how the gazes of the soldiers who saw the victims of such crimes differed from one another.

One photograph, taken by a German soldier in 1941 near Moscow, shows the body of Soviet resistance fighter Zoya Kosmodemyanskaya, who had been hanged and mutilated. She lies on the ground with her head twisted unnaturally; the picture shows her only to the waist. Her upper body is bare, and the viewer's gaze is drawn particularly to her nipple, which can be seen centre-right in the picture.[85] Another photograph from Klooga[86] (Estonia), dated 1942, shows a 'raped and murdered Jewish woman' according to the caption; the picture is of a nearly naked woman's corpse with spread legs, whose open jacket reveals her bare upper body. The viewer essentially looks down onto her bare breast; the shadow of the photographer can be seen at the bottom left of the picture.[87] Unlike the first example mentioned, the bodies of the women in these latter two photographs are in the centre of the picture, and their placement seems to hint at the photographers' desire and compulsion to look. Dieter Reifarth and Viktoria Schmidt-Linsenhoff, who have analysed numerous photos taken by soldiers of crimes in the Soviet Union, point out that taking pictures can be an escalation of the desire to look, an 'exponentiated, intensified kind of seeing'. They argue that the act of photography and the subsequent viewing of the pictures acquire an experiential quality.[88] In these pictures especially, it is not just the voyeuristic element but also the pornographic element that is blatantly centred.

A picture from Zwiahel in Poland reveals another kind of gaze. This photograph shows a woman's corpse on a bed frame, probably in a barn since the bed and room are laid with straw. The woman's skirt is pushed up, and her legs are bare and turned outwards. The soldier who took this picture in 1941 photographed the woman from a relatively great distance, which gives the image a documentary character. Unlike the pictures just described, the act of photography here seems to serve a distancing purpose.[89]

It is not possible to determine whether the women's bodies seen in these photos were actually found in the poses described or whether they were arranged after the fact – possibly even for the photos themselves. But the public display of half-naked or naked women's bodies in contorted positions is also mentioned in the oral accounts of former soldiers and testimonies of local residents.[90] In her study of the German occupation and the Holocaust in Ukraine, Wendy Lower describes a case from Zhytomyr[91] (Ukraine) in which members of the SS and police first raped a local woman, then murdered her and threw her body out of a car onto a street corner.[92] In an interview with Wendy Jo Gertjejanssen, a witness from the Cherkassy province[93] (Ukraine) related that, in February 1944, he saw the half-naked body of a woman on the side of the road. She was lying in a puddle of blood and had several bullet wounds. He assumed that she had been raped and then murdered.[94]

Some accounts and rumours suggest that there were also cases in which soldiers sexually abused a woman's body only after she had been murdered.[95] Occasionally they were mutilated as well. Some eyewitnesses report having seen women's bodies with their breasts cut off or bellies cut open.[96] There are also isolated accounts of German men in uniform hanging women.[97] Two witnesses recalled seeing the body of a girl with a bottle in her vagina.[98]

Sometimes genital mutilations were found on the corpses of men as well. In fact, the disfigurement of male bodies became the subject of military propaganda on both sides after the war started,[99] and many German soldiers wrote about it in their diaries and letters.[100] While the genital mutilation of men and boys was viewed first and foremost as an act of violence (though not sexual violence) and an attack on a country's national and military strength, the public display of naked or half-naked women's bodies was understood to be a sexual act that threatened to destroy the social basis of a country's existence, both actually and symbolically. This reflects the prevailing gender relations of the time, according to which men were regarded as protectors of the nation, while women were considered to be the custodians of culture and the next generation.[101]

The example of naked or half-naked female corpses makes it especially clear that sexual violence was directed not only against the immediate victims. The women's exposed bodies were meant to be seen, as they were proof of the occurrence of sexual violence and the powerlessness of the victims. During the war in the Soviet Union, they sent different messages to different groups. First, those who witnessed the acts were confronted with their own powerlessness and helplessness.[102] Second, the women's bodies – the proof of the deeds – affected the self-perception of the local population (particularly that of the men who were unable to protect 'their' women). And third, they demonstrated to fellow perpetrators in the male society of the Wehrmacht and SS that their comrades were resolutely aggressive.

There are two documented cases in which German men photographed themselves together with women's bodies in explicit poses of sexual violence. The first example is a series of four photographs discovered by Fabrice Virgili in the collection of the Resistance Museum in Champigny, France. The pictures show four Wehrmacht soldiers holding down a woman lying on a pile of planks. The photographer is positioned at the feet of the woman, aiming the camera at the height of the woman's genitals. The men are slightly bent down, looking either at their victim or into the camera. In the first photograph, the woman thrashes her legs as the soldiers take off her skirt. In the following two images, the men spread her bare legs, showing her genitals to the photographer. In the last image, one of the soldiers lowers his head for a closer look at the victim's vagina. In all of the images, we see the soldiers grinning. The woman's face, by contrast, is hidden, as is her upper body; we only see her lower half. She is reduced to her sex.[103]

The second case is a picture kept in the National Archives in Romania which has been analysed by Elissa Mailänder. It shows a group of fifteen Wehrmacht soldiers, loosely dressed and at ease in the bright light of the sun, carousing and laughing into the camera. At the centre of the picture are three men. Imitating a sex act, the first one is pushing himself up from the ground on his hands and feet to position his body above a woman lying on her back with bare legs. He is bare-chested, wearing only his uniform trousers and a cap, and he turns his head to the side to show off a victorious grin in the direction of the camera. Her face, by contrast, is not recognisable, and we do not know if she is alive or dead. The second soldier is standing at the woman's feet, pulling at his comrade's trousers at the buttocks – a gesture that could serve to steady his comrade's push-up position or encourage him to hurry, because he is next in line. A third man is squatting behind the two others, watching over the scene as if supervising it. The other twelve men stand in a semicircle around these three, most of them facing the photographer. At the centre of the photographic setting and the amusement of the men is the assault, degradation and humiliation of the woman.[104]

In both cases, we know neither who the men are, nor when and where they staged these explicit acts of sexual violence. In both cases, we have no clue as to the woman's identity. In both cases, we do not know what happened before or after the photographs were taken. Were the women penetrated, raped, murdered? The only thing we do know is that the men took these photographs of themselves – and, as photo historians such as Petra Bopp and Gerhard Paul have emphasised, the photographer was part of this act of sexual violence. He did not merely observe and capture a specific moment; he interacted with the men in front of the camera.[105]

Mailänder argues that taking this kind of group self-portrait was a highly self-affirmative and self-conscious act for the men, who aimed to retain a 'photographic trophy' that they could show off within a circle of comrades and that would serve in later life as a memory of the virility and transgressions of their youth.[106] As an unintended effect, these pictures are evidence of a rarely seen moment of male bonding that the men staged for and with the camera, illustrating that this form of violence is 'an interactive process that demonstrates highly sexualised social power'.¹⁰⁷ At the core of this interactive process seems to be a collective regression of the men. Like small children who are pulling out the wings of insects, they seem to be fascinated by their cruel transgression.

In addition, these pictures reveal a deep and far-reaching hostility towards women. Social psychologist Rolf Pohl has argued that the misogyny displayed by male soldiers is rooted in the male subject's conflict between autonomy and dependency. This goes back to childhood when the boy starts to appropriate the male position in the symbolic gender system. Masculinity represents independence and domination, while everything weak and dependent is split off from consciousness and associated with femininity. In the military, where hyper-masculinity is celebrated and the recruit is permitted to exert violence and kill, this splitting mechanism is radicalised.¹⁰⁸ The war situation then offers the subject the possibility of living out (gendered) fantasies in reality. Attacks against the enemy can thus be accompanied by what Alexander Mitschlerlich calls '*Grausamkeitslust*' (lust for cruelty) directed against everyone regarded as weak and feminine.¹⁰⁹

Statements from soldiers in different wars furthermore attest that bodily experiences of violence, cruelty, lust and sexuality can be deeply intertwined. The perpetration of violence can be accompanied by arousal and feelings of (sexual) pleasure.¹¹⁰ As Sala Pawlowicz described in her above-mentioned memoir, this can give rise to a 'hatred for one's own (sexual) desire [. . .], for which the woman is held responsible and therefore punished'.¹¹¹

*Everyday Wartime Life*¹¹²
As they advanced east, German troops encountered a society that had changed dramatically in its composition since 22 June 1941. This particularly applied to the inhabitants of cities. Both the Soviet leadership and general population had apparently been surprised by the German invasion, but they soon began making preparations to evacuate. First, senior officials from the party, the state, the NKVD and the army were to be brought to safety, then skilled workers with their families and businesses (in both cases, groups of people who mainly lived in cities) and, finally, children under the age of fifteen. Further evacuations were left at the discretion of regional administrators.

In the western regions close to the border, which were captured by the Germans in June, only around 10 per cent of city-dwellers were able to flee or reach an organised transport. The relocation of entire population groups did not start until July. In the regions farther east, where the Soviet authorities had more time, evacuations and refugee movements took place on a much larger scale. In Kharkiv[113] (Ukraine) and Bobruisk[114] (Belarus), population numbers had nearly halved by the winter of 1941–2, while in Gomel they had dwindled to a third. Farther north in Novgorod[115] (Russia) and Pskov, only about one in eight people remained. But in the rural areas where the majority of people lived, the decline in population was much less dramatic, at around 15 per cent. Government and party elites were evacuated from the countryside, too, but the reduced rural population numbers can be attributed primarily to the conscription of young men into the Red Army.[116] Threatened and embattled regions in particular thus lost both their Soviet leaders and most of their men between the ages of eighteen and thirty-five in a very short period of time. The population that came under German administration was therefore made up mainly of women, children and older people.[117]

Many people in the occupied territories were critical if not downright hostile towards the Soviets. At the start of the war, the German occupiers had ample opportunity to win them over – not least because the widely despised political leadership had disappeared in the evacuations, leaving behind a political vacuum. As varied as the conditions were in the different countries and territories of the Soviet Union, much of the population everywhere had suffered under the forced collectivisation and massive political persecution of the 1930s. The catastrophic famine of 1931 to 1934 in the southern Soviet Union, which had particularly devastating consequences in Ukraine and resulted in the decimation of entire villages, was also still very much alive in people's memory.[118]

But any hopes of improved living conditions associated with the arrival of the Germans were soon dashed. Though the nature of the direct personal interactions between locals and Germans differed depending on the time, region and the inhabitants' religion and 'racial' attributions, as well as the composition and discipline of the respective military units, the fact was that destruction and looting took place everywhere. Indeed, Germany's war plans called for the economic plundering of the Soviet Union right from the start in order to ensure provisions for the Wehrmacht and the 'people's community'.[119] Furthermore, even shortly after the invasion – as demonstrated by Omer Bartov and Christian Gerlach, among others – German soldiers ravaged businesses, farms and homes on their own authority, beyond what was called for in the context of military requisition measures. These raids increased when troop supplies ran low. The Wehrmacht leadership issued several military orders in an attempt to curb such solo actions, but the overall historical picture shows that looting was largely tolerated.[120] In an interview with Wendy Jo Gertjejanssen, a witness from Cherkassy described the excessive actions of the men:

> And they did whatever they wanted to here. They took our hope chest. They came in quickly and asked for eggs and milk, yelling, screaming, running after girls, taking everything. They were even killing pigs. They were eating. They destroyed everything and ate eggs, milk, running under the houses and yelling, 'Where are those eggs and milk?' They were already taken![121]

Women and girls could quickly become 'loot' themselves during such raids, as can also be seen in the reports and court decisions of the Wehrmacht and SS.[122] A case of forced oral sex was reported in this context as well.[123] Elena Kozhina, who experienced such raids as a young girl in Russia, had the following to say about what she remembered: 'It was no longer the seizure of something necessary, but purely an insulting reminder of the soldiers' unlimited power'.[124]

Such displays of power also took place when German soldiers were quartered in private houses and flats. In the countryside, individual soldiers were housed relatively often with farmers, despite a strict prohibition against this.[125] As a result, soldiers could spend days, weeks or months living right next door to – or, if it was a typical one-room wooden house,[126] even in the same room as – local women. Sometimes the soldiers felt quite comfortable in these accommodations and noted in their diaries that they always wanted to 'get home' as quickly as possible in the evening.[127] Under these circumstances, as we will see, consensual and romantic relationships could develop, but sexual assaults took place as well.

Anton Meiser, born in 1912, was a Wehrmacht infantryman stationed first in France and then, from the end of 1943, in Russia. In 1998 he published his war diary, *Die Hölle von Tscherkassy* (The Hell of Cherkassy). This book is based on diary entries he wrote during the war but later expanded upon, giving them subheadings and presenting them in the form of an account from memory. In a section entitled 'An Outrage', he describes an act of sexual violence:

> When I returned to my quarters [...], I immediately noticed a change in the Russians. [...] They were good people, they prayed [...] for an enemy! I was all the more surprised when they visibly steered clear of me. The father

scowled. The women sobbed. I couldn't make sense of it and even suspected that partisans might have worked over the father and tried to recruit him. [...] During the day I mostly kept to the fire control post. When I lay down to sleep in the house in the evening, they climbed into their sleeping area over the oven. I had requisitioned the only bed. While I was quartered there, the girl slept on the buttress under the oven. My bed was against the wall across from this. Everyone slept in their clothing. On this particular night, the girl also climbed on top of the oven. Her fear was unmistakeable. I had grown very suspicious and discreetly kept my pistol under the blanket, ready to fire. I pretended to sleep. Then the father carefully climbed down from the oven, went to the door and locked it. They had never locked the door before. It wasn't usual in Russian villages. Well, I didn't have anything against it, because then no one could come in from the outside. But I couldn't sleep because I was pondering the reason why. Suddenly I heard footsteps outside; they approached the door. I released the safety on my pistol again, got up and stood behind the door. The people were now praying loudly on top of the oven. The handle moved, but the door didn't open. Then a rifle butt slammed into the door, and I heard the familiar voice of Private Leo. He demanded that the girl immediately come to work. The women now cried loudly. The girl clung to her mother. Leo shouted again, loud and angry: 'Paninka, roboder, pistro, pistro!' There was loud wailing inside. I silently opened the door but remained hidden. Private Leo went to the oven and grabbed the girl's feet to pull her down. The father gnashed his teeth but did not dare fight back. Now everything was clear to me and I roared at Leo: 'Get back! Stand to attention!' He wheeled around and exclaimed in shock: 'You're here?' I demanded an immediate explanation. He had been sent by two *Oberwachtmeister* [senior NCOs]. Yesterday he had also fetched the girl on their behalf. They had raped her.[128]

In the context of his diary as a whole, Meiser uses this specific passage to present himself – as opposed to his comrades – as a responsible man and soldier. Like von Manstein and Göring at the Nuremberg trial, he believes his approach to dealing with sexual violence is a sign of his 'honour'. The woman, her father and the whole family are said to be 'decent' and eternally grateful to him from this point on. In Meiser's narrative, he is also the one to insist that the men be punished – although they receive only a disciplinary punishment because, ultimately, he does not want to do lasting harm to his comrades.

Birgit Beck has shown that men accused of such crimes were sometimes brought before a Wehrmacht court. In late March 1942, the gunner Heinz B. drove to the small village of Suglitz (Russia) to procure hay and potatoes. The men expected the mission to take several days, so they stayed in the cottage of a woman who lived together with her young daughter and a 23-year-old Russian woman who had been evacuated from Moscow. Even before the trip, Heinz B. had boasted to his comrades that he would 'acquire' a woman. During his stay in the cottage, he threatened the female inhabitants with his weapon and took several opportunities to rape a young woman. The court of the 339th Infantry Division sentenced Heinz B. to four years in jail. Its justification for this comparably harsh punishment was that this had been a 'heavily partisan-infested area' and Heinz B.'s deed had played a part in inciting the residents to join the ranks of the resistance – a fear that often played a role in the judgements of Wehrmacht courts.[129]

In the cities, by contrast, the headquarters would order residents to be evicted from their homes before the Germans moved in – due in part to limited space, but mainly to thwart friendly or sexual encounters between German soldiers and the local population and to prevent espionage. From the autumn of 1941, entire city districts were cleared,[130] forcing the residents to find accommodation elsewhere. For women, this often meant the loss of spaces that had served as refuges offering at least some protection from sexual assault. They were then forced to reorientate themselves and find new hiding places. Due to the shortage of space, and in order to not be alone, many women lived in groups together with their children. When German patrols stumbled across these communal accommodations, it offered them an opportunity to rape multiple women at once, sometimes repeatedly. As a result of such assaults, women sometimes decided to frequently change the place where they slept.[131]

When entire Wehrmacht or SS units were quartered in local buildings for a longer period of time, they employed women and girls from the area as maids whose job was to clean and cook. It is not clear whether the women chose these jobs or were forced to do them, or whether they received payment. This might have varied depending on the circumstances in a specific place at a given time as well as the decisions of the mid-level commanders. At any rate, these women and girls were often subjected to sexual violence. On 11 May 1944, for example, SS-*Obersturmführer* Oskar Paul Dirlewanger visited the quarters of the 1st company of the SS unit under his command and found the following:

> 22 Russian women were allegedly engaged in cleaning. In one room there was a recruit sitting at a table while 2 Russian women cleaned the floor. There were 6 native women in and for the kitchen alone. The 1st comp. is said to bring

20 women each morning to expand the military base. But nobody was busy with the construction of the base, every soldier brought the Russian woman he liked to his room.[132]

Dirlewanger's SS brigade was mainly made up of former prisoners – ranging from poachers and 'habitual criminals' (*Berufsverbrecher*) to expelled SS officers – and was notorious for its highly despotic and brutal leadership.[133] The large number of women mentioned here might be attributed to the habitual practices in this particular unit, but the employment of maids in general was common in all units.

In Dirlewanger's depiction, it appears self-evident that the women would also provide sexual services to the soldiers. He describes the particularity of the scenario in which a man could bring 'the Russian woman he liked to his room'. Ultimately, it seems to be this everyday 'privacy' that led Dirlewanger to change these conditions and order that only two women should be allowed to work in the kitchen in the future – otherwise the men would 'become sissies' (*verweichlichen*) and set a bad example for the new recruits.[134]

Dirlewanger feared that his men would develop affectionate feelings for and grow close to the 'local broads'. Since I do not have information about these women and girls, it is impossible to say how they positioned themselves. Some of them might actually have been interested in sexual experiences with the foreign men in uniform – a scenario I will discuss in more detail in Chapter 4. Even then, however, the power relations between the armed occupiers and the local women were unequal. The women's possibilities of choice were thus always limited. Ultimately, they had little opportunity to refuse the men.

In the relative 'privacy' of closed rooms, the men were not directly observed by their comrades. The only other person present in the room was the woman. This hints at the intimacy that could characterise acts of sexual violence. The women became witnesses to the ways the men (and their bodies) acted and reacted when they were on their own. They became witnesses to their power but also their fragility. Considering this, Gaby Zipfel has proposed that perhaps rape victims are murdered so often because the perpetrators feel they have exposed this side of themselves to their victims.[135]

In her analysis of witness testimonies before the ICTY, Gabriela Mischkowski observed that rape in the sense of forced sexual intercourse with the penis appears to have been perpetrated almost exclusively in 'private' settings, in which the victims were brought to another room or building. 'Even in cases of serial rapes, the first man would most often leave before the next came in.'[136] In public, by contrast, other forms of sexual violence seem to have been pervasive which did not reveal the intimacy between perpetrator and victim in the same way. Enforced undressing, sexual beatings, penetration with sticks or weapons, and mutilation unequivocally demonstrated to the audience the power of the perpetrators.

Due to the lack of detailed sources, we can only speculate on whether this private/public divide was also found during the German war in the Soviet Union. It is notable, however, that the demonstrative aspect of sexual violence in public did play a major role. The victims were meant to be seen, as demonstrated by another example from the Dirlewanger SS brigade. When the men were stationed in Lahoysk (Belarus) in the spring of 1944, a soldier named W.B. joined the unit for four weeks. In an affidavit after the end of the war, he described how the officers engaged in a brutal drinking bout: 'While I was standing guard one evening at the castle, which was used as the officers' quarters, I was told by an orderly that the officers, who were completely drunk, were whipping and maltreating eight naked women in the hall.'[137] W.B.'s statement was confirmed by Albin Vogels, who had been an employee of the Recruiting Office of the Waffen-SS and temporarily assigned to the Dirlewanger brigade for the purpose of 'probation'. When interrogated in March 1948, Vogels commented on this or a similar incident: 'I myself saw these naked women through the open door. The next morning three or four women were shot and beaten to death in front of the castle. These women were buried by us.'[138] We do not know what happened before or after the women were beaten. What we do know is that it was not enough for the men to violate them behind closed doors – they tortured and killed them in public.

Various accounts testify that German men went on the hunt for local women particularly in the evening hours, after darkness had fallen. On 6 December 1941, barely half a year after the Germans had occupied Riga, the Lithuanian eye specialist Dr Elena Buividaite–Kutorgene wrote in her diary that 'women are afraid to go out after eight in the evening, since the Germans attack them and take them away somewhere'.[139] Sometimes soldiers also threatened women by saying that they or their daughters would be 'next in line'.[140] In this atmosphere, taking precautions against sexual assault was a part of everyday life for many women. Eyewitnesses from various regions say that women would disguise themselves, spend the nights in lofts or cellars or permanently live in hideouts.[141] A few women feigned menstruation, typhoid or other illnesses to avoid physical assault.[142] A common motif in literary depictions is that of women stepping forward and volunteering to be raped so that others, usually sexually inexperienced 'virgins', daughters or sisters, would be spared this fate.[143] The sources indicate that women's fears were further stoked by Soviet media reports about the rape and abduction of women.[144]

Women were also very much at risk when they had to travel long distances to earn money or acquire food. In a letter written in 1999, a Ukrainian woman recalled her experiences with the German occupiers before she was deported to Germany as a forced labourer in 1942:

> In October 1941 in Dnipropetrovsk I went with some young people who were older than me to dig potatoes at the edge of the city. On the way back, German soldiers joined us. We conversed cheerfully in the foreign language ... But, oh no, suddenly as if on command the young people (rebjata) started to run away, but the rough hands of the soldier made it impossible for me to follow them. My cry for help went unheard because my mouth was held shut. For the first time I felt betrayed. [...] Mama took me to an old woman in the village and never even asked why I had come home at night and was all scratched up, in torn clothing and in tears.[145]

The author of the letter foregrounds her naïvety and inexperience. By highlighting the carefree conversation in a 'foreign language' that was unexpectedly interrupted by the crime, she emphasises that she had not been aware of her risk of being raped and was thus unable to take any protective measures. As explained earlier, this may be an indication of the pressure many women felt after the end of the war to justify themselves or prove that they had not encouraged the men in any way, but had instead been powerless and helpless.

Another illuminating aspect of the Ukrainian woman's account is the reaction of her mother, who was not at all surprised and asked her no questions, but apparently immediately took her to an 'old woman' for treatment – probably to prevent a pregnancy. It is clear here that sexual violence was a kind of open secret, one which everyone knew about but would only discuss abstractly or indirectly. The author of the letter herself perpetuates this approach in a way by leaving out the description of the actual act of violence and assuming the reader will know what she is talking about. It is likely that many women who had personally experienced sexual violence tried to completely conceal what had happened to them in order not to fall into disrepute. This was a major advantage for the German soldiers because it meant that many of their crimes remained hidden.

The transports that carried 'Eastern workers' (*Ostarbeiter*) to Germany were another opportunity for German men to sexually harass and rape women. After Germany invaded the Soviet Union, the focus was initially on putting the population to work locally. But in the spring of 1942, the occupying authorities began registering labourers on a large scale in order for them to work in the Reich, first on a more or less voluntary basis, but soon through forced recruitment. This particularly applied to the rural youth in Ukraine. Prior to being transported to the Reich, the women and men had to undergo a 'delousing' procedure. They were forced to wash themselves with special chemicals in communal shower rooms and submit to medical exams. Women also often had their hair cut off. The leader of the skilled workers' camp (*Facharbeiterlager*) in Kharkiv complained in the autumn of 1942 that, in the shower rooms of the delousing facilities, men regularly 'wandered around – even providing soaping services! – and [. . .] took photographs in the women's shower rooms'.[146] On the transports themselves, as one witness reported, some soldiers would pick out a woman during the journey and take her into their railway carriage.[147] In addition, the women had to reckon with the possibility of experiencing sexual violence at their place of work or residence in Germany. Reports and rumours spread quickly, and women in particular would try to evade the labour service by marrying a local collaborator or claiming to be pregnant.[148] The Reich Ministry for the Occupied Eastern Territories (*Reichsministerium für die besetzten Ostgebiete*, RMbO) attempted to quell the women's fear of sexual violence by launching an extensive propaganda campaign in April 1942.[149]

While many acts of sexual violence were apparently crimes of opportunity, there were also cases in which German men planned their attack and used deliberate ploys to lure women in.[150] Some men seem to have repeatedly followed the same pattern.[151] On 4 July 1942, SS-*Standartenführer* Rohde, who worked for the SS and Police Leader in Brest-Litovsk[152] (Belarus), took a statement from Axannder S., a dancer at the city theatre. She claimed that a German policeman had tried to rape her and other women. Rohde questioned other female witnesses, conducted further investigations and identified the perpetrator, Wehrmacht soldier Adolf H., who 'outright' admitted to the deeds and made excuses for himself by saying that he had been under the influence of alcohol.[153] The responsible military policeman arrested Adolf H. In his final report, Rohde described the course of events: on the night in question, a man in uniform had identified himself as a policeman to Axannder S., checked her papers and – although her documents were in order – demanded that she accompany him. When he did not take the expected route to the local headquarters, she tried to flee:

> In the same moment, he attempted to rape her by completely tearing off her coat and ripping parts of her dress as well. Because S. is extremely agile as a result of her profession, she was able to break away and fled to the front garden of a nearby house. She was able to conceal herself so cleverly there that the accused was unable to find her. [. . .] Because S. was extremely fearful, she continued hiding in the shrubbery and noticed after about 20 minutes that he had reappeared and was now wearing a field-grey uniform [. . .]. He was accompanied by another member of the Wehrmacht. [. . .] As these women had already been awakened by the dancer's cries for help, they stood in the doorway of their house, suspecting that something did not bode well. The perpetrator of the first crime now requested admittance and once again said he was a policeman. Since the two women did not immediately comprehend the situation, they were forced back, and while the elderly mother fled to the next room, Irene Sch. retreated to her bedroom. The accused followed her and apparently immediately tore the clothing from her body. A scuffle took place on the bed of Irene Sch., in which I. Sch. was severely injured on her left hand, left shoulder and both legs, as the accused behaved like a brute. No sexual intercourse took place as Sch. is exceptionally strong. When the mother Leokardia wanted to come to her daughter's aid and ran into the bedroom, the brute fell upon her and hit her in the right eye, as a result of which it is bloodshot and swollen shut. He also severely injured the woman's breast. Without taking anything and without having succeeded, the brute then left the house again. [. . .] It should be mentioned that the same accused had been in the same house 8 days earlier and had already attempted sexual intercourse. In this case, too, he posed as a police officer, and he additionally demanded vodka but was unable to achieve his goal. [. . .]
>
> It should also be mentioned that the dancer S. was seriously injured by H. on both legs, on the breast, on the neck and on the lips. Furthermore, H. is said to have gagged S. to prevent her from screaming.[154]

Rohde's report contains a number of incongruities. We are told neither when nor how the accused managed to 'seriously' injure and gag the first victim, the dancer S., since she was apparently able to immediately break free and hide, nor does the report mention the behaviour of the other Wehrmacht soldier present during the second attempted rape. Rohde's assessment of the people involved is clear, however: the women are honourable – fearful, but capable of protecting themselves and preventing the attempted rape – while Wehrmacht member H. is a drunken 'brute'. Rohde explains this dichotomous depiction by referring to his 'personal impression'. Adolf H. had not only damaged the reputation of the Wehrmacht, he had also brought the police into disrepute by taking on a false identity; this is likely to have played a significant role in Rohde's judgement. SS-*Standartenführer* Rohde also suspected that H. – who apparently spoke Russian well – had acquired counterfeit identity documents for 'elements [. . .] with whom we are currently engaged in fierce battle'.[155] He therefore demanded 'the severest punishment' for the accused. The records do not indicate whether a trial ever took place.

Acts of sexual violence could sometimes be associated with deliberate demonstrations of political power. Bernhard Chiari has shown that when 'minor rewards and benefits' were offered to the local population in the occupied territories, they were often followed by eruptions of violence from German men, including sexual assaults. He describes a case from the Chervyen raion near Minsk, where a future bonus system for farmers – which was to be introduced after the 'liberation of Belarus from the yoke of Bolshevism' – was announced at a German propaganda event in 1942. The following day, sixteen German men raped a fifteen-year-old girl in the middle of the street. The crime was extremely brutal; both of the victim's eyes were gouged out.[156] Just a few days later, a group of German men ordered several young women to undress on the market square and perform a Belarusian folk dance. When the women refused, they were shot.[157] Here, too, the acts of sexual violence conveyed the power of the occupiers to the local population.

Anti-Partisan Operations
In August 1941, the first signs emerged that organised resistance was forming outside of the Red Army. Partisan groups attacked German troops and infrastructure in the back country, particularly in the area of operations of the *Heeresgruppe Mitte* (Army Group Centre), and they assaulted locals suspected of collaboration.[158] These activities were initially not very coordinated, and most of the groups disbanded in the winter of 1941. But in the first months of 1942, the Soviet leadership, and especially the NKVD, began to systematically establish a Soviet partisan movement. By the summer of 1942, attacks were taking place on a much larger scale. In mid-1943, partisan units finally became a critically important military factor. They caused considerable economic and infrastructural damage, brought entire regions under their control and supported the increasingly successful Red Army.[159] Their campaigns against the Germans were frequently accompanied by acts of violence directed at the local population, often including sexual violence.[160]

Much of the population therefore felt trapped between the German and Soviet combatants.

The Wehrmacht did not consider the partisans to be a serious danger at first and instead viewed them primarily as a short-term problem for the supply lines. Moreover, German soldiers were neither trained nor equipped to fight underground groups. It was not until the spring and summer of 1942, after the first major actions against 'partisans' – some of which resulted in the indiscriminate mass murder of civilians – that the Army High Command (OKH) began to grapple intensively with how to respond to partisan warfare. The occupying forces were supposed to divide the population strictly along the lines of those who were favourably inclined towards the Germans and those who supported the partisans. But this distinction proved impossible to make, which is why the civilian population as a whole came under suspicion. In some cities, the headquarters actually ordered the internment of every single adult male.[161] The German Security Police and military officials generally assumed that the resistance was motivated by communism, but in keeping with the antisemitic stereotype of the Jews as 'puppet masters', they also believed that Jews were behind the organised movement.[162] According to a Wehrmacht High Command (OKW) order from December 1942, after interrogating partisans and those suspected of supporting them, German soldiers were required to shoot them immediately or hand them over to the Security Police. Additionally, partisan operations against Germans were to be punished with collective reprisals against the local population. The troops were 'to act ruthlessly, even against women and children, and no soldier [could] be punished for such action'.[163]

When 'combing through' villages on the hunt for 'corrosive elements' – i.e. Jews and communists – German soldiers would force their way into the private homes of local residents. According to a number of accounts, when members of the Security Service and Wehrmacht entered a house, they would order both men and women to strip to the waist.[164] Whether such attacks were perceived by the victims as sexually degrading or injurious was gender-specific and subjective. Men were often used to going bare-chested, but they might have felt a sense of sexual shame, especially if they had a physical ailment or were strictly religious. For women, however, even taking off a blouse in front of others was so uncustomary that it could be perceived as an attack on their sexual integrity. Young women in particular who had never been naked in front of a man before could feel this to be especially embarrassing. In any case, nakedness in front of an armed enemy –

especially when the victims had been forced to undress in their own home – generated feelings of humiliation, vulnerability and a particular defencelessness.[165]

In many cases, the intruders would touch the women in particular with their weapons while making sexualised and obscene comments about their figure or the size and firmness of their breasts. Sometimes they conducted strip-searches, which involved probing body cavities for hidden valuables or messages.[166] Men often had to drop their trousers and underwear to have their genitals inspected. If a man had been circumcised, he was considered a Jew. The sources indicate that the soldiers would also touch the men with weapons or canes, sometimes using them to lift their victim's penis for closer examination. This activity could also be accompanied by comments about the size of the sex organ or about the man's body.[167]

One special facet of the Germans' anti-partisan operations involved the treatment of women carrying weapons. It is estimated that there were a total of around one million women in the partisan units and the Red Army, about half of whom were armed.[168] The Belarusian staff of the partisan movement reported that the proportion of women in the Belarusian units in 1946 was 7.83 per cent.[169] While German soldiers may have occasionally shown respect for their male opponents, this generally did not apply to women bearing arms.[170] Armed women were typically a special source of irritation and provocation when it came to the masculine self-perception of the soldiers. The witness statements, diaries, letters and photographs of German soldiers reveal that, in the eyes of many of these men, female combatants were unnatural, savage and dangerous, but also fascinating – not least on account of the cliché that fighting women were sexually passionate.[171]

One former Wehrmacht soldier who visited the *War of Annihilation: Crimes of the Wehrmacht 1941–1944* exhibition in Vienna in 1995 found the idea of an armed Russian woman unsettling even fifty years after the end of the war:

> Much of what I've seen here today [in the exhibition] I witnessed myself, but I never saw anything happening that wasn't really . . . that happened without genuine reason. We never did anything out of malice, hatred or for kicks, or any other reason. That there were perhaps liquidations, behind the lines, we never heard anything like that. I really can't say. I can't say yes or no. I was in Russia, at the front and behind the lines, but I never heard anything about atrocities. Perhaps in some places, where there were several . . . where there were units that . . . What we found so terrible, was when a . . . a company of

Fig. 18 Anonymous album, female Red Army soldiers, Soviet Union, undated

women soldiers, where women were fighting ... that was so dreadful. Just dreadful.

How was that? Do you remember where that was?

Yes, I mean, for a woman ... it was so completely alien to us, against our concept of military order. We once witnessed ... My god, at the edge of the road there was a Russian woman in uniform. Her trousers had been taken off, her legs splayed apart, and she'd been dumped like that in the road. That was behavior which ... among rampaging soldiery ... after all, we were all men together ... could somehow spill over into hatred, lack of understanding and rage. Quite easily.

That means she was . . .
She had been shot.[172]

In view of the crimes documented in the exhibition, this former soldier apparently felt obliged to distance himself to the extent that he claimed to have 'never heard anything about atrocities'. The only crime about which he volunteers any information relates to the body of a 'Russian woman in uniform' displayed in an overtly sexual pose – and he tries to explain the way German soldiers had treated her by asserting that a 'company of women soldiers' had been against their 'concept of military order'. Indeed, during World War II, women fighting with the partisans and Red Army had broken into the exclusively male domain of the military.[173] This threatened both the character of the military as a 'place where masculinity is produced' (Ruth Seifert) and the stability of gender-specific power relations.[174] As the interview continues, the former soldier relativises the fact that German women were also deployed in every operational zone of the war as part of the retinue of the Wehrmacht and SS by saying that these *'Blitzmädels'* (signal girls, a term generally used for female Wehrmacht auxiliaries) were 'sometimes exposed to considerable danger, but they were never armed'.[175] This veteran therefore follows the official line of the Wehrmacht and SS, who carefully crafted the image of women as *Helferinnen* (auxiliaries) who were not actively involved in the fighting.[176]

Other accounts, too, indicate that the Wehrmacht and Security Police sometimes exhibited a special hatred for female partisans. Wendy Lower describes the case of one of the few female partisan leaders, Maria Kondratenko, who was persecuted with particular determination and disproportionate intensity by the German police in Ukraine.[177] Another interesting source is the protocols of conversations between German prisoners of war (POW) that were secretly recorded by the Allies in POW camps in Great Britain and the United States. Here the soldiers and SS men talked to each other idly and could not have even remotely imagined that their narratives would ever be used as a 'source' for explaining anything. They talked about the war and their impressions in real time, and we can assume that young men in particular also spoke about women and sex. Unfortunately, the Allies seldom considered this relevant enough to be recorded and transcribed, as one of the surveillance protocols indicates:

18:45   Women
19:15   Women

19:45   Women
20:00   Women[178]

Nevertheless, a number of such stories were actually noted down. As Sönke Neitzel and Harald Welzer show, these narratives reveal the intrinsic meaning of sexuality for the soldiers' understanding of themselves as military men.[179] On 22 March 1945, *Hauptmann* Franz Reimbold told a fellow prisoner with horror about the cruel maltreatment and murder of a woman who had been identified as a spy:

> In the first officers' quarters where I was held prisoner, there was a very stupid young lieutenant from Frankfurt, a real snot-nose. Eight of us were sitting around a table talking about Russia. And he said: 'We got hold of a female spy who was running around in the area. We hit her on the noggin [actually '*Äppelchen*' or 'little apples' in the original German; R. M.] with a stick and then flayed her behind with an unsheathed bayonet. Then we fucked her, threw her out, shot at her and, while she was lying on her back, lobbed grenades. Every time we got one close, she screamed. In the end, she died, and we threw her body away.' And imagine this! There were eight German officers sitting at the table with me all laughing their heads off. I couldn't stand it. I got up and said, 'Gentlemen, this goes too far.'[180]

Reimbold did not witness this act of sexual violence, he recounts a story he heard previously from a young lieutenant in another POW camp. Of course, this lieutenant might have embellished the details, bragging about his unflinching masculinity. Looking at the ensemble of sources, however, we can safely assume that incidents like this did happen.

It is noteworthy that this story did not elicit any particular reaction from the other officers. Apparently, they did not consider the cruelty towards the woman to be remarkable or unacceptable (or they did not dare to say so). In Reimbold's depiction, the officers show no sign of irritation and even seem to enjoy themselves. We have to take into consideration that Reimbold depicts the young Frankfurt lieutenant and the German officers as contrasting figures whose negative behaviour makes his own integrity all the more visible. Indeed, Reimbold himself exploited the shocking, pornographic story to make an impression on his interlocutor. Nevertheless, he seems to have been genuinely appalled by the story and wants to share his disgust.

When Reimbold had arrived at Fort Hunt, he was initially relieved to find that he could once again say 'whatever comes into your head' (this was a misjudgement, however, as he was beaten up some time later by a group of Nazis imprisoned in the same camp).[181] This indicates that Reimbold had often kept quiet about his opinions during the war situation before he was captured. Such different positions within the Wehrmacht units did not necessarily lead to a corrosion or lack of cohesion in the small units. On the contrary, in an institutional culture of hardened hypermasculinity, those who refuse to actively participate have a distinct function. As Thomas Kühne has shown, they bring the culturally shared and accepted ideal of hegemonic masculinity into sharp focus. Following Thomas Kühne, we can see that the silent but, ultimately, complicit bystanders not only facilitate but also empower the violent, hegemonic performances of military masculinity.[182] The fact that many men criticised the violence against women did not mean that they were not part of the setting for such violence.

Female relatives of men thought to be in the resistance were also generally suspected of supporting partisans and were quite often interrogated, imprisoned, tortured and murdered.[183] When female partisans or women suspected of helping partisans were taken prisoner by the Germans, the soldiers were allowed to torture them 'using all available means'.[184] None of the accounts found thus far from female former partisans in the Soviet Union address the sexual aspects of such torture, but we must assume that nudity and sexual humiliation played a major role – such as when women were forced to sit naked in the interrogation room and be questioned in front of multiple squad members.[185] Some witnesses in the Italian theatre of operations did report cases of rape during such interrogations.[186] In Russia, a female former partisan recalled enduring a 'fascist manicure', an extremely painful form of torture which involved needles being pushed under all of her fingernails at once. Reina Pennington, who documented this case, notes that rape was not necessarily the worst thing that could happen to a woman who had been captured.[187] Authors such as Marnia Lazreg additionally emphasise that torture always has a sexual dimension because it is associated with a physical and psychological intimacy that necessarily has sexual implications and effects.[188]

Female partisans were apparently occasionally held in women's prisoner-of-war camps intended for female Red Army soldiers, such as those that existed near Bobroisk and Baranovichi[189] (Belarus).[190] Women who were taken prisoner as *Flintenweiber* (a derogatory term literally meaning 'riflewomen') have recalled that members of the Security Service ripped the clothes from their bodies and took photographs of them naked.[191] I am not aware of any similar accounts from men. In general, the Wehrmacht viewed neither female partisans nor female Red Army soldiers as regular prisoners of war. German war propaganda spread stereotypes about the 'bestialised riflewomen' amongst the Bolshevists,[192] and in 1941 the OKW ordered female soldiers to be shot immediately after interrogation or handed over to the Security Police and Security Service.[193] It is apparent here that the military leadership viewed fighting women as a specific threat. They feared that soldiers would naïvely trust these women and not be aware that they might be dealing with spies or armed combatants.

Many partisan groups did, in fact, take advantage of the prevailing notions of femininity and opted to send young, harmless-looking women on what were often dangerous espionage missions and errands. The Soviet leadership also actively recruited women for the partisan movement. Belarusian partisan units mainly used women as reconnaissance scouts and couriers.[194] It was assumed that they would not be stopped as often when passing through military checkpoints and could distract the Germans if necessary by using their 'feminine charms'.[195]

The Wehrmacht and SS responded to this tactic. On 8 October 1941, the 2nd SS Infantry Brigade warned: 'The enemy is primarily using old men, women and children as agents [...]. These elements must be done away with using all available means.'[196] A leaflet for local commanders advised that female civilians who were encountered outside of towns should be checked thoroughly.[197] The 6th Infantry Division was instructed to carry out body searches if necessary, because young women in particular were known to hide the evidence of their espionage activity in their underwear.[198] Multiple reports exist of German soldiers groping women under their clothing during such searches, making derogatory comments while fondling their naked bodies, and scratching their breasts.[199] While the men had been instructed to check the women thoroughly, they had not been ordered to squeeze the women's nipples or grope their genitals. It is clear here that the men appropriated the regulations in their own 'wilful' way, in the sense of Alf Lüdtke's concept of *Eigen-Sinn*.[200] In an atmosphere in which members of the Wehrmacht, SS and police could never be sure whether they were facing an armed or unarmed woman, the men developed a specific kind of paranoia and animosity towards female members of the Red Army and the partisans.[201]

In this climate, German men could use 'anti-partisan operations' as a pretext for committing sexual violence against local women. For example, Birgit Beck recounts the case of a member of the 6th Panzer Grenadier Regiment. In the summer of 1943, the accused *Obergefreiter* had seen the twenty-two-year-old Russian woman Ekaterina G. near his quarters and demanded that she show him her papers. When she refused, he accused her of partisan activity, forced her to undress at gunpoint and tried to rape her. She resisted, so he shot at her – which prompted the court in his subsequent trial to sentence him to three years in prison for 'baseness' and 'exceptional violence'.[202]

Wolfgang Curilla documents a case from Reserve Police Battalion 65, which was formed in September 1939 and consisted of active-duty police officers and NCOs as well as reservists. When the war against the Soviet Union began, the battalion was ordered to secure the rear area of Army Group Centre and 'cleanse' it of scattered Soviet soldiers and units. Executions were one means of achieving this goal. In mid-January 1942, the battalion's three combat companies were transferred to the front and placed under the leadership of W. G., a police captain and head of the 1st Company. The battalion was stationed at the front until May 1942 in the region of Kholm[203] (Russia), where it was caught up in fierce fighting with the Red Army, which temporarily managed to encircle the German troops. During this blockade, a young woman of about eighteen was held prisoner in the cellar of the 'Red House', where the battalion had its command post. One day, W. G. subjected her to a kind of show trial in the presence of several other battalion members. He accused her of sympathising with the partisans and of having said that 'many German mothers will weep [because their sons were dying in the field; R. M.]'. He then stood her on a chair, hit her and pulled off her underwear. Probing her vagina, he remarked that female spies were known to hide messages there. Finally, he ordered the battalion members present to place their helmets on their heads, and he announced: 'In the name of the Führer, I sentence you to death by hanging.' He ordered police sergeant R. to hang the woman from the door frame. R. refused at first but ultimately followed the order. When the woman did not die immediately, W. G. pulled on her legs to hasten her death. In the course of investigations by the public prosecutor's office in the early 1970s, former battalion members distanced themselves from the sadistic acts of their battalion leader, saying that they had been sickening and unlawful.[204]

As part of their anti-partisan operations, German troops frequently burned down entire villages which had allegedly supported partisans. In some cases, all of the residents were executed in advance. On 22 January 1944, a Wehrmacht unit reached the small village of Bayki northeast of Brest-Litovsk. The soldiers ordered the inhabitants to assemble on the market square, took their valuables and checked their papers. Afterwards they herded all of the residents into three barns, leaving a few men to dig pits at the edge of the village. The villagers were executed in groups. The men were taken from the barn and led to the pit four at a time, while the women, who were expected to resist less, were taken in groups of seven or eight. Eyewitness Nikolai Stepanovich Shabonya, who managed to hide nearby, testified after the war that he had seen the guards pick out individual women from these groups and lead them to a building near the pit. He said the women were raped there and then shot in the house afterwards.[205]

Resistance against the German occupation sometimes prompted German soldiers and SS men to perpetrate demonstrative, ostentatious acts of sexual violence in public. Maren Röger cites some sources that refer to mass rapes during the violent suppression of the Warsaw Uprising in August 1944.[206] This was accompanied by orchestrated sexual violence. When the previously mentioned Dirlewanger brigade joined the Wehrmacht and the RONA (a Waffen-SS brigade composed of Russian collaborators) in Warsaw, they managed to break the line of resistance – a ruthless operation during which Polish civilians were indiscriminately targeted. At least 150,000 civilians died.[207] In 1988, Matthias Schenk, a Belgian of German descent who had joined the Wehrmacht at age eighteen, jotted down his memories of an evening after the Wehrmacht and SS had seized the military hospital, killing all non-German patients and subjecting the nurses to sexual violence, including rape. He remembered a tumult on the square where the gallows had been erected:

> Soldiers of all branches, SS, Ukrainians were whistling and catcalling. And then I witnessed – and I swear that every word is true – an event that is so disgusting and terrible that even today, after forty years, I can hardly describe it. The SS drove the Polish Red Cross nurses naked, hands above their heads, to the gallows. They had put a short shirt on the doctor, put a rope around his neck and pulled and pushed him towards a huge gallows, from which at least ten civilians were hanging. I overheard snippets of words, dirty jokes I don't want to reproduce.[208]

This kind of demonstrative sexual violence could substantiate the taking of control immediately after an attack. Mailänder cites the French anthropologist Veronique Nahoum-Grappe who argues that cruelty has the explicit aim not only of inflicting pain and suffering, but also of degrading the victim.[209] The performative character of such acts of cruelty lies not only in the fact that the perpetrators cross the boundaries of what is considered to be normal; the setting itself attributes an active role to the audience of this spectacle. By tacitly and sometimes reluctantly witnessing such acts, the spectators – comrades and accomplices as well as victims – provided a stage for sexual cruelty. Because the audience tolerated and even actively encouraged the spectacle in part by whistling, catcalling and making 'dirty jokes', the direct perpetrators could feel that their actions were approved and they were entitled to break taboos.

'Final Solution'
From the very start, the war against the Soviet Union was inextricably linked to the mass murder of Soviet Jews. Even in the early days of what was known as Operation Barbarossa, SS and police units following the Wehrmacht regularly shot able-bodied Jewish men.[210] In the subsequent weeks and months, the orders issued to the *Einsatzgruppen* (death squads) – made up of members of the SS and police – were gradually expanded, and a growing number of Jewish men and even women fell victim to shootings behind the front line. Finally, in August 1941, the *Einsatzgruppen* began killing women and children indiscriminately.[211] The first mass murder on a previously unsurpassed scale was carried out at the end of August in Kamenets-Podolsk[212] (Ukraine), where the staff of Higher SS and Police Leader Friedrich Jeckeln and a police battalion murdered over 23,000 Jewish men and women in the presence of several Wehrmacht officers. And at the end of September, the massacre that has come to symbolise all mass crimes under German occupation in the Soviet Union took place at the ravine of Babi Yar[213] near Kiev[214] (Ukraine) where German troops murdered around 34,000 people on 29 and 30 September 1941.[215]

Throughout the occupied territory, Jews were registered by the German military authorities, dispossessed, required to wear identifying badges and made to perform forced labour.[216] In some regions, Jews were driven from rural areas and smaller villages into the nearest large cities. In order to better control the Jewish population in the cities, the German military and civilian administration established hundreds of ghettos, in which the food situation was catastrophic and the hygienic conditions dismal.[217] Hunger, disease, excruciating overcrowding and death characterised the existence of the Jews living in these ghettos, as well as in the labour and concentration camps that were sometimes set up inside the ghettos themselves.

The *'Endlösung der Judenfrage'* (Final Solution to the Jewish question) was disclosed to government officials at the Wannsee Conference in Berlin on 20 January 1942. Once the details of it, including secrecy orders, had been worked out, the SS and police, along with the Wehrmacht in some places, began systematically clearing and liquidating the ghettos. They herded the residents together, took them to sites where Jewish forced labourers had previously dug pits, and murdered them following a standardised shooting procedure.[218] The cooperation between military command authorities, administrators, the SS and the police in these operations was largely seamless. In many places, the Germans could also count on the support of local collaborators.[219] In this context, too, acts of sexual violence were committed.

As I have shown in the section entitled 'Conquest', the prohibition against 'race defilement', which formally forbid German soldiers and SS men from having sexual contact with Jewish women, was apparently not considered much of an obstacle by the men in the Soviet Union. A number of sources show that SS men and Wehrmacht soldiers alike ignored these bans. Detained in a POW camp in Great Britain in 1943, two navy soldiers, the twenty-three-year-old mechanic Helmut Hartelt and the twenty-one-year-old sailor Horst Minnieur, believed they were unobserved – not knowing that the British had installed bugs to monitor the information they exchanged. At one point, Minnieur recounted a killing operation that he had witnessed in Vilnius (Lithuania) while serving with the *Reichsarbeitsdienst* (RAD, Reich Labour Service):

> Minnieur [. . .]: They had to strip to their shirts and the women to their vests and knickers and then they were shot by the 'Gestapo'. All the Jews there were executed.
> Hartelt: In their shirts?
> Minnieur: Yes.
> Hartelt: What was the reason for that?
> Minnieur: Well, so that they don't take anything into the grave with them. The things were collected up, cleaned and mended.
> Hartelt: They used them, did they?
> Minnieur: Yes, of course.
> Hartelt: (Laughs).
> Minnieur: Believe me, if you had seen it it would have made you shudder! ['*Ihnen wäre das Grauen gekommen*'; R. M.] We watched one of these executions once.
> Hartelt: Did they shoot them with machine guns?
> Minnieur: With tommy guns . . . We were actually there when a pretty girl was shot.
> Hartelt: What a pity.
> Minnieur: They were all shot ruthlessly ['*ratzekahl*'; R. M.]! She knew that she was going to be shot. We were going past on motor cycles and saw a

procession; suddenly she called to us and we stopped and asked where they were going. She said they were going to be shot. At first we thought she was making some sort of joke. She more or less told us the way to where they were going. We rode there and—it was quite true—they were shot.

Hartelt: Did she walk there in her clothes?

Minnieur: Yes, she was smartly dressed. She certainly was a marvellous girl ['*schneidiges Mädchen*'; R. M.].

Hartelt: Surely the one who shot her, shot wide.

Minnieur: No one can do anything about it. With . . . like that no one shoots wide. They arrived and the first ones had to line up and were shot. The fellows were standing there with their tommy guns and just sprayed quickly up and down the line, once to the right and once to the left with their tommy guns; there were six men there, a row of—

Hartelt: Then no one knew who had shot the girl?

Minnieur: No, they didn't know. They clipped on a magazine, fired to the right and left and that was that! It didn't matter whether they were still alive or not; when they were hit they fell over backwards into a pit. Then the next group came up with ashes and chloride of lime and scattered it over those who were lying down there; then they lined up and so it went on.

Hartelt: Did they have to cover them? Why was that?

Minnieur: Because the bodies would rot; they tipped chloride of lime over them so that there should be no smell and all that.

Hartelt: What about the people who were in there who were not properly dead yet?

Minnieur: That was bad luck for them; they died down there!

Hartelt: (Laughs.)

Minnieur: I can tell you, you heard a terrific screaming and shrieking!

Hartelt: Were the women shot at the same time?

Minnieur: Yes.

Hartelt: Were you watching when the pretty Jewess was there?

Minnieur: No, we weren't there then. All we know was that she was shot.

Hartelt: Did she say anything beforehand? Had you met her before?

Minnieur: Yes, we met her the day before; the next day we wondered why she didn't come. Then we set off on the motor-cycle.

Hartelt: Was she working there too?

Minnieur: Yes.

Hartelt: Making roads?

Minnieur: No, she cleaned our barracks. The week we were there we went into the barracks to sleep so that we didn't . . . outside—

Hartelt: I bet she let you sleep with her too? ['*Da hat sie sich gewiss hacken lassen noch?*' – 'I bet she let herself get banged'; R. M.]

Minnieur: Yes, but you had to take care not to be found out. It's nothing new; it was really a scandal, the way they slept with Jewish women. ['*die sind umgelegt worden die Judenweiber, dass es nicht mehr schön war*' – 'the Jewish broads got laid in a way that was not nice anymore'; R. M.]

Hartelt: What did she say, that she—?

Minnieur: Nothing at all. Well, we chatted together and she said she came from down there, from Landsberg on the Warthe, and was at Göttingen university.

Hartelt: And a girl like that let anyone sleep with her! ['*Da hat sie sich zur Hure machen lassen!*' – 'she let them turn her into a whore'; R. M.]

Minnieur: Yes. You couldn't tell that she was a Jewess; she was quite a nice type, too. It was just her bad luck that she had to die with the others. 75,000 Jews were shot there.[220]

The young submarine soldiers addressed each other in formal German, so they obviously were not well acquainted with one another. Nonetheless, they talked openly about the executions, extreme cruelty, sexual violence and 'race defilement'. It appears as if these subjects were not taboo or silenced. Instead, the men discussed them matter-of-factly, exchanging experiences and details from the Eastern Front. One can sense that Minnieur had initially been shocked by what he saw. The fact that he had known one of the victims and talked to her about her home in Germany might have further contributed to his wanting to 'shudder'. Ultimately, however, he presented the mass murder as well as the rapes as an unavoidable fate (and not a man-made atrocity) which the victims and perpetrators both had to endure: 'No one can do anything about it.'

The expression '*sich hacken lassen*' – a euphemism for sex that uses the word *hacken*, 'to chop' – reveals that the merging of violence and sexuality appeared natural to the men. It is worth noting that, in all the recorded conversations about sex, the language is characterised by this rough undertone as an assertion of male control. The men used terms like *ficken* (fuck), *bürsten* (screw), *vögeln* (getting a piece of ass), and *hacken* (meaning to 'bang' in this context).[221] Neitzel and Welzer emphasise that this kind of bragging is a 'normal' part of male bonding in non-war times. It is important, however, to decode this language in order to understand how sexual violence is normalised and legitimised, as Gaby Zipfel has pointed out: if a man were to say to a group of buddies

that he had beaten his wife until she collapsed the evening before, he would [. . .] disconcert his audience. However, if he described an incident in which he 'banged [*umlegen*] a woman until she couldn't take it any more', he would probably be able to count on a knowing sense of appreciation from one or the other.'²²²

As a matter of course, Hartelt assumed that female forced labourers were available to satisfy the sexual interests of German men. Minnieur confirmed this matter-of-factly and hinted at the violent nature of such practices; in the original German text, he explicitly notes that the women 'got laid in a way that was not nice anymore'. While he pointed out that sexual intercourse with Jewish women was forbidden, he alluded to the practice that these women were shot afterwards not least so that they could not incriminate the soldiers. What becomes clear is that the practice of mass executions in Eastern Europe and Russia opened up 'spaces of opportunity' (*Gelegenheitsräume*) in which soldiers and SS men perpetrated sexual violence against Jewish women and girls. If these women and girls were to be exterminated, then things could be done to them that would have been unthinkable under other conditions.

The process that led to the extreme conditions revealed by Minnieur and Hartelt was part of the war in the Soviet Union from the very first day. For example, Lwów (then in Poland, now Lviv in Ukraine) had already been occupied by German troops at the beginning of World War II in 1939, but it was then handed over to the Red Army. At the time, Jews made up between a quarter and a third of the population. With the 'annexation' of eastern Galicia to Soviet Ukraine, a rigorous policy of nationalisation and expropriation, prohibitions, arrests and deportations began. In this situation, large parts of the Polish and Ukrainian population started to blame the Jews for the new conditions. The Organisation of Ukrainian Nationalists (OUN) set a strong anti-Jewish course in April of 1941, publicly branding the Jews of the USSR as the 'most devoted supporters of the ruling Bolshevist regime and the vanguard of Muscovite imperialism in Ukraine'.²²³ When the Germans invaded the Soviet Union and eastern Galicia in 1941, Ukrainian nationalists, the OUN and civilians welcomed them with banners and flower arrangements. Shortly after, the Jews were caught in a wave of pogroms. For Timothy Snyder, this was the centre of what he describes as 'bloodlands', the territory of double occupation by Stalin and Hitler.²²⁴ One of the biggest pogroms took place in Lviv. The events are relatively well documented, as some dozen amateur photographers and filmmakers from the Wehrmacht and SS, as well as propaganda photographers, took pictures and films. Gerhard Paul has analysed this material and emphasises the sexual character of the violence that the pictures reveal, which is generally not handed down in oral or written testimony.²²⁵ While some survivors did testify to these events,[226] their descriptions tend to be observations of individual incidents. The pictures, by contrast, reveal the intrinsic meaning of this form of violence.

What the pictures show are different forms of cruelty: situations of public humiliation in which women and men are forced to 'clean up' a public square on their knees; beatings with pieces of wood and iron bars; women being dragged across a square by their hair; women and girls being forcibly undressed; women and men being driven through the streets half-naked; women, half-naked and naked, dragged in front of the camera and displayed as subjects for the photographers and amateur filmmakers. Research has shown that the victims of this violence were Jewish women, girls, men and boys from the Lviv middle class.[227] The perpetrators – apart from some Ukrainian militia members – seem to have been young and middle-aged men who also lived in the neighbourhood. In several photographs and a film sequence, we also see uniformed members of the Wehrmacht with photo and narrow-film cameras 'shooting' the violence, thereby not merely observing but also inciting it.[228]

What this visual material clearly illustrates is that Jews were subjected to sexual violence by their neighbours, who supported and actively collaborated with nationalist militias and German soldiers. The pogrom was a public collective act, and the pictures show crowds of spectators watching the events from the side of the street, including women, some of whom are wearing pretty summer dresses, others dressed in peasant clothing from the countryside. Some people laugh, others take an active part by posing in a demonstrative posture. Only a few behave passively—and only one photograph shows a woman whose face reflects the horror of the events and who seems to distance herself from the spectacle with her gestures and facial expressions.[229]

Five months after this pogrom, the Jewish population of Lviv was forced into a ghetto on the orders of the Higher SS and Police Leader (SSPF) Fritz Katzmann. Here as in other places, the conditions in the ghetto turned women into 'easy prey' for German soldiers and SS men as well as local militias, such as when searches were carried out.[230]

On 25 June 1941, Einsatzgruppe A marched into Kaunas. It carried out multiple pogroms – with the massive participation of the Lithuanian population – in which around 7,800 Jewish people, primarily men, were killed.[231] Two weeks later, the Lithuanian mayor of Kaunas and the military commander ordered the survivors to move within the space of one month to Vilijampolė, a part of the city in which around 12,000 people had lived. When the ghetto was sealed off with barbed wire on 15 August 1941 and surrounded by Lithuanian guards, it held nearly

30,000 registered Jews.²³² Three days after the ghetto was closed off, members of the German civilian administration and the 3rd Company of Reserve Police Battalion 11 began to systematically comb through it. For around four weeks, they appeared in Vilijampolė daily. In the postwar proceedings of the Frankfurt public prosecutor's office against the former head of the ghetto, SS-*Obersturmbannführer* Helmut Rauca, witnesses testified that the search for valuables had involved 'gynaecological examinations' for Jewish women.²³³ Body searches and the fingering of bodily orifices, particularly those of women, were reported from other ghettos as well. The perpetrators were Germans as well as local guards and policemen.²³⁴ Some of the guards watching over the ghettos and gangs of forced labourers ordered women and men to undress and swim, play ball, dance on tables, sing or act while naked. Scenes such as this were reported from various cities.²³⁵ The sexual humiliation of women (and men) seems to have been a distraction and stimulation for the guards in their often uneventful everyday duties.

In Pinsk²³⁶ (Belarus), the German administration established a ghetto for the remaining Jewish population on 1 May 1942.²³⁷ Testifying before the Soviet State Commission for the Investigation of the Crimes of the German-Fascist Aggressors in Pinsk, a rabbi who survived described the crimes of German and local policemen in the ghetto:

> Night. There's knocking at the door, they don't want to open it. They break down the door, three policemen force their way into the house. They illuminate everything with their torches, they're looking for young girls. Mama stands and cries, she pleads and begs to let her daughter go, but the bestial bandit pulls his pistol, he aims at her. Then he orders her to be quiet and rapes her daughter in front of her eyes. Then they leave, beat them bloody and order them not to tell anyone, otherwise they will come back tomorrow and kill everyone . . . This is the start of a series of rapes. The young girls hide, but there is no place they cannot be found.²³⁸

Sexual violence by policemen seems to have been pervasive and resulted in the spread of terror. Raping a young girl in front of her mother conveyed the men's ruthless cruelty to the ghetto's inhabitants. Women lived in fear of becoming the next victim, but there was hardly any way for them to avoid such acts of violence. For one thing, there were limited hiding places in the ghetto, and for another, the women always faced the risk of the Germans retaliating and abusing the rest of the ghetto's inhabitants. In light of the constant threat of death, it is possible that the experience of sexual violence lost some of the tremendous significance it held in normal everyday life. Joan Ringelheim has determined that experiences of sexual violence were played down and blocked out in the memory of female survivors, at least after the war. She argues that Jewish women often lived with the feeling that their experiences of sexual violence were trivial compared to the annihilation of the European Jews.[239]

Some sources indicate that boys and young men also became victims of sexual violence by armed men in uniform. The inspection of the penis in order to establish if a man was circumcised could be humiliating and threatening. Accounts testify to the fact that boys and men were ordered, sometimes at gunpoint, to drop their trousers and underwear and display their glans to uniformed German men and local collaborators.[240] Dorota Glowacka notes that Jewish boys and men also sometimes suffered genital mutilation. She quotes Bernhard Press, a Holocaust survivor from Latvia, who described 'the castration of fifty-six Jewish males, including ten boys aged from eight to fifteen years' during the German occupation of Bauska as one of 'the most appalling, maniacal ideas that National Socialist ideology ever had.'[241] In a diary entry dated 25 July 1944, written during his incarceration in the Klooga concentration camp in Estonia, Herman Kruk noted, 'Today new rumours are spreading: the men will be castrated, the women sent to Königsberg.'[242] As Louise du Toit and Elisabet le Roux have argued, 'Just as female bodies live under the constant threat of rape or other forms of sexual appropriation with impunity because of how patriarchy distributes sexual vulnerability, male bodies live under the constant threat of being feminised or castrated. This is one of the primary ways in which unruly men are either disciplined into, or otherwise expelled from, the privileged patriarchal masculine.'[243] In this way, the Germans effeminated and racialised Jewish men and boys, who thus ceased to be 'real men'.

When Michael Nutkiewicz spoke to S.B., a Jewish Holocaust survivor from Germany, the latter revealed an experience he had in 1941, when he was sixteen years old, in the ghetto in Riga. Two SS men appeared at his family home one evening and asked for him. While his family thought he was being summoned to work for the Germans, the SS men actually took him to an abandoned house where they raped him. S.B. had never told his family the truth. While he thought about this 'one or two times everyday', it was the first time he ever mentioned it to another person.[244] Stories from different theatres of war and armed conflict have shown how difficult it is for men to admit (to themselves and others) that they were raped, as this kind of violence effeminates them. They cease to be 'real men'. Furthermore, the stigma of homosexuality is a contributing factor in the concealment of these kinds of experiences.

Glowacka even claims, 'in conflict settings, attaching that stigma to the victim is often a principal motivation for the assault. Thus, survivors who have lived to tell the story fear that if they do not adequately explain what happened, they will be ostracised because of the association with homosexuality'.[245] Further research is needed to explore the dynamics of male–male sexual violence during the war of annihilation.

In some camps, the guards also forced prisoners to commit sexual violence against each other, as demonstrated by an example from the labour and concentration camp in Koldichevo (Belarus). The Command of the Security Police and Security Service (KdS) established this camp about 20 kilometres north of Baranovichi in December 1941. It held Jewish women and men from local villages and from the Baranovichi ghetto, along with Polish and Belarusian prisoners of war. One peculiarity of the Koldichevo camp was that, apart from a few supervising SS officers, the guards comprised around 100 Belarusian collaborators who were authorised to operate largely independently.[246] The post-war investigation files of the Belarusian public prosecutor's office include a witness statement from a former non-commissioned officer K., who testified that he heard noises one night in the camp's canteen. He discovered a few guards there who were forcing male and female prisoners to have sexual intercourse with one another. The guards beat the prisoners with sticks and ultimately killed them. K., who was their superior, had the bodies thrown out the window and buried the next day in a mass grave. No one responsible for the incident faced any consequences.[247] It is clear from this that acts of sexual violence could also serve to confirm the perpetrators' feeling of total power. The guards tried to coerce a libidinal reaction from the male prisoners so that they would rape the female prisoners.[248]

Another example from Koldichevo cited by Bernhard Chiari demonstrates how German SS officers and local guards took communal voyeuristic delight in the execution of prisoners. The Germans would offer local policemen the opportunity to watch the execution of female prisoners. Before being shot, the women had to undress and endure the obscene comments of the men. According to witnesses, some of the Belarusian guards relished this spectacle. In some cases where the women to be executed were young, a few guards apparently tried to convince their superiors to let them go.[249] The fact that the Germans brought in local guards particularly to watch women (and not men) being shot suggests that this was a deliberate act of male community-building which was achieved through the humiliation, torture and murder of women.

Some accounts indicate that members of the civilian administration also felt empowered to pick out Jewish women from the ghettos and bring them to their quarters. In August 1941, the Wehrmacht handed over the region around the city of Slonim[250] (Belarus) to German civilian administrators. The regional commissioner (*Gebietskommissar*) was Gerhard Erren, a sports instructor from Upper Silesia who had taught classes at the Ordensburg Krössinsee Nazi training centre. Erren was investigated by the Hamburg public prosecutor's office in the 1960s and 1970s. During questioning, he testified:

> The local commander of Slonim had a clique around him with whom he went drinking and played cards. B. from South Tirol also belonged to this clique. He had told us some of what went on, like that he always had to round up Jewish girls when the local commander was drunk.[251]

Excessive drinking, card games and sexual stimulation were permanent factors in the construction of soldierly masculinity, and they shaped the (desired or actual) 'leisure time' of the troops. The diaries of soldiers make it clear that evenings of boozing and card games often involved sexual boasting and obscene jokes as well.[252] In this situation, as we saw in the case of Willi Peter Reese mentioned earlier, the men might get the notion to turn their fantasies into reality. Erren's statement illustrates that this 'leisure time' was certainly not free of military hierarchies. Some superiors assigned their subordinates the task of 'acquiring' women for them. In doing so, they ran a risk of being denounced for 'race defilement' if the women were Jewish, as in the case cited above. But the casualness with which Erren talks about this suggests that the men generally did not have to hide their transgression of 'racial boundaries'. Instead, what we see here is a moment of complicity which could strengthen the cohesion of military units but also create a sense of competition. We can assume that the attitude of the higher-ranking soldiers was largely responsible for how a unit approached acts of sexual violence.

In some situations, Jewish women endured sexual violence in the hope of increasing their chance of survival – by receiving extra food in return, for example. A few sources hint that individual Jewish women offered sexual services to German men in order to save themselves and their family members.[253] The Polish survivor Felicia Berland Hyatt recalls that, in 1942, her mother advised her to do anything at all to save her life in a desperate situation.[254]

The recollections of a former Austrian Wehrmacht soldier, by contrast, imply that Jewish women sold their bodies in order to earn 'a few marks'. In an interview with the filmmaker Ruth Beckermann in 1995, he initially claimed that the soldiers 'didn't know anything about the

Jewish population. We didn't see the Jewish population'. But when she asked him about the existence of ghettos, he responded:

> Jewish ghettos? Yes, I saw some as we marched through. There were proper Jewish stretches, and the sight of them filled me with horror.
> *Were they ghettos that had existed before?*
> No, no, no! They were little towns and villages. On one side of the street were the houses of the Jews, which you could tell by the names or signs, and across from them were the houses of the farmers.
> *And why was that so terrible?*
> Once little Jewish boys came out of the houses and spoke to us: 'Hey you! Come, fuck, fuck.' His sister wanted to be shagged for a few marks, but we didn't do it. We were against Jews somehow. There was latent antisemitism in Austria too. Maybe especially Austria, even before 1938. Scenes like this made the antisemitism stronger.[255]

In the narrative of the former soldier, passing by the 'Jewish stretches' was a cause of 'horror' mainly because he was offered sex. The 'little Jewish boys' are characterised as accomplices of their sister. The fact that he and his comrades did not accept the offer is attributed by the narrator to the 'latent antisemitism' in Austria, according to which he, too, was 'against Jews somehow'. The widespread hatred towards Jewish women and men is held up here as a condition for and evidence of the soldier's sexual abstinence. He goes so far as to claim that 'scenes like this' stoked the antisemitism even more.[256] In fact, his narrative draws on common antisemitic clichés about 'the Jews' as pimps and the masterminds behind prostitution.[257]

A few members of the Security Police and Security Service, by contrast, entertained long-term contacts with Jewish women.[258] In the German section of the Jewish ghetto in Riga, *Oberwachtmeister* Neumann of the uniformed police had a 'girlfriend' whom he regularly visited in the garden behind the house at Berliner Strasse 17. Other members of the KdS Latvia office also met with 'Jewish girlfriends'.[259] In this situation of total dependency and mortal fear, some women apparently developed romantic feelings for their German 'boyfriend'/abductor.[260]

The men, by contrast, mostly did not hesitate to 'get rid of' these women in order to protect themselves, particularly if they were members of the SS or police. Kurt Christmann, who was later head of *Sonderkommando 10a*, had a relationship with a Jewish woman whose parents had been murdered by this same special squad. In the course of the squad's retreat, the woman disappeared. When Christmann was tried in 1971, the Munich public prosecutor concluded that he or his soldiers had shot the woman because she was a witness to his violation of the 'race laws'.[261] Klaus-Michael Mallmann presents the case of *Kriminaloberassistent* (senior criminal police assistant) Walter Thormeyer, who worked for the KdS Krakow. The head of the KdS field office in Mielec had denounced Thormeyer for having sexual relations with his female Jewish informant. Thormeyer subsequently shot the woman, claiming that she had been unreliable. He went unpunished.[262] The Ukrainian Anna Dychkant suspects that women would be executed immediately especially if they became pregnant.[263]

Some soldiers found such behaviour atrocious. In the early 1960s, the Munich public prosecutor's office investigated a massacre carried out in December 1941 near Kerch[264] (Ukraine). Former Wehrmacht soldier Josef F. was questioned as a witness. When asked about the days leading up to the organised mass shooting of Jews in Kerch, Josef F. related what transpired as he was looking for *Hauptsturmführer* Finger in the SS quarters:

> One day, when I was supposed to fetch tablecloths again for Lieutenant S. from *Hauptsturmführer* Finger, I couldn't initially find Finger in his quarters. I was in the SS quarters, a former school or public building in Kerch. Down a long corridor, many doors led to the individual rooms. So I went to the first floor and entered one of the first rooms. When I opened the door, I saw that an SS man was lying on the bed and he had a pretty young girl with him. Since this SS man couldn't tell me where Finger was, I went into a second room. In this room, too, I found another young girl with an SS man. Since I could not get any information from this man either, I went into a third room. In this third room, an SS man was lying on the bed without his uniform jacket, but wearing trousers. Next to him, sitting on the edge of the bed, there was another very pretty young girl, and I saw how she stroked the chin of the SS man. I also heard the girl say: 'You won't shoot me, will you, Franz!' The girl was very young and spoke German with no trace of an accent. [. . .] I waited in this room for *Hauptsturmführer* Finger. [. . .] I asked the SS man whether this girl, who I assumed was a Jew because the Russians weren't nearly as pretty, would actually be shot. The SS man told me that all the Jews would be shot, there were no exceptions. Then I asked him what would happen to the girls I had seen here in these rooms. The SS man essentially said that it was bitter. Sometimes they had the chance to hand these girls over to a different execution squad, but usually there was no time so they had to do it themselves. I was so appalled by this that I have never forgotten it. First these beautiful girls were the playmates of the SS men, then they were murdered by them.[265]

Josef F. was a former Wehrmacht soldier who testified against a former SS man at a time when the question of Nazi crimes and responsibility was a highly contested terrain. Institutional and personal rivalry and guilt were negotiated here. All the same, F.'s testimony is an indication that German men – in particular territories and at certain times – had the opportunity and the power to enslave Jewish women and girls.[266] Because they were about to be shot anyway, they could be raped. According to F.'s depiction, it was only the fact that they had to carry out some of these executions themselves that elicited an emotion from the SS man. He seemed to feel that killing a woman to whom he had revealed himself through sexual contact was a greater burden for him than other executions. This suggests that while he might or might not have felt sorry for the women, he mostly felt sorry for himself.

Various sources show that it was not unusual for Jewish women to be murdered after acts of sexual violence. Yaffa Eliach describes an episode from Ejszyszki (now Eišiškės in Lithuania), where, in September 1941, a local Pole gave the Germans a list of the names of all unmarried Jewish women in the town. The Germans ordered the women to assemble, then led them into a nearby forest, raped them and shot them.[267] Women who managed to escape such situations had to reckon with being sexually exploited even by the people who hid them or gave them food.[268]

The personal accounts of eyewitnesses also explicitly refer to acts of sexual violence during so-called *Judenaktionen* or 'Jewish operations'. Many of them mention nudity, for example, which generally played a major role during mass shootings. Prior to being executed, the men, women and children were ordered to disrobe and line up either in their underwear or completely naked. The guards collected their clothing next to the shooting pits in order to make use of it later.[269]

Regarding the previously mentioned massacre in the Ukrainian city of Kamenets-Podolsk at the end of August 1941,[270] the former commander of a uniformed police battalion told a Soviet commission after the war that the women often refused to take off their clothes. The guards would then tear them off violently, hit the women 'in the face and breasts' and kick them 'in the genitals with their boots'.[271] Similar accounts can be found in numerous reports from other places.[272] Men also sometimes refused to remove their clothing.[273] Male prisoners and even children were kicked in the genitals while the Germans made comments about their fertility. The Russian war correspondent Vladimir Germanovich Lidin reported that an SS man crushed a boy's genitals with his boots while shouting 'Try reproducing now!'[274]

Being forced to undress is always described as especially humiliating in the accounts of the victims.[275] For women in particular, this nudity seems to have been associated with feelings of shame. During the 'evacuation' of the Riga ghetto in December 1941, German troops executed Jews in the nearby forest of Rumbula with the assistance of Latvian units.[276] The young Jewish woman Frida Michelson survived. When the soldiers were not looking, she fell into a pit with corpses and pretended to be dead. She was able to escape the following night. In her memoirs entitled *I Survived Rumbuli*, she describes the procedure before the execution. 'Our column was broken up into sections,' she relates, 'and everyone was ordered to undress. I undressed to my underwear, and then I felt ashamed; there were men standing around, and all I had on was a slip.'[277]

For Michelson, nudity in front of her persecutors was not the only humiliation; exposing her body to the men and women she had lived with for years was also anguishing and embarrassing. As Marion Kaplan has suggested, this was probably especially true for Orthodox Jewish women who had grown up in a culture of strict separation of the sexes.[278]

The victims often had to stand naked for a long time before they were led to the shooting pits. This gave the execution squads an opportunity to indulge their voyeurism.[279] Some men blatantly stared at the naked women and commented on their supposed physical merits and shortcomings.[280] In a number of cases, men would stand at the edge of the pit with cameras.[281] There are also reports of German men stuffing trophies into their pockets, such as women's underwear, 'to remember a beautiful Jewish woman'.[282] The perpetrators' unlimited power in these situations could additionally entice them to live out sadistic sexual fantasies, as illustrated by an example from Poland: during the 'evacuation' of the ghetto in Tarnów on 11 June 1942, an 'ethnic German' shot a Jewish woman and urinated on her corpse.[283]

In some places, women were apparently raped immediately before the mass shootings. *Einsatzgruppe 9* marched into Vilnius in early August 1941, and over the next five months it murdered three quarters of the city's Jewish residents with the assistance of Wehrmacht units and Lithuanian militias (*Ypatingasis Būrys* or 'special squads').[284] On 23 August 1941, the Polish journalist Kazimierz Sakowicz noted that a group of Jewish women had arrived in the suburb of Ponary on a bus from Vilnius. About an hour passed between the women's arrival and 'the first shot'. Sakowicz later overheard a conversation between Lithuanian collaborators who had already participated in shootings. They insinuated that the Germans had spent this hour 'sullying their race with the Jewish women'. Sakowicz thought this was probably jealous gossip on the part of the Lithuanians, who would have liked to carry out these shootings themselves, but he was not certain that there was no truth to the claim. He emphasised that, in any case, the women had been naked before they were executed.[285]

Survivors of the Babi Yar massacre also reported that acts of sexual violence were committed right before the shootings. On 19 September 1941, the 6th Army captured Kiev. The German authorities had known for some time that, with an estimated Jewish population of 150,000, the city was home to the largest Jewish community in the territory of Germany's Eastern campaign. Soldiers from individual front-line units immediately began handing over Jewish men, and some Jewish women, to *Sonderkommando 4a*. On 24 September, bomb attacks were carried out on several buildings in the city centre, including military quarters. Four days later, 2,000 posters were hung all over Kiev calling for the Jewish population to assemble the next day at a road junction in the northwest of the city. From there, the people were forced to walk to the ravine of Babi Yar.[286] Elena Efimovna Borodyanskaya-Knysh recalls how a group of German men attacked a young woman when they arrived at the pit:

> I shall never forget one girl; her name was Sara, and she was about fifteen years old. It is hard to describe the beauty of this girl. Her mother was pulling at her own hair and crying out in a heart-rending voice, 'Kill us together!' They killed the mother with a rifle butt. Taking their time with the girl, five or six Germans stripped her naked, but I saw nothing more than that.[287]

Borodyanskaya-Knysh breaks off her account with the girl's forced nudity, saying that she did not see what happened next. This may or may not be true. It is notable that many accounts of sexual violence break off abruptly like this. The actual act remains unspoken. It occurs relatively often that a specific situation is described *en détail*, while the following act of violence is omitted.[288] Reference is made here to a collective imaginary, drawing on images of sexual violence that the recipients of the account have in their mind. The vision of what happened is left to their imagination.

Dina Mironovna Pronicheva survived this massacre by jumping into the pit before she was shot and pretending to be dead. While queuing up to hand over her clothing and valuables, she lost track of her parents. When she started looking for them, a German in uniform approached her and said 'come sleep with me and I'll let you out'. Pronicheva 'looked at him as if he were off his head and he went away'. She survived, but her parents were shot in the ravine of Babi Yar.[289]

The record of the proceedings of the Brest Regional Commission for the Investigation of Fascist Crimes[290] includes another witness statement that mentions rapes directly before executions. In the first days and weeks of the German occupation, Police Battalion 307 murdered around 4,000 Jews in Brest-Litovsk. In December 1941, the German occupying forces established a ghetto there. The ghetto was 'cleared' between 15 and 18 October 1942. The Police Company Nuremberg (*Polizeikompanie Nürnberg*), members of the SD, Polish guard squads and Police Battalion 310 sealed off the ghetto and rounded up its inhabitants. Many people were murdered on the spot during this operation. The survivors were transported by train to an area near Bronna Góra, around 110 kilometres east of Brest-Litovsk, where they were shot over the following days. After the war, Osher Moiseevich Zisman, one of the few survivors, described the 'cleansing' of the ghetto in a letter she wrote to the investigation commission:

> Through the ventilator I saw the German henchmen taunting their victims before they shot them. Under the threat of being buried alive, the people were forced to strip naked. [...] I contracted dysentery while staying in the cellar and could not get up, but from the ventilator I saw the Germans herd young girls into a shed next to the mass graves and rape them before shooting them. I heard one girl crying out for help; she punched the German in the snout, and in return they buried her alive.[291]

Statements such as this make it clear that rapes were certainly committed in the context of the institutionalised mass murder, even if we cannot conclude from these isolated accounts that rape was an inherent component of the mass shootings.[292]

Negotiations in the Military

On 13 May 1941, six weeks before the invasion of the Soviet Union, the OKW issued the 'Decree on Exercising Military Jurisdiction in the Territory of "Barbarossa" and Special Measures by the Troops' (known as the Military Jurisdiction or Barbarossa Decree), which allowed soldiers to shoot 'suspicious' civilians on the spot merely upon an officer's order. This decree also permitted various forms of collective violence against whole villages. About one month later, on 6 June 1941, the 'Directives on the Treatment of Political Commissars' (known as the Commissar Order) explicitly ordered the Wehrmacht not to take the Red Army's political functionaries as prisoners of war (in accordance with the Geneva Conventions) but rather to summarily execute them. Together with the 'Directives on the Conduct of the Troops in Russia', both decrees laid the foundation for conducting the impending war as a 'battle of annihilation', as Hitler had formulated it in front of his army commanders in March 1941.[293] Even from the perspective of the time, the unlawfulness of the decrees was unequivocal.[294] Ultimately, the Soviet Union was turned into a more or less extralegal territory.

Depending on when and how they were made aware of the decrees, the soldiers who marched into the Soviet Union could take them as an invitation to show no mercy – neither with regard to enemy soldiers nor the civilian population.[295] War diaries and daily division reports reveal that the Germans took hardly any prisoners in the first phase of the war. Instead, they executed enemy combatants – or, more precisely, people perceived as such – on the spot. As Felix Römer has demonstrated, the majority of German soldiers saw these executions as an acid test of their abilities and strength to overcome any doubts or scruples they might previously have had.[296]

The extensive impunity of both decrees did not mean, however, that absolutely everything was allowed at all times. The Military Jurisdiction Decree stipulated:

1. With regard to offenses committed against enemy civilians by members of the Wehrmacht or by its auxiliaries prosecution is not obligatory, even where the deed is at the same time a military crime or misdemeanor.
2. When judging such offenses, it will be taken into consideration in any type of procedure that the collapse of Germany in 1918, the subsequent sufferings of the German people and fight against National Socialism which cost the blood of innumerable followers of the movement were caused primarily by Bolshevist influence and that no German has forgotten this fact.
3. Therefore the judiciary will decide in such cases whether disciplinary punishment will be appropriate, or whether prosecution in court is necessary. In the case of offenses against indigenous inhabitants **the judiciary [*Gerichtsherr*] will order a prosecution before the military courts only if the maintenance of discipline or the security of the forces calls for such a measure. This applies for instance to serious deeds due to lack of self-control in sexual matters [*geschlechtlicher Hemmungslosigkeit*], which originate from a criminal disposition and which indicates that the discipline of the troops is threatening to deteriorate seriously [*zu verwildern droht*]**.[297]

Rather than having a guilty soldier tried and sentenced before a military court, the responsible *Gerichtsherr* (usually the division commander, who was invested with judicial authority) could independently decide to take disciplinary action instead. Only if crimes committed by German soldiers were regarded as dangers to the military discipline or safety of the troops should they be tried before a military court.

Ultimately, this decree reveals that the German military command regarded criminal offences against civilians, including rape and other types of sexual violence, as legitimate and reasonable forms of revenge against 'Bolshevism.' Only if soldiers lost sight of the military aims of the campaign or their efforts to satisfy their personal lusts (for sex or blood) or enrich themselves displayed a complete lack of self-control, then they were to be subjected to the punishments of military justice.

This reading of the Military Jurisdiction Decree makes it clear that it was in no way the intention of Hitler or the Wehrmacht High Command to give German soldiers licence to pillage and rape at will or to take advantage of the mayhem of war to act solely out of individual personal interest or desire. Instead, the decree was designed to exempt German soldiers from punishment for acts normally subject to prosecution if they were carried out in the context of a battle meant to advance the political interests of Germany. In this sense, sexual violence was included in the 'German soldier's kit bag of weapons' (Susan Brownmiller) in the military warfare against the 'Bolshevist enemy'.

The wording 'serious deeds due to lack of self-control in sexual matters' furthermore reveals the assumption, common among both military and civilian policymakers since the mid-nineteenth century, that men could become objects of their biology or be overpowered by their urges. In 1919, for instance, at the meeting of the *Reichsgesundheitsrat* (Reich Health Council) to discuss problems of sexually transmitted diseases caused by returning soldiers, Max von Gruber, president of the German *Gesellschaft für Rassenhygiene* (Society for Racial Hygiene), had argued that 'most men are entirely without will against the power of their sexual urges'.[298]

Some military doctors and psychologists also suspected that the brutality of modern warfare could change the sexuality of soldiers regardless of their class or 'race'. In the wake of World War I, military doctors had diagnosed around 600,000 soldiers and reserve officers as suffering from various forms of 'war hysteria' or 'war neurosis', conditions thought to manifest themselves in impotence and 'perversions' (autoeroticism, uncontrollable masturbation, fetishism, homosexuality), among other things.[299] After surveying veterans, the psychologist Paul Plaut concluded in 1920 that many soldiers were deadened by the brutality and could become addicted to the emotional or sexual sensations they experienced when committing massive acts of violence (bloodlust).[300]

The Wehrmacht took note of such observations. In 1943, the military medicine journal *Medizinische Welt* published an article on 'Sexual Problems in the Field', which examined the connection between the 'male reproductive instinct' and the 'aggressive instinct'.[301] While many soldiers apparently experienced sexual sensations like arousal in battle, the consultant psychologist at the Army Medical Inspectorate registered a growing number of cases in which men complained of impotency while on home leave.[302] Male sexuality was consequently viewed as something uncanny that could unleash uncontrollable energies even in 'healthy', soldierly, strong men. The fact that 'serious deeds due to lack of self-control in sexual matters' were not exempt from punishment according to the Military Jurisdiction Decree – even in the war of annihilation – reveals that the military leadership feared losing control over its soldiers if sexual lust were coupled with extreme violence.

Felix Römer has described in detail how the command authorities of the German army in the East by and large supported the Military Jurisdiction Decree, while many troop leaders feared that abolishing the obligation to prosecute crimes would result in a loss of discipline that would erode their units.[303] When they voiced such concerns, they explicitly mentioned sexual violence. The commander of the 134th Infantry Division, who largely supported the decree, said five days before the invasion of the Soviet Union that the soldiers were not to engage in 'any looting, rape or other filthy business' because 'whoever rapes can also mutiny'.[304] Rape was interpreted here as an individual act that ran counter to the military's sense of community. Sexual desires were effectively seen as a temptation that could incite men to refuse orders or even to desert.[305]

The leaders of the 299th Infantry Division, who interpreted the military jurisdiction decree relatively restrictively, also thought rape was a danger to discipline: 'Discipline and *Mannszucht* are essential foundations for success. Take immediate rigorous action against violations. The strictest intervention is called for immediately in the case of looting, excessive alcohol consumption, rape'.[306] The term *Mannszucht* (meaning masculine discipline and restraint) harked back to Prussian military tradition.[307] A man was considered a good soldier when 'unconditional obedience [. . .] had become habit'.[308] Following this thinking, the ability to subordinate oneself was not innate in all men; it had to be cultivated and perfected instead.[309] Under the Nazis, this concept of masculine (self-)control was linked to the notion of the *Volksgemeinschaft* or 'people's community'. In accordance with this, the 1939 edition of the *Meyers Lexikon* encyclopaedia proclaimed that *Manneszucht* was 'important to the education of the people and success in battle'.[310] Klaus Naumann and Hannes Heer argue that this fusion of military and ideological mobilisation aimed 'to establish the martial spirit as the primary social virtue and thus transform the national community into a military community'.[311] Men who were classified as *fremdvölkisch* ('ethnically alien') or as *artfremd* ('of alien races') were thus automatically excluded from the 'military community'. Consequently, *Manneszucht* was considered an essential condition for military success,[312] while the male sex drive posed a danger – as it threatened to govern a man 'against his will' and cause him to forget his *Manneszucht*.

In light of this, even before the start of the Eastern campaign, some military staff ordered that sexual excesses amongst the soldiers were not to be tolerated under any circumstances. When the military jurisdiction decree was announced within the VI Corps of the Wehrmacht, General Otto-Wilhelm Förster made it absolutely clear to the troop leaders that 'anyone who loots, anyone who rapes, will face a court-martial or special court'.[313] In some units, the commanders also explicitly mentioned the danger of sexually transmitted diseases when the Commissar Order was conveyed.[314]

However, pronouncements such as these were apparently not widespread and did not dissuade the men from committing acts of sexual violence. In August 1941, the 9th Army Command complained of 'alarming signs of a decline in discipline', evidenced in part by the fact that the number of rapes had 'risen' significantly.[315] Rape was also mentioned in some situation reports, often in lists of other offences including looting, livestock theft and excessive alcohol consumption.[316] Troop leaders occasionally commented on such incidents, such as when entire units were implicated in orgies of sexual violence.[317] On 13 November 1941, the 2nd Adjutant of the LV Corps in Kharkiv wrote in his personal notes: 'A Russian woman was locked in the cellar and raped by 6! soldiers, one after the other'.[318]

The military leadership responded to such reports. On 10 November 1941, Field Marshal Erich von Manstein called for 'restraint towards [...] the other sex'. He demanded that superior officers take the 'severest action' against 'lawlessness and lack of discipline' amongst German soldiers.[319] Other orders, too, called for the 'maintenance of *Manneszucht*'.[320] The punishment book for non-commissioned officer A., who was sentenced to ten days' detention in September 1941 for having attempted to rape a Russian woman while intoxicated, indicates that soldiers did sometimes face disciplinary action for violent sexual offences.[321] In general, however, it can be assumed that most cases of sexual violence did not result in disciplinary consequences. Christian Thomas Huber believes that, due to the concerns outlined above, acts of sexual violence were seldom punished with disciplinary action, but were instead immediately prosecuted.[322] However, the research by Birgit Beck and David Raub Snyder into sexual offences brought before Wehrmacht courts suggests that such proceedings were relatively uncommon.[323]

On 5 July 1940, at the beginning of the German occupation of France, Commander-in-Chief of the Army Walther von Brauchitsch decreed that while 'Notzucht' (rape) should indeed be punished, it was necessary to consider that

> during the operations and period of occupation, the soldiers will experience situations that deviate considerably from those at home. Life under entirely different conditions, powerful emotional impressions and excessive alcohol consumption from time to time will lead to the occasional loss of inhibition amongst otherwise reliable and impeccable soldiers. [...] It does not seem feasible to always punish one-time lapses in morality as would be appropriate under normal circumstances.[324]

With this decree, which was also disseminated amongst commanders at the Eastern Front, von Brauchitsch steered against the Wehrmacht courts that had previously sometimes imposed severe penalties on soldiers found guilty of rape.[325] According to paragraph 177 of the Reich Criminal Code, rapists were to be sentenced to imprisonment with hard labour, or to no less than one year in jail if there were mitigating circumstances. When the Special Wartime Penal Code (*Kriegssonderstrafrechtsverordnung* or KSSVO) was introduced on 1 November 1939, paragraph 5a stipulated that the death penalty could even be imposed if *Manneszucht* demanded it.[326] But the military commanders considered such drastic punishments to be counterproductive in the occupied territories. Von Brauchitsch claimed that imprisonment with hard labour was a 'disgrace' that branded a soldier for life, so this was only appropriate when the crime had involved exceptional 'baseness, brutal behaviour and savagery'. The death penalty, then, was called for only in 'exceedingly vicious, rare cases in which the perpetrator acted in an inhumane and bestial way in every respect'.[327] The divisional courts in the occupied territories and the legal authorities that reviewed the sentences took note of this decree, and some of them continued to refer to it explicitly until the end of the war.[328]

As Birgit Beck has shown, many military judges in the occupied territories of the Soviet Union tended to impose relatively light penalties for crimes of sexual violence. While soldiers accused of rape on the Western Front often served sentences of several years' imprisonment with hard labour, perpetrators on the Eastern Front usually got away with a few months to two years in jail. According to Beck, the judges' behaviour reinforced the soldiers' rigorous and brutalising contempt for the population of the Soviet Union, the foundations for which had been laid by the 'Barbarossa decree'.[329] David Raub Snyder points out that sentencing could vary widely between different divisional courts, and some courts on the Eastern Front did impose severe punishments. But in the end, even the soldiers who received harsh sentences usually did not have to serve the whole time. Particularly as the military situation escalated, no one wanted the offenders to be catered to in prison while other soldiers risked their lives at the front.[330]

The fact that soldiers who committed rape in the Soviet Union were often violating the Nazis' 'race laws' seems to have played only a subordinate role in convictions for acts of sexual violence, at least according to the research to date. If the 'race' of the victim was addressed at all during a trial, the judges would focus on assessing the victim's '*Geschlechtsehre*' or 'sexual honour', with a distinction being made between 'honourable' and 'dishonourable' women.[331] In May 1944, the court of the 6th Panzer Division heard the case of nine soldiers accused of raping or aiding and abetting the rape of a Polish woman and a Ukrainian woman. In the first trial, all of the accused received sentences of imprisonment with hard labour or time in jail. However, the author of a legal opinion expressed serious concerns about this and suggested a reversal of the judgement, which he considered disproportionately harsh. In a second trial, the judges imposed much lighter sentences, asserting that the accused had been inebriated and that, in their assessment, though the Ukrainian woman was young, she was already 'morally corrupt'. Ironically, the basis for this appraisal was the fact that she had previously been in a relationship with a Wehrmacht NCO and had frequently met with German soldiers at dances.[332]

Wehrmacht judges passed sentences in accordance with the notion that the 'sexual honour' of women in the Soviet Union was to be considered much lower or of a different quality than that of German women. In one case in Russia, a judge claimed

> that the threat of severe punishment under paragraph 176 [sexual assault; R. M.] is justified by the German understanding of the sexual honour of the

German woman, but this sentence cannot be fully applied when, as is the case here, the injured female belongs to a people who have almost entirely lost the concept of woman's sexual honour.[333]

Even when soldiers raped women who were considered Jews under the 'race laws', the perpetrators rarely faced consequences. Although the previously mentioned leaflet distributed by the OKH on 26 June 1942 to soldiers in the 'occupied Eastern territories' stated that 'sexual intercourse with Jewish women violates the Race Law and will result in legal punishment', this dictum was not followed in any of the trials we know of to date.[334] It must be assumed that these cases were generally never prosecuted – particularly as brutal violence against Jewish women was already the rule, and in most instances the victims were probably murdered after being raped.[335]

If a soldier was actually convicted of rape, the judges would make of point of emphasising in their written decisions that the accused had damaged the military discipline or reputation of the Wehrmacht and thus endangered the success of the military operation. The fear here was that sexual assaults would stoke anti-German sentiment amongst the local population, which in turn could encourage people to join the partisans.[336] In this respect, the focus of the Wehrmacht judges was on the long-term consequences for occupation policy and the military situation. The OKH shared this view. As early as November 1941, the Commander-in-Chief of the 11th Army, General Erich von Manstein, pointed out that 'the conduct of every soldier [. . .] is always being observed' and could provide fodder for enemy propaganda.[337] An OKH leaflet with guidelines for soldierly conduct explicitly advised that 'disregarding the sense of honour of women and girls' would foster a hostile attitude amongst the population, thus increasing partisan support and acts of sabotage and generally compromising the situation of the Wehrmacht in the rear area.[338] In fact, complaints were submitted to German offices by interpreters, for example, who warned that the soldiers' shamelessness would have repercussions for Germany's occupation policy.[339]

The civilian occupation authorities, too, feared the reaction of the local population. In the summer of 1942, the RMbO sent an article on 'The Position of Women in Soviet Russia' to the OKH, which stressed that the pride and honour of Russian women were to be respected.[340] And in May 1943, the OKH noted that the Soviet leadership had called upon Soviet citizens to report all German atrocities, especially rape, so that the information could be used 'for propaganda purposes'. The

OKH said it was therefore all the more important for German soldiers to provide no cause for such reports.³⁴¹

While the growth of the partisan movement was one reason for the Wehrmacht leadership to curb acts of sexual violence and keep them under control, Omer Bartov has shown that the pretence of '"anti-partisan" operations' gave ordinary soldiers 'endless opportunities for committing authorised and unauthorised acts of murder and destruction, robbery and plunder, rape and torture'.³⁴² The increasingly rigorous general orders from the command headquarters were accompanied by demands that the soldiers show 'no mercy' towards the 'Bolshevist sub-humans, not even women and children. Hang partisans and their accessories from the nearest tree!'³⁴³ Wolfgang Petter has pointed out that the order issued in December 1942 by the OKW 'to act ruthlessly, even against women and children'³⁴⁴ could certainly have been taken by the soldiers involved as an 'authorisation to rape women'.³⁴⁵ Subsequent directives opened up similar spaces of action. On 2 April 1943, for example, the 2nd Army High Command suggested to the Army Group Centre High Command that the following line be added to the 'Combat Instructions for Fighting Partisans in the East': 'When interrogating bandits, even women, use all possible measures to get the necessary statements'. One week later, the Army Group Centre High Command adopted this wording.³⁴⁶

Members of the SS as well as policemen, who had in any case already embarked on an ideological campaign of extermination against 'Jews and communists', are likely to have interpreted these kinds of regulations in their own favour and taken them as a warrant to commit acts of sexual violence. On 12 November 1941, Reichsführer-SS Heinrich Himmler demanded to be notified of 'every case of sexual intercourse between members of the SS or police with females from the occupied Russian territories who are not ethnically German, after thorough investigation'. The cases were first supposed to be investigated by way of a disciplinary procedure, without initiating legal proceedings.³⁴⁷ In mid-1942, Himmler revised this order and stipulated that all cases of 'sexual intercourse' – including rape – 'with members of a population of a different race' should be 'legally punished as military disobedience'.³⁴⁸ Whether, how and to what extent cases of rape were actually prosecuted before SS courts has yet to be established.

Fundamentally, however, the men on the ground seem to have assumed that the regulations would be applied relatively loosely in the Soviet Union. For example, in early 1943, several SS men in Minsk publicly declared that the provisions against 'race defilement' only applied in the Reich and had been suspended 'in the East'; tellingly, they faced no consequences for doing so.[349] When he was questioned in 1964, a former member of an SS unit known as 'Butcher Company 34' who had been stationed in Pinsk claimed that he and his comrades had been informed by their company commander 'that the majority of the residents of Pinsk are Jews, and no race defilement should be committed'.[350] However, further hearings revealed that some men clearly did not heed this order, and that SS men regularly raped women in the ghetto without being punished for it.[351] In general, some superior officers appear to have simply accepted that such violent excesses would take place.[352] In May 1943, the presiding judges of the SS and police courts in Poland and the 'occupied Eastern territories' finally decided to advise Himmler to temporarily suspend the prohibition against 'undesirable sexual intercourse' – because otherwise they would have to convict too many members of the SS.[353]

Sexual violence was also a frequent topic of discussion in the correspondence between German and local officials concerning occupation policy. On 30 October 1942, the chairman of the regional administration forwarded the translation of a report to the SD in Vinnitsa[354] (Ukraine). In this document, Ukrainian militiamen reported on the rapes of local women by German soldiers:

> During our watch on 27 October at 10 in the evening, a drunk officer from the agricultural headquarters and the commandant himself came to the militia meeting. They demanded that we find girls for them and gave us a 20-minute deadline, and if we could not find any, they swore to beat us and showed us a whip. We all went into town, leaving only SAWALNIJ Mikola on guard. The unknown officer and the commandant then went to where the weapons were and started to shoot. When we had not come back after 20 minutes, the officer took Sawalnij [. . .] off guard duty and sent him to find girls. Sawalnij went to the cleaning woman Gorelizka, who he brought to the commandant in his flat, where they were drinking. After 10 minutes Gorelizka ran from the commandant, terrified, tattered and crying, we do not know what was wrong with her. After that they came to the militia many more times and demanded that girls be found.[355]

The militiamen complained to their superiors not primarily about the rapes themselves, but about the fact that they had been caught up in them. In accordance with this, the Vinnitsa regional administration did not make any direct accusations, it merely raised the point that, under these circumstances, the SD could not expect 'good work' from the Ukrainians.

Elsewhere the authorities tried to ensure discipline on the part of German officials when it came to dealing with local women. Bernhard Chiari cites a case from Belarus in which German and local policeman conducted interrogations together. The treatment of local women was regulated jointly between the Germans and their Belarusian colleagues in the interests of close cooperation; the German policemen were not allowed to ask 'voyeuristic questions', and 'suspect women' were to be questioned 'chivalrously'.[356]

In some cases, local authorities in the occupied territories accused collaborators of sexual violence. Local mayors repeatedly complained to the responsible regional commissioners about residents who had joined the Wehrmacht or SS as volunteers and then committed acts of sexual violence.[357] It is impossible to prove whether such claims were always truthful or instead served to damage the collaborators' reputation. The staff of the German occupation authorities occasionally responded to such complaints by telling the military units to treat their 'foreign volunteers' better so that they would be less inclined to commit crimes for 'personal gain'.[358]

Acts of sexual violence could also become a flashpoint for institutional differences between the SS and Wehrmacht. On 10 August 1943, the head office of the Wehrmacht sent a letter to SS-*Obergruppenführer* Karl Wolff listing eighteen cases of rape by members of the SS. The letter claimed that, on account of the constant threat of being raped, women were leaving their places of work, fleeing and even joining the partisans. It went on to say that since the local population was unable to distinguish an SS officer from a Wehrmacht soldier, the SS was casting the Wehrmacht's warfare in an unfavourable light. In doing so, the SS was damaging the army's military strategy and jeopardising Germany's victory.[359] This is the same argument put forward by the previously mentioned SS-*Standartenführer* Rohde, who complained that Wehrmacht member Adolf H. had damaged the reputation of the SS and the German police by posing as a policeman during multiple attempted rapes.[360]

From the viewpoint of the soldiers and members of the SS and police, at least, the situation was unequivocal: there were clear prohibitions against sexual contact with women of a 'different race', but they were rarely put into practice. The military leaderships viewed sexual violence as a threat to the military discipline, health and reputation of the troops, but they also considered such violence to be a normal and practically unavoidable part of war.[361] Furthermore, since virility was taken as an expression of soldierly strength, the troop commanders and the leadership of the Wehrmacht and SS alike seem to have largely accepted that acts of sexual violence would take place. The extent to which they approved or disapproved of such acts would have to be investigated on a case-by-case basis. But in any event, the military authorities opened up 'windows of opportunity' (Bernd Greiner)[362] for sexual violence, which the men in the field could 'seize' – particularly since the Barbarossa decree fostered such opportunities.

Whether and how individual men took advantage of these opportunities depended on their respective sexual and gender-specific pre-war experiences, their assessment of the 'women of the enemy', their reaction to the dynamics of violence in the field and the peer pressure in their units. Officers and NCOs, through their hostile, tolerant or complicit attitude, also contributed significantly to whether sexual violence was deemed normal or not in a specific unit. All of this could lead members of the Wehrmacht, SS and police to increasingly consider acts of sexual violence to be acceptable, even if such acts had been unthinkable to many before the war.

In most cases, commanders tacitly tolerated and overlooked sexual violence, in some cases they actively supported and instigated such acts. In either case, this form of violence was part of the everyday military calculations. Sexual violence might not have been explicitly spelled out, let alone ordered, but it was part of military knowledge and thus – at least implicitly – included in operational calculations.

Notes

1. City in southeastern Belarus invaded by German troops on 19 December 1941.
2. Reese, *A Stranger to Myself*, p. 149.
3. Kühne, *Kameradschaft*, pp. 161f.; Kühne, *The Rise and Fall of Comradeship*, pp. 173f., and Steinkamp, *Zur Devianz-Problematik in der Wehrmacht*.
4. Zipfel, 'Ausnahmezustand Krieg?', p. 73.
5. Published in *Trial of the Major War Criminals*, vol. 7, pp. 455ff.
6. The Germans also engaged in propaganda during the campaign against the Soviet Union by spreading stories about the alleged sexual 'atrocities of Jewish Soviet commissars'; see 'Neue Funde: Sowjet-Opfer in Lettland' in the *Illustrierter Beobachter* propaganda magazine, 17 July 1941, and 'Bolschewistischer Blutrausch in Kischinew', *Illustrierter Beobachter*, 10 December 1941.
7. See the summary of witness statements in *Trial of the Major War Criminals*, vol. 7, p. 497, as well as the film shown as evidence by the Soviet prosecutor (*The Atrocities by the German Fascist Invaders in the USSR* [USSR-81], shown on 19 February 1946 to the International Military Tribunal in Delage, *Nuremberg*, documentary film, DVD 2, track 3). Also see the opening statements by chief

British prosecutor Sir Hartley Shawcross, in *Trial of the Major War Criminals*, vol. 3, p. 144, and chief Soviet prosecutor Lieutenant-General Roman Andriyovych Rudenko, in *Trial of the Major War Criminals*, vol. 7, pp. 149, 179, as well as the evidence presented by assistant Soviet prosecutor M. Y. Raginsky, in *Trial of the Major War Criminals*, vol. 8, p. 54. In the Smolensk military district, at least two members of the Wehrmacht, named Gaudian and Müller, were found guilty of numerous rapes ('Verdict of the trial held in the town of Smolensk by the district military tribunal against a group of former members of the German Army', Exhibit Number USSR-87, published in *Trial of the Major War Criminals*, vol. 7, pp. 465ff.).
8. Henry, *War and Rape*, p. 34.
9. *Trial of the Major War Criminals*, vol. 20, p. 610. Also see Manstein, *Lost Victories*, p. 222. The lengths that Manstein went to after World War II to assert a 'purified memory' of the war and rehabilitate the Wehrmacht elite are described by Wrochem, *Erich von Manstein*, p. 109.
10. *Trial of the Major War Criminals*, vol. 9, pp. 564, 361.
11. Such death sentences were the exception, as demonstrated by Beck, *Wehrmacht und sexuelle Gewalt*, pp. 308ff.
12. The Nuremberg Charter listed murder, extermination, enslavement and 'other inhumane acts' as 'crimes against humanity'. Theoretically, rape and other types of sexual violence could have been covered by this formulation and prosecuted had the court followed this interpretation; see Askin, *War Crimes*, p. 163. The text of the charter can be found in *Trial of the Major War Criminals*, vol. 1, pp. 10ff. Regarding the options available under the case law of the time, see the detailed explanation in *The Women's International War Crimes Tribunal*.
13. In fact, there were no female witnesses at the Nuremberg Trials (Moodrick-Even Khen and Hagay-Frey, 'Silence at the Nuremberg Trials', pp. 60f.).
14. Moodrick-Even Khen and Hagay-Frey, 'Silence at the Nuremberg Trials', p. 60.
15. IMTFE Judgment, quoted in Henry, *War and Rape*, p. 38.
16. Henry, *War and Rape*, p. 39.
17. 'Trial of Washio Awochi, Netherlands Temporary Court-Martial at Batavia (Judgment delivered on 25th October 1946)', in *Law Reports*, vol. 13, case no. 76, pp. 122ff. It is interesting to note that enforced prostitution was construed not as a crime against humanity here, but rather explicitly as a war crime. The legal basis for the judgment was article 1, paragraph 7 of Statute Book Decree No. 44 of 1946, which prohibited the 'abduction of girls and women for the purpose of enforced prostitution' (ibid. p. 124).
18. 'Trial of Shigeki Motomura and 15 Others, Netherlands Temporary Court-Martial at Macassar (Judgment delivered 18th July 1947)', in *Law Reports*, vol. 13, case no. 79, pp. 138ff. Also see Möller, 'Sexuelle Gewalt im Krieg', pp. 286f.
19. Regarding the organisation of the 'comfort stations' in which the Japanese Army sexually enslaved up to 200,000 women and girls between 1932 and 1945, see in particular Yoshimi, *Comfort Women* (regarding Indonesia, see ibid. pp. 127f.); *The Women's International War Crimes Tribunal*.

20. Regarding the legal and socio-political battles that have been fought since the 1990s by Asian women who were raped by Japanese soldiers or sexually enslaved at their 'comfort stations' during the war, see Buckel, 'Feministische Erfolge'; Dudden, '"We Came to Tell the Truth"'; Watanabe, 'Passing on the History'; Yang, 'Revisiting the Issue'.
21. Tanaka, *Japan's Comfort Women*, p. 86.
22. Ibid. 110ff., 133ff.; Tanaka, 'War, Rape and Patriarchy', pp. 41ff. This was also true for the European theatre of war (see, e.g., Kuber, '"Frivolous Broads"'; Gebhardt, *Als die Soldaten*; Roberts, *What Soldiers Do*; Lilly, *Taken by Force*).
23. See, e.g., Möller, 'Sexuelle Gewalt im Krieg', pp. 284f.; Mühlhäuser, 'Sexuelle Gewalt als Kriegsverbrechen', p. 33; Seifert, 'War and Rape', p. 58. This view was shared by soldiers in the Soviet Army, as demonstrated by former Red Army member Fyodor Zverev, who appears in the 1992 documentary *BeFreier und Befreite* (*Liberators Take Liberties*), directed by Helke Sanders and Barbara Johr. Zverev says: 'A war is a war. [. . .] A man is still a man, and when the man saw a young woman in front of him, he could feel the need to rape her' (Johr and Sander, *BeFreier und Befreite*, p. 118).
24. On these early theoretisations, see Mühlhäuser, 'Reframing Sexual Violence as a Weapon and Strategy of War'.
25. See, e.g., Brownmiller, *Against Our Will*; Millett, *Sexual Politics*; Griffin, 'Rape: The All-American Crime'; Greer, *The Female Eunuch*; Edwards, *Rape, Racism and the White Women's Movement*; Crenshaw, 'Demarginalizing', p. 158.
26. See, e.g., Schwendinger and Schwendinger, *Rape and Inequality*.
27. See, e.g., Eisen Bergman, *Women of Viet Nam*.
28. See *Rome Statute of the International Criminal Court*. For a precise definition of the different offences, see the Women's Caucus for Gender Justice, *Definitions of Crimes of Sexual Violence in the ICC*. 'Persecution on gender grounds' is now also considered a crime against humanity. For a more fundamental evaluation of the ICC statute and the approach to dealing with these crimes, see De Brouwer, *Supranational Criminal Prosecution of Sexual Violence*, pp. 410ff.; Möller, *Völkerstrafrecht und Internationaler Strafgerichtshof*, pp. 376ff.; Mischkowski, 'Damit die Welt es erfährt', pp. 154ff.
29. See, e.g., Bos, 'Feminists Interpreting Wartime Rape'; Mibenge, *Sex and International Tribunals*, pp. 41ff.; Mühlhäuser, 'Reframing Sexual Violence as a Weapon and Strategy of War', pp. 368ff.
30. Jarvis and Vigneswaran, 'Challenges to Successful Outcomes', p. 35–39.
31. Buss, 'Making Sense of Genocide'.
32. Copelon, 'Surfacing Gender', pp. 246f. See also Mischkowski, '"Ob es den Frauen"', p. 245; Mibenge, *Sex and International Tribunals*, p. 147; Buss, 'Rethinking "Rape as a Weapon of War"', pp. 153ff.; Buss, 'Making Sense of Genocide'.
33. Jarvis and Vigneswaran, 'Challenges to Successful Outcomes', p. 40.
34. My analysis is based in part on the deliberations of Elisabeth Heineman and Dagmar Herzog regarding the coupling of sexuality, racial concepts and

violence; see Heineman, 'Sexuality and Nazism', pp. 55, 65; Herzog, *Sex After Fascism*, pp. 59f.
35. After Lithuania was annexed by the Soviet Union on 3 August 1940, Vilnius temporarily became the capital of the Lithuanian Soviet Socialist Republic. The German occupation of the city began on 23 June 1941 and ended on 13 July 1944.
36. Kaunas was captured by German troops on 24 June 1941 and remained occupied until 1944.
37. Originally a Polish city, Bialystok briefly belonged to the Soviet Union following the Hitler-Stalin Pact before German troops marched in on 27 June 1941.
38. The SS and Wehrmacht captured Minsk on 28 June 1941, just six days after the start of the war.
39. The first German regiment invaded the Latvian capital on 29 June 1941; see Angrick and Klein, *The 'Final Solution' in Riga*, pp. 61ff.
40. While it was strictly forbidden for Red Army soldiers and officers to have cameras (Jahn, 'Vorwort', p. 7), Wehrmacht soldiers were explicitly encouraged to document their 'war experiences' in 'true-to-life snapshots'. However, pictures of weapons, equipment or terrain that could provide information to the enemy had been prohibited since 1 April 1940. Violations of this rule could result in the negatives being destroyed by a soldier's disciplinary superior. Photographs of executions were also strictly prohibited by order of the Waffen-SS; see Reifarth and Schmidt-Linsenhoff, 'Die Kamera der Täter', p. 485; Schmiegelt, '"Macht Euch um mich keine Sorgen"', p. 25. Petra Bopp notes that the men often acquired their cameras through looting (Bopp, *Fremde im Visier*, p. 40).
41. Regarding the situation of the local population prior to the German invasion, see Pohl, *Die Herrschaft der Wehrmacht*, pp. 117ff., 129ff., 135f.
42. Regarding historically evolved nationalist and fascist structures in the Baltic countries, see Hiden and Salmon, *The Baltic Nations*. Regarding cooperation between the Wehrmacht, SS and local nationalists, see Müller, *The Unknown Eastern Front*, pp. 170ff.
43. Epelfeld, 'May my memory keep me from forgetting', p. 366. Regarding such incidents, also see Bortniker, 'We Were in Distress', p. 24, and Feld, 'The Town was Invaded by Germans', pp. 294ff.; Gekhtman, 'Riga', p. 382.
44. Seifert, 'War and Rape'.
45. See, e.g., Essner, *Die 'Nürnberger Gesetze'*, pp. 219ff.; Przyrembel, *'Rassenschande'*, pp. 127ff.
46. See, e.g., the description of the first encounter with German soldiers in Pawlowicz, *I Will Survive*, p. 29.
47. Registering the population is common in the context of military occupation. In the case of the Nazi occupation, however, the lists were used to 'racially' and politically classify people in preparation for corresponding persecution measures; see Pohl, *Die Herrschaft der Wehrmacht*, pp. 134f.
48. 'Hauptamt SS-Gericht, SS-Reichsamt, 4. Sammelerlass', 1.4.1941, order from 19.4.1939, BArch, NS 7/3, pp. 84–129, here p. 90.

49. This will be covered in detail in the next chapter.
50. 'OKH, Merkblatt für das Verhalten der deutschen Soldaten in den besetzten Ostgebieten', 26.6.1942, BA-MA, RH 26-6/67.
51. Simon Geissbühler has started to describe this more systematically for the Romanian soldiers who collaborated with the German Wehrmacht and SS (Geissbühler, 'The Rape of Jewish Women'). The sources indicate that this was true in other territories, too; see, e.g., Podolsky, 'The Tragic Fate'.
52. Testimony of Anton S., former medical NCO with the 7th Company of Infantry Regiment 81, concerning Mogilev (Belarus) in July 1941, ZStdLJV, 202 AR-Z 589/63, vol. 1, pp. 176f., here p. 177, excerpts quoted in Hamburger Institut (ed.), *Verbrechen der Wehrmacht*, p. 153.
53. Cited in Rossino, 'Destructive Impulses', p. 357.
54. Szobar, 'Prosecution of Jewish–Gentile Sex'.
55. Rossino, 'Destructive Impulses', p. 358.
56. Katz, 'Thoughts on the Intersection of Rape and "Rassenschande" During the Holocaust'.
57. Interview with Barbara Stimler, 28 May 1997, IWM, 17475. Stimler had already related a version of the story in another interview in 1988, IWM, C410/004.
58. Regarding the German law, see Kieler, 'Tatbestandsprobleme'. Also see Mühlhäuser, 'Vergewaltigung', pp. 164ff.
59. See, e.g., Inciuriene, 'Rettung und Widerstand in Kaunas', p. 208; the scene described in this account took place later, however, after the establishment of the ghetto in Kaunas. Also see Brusch, 'One Hundred and Six Members,' p. 30.
60. German troops invaded this district capital in what was then western Poland on 6 September 1939.
61. Pawlowicz, *I Will Survive*, pp. 32ff.
62. See, e.g., the statement by *Obergefreiter* Arno Schwager, quoted in Bordjugov, 'Terror der Wehrmacht', p. 62; the diary of former soldier Lothar-Günther Hochschulz, quoted in Heer, 'Einübung'; or the recollections of the survivor Inciuriene, 'Rettung und Widerstand in Kaunas', p. 208.
63. See, e.g., 'In Bialystock', p. 203.
64. See, e.g., Stabholz, *Seven Hells*; *Verbrechen und Strafe*, p. 55. Also see Bergen, 'Sexual Violence in the Holocaust', pp. 182f.
65. Krog, *Country of My Skull*, p. 277. This thinking is driven by gender-specific stereotypes, according to which men control their sexuality while women are at the mercy of their sexuality.
66. See Heer, 'Einübung', p. 420. For a corresponding account from Latvia, see Inciuriene, 'Rettung und Widerstand in Kaunas', p. 202.
67. Testimony of Ella Medalje, 15 January 1979, Sta Hamburg, SB 37, 141 Js 534/60, pp. 6310ff., quoted in Angrick and Klein, *The 'Final Solution' in Riga*, p. 70. Thunder Cross (*Pērkonkrusts* in Latvian) was a Latvian fascist organisation founded in 1933. It is uncertain whether Medalje identified the men accurately, however; Angrick and Klein point out that Jewish witnesses often referred to both Arajs's men and militia men as Thunder Cross members (ibid. p. 69).

Regarding the rape of Jewish women at the police headquarters in the first days after the occupation of Riga, also see Press, *The Murder of the Jews in Latvia*, p. 45. Regarding corresponding cases in other regions, see, e.g., Dean, *Collaboration in the Holocaust*, p. 70, and Birn, *Die Sicherheitspolizei in Estland*, p. 54.

68. See, e.g., 'From the Diary of Doctor Elena Buividaite-Kutorgene', p. 354; Inber, 'Odessa', p. 58; Chiari, *Alltag hinter der Front*, pp. 167, 193.
69. Regarding sexual violence as a means of power and communication, see, e.g., Card, 'Rape as a Weapon', pp. 6ff.; Seifert, 'War and Rape', p. 59.
70. See Gekhtman, 'Riga', p. 382; Sabina Lustig, Testimony #03/8792, Yad Vashem archives, quoted in Ní Aoláin, 'Sex-Based Violence and the Holocaust', p. 53.
71. Goldstein, *War and Gender*, p. 365; Alison, 'Wartime Sexual Violence', p. 77.
72. Seifert, 'War and Rape', p. 56; Pohl, *Feindbild Frau*, pp. 478ff. This process of male bonding carries homoerotic elements that are denied and negated (Pohl, 'Massenvergewaltigung', pp. 67ff.).
73. See, e.g., Röger, *Kriegsbeziehungen*, 180.
74. Pskov (Pleskau in German) was occupied by the Germans from 9 July 1941 to 23 July 1944. For more precise details, see Kormina and Styrkov, 'Niemand und nichts'.
75. Demianova, *Comrade Genia*, pp. 54–9, also quoted in Gertjejanssen, *Victims, Heroes, Survivors*, pp. 297ff.
76. Regarding the central importance of the virginity myth in Russia, see Greku, 'Die Deutschen in sowjetischen Lehrbüchern', pp. 134, 137.
77. Regarding the connection between purity, femininity, nation and honour, see Yuval-Davis, *Gender and Nation*, pp. 6, 44ff.
78. Regarding the tension between hegemonial, authorised, contested and taboo accounts by women, see Lenz, *Haushaltspflicht und Widerstand*, pp. 90ff. Her analysis also shows that the limits of what is authorised can shift on account of social developments (ibid, pp. 224ff.).

    In this context, it is interesting to note that the figure of the helpless, defenceless 'little girl' who was at the mercy of 'many fascists' who raped and killed her played an important role in Soviet textbooks after 1945 (Greku, 'Die Deutschen', pp. 134, 137).
79. Area in western Russia that was invaded by German troops in late September 1941.
80. Jürgen W., 'Tagebuch in Russland', HIS-Arch, NS-O 22, box 4.
81. Ibid. passim.
82. Hockey, 'No More Heroes'.
83. Siebold, 'The Essence of Military Group Cohesion', p. 287.
84. Ibid. box 5. 'Jeziornico' probably refers to the formerly Polish town of Jeziornica, which passed to the Soviet Union under the Hitler–Stalin Pact of August 1939. It is now the town of Ozernitsa in Belarus. Heavy fighting took place in this region in the last week of June 1941.
85. Reproduced in Reifarth and Schmidt-Linsenhoff, 'Die Kamera der Täter', p. 501.

86. The village of Klooga in northern Estonia was captured by the Germans in June 1941. In September 1943, the occupying forces established the Klooga concentration camp, one of a total of over twenty satellite camps of the Vaivara concentration camp. Most of the prisoners were Jewish men and women who had been deported from the ghettos of Kaunas, Vilnius and Salaspils.
87. This picture is held in the image archive of the Prussian Cultural Heritage Foundation (bpk-Bildagentur) and is reproduced in Johr and Sander, *BeFreier und Befreite*, p. 132. There is also a photograph of a naked female corpse in the Heinz Bergschicker image archive. The woman in this photo is twisted unnaturally to the side with her arms above her head, leaving her breasts bare, and there is a long object in front of her stomach, probably an instrument of torture. Unfortunately, it is not possible to determine exactly when or where the photograph was taken; published in Engert (ed.), *Soldaten für Hitler*, p. 131. Regarding similar photographs, also see Gertjejanssen, *Victims, Heroes, Survivors*, p. 272.
88. Reifarth and Schmidt-Linsenhoff, 'Die Kamera der Täter', pp. 499ff.
89. See Jahn and Schmiegelt (eds), *Foto-Feldpost*, p. 121. I would like to thank Gudrun Schwarz for pointing me to this.
90. Regarding the accounts of former soldiers, see, e.g., the memory interview with a former soldier in Beckermann, *East of War*, documentary film.
91. The first German ground troops reached the capital of Zhytomyr province in western Ukraine on 9 July 1941. Regarding the history of the occupation here, see Lower, *Nazi Empire-Building*, pp. 32ff.
92. In Berdychiv, too, members of the SS and police murdered a Ukrainian woman after they had raped her; regarding these two incidents, see ibid. p. 111 and note 38 on p. 245.
93. Region in central Ukraine that was occupied by the Germans in September 1941.
94. Gertjejanssen, *Victims, Heroes, Survivors*, pp. 253f.
95. Verdict of the trial in the Smolensk military district against a group of former German Army members, Exhibit Number USSR-87, in *Trial of the Major War Criminals*, vol. 7, p. 467; Beck, *Wehrmacht und sexuelle Gewalt*, p. 234.
96. See the diary of Fritz Gradner, member of a mountain infantry battalion, from 1 July 1941 (excerpt), published in Mallmann, Riess and Pyta (eds), *Deutscher Osten*, pp. 80ff., here p. 81; report of Jewish survivor Menasche F. from 21 June 1963 (excerpt), in ibid. p. 92; *Trial of the Major War Criminals*, vol. 1, p. 49, vol. 2, p. 63, and vol. 7, p. 494; Pikman, 'The Story of Engineer Pikman', p. 170; Chernyakova, 'Liozno', p. 187; Besl, 'Eröffnungsrede', p. 22.
97. *Trial of the Major War Criminals*, vol. 7, p. 457; Kohl, *Der Krieg der deutschen Wehrmacht*, p. 136; Gertjejanssen, *Victims, Heroes, Survivors*, p. 296; Klausch, *Antifaschisten in SS-Uniform*, p. 114.
98. Gertjejanssen, *Victims, Heroes, Survivors*, p. 296. A similar witness statement was made in connection with the massacre in Kommeno (Greece); see Hamburger Institut (ed.), *Verbrechen der Wehrmacht*, p. 568.

99. See, e.g., 'Neue Funde: Sowjet-Opfer in Lettland', *Illustrierter Beobacher* (Nazi propaganda magazine), 17 July 1941, as well as 'Bolschewistischer Blutrausch in Kischinew', in ibid. 10 December 1941; Boll and Safrian, 'On the Way to Stalingrad', p. 247; Heer, *Tote Zonen*, p. 116; report from inhabitants of Kharkiv submitted to the Central Commission for Investigating the Atrocities of the German Occupiers on the Shooting of Wounded Prisoners of War, with twelve signatures, 12/1943, published in *Wehrmachtsverbrechen*, p. 172.
100. See, e.g., Maeger, *Lost Honour, Betrayed Loyalty*, p. 144; Beckermann, *Jenseits des Krieges*, p. 30.
101. See, e.g., Lentin, 'Introduction'.
102. Regarding the 'triad of violence' between perpetrators, victims and third parties, see Reemtsma, 'Die Natur der Gewalt', pp. 17f. Regarding the communication function of violence, see Reemtsma, *Trust and Violence*.
103. Virgili, 'Le Sexe Blessé', p. 140.
104. Mailänder, 'Making Sense of a Rape Photograph', p. 489.
105. Paul, '"Bloodlands" 41', p. 176; Bopp, 'Images of Violence'.
106. Mailänder, 'Making Sense of a Rape Photograph', pp. 513ff.
107. Ibid. pp. 495ff.
108. Pohl, 'Massenvergewaltigung'.
109. Mitscherlich, 'Zwei Arten', p. 337. See also Reemtsma, *Trust and Violence*.
110. Zipfel, 'What Do Bodies Tell?'.
111. Pohl, 'Massenvergewaltigung', p. 71.
112. Peter Knoch has shown that everyday life (in the sense of familiar experiences) and war (in the sense of extraordinary and critical experiences) are not necessarily a contradiction. Knoch argues that war is integrated into the practices of everyday life, meaning that even existential danger eventually becomes familiar; see Knoch, 'Kriegsalltag', p. 241.
113. The Wehrmacht captured this city in northeastern Ukraine in October 1941.
114. German soldiers invaded this city in central Belarus on 21 July 1941.
115. The German occupation of this city in northeastern Russia lasted from August 1941 to February 1944.
116. Regarding evacuation measures and population numbers, see Pohl, *Die Herrschaft der Wehrmacht*, pp. 122f.; Arad, *The Holocaust in the Soviet Union*, pp. 72ff.
117. Pohl, *Die Herrschaft der Wehrmacht*, p. 124.
118. Regarding the structure of the population in the western part of the Soviet Union, see ibid. pp. 117ff.
119. Hamburger Institut (ed.), *Verbrechen der Wehrmacht*, pp. 287ff.
120. Bartov, *Hitler's Army*, pp. 67ff.; Gerlach, *Kalkulierte Morde*, pp. 260ff.; Oldenburg, *Ideologie und militärisches Kalkül*, pp. 68ff.
121. Quoted in Gertjejanssen, *Victims, Heroes, Survivors*, p. 267.
122. See, e.g., 'Oberbefehlshaber der 4. Panzer-Armee, betr.: Plünderungen', 22.7.1941, BA-MA, RH 27-7/156; 'SS- und Polizeiführer Brest-Litowsk, Lagebericht für die Zeit vom 15. Juni bis 15. Juli 1942', BArch, R 94/6; 'Feld-

kriegsgericht der 7. Panzer-Division, Urteil', 19.8.1941, BA-ZNS, S 269, quoted in Ibid. pp. 109f.; 'Feldkriegsgericht der 7. Panzer-Division, Urteil', 27.8.1941, BA-ZNS, S 243, quoted in Ibid. pp. 110f.; 'Feldkriegsgericht der 88. Inf.-Division, Urteil', 30.1.1944, BA-ZNS, S 313, quoted in Huber, *Die Rechtsprechung*, pp. 112f.

123. 'Anklage zum Hauptverhandlungsprotokoll', 29.5.1943, BA-ZNS, 'Gericht der 6. Pz.Div./19', p. 28, quoted in Beck, *Wehrmacht und sexuelle Gewalt*, pp. 13f.
124. Kozhina, *Through the Burning Steppe*, p. 80.
125. 'Korpsbefehl Nr. 95 Berück Mitte', 1.3.1942, BA-MA, RH 22/230, p. 133.
126. Regarding architecture in Belarus, see Chiari, 'Die Büchse der Pandora', p. 884.
127. See Jürgen W., 'Tagebuch in Russland', HIS-Arch, NS-O 22, box 4.
128. Meiser, *Die Hölle von Tscherkassy*, pp. 141f.
129. 'Feldkriegsgericht der 339. Inf.-Division, Feldurteil', 28.4.1942, BA-ZNS, S 334, pp. 19–25, quoted in Beck, *Wehrmacht und sexuelle Gewalt*, pp. 229, 258; Snyder, *Sex Crimes*, p. 139. Beck mentions two other cases as well: a Wehrmacht soldier in Russia was tried by the court of the 9th Army Corps for the attempted rape of the twelve-year-old daughter of the house (BA-ZNS, S 250), and five members of the Wehrmacht were brought before the court of the 95th Infantry Division for raping a Belarusian women with whom they had been quartered (BA-ZNS, S 150). See Beck, *Wehrmacht und sexuelle Gewalt*, p. 229; for more examples, see Gertjejanssen, *Victims, Heroes, Survivors*, pp. 267f.
130. Pohl, *Die Herrschaft der Wehrmacht*, p. 131.
131. See the witness statements in Gertjejanssen, *Victims, Heroes, Survivors*, p. 293.
132. SS-Sdr. Rgt Dirlewanger, 11.05.1944, BA-MA, RS 3-36/10, cited in Klausch, *Antifaschisten in SS-Uniform*, p. 87.
133. Ingrao, *The SS Dirlewanger Brigade*; Auerbach, 'Die Einheit Dirlewanger'.
134. SS-Sdr. Rgt Dirlewanger, 11.05.1944, BA-MA, RS 3-36/10, cited in Klausch, *Antifaschisten in SS-Uniform*, p. 87.
135. Zipfel, '"Blood, Sperm, and Tears"', p. 9.
136. Mischkowski, quoted in Bergoffen, Bos, Bourke et al., 'Gaps and Traps', p. xxx.
137. Affadavit of W.B., 22 September 1946, IfZ, NO 867, cited in Klausch, *Antifaschisten in SS-Uniform*, p. 86f.
138. 'Niederschrift der Vernehmung des Albin Vogels vom 19.3.1948', IfZ, Zeugenschrifttum 1560, p. 7, cited in Klausch, *Antifaschisten in SS-Uniform*, p. 87.
139. 'From the Diary of Doctor Elena Buividaite-Kutorgene', p. 365. Similar recollections are quoted in Gertjejanssen, *Victims, Heroes, Survivors*, p. 269.
140. See Ida M. B., interview, 1995, USHMM, RG-50.378*0006; 'From the Diary of Doctor Elena Buividaite-Kutorgene', p. 366. See also Bergen, 'Sexual Violence in the Holocaust', p. 181.
141. Gertjejanssen, *Victims, Heroes, Survivors*, pp. 267ff., 274ff.; Cohen and Kagan, *Surviving the Holocaust*, p. 43.
142. Claudia R. L., interview, 16 March 2004, USHMM, RG-50.030*0484; Gertjejanssen, *Victims, Heroes, Survivors*, p. 275.

143. See, e.g., the memoirs of the Latvian writer Agate Nesaule, *Woman in Amber*, pp. 59ff.; Gertjejanssen, *Victims, Heroes, Survivors*, pp. 256f.
144. See, e.g., Interradio AG monitoring service, Sonderdienst Seehaus, Radio Moscow, originally in Russian, 26 September 1943, 15:00–15:15, BArch, R 6/684, p. 101; Interradio AG monitoring service, Sonderdienst Seehaus, Radio Moscow, originally in Russian, 17 November 1943, 17:20–17:40, BArch, R 6/684, p. 61.
145. Quoted in Nolte, 'Vergewaltigungen durch Deutsche im Russlandfeldzug', p. 124. For similar accounts, see Gertjejanssen, *Victims, Heroes, Survivors*, p. 262.
146. 'Leiter des Facharbeitersammellagers Charkow über die ungerechte Behandlung der Ukrainer (Herbst 1942)', quoted in Klee and Dressen (eds), *'Gott mit uns'*, pp. 172–6, here p. 175.
147. Quoted in Nolte, 'Vergewaltigungen durch Deutsche', p. 123.
148. Gertjejanssen, *Victims, Heroes, Survivors*, p. 284.
149. Quinkert, *Propaganda und Terror*, pp. 260ff.
150. Beck, *Wehrmacht und sexuelle Gewalt*, p. 220.
151. See, e.g., 'Feldkriegsgericht der 35. Division, Urteil', 24.10.1943, BA-ZNS, p. 152, quoted in Huber, *Die Rechtsprechung*, pp. 111f.
152. German troops captured this city in southwestern Belarus on 29 June 1941.
153. Intoxication was generally accepted as an excuse and mitigating factor in the prosecution of acts of sexual violence in Wehrmacht courts; see Beck, *Wehrmacht und sexuelle Gewalt*, pp. 266ff.; Snyder, *Sex Crimes*, pp. 219ff.
154. 'SS- und Polizeiführer in Brest-Litowsk, gez. Rohde, Bericht an den Stadtkommissar in Brest Litowsk', copy, 5.7.1942, BArch, R 94/6, unpaginated. See also 'SS- und Polizeiführer in Brest-Litowsk, Lagebericht für die Zeit vom 15. Juni bis 15. Juli 1942', 15.7.1942, BArch, R 94/6, unpaginated.
155. 'SS- und Polizeiführer in Brest-Litowsk, gez. Rohde, Bericht an den Stadtkommissar in Brest-Litowsk', copy, 5.7.1942, BArch, R 94/6.
156. Chiari, *Alltag hinter der Front*, p. 146.
157. Ibid. p. 146.
158. Regarding the multifaceted experiences of the partisans, see Cerovic, 'Fighters Like No Others'.
159. Regarding the establishment of Soviet partisan groups, see Hill, *The War Behind the Eastern Front*, pp. 70ff.
160. Gertjejanssen, *Victims, Heroes, Survivors*, pp. 45ff., 326ff.; Musial, *Sowjetische Partisanen*, pp. 350ff.; Tec, *Defiance*, pp. 156ff.
161. Pohl, *Die Herrschaft der Wehrmacht*, pp. 285ff.
162. Anti-partisan operations were repeatedly used as a pretext for the mass murder of Jews; individual massacres are not the only evidence of this. See, e.g., Longerich, *Heinrich Himmler*, pp. 485, 526, 553; Hamburger Institut (ed.), *Verbrechen der Wehrmacht*, pp. 83, 469ff.; Heer, 'The logic of the war of extermination', p. 97. Hill rejects the interpretation that the fight against Soviet partisans was shaped by antisemitic ideology and language, but he pro-

vides no information to back this up (Hill, *The War Behind the Eastern Front*, pp. 3f.).
163. 'Chef des OKW, gez. Keitel, betr.: Bandenbekämpfung', 16.12.1942, published in *Trial of the Major War Criminals*, vol. 39, pp. 125ff.; 'OKW, WFSt., Kampfanweisung für die Bandenbekämpfung im Osten', 11.11.1942, and 'Befehl OKW', 16.12.1942, published (in abbreviated form) in Müller, *Deutsche Besatzungspolitik*, pp. 136–40. Also see Heiber (ed.), *Hitler and His Generals*, pp. 14ff.
164. Schulman, *A Partisan's Memoir*, p. 65.
165. Regarding the significance attributed to naked helplessness, see Scarry, *The Body in Pain*.
166. Gross, 'The Jewish Community', p. 169; Hilberg, *The Destruction of the European Jews*, p. 191; Mallmann, '"Mensch, ich feiere heut"', p. 123.
167. Many families decided during the war to no longer have their boys circumcised to protect them. See, e.g., the recollections of Anna Dychkant in Desbois, *The Holocaust by Bullets*, pp. 124–8, here p. 127. The historian Emanuel Ringelblum, who documented German crimes while hiding in a cellar in the Warsaw Ghetto until he was discovered in March 1944 and shot, noted that Jews could have an operation to 'reverse' their circumcision, but 'on account of the sexual impairment associated with this very costly operation, it was mostly eschewed'; see Ringelblum, *Ghetto Warschau*, p. 119.
168. Conze and Fieseler, 'Soviet women as comrades-in-arms', p. 212. Jörg Friedrich says there were around 800,000 armed Soviet women (Friedrich, *Das Gesetz des Krieges*, p. 747). According to Beate Fieseler, the precise numbers are still not clear, but women accounted for at least 8 per cent of the Soviet forces (Fieseler, 'Der Krieg der Frauen', p. 11). Regarding the experiences of women in the Red Army, also see Fieseler, 'Rotarmistinnen im Zweiten Weltkrieg'.
169. Musial, *Sowjetische Partisanen*, p. 329. More recent studies have shown that male partisans rarely viewed women as combatants on an equal footing with them (see Bischl, *Frontbeziehungen*, pp. 139ff.). In fact, former female partisans have reported that women were sexually exploited and raped in the hideouts and camps of the resistance fighters. According to Nechama Tec, partisan units would often only accept a woman if she entered a relationship with one of the head fighters. The Soviet leadership occasionally tried to curb these demoralising and corrupting excesses; see, e.g., Tec, 'Women among the Forest Partisans'; Musial, *Sowjetische Partisanen*, pp. 331ff.; Chiari, *Alltag hinter der Front*, p. 256.
170. See the statement of a veteran in Beckermann, *Jenseits des Krieges*, pp. 103, 107f.
171. See, e.g., Gercke, *Nach Hause geschrieben*, p. 43, also quoted in Schwarz and Zipfel, 'Die halbierte Gesellschaft', pp. 82f.; Marszolek, '"Ich möchte Dich zu gerne mal"', pp. 53f.; Freytag, 'Kriegsbeute "Flintenweib"', p. 32; Schäfer, 'Jedenfalls habe ich auch mitgeschossen', p. 199; Heer, *Tote Zonen*, p. 143. Soldiers in other wars have also described how female combatants were particularly frightening to them because they felt unable to gauge how these

women would act. See, e.g., the testimony of a Vietnam War veteran in Bourke, *Rape*, p. 375.
172. Beckermann, *East of War*, documentary film, available at <https://www.youtube.com/watch?v=l2U4m49mmy8>; also quoted in Beckermann, *Jenseits des Krieges*, p. 126. Also see Schwarz and Zipfel, 'Die halbierte Gesellschaft', pp. 83f.
173. Interviews with female former Red Army soldiers indicate that they sometimes consciously or unconsciously strove to cast off prevailing definitions of femininity. See Cottam, *Women in War and Resistance* and Cottam, *Women in Air War*.
174. Seifert, *Militär – Kultur – Identität*, p. 88. Also see Bopp, *Fremde im Visier*, p. 95. Regarding more recent research into this phenomenon, see Seifert, 'Weibliche Soldaten', pp. 236ff.; Keller, 'Küss' die Hand gnäd'ge Frau'; Yuval-Davis, 'Militär, Krieg und Geschlechterverhältnisse', pp. 28ff.; Barrett, 'The Organizational Construction of Hegemonic Masculinity', pp. 72ff.
175. Beckermann, *East of War*, documentary film, available at <https://www.youtube.com/watch?v=XFflc3H3u6w>; also quoted in Beckermann, *Jenseits des Krieges*, p. 127. Similar interpretations can also be found in the statements of other former soldiers (ibid. p. 135).
176. See Maubach, 'Expansionen weiblicher Hilfe', pp. 96f. Regarding the real deployment sites, activities and self-perception of women in the Wehrmacht and SS, see Maubach, *Die Stellung halten*, pp. 128ff.; Mühlenberg, *Das SS-Helferinnenkorps*.
177. Lower, *Nazi Empire-Building*, pp. 192f.
178. Neitzel and Welzer, *Soldaten – On Fighting, Killing and Dying*, pp. 170f.
179. Ibid. pp. 164ff.
180. Ibid. p. 173.
181. Römer, *Kameraden*, p. 107.
182. Kühne, 'The Pleasure of Terror', p. 242.
183. Pressure was put on these women in an attempt to convince the men to give themselves up. When the German police were searching for a man, they would generally first interrogate his wife, mother or daughters and subject them to severe and brutal treatment (Schäfer, 'Jedenfalls habe ich auch mitgeschossen', pp. 136ff.). In some cases, the Germans would murder family members to dissuade others from joining the partisans. For example, Wendy Lower describes the case of two Ukrainian auxiliary policemen who had been accused of desertion by the German police. During the first interrogation, the Germans shot their wives and children (Lower, *Nazi Empire-Building*, p. 191).
184. Gerlach, *Kalkulierte Morde*, pp. 873, 954, 1108; Streim, *Sowjetische Gefangene*, pp. 107ff.
185. Angrick, *Besatzungspolitik und Massenmord*, p. 150.
186. Interviews with former female partisans in Reggio Emilia and Venice (Italy); recordings in possession of the author.
187. Pennington, 'Offensive Women', pp. 255, 260.

188. Lazreg, *Torture and the Twilight of Empire*, p. 269.
189. Before German troops invaded in July 1941, this city in western Belarus had 12,000 Jewish residents, accounting for about half the total population; see Bauer, 'Jewish Baranowicze in the Holocaust', p. 1.
190. Gerlach, *Kalkulierte Morde*, p. 778.
191. Friedrich, *Das Gesetz des Krieges*, pp. 747f.
192. Freytag, 'Kriegsbeute "Flintenweib"', p. 32.
193. On 29 June 1941, an order signed by Field Marshal Günther von Kluge was issued which stated: 'All women in uniform are to be shot' ('AOK 4, Armeebefehl Barbarossa Nr. 3, in Einzelbefehlen voraus', 29.6.1941, BA-MA, WF 03/15648, pp. 2321f.). On 3 July, the 286th Security Division received a counter-order from the OKH stating that women in uniform were to be recognised as prisoners of war. The orders continued to change, however, and both female partisans and female Red Army soldiers were sometimes persecuted with particular hatred. See Gerlach, *Kalkulierte Morde*, pp. 777f. Also see Schwarz and Zipfel, 'Die halbierte Gesellschaft', p. 85; Heer, *Tote Zonen*, pp. 114f., 228, 286.
194. Musial, *Sowjetische Partisanen*, pp. 329f.; Margolis, *A Partisan from Vilna*, pp. 403f., 417ff. This was common in other places as well. Regarding the activities of female partisans in Yugoslavia, see Wiesinger, *Partisaninnen*, p. 35; regarding Italy, see Weber, *PartisanInnen in Piemont*, pp. 60, 66.
195. Successfully playing with concepts of femininity is a common topos in the narratives of female former partisans. See, e.g., the audio recordings of interviews with female former partisans in Reggio Emilia and Venice, in possession of the author, or Markovna, *Nina's Journey*.
196. '2. SS- Infanteriebrigade (mot), Brigadebefehl Nr. 20', 8.10.1941, excerpts published in Mallmann, Riess and Pyta (eds), *Deutscher Osten*, p. 29. In Greece, too, the Wehrmacht warned against this tactic of 'deceit', which took advantage of the soldiers' 'humanitarian instincts'; see Mazower, 'Military Violence', p. 165.
197. 'Merkblatt für Ortskommandanten', 26.11.1941, BA-MA, RH 26-12/245; also see Beck, *Wehrmacht und sexuelle Gewalt*, p. 222.
198. 'Anlagenband IV zu KTB Nr. 6, 6. Div., Anlage 63, Abt. Ic, Nr. 141/42, geh., 2. Juni 1942', BA-MA, RH 26-6/28; also see Beck, *Wehrmacht und sexuelle Gewalt*, p. 222; Richter, 'Die Wehrmacht und der Partisanenkrieg', p. 845.
199. See, e.g., 'From the Notebook of the Sculptor Elik Rivosh', p. 399; Curilla, *Die deutsche Ordnungspolizei*, p. 176.
200. Regarding the theoretical concept of *Eigen-Sinn* (wilful self-affirmation), see Lüdtke, *Eigen-Sinn*, p. 377, and Lüdtke, *The History of Everday Life*, pp. 313f.
201. See, e.g., Gerlach, *Kalkulierte Morde*, pp. 104, 472ff., 560, 777, 938.
202. BA-ZNS, 'Gericht der 6. Pz.Div./4, Feldurteil', 23.10.1943, pp. 21f., here p. 22, also quoted in Beck, *Wehrmacht und sexuelle Gewalt*, p. 222. Regarding other cases, see ibid.; Cottam, *Defending Leningrad*, p. 90.
203. This small town in southwestern Russia was captured by the Wehrmacht on

3 August 1941 and retaken on 21 February 1944 by the 2nd Baltic Front of the Red Army.
204. 'ZStD gegen Res.Pol.Bat 65', pp. 101f., quoted in Curilla, *Die deutsche Ordnungspolizei*, pp. 185f.
205. Quoted in Kohl, *Der Krieg der deutschen Wehrmacht*, p. 52; Kohl, 'Ich wundere mich', p. 44.
206. Röger, *Kriegsbeziehungen*, pp. 195–197.
207. Borodziej, *Der Warschauer Aufstand*.
208. 'Bericht Matthias Schenk, Brieflicher Bericht an Hans-Peter Klausch', January 1988, quoted in Klausch, *Antifaschisten in SS-Uniform*, p. 114.
209. Mailänder, 'Making Sense of a Rape Photograph', p. 500.
210. See, e.g., Pohl, *Die Herrschaft der Wehrmacht*, pp. 256f.
211. Regarding the development of this policy of mass murder and the continually changing orders that were issued, see, e.g., Longerich, *Heinrich Himmler*, pp. 530–32; Gerlach, *Kalkulierte Morde*, pp. 566f.; Pohl, *Die Herrschaft der Wehrmacht*, pp. 256ff.
212. German troops captured this city at the edge of the Carpathians in early July 1941.
213. On 29–30 September 1941, members of the Wehrmacht, Security Service, regular police, Secret Field Police, Sonderkommando 4a and Einsatzgruppe C murdered more than 33,700 Jewish men and women within thirty-six hours; see, e.g., Pohl, 'Die Einsatzgruppe C 1941/1942'.
214. The capital of Ukraine was occupied by German troops from 19 September 1941 to 6 November 1943. During this time, 120,000 to 160,000 Jews and Soviet prisoners of war were murdered.
215. Regarding the circumstances of these mass crimes, see Pohl, *Die Herrschaft der Wehrmacht*, pp. 257ff.; Lower, *Nazi Empire-Building*, pp. 74, 77.
216. Pohl, *Die Herrschaft der Wehrmacht*, p. 249. Regarding Jewish forced labour in Belarus, see Gerlach, *Kalkulierte Morde*, pp. 658ff.
217. Regarding the establishment of ghettos in Belarus, see Gerlach, *Kalkulierte Morde*, pp. 521ff.
218. The development of this unbounded violence has been described and analysed by many scholars. See, e.g., Wildt, 'Sind die Nazis Barbaren?'; Welzer, *Täter*; Reemtsma, 'Über den Begriff "Handlungsspielräume"'; Browning, *Ordinary Men*.
219. For overviews and studies of individual aspects of the Holocaust in the Soviet territories under German occupation, see, e.g., Hamburger Institut (ed.), *Verbrechen der Wehrmacht*; Hamburger Institut (ed.), *Vernichtungskrieg*; Arad, *The Holocaust in the Soviet Union*; Hilberg, *The Destruction of the European Jews*; Yahil, *The Holocaust*; Pohl, *Die Herrschaft der Wehrmacht*; Krausnick and Wilhelm (eds), *Die Truppe des Weltanschauungskrieges*; Angrick, *Besatzungspolitik und Massenmord*; Longerich, *Heinrich Himmler*; Gerlach, *Kalkulierte Morde*; Curilla, *Die deutsche Ordnungspolizei*; Lower, *Nazi Empire-Building*; Klein, *Die 'Gettoverwaltung Litzmannstadt'*.

220. Quoted in Neitzel and Welzer, *Soldaten – On Fighting, Killing and Dying*, pp. 115f.
221. Ibid. pp. 164–75. This was first observed by Mailänder, 'Making Sense of a Rape Photograph', p. 503.
222. Zipfel, 'Liberté, Egalité, Sexualité', pp. 98f.
223. Quoted in Mallmann, Riess and Pyta (eds), *Deutscher Osten*, p. 79.
224. Snyder, *Bloodlands*.
225. Paul, '"Bloodlands 41"', p. 173.
226. See, e.g., Podolsky, 'The Tragic Fate', p. 101.
227. Paul, '"Bloodlands 41"', pp. 168ff.
228. Ibid. pp. 41, 176.
229. Ibid. p. 174.
230. Podolsky, 'The Tragic Fate'. For similar observations regarding collaboration in Transnistria, see Geissbühler, 'The Rape of Jewish Women'.
231. Mallmann, Riess and Pyta (eds), *Deutscher Osten*, p. 62.
232. Matthäus, 'Das Ghetto Kaunas', pp. 103f.
233. Curilla, *Die deutsche Ordnungspolizei*, p. 156.
234. Ibid. p. 176; Abramowitch, *To Forgive . . . But Not Forget*, p. 65; Tory, *Surviving the Holocaust*, p. 245; Angrick and Klein, *The 'Final Solution' in Riga*, p. 114; interrogation of Hans Mack, head of the KdS field office in Reichshof, from 21 November 1961, concerning 'resettlement' (excerpts), published in Mallmann, Riess and Pyta (eds), *Deutscher Osten*, pp. 105f., here p. 106. We know of a few cases in Poland in which women were forced during these searches to bend over or clean stairs while not wearing underwear as German policemen looked on. This reveals the entanglement of wartime sexual violence and pornographic fantasies. See Republic of Poland/Ministry of Foreign Affairs (ed.), *German Occupation* (1941), p. 21.
235. Interview with Barbara Stimler, 28 May 1997, IWM, 17475; Gekhtman, 'Riga', p. 392; Chiari, *Alltag hinter der Front*, p. 146; Gross, 'A Tangled Web', p. 96; Gross, 'The Jewish Community', p. 169; Porudominskij, *Die Juden von Wilna*, p. 129. *The Black Book of Polish Jewry* documents similar cases from the Warsaw Ghetto; in some of these cases, the women were raped (Apenszlak, *The Black Book*, p. 29).
236. In the summer of 1941, German troops murdered around 11,000 Jews in this city in southwestern Belarus.
237. Half a year later, the ghetto was 'liquidated' on Himmler's personal order (Gerlach, *Kalkulierte Morde*, pp. 715, 719ff.).
238. Testimony of B. R., StA Frankfurt/Main, 4Ks1/71, vol. 107, special volume F, pp. 42f., quoted in Schäfer, 'Jedenfalls habe ich auch mitgeschossen', p. 280. A similar depiction can be found in Pawlowicz, *I Will Survive*, pp. 109f.
239. See Ringelheim, 'The Split Between Gender and the Holocaust,' pp. 343ff. Regarding the questions that such deliberations pose for researchers, see Ní Aoláin, 'Sex-Based Violence', p. 47; Grossmann, 'Women and the Holocaust', pp. 96ff.
240. Mühlhäuser, 'Sex, Violence, Volksgemeinschaft'.

241. Press, *The Murder of the Jews in Latvia 1941–1945*, p. 47, quoted in Glowacka, 'Sexual Violence Against Men and Boys'.
242. Kruk, *The Last Days of the Jerusalem of Lithuania*, p. 697, quoted in Glowacka, 'Sexual Violence Against Men and Boys'.
243. DuToit and LeRoux, 'A Feminist Reflection', p. 9.
244. Nutkiewicz, 'Shame', pp. 1f.
245. Glowacka, 'Sexual Violence Against Men and Boys'.
246. Gerlach, *Kalkulierte Morde*, p. 771; Bauer, 'Jewish Baranowicze in the Holocaust', p. 27; Chiari, *Alltag hinter der Front*, pp. 190ff.
247. Other witness statements verify that rapes often occurred here; see KGB RB, File 19592-9, N.A.K., pp. 55, 57, 62, quoted in Chiari, *Alltag hinter der Front*, pp. 192f. A similar description can be found in Pawlowicz, *I Will Survive*, p. 109.
248. Regarding the instrumentalisation of libidinosity, see Zipfel, 'Ausnahmezustand Krieg?', pp. 70ff.
249. Chiari, *Alltag hinter der Front*, p. 193. For other references, also see Grossman, 'Treblinka'.
250. Regarding the history of this region, the ghettos located there and the executions, see Abramowitsch, *Die Leere in Slonim*.
251. 'LG Hamburg, 147 Js 29/67, Strafsache Erren', pp. 3138f., quoted in Heer, 'Killing fields: the Wehrmacht and the Holocaust', p. 63. The proceedings before the Hamburg State Court ended in 1974 with a sentence of life imprisonment. A similar case is recounted in Schäfer, 'Jedenfalls habe ich auch mitgeschossen', p. 279.
252. See, e.g., Jürgen W., 'Tagebuch in Russland', HIS-Arch, NS-O 22, box 4. Also see Kühne, *Kameradschaft*, p. 132, and Kühne, *The Rise and Fall of Comradeship*, p. 174.
253. See, e.g., Berkhoff, *Harvest of Despair*, pp. 182ff.
254. Berland Hyatt, *Close Calls*, pp. 76f., also quoted in Goldenberg, 'Lessons Learned from Gentle Heroism', p. 84.
255. Interview published in Beckermann, *Jenseits des Krieges*, p. 131.
256. Regarding the trope of the reversal of perpetrator and victim, according to which Jews are responsible for antisemitism because of their behaviour, see, e.g., Haury, *Antisemitismus von links*, pp. 115f.; Achinger, *Gespaltene Moderne*, pp. 41f.
257. See Roos, 'Backlash Against Prostitutes' Rights', p. 79; Herzog, *Sex After Fascism*, pp. 19f.; Henschel, *Neidgeschrei*, pp. 103ff.
258. Angrick, *Besatzungspolitik und Massenmord*, pp. 359, 450; Wilhelm, 'Die Einsatzgruppe A', p. 480; Dean, *Collaboration*, p. 110.
259. See Schneider, *Journey into Terror*, p. 61, also quoted in Curilla, *Die deutsche Ordnungspolizei*, p. 240; Reichelt, 'Profit and Loss', p. 181; Scheffler, 'The Fate', p. 71.
260. See, e.g., the account in Abramowitch, *To Forgive*, p. 53. In their study of sexual violence in concentration and extermination camps, Helga Amesberger,

Katrin Auer and Brigitte Halbmayr discuss cases such as this and relate them to Stockholm syndrome, a condition described by psychologists in which victims develop feelings of affection for those committing violence against them. See Amesberger, Auer and Halbmayr, *Sexualisierte Gewalt*, pp. 43f.; Harnischmacher and Muether, 'Stockholm-Syndrom'.

261. StA München I (Munich Public Prosecutor's Office), 'Anklageschrift gegen Kurt Christmann', 29.9.1971, 22 Js 202/61, p. 5; also quoted in Angrick, *Besatzungspolitik und Massenmord*, p. 450. Other officers in his squad were said to have taken women prisoner and 'sometimes raped the victim until she lost consciousness' (ibid).
262. Mallmann, '"Mensch, ich feiere heut' den tausendsten Genickschuss"', p. 123.
263. Interview published in Desbois, *The Holocaust by Bullets*, p. 126.
264. This city in Crimea was first taken by the Wehrmacht in November 1941. On 30 December 1941, after the naval landing of the Red Army, Kerch became a Soviet bridgehead. In May 1942, the Wehrmacht recaptured the city.
265. Interrogation of Josef F., stationed in Kerch in Crimea in December 1941 with the 46th Infantry Division, speaking on 13 February 1965 about the days before the planned shooting of Jews, quoted in Mallmann, Riess and Pyta (eds), *Deutscher Osten*, pp. 154f.; Source 22 Js 203/61 of StA München I (Munich Public Prosecutor's Office), vol. 7, p. 1665, mentioned in Angrick, *Besatzungspolitik und Massenmord*, pp. 359, 449f. Regarding similar incidents, see Wolff, *Sadismus oder Wahnsinn* (excerpts), published in Mallmann, Riess and Pyta (eds), *Deutscher Osten*, p. 93; Schwan and Heindrichs, *Der SS-Mann*, pp. 114ff.
266. Also see Podolsky, 'The Tragic Fate'.
267. Eliach, 'Women of Valor', section on 'Historical Background', unpaginated. From Czechoslovakia, former Wehrmacht soldier L. reported having heard that a group of girls had first been raped and then shot; their bodies were buried in a mass grave; see Heer, *Tote Zonen*, p. 241. In some places, the Germans apparently specifically demanded lists of all unmarried Jewish women; see, e.g., Gustav Hörmann, 'Das Ghetto in Kowno: Schriftliche Aussage vor der Historisze Komisje Landsberg, 2.9.1946', in Friedmann, *Die Drei SS- und Polizeiführer*, unpaginated.
268. Account of Jewish survivor Bezalel S. about the behaviour of the Ukrainian population in Kremenez (Krzemieniec) during the ghetto liquidation in August 1942 (undated, excerpts), published in Mallmann, Riess and Pyta (eds), *Deutscher Osten*, pp. 44f., here p. 45.
269. As early as the 1980s, Susanne Heim and Götz Aly revealed the extent to which the annihilation of the European Jews followed a logic of utilisation down to the smallest detail (Heim and Aly, 'Die Ökonomie der "Endlösung"').
270. Hamburger Institut (ed.), *Verbrechen der Wehrmacht*, p. 128; Pohl, *Die Herrschaft der Wehrmacht*, pp. 257f.
271. Quoted in 'From the Deposition of Captain Salog', p. 571.
272. See, e.g., 'Ponary', p. 442.

273. Testimony of Rivka Yosselevska during the trial of Adolf Eichmann in Jerusalem on 8 May 1961, quoted in Laska, *Women in the Resistance*, p. 267.
274. Lidin, 'Talnoe', p. 21. In July 1941, 56 Jewish men were castrated in Bauska (Latvia). The men responsible were the local commander Nepil, a native of Vienna; the city's Latvian police chief, Druveskalns; and a doctor named Steinharts, who apparently carried out the procedure; see Press, *The Murder of the Jews in Latvia*, pp. 47f.
275. See, e.g., Grossman and Ehrenburg (eds), *The Complete Black Book*, passim; Kohl, *Der Krieg der deutschen Wehrmacht*, p. 49; Margolis and Tobias (eds), *Die geheimen Notizen*, pp. 57, 59, 106, 113; Lozansky Bogomolnaya, *Wartime Experiences*, p. 30.
276. See Curilla, *Die deutsche Ordnungspolizei*, pp. 248ff.; Angrick and Klein, *The 'Final Solution' in Riga*, pp. 141ff. 155ff.
277. Michelson, *I Survived Rumbuli*, pp. 88-93; quoted in Gekhtman, 'Riga', p. 390.
278. Kaplan, *The Making of the Jewish Middle Class*, p. ix.
279. Welzer, *Täter*, pp. 203ff.
280. Eyewitnesses have repeatedly reported that German men and foreign volunteers would remark that a particular Jewish woman was actually much too pretty to die; see Sutzkever, 'The Vilna Ghetto', p. 251; Curilla, *Die deutsche Ordnungspolizei*, p. 174; Chiari, *Alltag hinter der Front*, p. 193; Margolis and Tobias (eds), *Die geheimen Notizen*, p. 57.
281. See Hüppauf, 'Emptying the Gaze', p. 27; Reifarth and Schmidt-Linsenhoff, 'Die Kamera der Täter', pp. 499ff.
282. See, e.g., Grossman, 'The Minsk Ghetto', p. 133.
283. Statement by Dr Josef K. (undated), BAL, 206 AR-Z 232/60, vol. 2, pp. 230ff., quoted in Mallmann, '"Mensch, ich feiere heut'"', p. 121.
284. Mackiewicz, 'Der Stützpunkt Ponary'; Margolis, 'Einführung'; Tobias, 'Die Massenexekutionsstätte Ponary'.
285. Margolis and Tobias (eds), *Die geheimen Notizen*, p. 57.
286. Hamburger Institut (ed.), *Verbrechen der Wehrmacht*, pp. 160ff.; Pohl, *Die Herrschaft der Wehrmacht*, pp. 259f.
287. Quoted in 'Kiev: Babi Yar', p. 9.
288. Some women who were raped report that they lost conciousness right before the act of penetration. This can describe an actual physical reaction, but it can also be a protective assertion made after the fact; see, e.g., Pawlowicz, *I Will Survive*, p. 36.
289. Anatoli, *Babi Yar*, p. 105. A Ukrainian woman named Petrivna reported that, right before a shooting near Ternivka in Ukraine, 'the German commander' Hummel picked out two Jewish girls from the line: 'They were taken to Hummel's house and were not killed that day'; quoted in Desbois, *The Holocaust by Bullets*, p. 85.
290. The Commission convened after the end of the war and comprised representatives of the Soviet authorities, partisans and residents of the Brest region.
291. 'Brest', pp. 182f.

292. Very little is known about this, probably in part because witnesses who wanted to testify before Soviet investigation commissions were directly threatened by former collaborators (Birn, *Die Sicherheitspolizei in Estland*, p. 83).
293. Hürter, *Hitlers Heerführer*, pp. 5–13.
294. Römer, '"Im alten Deutschland"', p. 57; Römer, *Der Kommissarbefehl*, p. 74.
295. Förster, 'Das Unternehmen "Barbarossa"'.
296. Römer, *Kameraden*, pp. 120–22. Also see Werner, '"Noch härter"'.
297. 'Erlaß über die Ausübung der Kriegsgerichtsbarkeit im Gebiet "Barbarossa" und über besondere Maßnahmen der Truppe', 13 May 1941, with an introduction by Felix Römer, <http://www.1000dokumente.de/index.html?c=dokument_de&dokument=0093_kgs&object=translation&st=&l=de>. English translation published in Trials of War Criminals, vol. 11, pp. 521–3, here p. 522. Facsimile in Hamburger Institut (ed.), Verbrechen der Wehrmacht, pp. 46ff.
298. Timm, *Politics of Fertility*, p. 72. See also Sauerteig, 'Militär, Medizin', p. 202.
299. Kienitz, *Beschädigte Helden*, pp. 271ff.; Crouthamel, 'Male Sexuality and Psychological Trauma', pp. 62ff., 69, 77f.; Bröckling, *Disziplin*, pp. 297ff. Impotence as a consequence of war was a topic of discussion in Great Britain as well after World War I; see McLaren, *Impotence*, pp. 150ff.
300. Plaut, 'Psychografie des Kriegers' (1920), pp. 34, 46f.; Crouthamel, 'Male Sexuality and Psychological Trauma', p. 69. Regarding this issue in the British and French armies, see Ferguson, *The Pity of War*, pp. 357ff., 380ff.
301. 'Wehrmediziner Dr. Joachim Rost, Oberfeldarzt im Stabe eines Befehlshabers, Sexuelle Probleme im Felde', 14.4.1943, published in *Medizinische Welt* (1943), 18, BArch, NS 7/267, pp. 1–6.
302. 'Beratender Psychiater beim Heeressanitätsinspekteur, Sammelbericht Nr. 9', Berlin, August 1944, NARA, RG-242, T 78/R 192, pp. 6135462–83, here p. 6135480.
303. Römer, '"Im alten Deutschland"', pp. 57f.
304. 'Manuskript der Schlussansprache des Kdr. der 134. Div. vom 16. 6. 1941', BA-MA, RH 26-134/5, attachment 7, also quoted in Römer, '"Im alten Deutschland"', p. 67.
305. Koch, *Fahnenfluchten*.
306. 'Befehl der 299. Inf.Div/Abt. Ib, Nr. 14/41, g.Kdos.', 16.6.1941, BA-MA, RH 26-299/29, quoted in Römer, '"Im alten Deutschland"', p. 67.
307. Haase, 'Gefahr für die Mannszucht', p. 47.
308. *Meyers Konversations-Lexikon* (1888), volume 11, p. 198. In keeping with this, the goal of disciplinary punishments for minor infractions was 'the preservation of unconditional obedience and *Mannszucht*' (ibid. p. 616).
309. To use Foucault's terminology, the male individual disciplined himself by applying 'technologies' for his own improvement. The army supplied these 'technologies of the self', and society expected a man to use them because they were associated with the hope of empowerment and increased scope for action; see Foucault, 'Technologies of the Self', pp. 18ff.
310. *Meyers Lexikon* (1939), p. 970.

311. Heer and Naumann, 'Introduction', p. 5.
312. Haase, *'Gefahr für die Manneszucht'*, p. 47.
313. 'Notizen zur Kdr.-Besprechung am 18.6.1941', BA-MA, RH 24-6/27b, pp. 107–119, here p. 108, quoted in Römer, *Der Kommissarbefehl*, p. 169.
314. See ibid. p. 149.
315. 'AOK 9/Abt. IC, Armeebefehl, betr.: Überwachung der Disziplin', 10.8.1941, NARA, RG-242 314/679, p. 649; also quoted in Rass, 'Menschenmaterial', p. 268.
316. See, e.g., 'Oberbefehlshaber der 4. Armee, gez. von Kluge, betr.: Aufrechterhaltung der Manneszucht, geh.', 11.9.1941, BA-MA, RH 21-2/v. 656, also quoted in Krausnick, 'Die Einsatzgruppen', p. 230.
317. '252. ID Merkpunkte für Kommandeur-Besprechung', 14.9.1941, BA-MA, RH 26-252/76; Heer, 'The Logic of the War of Extermination', p. 110.
318. 'Private Aufzeichnungen des 2. Adjutanten (Abt. IIb) beim LV. Armee Korps, Charchow', 13.11.1941, quoted in Hamburger Institut (ed.), *Vernichtungskrieg*, p. 100.
319. 'AOK 11, geh., gez. von Manstein', 20.11.1941, published in *Trial of the Major War Criminals*, vol. 20, p. 643, also quoted in Beck, *Wehrmacht und sexuelle Gewalt*, p. 280.
320. 'AOK 4, Abt. O. Qu./III/IIa/Ic, geh., gez. Kluge, Sonderbefehl zur Aufrechterhaltung der Manneszucht', 11.09.1941, BA-MA, RH 23/127, p. 25.
321. 'Auszug aus dem Strafbuch von August A.', BA-ZNS, 'Gericht der 254. Inf. Div./9', p. III. Regarding a different case, see Meiser, *Die Hölle von Tscherkassy*, pp. 141f.
322. Huber, *Die Rechtsprechung*, p. 244.
323. Also see the discussion of unrecorded cases of acts of sexual violence in Beck, 'Sexual Violence and its Prosecution'; Huber, *Rechtsprechung*, p. 95.
324. 'Oberbefehlshaber des Heeres, gez. v. Brauchitsch, betr.: Notzuchtverbrechen', 5.7.1940, BA-MA, RH 14/v.30.
325. Beck, *Wehrmacht und sexuelle Gewalt*, pp. 161ff.
326. According to the first supplementing regulation to the KSSVO, RGBl. 1939, vol. 1, p. 2131. Regarding the development of criminal offences defined by the Reich Criminal Code, see Beck, *Wehrmacht und sexuelle Gewalt*, pp. 154ff.
327. 'Oberbefehlshaber des Heeres, gez. v. Brauchitsch, betr.: Notzuchtverbrechen', 5.7.1940, BA-MA, RH 14/v.30.
328. Huber, *Die Rechtsprechung*, p. 15.
329. Beck, *Wehrmacht und sexuelle Gewalt*, pp. 247ff.; Beck, 'Sexual Violence and its Prosecution', p. 329.
330. Snyder, *Sex Crimes*, p. 138.
331. Beck, *Wehrmacht und sexuelle Gewalt*, p. 194.
332. BA-ZNS, 'Gericht der 6. Panz.Div./173', pp. 67f.; 'Rechtsgutachten', 2.6.1944, ibid. pp. 91–4; 'Feldurteil des Gerichts des Ersatz-Brigade 999', 12.9.1944, ibid. p. 94; Beck, *Wehrmacht und sexuelle Gewalt*, p. 194.
333. 'Feldkriegsgericht der 7. Panzer-Division, Urteil', 19.8.1941, BA-ZNS, p. 269,

quoted in Huber, *Die Rechtsprechung*, p. 110. Also see Beck, *Wehrmacht und sexuelle Gewalt*, pp. 272ff., 285ff.

334. 'Merkblatt für das Verhalten der deutschen Soldaten in den besetzten Ostgebieten, Anlage 62 zu 6. Div., Abt. 1c, Nr. 169/42, geh.', 26.6.1942, BA-MA, RH 26-6/67, unpaginated. Regarding the secondary importance of 'race defilement' in these criminal proceedings, see Beck, *Wehrmacht und sexuelle Gewalt*, pp. 277ff.

335. Even when a soldier was tried for the rape of a Jewish woman, any suspected 'race defilement' did not necessarily result in a conviction. Beck cites a case from France, for example, in which the accused justified himself by saying he had not known his victim was Jewish. The court found this argument convincing. See Beck, *Wehrmacht und sexuelle Gewalt*, p. 278.

336. Ibid. pp. 251ff., 258f.; Snyder, *Sex Crimes*, pp. 141f.; Huber, *Die Rechtsprechung*, p. 102.

337. 'AOK 11, geh., gez. von Manstein', 20.11.1941, in *Trial of the Major War Criminals*, vol. 34, pp. 129-2, here p. 131.

338. 'Merkblatt für das Verhalten des deutschen Soldaten in den besetzten Ostgebieten, Anlage 62 zu 6. Div., Abt. Ic, Nr. 169/42, geh.', 26.6.1942, BA-MA, RH 26-6/67.

339. Quoted in Scherstjanoi, 'Das Bild vom feindlichen Fremden', pp. 97f. Also see 'Sof. (Z) Anatol Herlitz, Dolm.Ers.Komp. 16, Die Verwaltungsprobleme im Osten', 13.9.1943, BArch, R 93/6, fol 1, unpaginated.

340. 'Die Stellung der Frau in Sowjetrussland', BArch, NS 33/4, pp. 17–23.

341. 'OKH GenStdH, Nachrichten über Bandenkrieg Nr. 1', 3.5.1943, BA-MA, RHD 18/205.

342. Bartov, *Hitler's Army*, pp. 92f.

343. '4. Pz.Div., Parolen des Tages, 18.1. und 4.2.1942, Anlage zum Schreiben der 4. Pz.Div. an das XXXXVII. AK', 20.3.1942, BA-MA, RH 24-47/113.

344. 'Chef des OKW, Befehl zur Bandenbekämpfung', 16.12.1942, in Müller, *Deutsche Besatzungspolitik*, pp. 139–40, here p. 140; also see 'OKW, Kampfanweisung für die Bandenbekämpfung im Osten', 11.11.1942, in Ibid. p. 137.

345. Petter, 'Militärische Massengesellschaft', p. 370, note 50. Also see Beck, *Wehrmacht und sexuelle Gewalt*, p. 223.

346. 'AOK 2, Schreiben andas OK Heeresgruppe Mitte betr.: Erfahrungen über Bandenbekämpfung im Osten', 2.4.1943, BA-MA, WF 03/5365, pp. 849f., here p. 849; 'Oberkommando der Heeresgrupp Mitte, Ergänzungs- und Änderungsvorschläge zu dem Merkblatt "Kampfanweisung für die Bandenbekämpfung im Osten"', 9.4.1943, BA-MA, WF 03/5365, pp. 928f., here p. 929.

347. 'SS-Richter beim Reichsführer-SS und Chef der deutschen Polizei, Schreibn an das Hauptamt SS-Gericht betr.: Geschlechtsverkehr von Angehörigen der SS und Polizei mit einer anders rassigen [sic] Bevölkerung', 12.11.1941, BArch, NS 7/265, pp. 21f.

348. 'Reichsführer-SS und Chef der deutschen Polizei, Schreiben an den Höheren SS- und Polizeiführer Ost, SS-Gruppenführer Krüger, betr.: Geschlechtsverkehr von Angehörigen der SS und Polizei mit Frauen einer andersrassigen Bevölkerung', 30.6.1942, BArch, NS 7/265, pp. 21f., here p. 21.
349. Wilhelm, 'Die Einsatzgruppe A', p. 479.
350. A. K., StA Frankfurt/Main, 4Ks1/71, vol. 31, interrogation from 13.10.1964, p. 6418, quoted in Schäfer, '"Jedenfalls habe ich auch mitgeschossen"', p. 279.
351. B. R., StA Frankfurt/Main, 4Ks1/71, vol. 107, special volume F, pp. 42f., quoted in ibid. p. 280.
352. See Wilhelm, 'Die Einsatzgruppe A', pp. 480, 540, 560.
353. 'Richtertagung in München am 7.5.1943, Bericht und Vermerk zu diversen Besprechungspunkten', BArch, NS 7/13, pp. 1–21, here pp. 7f.
354. City in central Ukraine that was captured by the 6th Army in mid-July 1941. Himmler, as Reich Commissioner for the Consolidation of the Ethnic German Nation, had planned to establish a colony named 'Hegewald' not far from the city, which was to be the core of future German settlements in Ukraine.
355. 'Milizionäre der Machniwski Miliz, Rapport an den Vorgesetzten der Machniwski ukrainischen Miliz, Winniza', 30.10.1941, translation forwarded by chairman of the Vinnitsa regional administration to the German SD Vinnitsa, USHMM, RG-31.011M, reel 1, P-1311c/1c/2 (3.9.1941–18.11.1941), pp. 12f.
356. Chiari, *Alltag hinter der Front*, p. 167.
357. 'The trek of Caucasians and Cossacks from the Kuban region through the area also resulted in many assaults. The mayor of one municipality said the following to me verbatim: "Not only do the Caucasians steal our horses and livestock, they steal our women and girls too!"' ('Gebietskommissar in Brest-Litowsk, Schreiben an den Generalkommissar für Weissruthenien, betr.: Lagebericht für die Monate Januar–März 1944', 21.03.1944, BArch, R 94/8, unpaginated, p. 2 of the document).
358. See, e.g., 'SS- und Polizeiführer in Brest-Litowsk, Lagebericht für die Zeit vom 15. Juni bis 15 Juli 1942', 15.7.1942, BArch, R 94/6, unpaginated.
359. 'Chef des Allgemeinen Wehrmachtsamts im Oberkommando der Wehrmacht, Schreiben an SS-Obergruppenführer Wolff', 2.8.1943, BArch, NS 19/3717, vol. 10, pp. 38–42.
360. 'SS- und Polizeiführer in Brest-Litowsk, gez. Rohde, Bericht an den Stadtkommissar in Brest-Litowsk', copy, 5.7.1942, BArch, R 94/6. Also see 'SS- und Polizeiführer in Brest-Litowsk, Lagebericht für die Zeit vom 15. Juni bis 15 Juli 1942', 15.7.1942, BArch, R 94/6.
361. See Mühlhäuser, 'Between "Racial Awareness" and Fantasies of Potency'.
362. In his study of the Vietnam War, Greiner uses the term 'windows of opportunity' to define the contingent space in which certain actions and decisions take place which would not otherwise be expected or logical given the military circumstances; Greiner, *War Without Fronts*, pp. 13f.

CHAPTER 3

Sexual Transactions

In March 1995, the Hamburg Institute for Social Research opened its travelling exhibition entitled *Vernichtungskrieg: Verbrechen der Wehrmacht 1941–1944* (War of Annihilation: Crimes of the Wehrmacht 1941–1944).[1] The visitors included many former soldiers who had been stationed in the Soviet Union during the war and now suddenly found themselves confronted with their own past. Their expectations and reactions varied. Most of those who spoke publicly complained that the exhibition was a blanket condemnation of all soldiers. But some felt that addressing the long-concealed crimes of the Wehrmacht was a necessary reckoning with the past. The exhibition often seemed to exert a pull on both sides, which filmmaker Ruth Beckermann describes as follows: 'They went there like it was a peep show. And then there was the fear/desire to see whether they would recognise themselves or a friend in one of the photos'.[2] When it was shown in Vienna in the autumn of 1995, Beckermann spent days at the exhibition and asked eyewitnesses for interviews.[3] One of the men she speaks with on camera had been imprisoned before the war for 'resistance against fascism'. He was only released after a childhood friend who had joined the Nazi Party interceded on his behalf; however, he was immediately forced to enlist in the Wehrmacht, where he became a medic. Even in 1995, his comments reflect a critical attitude towards Nazi regime, such as when he speaks of the German 'invasion' of the Soviet Union. When Beckermann asks whether he witnessed any violence against women, he responds:

> I don't think there was ever a rape where I was. The population was starving, so it wasn't necessary. You have to understand: if the women wanted to stay alive, they actually had to prostitute themselves. I saw that on the Kerch

Peninsula, in Crimea. We were assigned to coastal defence there for a while. The railway line that ran in there from Ukraine was very often destroyed. We had very little to eat. There were always children waiting when food was distributed. The soldiers who were a bit sympathetic would give them half their food, even though they didn't have much themselves. They gave the children the pots to wash up. That's what we made it look like, anyway, so the officers wouldn't notice that we were giving the children food, because it was forbidden. There was a sweet girl there, too, and sometimes I gave her mother my dishes to 'rinse out'. I saw a soldier with her and asked her why she was doing that, meaning why she was involved with a German soldier. She said she was doing it because she was hungry. 'But you were just given bread!' I said. She showed me the bread: it was inedible. It was all sawdust and a bit of flour. So the women were forced . . .

  . . . *to prostitute themselves?*

Yes, for food and bread. I never saw a rape. As I said, it wasn't necessary.[4]

The account of this former soldier illuminates the plight in which local women could find themselves, and it highlights the moment of structural violence that prompted some to engage in occasional sexual bartering. The food situation in Crimea[5] (Ukraine) was indeed catastrophic. The 11th Army harboured great economic expectations when it occupied the peninsula (which was one of the Soviet Union's agricultural surplus areas), but it soon realised that the Red Army had managed to carry off grain and livestock and blow up storehouses, mills and food factories. Military requisition measures and unauthorised plundering by German soldiers quickly exacerbated the situation for the local population. In February 1942, fifteen to seventeen people were dying of starvation every day.[6]

The former Wehrmacht soldier interviewed by Beckermann certainly exhibits sympathy for the women who had to fight for survival in this situation. But despite his unusually open and critical perspective, he never actually questions the men's behaviour. As he portrays it, the link between soldiers and prostitution – particularly as distinct from rape – is an unpleasant but somehow natural part of military life. The subtext here is that sexual urges had to be satisfied in this predicament just like hunger. This soldier was drawing on a long history of prostitution and the German military. In Prussia, for example, visiting prostitutes and 'whorehouses' was a regular part of soldierly life,[7] despite various prohibitions against this. In the German imperial army, too, warnings against consorting with prostitutes were rarely heeded. 'Among the soldiers of all ranks and branches of service, it was customary to visit brothels, often together with comrades'.⁸ For many sexually inexperienced men, serving in military barracks became a kind of sexual initiation. When World War I started, soldiers were given a new opportunity for sexual transactions alongside occasional sexual bartering and visiting professional prostitutes: mainly to prevent the spread of sexually transmitted diseases, the army began to establish military-run brothels, with separate facilities for infantrymen and officers, sometimes housed in mobile wagons that accompanied the units as they moved.⁹ In general, the German army's view of the local women in Eastern Europe seems to have been shaped by this approach. German soldiers' newspapers such as the *Kriegs-Zeitung von Baranowitschi* (War Newspaper of Baranovichi) depicted 'Slavic' women as 'whores' and sexually available 'easy-going girls'.¹⁰ Very similar images can be found in the first-hand accounts of German soldiers stationed in Eastern Europe during World War I.¹¹

As demonstrated by the interview with the former soldier stationed in Crimea, the Wehrmacht and its men followed in the footsteps of such traditions. Granted, in 1924 Hitler had written in *Mein Kampf* that the National Socialists were to strictly reject all forms of prostitution, as the 'prostitution of love' was one of the main reasons for Germany's 'decay' during the Weimar Republic.¹² And in the first years after taking power, the Nazi regime cracked down hard on prostitution, not least in order to win over Christian women and men by proclaiming rigid attitudes towards morality.¹³ But by the start of World War II at the latest, Hitler no longer publicly advocated this position. In keeping with the prevailing notion of the victorious, virile soldier who developed fighting strength in part by satisfying his urges, it seemed counterproductive to deny men access to heterosexual services.¹⁴ The soldiers who stayed behind as occupying forces in the conquered territories after the fighting ended were not actually supposed to enter into personal relationships with the local population on 'racial' grounds and for reasons of military policy. As the Wehrmacht saw it, however, this did not amount to a strict prohibition against prostitution; instead it meant that sexual transactions should be controlled and regulated.

The sexual policies of both the Wehrmacht and the SS will be outlined in the following. The first aspect to explore is the situation that the soldiers encountered in the Soviet Union and how they reacted to it. Which different forms of prostitution were used by the men of the Wehrmacht, SS, Security Police and SD? Based on this, the middle section of the chapter will look at aspects of military policy and control. Which measures were employed to discipline the men, and how did they differ between the Wehrmacht and SS? The Wehrmacht's farthest-reaching measure for controlling the sexuality of its soldiers involved the establishment of military brothels. The last part of the chapter will look at how these brothels were structured and run. What difficulties were faced by the OKH, OKW and Wehrmacht medical services, and how did they try to resolve them?

Occasional Sexual Bartering

In her autobiographical novel *Kharkiv* published in Ukraine in 1947, Olena Zvychaina describes the situation in the Ukrainian city of the same name shortly after it was occupied by German troops in October 1941:

> Oh, how many armed people there are here, that walk in green-blue uniforms and converse in a language incomprehensible to most people! ... Entire army regiments come to the large city from the front, to rest ... They look for amusement, and young female bodies ... And these they find easily, because they can pay, with bread, food ... [15]

Kharkiv was the fourth-largest city in the Soviet Union at the time, and the fight for it was fierce. It was home to 430,000 people who found themselves confronted with a systematic policy of plundering under the German occupation. The ruthless requisition of food, livestock and grain by the 6th Army soon unleashed a hunger crisis that took nearly 12,000 lives by the end of September 1942 (according to the lowest estimates). The city was sealed off, and the surrounding area deteriorated into a *Kahlfrasszone* or 'defoliation zone' for the Wehrmacht.[16] Zvychaina's description illustrates the power relations that emerged in this situation. The German occupiers who sought distraction in Kharkiv from everyday life at the front were well aware of the inhabitants' desperation. They also knew that most of the women were alone, as their fathers, husbands and sons were fighting either in the army or with the partisans. In light of this, many soldiers felt that they had almost unlimited access to these women.

In other territories, too, the local population suffered food shortages after the German invasion.[17] Rumours of cannibalism even circulated in Kiev. Under these conditions, women might agree to provide heterosexual services in exchange for food and other essentials, sometimes offering up their bodies of their own accord.[18] Their circumstances and strategies varied. Some women would agree to a single sexual transaction if they were in dire need, while others maintained regular contact with men in order to improve their own food situation or that of their children and relatives.

Opportunities for such transactions could arise when the men were quartered in private houses and lived in direct proximity to local women. On 19 January 1942, Otto Hilger wrote to his wife:

> F. has shown his true colours as regards consorting with the ladies. Several nights in a row he scurried off, and not always to the same one, last night he wanted to go again, but the position was occupied, there's a woman whose husband was deported to Siberia, and he worked on her until he got his way, and he's visited others as well, who we call prostitutes. He probably doesn't need to talk about them in front of his wife, don't you agree?[19]

Hilger was born in June 1901, meaning that he was forty years old and long married when he wrote this letter. By describing the sexual debaucheries of his comrade, who was also married, he may have been trying to dissociate himself from such activities and emphasise his own loyalty. This remained ambiguous, however, as he was also indirectly letting his wife know what opportunities were open to the soldiers. His writing furthermore suggests that he was aware of the difficult position the women were in, women 'who *we call* prostitutes'.

Herbert Maeger, who joined the *Leibstandarte Adolf Hitler* division as a sixteen-year-old and marched into the Soviet Union with his unit in mid-December 1941, published a memoir in 2000 on the basis of his war diary. In this book, he recalls the weeks following a particularly successful looting run near Kharkiv in the spring of 1942:

> In our billets there were often enough pretty but absolutely cool girls and young women. We were all naturally interested in them but I never knew a case in which one of us got his way. Babucke [the corporal responsible for the food supply; R. M.], on the other hand, looked for and found suitable to his taste the fuller-figured, more mature and correspondingly more realistic and accessible partners who knew how to use his military position to their own advantage.[20]

Maeger's description speaks mainly to the envy he felt towards his comrade, an element that appears in the accounts of other soldiers as well.[21] Opportunities for sexual transactions could be found not only in their accommodations, but also in the workplaces where Germans had either hired or forcibly recruited local women. A witness from Kolomyia[22] (Ukraine) said in an interview with Wendy Jo Gertjejanssen that some women gave their addresses to German men while at work (digging trenches, for example) so the men could visit them at night.[23] A number of sources additionally mention that women used special events such as village festivals, music recitals and markets to initiate such transactions. Andrej Angrick has described how members of the Security Police and SD frequently attended local celebrations to get drunk and meet women from the area. Such evenings could end with sexual assaults, affairs or romances, or with the exchange of sexual services for goods.[24]

Some women apparently engaged in occasional sexual bartering over the course of several days or weeks. When Einsatzgruppe D was stationed in Taganrog[25] (Russia), a few members of the detachment established a theatre group consisting primarily of 'pretty Russian women and girls' who performed in order to 'improve their food rations'. After the war, one witness recalled that the regular evening programmes were attended by SS officers from the Leibstandarte division as well. Following the performance, there would be 'dancing and drinking and the girls would then somehow come to an agreement [with the SS men]'. They would meet in houses at the edge of the city that had been taken over by the detachment commanders.[26]

The German military authorities were well aware that the soldiers were trading military provisions for sex. On 20 March 1942, the Quartermaster General of the OKH complained that food was 'very often' being used as payment for prostitution.[27] One year later, the Security Police and SD reported from the 'occupied Eastern territories' that local women were trying to 'flirt with' German men to ensure their supply of food.[28] Even prior to this, however, the Wehrmacht had expressed fears that bartering and 'sympathetic hand-outs' would cause much of the army's supplies to fall into enemy hands, thus weakening the German campaign. The Commander-in-Chief of the 6th Army, Field Marshal Walter von Reichenau, therefore issued an order on 10 October 1941 concerning the 'Conduct of Troops in Eastern Territories', in which he declared: 'Feeding local inhabitants and prisoners of war [. . .] from army kitchens is just as misconceived an act of humanity as handing out cigarettes and bread'.[29] On 4 November 1941, the Quartermaster General also forbid 'any distribution of troop rations to the population of the occupied Eastern territories'. And just a few weeks later, on 20 November 1941, Field Marshal Erich von Manstein adopted Reichenau's formulation and warned the soldiers of the 11th Army to be wary of a 'misguided sense of humanity' and not dispense any goods to the civilian population. Von Manstein's order was reiterated multiple times in the following months, which Manfred Oldenburg interprets as an indication that 'ordinary soldiers' repeatedly disregarded it.[30]

The German civilian administration in the 'occupied Eastern territories' additionally criticised Wehrmacht soldiers for supposedly trying to protect 'their girls' from deportation. The German labour office in Novograd-Volynski[31] (Ukraine) complained to headquarters on 13 July 1942 that Wehrmacht members were promising to spare their 'girlfriends' from being transported to Germany to work.[32] Very similar stories were reported from other regions as well right up until the end of the war. For example, a letter from the German labour office in Brest-Litovsk from August 1944 said that in the offices of the Wehrmacht in particular, there were a number of 'protective relationships' which ran counter to German interests.[33]

Professional Prostitution

The line between occasional sexual bartering – offered on a situational basis – and professional sexual transactions was blurry. This distinction is especially difficult to make in any analysis of the 'occupied Eastern territories' because prostitution was officially forbidden there before the German invasion. The trade was carried on in secret, often in private spaces. Commercial sexual services had a chequered history in Russia from the start of the 20th century. In Imperial Russia, state officials viewed prostitution as a necessary part of social life. According to communist theory, however, it was a perversion of the bourgeoisie.[34] The fight against prostitution was not supposed to be directed against the women themselves, but after the October Revolution of 1917 and the establishment of the new labour camps by the Petrograd Soviet in 1919, women in prostitution were some of the first people to be sentenced to forced labour. They were convicted of 'labour desertion' because they did not work in the state economic sector.[35]

By the time the New Economic Policy (NEP) was introduced in 1921, however, the state was already incapable of guaranteeing employment that would have been an alternative to prostitution.[36] Sex workers were no longer convicted of being 'labour deserters', and prostitution as a trade began to thrive again.[37] To control this development, the state formed a commission against prostitution, established medical programmes for treating sexually transmitted diseases and pronounced a ban on hiring women as waitresses in private rooms, taverns or drinking halls. Men who were known to frequent prostitutes could be excluded from the Communist Party,[38] and 'medical asylums' were set up to rehabilitate 'fallen women' and turn them into 'productive member[s] of society'.[39]

Prostitution was generally prohibited in the early 1930s under Stalin. After the USSR annexed the Baltic countries in June 1940, the Soviet leadership expanded this policy of criminalisation to Estonia, Latvia and Lithuania.[40] We can roughly trace the effects of this by looking at the example of Estonia. In the 1930s, prostitution had been legal in principle in Estonia. The Estonian authorities had registered around 1,200 women as prostitutes, though the unreported number was probably twice as high.[41] During this period, policing measures were limited to the enforcement of regular medical exams for the women.[42] When Estonia was recognised as a Soviet republic, a new criminal code was introduced, according to which running a brothel, begging, vagrancy and any type of 'parasitic lifestyle' (including prostitution) was a criminal offence.[43] The Soviet secret service – the NKVD – used informers as waiters in public spaces such as restaurants, and a newly established 'Workers and Farmers' militia registered people thought to be prostitutes or thieves so they could be expelled from the cities.[44]

By the time the first German units marched into Estonia in June 1941, sex workers were being forced to ply their trade secretly, in closed, non-public spaces, where transactions for sexual services could not be observed by militia members or informers. This drove prostitution into a semi-private sphere which offered the women very little protection. To initiate a transaction with a woman, a man would either have to be familiar with the local situation, receive help from a third party or be approached directly by a woman.[45] Markets were an obvious place for German soldiers to look for prostitutes. In early 1944, Heinrich Böll wrote to his wife about the black market in Odessa[46] (Ukraine):

> At the bazaar, you can buy anything you want, and you can sell anything too. There is mad haggling between soldiers and sleazy 'local characters', all of whom have tens of thousands of marks in their pocket. You can eat as many 'grilled sausages' as you want, you can buy chocolate, cigarettes, bacon, butter, ham, wonderful sunflower oil, spirited and beautiful Russian and French women, vodka and radios, 'Thuringian liver sausage' and 'Eckstein No. 5'.[47]

As Böll describes it, soldiers could seek distraction from everyday wartime life at the black markets with the help of luxurious foods and purchased intimacies. The presence of the French women mentioned by Böll can be attributed largely to the fact that port cities such as Odessa traditionally had an international market for prostitution aimed especially at sailors. Under the German occupation, the women's pool of clients expanded and changed. German soldiers increased the demand for prostitutes, and they offered the women not only money but also food and other products that were otherwise difficult to acquire. In light of this, more women probably decided in the course of the occupation to ensure their subsistence by engaging in the trade professionally. In general, however, sex work during the war posed a major risk for women. First, they faced the brutality of armed soldiers who sometimes visited them straight after combat, and with whom they could often barely communicate due to the language barrier. And second, they faced persecution by both the local police and the German occupation authorities.

Persecution of Women 'Suspected of Prostitution'

Ultimately, any woman suspected by a German of engaging in occasional sexual bartering or professional prostitution could attract the attention of the authorities. Just a few months after Germany invaded the Soviet Union, the military and civilian occupation authorities began registering local women who offered their bodies in exchange for food or money. In many places, some of the first garrison orders issued by the headquarters after a city had been captured called for 'secret prostitution' to be brought under control. For example, on 3 September 1941, the German city commander of Kaunas (Lithuania) published the following order:

> The increase in venereal diseases demands strict monitoring of secret prostitution. Every soldier and every patrol is required to report any incident of secret prostitution (street, inns, houses).[48]

All patrols were instructed to take the details of 'suspect women' and forward them to the commander, the unit leader or the regional commissioner. In the view of *Reichsleiter* Martin Bormann, women were to be considered suspect merely for wearing short trousers, smoking on the street or using lipstick.[49] It was the responsibility of the police to 'eliminate' prostitution from the cityscape.[50] In Vitebsk[51] (Belarus) alone, ten 'secret brothels' were closed by May 1943, and seventeen women who had worked in them were transferred to a labour camp 'for regulated work'.[52] Sometimes the women in question could be punished even more harshly, as Ruth Bettina Birn has shown in the case of Estonia, where the German Security Police and the country's own criminal investigation department jointly took action against women considered to be prostitutes in the context of the Nazis' *'Vorbeugende Verbrechensbekämpfung'* (crime prevention) measures.[53] In at least one case, a woman was even admitted to a 'facility for the mentally ill' and it was recommended that she be sentenced to death. It is not known whether the sentence was carried out in the end.[54]

In general, any woman so much as suspected of being a 'secret prostitute' had to undergo a medical examination.[55] As will be discussed later, Wehrmacht doctors amongst themselves often held the soldiers responsible for introducing and spreading sexually transmitted diseases,[56] but in daily practice women were almost always blamed as the 'source of infection'.[57] The notices issued by the Wehrmacht claimed that prostitutes offered their services in order to infect German men with sexually transmitted diseases. The image presented here is of a specifically female, insidious form of resistance that played on much older notions of female sexuality as a source of corruption, disease and decay.[58]

Once the office of the *Generalkommissariat* (general commissariat, a regional administrative unit in the occupied territories) had determined the identity and address of a woman suspected of prostitution, she would be questioned and summoned to an examination at the local hospital. These examinations were probably a very unpleasant procedure for many women. Medical staff would palpate the woman's genitals externally and internally to identify any potential swelling or changes to the skin texture, and the doctors usually not only took blood samples but also performed smear tests and asked the women about their sexual history.[59] If a woman refused to attend her appointment, she would be picked up by the police and taken straight to the outpatient clinic. Even the wives of Wehrmacht soldiers were subjected to these forced examinations. In November 1942, *Gefreiter* Martin P. reported that he had contracted gonorrhoea from his wife, who worked as a secretary at the Bank of German Labour in Riga. When questioned by the doctor, the woman said 'with certainty that she had not had extramarital sexual intercourse'. Nonetheless, she was forced to undergo an examination in early January 1943. The results supported her account, as she was found to be healthy.[60]

If the test results were positive, however, a woman could be kept at the hospital for treatment against her will, without even being allowed to go home first.[61] On 4 November 1941, the Wehrmacht headquarters in Minsk noted that 'prostitutes' were to be 'taken to a civilian hospital, dept. for venereal diseases, until completely healed'.[62] In an activity report sent to the army physician of the 6th Army Command on 17 July 1942, the head medical officer for the commander of Rear Army

Area 585 explicitly mentioned the 'forced treatment of women with venereal disease' and praised the 'good results' of this method in the region covered by *Feldkommandantur* 765 (the area headquarters).[63] Other officials also made no secret of the fact that a woman's refusal to cooperate would result in her 'forced admission' to a hospital.[64] The 'General Orders for the Medical Service' issued in May 1943 additionally advised that sick women should have their hair shorn so they could be identified on sight.[65] It has yet to be established whether this plan – which would have stigmatised women not just as being infected but also as prostitutes and collaborators – was ever actually implemented anywhere.

Generally speaking, women had ways of influencing the exam results. If a woman took a sulphonamide one day before the exam, it would not be possible to diagnose a gonorrhoea infection.[66] The local staff members of city hospitals were another element of uncertainty, as they were not always willing to follow German orders. For example, the head medical officer under the commander of Army Area B complained that various hospitals in Ukraine were only treating infected women on an outpatient basis and refusing to 'investigate the source of infection'.[67] The interests of the women themselves varied as well. While some were held in hospital against their will, others agreed to extensive treatment. The activity report of Feldkommandantur 608 from 14 June 1942 indicates that the women's compliance could vary from place to place. The report stated that, in the troops' current location, 'women infected with lues or gonorrhoea or suspected of such' would 'seek out the doctor for clarification and, in the event of a positive finding' would be 'very anxious to carry out the treatment'. But where the area headquarters had been stationed previously, 'forced admissions to the hospitals' had been necessary.[68] In cases such as this, some area and local headquarters recorded these forced admissions in their activity reports as occupation policy successes.[69]

Reports from Wehrmacht and SS members tended to depict the women either as deceitful seductresses who deliberately instrumentalised their sexuality, or as naïve girls who had fallen victim to scheming. In early February 1942, for instance, the uniformed police in Libau (now Liepāja, in Latvia) issued a report concerning 'procuration' which said that a brothel that had already existed 'in Latvian times' had recruited some 'very young' women 'with lies and false promises'. Though the policeman who wrote the report suspected that only two of the women were infected with a sexually transmitted disease, he recommended that all of the women be detained and forced to undergo an examination.[70]

It appears that forced examinations were often carried out even when the German authorities actually assumed that the woman in question was healthy or they had pinpointed the wrong person. This enabled the occupiers to eliminate all traces of doubt while simultaneously demonstrating their position of power. For example, Reserve Military Hospital II in Königsberg (now Kaliningrad) registered Grenadier Hermann M. as a 'luetic' at the start of May 1943. When questioned, M. said he had been infected in early January by a nurse at the Riga War Hospital. However, based on the stage of the soldier's disease, the attending doctor suspected the infection had been acquired later. He assumed there had been a different 'source of infection', but he recommended nonetheless that the nurse be examined against her will. It is not clear whether the woman who was eventually identified as the nurse was actually the person accused by the soldier. Her name was similar to the one mentioned by the infected man, but only vaguely. She was summoned to a mandatory examination all the same.[71]

A variety of factors determined when or why a woman would come under suspicion. In June 1942, the military police in Kerch ordered not only the detention of infected individuals but also 'the registration of anyone even suspected of having a venereal disease'.[72] The authorities focused in particular on women residing near potential 'sources of infection'. On 23 September 1943, a Wehrmacht staff physician reported that soldier Alfred F. had identified 'the Russian woman Anni', who worked in a furnishing warehouse in Riga, as a 'source of infection'.[73] The person responsible for this warehouse in the central department of the general commissariat subsequently wrote:

> Non-commissioned officer Alfred F[...] spent a few days in mid-September visiting the manager of my warehouse for furnishings at Karl Schirrenstrasse 141. By his own account, he had sexual intercourse with the Russian woman Anni P[...], who is employed in my warehouse, and thus became infected. P. denies that sexual intercourse took place.
>
> I request the arrangement of an immediate examination of P. by the Latvian health authority. Please inform me of the result of the examination.
>
> If P. is found not to be infected, I recommend that all of the 21 Russian women at the warehouse undergo a health check.[74]

The director of the health authority reported in mid-December 1943 that Anni P. was 'healthy', but the records do not indicate whether the planned group examination took place.[75] In general, however, it is apparent that medical concerns were not necessarily the priority when it came to such measures. Military commanders considered every local woman of a sexually active age to be a potential threat to the unrestricted operational readiness of 'their' men. The measures taken against these women, up to and including criminalisation – ostensibly to 'block the source of infection' as one troop doctor put it[76] – therefore simultaneously served as a warning to all women, regardless of whether they had sexual contact with a German or not.

Disciplining Wehrmacht Soldiers

The Wehrmacht not only concerned itself with local women; it also put considerable effort into controlling German men and encouraging them to exhibit restraint. On 31 July 1940, one month before the German occupation of France, Commander-in-Chief of the Army Walther von Brauchitsch addressed the 'sex life of soldiers in the field' in a letter with the subject of '*Selbstzucht*' ('self-discipline'). In connection with an OKH order concerning 'alcohol abuse' from 6 September 1941, his remarks were also disseminated on the Eastern Front:

> The longer German troops spend in the occupied territories, the more orderly and peaceable the conditions will become under which the soldier lives and serves, the more serious thought will need to be given to the sexual issue in all of its circumstances and consequences.
>
> Frank words are called for here.
>
> I have already said on another occasion that the situation faced by the soldier in the occupied territory, not just during operations but also [...] after the end of combat, is peculiar in nature and sometimes deviates significantly from that at home.
>
> As the dispositions of the men are diverse, it is inevitable that tensions and needs [*Spannungen und Nöte*] will arise now and then in the sexual realm, to which we cannot and must not turn a blind eye.
>
> Prohibiting sexual activity in the occupied territories will not solve the problem in any case. Besides other negative consequences, such a prohibition would undoubtedly increase the number of sexual offences [*Notzuchtverbrechen*] and the risk of violations of paragraph 175 [criminalising homosexuality; R.M].[77]

Von Brauchitsch considered the sexuality of the soldiers to be a central military policy problem. He assumed that, depending on the men's individual dispositions, their sexual 'tensions and needs' would build up and potentially erupt in sexual violence or homosexual acts if no moderated heterosexual opportunities were available. As both sexual violence and homosexual activities were undesirable in the view of the military leadership, von Brauchitsch advised the establishment of 'suitable brothels under medical supervision for German soldiers'.[78]

Von Brauchitsch's notion that a soldier was at the mercy of his urges in certain situations – not a subject making conscious decisions, but rather the object of his own biology – was widely shared in the Wehrmacht. This is clear from the criminal proceedings initiated by the Wehrmacht in some cases against soldiers who had been accused of rape. Wehrmacht courts would not hold a soldier fully liable if they determined that he had suffered from 'sexual distress' ('*sexueller Notstand*') or a 'build-up of sexual urges' ('*Triebstau*') at the time of the offence.[79] However, this condition would not be taken into account if the judges believed that other opportunities for the man to satisfy his 'sexual needs' ('*sexuelle Nöte*') had been available. In a case tried before the court of the Riga local headquarters in April 1944, the judges provided the following justification for convicting a soldier of the attempted rape of two Latvian women:

> It is [. . .] out of the question that the accused acted in a state of sexual distress. The Wehrmacht has established sanitation facilities in Riga, and furthermore, any soldier can easily engage in sexual intercourse in Riga, as in nearly all large cities.[80]

The judges' argument was based on the assumption that sexual lust would usually only be expressed in the form of violence if a man had no opportunity to engage in 'normal' heterosexual activity. The diverse motives underlying the coupling of sexuality and violence[81] play no role in this perspective. A very similar line of thinking can be found in the proceedings of soldiers accused of homosexual acts. Here, too, the lack of specifically female sexual partners was blamed for the men's deeds.[82] Following this logic, prostitution was a means of preventing potentially 'deviant' sexual behaviour by soldiers and thus guaranteeing the stability of the German occupation.

At the same time, however, the OKH and OKW believed that both occasional sexual bartering and professional prostitution posed significant military risks. The most obvious risk was the rapid spread of sexually transmitted diseases. In advance of the war, the Wehrmacht had been curious about the conditions it would encounter in the Soviet Union. The records of the OKH from the spring of 1941 include the German translation of an article from the Russian newspaper *Isvestia* about the efforts of the NKVD to combat prostitution and sexually transmitted diseases in the Polish territory annexed by the Soviet Union.[83] After German troops invaded the Soviet Union, the Wehrmacht's medical authorities increasingly reported cases of communicable diseases that had been transmitted through sexual contact.[84] On 20 April 1943, the Deputy General Command of the VII Army Corps stated that:

> The spread of venereal diseases is increasing, not only at home but also in France, in the Balkan countries and in Russia. That our soldiers are playing a significant role in the spread of venereal diseases unfortunately cannot be ruled out.[85]

Sexually transmitted diseases were a military concern, first, because they endangered the health of the soldiers and thus the fighting power of the army. Before World War I, more soldiers had been put out of action or killed by infectious diseases than by combat itself.[86] Though treatment methods had become much more sophisticated by World War II, the therapy was expensive and often inadequate in the military hospitals at the front and in the occupied territories, not least because the necessary medicines were unavailable in many places.[87] Furthermore, since sexually transmitted diseases often became chronic, those suffering from them would be out of action for long periods of time. The loss of the 'military strength of our *Volk*' due to 'recklessly acquired venereal diseases' became a matter of particular concern to the Army Medical Inspectorate in 1944, as the war began to look increasingly hopeless.[88]

Second, Nazi physicians viewed sexually transmitted diseases as a danger to the '*deutschen Volkskörper*' or 'body of the German people'. As had been the case in World War I,[89] military doctors warned that soldiers who had not been fully cured of a disease could infect their wives, fiancées or girlfriends while on leave or after returning home, and might even endanger their unborn children. Gonorrhoea ('the clap') could harm the entire organism if treated inadequately,[90] while syphilis (lues) could result in chronic inflammation of the brain and, in its final stage, the destruction of the central nervous system.[91] In antisemitic thinking, syphilis was additionally considered a Jewish disease. As the historian Sander Gilman has shown, scientists and wide swathes of the population in Europe had closely associated Jews with the emergence and spread of syphilis ever since the late nineteenth century.[92] Hitler also related the infection to Jews. In 1925 he wrote in *Mein Kampf* that the Jews ran brothels and infected prostitutes with syphilis in order to weaken the German 'national body'.[93]

Third, the commanders of the Wehrmacht feared that soldiers who had contact with women from an enemy population would give away military secrets. The OKH though that soldiers who visited prostitutes would be seduced into trusting the women and speaking carelessly. Numerous posters and leaflets were therefore distributed warning against female spies who might pump the men for information and pass on secret plans to the partisans.[94]

Finally, in the eyes of the commanders, there was a danger that sexual contact between German soldiers and local women could lead to relationships that threatened to eliminate the distance from the enemy civilian population that was deemed necessary for the purposes of military and 'ethnic' policy. A soldier who became 'intimately acquainted' with a prostitute not only damaged the image of the Wehrmacht and the 'dignity of the master race'; his personal insight into the life of the enemy population could also impact his willingness to fight. A dangerous power was sometimes attributed to enemy women. For example, the commander of the Army Patrol Service (*Heeresstreifendienst*) in the 'Ostland' administrative area said in September 1942 that 'secret prostitutes' could influence German soldiers and 'entice them into desertion'.[95]

To keep the soldiers' sexual activities under control and minimise the risks, the OKH and OKW as well as the civilian occupation authorities relied on a tiered system of disciplinary measures: instruction, sanitation, treatment, interrogation and punishment.

Instruction
Soldiers usually received a leaflet during their training urging them to exercise sexual discipline. The most widely circulated text, entitled *Deutscher Soldat!* (German Soldier!), was first issued on 6 February 1936 by the Reich Ministry of War. Slightly modified versions of it were subsequently distributed in France and the occupied Polish and Soviet territories. One version that was circulated in Ukraine in 1943 read as follows:

> German soldier!
> Beware of sexual excesses! They diminish your performance and are not beneficial to your health.
> A soldier with venereal disease is unfit for duty. Self-inflicted invalidity is unworthy of a German soldier!
> Venereal diseases can make you unfit for marriage and unable to reproduce. The Fatherland not only expects the maximum soldierly performance from

you, it also wants you to start a healthy German family and provide it with healthy offspring one day.[96]

This leaflet appealed to both the military and the 'ethnic-nationalist' ('*volkstumspolitisch*') responsibilities of the men. It focused once again on the concept of *Manneszucht*, which was discussed earlier in the context of sexual violence, according to which a man was expected to moderate himself to ensure the combat effectiveness of the troops and the 'health of the *Volk*'. The Reich Ministry of War had begun pursuing 'racial hygiene' goals long before the start of the war, as illustrated by the 'Guide to racial hygiene instruction' that was first published in 1936. The chapter on 'The importance of race and heredity for the *Volk*' warns against sexually transmitted diseases:

> Contracting a venereal disease is no longer a matter that only affects the individual personally, it affects the people's community as a whole. Every reasonable person knows that, when it comes to sexual issues, it is not possible to measure all men against the same standard. But if someone recklessly jeopardises the health of his national comrades [*Volksgenossen*] by engaging in intercourse in the knowledge that he is sick, we consider him a pest [*Schädling*] who has placed himself outside of the community. If someone teases or disparages the young people entrusted to him to the point that they compromise their health in a misunderstood notion of manliness merely to be seen as 'men' in the eyes of others, he is acting in an uncomradely and base way! The freedom of the individual, even in sexual matters, reaches its limit where it touches on the interests of the whole.[97]

In this brochure, infection with a sexually transmitted disease was referred to as a threat to the entire 'body of the German people'. A careless approach to the disease – and, in particular, the conscious endangerment of one's 'national comrades' – could quickly turn an allegedly 'Aryan' man into a '*Volksschädling*', or pest harmful to the people. The Reich Ministry of War considered young men to be a special danger. It was assumed that they would take extreme risks to gain sexual experience and prove their masculinity to themselves and those around them. For this reason, higher-ranking soldiers were specifically called upon to minimise the social pressure on their subordinates as much as possible.

The 'Guide to racial hygiene instruction' was one of the foundations for the oral 'troop lectures' that head medical officers were expected to hold regularly in all Wehrmacht units, including the navy and air force, by order of the OKH. Medical officers were also required to specifically inform the soldiers of the dangers of prostitution and sexually transmitted diseases.[98] From the spring of 1942, the situation reports and correspondence of the medical units in the occupied Soviet territories repeatedly included warnings not to let such lectures slide.[99] In the spring of 1943, the commander of Army Area South ordered these briefings to be held every fourteen days, with interpreters on hand for the foreign Wehrmacht volunteers if necessary.[100] Although women in the retinue of the Wehrmacht also contracted gonorrhoea and syphilis, this type of group instruction was intended only for the men. The sources indicate that if female Wehrmacht auxiliaries received any instructions at all regarding the dangers of 'extramarital sexual intercourse', it was only during the Wehrmacht's 'gynaecological consultation hour' or in the context of individual gynaecological exams by the public health officer.[101]

The content of the lectures for the soldiers was based on guidelines that had been issued by the Prussian Ministry of War during World War I.[102] First, the men were supposed to be encouraged to practice sexual abstinence, which deliberately ran counter to the widespread belief that sexually inactive men or men who engaged in autoerotic practices were physically ill and weak of character.[103] The dangers of alcohol were also on the agenda, as drunken soldiers generally had a more reckless attitude towards the risks of prostitution.[104]

In addition to explaining the symptoms and dangers of sexually transmitted diseases, the troop lectures focused on medical and military prophylactic measures.[105] Medical officers were required to make it clear to the soldiers that it was their duty to use condoms. The Wehrmacht had condoms produced which came with an enclosed leaflet that said 'For the German Wehrmacht only. Destroy immediately after use'; the packs could be distributed by the medical officers.[106] The use of condoms was actually extremely contentious within the borders of the Reich, since they not only provided welcome protection against infection but were also an undesirable form of birth control that could prevent the conception of 'Aryan' children.[107] But such matters were of no concern to the armed forces engaged in combat. On the contrary, it was precisely because of their dual function of preventing both infection and conception that Reich Health Leader Leonardo Conti called for condoms to be distributed to German men in the occupied territories of the Soviet Union in November 1942 – as this would prevent the conception of children between 'German military members and civilians and ethnically alien [fremdvölkisch] women'. However, military medical officers were expected to ensure that when the men visited their wives and girlfriends on leave, they did not take along the condoms that had been issued to them.[108]

Sanitation

The obligation to take preventive measures was supplemented with a requirement to take follow-up measures. In larger cities such as Riga and Minsk, the military medical services established what were known as *Sanierstuben* or sanitation stations, which were to be 'clearly identified by signs'.[109] Within two hours after sexual contact, soldiers were supposed to receive treatment from the medical staff there so that any potential pathogens would be killed. This 'sanitation' involved washing with soap and water, rinsing with a sublimate solution and the insertion of a disinfectant swab in the urethra. An ointment was additionally used to prevent syphilis.[110] Finally, the medic would record the treatment in the 'troop sanitation book' and issue a 'sanitation certificate' to the soldier, which proved that he had done his duty.[111]

Medical officers were very concerned with the location of these 'sanitation stations'. There had to be a good number of them so soldiers would not have to cross an entire city to reach one after a sexual encounter, but at the same time they could not be too close to the troop accommodations so the men could undergo the intimate procedure without being seen.[112] When new sanitation stations opened or established ones moved, this was sometimes announced in the headquarters orders (*Kommandanturbefehlen*) issued by the local headquarters; in general, however, it was the responsibility of the medical officers to ensure that soldiers knew where to go.[113]

The establishment of 'sanitation stations' and distribution of condoms was not unanimously supported by all Wehrmacht officers. This particularly applied to the military leadership in the Reich. The commander of Military District VII, who was responsible for recruiting and training soldiers in southern Bavaria, warned on 20 April 1943 that while the Wehrmacht should not 'turn a blind eye to the dangers out of prudery or take the problem of venereal diseases too lightly', it also had to make sure that the 'protective sanitary measures' were not 'taken by the soldiers as tacit approval or even encouragement to engage in extramarital sexual intercourse'.[114] Young men especially seem to have sometimes viewed such infections as proof of their sexual adventurousness and virility, almost like a trophy. In a training letter from 15 July 1942, the Naval Office made it clear that it was necessary to 'strictly counter' the notion that 'venereal diseases were not dishonourable but actually a symbol of particular manliness' – an attitude that had been widespread since the start of the war.[115]

The OKH was constantly concerned that the instructions were not being conveyed with the necessary 'moral seriousness'.[116] Judging by the memoirs of Wolfgang von Buch, who was conscripted into the Wehrmacht in 1944 at the age of fifteen, there was good reason to worry:

> We regularly had to sign papers confirming that we'd been taught this or that. There was a list of two dozen topics, none of which we'd been taught, of course. To this day I'm not sure what you were supposed to do about a syphilis or gonorrhoea infection. They said soldiers had to visit the medic for 'sanitation', and that it was very unpleasant. But we didn't really know how everything was connected. Our knowledge was limited to a medical student rhyme that had inexplicably found its way to us:
>
>> *The gonococcus holds fast*
>> *as the urine rushes past.*
>> *While over there – hum de dum –*
>> *is Spirochaeta pallidum.*
>
> We thought it was very dirty. [. . .] It [the lectures; R. M.] would have been a tough job for our superiors and a big joke to us.[117]

The troop lectures apparently became more and more of a formality especially towards the end of the war. In particular, young men who joined the Wehrmacht in the last year of the war seem not to have been thoroughly briefed. Sometimes they had no idea what conduct was expected of them. Buch's anecdote also makes it clear that the men could feel ashamed to discuss apparently indecent subjects. For many, talking about sex involved breaking a bourgeois taboo, which they tried to downplay by making jokes and showing off.[118]

Many men obviously shared the ignorance, shame and fear of potentially painful examinations and treatments, as well as the associated flippancy described by Buch. The files of the public health officer in Riga reveal that a number of soldiers neither used condoms nor visited the sanitation stations.[119] After being diagnosed with an infection, some men would admit to the responsible doctor that they had not gone for 'sanitation' because they had used a condom and believed that this would protect them.[120] On 6 February 1942, the headquarters of Rear Army Area 585 complained of a growing number of cases 'in which it was proven that no sanitation took place following sexual intercourse'. The infected men were said to pass this off 'with flimsy excuses'.[121] In response to this negligence, the OKW expanded its 'sanitation' regulations in January 1943. From this point on, even the smallest military units were supposed to offer access to genital disinfection treatment at all times. If no trained medics were available for this, the troops were to be trained accordingly. The unit leaders were responsible for ensuring compliance with these regulations.[122] But smaller units in rural areas, where materials were often in short supply, continued to face problems.[123]

Treatment

If a man fell ill, he was to report immediately to the responsible troop doctor or medic. Members of the Wehrmacht and its retinue were to be treated exclusively by medical personnel 'especially in the case of venereal diseases!'.[124] Gonorrhoea was considered relatively quick and easy to treat, at least in men. If a soldier was infected for the first time, he would usually have to take sulphonamide for two to four weeks. He would be unfit for duty during this period, but afterwards he was considered cured.[125] In some regions, however, there was a very high resistance to sulphonamide, so other methods of treatment had to be tried – though these had a reputation for being very painful.[126] The treatment for syphilis was much lengthier and riskier. The most promising approach consisted of a combination of the arsenic-based drug Salvarsan along with bismuth or mercury. The therapy involved three to six courses of treatment, with one treatment comprising twelve to fifteen injections. Since the treatments took place at intervals of four to six weeks, the affected individual would be absent from military duty for up to half a year.[127] The therapy could be very unpleasant and result in severe side effects, including nausea, fever, hair loss and jaundice. The mortality rate was also relatively high.[128] It was possible to cure syphilis completely if the treatment began as soon as possible.[129] In milder cases, after the first treatment, soldiers would be sent from the military hospital back to the front line, where the subsequent treatments would be administered on an outpatient basis. From the end of 1942 in particular, however, the military medical services reported more and more failed attempts to cure venereal diseases.[130]

In occupied France, military commanders had realised that many infected soldiers tried to treat themselves by acquiring sulphonamide from a chemist, a local doctor or on the black market.[131] In the 'occupied Eastern territories', however, the relevant medicines were much harder to come by. Official warnings were occasionally even issued about drug shortages.[132] But clearly there were ways for the soldiers to get hold of the preparations nonetheless. In May 1943, the medical service circulated a notice that

> sulphonamides that fell into the hands of the troops during the clearance and recapture of Kharkiv and remained in their possession were ingested in a

completely uncontrolled way, without the knowledge of the troop doctor, in abnormally large amounts of up to 300! tablets'.[133]

In the wake of this, the doctors reported increased resistance to the active ingredient and an accompanying 'delay in recovery'. The soldiers stationed near Kharkiv were ordered to hand in any sulphonamide tablets still in their possession and undergo a 'health inspection' every eight days. The incident resulted in no further consequences, however.[134]

There were various reasons for men to hide the fact that they had acquired a sexually transmitted disease. Just the thought of having to show one's penis to the troop doctor or orderly and talk about sexual practices could be so embarrassing for a soldier that he would keep quiet about his disease. He might also fear the consequences of a positive diagnosis; troop doctors usually sent infected soldiers to a military hospital for treatment,[135] and the prospect of spending weeks or months with other sick, injured or dying soldiers could – depending on the war situation at the time – be horrifying in its own way. Furthermore, soldiers would be denied all home leave for the duration of their illness to prevent the spread of the disease within the borders of the Reich. Men therefore probably sometimes concealed their illness to avoid missing out on visiting friends and family.[136] In general, an infection was proof of sexual activity, a circumstance that married men and those in permanent relationships would probably want to hide.[137] Such conflicts could apparently escalate severely for a significant number of those affected. On 6 October 1942, the Inspector of the *Luftwaffe* Medical Service issued a warning to troop doctors in his 'Instructions for preventing suicide':

> Married and engaged men with venereal diseases must be monitored carefully. A man who is not fully healed must not be sent on leave. [. . .] Soldiers are often torn between the understandable desire not to miss out on leave and their fears. The doctor must help them find the right path and make a decision that soothes their conscience and ensures that the leave is truly recuperative and they will return with increased operational readiness. The number of cases in which an actual or supposed venereal disease has been the cause of suicide is relatively large.[138]

Infection with a sexually transmitted disease apparently compelled some men to start mentally connecting the realities in their area of operations with those back home, which were usually only partially correlated in their Feldpost letters.[139] Merely the thought that knowledge of their illness might cause them to lose contact with the people who supported them and for whom they believed they were fighting[140] could, in extreme cases, drive soldiers to suicide. Others felt compelled to take their own lives because they had actually lost such contact. Therefore, when soldiers contracted sexually transmitted diseases, the military commanders placed value in secrecy and confidential consultation with the troop doctor. The instructions and orders issued to soldiers encouraged them to 'confide in' their troop doctor, which suggested that he could provide not only medical but also 'emotional' relief.[141]

It seems to have been difficult for medics to establish the necessary trusting relationships with the soldiers in the male society of the Wehrmacht, however. In one-on-one conversations, many soldiers gave no indication of who might have infected them or whether they had gone for 'sanitation'.[142] It is not possible to determine whether the troop doctors and medics simply did not ask the men about this, or whether the infected men refused to provide the information when questioned. In any case, the doctors and medics generally do not seem to have put any pressure on men who preferred to keep a low profile. 'Chumminess' with the men may have been responsible for this in some cases, while in others it was probably the desire to avoid an embarrassing situation or gloss over the fact that no proper health guidance had been given to the men beforehand.

Interrogation
As mentioned earlier, one key measure for halting the spread of sexually transmitted diseases involved tracing the '*Ansteckungsquelle*' or source of infection. On 20 September 1941, the Wehrmacht headquarters in Minsk noted that every infected soldier was to report to headquarters 'immediately with information about the source of infection'.[143] Following a standard procedure, the troop doctor would first ask a soldier diagnosed with syphilis or gonorrhoea about the details of his last heterosexual encounter – disregarding the fact that the infection could have been acquired months earlier, since soldiers often did not report an illness until it had broken out fully. The responses were recorded on a pre-printed questionnaire, various versions of which were in circulation.[144] The Wehrmacht wanted to know the name of the woman, where she lived and what she looked like (height, hair and eye colour, age, clothing), and the details of the sexual encounter: Where had the infected soldier met the woman? When and where did they have sexual intercourse? Some versions of the questionnaire also asked whether the infected soldier had used prophylactics and whether the 'sexual intercourse had taken place in exchange for payment'.[145] Whether the soldier

had violently coerced the woman into sexual contact was not addressed, nor was the 'racial evaluation' of the respective woman.

Once the medic had taken this information, he was obligated, first, to inform the health authority in the soldier's hometown; second, to regularly update the head medical officer,[146] who would note the total number of infected and cured men in his reports;[147] and, third, to notify the respective local commissariat, which was responsible for finding the woman in question and summoning her to an examination. The files of the public health officer of the general commissioner in Riga include sixty-nine cases concerning men infected with gonorrhoea or syphilis from the end of 1942 to the end of 1943. The majority of these men were between twenty and thirty years old.[148] Around half of them said they were married, and a few of them were Latvian Wehrmacht or SS volunteers.[149]

It is not possible to draw any reliable conclusions from these questionnaires about the men's actual sexual encounters, but they do offer interesting insights into certain narratives that were apparently commonplace amongst the infected men – such as how they had met the women in question and how the sexual intercourse had come about. In general, the information provided by the sick men was extremely meagre. For example, a number of reports simply say 'source of infection unknown'.[150] Some men explained this by saying that they had been very drunk and could therefore no long remember anything.[151] When asked about the details of the 'source of infection', very few of the infected men gave a woman's full name; in most cases, they mentioned a first name or nickname,[152] if they gave any name at all.[153] It is notable that many men claimed the women had been of medium height, slender, blonde, blue-eyed, young, pretty, neatly dressed and well-groomed.[154] *Obergefreiter* Franz C. went so far as to say that the Latvian woman who called herself 'Julie or something similar' had 'good teeth'.[155] Several men stated that the women had spoken 'broken German'.[156]

The historian Wendy Jo Gertjejanssen suspects that many men were expressing their fantasies with these descriptions.[157] They may also have been attempting to avoid the appearance of carelessness or delinquency. When a soldier described the woman with whom he had had sexual intercourse as looking 'Aryan' and healthy, he was implying that he could not have known she was infected with a sexually transmitted disease. If she spoke 'broken German' on top of that, he could assume that she was friendly towards the Germans. If this were the case, the soldier could not be said to have acted irresponsibly; instead, he had fallen victim to the woman because he was, at worst, naïve.

The location of the encounter or sexual intercourse was often unspecific: 'in the street',[158] 'on a bench in the park',[159] 'cinema',[160] or 'hotel, name forgotten'.[161] Sometimes more detailed information was provided, however, and two questionnaires even included drawings. Gonorrhoea patient Georg Sch. claimed to have had sexual intercourse on 9 May 1943 at around ten in the evening at the Libau (Liepāja) railway station. He provided a pencil drawing to pinpoint the 'location of intercourse' in a complex near the main building.[162] *Obergefreiter* Rudolf T. also sketched the section of the beach in Riga where he said he met an eighteen-year-old Latvian woman named Deina.[163] But more substantial information, such as the surnames or addresses of the women, was not provided in either of these cases. We can only speculate as to whether these soldiers actually believed they were helping the military authorities in their search for the 'source of infection' or whether they merely wanted to appear cooperative. In any case, the responsible medics were unable to glean any information from these drawings that would help them prosecute the women. In the end, the questionnaires were simply 'filed away'.

The health authority in Riga often added a handwritten note to the margins of such reports: 'filed away on account of imprecise information', 'no further investigation possible' or 'insufficient information'. It is not clear whether the local headquarters even tried to investigate cases such as these.[164] In May 1943, however, the military medical services were explicitly reminded to 'send the afflicted man with a non-commissioned officer or *Feldwebel* to the quarters used' so that the 'incriminated civilian' could be identified and apprehended.[165]

If an infected man supplied the home or work address of the woman in question, the responsible authorities could report that they were successful in 'locating the source of infection'.[166] Sometimes this information also proved to be false, however – such as when the names of non-existent streets were given.[167] Whether the men were trying to protect themselves or the women with this false information – perhaps in the hope that they would be out of reach by the time the deception was discovered – is something to be determined on a case-by-base basis.

Even when the authorities did manage to identify an incriminated woman, this did not automatically mean they had found the actual 'source of infection'. In fact, a relatively large number of men accused women who proved upon examination not to be infected at all. *Oberfeldwebel* Hugo F. claimed in late 1942 that he had contracted gonorrhoea from a Latvian maid. After the woman had been tracked down and examined, the director of the health authority in Riga reported that the physician had found the woman to be healthy.[168] What the women themselves said in such cases was irrelevant. For instance, if a woman asserted that the soldier had lied, she did not know him or had not had sexual intercourse with him, this had no influence on the procedure.

Even if the test results were negative, the authorities could summon the women to additional doctor's appointments, often for months on end.[169] When an unnamed Wehrmacht soldier in July 1943 accused Anna W., a nurse at the municipal hospital in Cēsis[170] (Latvia), of having infected him with syphilis, the woman was forced to undergo a series of examinations in the autumn of 1943, all of which produced the same result: the patient was healthy.[171] The soldier F. A. Xcaver G. also reported a healthy woman to the military authorities. In May 1943, he named the Latvian woman Lisa Sch. as his 'infector'. The woman was subsequently examined every two to three weeks for the next three months. On 5 July, the head of the health authority finally informed the public health officer that Lisa Sch. had been 'tested for gonorrhoea 3x by means of challenge with negative findings'.[172]

False statements such as these were not a rarity. On the one hand, men might make such statements because they actually believed they had been infected by the woman they named, even though a different sexual encounter had been responsible for the infection. On the other hand, we must assume that the majority of the men lied for tactical reasons, perhaps to conceal the fact that they had visited a 'secret prostitute' or had raped a woman. In general, it is noteworthy that the soldiers often cooperated insufficiently, if at all, in the official search for the 'source of infection'. This hints at how helpless the military and official bodies often were when it came to dealing with this issue.

Punishment
The men could face consequences for remaining silent, however. If a man was infected and it emerged that he had not fulfilled his 'sanitation duty' or was not willing to provide 'information about the source of infection as ordered', he would be threatened with disciplinary measures under the *Gesundheitspflicht* or 'duty to remain healthy' that had been introduced in 1939. These measures were generally tiered, ranging from a reprimand to a severe reprimand, pay management, curfews, arrest, demotion and fines. Additionally, time spent in the military hospital was counted as part of the soldier's annual leave. In repeat cases, or when the disease had been passed on to someone else, the offender might also be 'reported for disobedience'. If a member of an air force unit or the crew of a submarine or speedboat contracted an infection

through reckless behaviour and thus 'endangered the operational readiness of his combat unit' on account of his subsequent absence, he might even be charged with 'self-mutilation' (*Selbstverstümmelung*) or 'subversion of military power' (*Wehrkraftzersetzung*) under the Special Wartime Penal Code.[173]

This was the legal situation on paper, anyway. No research has been conducted to date into the extent to which the men were actually called to account by their disciplinary superiors, but the sources suggest that there were no consequences for inadequate 'sanitation' in many units.[174] It can generally be assumed that many superiors were sympathetic towards their soldiers. Extramarital sexual contact was considered an inevitable part of war for most of them, regardless of whether they took a positive or negative view of it. Insufficient 'sanitation' after such contact was indeed considered a serious breach of duty, but the reasons for it were easy to understand, and the unit leaders probably had little interest in antagonising their men because of it.

This was likely to be especially true when the war situation began to deteriorate for the German army at the end of 1943. On 25 October 1943, head of the OKW Wilhelm Keitel once again explicitly stated that all members of the Wehrmacht, Waffen-SS and associated organisations in the 'territories outside of the Greater German Reich' were to be held to account for failing to take disinfectant measures after sexual contact. However, he recommended 'judging such cases leniently, particularly on their first occurrence'.[175] The leaflet on the 'Punishment of men with venereal disease' declared that a man who 'carelessly neglects sanitation or hides his illness' was to be reported to the troop leader for 'correctional disciplinary measures'.[176] On 30 August 1944, the OKW expanded this regulation to cover the territory inside the Reich as well.[177]

As Keitel's vacillation in his order of 25 October 1943 indicates, military commanders faced a dilemma when it came to imposing disciplinary punishments. If a man fell ill, his fear of punishment could lead him to ignore his infection or keep it secret for as long as possible and thus not receive the necessary medical treatment. The commander-in-chief of the *Luftwaffe* had therefore ordered his military leaders as early as December 1941 to 'desist from all threats of punishment' and rescind any penal provisions that had already been enacted.[178] The consultant dermatologist at the Army Medical Inspectorate attempted to solve the problem by suggesting that the degree of punishment should be tailored to the 'personal and soldierly' characteristics of the individual.[179] In any case, the military leadership was interested primarily in treating the infected men as quickly as possible and returning them to duty.[180]

The soldiers were clearly not very daunted by the threat of reprimand, particularly when they were involved in rearguard action. In the last year of the war, the Wehrmacht Medical Service increasingly expressed concern that the soldiers were refusing to take hygienic and protective measures. *Oberfeldarzt* Hans von Hattinberg, the consultant hygienist working under the physician in Military District XX, reported that over 90 per cent of infected men had not undergone sanitation. In the *Ersatzheer* (replacement army), too, many soldiers refused to name the women with whom they had sexual contact.[181] In September 1944, the High Command of Army Group Centre complained that 'the [recent] provisions issued for combatting venereal diseases' were no longer 'being observed with the urgently necessary diligence'.[182] Franz Seidler attributes this to the fact that the soldiers had developed a 'certain indifference' towards infectious diseases, which were less terrifying to the individual than the thought of injury or mutilation and could additionally offer the opportunity to spend time in a military hospital far from the front.[183] In fact, Wehrmacht doctors did record a few cases in which soldiers had deliberately infected themselves using pus from a fellow infected comrade.[184]

Despite this, the Army Medical Inspectorate did not do away with the disciplinary measures. Following the revision of the Wehrmacht's disciplinary regulations in November 1944, the head doctors at the reserve military hospitals were granted disciplinary authority over soldiers who had neglected their prescribed 'sanitation'.[185] From January 1945, the men in Military District XVIII even faced legal punishment for such neglect.[186] However, it is doubtful that such punishment was ever actually imposed.

Appeals to SS Men

While the Wehrmacht tried to raise its soldiers' awareness of both the military aims and 'racial hygiene' goals of its approach to dealing with 'secret prostitution' and 'undesirable sexual intercourse', the inextricable link between military and 'racial' goals was openly programmatic from the outset for the men of the SS. The SS thought of domination in terms of race relations and pursued a vision of the 'racial restructuring of Europe' in its war against the Soviet Union.[187] Reichsführer-SS Heinrich Himmler viewed the SS '*Sippengemeinschaft*' or 'kinship community' as the realisation of a programme of 'racial selection' that was to be the foundation of selective breeding for the refinement of the 'Aryan race'. Drawing on nineteenth-century racial theories, eugenics, the life reform movement, and ariosophist and esoteric elements, Himmler believed the 'Aryan' men he wanted to recruit for the SS were the physical and mental manifestation of 'racial selection' within the '*Volksgemeinschaft*'. Gender-specific, eugenic and political ambitions came together in the ideal of the SS man.[188]

In accordance with this fundamental notion of 'racial breeding', the individual SS man was expected to control his sexual desires in the interest of the 'SS clan' and the German 'people's community'. The 'Sanitary Regulation for the General SS' from 1935 illustrates this expectation:

> It must be clear to every SS man that his body and his life do not belong to him but rather to the future of his people. If an SS man destroys or weakens his ability to fight and to reproduce through careless actions, he has betrayed his loyalty to his Führer. [. . .]
>
> The desire to demonstrate brashness through unbridled indulgence with respect to sex and alcohol can only be viewed as a relapse into reactionary and liberalist standards.[189]

An SS man was supposed to consider himself the property of the people. If he harmed his own body by contracting a sexually transmitted disease, thus weakening his ability to fight and reproduce, he was not only committing an offence against the 'body of the people', he was also violating the prime moral precept of the SS, namely, loyalty to the '*Führer*'.[190] By rejecting a life of excess, the SS wanted to distinguish itself not only from the freewheeling Weimar Republic but also from the SA (*Sturmabteilung*), its inner-party competitor in the so-called 'time of struggle' and an organisation that had become a talking point not only on account of its combat strength but also due to its 'indulgence with respect to sex and alcohol'. By contrast, Himmler had deliberately conceived of the '*Schutzstaffel*' as a 'racial' and moral elite, and this self-image shaped every part of the life of the men in this organisation.[191] For example, from 1931, SS members were subject to an 'Engagement and Marriage Order', which was meant to ensure that their life partners were selected according to 'racial' criteria.[192] Long-term intimate relationships with women considered 'ethnically alien' ('*fremdvölkisch*') or 'racially alien' ('*artfremd*') according to Nazi ideology were viewed as a kind of contamination – of both the individual man and the 'body of the people'.

SS men were exposed to this ideal of the 'new man' through a number of 'ideological training materials'.[193] For example, in the dormitories of what were known as SS-*Mannschaftshäuser* or 'team houses' (which functioned as a kind of 'SS academic foundation'),[194] the SS medical service placed posters with slogans such as 'Your urges shall not master you – you shall master your urges. Remember – any intercourse outside of marriage harbours the danger of a venereal disease'.[195] In the combat zone, however, this ideal of self-control collided with the notion that men had to act on their urges in order to fully realise their fighting power.[196] The SS leadership was aware of the contradiction, so it warned individuals to restrain themselves while simultaneously assuming that the SS men would engage in uncontrolled sexual contact anyway, thereby infecting themselves with sexually transmitted diseases. For this reason, SS candidates received the following training text at the end of 1938:

Leaflet
1. Sexual abstinence is not harmful to your health.
2. *Every* act of extramarital sexual intercourse can lead to a venereal disease.
3. Excessive alcohol consumption leads to sexual debauchery and thus to numerous infections.
4. Never engage in extramarital intercourse without protection. The best protection is provided by a condom.
5. Visit the troop infirmary after having unprotected intercourse. Even 12 hours after intercourse, medical attention can prevent the clap.
6. The slightest change to the genitals (burning, discharge, soreness, ulcers, etc.) requires that you report immediately to the troop doctor.
7. Early treatment can quickly and fully cure gonorrhoea and syphilis.
8. The clap and chancroid appear 2–6 days after infection, syphilis 10–20 days.
9. The doctor will determine when you have been cured and can resume sexual activity.
10. Before marrying, another examination by a doctor is required in the interest of the woman and your offspring.
11. Recovery from venereal diseases does not protect against further infections.[197]

The SS medical service was concerned less with the sexual contact itself than with its potential negative consequences and how to prevent them. It therefore banked mainly on educating the men about medical facts and sexual myths, such as the widespread rumour that recovering from an infection made one immune to further illness. The moralising tone found in the Wehrmacht, at least until 1944, is absent here. In contrast to the Wehrmacht leaflet mentioned earlier ('German soldier!'), the educational paper issued by the SS did not address the men's duty, honour or morality, nor did it appeal to their sense of reason. Instead, the list is more like an instruction manual. In a pragmatic tone, it mentions the possible side effects of sexual encounters and offers tips on how to identify and treat them.

In the combat units of the SS, this leaflet – which was distributed at least until 1943 – was supplemented with regular instructional lectures. The SS medical service wanted all *Waffen-SS* units to receive instructions once a month.[198] Furthermore, the men were supposed to be individually instructed prior to going out for the first time and on special occasions, such as before taking leave or being re-stationed. It is not possible to determine whether such measures were actually carried out, however.

Even during training, the SS conducted inspections to teach the men hygienic principles. In his wartime memoir, Franz Schönhuber writes that newly recruited SS men had to line up at five o'clock one morning during their training for a 'prick parade' ('*Schwanzappell*'):

> We stood there in a line, naked, and the sergeant went from recruit to recruit, looked at their penis, pushed back a foreskin here and there, to check – just like a rifle inspection – that there weren't any specks in the barrel.[199]

The way Schönhuber describes this procedure speaks to everyday life in the male society of the SS as well as to the sense of shame with which SS recruits reluctantly submitted to the measures designed to control their sexuality. Both the term 'prick parade' and the comparison between the hygienically clean penis and the cleaned rifle appear in the memoirs of former SS man Heinz Maeger as well.[200]

It is noteworthy that the sexual instructions given to the SS men apparently did not involve any threat of punishment.[201] Even while they were being trained, SS doctors were explicitly told that 'a man with venereal disease is not a second-rate man. [. . .] A second-rate man is an SS man who knows or suspects that he has been infected and nonetheless does not report to the troop doctor for an examination'.[202] The SS medical service had clearly set its sights not on the men who had unprotected extramarital sexual contact without 'sanitising' themselves, but on those who covered up their illness. It was not so much the sexual debauchery itself that was considered a breach of duty, but rather the hygienic and 'racial' betrayal of one's 'Aryan' sexual partners, comrades and the 'people's community'. As early as 1937, Himmler had clearly stated that he believed it was necessary to be 'generous' when it came to the 'prostitute issue' because 'you cannot want to prevent the youth from turning to homosexuality on the one hand while closing off every other avenue on the other'.[203] And in Poland in June 1942, he emphatically declared that 'it is possible to have a healthy encounter with girls without the risk of children being brought into the world, the men falling ill or a social bond being formed with the Polish people.'[204]

This approach apparently also applied to the occupied territories of the Soviet Union. Even before the start of the war, the Security Police and SD had become aware that syphilis was 'very common' in the Ukrainian territories captured by the Red Army.[205] One year later, on 25 February 1942, the 'Reports from the occupied territories of the USSR' noted that 'venereal diseases' had been 'brought to Russia by German soldiers', in part through contact with 'secret' prostitutes.[206] In June 1943, Himmler responded to such reports by emphasising once again that the men had a duty to disinfect themselves after sexual contact. But this certainly did not mean that SS men who disobeyed this order would generally face punishment – as is clear from the letter of an SS judge who, in the second half of 1943, argued in favour of dropping the proceedings against an SS man who had been accused of *'mangelnde Sanierung'* ('lack of sanitation'):

> In his decree of 11 June 1943, the Reichsführer-SS once again made it the duty of every member of the SS and police to undergo sanitation immediately after any sexual intercourse. However, according to this order, as expressed in the as yet unpublished addendum of the SS Court Main Office, one should 'deliberately refrain from any threat of punishment', meaning that no punishment for military disobedience is possible in the event of contraventions of this order.[207]

In keeping with this, the Head of the SS Race and Settlement Main Office (RuSHA), SS-*Obergruppenführer* Richard Hildebrandt, informed the disciplinary superiors of the SS and German police in September 1943 that they should tell their men there would be no punishment for 'neglecting sanitation'. Instead, punishment would be faced by those who 'did not promptly report sick'.[208] Within the borders of the Reich, too, the SS seems to have refrained from threats of punishment so that infected men would not be afraid to report their illness.[209] The regulatory measures of the SS largely aimed to maintain productivity, meaning the health of both the individual and the 'body of the people'.

When an SS man contracted a sexually transmitted disease, the SS would follow a procedure similar to that of the Wehrmacht and inform the public health officer of the respective general commissariat.²¹⁰ In some cases, the public health officer would be the first to hear of a suspected illness and he would then inform the SS medical service. For example, the twenty-five-year-old Inge O., who was born in Erfurt but lived in Kaunas, told the public health officer of the general commissariat in Riga that she had been infected with gonorrhoea by SS-*Obersturmführer* Hans Sch. She said she had met the SS man through acquaintances in Kaunas and spent a few nights in a hotel with him in late September and early October 1942. The SS informed the public health officer that the man had been transferred and his new post could not be determined.²¹¹ Whether this was actually true or the SS just wanted to handle the case itself without updating the public health officer is not clear.

Sometimes the SS and Wehrmacht worked together to treat infected men. For example, SS men who contracted infections were occasionally treated by Wehrmacht doctors and admitted to Wehrmacht hospitals.²¹² This led to difficulties, however. In February 1944, the SS Leadership Main Office asked the head of the Wehrmacht medical service to ensure that SS men being treated on an inpatient basis in the reserve hospitals of the Wehrmacht were not punished in accordance with the Wehrmacht's regulations against 'neglected sanitation', as this went against the orders of the SS.²¹³ If such a distinction was actually made in the military hospitals, it was probably a source of resentment. This may also explain why the Wehrmacht Medical Inspectorate made no mention of disciplinary punishments in its 'Guidelines for lectures on venereal diseases' published in April 1944.

Wehrmacht Brothels

In its most far-reaching attempt to influence the sexuality of its soldiers, the Wehrmacht established its own brothels. On 25 February 1942, eight months after the German army invaded the Soviet Union, the 'Reports from the occupied territories of the USSR' published by the Security Police and SD first mentioned that the Wehrmacht planned to set up brothels under military control:

> For the purposes of preventing the growth of venereal diseases and the resulting opportunities for activity by enemy agents in daily interactions between German people and Russian people, leading to the elimination of the necessary distance from the people in the Russian territory, the prospect has been raised in various cities of establishing brothels for the Wehrmacht.²¹⁴

The Wehrmacht hoped that military brothels would make it possible to discipline the clients and permanently monitor the prostitutes. The military trappings in the brothels were expected to have a moderating influence on the soldiers and prevent drunkenness, reckless talk and confiding relationships. The women were to be registered so the medical service could ensure that they were examined regularly, their test results were archived and even minor changes in their health would be noticed immediately. Last but not least, the OKH and OKW wanted to prevent the 'conception of undesirable bastards' in whom Germany had 'absolutely no interest', as head of the OKW Wilhelm Keitel put it in September 1942.[215]

The 'prospect' of establishing brothels under military control institutionalised and centralised a development that was already under way by this point. In late 1941, the RMbO and RKO had sought contact with the Wehrmacht commander of the Ostland territory and the Higher SS and Police Leader in order to clarify 'whether the prostitutes in the cities permanently occupied by Wehrmacht units' should be 'quartered in barracks and monitored by doctors'. During these discussions, the representative of the Higher SS and Police Leader declared that establishing brothels for members of the SS and police was out of the question 'for ideological reasons', but it might make sense for the Wehrmacht. This distinction once again reflects the notion that the SS occupied a more prominent position. As a 'racial elite', the SS could not be involved in the organisation of brothels, which were considered 'undignified'.[216] In early 1943, Carl Oberg, the Higher SS and Police Leader in France, ordered the establishment of military-controlled brothels near all Waffen-SS posts in France (not least as a way of mollifying the 'sexually starving' troops coming 'from the East'), but no such regulation seems to have been issued for the SS in the occupied Soviet territories before the end of the war.[217]

In the correspondence mentioned above, however, the Wehrmacht commander for the Ostland territory called for just such a step to be taken, because experience from World War I had shown that military brothels could prevent the spread of diseases.[218] Individual Wehrmacht units in Latvia appear to have begun independently establishing prostitution structures at this time. In March 1942, in any case, Dr Ernst Wegner, the official responsible for health affairs, and Friedrich Trampedach, the senior civil servant who was head of the Political Affairs department in the RKO, complained that an 'officers' brothel' in Riga had to be closed temporarily because it had become a centre of infection for sexually transmitted diseases. The description of this brothel's closure suggests that the degree of military organisation and medical supervision in these first brothels in the Soviet Union was relatively low.[219]

As this discussion was going on, medically supervised Wehrmacht brothels had already become a part of everyday military life in other occupied territories. Immediately after the invasion of Poland on 9 September 1939, Reinhard Heydrich – acting as Himmler's deputy and head of the Security Police Main Office – had countersigned a decree on the 'Handling of prostitution by the police' issued by the Reich Minister of the Interior. This declared that the establishment and supervision of brothels in the army's area of operations within the Reich was to be placed under the authority of the criminal investigation department and health authorities. The decree stated that 'to guarantee effective defence against the dangers posed by prostitution for Wehrmacht members and the civilian population', all prostitutes were to be registered and continually medically supervised. This advanced the dual strategy behind the prostitution policy, namely, the restriction and criminalisation of prostitution outside of brothels, and the administrative organisation of a supervised brothel system.[220]

On 16 March 1940, this decree was extended to the entire Reich, with the exception of the Protectorate of Bohemia and Moravia.[221] It also served as a guideline for the Wehrmacht's prostitution policy in the occupied territories.[222] In July 1940, immediately following the occupation of France, the OKH issued two orders calling for the prosecution of prostitutes and the establishment of supervised brothels for the entire French territory under German control.[223] The list of rules governing the operation of such brothels covered everything from their opening hours and hygienic facilities to a prohibition against serving alcohol. The influence that the OKH wielded when it came to controlling prostitution was 'important in two respects', according to Insa Meinen. First, the establishment of Wehrmacht brothels in the occupied territories can be traced back to plans and instructions formulated at the highest level of the army, and second, benchmarks were defined by the OKH headquarters that ultimately resulted in the creation of a kind of 'standard brothel for occupation purposes'.[224] In his decree on 'Combatting venereal diseases' issued on 27 January 1943, head of the OKW Keitel additionally portrayed medically supervised brothels as an effective military policy measure and made the establishment of such facilities the norm in all of the Wehrmacht's areas of operations – in France as well as Norway and Russia.[225]

By this point, the Wehrmacht already had almost a year of experience with military brothels set up as directed in the occupied Soviet territories. The practice soon proved to be controversial, however. The previously mentioned reports sent from the occupied territories of the USSR in February 1942 – before the first official military brothels had even been established – stated:

> Opinions are sharply divided as to the necessity and expediency of establishing brothels, not least because, in its time, even the Bolshevist regime, when it introduced the Bolshevist order of life, dissolved the houses of pleasure that had existed in the tsarist period with the justification of the 'elimination of a stratum of women and girls evading professional life and thus the creation of the socialist state'.[226]

The mention of disagreement regarding the 'necessity and expediency' of the brothels refers to the differing positions of various military representatives, some of whom doubted the brothels would do much to lower the infection rates and worried that they would instead damage the reputation of the Wehrmacht.[227] In the occupied territories of the Soviet union, such objections were shared by the civilian occupation authorities. The RKO insisted that the 'maintenance of troop brothels' could only be justified on a military basis, if at all. If responsibility for such brothels were transferred to the civilian occupation authorities, it would endanger the 'standing of the German Reich'. The responsible officials apparently assumed that the local population would initially accept military brothels as a necessary by-product of the war, but that prostitution organised by the civilian authorities – representing longer-lasting institutionalisation – would negatively impact the occupying power and the nation as a whole.[228]

In addition to these general objections, the SD report hinted at the organisational challenges facing the army leadership. By mentioning the official abolition of prostitution in the Soviet Union, there was an implication that, unlike in France, the army units in the East would not be able to fall back on existing brothels or police card indexes with the names and addresses of prostitutes. Instead, they would either have to track down prostitutes working illegally, which would require detailed knowledge of the respective region or contact with local intermediaries, or they would need to set up a whole new system and 'acquire' women for their brothels – either voluntarily or by force.

In general, establishing a system of prostitution controlled by the military was a complex organisational task for the army units. Nonetheless, on 20 March 1942, the Quartermaster General of the OKH issued an order calling for the creation of military brothels in the occupied territories of the Soviet Union:

> There is no other way of countering the dangers [of hidden prostitution; R. M.] that threaten the clout of the German Wehrmacht than by establishing strictly monitored and properly medically supervised brothels. [. . .] In such larger cities and towns where there is a need for them, the local headquarters are to set up suitable houses approved for the exclusive use of German soldiers. The use of these houses by locals is to be forbidden, and signs should be posted to this effect.[229]

Responsibility for setting up the brothels was assigned to the local headquarters, which were expected to come to an agreement with the medical officers and company leaders regarding the number, location and management of the facilities.[230] The key point here, as the decree from the Quartermaster General went on to say, was to consider the reputation of the Wehrmacht every step of the way and ensure the 'necessary distance from the people of the Russian territory'.

The placement and configuration of the brothels varied from region to region and depended first and foremost on how prostitution had been organised in the respective area prior to the German occupation. The general rule, however, was that 'brothels should be on side streets and [. . .] not in the immediate vicinity of soldiers' recreation centres or accommodations'.[231] The degree of collaboration with the local authorities and the tactics behind Germany's occupation policy also played a role. In Riga, for example, the medical service considered the task to be relatively easy because Latvia had a long-established system of registering prostitutes by the police even before the country was annexed by the USSR, and much of Latvian society was 'favourably disposed towards' the German occupying forces.[232]

The reports of the Commander of the Army Patrol Service Ostland hint that the brothels in larger cities in the occupied back country might have become permanent establishments. From September 1942 to March 1944, these reports included a monthly section covering the operation of the facilities, which addressed aspects such as the condition of the brothels – particularly their (lack of) cleanliness[233] – and the appropriate placement of posters warning against enemy espionage, which were to be hung in a prominent position in the foyer of each facility.[234] The Army Patrol Service also gave some thought to potentially desirable locations for additional brothels. The report from 15 September 1942 stated:

The brothels in Kaunas and Vilnius were [...] acceptable; it is urgently necessary to establish a brothel in Minsk so that the soldiers stay away from the dirty local brothels, where they might be tempted to desert or subjected to enemy espionage. The establishment of a brothel for Baranovichi is also recommended.[235]

The need for a new brothel was apparently not always determined on the basis of clear standards, such as the number of men stationed in an area. In any case, none of the sources mention any objective criteria. Instead, it seems the troop leaders or area headquarters would consider the situation and the conduct of their units and then spontaneously decide to set up facilities locally. For example, a brothel might be established if there were reports of homosexual encounters taking place between the soldiers.[236] The court of the 122nd Infantry Division, which was deployed in the operations area of Army Group North near Staraya Russa early in the summer of 1942, sentenced two non-commissioned officers for violating Paragraph 175, and two others were accused of the same offence. In light of this, a troop leader suggested to the division commander that a brothel be set up in Staraya Russa.[237] The thinking behind this was the widespread view mentioned earlier, namely, that regularly satisfying heterosexual urges would nip homosexual desires in the bud. In the end, the division commander decided against a brothel in Staraya Russa, however. Malaria and typhus were rampant in the region at the time, and it was feared that a brothel would cause the diseases to spread even further.[238]

Once a brothel had been set up, medical officers had to keep the area headquarters updated on whether the establishment was working to capacity. This was not always the case; for example, in March 1944, the Wehrmacht Patrol Service reported that the brothel in Libau (Liepāja) had 'folded'.[239] The orders issued by the local headquarters also announced the closure of old brothels, the opening of new ones and the brothels' business hours.[240]

Individual sources indicate that the occupation authorities sometimes seized private property for use as a brothel. Antonina Ivanovna from Novomoskovsk[241] (Ukraine) recalled how her family home was turned into a military brothel after the Germans discovered that her father had joined the partisans.[242] In cases such as this, the establishment of a brothel could have a strong symbolic effect; the conquerors were demonstrating to their enemy that they had seized their territory in sexual terms as well. The punitive or deterrent effect of such actions is also likely to have played a role. And, as Ivanovna's account clearly shows, this effect not only impacted the people who owned or lived in the house: 'They [the women; R. M.] didn't necessarily come from Novomoskovsk, but were from the surrounding villages. [. . .] They were able to recruit some of the girls. Others were forced to go to the brothel'.[243] Since any woman could, in principle, fall into the hands of the soldiers, all women in the area were massively restricted in their freedom of movement. The more accounts circulated about the abduction and sexual enslavement of women, the more fear spread among the women and girls, even if they lived some distance from the brothels.[244] Witnesses from the time have reported relatively often that the Germans captured the women for their 'houses' during raids in the street, outside of labour offices, in cafés and in cinemas.[245] Similar accounts were publicised in the Soviet press.[246]

The fact that these depictions are remarkably similar in terms of both structure and vocabulary could indicate that the witnesses were not always necessarily reporting actual cases but were instead referring to the warnings that were spread to keep women and girls from leaving the house. It was also said relatively often that women had been deported from Czechoslovakia, Poland or the concentration camps to work in brothels in the Soviet Union.[247] Siegfried von Vegesack, a German who worked as an interpreter for the Wirtschaftsstab Ost economic authority in Ukraine in 1942–3, wrote in his memoirs in 1965 that most of the women who were 'requisitioned' for the Wehrmacht brothel in Poltava (Ukraine) were very young. After being examined by a doctor, he said that around 85 per cent of them were reported as being 'untouched'.[248]

While Vegesack's account indicates that the women were sexually enslaved, another German soldier claimed they were prostitutes by trade: 'that was their profession'.[249] To this day, very little is known about the actual circumstances under which women wound up in the brothels. Presumably many women were sexually enslaved while some did report to the brothels of their own volition, particularly if they had previously worked as prostitutes or saw no other way of saving themselves and their families from starvation.[250] But the line between voluntary action and coercion was blurry here. Fritz Seidler believed that young women in particular preferred to work in military brothels in lieu of the forced labour they feared in Germany.[251] Horrifying stories did circulate about what could happen when young women went to Germany alone to work: they faced the threat of rape, sexual enslavement, sterilisation, impregnation and even murder.[252] These terrifying prospects might well have compelled some young women to want to stay in familiar surroundings, near their mothers and friends.

Overall, the recruitment of the women seems to have depended largely on the approach of the responsible men in the area. Based on a Wehrmacht document found in the central archives of Ukraine, Wendy Lower has shown that the Wehrmacht in Zhytomyr contemplated using 'more racially acceptable' women – such as Dutch women – in the local military brothel.[253] But generally, the women in these brothels would have been considered 'ethnically alien' according to Nazi racial ideology. The sources show that the transgression of 'racial boundaries' in the brothels was at least tolerated because 'the relationships of the prostitutes with their changing visitors' was of an 'impersonal and economic nature', with no 'social interaction' or 'mutual esteem' involved.[254] Even Himmler had explicitly condoned such encounters for SS men in 1942, arguing that they took place outside the context of personal connection and reproduction.[255]

This casual approach did not apply to 'sexual intercourse with Jewish women', however. In his order of 20 March 1942, the head medical officer of the OKH explicitly stated that Jewish women were to be 'expelled'.[256] All of the other military proclamations also leave no doubt that Jewish women were strictly prohibited from working in Wehrmacht brothels.[257] However, a number of narratives suggest that this prohibition might have been violated in isolated cases.[258] It remains to be determined whether this corresponds to historical reality or is more a product of post-war depictions that exhibited a fascination with the potential interplay between sex, violence and antisemitism.[259]

When women arrived at the Wehrmacht brothels, they were given an alias and a control number and were registered by the responsible medical officer or NCO for their weekly examination. In principle, the OKH had entrusted the army medical service with the medical supervision of the brothels. But the *Heeresarzt* (army doctor) of the OKH decided that brothel operations should be organised largely in cooperation with local personnel:

> The only option for successfully monitoring the prostitutes lies with the residents of the brothels, assuming that the regular examinations are conducted by suitable Russian doctors and supervised by German medical officers. If no Russian doctors are available, the necessary examinations must be carried out by suitable medical officers themselves.[260]

The thinking behind this was that the women could only receive optimal medical supervision if the examinations were conducted by doctors who spoke their language. German medical officers were present solely for monitoring purposes. The Germans themselves were only supposed to take over if no local doctors were available – in fact the medical officers were often not trained to treat female patients, and it could be difficult to diagnose sexually transmitted diseases in women.

In some places, including the Wehrmacht brothel on Parkstrasse in Riga, the women had to visit the doctor up to three times a week.[261] If the doctor diagnosed a sexually transmitted disease, he would admit the woman to the local hospital. At least in some cases, the women were taken back to the brothel afterwards.[262] Little is known about the lives of the women and girls in the brothels, the different conditions for those sexually enslaved and those who had volunteered, their freedom of movement, and whether or how the latter were paid.[263] At any rate, none of the women could reject a client and all of them were confronted with men who had been brutalised by the war. The 'direct supervision of the girls' was usually the responsibility of a local civilian who could speak the language. Some of these 'brothel hosts' ('*Bordellwirte*') were women themselves.[264] The military units thought such regulations were sensible, not least because in Riga, for instance, the soldier who was entrusted with this job had proved to be hopelessly out of his depth.[265]

How the brothel operations were financed is a subject for future study.[266] The fees for visiting a brothel were probably not set by the 'brothel hosts' or the women themselves, but rather by the military administration.[267] Not much is known about the prices. According to the notes of the head doctor of the general commissariat in Latvia, one Wehrmacht soldier said he paid 15 Reichsmarks in May 1943 to visit the Wehrmacht brothel in Riga.[268] This price seems very high, however, since the German authorities assumed that visiting a 'secret prostitute' only cost between two and three Reichsmarks.[269]

The question of how many men visited the brothels run by the Wehrmacht and who they were is a matter of speculation. However, the sources show that the mere existence of the brothels could be used as a pretence for soldiers to explain how they had contracted a sexually transmitted disease. For example, at the end of April and start of May 1943, two men in different military hospitals claimed to have contracted infections in the military brothel in Riga.[270] A few days later, however, the head of the Wehrmacht brothel reported that 'the girl in question' had been 'examined [. . .] and found to be healthy'. He recommended further investigation, since one of the soldiers had previously been put up 'in a private hotel', where he might have picked up the infection.[271] In other similar cases, when the examinations returned negative results each time, the garrison doctor would usually order the respective soldiers to be questioned once again.²⁷² Nonetheless, the doctors involved could never prove conclusively that a soldier had lied, as it was always theoretically possible for the accused woman to have taken a sulphonamide preparation on the day of the exam in order to falsify the results and avoid any trouble.²⁷³ Ultimately, Wehrmacht brothels gave soldiers the opportunity not only to engage in sexual intercourse but also to cover up sexual encounters that took place elsewhere.

The effects of the operation and specific organisation of the brothels extended far beyond the original aims of the Wehrmacht leadership. Hierarchies and distinctions within the troops often played a role in this. Additionally, the Wehrmacht and civilian authorities alike were concerned with the image that soldiers acquired when they visited the brothels and the potential long-term impact of the institutionalisation of official military brothels. For example, brothel visits could serve to remind the German women serving alongside Wehrmacht soldiers that the military was a male society. Former Wehrmacht auxiliary Ilse Schmidt recalled how one of her superiors announced the opening of an officers' brothel during dinner one evening:

> They talk in detail about the encirclement battle of Smolensk in August 1941. [. . .] While this is still being discussed, Major L. smoothly changes the subject, turns to the officers and asks: 'By the way, gentlemen, have you heard about the new officers' brothel? Apparently it's run by a lady! Very classy! They say there's good wine to be had there!' The table grows quiet. No one seems to have heard of the place, and if they have, they don't admit it. Major L. continues: 'What if we took a look at the establishment? The furnishings are apparently expensive and elegant. Really something special!!' A few of the men grin, including Dr. Sch. Sonja sneaks a side glance at her boyfriend. Everyone knows that if the Head of Brothel Inspection gives an order, no one can defy him. [. . .] Then I feel a creeping sense of unease. A brothel visit is being arranged in our presence. The major's crude behaviour, his contempt for women, appals me.²⁷⁴

One of the functions of visiting a brothel with comrades was to exclude women.²⁷⁵ Schmidt's account indicates that this also played a role for the German men and women stationed in the occupied territories. Her description additionally illustrates that even brothel visits were governed by military hierarchies. This applied both to the communal visits sometimes 'ordered' by military superiors and to the overall organisation of the brothels. Witnesses have repeatedly reported that certain brothels were only open to German officers.²⁷⁶ The parody

'Tünnes and Schäl' letter that circulated in a Wehrmacht unit in December 1941 also hints that this was the case. The letter claimed that the 'live girls' in Russia were 'mostly there for the officers'; ordinary soldiers had to go to the cinema instead.[277] The tensions this could produce are reflected in the experiences of Hildegard Klemm, a singer who participated in a 'Strength-through-Joy' tour for the Wehrmacht in the occupied Soviet territories. In a letter dated 26 February 1943, she wrote to her former colleagues that physical altercations often took place after the shows between officers and ordinary infantrymen because each believed they had the privilege of the singers' company.[278] Similar competition is likely to have occurred between the SS and the Wehrmacht. It has yet to be determined whether the SS set up its own brothels[279] – and, if so, where – but witnesses from the time report that SS men definitely visited the Wehrmacht brothels, particularly the ones for officers.[280]

The international composition of the military units further complicated the situation. Local headquarters repeatedly voiced concerns about 'frictions' inside and outside the brothels. Their reports suggest that fights took place above all when men of different nationalities visited a brothel at the same time. On 1 January 1944, the Wehrmacht Patrol Service in Riga noted:

> In Riga, visiting the German military brothel is prohibited for anyone other than German soldiers. This rule has eliminated the frictions that previously existed.
>
> In other places, such as Kaunas, this separation has not been implemented, meaning that disagreements are the order of the day. In particular, preference is naturally given to the native soldiers by the native brothel occupants. A separation would be generally desirable [. . .].[281]

From the perspective of the Wehrmacht Patrol Service, the prospect of soldiers of different nationalities running into one another at a brothel was problematic for two reasons. First, the fact that the visitors encountered each other as men seeking to satisfy their sexual needs suggested a moment of equality, but the soldiers' special emphasis on hierarchy apparently repeatedly led to 'disagreements'. And second, the purported or actual 'preference' given to 'native Wehrmacht volunteers' by the prostitutes could be seen as particularly humiliating in the eyes of German soldiers. The national hierarchy was not just blurred here, it was turned completely upside down. To eliminate the breeding ground for such conflicts, the Wehrmacht Patrol Service made a case for at least establishing different opening hours for soldiers of different nationalities.²⁸²

This example makes it clear that the above-mentioned OKH order from March 1942, which called for brothels to be opened in the Soviet Union exclusively for German members of the army, became obsolete at least in some regions in the course of the war.²⁸³ During medical examinations, foreign Wehrmacht volunteers also reported having contracted sexually transmitted diseases in German military brothels, which implies that the envisioned exclusivity of the brothels was not strictly maintained.²⁸⁴ The OKH could not completely deny access to the brothels for non-German Wehrmacht and SS volunteers; after all, as an adjutant of the *'Ostbatallion'* wrote in December 1943, a man who was 'willing to die for Germany [. . .] should also be given access to the brothels'.²⁸⁵

This seemed to be all the more necessary for the Wehrmacht, as the percentage of non-German men serving in its combat units was relatively high; there were nearly one million foreign volunteers at the start of the Eastern campaign, a number that doubled in the course of the war.²⁸⁶ The doctor of the Army Group D High Command therefore ordered in April 1944 that 'special brothels' be established for the 'foreign volunteers', as was already the case in France:

> Special brothels for members of the Eastern peoples etc. are [. . .] to be set up if there is an urgent need for them. This is the case if many such members are present at a site. If it is not worth setting up a special brothel, Wehrmacht brothels can be opened for certain hours if required while being closed to Wehrmacht members during the same period. The area headquarters physician is to specify times during which visits by German Wehrmacht members are known to be infrequent (early hours of the afternoon). The area headquarters physician will make the necessary arrangements in agreement with the brothel owners.²⁸⁷

The approach to dealing with military prostitution for foreign volunteers could apparently vary depending on the army group. This order from the doctor of the Army Group D High Command was probably not implemented to any notable degree, however, because in the spring of 1944 the Germans were already engaged in rearguard action.

The obviously large number of visitors to the brothels was also occasionally a cause of concern for the Wehrmacht. In some regions, medical officers complained that the demand for sexual services exceeded the number of available prostitutes.²⁸⁸ In March 1943, for example, the head medical officer in Lemberg (Lviv) reported that queues stretching across the street were forming at lunchtime and in the evenings. He said the civilian population responded to this with a 'lack of comprehension'. In the 'present situation', he concluded, the 'whole military brothel business' had to be considered 'unworthy of the Wehrmacht'.[289] The interpreter Anatol Herlitz, a so-called 'ethnic German' who worked for the occupation authorities, also felt it was incompatible with the 'dignity of a master race' for a German man to 'let himself go while drinking' and 'amuse himself with Russian whores'.[290] And Lieutenant-General Max von Viebahn called upon his men to intervene with the non-commissioned officers in order to curb their brothel visits and excessive drinking and prevent them from exploiting the 'dominance of the Germans' in the 'manner of a pasha'.[291] The reference to the 'manner of a pasha' presents an ambivalent image. Pashas were thought of as domineering and ruthless warriors who were pampered by women every day, as a consequence of which – according to the widespread cliché – these Eastern despots quickly grew lazy, soft, effeminate and fixated on luxury goods and sensual pleasures. In Viebahn's metaphor, the masculinity of the sexually active soldier threatened to tip into libidinal and irrational femininity.

While complaints such as this revolved primarily around the reputation of the Wehrmacht, other authorities were more concerned with the morals and discipline of the men. As early as July 1940, Commander-in-Chief of the Army Walther von Brauchitsch remarked that the troop leaders in France had to take action against the 'vile and unworthy excesses' that mainly occurred when 'younger soldiers and even subordinates' were 'enticed by older comrades to visit brothels'.[292] Other commanders concluded from such incidents that the brothels should be closed altogether. For example, the head doctor in Military District XVIII, who was responsible for the soldiers being trained in the Austrian administrative regions of Salzburg, Tirol/Vorarlberg, Kärnten and Steiermark, wrote to the Army Medical Inspectorate on 3 January 1945:

> The disadvantages of a brothel, the altogether unsavoury masses of visitors and the non-negligible fact that large numbers of young soldiers and those who would not otherwise have done such a thing are being taken along by comrades and practically forced into intercourse with prostitutes – these unequivocal disadvantages are in no way balanced out by the control function, so in the opinion of this office, it would be correct to forbid the establishment of brothels by the Wehrmacht and make brothel visits by soldiers a punishable offence.[293]

The author's revulsion for the serial 'masses of visitors' is clear here. He viewed the brothels as a long-term danger to the 'people's community', since an entire generation of young men were having their first sexual experiences in brothels, possibly under peer pressure and with women who were considered 'anti-social' from a 'racial hygiene' point of view. The men were thus learning to view an actually undesirable experience as something normal. Granted, this letter was written in early 1945 and was not likely to have been met with any great response. But the notion that loose morals on the front could later give rise to problems back home was not new. Even in 1942, the head medical officer in southwest France had claimed that the brothels were teaching the soldiers to be 'sissies' and leading to their moral decline.[294] And in May 1943, troop doctor Walther Camerer raised the following point:

> In all of Bolshevist Russia, for example, I have not seen nude pictures of any kind in any newspaper, in any home. But you only need to open a single German glossy, a magazine or a soldiers' newspaper (though the latter have been much improved for some time now!) or step into a bunker or other accommodation – they are full of them. This degradation of woman to wench, this deliberate stimulation of sensuality, is bound to have an effect.[295]

Camerer feared that the rampant use of pornographic imagery by German men would have negative consequences for gender relations as a whole, because the 'degradation of woman to wench' meant that women were being viewed first and foremost as sexual objects. This was problematic enough in Russia, he believed, because it damaged the image of the Wehrmacht – but the effects were thought to be positively disastrous in Germany. If the men did not learn to respect an 'honourable' woman, then good, 'racially desirable' relationships and 'normal' family life would be impossible.

The medical benefits of the brothels were also increasingly called into question in the last years of the war. In September 1944, the High Command of Army Group South-Ukraine contended that the brothels were actually 'conducive to the spread of venereal diseases' because the men were infecting each other through their contact with the women.[296] The high command was largely alone in this assessment, however. The troop leaders themselves reported that 'venereal diseases almost never appear in the Wehrmacht brothels'.[297] And in early January 1945, the consultant dermatologist for the Army Medical Inspectorate, Dr Heinrich Löhe, responded to the concerns of the High Command of Army Group

South-Ukraine by providing the following summary of the military's programme of controlled prostitution:

> On my many inspection tours, I always checked the hygienic conditions in all the brothels in the Wehrmacht billets and reviewed the operation of these houses and determined that [. . .] infections only very rarely emerged from the brothels. Based on the books that were kept, it was possible to determine that in France, Italy, Greece and Romania, for example, [. . .] the disease had been brought in by German Wehrmacht members and the sick prostitute could be rendered harmless very quickly be being transferred to hospital [. . .].
>
> The conditions are very different where there is a predominance of free prostitution [. . .], because there are great difficulties in registering these women, most of whom are sick. But even this problem can be solved successfully, as seen in the exemplary results of carefully conducted investigations into the sources of infection in Belgrade, Oslo and Paris, for example, where very good results were able to be achieved through conscientious cooperation between doctor, troop leadership, field police and local authorities.
>
> In my view, therefore, the Wehrmacht brothels must continue to be maintained [. . .], and the basic order issued by the head of the Wehrmacht Medical Service on 27 January 1943 must remain in full effect.[298]

In the eyes of the consultant dermatologist, the Germans' attempts to control prostitution on a European level had generally been successful. The Army High Command in Berlin also continued to support the centrally organised system of military prostitution until the end of the war. The question of how many brothels the Wehrmacht established in the occupied territories of the Soviet Union will have to be answered by future researchers. But we can already say with some certainty that there were military-run brothels in the following locations: one in Vilnius (Lithuania); two in Riga and one in Liepāja (Latvia); one each in Kharkiv, Lviv, Zhytomyr, Baranovichi, Poltava, Moshny, Yasnoziria, Bezobrazia and Novomoskovsk (Ukraine); and one each in Gomel and Mogilev (Belarus) and in Smolensk (Russia).[299]

On the whole, the establishment of brothels and sanitation stations, the distribution of condoms, and lectures on the symptoms and risks of sexually transmitted diseases demonstrate that the military leadership did not try to control the soldiers' sexuality in a purely repressive fashion. Instead, the OKH, OKW and RF-SS created opportunities for the men to engage in relatively convenient, unrisky and economical sexual contact. While the military viewed these measures for relieving 'sexual needs' and curbing sexually transmitted diseases as a normal, everyday aspect of the war and thus took a pragmatic approach to managing them, the policy towards consensual relations proved to be much more complicated. In this case, it was not possible to reduce the soldiers' behaviour to their biological instincts alone. Instead, the military and civilian occupation authorities alike were forced to engage with the emotional needs and ties of the men.

Notes

1. Regarding the debate triggered by this exhibition about the responsibility of German soldiers, see Donat and Strohmeyer, *Befreiung von der Wehrmacht?*; Prantl (ed.), *Wehrmachtsverbrechen*; Hamburger Institut (ed.), *Eine Ausstellung und ihre Folgen*.
2. Beckermann and Wulff, 'Vom Mangel an Herzensbildung', p. 21. Also see Bopp, 'Wo sind die Augenzeugen, wo ihre Fotos?', pp. 202f.
3. Over the course of five weeks, Beckermann and her team conducted more than 200 interviews. The resulting documentary film illustrates the process of remembering and recounting, making the decades of silence about the crimes even more powerful an issue. Beckermann, *East of War (Jenseits des Krieges)*, documentary film.
4. Published in Beckermann, *Jenseits des Krieges*, pp. 102f.
5. Peninsula on the northern coast of the Black Sea. After fierce fighting for the southern port city of Sevastopol, the Wehrmacht occupied Crimea from 1941 to 1944.
6. Oldenburg, *Ideologie und militärisches Kalkül*, pp. 68ff., 87.
7. There was a sometimes-blurry distinction between prostitutes and 'soldiers' sweethearts' who lived in long-term non-marital relationships with soldiers. The latter were granted a specific legal status, at least in Berlin and Potsdam; see Engelen, *Soldatenfrauen*, pp. 109ff., 439ff.
8. Frevert, 'Militär als Schule der Männlichkeiten', p. 66.
9. See the discussions in the journal *Zeitschrift zur Bekämpfung von Geschlechtskrankheiten*, volumes 15 (1914), 16 (1915/16) and 19 (1919/20); I would like to thank Robert Sommer for this reference. Also see Hirschfeld, *The Sexual History of the World War*, pp. 141ff.; Frischauer, 'The Brothel Brigade'; Liulevicius, *War Land on the Eastern Front*, p. 133; Rother, *Der Weltkrieg*, pp. 179f. While it was considered normal for soldiers to visit brothels and have sexual affairs, women were increasingly accused of 'moral decline' and prostitution during World War I. See Kundrus, *Kriegerfrauen*, pp. 212ff.
10. Nelson, 'German Comrades – Slavic Whores', pp. 79f.
11. Wurzer, 'Die Erfahrung der Extreme', pp. 117f.
12. Hitler, *Mein Kampf*, pp. 247f., 251ff.
13. Roos, 'Backlash Against Prostitutes' Rights', pp. 69, 80ff.; Herzog, *Sex After*

Fascism, p. 25ff.; Sommer, *Das KZ-Bordell*, pp. 34ff.; Alakus, Kniefacz and Vorberg (eds), *Sex-Zwangsarbeit*, pp. 49ff.
14. Hitler, by contrast, embraced the ideal of the 'race-conscious man of the master race' whose masculinity was characterised by strength of will and sexual self-control. Regarding the image of the 'self-controlled member of the master race', see Diehl, *Macht – Mythos – Utopie*, pp. 162ff.
15. Zvychaina, *Kharkiv*, pp. 20f., also quoted in Gertjejanssen, *Victims, Heroes, Survivors*, p. 92.
16. Hamburger Institut (ed.), *Verbrechen der Wehrmacht*, pp. 287, 328; *Crimes of the Wehrmacht*, pp. 14f.
17. Regarding the food situation in different regions of the Soviet Union, see Oldenburg, *Ideologie und militärisches Kalkül*, pp. 68ff., 228ff., 267ff., 308.
18. Regarding sexual bartering in Kiev, see Berkhoff, *Harvest of Despair*, pp. 182f.
19. The name has been anonymised. Otto Hilger, Feldpost, 19.1.1942, BfZ, Sterz collection, quoted in Humburg, *Das Gesicht des Krieges*, p. 113.
20. Maeger, *Lost Honour, Betrayed Loyalty*, p. 102.
21. See, e.g., Jürgen W., 'Tagebuch in Russland', HIS-Arch, NS-O 22, box 4.
22. City in western Ukraine that was annexed by the Soviet Union in September 1939 and occupied by the Wehrmacht in August 1941.
23. It is not clear whether the witness saw this happen once or many times, and whether it was common practice or primarily something that he imagined; see Gertjejanssen, *Victims, Heroes, Survivors*, pp. 92f.
24. Angrick, *Besatzungspolitik und Massenmord*, p. 448.
25. Port city in southern Russia, west of the mouth of the Don, which was taken by SS units in October 1941. On 30 August 1943, the Red Army recaptured Taganrog.
26. BAB, BDC-SSO Seetzen; 'Schreiben Dr. Heinrich Görz an RA Dr. Aschenauer', green notebook, unpaginated, BA-MA, N 642, box 29, quoted in Angrick, *Besatzungspolitik und Massenmord*, p. 448.
27. 'OKH Generalquartiermeister, betr.: Prostitution und Bordellwesen in den besetzten Ostgebieten', 20.3.1942, BA-MA, RH 12-23/1818.
28. 'Meldungen aus den besetzten Ostgebieten 41', 12.2.1943, p. 17, NARA, RG-242 175/236.
29. Quoted in Hamburger Institut (ed.), *Verbrechen der Wehrmacht*, p. 331.
30. 'Oberbefehlshaber der 11. Armee, Generaloberst von Manstein, Befehl', 20.11.1941, published in *Trial of the Major War Criminals*, vol. 20, p. 642, and Ueberschär and Wette (eds), '*Unternehmen Barbarossa*', p. 246. Also see Oldenburg, *Ideologie und militärisches Kalkül*, pp. 104f.
31. City in the province of Zhytomyr in western Ukraine. Before German troops occupied it in the summer of 1941, Novograd-Volynski had been part of the Ukrainian Soviet Socialist Republic.
32. 'Arbeitsamt, Gebietskommissar Nowograd-Wolynsk', 13.2.1942, State Archives of Zhytomyr Oblast (ZSA), PI465-I-6, quoted in Lower, *Nazi Empire-Building*, p. 111.

33. 'Tätigkeitsbericht des Arbeitsamtes Brest-Litowsk für die Jahre 1941–1944', 24.8.1944, BArch, R 93/14, fol 1, unpaginated.
34. See Lenin, 'Capitalism and Female Labour' (1913), pp. 682f. Regarding prostitution in Russia in the nineteenth and early twentieth centuries, see, e.g., Bernstein, *Sonia's Daughters*; Fieseler, '"Stell dich doch auf den Nevskij!"'. Regarding the assessment of prostitution against the backdrop of socialist policies on marriage and family, see Schmitt, 'Regulieren, tabuisieren, kriminalisieren', pp. 42ff.
35. Wood, 'Prostitution Unbound', p. 131.
36. For a short introduction to the circumstances and effects of the NEP, see Berend, *Decades of Crisis*, p. 207.
37. Eliot Borenstein has shown that prostitution also flourished as a cultural phenomenon. In Russia under the NEP, prostitutes 'functioned as a kind of shorthand for the moral and physical diseases brought on by the partial return to a market economy'; Borenstein, 'Selling Russia', pp. 191f., note 7.
38. Wood, 'Prostitution Unbound', p. 115.
39. The women were given a room, food, clothing and medical treatment. They were not allowed to leave the facility between 3:00 and 10:00 p.m. to prevent them from being 'drawn back' into prostitution. Once a woman was considered 'cured' she would be assigned to a new workplace, but her employer would be notified of her former profession so she could be carefully monitored. Elizabeth Wood concludes that the Bolshevist regime that had initially rejected such policing measures ultimately landed on 'forms of institutional solutions that in many ways resembled precisely the lock wards and Magdalene Societies of Victorian England' (Wood, 'Prostitution Unbound', p. 132). Also see Bernstein, 'Prostitutes and Proletarians', p. 115.
40. Regarding the annexation of the Baltic countries by the Soviet Union, see Hiden and Salmon, *The Baltic Nations*, pp. 110–15.
41. Registered prostitutes often worked out of homes shared by four to nine women. In early 1940, there were forty-seven such homes registered in Estonia; see Kalikov, *Prostitution in Estonia, Latvia and Lithuania*, available at <http://pdc.ceu.hu/archive/00002057/01/kalikov.pdf> (last accessed 1 April 2019).
42. In Tallinn (known as Reval under the German occupation), a special department was established for moral policing and the outpatient treatment of sexually transmitted diseases; see ibid.
43. Ibid.; see paragraphs 200 and 201, section 3, of the Criminal Code of the Estonian Soviet Socialist Republic.
44. Birn, *Die Sicherheitspolizei in Estland*, pp. 107, 109.
45. It would be interesting to know whether Red Army soldiers were also clients of these women. They probably were, but as far as I know this has not yet been researched.
46. Port city in southern Ukraine on the Black Sea, which was occupied by the German and Romanian armies from 5 August 1941.
47. Heinrich Böll, letter to Annemarie Böll, 7 January 1944, in Heinrich Böll, *Briefe*

aus dem Krieg, vol. 2, p. 975, also quoted in Vossler, *Propaganda in die eigene Truppe*, p. 353. Similarly, in a letter dated 30 January 1944, Böll describes the availability of the 'most beautiful, spirited southern Russian women' (ibid. p. 987).

48. 'Stadkommandant Kauen, Feldkommandantur 821, gez. Generalmajor Pohl, Standortbefehl', Kaunas, 3.9.1941, USHMM, RG-18.002M, reel 7, 80/3/2, pp. 4–5. Regarding similar orders in other places, see 'Wehrmachtskommandantur Minsk, Feldkommandantur 812, Kommandantur-Befehl Nr. 12', Minsk, 4.11.1941, USHMM, RG-53.002M, reel 3, 37/2/45, unpaginated; 'Stadtkommissar in Grodno, Bekanntmachung', 19.12.1941, USHMM, RG-53.004M, reel 6.
49. 'Bormann, Schreiben an Koch', 23.7.1942, NARA, RG-242 454/92, pp. 000894–000897. Also see Lower, *Nazi Empire-Building*, p. 112.
50. See, e.g., Wilhelm, 'Die Einsatzgruppe A', p. 478; Lower, *Nazi Empire-Building*, p. 112; Birn, *Die Sicherheitspolizei in Estland*, pp. 198f.
51. City in northern Belarus near the Russian border. Before the war, around 34,000 Jews lived here, accounting for more than half the total population. Most of them were murdered in 1941 and 1944 in the Vitebsk ghetto.
52. Stabsarzt Karies, 'Erfahrungsbericht Februar bis Mai 1943', BA-MA, RH 12-23/193, p. 146.
53. Birn, *Die Sicherheitspolizei in Estland*, pp. 198f. The activities of the criminal investigation department in Minsk, as described by Hans-Heinrich Wilhelm, suggest that the situation was similar in Belarus (Wilhelm, 'Die Einsatzgruppe A', p. 478).
54. Birn, *Die Sicherheitspolizei in Estland*, pp. 198f.
55. 'SS- und Polizeistandortführer Libau, verschiedene Bekanntmachungen, betr.: Bekämpfung von Geschlechtskrankheiten', USHMM, RG-18.002M, reel 11, R-83/1/237, pp. 17–21.
56. 'Chef der Sicherheitspolizei und des SD, Kommandostab, Meldungen aus den besetzten Gebieten der UdSSR', 25.2.1942, USHMM, RG-31.002M, reel 11, 3676/4/105, p. 16.
57. This approach had a long tradition behind it. Even in the early sixteenth century, when a growing number of works on the spread of syphilis were being published in Europe, women were accused of deliberately spreading the disease and were punished for it. Men, by contrast, could often move about freely without having to fear so much as a medical exam; see, e.g., Haberling, 'Army Prostitution and its Control', p. 30.
58. See, e.g., 'XXVI Armeekorps, Richtlinien für die Behandlung schädlicher und verdächtiger Teile der Zivilbevölkerung', 26.12.1941, in Müller, *Deutsche Besatzungspolitik*, pp. 81–7, here p. 84.
59. Regarding the symptoms of disease among women, see Meinen, *Wehrmacht und Prostitution*, pp. 116f. These thorough exams required well-equipped laboratories with microscopes.
60. 'Reservelazarett II, Vordruck Fragebogen an das Deutsche Gesundheitshamt

in Riga', 30.12.1942, BArch, R 92/10036, unpaginated; 'Amtsarzt, Schreiben an Irmgard P., Vorladung zur Untersuchung', 11.1.1943, BArch, R 92/10036, unpaginated; 'Gesundheitszeugnis Irmgard P.', 13.1.1943, BArch, R 92/10036, unpaginated.

61. 'Vermerk, Feldwebel Mai über Alma M.', 5.8.1943, BArch, R 92/10036, unpaginated. Also see 'Ortskommandantur I (V) 277, Schreiben an die Kommandantur rückw. Armeegebiet 533, Qu., St.Qu., Tätigkeitsbericht für die Zeit vom 16.–30. Juni 1942, über Feldkommandantur (V)810', Eupatoria, 28.6.1942, NARA, RG-242 501/65, pp. 260f.

62. 'Wehrmachtskommandantur Minsk, Feldkommandantur 812, Kommandanturbefehl Nr. 12', Minsk, 4.11.1941, USHMM, RG-53.002M, Reel 3, 37/2/45, unpaginated.

63. 'Leitender Sanitätsoffizier beim Kommandanten rückw. Armeegebiet 585, Tätigkeitsbericht an den Armeearzt AOK 6, betr.: Erfahrungen im San.-Dienst des Kriegs vom 1.5.–30.6.1942', 17.7.1942, NARA, RG-242 501/65, pp. 531–4, here p. 531.

64. 'Feldkommandantur 608, Schreiben an Korück 553, Simferopol, Tätigkeitsbericht für die Zeit vom 30. Mai bis 13. Juni 1942', NARA, RG-242 501/65, pp. 135–8, here p. 138.

65. 'Allgemeine Anordnungen für den San.-Dienst Nr. 5/1943', published in Fischer, *Der deutsche Sanitätsdienst*, supplemental vol. 1, pp. 4909–12, here p. 4910.

66. 'Beratender Dermatologe beim OKH, gez. Löhe, Notiz zum Schreiben des Leit.-San.-Offz. der Deutschen Heeresmission in Rumänien', 6.10.1941, BA-MA, H 20/1082-2, unpaginated.

67. 'Leitender Sanitätsoffizier beim Befehlshaber im Heeresgebiet B, Bericht über die Dienstreise vom 29.12.42–13.1.1943', BA-MA, RH 22/195, pp. 195–206, esp. pp. 195, 200f., 206. Also see 'Generalkommissar für die Ukraine, Lagebericht des Generalkommissars Shitomir für Monat Mai', 3.6.1942, BA-MA, FPF 01/7841, pp. 427–38, here p. 437. Similar complaints were lodged in Romania ('Leitender Sanitätsoffizier bei der deutschen Heeresmission Rumänien, Schreiben an den Heeresarzt beim Oberkommando des Heeres', 30.5.1941, BA-MA, RH 12-23/1819).

68. 'Feldkommandantur 608, Schreiben an Korück 553, Simferopol, Tätigkeitsbericht für die Zeit vom 30. Mai bis 13. Juni 1942', NARA, RG-242 501/65, pp. 135–8, here p. 138.

69. See, e.g., 'Ortskommandantur II/937/V, Schreiben an die Feldkommandantur 751, Tätigkeitsbericht für die Zeit vom 1.–15. 6. 1942', Karasubazar (Bilohirsk), 12.6.1942, NARA, RG-242 501/65, pp. 196f.; 'Ortskommandantur I (V) 277, Schreiben an die Kommandantur rückw. Armeegebiet 533, Qu., St.Qu., Tätigkeitsbericht für die Zeit vom 1.–15. Juni 1942, über. Feldkommandantur (V)810', Eupatoria, 14.6.1942, NARA, RG-242 501/65, pp. 176f.; 'Ortskommandantur I (V) 277, Schreiben an die Kommandantur rückw. Armeegebiet 533, Qu., St.Qu., Tätigkeitsbericht für die Zeit vom

16.–30. Juni 1942, über. Feldkommandantur (V)810', Eupatoria, 28.6.1942, NARA, RG-242 501/65, pp. 260f., here p. 260; 'Feldkommandantur I (V) 237, Feldgendarmerie, Tätigkeitsbericht der Feldgendarmerie für die Zeit vom 15. bis 30. Juni 1942', Kerch, 30.6.1942, NARA, RG-242 50/65, pp. 284–7, here p. 286; 'Stadt-Verwaltung Brest-Litowsk, Bericht über den Arbeitsverlauf der Stadtverwaltung in der Zeit vom 20.9. bis zum 10.10.1943', 22.10.1943, BArch, R 94/8, unpaginated, p. 1 of the document.
70. 'Schutzpolizei, Dienstabteilung Libau, Bericht, betr.: Kuppelei', 11.2.1942, USHMM, RG-18.002M, reel 11, R-83/1/207.
71. 'Reservelazarett II, Königsberg, Meldung an den Leitenden Arzt beim Generalkommissariat in Riga', 8. 5. 1943, BArch, R 92/10036, p. 32; 'Direktor des Gesundheitsamtes, Kirschentals, Meldung an den Kommissarischen Oberbürgermeister der Stadt Riga, betr.: Ansteckungsquelle', 19.7.1943, BArch, R 92/10036, unpaginated.
72. 'Feldkommandantur I (V) 237, Feldgendarmerie, Tätigkeitsbericht der Feldgendarmerie für die Zeit vom 15. bis 30. June 1942', Kerch, 30.6.1942, NARA, RG-242 50/65, pp. 284–7, here p. 286.
73. 'Stabsarzt San.Komp. 1/30, Dienststellt Feldpostnummer 34218, Meldung von Geschlechtskrankheiten!, Alfred F.', 23.9.1943, BArch, R 92/10036, unpaginated.
74. 'Zentralabteilung, gez. Bornheim, Schreiben an die Abteilung II Gesund, betr.: Meldung der Einheit Feldpostnummer 34218 über Erkrankung des Unteroffiziers Alfred F. an Gonorrhoe, 4.10.1943, beglaubigt vom Reichskommissar für das Ostland', BArch, R 92/10036, unpaginated.
75. 'Direktor des Gesundheitsamtes, Dr. H. Kirschentals, Meldung an den Kommissarischen Oberbürgermeister der Stadt Riga, betr.: Ansteckungsquelle', 15.12.1943, BArch, R 92/10036, unpaginated.
76. 'Dienststelle der Feldpostnummer 43500, Truppenarzt, gez. SS-Sturmbannführer Gruhner, Schreiben an das Gesundheitsamt Riga, betr.: Erfassung von Ansteckungsquellen (Geschlechtskrankheiten)', 9.12.1943, BArch, R 92/10036, unpaginated. Also see 'Beratender Dermatologe beim OKH, gez. Löhe, Notiz zum Schreiben des Leit.-San.-Offz. der Deutschen Heeresmission in Rumänien', 6.10.1941, BA-MA, H 20/1082–2, unpaginated.
77. 'OKH, von Brauchitsch, Schreiben an Generalquartiermeister, betr.: Selbstzucht', 31.7.1940, BA-MA, RH 53-7/v. 233a/167; also 'Anl. 1 zu OKH-Befehl, betr.: Alkoholmissbrauch', 6.9.1941, BA-MA, H 20/825 and BA-MA, RH 53-7/709; also quoted in Seidler, *Prostitution, Homosexualität, Selbstverstümmelung*, pp. 136f. Regarding similar remarks, see, e.g., 'Stellvertretendes Generalkommando VII A.K., betr.: Bekämpfung von Geschlechtskrankheiten', 20.4.1943, NARA, RG-242 78/189, pp. 6130737f.
78. 'OKH, von Brauchitsch, Schreiben an Generalquartiermeister, betr.: Selbstzucht', 31.7.1940, BA-MA, RH 53-7/v. 233a/167, also 'Anl. 1 zu OKH-Befehl, betr.: Alkoholmissbrauch', 6.9.1941, BA-MA, H 20/825 and BA-MA, RH 53-7/709; also quoted in Seidler, *Prostitution, Homosexualität, Selbstverstümmelung*,

pp. 136f. Even today, it is a common perception that prostitution is a means of preventing rape; see Grenz, 'Prostitution, eine Verhinderung oder Ermöglichung sexueller Gewalt?', pp. 330ff.
79. Regarding the term '*Geschlechtsnot*' (a legal and archaic term for rape), also see Beck, *Wehrmacht und sexuelle Gewalt*, pp. 272ff.
80. 'Gericht der Wehrmachts-Ortskommandantur Riga, Feldurteil', 13.4.1944, BA-ZNS, S 264, pp. 31–8, here p. 37, also quoted in Beck, *Wehrmacht und sexuelle Gewalt*, p. 273. Regarding similar arguments, see, e.g., 'RF-SS Himmler, Rede vor SS-Führern', 18.2.1937, excerpts published in Himmler, *Geheimreden*, p. 98.
81. Pohl, *Feindbild Frau*; Zipfel, 'Ausnahmezustand Krieg?'; Alison, 'Wartime Sexual Violence'.
82. Regarding how homosexuality was dealt with by the Wehrmacht and SS, see, e.g., Snyder, *Sex Crimes*, pp. 103ff.; Giles, 'The institutionalization of homosexual panic'; Seidler, *Prostitution, Homosexualität, Selbstverstümmelung*. For an overview of the research into homosexuality under the Nazis, see Heineman, 'Sexuality and Nazism', pp. 33ff.
83. Translation from *Isvestia*, No. 35 (7107), from 12.2.1940, 'Bekämpfung des Verbrechertums in den westlichen Gebieten der Ukraine und Weissrusslands', USHMM, RG-31.002M, reel 11, 3676/4/133, pp. 41ff., here p. 43.
84. 'Allgemeine Anordnungen für den San.-Dienst Nr. 5/1943', published in Fischer, *Der deutsche Sanitätsdienst*, supplemental vol. 1, pp. 4909–12, here esp. p. 4910.
85. 'Stellvertretendes Generalkommando VII A.K., betr.: Bekämpfung der Geschlechtskrankheiten', 20.4.1943, NARA, RG-242 78/189, pp. 6130737f., here p. 6130737. The fact that the men themselves were spreading existing infections as they continually moved around was common knowledge in all armies at the time and had been a topic of discussion even in the nineteenth century. Sailors of the fleet, in particular, were traditionally held responsible for spreading venereal diseases. As early as 1869, the French doctor Julien Jeannel published a 'draft of international regulations for fighting the spread of venereal diseases by seafarers' (Jeannel, *Die Prostitution*, pp. 287ff.).
86. Seidler, *Prostitution, Homosexualität, Selbstverstümmelung*, pp. 59ff. Regarding the spread of sexually transmitted diseases in the Wehrmacht before the start of the war, see 'OKH, Gesundheitszustand und Krankenbewegung des Heeres im ersten Jahre der neuen Wehrpflicht', 29.6.1937, NARA, RG-242 78/189, pp. 6131307–75.
87. See, e.g., 'Generalkommissar für die Ukraine, Lagebericht des Generalkommissars Shitomir für Monat Mai', 3.6.1942, BA-MA, FPF 01/7841, pp. 427–38, here p. 437; 'Feldkommandantur (V) 810, Abt. IV b, Schreiben an den leitenden Sanitätsoffizier b. Kdt. rückw. Armeegebiet 553, betr.: Tätigkeitsbericht', 14.6.1942, NARA, RG-242 501/65, pp. 000164f.; 'Reichskommissar für die Ukraine, Lagebericht für die Monate März und April 1943', 14.5.1943, BArch, R 94/18, p. 4; 'beratender Dermatologe beim Wehrkreis XII, Oberstabsarzt

Prof. Schoenfeld, Schreiben an die Berichtssammelstelle der Militärärztlichen Akademie und an den Wehrkreisarzt XIII, betr.: Tagebuchdurchschrift für März 1944', 1.4.1944, NARA, RG-242 78/189, p. 6130580; 'beratender Dermatologe beim Heeressanitätsinspekteur, Sammelbericht Nr. 1', 5.8.1944, NARA, RG-242 78/189, pp. 6131227–35.

88. 'Heeressanitätsinspektion, Abteilung Wissenschaft und Gesundheitsführung Ib, Bekämpfung der Geschlechtskrankheiten', 18.9.1944, BA-MA, RH 12-23/1849. The treatment of gonorrhoea was also an important topic of discussion at the 4th Working Conference of Consulting Physicians in May 1944 ('Bericht über die 4. Arbeitstagung der beratenden Ärzte', 16–18.5.1944, BA-MA, RHD 43/54).

89. See, e.g., Finger, *Der Krieg und die Bekämpfung der Geschlechtskrankheiten* (1916); Freund, *Wie bewahrt ihr euch vor Syphilis?* (1916); Fischer, 'Zweites Sammelreferat' (1917), pp. 67ff. Also see Sigusch, *Geschichte der Sexualwissenschaft*, pp. 247ff., 253.

90. It can lead to inflammation of the conjunctiva, iris, muscles, joints and heart; long-term gonorrhoea infections can often result in infertility in both women and men.

91. In the 1940s it was still difficult to diagnose syphilis in its early stages. The disease usually starts with painless sores in the mucous membranes and swelling of the lymph nodes. In some people, the disease becomes chronic and attacks the skin and organs. Syphilitic infections can be accompanied by a decline in intellectual abilities, impaired speech and psychosis. Syphilis is not hereditary, but it can be transmitted to unborn children through the placenta. Many infected children die in their first years of life. Under the Nazi dictatorship, children who survived longer than this were considered 'physically, mentally and psychologically inferior' (Lutz, 'Erbkrankheit oder angeborene Syphilis' [1942], p. 36). Regarding the discussion of the diagnosis and consequences of 'congenital syphilis' in the 1940s, see Gottschalk, 'Die Syphilis in der amtlichen Todesursachenstatistik' (1942), pp. 33–6; Spiethoff, 'Die Behandlung der konnatalen Syphilis' (1941), pp. 1071ff.; Dringenberg, 'Untersuchungen an Hilfsschülern' (1941), pp. 35f.; Lutz, 'Über einen klinisch eindrucksvollen Fall' (1940). Regarding the myth of heritable syphilis, see Meinen, *Wehrmacht und Prostitution*, pp. 38ff.; Adam, *Die Strafe der Venus*, pp. 17ff.

92. Gilman, *Freud, Race and Gender*, pp. 61ff.; Bristow, *Prostitution and Prejudice*, pp. 45ff. In Imperial Russia, too, the image of the Jewish brothel owner who forced women into prostitution and thus exposed them to syphilis was widespread; see Bernstein, *Sonia's Daughters*, pp. 161ff. Other racist constructs circulated alongside these antisemitic attributions. For example, the German 'Campaign against the Black Shame' repeatedly addressed the supposed transmission of syphilis by Black colonial soldiers. The children born of sexual encounters between German women and French colonial soldiers were referred to as 'syphilitic bastards' (Koller, *'Von Wilden aller Rassen niedergemetzelt'*, pp. 243ff.).

93. Hitler, *Mein Kampf*, pp. 59, 246f. Also see Bristow, *Prostitution and Prejudice*, p. 304; Gilman, *Freud, Race and Gender*, p. 62.
94. See, e.g., 'Chef der Sicherheitspolizei und des SD, Kommandostab, Meldungen aus den besetzten Gebieten der UdSSR', USHMM, RG-31.002M, reel 11, 3676/4/105, pp. 8–25, here p. 8; 'Wehrmachtsbefehlshaber Ostland, Kommandeur Wehrmachtsstreifendienst (Aufgabengebiet General z. b.V.), Bericht Nr. 9, umfassend die Zeit vom 11.1.1944 bis 15.3.1944', Riga, 18.3.1944, BA-MA, RW 41/57, p. 3.
95. 'Wehrmachtsbefehlshaber Ostland, Kommandeur Wehrmachtsstreifendienst (Aufgabengebiet General z. b.V.), Bericht, betr.: Reiseverkehr und Betreuungseinrichtungen', Riga, 15.9.1942, BA-MA, RW 41/57, unpaginated, p. 8. In France, after photographs of soldiers were found in the rooms of prostitutes, all field commanders were instructed to promptly inform their men that no photos should be given to prostitutes, as this was an expression of an inappropriate 'inner bond'. See 'Militärbefehlshaber in Frankreich IIa (Z), betr.: Fotografien deutscher Soldaten in Bordellen', 31.10.1943, BA-MA, RH 36/v. 317, quoted in Seidler, *Prostitution, Homosexualität, Selbstverstümmelung*, p. 180.
96. 'OKH, Merkblatt Deutscher Soldat!', undated (1939), NARA, RG-242 78/189, pp. 654f., published in Seidler, *Prostitution, Homosexualität, Selbstverstümmelung*, p. 172.
97. Reichskriegsministerium (ed.), *Wegweiser* (1936), pp. 21f., excerpts published in Seidler, *Prostitution, Homosexualität, Selbstverstümmelung*, pp. 101f.
98. Ibid., pp. 100ff.; Meinen, *Wehrmacht und Prostitution*, pp. 48f.; Gertjejanssen, *Victims, Heroes, Survivors*, pp. 127ff.
99. 'Leitender Sanitätsoffizier beim Kommandanten rückw. Armeegebiet 585, Tätigkeitsbericht an den Armeearzt AOK 6, betr.: Erfahrungen im San.-Dienst des Kriegs vom 11.3.–30.4.1942', 19.5.1942, NARA, RG-242 501/65, pp. 321f., here p. 321.
100. 'Befehlshaber Heeresgebiet Süd, Besondere Anordnungen für die Versorgung und die Versorgungstruppen', 21.3.1943, BA-MA, RH 22/195, pp. 38–41, here p. 39.
101. 'Wehrmachtsbefehlhaber Ostland, Besondere Anordnungen Nr. 6/41', Kaunas, 11.9.1941, USHMM, RG-18.002M, reel 7, R-80/3/4, pp. 51–63, here p. 61; 'Gesundheitsamt der Hansestadt Danzig, Städtische Medizinalrätin, Meldung an den leitenden Arzt des Generalkommissariats in Riga, betr.: Luftnachrichtenanwärterin Ursula M.', 10.5.1943, BArch, R 92/10036, unpaginated; 'Amtsarzt, Meldung an den Gebietskommissar Riga, betr.: Gefolgschaftsmitglied der Landbewirtschaftungsgesellschaft Ostland Natalie W.', 27.1.1943, BArch, R 92/10036, unpaginated; 'Beratungsstelle des Städtischen Gesundheitsamtes, Schreiben an den Amtsarzt beim Generalkommissar in Riga, betr.: Frau Ursula v.H.', 28.1.1943, BArch, R 92/10036, unpaginated; 'Amtsarzt in Riga, Schreiben an das Hauptgesundheitsamt der Reichshauptstadt Berlin, betr.: Margot B. [Angestellte der Reichsbahn]', 23.2.1943, BArch, R 92/10036,

unpaginated; 'Zentral-Handelsgesellschaft Ost, Schreiben an den Amtsarzt Dr. Marnitz, betr.: Unser Gefolgschaftsmitglied Erika Sch.', 15.7.1943, BArch, R 92/10036, unpaginated; 'Amtsarzt, gez. Dr. Marnitz, Schreiben an die Zentral-Handelsgesellschaft Ost, betr: Amtsärztliche Untersuchung von Erika Sch.', 21.7.1943, BArch, R 92/10036, unpaginated.

102. Ellenbrand, *Die Volksbewegung und Volksaufklärung*, p. 100. Also see the text by Navy Chief Staff Physician Rost, 'Die Verhütung der venerischen Krankheiten' (1914).

103. Regarding the menacing fantasies of degeneration that were and are associated with male masturbation, see Laqueur, *Solitary Sex*. Regarding various autoerotic practices in the Wehrmacht, see Steinkamp, 'Ungewöhnliche Todesfälle bei der Wehrmacht'.

104. See, e.g., Gertjejanssen, *Victims, Heroes, Survivors*, pp. 64ff.; Steinkamp, *Zur Devianz-Problematik in der Wehrmacht*, pp. 304f.

105. References to the consequences of sexually transmitted diseases can be found in Wehrmacht medical publications from before the start of the war until 1944; see, e.g., Jaeckel, 'Geschlechtskrankheiten' (1936), p. 583; Löhe, 'Die Geschlechtskrankheiten' (1944), p. 160.

106. A photo of a package with its enclosed leaflet can be found in Dücker and Museum der Arbeit (eds), *Sexarbeit*, p. 305. Since rubber was in short supply, there were fears at the end of 1942 that it would soon be impossible to produce enough condoms; see 'Brief des Reichsgesundheitsführers Conti an den RF-SS', 9.11.1942, BArch, NS 19/1886, pp. 1–3, here p. 1.

107. See, e.g., Aly and Sontheimer, *Fromms*; Ellenbrand, *Die Volksbewegung und Volksaufklärung*.

108. To keep the number of 'ethnically alien' children low, Conti suggested using chemical contraceptives. This implied that it was not deemed necessary to protect the local population from sexually transmitted diseases; see 'Brief des Reichsgesundheitsführers Conti an den RF-SS', 9.11.1942, BArch, NS 19/1886, pp. 1ff., here p. 1.

109. 'Wehrmachts-Ortskommandantur Riga, Kommandanturbefehl Nr. 3', Riga, 26.1.1942, USHMM, RG-18.002M, reel 7, 80/3/2, p. 16; 'Wehrmachtskommandantur Minsk, Kommandanturbefehl Nr. 18', Minsk, 11.7.1942, USHMM, RG-53.002, reel 3, 37/2/45, pp. 34ff., here p. 34.

110. Ellenbrand, *Die Volksbewegung und Volksaufklärung*, p. 99. Also see Mai, *Geschlechtskrankheiten*, pp. 81ff.

111. 'Befehlshaber Heeresgebiet Süd, Besondere Anordnungen für die Versorgung und die Versorgungstruppen', 21.3.1943, BA-MA, RH 22/195, pp. 38–41, here p. 39. Some soldiers who fell ill would claim that they had received treatment but lost their 'sanitation certification'. See 'Reservelazarett Darmstadt, Meldung an den leitenden Arzt des Generalkommissariats Riga, Peter A.', 19.5.1943, BArch, R 92/10036, p. 11.

112. As early as 20 April 1940, the commander in Military District VII had advised that the 'preservation of confidentiality' should be taken into account when

sanitation stations were established in occupied France ('Stellvertretendes Generalkommando VII A.K., betr.: Bekämpfung der Geschlechtskrankheiten', 20.4.1943, NARA, RG-242 78/189, pp. 6130737f., here p. 6130737).
113. See, e.g., 'Wehrmachts-Ortskommandantur Riga, Kommandanturbefehlt Nr. 3', 26.1.1942, USHMM, RG-18.002M, reel 7, 80/3/2, pp. 16a–b, here p. 16b.
114. 'Stellvertretendes Generalkommando VII A.K., betr.: Bekämpfung der Geschlechtskrankheiten', 20.4.1943, NARA, RG-242 78/189, pp. 6130737f., here p. 6130737.
115. 'Oberbefehlshaber der Kriegsmarine, Schulungsbrief, 15.7.1942, Anlage Soldat und Frau', pp. 8ff., quoted in Seidler, *Prostitution, Homosexualität, Selbstverstümmelung*, p. 102. Also see 'Heeressanitätsinspektion, Abteilung Wissenschaft und Gesundheitsführung Ia, Zusätze zu "Hygiene der jungen Jahrgänge"', 7.6.1944, BA-MA, RH 12-23/1844.
116. See, e.g., 'Befehl des Oberbefehlshabers Süd-West', 11.1.1945, BA-MA, H 20/1093.
117. Buch, *Wir Kindersoldaten*, p. 54.
118. In his study of comradeship in the Wehrmacht, Thomas Kühne has shown that talking about sex usually involved obscenities (Kühne, *Kameradschaft*, pp. 132, 163; Kühne, *The Rise and Fall of Comradeship*, pp. 122, 173).
119. See, e.g., 'leitender Sanitätsoffizier, Meldung an den leitenden Arzt beim Generalkommissariat Riga, Matrose Heinrich D.', 24.6.1943, BArch, R 92/10036, pp. 25f.
120. 'Reservelazarett Marburg, Meldung an das Gesundheitsamt in Riga, Paul W.', 14.7.1943, BArch, R 92/10036, unpaginated; 'Reservelazarett Riesenburg, Meldung an das Gesundheitsamt in Riga', no patient name, 2.5.1943, BArch, R 92/10036, unpaginated; 'Reservelazarett Wien, Meldung an den leitenden Arzt des Generalkommissariats in Riga, Feldwebel Wilhelm B.', 28.5.1943, BArch, R 92/10036, p. 19; 'leitender Sanitätsoffizier, Meldung an den leitenden Arzt beim Generalkommissariat Lettland, betr.: Go.-Infektion Peter S., SS-Schütze (Erika L.)', 6.7.1943, BArch, R 92/10036, unpaginated.
121. 'Kommandanturrückwärtiges Armeegebiet 585, Abt. Qu., Kommandanturbefehl Nr. 5,' 6.2.1942, NARA, RG-242 501/65, pp. 334–8, here p. 337.
122. 'OKW, Chef W.San.' 27.1.1943, BA-MA, H 20/840. The lack of qualified medical personnel also led to conflicts between German institutions. For example, the regional commissioner in Brest-Litovsk complained that the Wehrmacht had requisitioned three prisoners of war who were working as doctors at the local hospital. The commissioner objected to this 'because otherwise I will have to close the hospital' ('Gebietskommissar Brest-Litowsk, Monatsbericht!', 24.2.1942, BArch, R 94/7, fol 1, unpaginated). Also see 'Generalkommissar für Wolhynien und Podolien, Lagebericht für März–April 1943, VIII. Gesundheitswesen', 30.4.1943, BArch, R 94/17, pp. 1–36, here p. 9.
123. 'Chef des OKW, gez. Keitel, Befehl zur Bekämpfung von Geschlechtskrankheiten', 25.10.1943, in Oberkommando des Heeres (ed.), *Heeresverordnungsblatt* (1943), pp. 358ff., and Reichsminister der Luftwaffe

(ed.), *Luftwaffenverordnungsblatt* (1943), p. 1164. Also see Seidler, *Prostitution, Homosexualität, Selbstverstümmelung*, pp. 108f.
124. 'Wehrmachtsbefehlshaber Ostland, Oberquartiermeister, Besondere Anordnungen Nr. 6/41', 11.9.1941, USHMM, RG-18.002M, reel 7, R-80/3/4, pp. 51–63, here p. 63; 'Merkblatt Bestrafung der Geschlechtskranken', undated, NARA, RG-242 78/189, p. 6130734. The same applied to the air force ('Reichsminister und Oberbefehlshaber der Luftwaffe, Verfügung, betr: Bestrafung wegen Geschlechtskrankheiten', 22.12.1941, BA-MA, RL 19/64, fiche 4).
125. Mai, *Geschlechtskrankheiten*, pp. 34ff.
126. 'Beratender Dermatologe, Prof. Dr. Schreuz, Schreiben an den Wehrkreisarzt VI, betr.: Erfahrungsbericht vom 15. Juli bis 15. Oktober 1944', 10.10.1944, NARA, RG-242 78/189, pp. 6130739–42, here p. 6130740; 'Stabsarzt Prof. Dr. Nagel, beratender Dermatologe der Heeresgruppe A, Erfahrungsbericht über das 3. Quartal 1944', 16.10.1944, NARA, RG-242 78/189, pp. 6130757–9. For a comprehensive documentation of gonorrhoea diagnosis and treatment, see Mai, *Geschlechtskrankheiten*, pp. 20ff.; Seidler, *Prostitution, Homosexualität, Selbstverstümmelung*, pp. 84ff.
127. Mai, *Geschlechtskrankheiten*, pp. 46ff.; Seidler, *Prostitution, Homosexualität, Selbstverstümmelung*, pp. 82f. Today syphilis can be cured by administering antibiotics such as penicillin. The discovery and testing of penicillin led to a significant decline in the disease immediately after World War II. Since the 1990s, however, the number of cases has been rising again, particularly in the context of sex tourism in Asia, South America and Eastern Europe. To this day, syphilis is a notifiable disease (Adam, *Die Strafe der Venus*, pp. 107ff.).
128. In 1941, the doctor Alfred Brauchle suggested that the use of more naturopathic methods would be less damaging to the health and lead to lower mortality rates. However, this was opposed by the head of the German Society for Combatting Venereal Diseases, Professor Bodo Spiethoff, and the chairman of the German Dermatological Society, Professor Karl Zieler, who believed that drug treatment was the only sensible approach; see Spiethoff and Zieler, 'Erklärung zur Frage der "naturgemässen" Behandlung der Syphilis' (1942).
129. Seidler, *Prostitution, Homosexualität, Selbstverstümmelung*, pp. 82f.
130. See, e.g., 'OKH, Sammelbericht Nr. 1, Berlin', 5.8.1944, NARA RG 242, 78/189, pp. 6131227–35, here pp. 6131234f.
131. Gonorrhoea could be cured this way, but in the case of syphilis, the symptoms would merely be suppressed; see Mai, *Geschlechtskrankheiten*, p. 54; Seidler, *Prostitution, Homosexualität, Selbstverstümmelung*, pp. 97f.
132. See, e.g., 'Feldkommandantur (V) 810, Abt. Ivb, Schreiben an den leitenden Sanitätsoffizier bei der Kommandantur rückw. Armeegebiet, betr.: Tätigkeitsbericht', Eupatoria, 14.6.1942, NARA, RG 242, 501/65, pp. 000164f.; 'Reichskommissar für die Ukraine, betr.: Lagebericht für die Monate März und April 1943', 14.5.1943, BArch, R 94/18, p. 4.

133. 'Allgemeine Anordnungen für den San.-Dienst Nr. 5/1943', published in Fischer, *Der deutsche Sanitätsdienst*, supplemental vol. 1, pp. 4909–12, here p. 4910.
134. Ibid.
135. This arrangement persisted until the final days before Germany's defeat; see, e.g., 'Chef des Sanitätswesens der Luftwaffe, gez. Schröder, Anweisung für Truppenärzte, Einzelanordnung Nr. 11', 06.12.1944, NARA, RG-242 78/192, pp. 6135754–64.
136. 'Beratender Hygieniker beim Heeressanitätsinspekteur, gez. Zeiss, Schreiben an den beratenden Hygieniker des Feld- und Ersatzheeres, betr.: Sammelbericht über Kriegserfahrungen der beratenden Hygienikers', 20.1.1944, NARA, RG-242 78/189, pp. 6131272f.; 'OKH, Gen.St.d.H., betr.: Urlaubssperre nach überstandener Geschlechtskrankheit und Untersuchung von Urlaubern auf Geschlechtskrankheiten', 20.4.1941, BA-MA, H 20/280. Also see Seidler, *Prostitution, Homosexualität, Selbstverstümmelung*, pp. 97, 107, 122; Gertjejanssen, *Victims, Heroes, Survivors*, p. 135.
137. Generalstabsarzt, Wissmann, Schreiben an den beratenden Dermatologen des Heeres-Sanitätsinspekteurs, Prof. Dr. Löhe', Berlin, 20.1.1945, NARA, RG-242 78/189, pp. 6130752–5.
138. 'Inspekteur des Sanitätswesens der Luftwaffe, Anweisung für Truppenärzte über Verhütung von Selbstmord', Berlin, 6.10.1942, NARA, RG-242 78/192, pp. 6135832–7, here p. 6135834.
139. As 'conversational media' (*'Gesprächsmedien'*, as Klaus Latzel says), these letters gave the men and their points of reference back home the opportunity to attribute some meaning to the new reality of the war by writing about it. The men mostly wrote about the ideals that seemed to be at stake and the hardship of being separated from family and loved ones so far from home. Acts of violence and sexual encounters with the local population were generally not mentioned; see Latzel, *Deutsche Soldaten*, pp. 31ff.; Müller, *Deutsche Soldaten*, pp. 116ff.
140. A soldier's desire to return home to his family and friends threatened his total devotion to the regime. In his dissertation on troop welfare in the Wehrmacht, Frank Vossler shows that military commanders tried to address this inner conflict by holding cultural events such as film screenings and concerts, which were supposed to 'create the illusion of contact between the front and home'. As the war dragged on, however, this became increasingly difficult (Vossler, *Propaganda in die eigene Truppe*, pp. 55ff., here esp. p. 61).
141. OKH, 'Deutscher Soldat!', undated (1939), NARA, RG-242 78/189, pp. 654f., published in Seidler, *Prostitution, Homosexualität, Selbstverstümmelung*, p. 172; Gesterding, *Unteroffizierthemen* (1943), p. 71.
142. See the questionnaires in the files of the public health officer in Riga, BArch, R 92/10036.
143. 'Wehrmachtskommandantur Minsk, Feldkommandantur 812, Kommandanturbefehl Nr. 12', Minsk, 4.11.1941, USHMM, RG-53.002M, reel 3, 37/2/45, unpaginated. Regarding the importance of determining the 'source of infec-

tion', also see 'Allgemeine Anordnungen für den San.-Dienst Nr. 5/1943', published in Fischer, *Der deutsche Sanitätsdienst*, supplemental vol. 1, pp. 4909–12, here esp. p. 4910; 'Stellv Gen.Kdo IV. A.K., betr.: Geschlechtskrankheiten', January 1945, NARA, RG-242 78/189, pp. 6130753–6.

144. In some cases, this was the same form that was used in France in 1940. The most widely used questionnaire was published by the Reich Working Group for Combatting Venereal Diseases.

145. Various versions of this questionnaire can be found in BArch, R 92/10036, passim.

146. 'Feldkommandantur (V) 810, Schreiben an den leitenden Sanitäts-Offizier beim Kommandanten rückw. Armeegebiet 553, betr.: Tätigkeitsbericht', Eupatoria, 14.6.1942, NARA, RG-242 501/65, pp. 164f.; 'Feldkommandantur (V) 810, Schreiben an den leitenden Sanitäts-Offizier beim Kommandanten rückw. Armeegebiet 553, betr.: Tätigkeitsbericht', Eupatoria, 28.6.1942, NARA, RG-242 501/65, p. 250.

147. 'Leitender Sanitätsoffizier beim Kommandanten rückw. Armeegebiet 585, Tätigkeitsbericht an den Armeearzt AOK 6, betr.: Erfahrungen im San.-Dienst des Kriegs vom 11.3.–30.4.1942', 19.05.1942, NARA, RG-242 501/65, pp. 321f.; 'leitender Sanitätsoffizier beim Kommandanten rückw. Armeegebiet 585, Tätigkeitsbericht an den Armeearzt AOK 6, betr.: Erfahrungen im San.-Dienst des Kriegs vom 1.5.–30.6.1942', 17.7.1942, NARA, RG 242 501/65, pp. 531–4, here p. 531; 'leitender Sanitätsoffizier beim Kommandanten rückw. Armeegebiet 585, Tätigkeitsbericht an den Armeearzt AOK 6, betr.: Erfahrungen im San.-Dienst des Kriegs vom 1.7.42.–31.8.1942', 20.9.1942, NARA, RG-242 501/65, pp. 499–502, here p. 499.

148. One exception was Franz Sch., born in 1882, who contracted gonorrhoea in 1943 at the age of 61 ('Deutsche Klinik Riga, Dr. Fritz Zmugg, Anzeige eines Verdachts einer Erkrankung an Tripper, Franz Sch.', 8.7.1943, BArch, R 92/10036, p. 28).

149. See 'Sanitätskompanie 10, Ortslazarett Lamocha, Meldung an den Divisionsarzt 10. Lw. Felddivision, Stanislaus W.', 10.6.1943, BArch, R 92/10036, p. 21; 'Sanitätskompanie 10, Ortslazarett Lamocha, Meldung an den Divisionsarzt 10. Lw. Felddivision, Laimons D.', 2.7.1943, BArch, R 92/10036, unpaginated; 'Dienststelle L18089, Schreiben an den leitenden Sanitätsoffizier beim Generalkommissariat Lettland, betr.: Bekämpfung der Geschlechtskrankheiten', 3.8.1943, BArch, R 92/10036, unpaginated; 'SS-Lazarett Riga, Meldung einer Ansteckungsquelle, Jonas P.', 13.5.1943, BArch, R 92/10036, unpaginated.

150. See, e.g., 'Dr. med. Arnulf Scholz, Anzeige an den Amtsarzt beim Generalkommissar in Riga, Dr. Marnitz, Alfred G.', 15.7.1943, BArch, R 92/10036, unpaginated; 'Deutsche Klinik Riga, Dr. med. Rudolf Paetsch, Meldung an das staatliche Gesundheitsamt Riga, Fritz K.', 21.9.1943, BArch, R 92/10036, unpaginated.

151. 'Leitender Sanitätsoffizier, Meldung an den leitenden Arzt beim Generalkommissariat Riga, Matrose Heinrich D.', 24.6.1943, BArch, R 92/10036,

pp. 25f.; 'SS-Lazarett Riga, Meldung einer Ansteckungsquelle, Jonas P.', 13.5.1943, BArch, R 92/110036, unpaginated.
152. See, e.g., 'Deutsche Klinik in Riga, Dr. Arnulf Scholz, Vordruck Fragebogen an das Gesundheitsamt in Riga', 13.5.1943, BArch, R 92/10036, p. 8.
153. See, e.g., 'Reservelazarett Riesenburg, Meldung an das Gesundheitsamt in Riga, ohne Patientenname', 2.5.1943, BArch, R 92/10036, unpaginated; 'Armeearzt AOK 20, Meldung an den leitenden Arzt beim Generalkommissariat in Riga, August W.', 25.5.1943, BArch, R 92/10036, pp. 18f.; 'Armeearzt AOK 20, Meldung an den leitenden Arzt beim Generalkommissariat in Riga, Georg Sch.' 25.5.1943, BArch, R 92/10036, pp. 18ff.; 'Sanitätskompanie 10, Ortslazarett Lamocha, Meldung an den Divisionsarzt 10. Lw. Felddivision, Stanislaus W.', 10.6.1943, BArch, R 92/10036, p. 21; 'leitender Sanitätsoffizier, Meldung an den leitenden Arzt beim Generalkommissariat Riga, Matrose Heinrich D.', 24.6.1943, BArch, R 92/10036, pp. 25f.; 'Deutsche Klinik Riga, Dr. Fritz Zmugg, Anzeige eines Verdachts einer Erkrankung an Tripper, Franz Sch.', 8.7.1943, BArch, R 92/10036, p. 28; 'Sanitätskompanie 10, Ortslazarett Lamocha, Meldung an den Divisionsarzt 10. Lw. Felddivision, Laimons D.', 2.7.1943, BArch, R 92/10036, unpaginated; 'Meldung an den leitenden Arzt beim Generalkommissariat in Riga, Fritz M.', 16.7.1943, BArch, R 92/10036, unpaginated.
154. See, e.g., 'Deutsche Klinik in Riga, Dr. Arnulf Scholz, Vordruck Fragebogen an das Gesundheitsamt in Riga', 13.5.1943, BArch, R 92/10036, p. 8.; 'Reservelazarett Neulengbach, Meldung an den leitenden Arzt beim Generalkommissariat in Riga, Johann Sch.', 20.5.1943, BArch, R 92/10036, unpaginated.
155. 'Stabsarzt der Feldpostnummer 18061, Meldung an den leitenden Arzt im Generalkommissariat Riga, Franz C.', 17.5.1943, BArch, R 92/10036, p. 10. Other references to women's teeth can be found in 'Reservelazarett Marburg, Meldung an das Gesundheitsamt in Riga, Paul W.', 14.7.1943, BArch, R 92/10036, unpaginated; 'Armeearzt beim AOK 18, Meldung über Geschlechtskranke, Heinrich B.', 13.11.1943, BArch, R 92/10036, unpaginated.
156. See, e.g., 'Reservelazarett Riesenburg, Meldung an das Gesundheitsamt in Riga, ohne Patientennamen', 2.5.1943, BArch, R 92/10036, unpaginated; Armeearzt AOK 20, Meldung an den leitenden Arzt beim Generalkommissariat in Riga, Georg Sch.', 25.5.1943, BArch, R 92/10036, pp. 18ff.; 'Reservelazarett Wien, Meldung an den leitenden Arzt des Generalkommissariats in Riga, Feldwebel Wilhelm B.', 28.5.1943, BArch, R 92/10036, p. 19.
157. Gertjejanssen, *Victims, Heroes, Survivors*, p. 84.
158. 'Deutsche Klinik in Riga, Dr. Arnulf Scholz, Meldung an das Gesundheitsamt in Riga, Rudie L.', 13.5.1943, BArch, R 92/10036, p. 8; 'leitender Sanitätsoffizier, Meldung an den leitenden Arzt beim Generalkommissariat Riga, Matrose Heinrich D.', 24.6.1943, BArch, R 92/10036, pp. 25f.
159. 'Deutsche Klinik Riga, Dr. Fritz Zmugg, Anzeige eines Verdachts einer Erkrankung an Tripper, Franz Sch.', 8.7.1943, BArch, R 92/10036, p. 28.
160. 'Standortarzt Wenden, Meldung an das Gesundheitsamt Riga, Gefreiter Josef B.', 30.12.1942, BArch, R 92/10036, unpaginated; 'Armeearzt AOK 20,

Meldung an den leitenden Arzt beim Generalkommissariat in Riga, August W.', 25.5.1943, BArch, R 92/10036, pp. 18f.; 'Reservelazarett Neulengbach, Meldung an den leitenden Arzt beim Generalkommissariat in Riga, Johann Sch.', 20.5.1943, BArch, R 92/10036, unpaginated.
161. 'Reservelazarett II Königsberg, Meldung an den leitenden Arzt beim Generalkommissariat in Lettland, Fritz N.', 20.7.1943, BArch, R 92/10036, p. 35.
162. 'Armeearzt AOK 20, Meldung an den leitenden Arzt beim Generalkommissariat in Riga, Georg Sch.', 25.5.1943, BArch, R 92/10036, pp. 18ff.
163. 'Stabsarzt, Meldung beim leitenden Arzt beim Generalkommissariat in Riga', 14.9.1943, BArch, R 92/10036, unpaginated.
164. 'Deutsche Klinik Riga, Dr. Arnulf Scholz, Meldung an das Gesundheitsamt in Riga', 13.5.1943, BArch, R 92/10036, p. 8; 'Sanitätskompanie 10, Ortslazarett Lamocha, Meldung an den Divisionsarzt 10. Lw. Felddivision, Stanislaus W.', 10.6.1943, BArch, R 92/10036, p. 21; 'leitender Sanitätsoffizier, Meldung an den leitenden Arzt beim Generalkommissariat Riga, Matrose Heinrich D.', 24.6.1943, BArch, R 92/10036, pp. 25f.; 'Truppenarzt Panzerjägerabteilung 10, Meldung an das Generalkommissariat Riga, ohne Patientennamen', 30.6.1943, BArch, R 92/10036, p. 26; 'Deutsche Klinik Riga, Dr. Fritz Zmugg, Anzeige eines Verdachts einer Erkrankung an Tripper, Franz Sch.', 8.7.1943, BArch, R 92/10036, p. 28.
165. 'Allgemeine Anordnungen für den San.-Dienst Nr. 5/1943', published in Fischer, *Der deutsche Sanitätsdienst*, supplemental vol. 1, pp. 49094912, here p. 4910.
166. See, e.g., 'Reservelazarett Berlin-Tempelhof, Dr. Schwarzkopf, Meldung an das Gesundheitsamt im Riga, Willi J.', 10.4.1943, BArch, R 92/10036, p. 22; 'Vermerk über Else K.', 24.5.1943, BArch, R 92/10036, p. 23; 'kommissarischer Direktor des Gesundheitsamts, Dr. H. Kirschentals, Meldung an den Oberbürgermeister der Stadt Riga, betr.: Ansteckungsquelle Elsa K.', 18.6.1943, BArch, R 92/10036, unpaginated; 'Dr. Lange, Meldung an das Gesundheitsamt Riga, betr.: Gerhard O.', 2.4.1943, BArch, R 92/10036, unpaginated; 'Vermerk über Anni', 8.4.1943, BArch, R 92/10036, unpaginated; 'kommissarischer Direktor des Gesundheitsamts, Dr. H. Kirschentals, Meldung an den kommissarischen Oberbürgermeister der Stadt Riga, betr.: Ansteckungsquelle Anni, mit richtigem Namen Biruta R.', 18.6.1943, BArch, R 92/10036, p. 24; 'Reservelazarett Tapiau, Meldung an den leitenden Arzt beim Generalkommissariat in Riga, F. A. Xcaver G.', 4.5.1943, BArch, R 92/10036, p. 27; Amtsarzt, Mitteilung an das Gesundheitsamt Mitau, Lisa Sch.', 12.5.1943, BArch, R 92/10036, unpaginated; 'Gesundheitsamt, Stadtverwaltung Mitau, Mitteilung an den Amtsarzt beim Generalkommissar in Riga, Lisa Sch.', 5.7.1943, BArch, R 92/10036, unpaginated.
167. See, e.g., 'Sanitätsabteilung Libau, Schreiben an den leitenden Arzt beim Generalkommissariat in Riga, gez. Dr. J. Vedigs', 24.5.1943, BArch, R 92/10036, unpaginated.
168. 'Truppenarzt, Einheit der Feldpostnr. L 51837 A, Schreiben an den Amtsarzt in

Riga, betr.: Meldung von Geschlechtskrankheiten', 1.1.1943, BArch, R 92/10036, unpaginated (previously p. 2); 'kommissarischer Oberbürgermeister der Stadt Riga, Gesundheitsamt, fernmündliche Meldung an den kommissarischen Oberbürgermeister der Stadt Riga, betr.: Ansteckungsquelle', 2.2.1943, BArch, R 92/10036, unpaginated.

169. See, e.g., 'Gesundheitsdepartment Riga, Schreiben an den Generalkommissar in Riga, betr. Pauline A.', 12.2.1943, BArch, R 92/10036, p. 4; ' Gesundheitsdepartment Riga, Schreiben an den Generalkommissar in Riga, betr. Valija S. und Marta P.', 16.7.1943, BArch, R 92/10036, unpaginated.
170. German troops invaded this city (known as Wenden in German) in the Livonian region of northern Latvia on 5 July 1941.
171. 'Reservelazarett III, Hannover, Meldung an den leitenden Arzt beim Generalkommissariat in Riga', 16.7.1943, BArch, R 92/10036, unpaginated; 'Amtsarzt, Dr. Marnitz, Schreiben an das Gesundheitsamt in Riga, Anna W.', 27.7.1943; 'Direktor des Gesundheitsdepartments, Dr. T. Wankin, Schreiben an den Amtsarzt, Dr. Marnitz', 10.9.1943, BArch, R 92/10036, unpaginated. For a similar case, see 'Meldung an den leitenden Arzt beim Generalkommissariat in Riga', Fritz M.', 16.7.1943, BArch, R 92/10036, unpaginated; 'Direktor des Gesundheitsdepartments, Dr. Th. Wankin, Schreiben an den Generalkommissar in Riga, Amtsarzt, Dr. Marnitz', 15.9.1943, BArch, R 92/10036, unpaginated.
172. 'Reservelazarett Tapiau, Meldung an den leitenden Arzt beim Generalkommissariat in Riga, F. A. Xcaver G.', 4.5.1943, BArch, R 92/10036, p. 27; 'Amtsarzt, Mitteilung an das Gesundheitsamt Mitau, Lisa Sch.', 12.5.1943, BArch, R 92/10036, unpaginated; 'Gesundheitsamt, Stadtverwaltung Mitau, Mitteilung an den Amtsarzt beim Generalkommissar in Riga, Lisa Sch.', 5.7.1943, BArch, R 92/10036, unpaginated.
173. 'Chef des OKW, gez. Keitel, Befehl zur Bekämpfung von Geschlechtskrankheiten', 25.10.1943, in Oberkommando des Heeres (ed.), *Heeresverordnungsblatt* (1943), pp. 358ff., and Reichsminister der Luftwaffe – Luftwaffenverwaltungsamt (ed.), *Luftwaffenverordnungsblatt* (1943), p. 1164; also see Seidler, *Prostitution, Homosexualität, Selbstverstümmelung*, pp. 108f.
174. 'Stellvertretendes Generalkommando VII A.K., betr.: Bekämpfung der Geschlechtskrankheiten', 20.4.1943, NARA, RG-242 78/189, pp. 6130737f., here p. 6130738.
175. 'Chef des OKW, gez. Keitel, Befehl zur Bekämpfung von Geschlechtskrankheiten', 25.10.1943, in Oberkommando des Heeres (ed.), *Heeresverordnungsblatt* (1943), pp. 358ff., and Luftwaffe – Luftwaffenverwaltungsamt (ed.), *Luftwaffenverordnungsblatt* (1943), p. 1164; also see Seidler, *Prostitution, Homosexualität, Selbstverstümmelung*, pp. 108f.
176. 'Bestrafung der Geschlechtskranken', undated, NARA, RG-242 78/189, p. 6130734. Also see 'Heeressanitätsinspektion, Abteilung Wissenschaft und Gesundheitsführung Ib, Schreiben an Allgemeines Heeresamt, Abwickl. Stab 6. Armee', 10.1.1944, BA-MA, RH 12-23/1136.

177. 'OKW/Chef W.San., Verfügung Nr. 3761/44', 30.8.1944, quoted in 'Chef des Sanitätswesens der Luftwaffe, gez. Schröder, Anweisung für Truppenärzte, Einzelanordnung Nr. 11', 6.12.1944, NARA, RG-242 78/192, pp. 6135754–64, here p. 6135756.
178. 'Reichsminister der Luftfahrt und Oberbefehlshaber der Luftwaffe, Verordnung, betr.: Bestrafung von Geschlechtskrankheiten', 22.12.1941, BA-MA, RL 19/64, fiche 4, unpaginated.
179. 'Beratender Dermatologe beim Heeressanitätsinspekteur, gez. Löhe, Schreiben C der militärärztlichen Akademie, betr.: Stellungnahme zu dem Thema: Bekämpfung der Geschlechtskrankh.', 18.3.1943, BA-MA, RH 12-23/1809.
180. In view of the absence rate due to gonorrhoea and syphilis, the consultant dermatologist in Military District VIII actually proposed in October 1944 that so-called 'venereal disease battalions' should be established, analogous to the existing *Magenbataillonen* ('stomach battalions', for soldiers with stomach problems who needed a special diet) and *Ohrenbataillonen* ('ear battalions', for soldiers receiving special treatment for ear issues). He said that this would ensure targeted medical care throughout the soldiers' deployment and thus prevent the further spread of disease. For various reasons, the OKH rejected this idea; see Seidler, *Prostitution, Homosexualität, Selbstverstümmelung*, pp. 115f.; Neumann, *'Arzttum ist immer Kämpfertum'*, p. 249.
181. 'Oberfeldarzt Ritter von Hattinberg, Erfahrungsbericht 1. Quartal 1944', 31.3.1944, BA-MA, RH 12-23/1818.
182. 'Oberkommando der Heeresgruppe Mitte, betr.: Bekämpfung der Geschlechtskrankheiten', 11.9.1944, BA-MA, H 20/447, also quoted in Seidler, *Prostitution, Homosexualität, Selbstverstümmelung*, pp. 104f. The senior staff medical officer Dr Greinl, however, claimed in January 1945 that while the rate of infection for sexually transmitted diseases had risen in the civilian population, there had been no 'noticeable increase' amongst the troops ('Oberstabsarzt Prof. Dr. Greinl, beratender Dermatologe beim Wehrkreisarzt Böhmen und Mähren, Schreiben an Generalarzt Prof. Dr. Loehe', Prague, 25.1.1945, NARA, RG-242 78/189).
183. Seidler, *Prostitution, Homosexualität, Selbstverstümmelung*, p. 78.
184. Schneider-Janessen, *Arzt im Krieg*.
185. 'Heeressanitätsinspektion, Abteilung Wissenschaft und Gesundheitsförderung, Schreiben an den Heeressanitätsinspekteur', 6.11.1944, BA-MA, RH 12-23/1848.
186. 'Wehrkreisarzt XVIII an die Heeressanitätsinspekteur', 3.1.1945, BA-MA, RH 12-23/1825.
187. Heinemann, *'Rasse, Siedlung, deutsches Blut'*; Wildt, *An Uncompromising Generation*, pp. 242ff.
188. Regarding the notion of 'racial selection and 'racial breeding' in the SS, see Diehl, *Macht – Mythos – Utopie*, pp. 56ff., 99ff.
189. 'Sanitätsvorschrift für die Allgemeine SS (SS-San.V.)', 16.8.1935, quoted in Seidler, *Prostitution, Homosexualität, Selbstverstümmelung*, p. 105.

190. Regarding the catalogue of virtues and interpretation of loyalty in the SS, see, e.g., Longerich, *Heinrich Himmler*, pp. 118, 304ff.
191. See Longerich, *Heinrich Himmler*.
192. Schwarz, *Eine Frau an seiner Seite*, pp. 17ff.; Heinemann, 'Rasse, Siedlung, deutsches Blut', pp. 50ff.
193. Regarding the ideal of the 'new man', see Diehl, *Macht – Mythos – Utopie*, p. 71. Regarding the training materials for the SS, see Heinemann, 'Rasse, Siedlung, deutsches Blut', pp. 91ff.
194. Heinemann, 'Rasse, Siedlung, deutsches Blut', p. 92.
195. 'Sanitätsvorschrift für die Allgemeine SS (SS-San.V.)', 16.8.1935, quoted in Seidler, *Prostitution, Homosexualität, Selbstverstümmelung*, p. 106.
196. Mühlhäuser, 'Between "Racial Awareness" and Fantasies', pp. 198, 205.
197. 'Chef des SS-Hauptamtes, SS-Sanitätsamt, Ausbildungsbrief Nr. 5', 15.11.1938, BArch, NS 31/292, pp. 62–95, here p. 78, also found in BArch, NS 31/183, pp. 60–79, and BArch, R 187/442.
198. Isolated cases of gonorrhoea were reported in the SS Female Auxiliary Corps, too. Records show that three women were dismissed from the basic training course of the Reichsschule-SS (the school for female auxiliaries) on account of this disease. Sexually transmitted diseases were mentioned in the context of first-aid courses during the women's training. The extent to which the women were taught about the risks, symptoms and treatment of these diseases is not known. See Mühlenberg, *Das SS-Helferinnenkorps*.
199. Schönhuber, *Ich war dabei*, p. 51.
200. Maeger, *Lost Honour, Betrayed Loyalty*, p. 72.
201. See, e.g., 'Verordnungsblatt der Waffen-SS Nr. 20', BArch, R 187/459.
202. 'Chef des SS-Hauptamtes, SS-Sanitätsamt, Ausbildungsbrief Nr. 5', 15.11.1938, BArch, NS 31/292, pp. 62–95, here pp. 76f., also found in BArch, NS 31/183, pp. 60–79, and BArch, R 187/442.
203. 'RF-SS Himmler, Rede vor Gruppenführern', 18.2.1937, published in Himmler, *Geheimreden*, p. 98.
204. Rübel, the troop doctor, had informed him that 90 per cent of all SS men stationed in Warsaw were infected with a sexually transmitted disease. Rübel suggested that the women – most of whom, according to him, were German – be quartered in the barracks and subjected to regular examinations. Himmler agreed to this plan, but whether it was actually implemented is not known. See 'Aktennotiz Rübel', 17.7.1942, BArch, NS 19/2491.
205. 'Nachrichten aus den von den Russen besetzten ukr. Gebieten', undated (spring 1941), USHMM, RG-31.002M 3676/4/133, pp. 75f.
206. 'Chef der Sicherheitspolizei und des SD, Kommandostab, Meldungen aus den besetzten Gebieten der UdSSR', 25.2.1942, USHMM, RG-31.002M, reel 11, 3676/4/105, p. 16.
207. 'SS-Richter, unvollständiges Schreiben, betr.: Strafandrohung gegen einen SS-Angehörigen', undated (after June 1943), BArch, NS 19/0536, p. 1.
208. 'Chef des Rasse- und Siedlungshauptamtes-SS, betr.: Verhütung von

Geschlechtskrankheiten', 23.9.1943, quoted in Seidler, *Prostitution, Homosexualität, Selbstverstümmelung*, p. 113.
209. 'Genzken an Handloser', 21.2.1944, BA-MA, RH 12-23/1855.
210. 'SS-Lazarett Riga, Meldung, betr.: Infektionsquelle zur beiliegenden Meldung eines Go.-Kranken', 3.9.1942, BArch, R 92/10036, unpaginated.
211. 'Amtsarzt für den Generalbezirk Litauen, Vordruck Fragebogen an den deutschen Amtsarzt für den Generalbezirk in Lettland beim Reichskommissar in Riga', 4.12.1942, BArch, R 92/10036, unpaginated; 'Amtsarzt in Riga, Schreiben an den Amtsarzt beim Generalkommissar in Kauen, betr.: Ansteckungsquelle Hans Sch.', 12.1.1943, BArch, R 92/10036, unpaginated; 'Amtsarzt beim Generalkommissar in Kauen, Schreiben an den Amtsarzt beim Generalkommissar in Riga, betr.: Go.-Ansteckungsquelle Hans Sch.', 8.2.1943, BArch, R 92/10036, p. 3.
212. 'Leitender Sanitätsoffizier, Meldung an den leitenden Arzt beim Generalkommissariat Lettland, betr.: Go.-Infektion Peter S., SS-Schütze (Erika L.)', 6.7.1943, BArch, R 92/10036, unpaginated.
213. 'SS-Führungshauptamt, Amtsgruppe D', 21.2.1944, BA-MA, H 20/57.
214. 'Chef der Sicherheitspolizei und des SD, Kommandostab, Meldungen aus den besetzten Gebieten der UdSSR', 25.2.1942, USHMM, RG-31.002M, reel 11, 3676/4/105, pp. 16f.
215. 'Oberkommando der Wehrmacht, Keitel, betr.: Verkehr des deutschen Soldaten mit der Zivilbevölkerung in den besetzten Ostgebieten', 12.9.1942, copy, BA-MA, RH 12-23/1371. In Berlin at the same time, very different conclusions had been reached about such children; see Chapter 5 on 'Occupation Children'.
216. 'RMbO, gez. Dr. Runte, Schreiben an den RKO, betr.: den ausserehelichen Verkehr zwischen Deutschen und Angehoerigen eines fremden Volkstums', 24.11.1941, BArch, R 90/460, pp. 170f., here p. 170. However, this did not mean that the brothels set up by the Wehrmacht were not frequented by SS members as well.
217. 'Höherer SS- und Polizeiführer in Frankreich, gez. Oberg', 20.1.1943, BArch, NS 19/264, unpaginated. Also see 'RF-SS, gez. Himmler, Schreiben an Oberg', 5.1.1943, BArch, NS 19/264, unpaginated.
218. 'RMbO, gez. Dr. Runte, Schreiben an den RKO, betr.: den ausserehelichen Verkehr zwischen Deutschen und Angehoerigen eines fremden Volkstums', 24.11.1941, BArch, R 90/460, pp. 170f., here p. 170.
219. 'RKO, gez. Wegner und Trampedach, Schreiben an den RMbO, betr.: Ausserehelicher Verkehr Deutscher mit Angehörigen fremden Volkstums', undated (March 1942), BArch, R 90/460, pp. 167ff., here pp. 168f.
220. The decree also curtailed forms of prostitution that were not organised by the military but were approved by the police. For example, women, pimps and brothel owners were not permitted to proposition clients on the street and producing or possessing accessories for sadomasochistic practices was also forbidden. While Jewish women were fundamentally prohibited from working in brothels, prostitutes with 'non-German blood' were permitted 'in port cities'

('Reichsministerium des Innern, Erlass, betr: Zur polizeilichen Behandlung der Prostitution, Berlin, 9.9.1939, verschickt an die Landesregierungen, den Reichskommissar für die Wiedervereinigung Österreichs mit dem Deutschen Reich, den Reichskommissar für das Saarland, den Reichsstatthalter im Sudetengau, den Reichsstatthalter in Hamburg, das Reichskriminalpolizeiamt, die Regierungspräsidenten und Kriminalpolizei[leit]stellen', BArch, R 22/1515, pp. 8f., also published in Ayass, *'Gemeinschaftsfremde'*, document no. 94, and Seidler, *Prostitution, Homosexualität, Selbstverstümmelung*, pp. 284–7).
221. Seidler, *Prostitution, Homosexualität, Selbstverstümmelung*, p. 135.
222. Meinen, *Wehrmacht und Prostitution*, pp. 22f.
223. 'Generalquartiermeister im Generalstab des Heeres, Befehl', 29.7.1940, BA-MA, H 20/825; 'Oberbefehlshaber des Heeres, gez. von Brauchitsch, Erlass', 31.7.1940, BA-MA, H 20/825. For a detailed discussion of this, see Meinen, *Wehrmacht und Prostitution*, pp. 21f.
224. Meinen, *Wehrmacht und Prostitution*, p. 22.
225. The decree applied to the occupied territories in Denmark, Norway, Croatia, Serbia, Greece, France, Belgium, Holland, Poland, Lithuania, Latvia, Estonia, Belarus, Volhynia, Ukraine and Russia as well as other 'allied and friendly countries', namely, Romania, Italy, Finland, Slovakia, Hungary and Bulgaria. In terms of 'racial policy', the decree stipulated that, first, the soldiers were to be taught the 'impact of venereal diseases on the development of the population' and, second, Jewish women were not allowed to be prostitutes ('OKW, gez. Dr. Handloser, Rundschreiben, betr.: Bekämpfung von Geschlechtskrankheiten', 27.1.1943, BA-MA, H 20/58, unpaginated). The OKH printed 8,800 copies of the decree so they could be distributed to all military district headquarters, military hospitals and medical facilities ('OKH, gez. Schmidt-Brücken, betr.: Abdruck zur Kenntnisnahme', undated [January 1943], BA-MA, H 20/58, unpaginated). Also see 'OKW, Az. B 49, TgbNr. 71/42 ChW San', 27.1.1943, BA-MA, H 20/840, quoted in Seidler, *Prostitution, Homosexualität, Selbstverstümmelung*, p. 140.
226. 'Chef der Sicherheitspolizei und des SD, Kommandostab, Meldungen aus den besetzten Gebieten der UdSSR', 25.2.1942, USHMM, RG-31.002M, reel 11, 3676/4/105, pp. V–VI, sheets 16f.
227. 'Heeresarzt im OKH, Mitteilungen an die Sanitätsoffiziere', 10.12.1940, BA-MA, RH 36/329; 'leitender Sanitätsoffizier im Militärverwaltungsbezirk A, betr.: Bordellwesen', 12.9.1942, BA-MA, RW 35/1221; 'Wehrkreisarzt XVIII, Schreiben an den Heeressanitätsinspekteur in Berlin', 3.1.1945, NARA, RG-242 78/189, pp. 761f., here p. 761.
228. 'RKO, gez. Wegner und Trampedach, Schreiben an den RMbO, betr.: Aussereheliches Verkehr Deutscher mit Angehoerigen fremden Volkstums', undated (March 1942), BArch, R 90/460, pp. 167ff., here pp. 168f.
229. 'OKH, Generalquartiermeister, betr.: Prostitution und Bordellwesen in den besetzten Ostgebieten', 20.3.1942, BA-MA, RH 12-23/1818, also published in Seidler, *Prostitution, Homosexualität, Selbstverstümmelung*, p. 139.

230. Regarding the cooperation between various institutions in the establishment of Wehrmacht brothels in France, see Meinen, *Wehrmacht und Prostitution*; Plassmann, 'Wehrmachtsbordelle'. Responsibilities were assigned differently only in the General Government, where civilian administrators were responsible for brothel operations. The military units there only supplied the medical personnel, while the local commanders handled the monitoring of the brothels (Seidler, *Prostitution, Homosexualität, Selbstverstümmelung*, p. 145).
231. 'Wehrmachtsbefehlshaber Ostland, Kommandeur Heeresstreifendienst (Aufgabengebiet General z. b.V.), Bericht, betr.: Reiseverkehr und Betreuungseinrichtungen', Riga, 15.9.1942, BA-MA, RW 41/57, unpaginated, p. 8 of the document.
232. 'Beratender Hygieniker beim Heeres-Sanitätsinspekteur, gez. Zeiss, Schreiben an den beratenden Hygieniker des Feld- und Ersatzheeres', Berlin, 10.2.1943, NARA, RG-242 78/189, pp. 1247f. Similar sentiments can be found in a letter from senior physician Dr Wendt with respect to Romania (*Oberarzt* Dr. Wendt, Bucharest, 'Bericht an den Heeressanitätsinspekteur', 28.8.1941, BA-MA, H 20/1082-2, unpaginated).
233. 'Wehrmachtsbefehlshaber Ostland, Kommandeur Wehrmachtsstreifendienst (Aufgabengebiet General z. b.V.), Bericht Nr. 8, umfassend die Zeit vom 5.6.1943 bis 10.1.1944', Riga, 11.1.1944, BA-MA, RW 41/57, p. 5. Also see the sources in the following notes.
234. 'Wehrmachtsbefehlshaber Ostland, Kommandeur Wehrmachtsstreifendienst (Aufgabengebiet General z. b.V.), Bericht Nr. 9, umfassend die Zeit vom 11. 1. 1944 bis 15. 3. 1944', Riga, 18.3.1944, BA-MA, RW 41/57, p. 3.
235. 'Wehrmachtsbefehlshaber Ostland, Kommandeur Heeresstreifendienst (Aufgabengebiet General z. b.V.), Bericht, betr.: Reiseverkehr und Betreuungseinrichtungen', Riga, 15.9.1942, BA-MA, RW 41/57, p. 8.
236. Regarding homosexuality in the Wehrmacht, see Snyder, *Sex Crimes*, pp. 103ff.; Steinkamp, *Zur Devianz-Problematik in der Wehrmacht*, pp. 302ff.; Fout, 'Homosexuelle in der NS-Zeit'; Seidler, *Prostitution, Homosexualität, Selbstverstümmelung*, pp. 193ff. The lines between tender, comforting comradeship and homosexuality were sometimes blurry, as demonstrated by Kühne, *Kameradschaft*, p. 159.
237. '122. Infanteriedivision, Tagebuch Abt. III, TB Nr. 5 für die Zeit vom 1.–31.5.1942', 1.6.1942, BA-MA, RH 26-122/55, also quoted in Steinkamp, *Zur Devianz-Problematik in der Wehrmacht*, p. 305.
238. '122. Infanteriedivision, Tagebuch Abt. III, TB Nr. 6 für die Zeit vom 1.–30.6.1942', 1.7.1942, BA-MA, RH 26-122/55, also quoted in Steinkamp, *Zur Devianz-Problematik in der Wehrmacht*, p. 305.
239. 'Wehrmachtsbefehlshaber Ostland, Kommandeur Wehrmachtsstreifendienst (Aufgabengebiet General z. b.V.), Bericht Nr. 9, umfassend die Zeit vom 11. 1. 1944 bis 15. 3. 1944', Riga, 18.3.1944, BA-MA, RW 41/57, p. 3.
240. 'Wehrmacht-Ortskommandantur Riga, Kommandanturbefehl Nr. 59/42',

Riga, 17.12.1942, USHMM, RG-18.002M, reel 14, 752/2/1, p. 58: 'The troop brothel on Parkstrasse is open from 16:00–21:30 as of today'.
241. City in central Ukraine on the Samara River. Novomoskovsk was occupied by the Germans in September 1941.
242. Witness interview in Gaevert and Hilbert, *Women as Booty*, documentary film. Regarding the appropriation of a house in Warsaw, see Apenszlak (ed.), *The Black Book*, p. 28.
243. Witness interview in Gaevert and Hilbert, *Women as Booty*, documentary film.
244. See, e.g., 'From the diary of Doctor Elena Buividaite-Kutorgene', p. 365; Sutzkever, 'The Vilna Ghetto', p. 251.
245. Sutzkever, 'The Vilna Ghetto'; *Trial of the Major War Criminals*, vol. 7, p. 456.; Werth, *Russia at War*, p. 609; Gertjejanssen, *Victims, Heroes, Survivors*, pp. 180f. Gertjejanssen also quotes a number of literary depictions (ibid.). For similar accounts from Poland, see, e.g., Republic of Poland/Ministry of Foreign Affairs (ed.) *German Occupation*, pp. 229ff.
246. A radio broadcast about German crimes in Kharkiv claimed: 'The people were captured like dogs. On busy streets and the market square, a lorry suddenly appeared which was divided into compartments inside. The people were herded into it and taken to the railway station. The pretty girls were taken to brothels. The soldiers received admission tickets for the brothels' (Interradio AG monitoring service, Sonderdienst Seehaus, Radio Moscow, originally in Russian, 17.11.1943, 17:20–17:40, BArch, R 6/684, p. 61).
247. See, e.g., Peter O. Vlcko, Righteous Among Nations, USHMM, RG-20.015*01, p. 3. Some military leaders were, in fact, thinking along these lines. The reports from the occupied territories of the Soviet Union in early 1942 stated: 'It is indicative of this attitude [viewing prostitution as a bourgeois perversion; R. M.] that Russian girls are known to have said "they would rather kill themselves than work in a brothel". In view of this situation, many are of the opinion that, when brothels are established, their residents should be taken from the Polish population of the General Government' ('Chef der Sicherheitspolizei und des SD, Kommandostab, Meldungen aus den besetzten Gebieten der UdSSR', 25.2.1942, USHMM, RG-31.002M, reel 11, 3676/4/105, pp. 16f.).
248. Vegesack, *Als Dolmetscher im Osten*, p. 262.
249. Quoted in Beckermann, *Jenseits des Krieges*, p. 115.
250. Seidler, *Prostitution, Homosexualität, Selbstverstümmelung*, p. 138; Vossler, *Propaganda in die eigene Truppe*, p. 353; Gertjejanssen, *Victims, Heroes, Survivors*, p. 183.
251. Seidler provides no evidence for this argument, however; Seidler, *Prostitution, Homosexualität, Selbstverstümmelung*, p. 154.
252. See Interradio AG monitoring service, Sonderdienst Seehaus, Radio Moscow, originally in Russian, 24.10.1943, 17:15, BArch, R 6/684, p. 89; Interradio AG monitoring service, Sonderdienst Seehaus, Radio Shevchenko, originally in Russian, 1.10.1943, 19:20, BArch, R 6/678, p. 21; Republic of Poland/Ministry

of Foreign Affairs (ed.), *German Occupation*, p. 229. Regarding forced labour by women in general, see Herbert, *Hitler's Foreign Workers*.
253. Lower, *Nazi Empire-Building*, pp. 110f.
254. 'Leitender Sanitätsoffizier im Generalgouvernement, Bericht über Bordelle für Heeresangehörige im Gen.-Gouv.', 2.10.1940, BA-MA, RH 12-23/1818. Though the head medical officer who wrote this was referring to brothels in the General Government, the assessment is likely to have been similar in the Reich Commissariat Ostland and Reich Commissariat Ukraine.
255. 'RKF Himmler an SS-Obergruppenführer Friedrich Wilhelm Krüger, betr.: Geschlechtsverkehr von Angehörigen der SS und Polizei mit Frauen einer andersrassigen Bevölkerung', 30.6.1942, BArch, NS 19/1913, pp. 3f., here p. 4, also published in Himmler, *Reichsführer!*, pp. 156f., document 120. It would also be interesting to investigate how the Wehrmacht and SS viewed the contact between German men and Black women in brothels in Libya, for instance. In reference to this, Neumann quotes a Wehrmacht doctor who wrote in July 1941 that there was a kind of 'natural emotional disconnection' between 'two worlds'. Consequently, it was thought that German soldiers would seek out Black prostitutes relatively infrequently, while Italian soldiers would relish such contact (Neumann, *'Arzttum ist immer Kämpfertum'*, pp. 244, 242).
256. 'Heeresarzt im OKH, gez. Dr. Handloser, Prostitution und Bordellwesen im besetzten Gebiet in Sowjetrussland', 20.3.1942, BA-MA, RH 12-23/1371.
257. See, e.g., 'OKH, Merkblatt für das Verhalten des deutschen Soldaten in den besetzten Ostgebieten', 8.6.1942, BA-MA, RH 12-23/1371; 'OKW, gez. Dr. Handloser, Rundschreiben, betr.: Bekämpfung von Geschlechtskrankheiten', 27.1.1943, BA-MA, H 20/58, unpaginated.
258. Gertjejanssen, *Victims, Heroes, Survivors*, pp. 191ff.; Brownmiller, *Against Our Will*, pp. 51ff.; D.V. Galperns, witness statement, 27.12.1945, USHMM, RG-06.025*1 RIGA N-18313, 3/46, p. 2. Also see the literary depictions in Lustig, *Lovely Green Eyes*, and Ka-Tzetnik, *House of Dolls*.
259. Sybil Milton has pointed out that the sources dealing with this issue must be approached with caution, not least because a number of sensationalist myths about Jewish women in SS brothels circulated in the early post-war period (Milton, 'Women and the Holocaust', pp. 230f.).
260. 'Heeresarzt im OKH, gez. Dr. Handloser, betr.: Prostitution und Bordellwesen im besetzten Gebiet in Sowjetrussland', 20.3.1942, BA-MA, RH 12-23/1371.
261. 'Wehrmachts-Ortskommandantur Riga, Standortarzt, Schreiben an das Reservelazarett III, Königsberg, betr.: Go.-Meldung Uffz Rich. L.', 23.7.1943, BArch, R 92/10036, unpaginated; 'Wehrmachts-Ortskommandantur Riga, Standortarzt, Schreiben an das Staatliche Gesundheitsamt Rostock, betr.: Bordellmädchen Vera', 17.8.1943, BArch, R 92/10036, unpaginated; 'Wehrmachts-Ortskommandantur Riga, Standortarzt, Schreiben an das Reservelazarett 116 in Berlin-Lichtenrade, betr.: Go.- Meldung Oskar Mrocek', 17.8.1943, BArch, R 92/10036, unpaginated.
262. 'Löhe, Schreiben an die Lehrgruppe C der militärärztlichen Akademie, betr.:

Stellungnahme zu dem Thema: Bekämpfung der Geschlechtskrankh.', BA-MA, RH 12-23/1809.
263. Only the situation of the women in the Wehrmacht brothels in France has been researched in more detail (Meinen, *Wehrmacht und Prostitution*, pp. 84ff.). Individual sources from various regions of the Soviet Union indicate that this was handled differently in urban and rural areas, and that the situation could change over time. Regarding Romania, see *Oberarzt* Dr Wendt, Bucharest, 'Bericht an den Heeressanitätsinspekteur', 28.8.1941, BA-MA, H 20/1082-2.
264. 'Heeresgruppenarzt beim Oberkommando Heeresgruppe D, betr.: Bordelle für Osttruppen', 28.4.1944, BA-MA, RH 36/ v. 491, also quoted in Seidler, *Prostitution, Homosexualität, Selbstverstümmelung*, p. 183.
265. 'Wehrmachtsbefehlshaber Ostland, Kommandeur Heeresstreifendienst (Aufgabengebiet General z. b.V.), Bericht, betr.: Reiseverkehr und Betreuungseinrichtungen', Riga, 15.9.1942, BA-MA, RW 41/57, p. 8.
266. For some isolated findings, see Gertjejanssen, *Victims, Heroes, Survivors*, pp. 207ff. In occupied France, the Wehrmacht brothels were a significant economic factor; see Plassmann, 'Wehrmachtsbordelle', p. 163.
267. This was the arrangement in France, in any case; see Meinen, *Wehrmacht und Prostitution*, pp. 209f.
268. 'Leitender Arzt beim Generalkommissariat in Lettland mit Sitz in Riga, Fragebogen', 19.5.1943, BArch, R 92/10036, unpaginated.
269. 'Hauptwachtmeister der Schutzpolizei-Dienstabteilung, Lemke, Polizeibericht', Libau (Liepāja), 11.2.1943, USHMM, RG 18.002M, reel 11, 83/1/207, pp. 107f. Also see Gertjejanssen, *Victims, Heroes, Survivors*, p. 151. In France, it cost between three and ten Reichsmarks to visit a Wehrmacht brothel; see Meinen, *Wehrmacht und Prostitution*, pp. 209ff.
270. See, e.g., 'Reservelazarett Darmstadt, Meldung an den leitenden Arzt des Generalkommissariats in Riga, Peter A.', 19.4.1943, BArch, R 02/10036, p. 11; 'Reservelazarett Tapiau, Meldung an den leitenden Arzt beim Generalkommissariat in Riga, Karl K.', 19.5.1943, BArch, R 02/10036, p. 14. Insa Meinen has shown that this strategy was also used in occupied France; see Meinen, *Wehrmacht und Prostitution*, pp. 95f.
271. 'Reservelazarett Darmstadt, Meldung an den leitenden Arzt des Generalkommissariats in Riga, Peter A.', 19.4.1943, BArch, R 02/10036, p. 11; 'Reservelazarett Tapiau, Meldung an den leitenden Arzt beim Generalkommissariat in Riga, Karl K.', 19.5.1943, BArch, R 02/10036, p. 14.
272. 'Wehrmachts-Ortskommandantur Riga, Standortarzt, Schreiben an das Reservelazarett III, Königsberg, betr.: Go.-Meldung Uffz Rich. L.', 23.7.1943, BArch, R 92/10036, unpaginated; 'Wehrmachts-Ortskommandantur Riga, Standortarzt, Schreiben an das Staatliche Gesundheitsamt Rostock, betr.: Bordellmädchen Vera', 17.8.1943, BArch, R 92/10036, unpaginated; 'Wehrmachts-Ortskommandantur Riga, Standortarzt, Schreiben an das Reservelazarett 116 in Berlin-Lichtenrade, betr.: Go.- Meldung Oskar Mrocek', 17.8.1943, BArch, R 92/10036, unpaginated.

273. 'Beratender Dermatologe beim OKH, gez. Löhe, Notiz zum Schreiben des Leit.-San.-Offz. der Deutschen Heeresmission Rumänien', 6.10.1941, BA-MA, H 20/1082–2.
274. Schmidt, *Die Mitläuferin*, pp. 47f. The episode she describes took place during her time in Yugoslavia.
275. Also see Kühne, *Kameradschaft*, pp. 163, 165f, and Kühne, *The Rise and Fall of Comradeship*, pp. 173f. This is the case even today, as can be seen when company executives celebrate a business success by visiting a brothel; see Grenz, *(Un)heimliche Lust*.
276. See, e.g., 'From the diary of Doctor Elena Buividaite-Kutorgene', p. 365; Sutzkever, 'The Vilna Ghetto', p. 251. Hierarchical divisions also governed brothel operations in France. See Meinen, *Wehrmacht und Prostitution*, pp. 199f.; Plassmann, 'Wehrmachtsbordelle', p. 170.
277. Tünnes and Schäl are two traditional characters from the puppet theatre of Cologne; 'Brief Tünnes an Schääl, Russland, om hillige Ovend 1941', BA-MA, RH 22/255, p. 8.
278. Hildegard Klemm, handwritten letter to her former work colleagues at the Reich Institute for the History of the New Germany, 26.2.1943, BArch, R 1/38, unpaginated, also quoted in Vossler, *Propaganda in die eigene Truppe*, p. 345.
279. In January 1943, SS-*Obergruppenführer* Dietrich reported that 7,000 of the men stationed in Frankfurt with the Leibstandarte Adolf Hitler had contracted sexually transmitted diseases. Although the medical exams that were subsequently carried out revealed that actually only 244 men were infected, Himmler recommended that brothels be established at all Waffen-SS sites. The response to this directive is unknown. See 'RF-SS Himmler, Schreiben an Obergruppenführer Carl Albrecht Oberg', 5.1.1943, BArch, NS 19/264.
280. Gaevert and Hilberg, *Women as Booty*; Gertjejanssen, *Victims, Heroes, Survivors*, p. 175.
281. 'Wehrmachtsbefehlshaber Ostland, Kommandeur Wehrmachtsstreifendienst (Aufgabengebiet General z. b.V.), Bericht Nr. 8, umfassend die Zeit vom 5.6.1943 bis 10.1.1944', Riga, 11.1.1944, BA-MA, RW 41/57, unpaginated, p. 5 of the document.
282. Ibid. This 'differentiation of the brothel system' was put into practice by the Wehrmacht in occupied France as well (Meinen, *Wehrmacht und Prostitution*, pp. 200f.). Further research is needed to determine whether the members of allied armies – such as the Spanish divisions or men from 'Nordic' countries, including Norwegian SS volunteers – could visit Wehrmacht brothels at the same time as German soldiers.
283. Neither foreign Wehrmacht volunteers nor German civilians were supposed to have access to the brothels ('OKH, Generalquartiermeister, betr.: Prostitution und Bordellwesen im besetzten Gebiet in Sowjetrussland', 20.3.1942, BA-MA, RH 12-23/1818).
284. See, e.g., 'SS-Lazarett Riga, Meldung einer Ansteckungsquelle, Jonas P.', 13.5.1943, BArch, R 92/10036, unpaginated; 'Sanitätskompanie 10,

Ortslazarett Lamocha, Meldung an den Divisionsarzt 10. Lw. Felddivision, Stanislaus W.' 10.6.1943, BArch, R 92/10036, p. 21; 'Sanitätskompanie 10, Ortslazarett Lamocha, Meldung an den Divisionsarzt 10. Lw. Felddivision, Laimons D.', 2.7.1943, BArch, R 92/10036, unpaginated; 'Dienststelle L18089, Schreiben an den leitenden Sanitätsoffizier beim Generalkommissariat Lettland, betr.: Bekämpfung der Geschlechtskrankheiten', 3.8.1943, BArch, R 92/10036, unpaginated.

285. Memo, 6.12.1943, Düsseldorf University Archives (UAD) 8/4, 19, quoted in Plassmann, 'Wehrmachtsbordelle', p. 162.
286. Recent studies estimate that the Wehrmacht's allies and volunteers from all over Europe numbered nearly one million even in the first phase of the war against the Soviet Union, compared to three million German Wehrmacht soldiers. In the following years, the average size of the Wehrmacht shrank to 2.5 million, but the number of foreigners rose by another million. Most of these men were volunteers from the Soviet Union who wanted to fight Bolshevism or provide auxiliary services (Müller, *The Unknown Eastern Front*, pp. 255).
287. 'Heeresgruppenarzt beim Oberkommando Heeresgruppe D, betr.: Bordelle für Osttruppen', 28.4.1944, BA-MA, RH 36/v. 491, also quoted in Seidler, *Prostitution, Homosexualität, Selbstverstümmelung*, p. 183. Regarding the brothels set up in France specially for members of the 'Eastern troops', cf. Plassmann, 'Wehrmachtsbordelle", pp. 161f.
288. Gertjejanssen, *Victims, Heroes, Survivors*, pp. 198ff.; Vossler, *Propaganda in die eigene Truppe*, pp. 356ff.
289. 'Leitender San.-Offizier, OFK 365, Az. 49s (I/F) Monatsbericht, geheim, Anlage 3 zu OFK 365 Ia Nr 1286/43', pp. 1f., Lemberg (Lviv), 15.3.1943, NARA, RG-242 501/217, p. 338, also quoted in Gertjejanssen, *Victims, Heroes, Survivors*, pp. 199f. Standing in a queue was generally considered unworthy of a German soldier. In March 1944, Wehrmacht members in Riga were even forbidden from standing in line outside the cinema ('Wehrmachtsbefehlshaber Ostland, Kommandeur Wehrmachtsstreifendienst, [Aufgabengebiet General z. b.V.], Bericht Nr. 9, umfassend die Zeit vom 11.1.1944 bis 15.3.1944', Riga, 18.3.1944, BA-MA, RW 41/57, unpaginated, p. 3 of the document).
290. 'Sof. (Z) Anatol Herlitz, Dolm.Ers.Komp. 16, Die Verwaltungsprobleme im Osten', 13.9.1943, BArch, R 93/6, p. 1, unpaginated. Also see Vegesack, *Als Dolmetscher im Osten*, pp. 262f.
291. Kruse, 'Major Kurt Werner', p. 278.
292. 'OKH, von Brauchitsch, Schreiben an den Generalquartiermeister', 31.7.1940, BA-MA, RH 53-7/v. 233a/167, also 'Anl. 1 zu OKH, betr.: Selbstzucht', 6.9.1941, BA-MA, H 20/825; quoted in Seidler, *Prostitution, Homosexualität, Selbstverstümmelung*, pp. 136f.
293. 'Wehrkreisarzt XVIII, Schreiben an den Heeressanitätsinspekteur in Berlin', 3.1.1945, NARA, RG-242 78/189, pp. 761f., here p. 761.
294. Quoted in Plassmann, 'Wehrmachtsbordelle', p. 160.
295. Quoted in Vossler, *Propaganda in die eigene Truppe*, p. 340.

296. Quoted in 'OKH, Heeressanitätsinspektion, Abt. Wissenschaft und Gesundheitsführung, Schreiben an Lehrgruppe C der militärärztlichen Akademie, betr.: Stellungnahme zu dem Thema: Bekämpfung der Geschlechtskrankh.', Berlin, 9.1.1945, BA-MA, H 20/447, unpaginated. Also see the comments of *Standartenführer* Joachim Mrugowsky, who considered sexually transmitted diseases to be the worst wartime epidemic in Ukraine (Mrugowsky, 'Bericht über die Besichtigung von Seuchenlazaretten in der Ukraine', BA-MA, RG 12–23/193, p. 146).
297. 'Marinegruppenkommando Süd, betr.: Bekämpfung von Geschlechtskrankheiten', 12.3.1943, BA-MA, H 20/1082-2; also see 'Wehrmachtsbefehlshaber Ostland, Kommandeur Wehrmachtsstreifendienst (Aufgabengebiet General z. b.V.), Bericht Nr. 8, umfassend die Zeit vom 5.6.1943 bis 10.1.1944', Riga, 11.1.1944, BA-MA, RW 41/57, unpaginated, p. 5 of the document.
298. 'OKH, Heeressanitätsinspektion, Abt. Wissenschaft und Gesundheitsführung, Schreiben an Lehrgruppe C der militärärztlichen Akademie, betr.: Stellungnahme zu dem Thema: Bekämpfung der Geschlechtskrankh.', Berlin, 9.1.1945, BA-MA, H 20/447, unpaginated.
299. See the sources used in this chapter as well as Gertjejanssen, *Victims, Heroes, Survivors*, pp. 221f.

CHAPTER 4

Consensual Relations

Jürgen W. was born in 1916 and conscripted into the Wehrmacht in 1935 when compulsory military service was reintroduced. He was stationed in Austria and the Sudetenland in 1938, Poland in 1939, and then in France, the Soviet Union and Italy. Even before the start of World War II, Jürgen W. had begun documenting his experiences in a diary. In the Soviet Union, he used loose paper and pencil to record where he was almost daily. Two days before the invasion, Jürgen W. – now a General of the Artillery – noted how excited his men had been when the attack was announced. As a superior officer, he always tried to keep tabs on the mood in his unit. He meticulously recorded whether letters were expected from home, how the food tasted and what his impressions were of the physical constitution of his men. Shortly before his unit reached Stalingrad, Jürgen W. went back to attend an artillery training course in the Reich. Instead of returning to the Soviet Union afterwards, he was sent straight to Italy. After the war, Jürgen W. was active in veterans' associations. He also produced a verbatim typed copy of his wartime notes, and he illustrated this 'Diary in Russia' with painstakingly drawn maps and carefully captioned photographs. While keeping a diary is, in itself, a communicative act – one addressed to an imaginary or real audience[1] – Jürgen W.'s 'reworking' of his journal reveals all the more clearly that he was explicitly addressing a third party. In various places in his diary, there are references to sexual encounters between his subordinates and local women – such as on 25 June 1942:

> Kh[arkiv is] a typical rear echelon city. Heavy lorry traffic, trams, cinemas, coffee houses, soldiers everywhere, some in fancy suits, and in between them Labour Service, Italians, Hungarians, Croats, Slovaks, nurses and more or less

pretty, sometimes very well-dressed Russian girls. Soldiers arm in arm with them, officers somewhat more reserved but clearly also not averse, paymasters with girls in their car. The front-line soldiers are disgusted, the nurses angry that the Russian girls are given preference.[2]

German men in the rear echelon often spent weeks or months in the same place. Most of them were soldiers serving in logistics, headquarters and support units, recuperating in military hospitals or temporarily stopping off on their advance with their unit. There were also hundreds of thousands of German railway employees and builders working for Organisation Todt, postal workers, administrative assistants, SS men and police, business officials and employees of private and state-owned companies. In occupied Belarus, according to Christian Gerlach, the Germans comprised the 'upper class in terms of politics, economics, standard of living, law and culture' from 1941 to 1944.[3] They lived in private houses and worked in the immediate vicinity of the local population. Since the military and civilian authorities also relied on staff from the region, German men were sometimes in daily contact with local women. When they were off-duty, too, the men did not always keep to themselves. Many visited local pubs, film screenings and parks where they met women. Over time, this led to friendly relations and intimate contact.[4] This contact could take the form of short-term flirtations, sexual flings, longer-term relationships or even serious love affairs. Ludwig Runte, head of the administrative department in the RKO, complained in 1942 that Germans were increasingly even spending their holidays in Belarus.[5] Jürgen W.'s diary entry illustrates that these consensual relations were not equally available to all soldiers, however, and that they could also lead to competition and tension between the men.

The boundaries between consensual relations and sexual bartering were often blurry. The eleven-part television mini-series entitled *Štrafbat* (*Penal Battlion*), first broadcast in Russia in 2004, addresses the complexity of this situation. One episode features a Russian woman who is living with a German officer. Not knowing whether her husband is still alive, she enters into a relationship with the German, who provides food for her and her young daughter. Over time, a serious romance develops between the two. In one scene, the German hits her because he suspects she has been unfaithful to him. He could not bear this, he says, because he loves her.[6] The episode hints that the women in this situation had a different perspective on such relationships than the men. This also becomes apparent when Jürgen W.'s notes are compared with the description in the post-war novel *Kharkiv* by Olena Zvychaina (see section on 'Occasional Sexual Bartering'). At first glance, the two depictions of the city of Kharkiv seem very similar. But while Jürgen W. decries the rear-echelon soldiers who seem more concerned with pleasure than war, Zvychaina grapples with the desperation and fear that drove many women into the arms of Germans.

More or less consensual heterosexual relationships between German soldiers and local women in the occupied territories have become the focus of increased public and academic attention in recent years.[7] Journalists and scholars often interpret these couples' encounters as moments in which young people fell in love, with love being depicted as a fateful, romantic feeling that overcame and overwhelmed the individuals despite the horrific war.[8] More recent studies, however, emphasise that emotions themselves are contingent concepts. For example, in her overview of intellectual analyses of love affairs in history, Claire Langhamer writes that love is an extremely mutable and elastic term, the meaning and use of which varies depending on historical moment, gender, status and age group.[9] From this perspective, it was not that an eternally unchanged, purely human emotion was able to take hold during the war of annihilation despite the brutal situation; instead, the war and occupation created the conditions in which intimate relationships would develop in the first place.[10] These relationships could involve feelings of infatuation, affinity, fascination and pleasure without necessarily involving romance or love, which is why they are referred to here as *consensual relations* or *romantic relationships*.

The sources show that men and women had different and diverse motivations for engaging in consensual relations. The desire for normality and distraction, the longing for a feeling of comfort and security, and distance from one's family played a role as well as the fulfilment of sexual curiosity and desire. In the following, I will first examine the different perspectives of the men and women. What did these consensual relations mean to them, and how were their experiences shaped by their respective position during the war and occupation? I will also look at the measures employed by the Wehrmacht and SS in their attempt to intervene in the men's 'private life'. What conflicts of interest arose here in terms of military and occupation policy? The civilian occupation authorities were particularly concerned with the marriage applications submitted by Wehrmacht and SS members in the Baltic countries and Ukraine. Finally, I will explore how the different actors dealt with the prospect of long-term occupation.

The Men's Desire for Normality

In the summer of 2000, the German-Russian Museum in Berlin-Karlshorst opened an exhibition entitled *Foto-Feldpost: Geknipste Kriegserlebnisse 1939–1945* (Photo Feldpost: Snapshots of wartime experiences 1939–1945). The curators said their goal was to convey an impression of how German soldiers captured their war experiences in photographs of themselves and their comrades, their activities, the Wehrmacht's tools of power, foreign countries and peoples, the destruction of the war, fallen and executed enemies, and the graves of German 'heroes'.[11] The exhibition included photos of the local population in the Soviet Union. Ulrike Schmiegelt points out that a relatively large number of these pictures are of young women, often in skilfully arranged scenes. In many cases, these women were the daughters of the families with whom the soldiers lived. Some of them seem to have posed for the photographs, and in a few images they smile directly at the camera. A large number of pictures show local women together with German soldiers – dancing, for example.[12] Some photos reveal the photographers' fascination with the foreign women and their attempts to capture the specifics of their facial expressions, clothing and way of presenting themselves.

The Wehrmacht leadership had told the soldiers that they would be dealing with 'Bolshevist sub-humans'. The women of the Soviet Union were generally described as 'peasant-like', 'coarse' and prone to 'prolific breeding'.[13] German propaganda had also carefully fostered the cliché of the fanatic, devious female Bolshevist. For example, on 20 July 1941, the *Völkische Beobachter* newspaper published a report on a successful German campaign, during which a female Red Army soldier had been killed: 'a woman – though a creature like this no longer deserves the name. A bestial apparition whose features no longer had anything feminine about them.'[14] While many soldiers in the Soviet Union looked for such 'apparitions' and apparently had their suspicions confirmed,[15] others expressed astonishment because their first impressions of the country and its people were nothing like they expected.[16] Jürgen W., the artillery general mentioned earlier, wrote about Latvia on 26 June 1941, five days after the invasion: 'The landscape is much more beautiful than in Poland, more varied, more friendly, the villages cleaner. Above all things, the population is mostly clean, and some of the girls are even nicely dressed.'[17] Some soldiers additionally felt it worth mentioning that many women in the formerly Polish and Soviet territories corresponded to the beauty ideals that prevailed in Germany. In their letters and diaries, the men often noted with surprise that a large number of the women were blonde – an indication of high 'racial value', according to their standards. For example, Wehrmacht judge Hans Meier-Brennecke wrote to his wife in July 1941:

> Incidentally, all of the men are astonished how many very pretty girls (nearly all blonde) there are in the formerly Polish territories. They are full of national pride and are very attached to their crushed fatherland. Nonetheless, they are pleased with our arrival because we have driven away the hated Muscovites.[18]

Meier-Brennecke draws a connection between his positive impression of the women's appearance and their love of their fatherland and friendliness towards the Germans, and he portrays himself as the 'liberator' of these 'proud' and 'pretty girls'. Others, however, found the appearance of the local woman to be an 'empty shell'. A soldier in Ukraine expressed his incomprehension as follows: 'They look as though they're made of flesh. But when you feel them, then they're like wood. I just wonder how they wind up with so many children!'[19] The men sometimes felt deceived by the women's appearance and behaviour, as illustrated by a note written by a soldier on the back of a photograph showing a Crimean Tatar[20] woman in traditional clothing: 'These women were pretty and proud, and they spit at the feet of many a soldier who wanted to get close to them'.[21] Soldiers who believed they were confronting the 'women of the enemy' as military victors could have been prompted by such actions to attempt to 'conquer' them as well.

But in the memoirs of German Wehrmacht members in the Soviet Union, the motif of flirtatious encounters and 'harmless relations' with local women plays the most prominent role. A passage from the diary-based memoirs of Fritz Hahl is a good example of this. Describing a two-week break spent by his regiment in Amvrosiivka (Ukraine) in the autumn of 1941, he writes: 'The Ukrainian population was well-disposed towards us. A few men, myself included, had wonderful, harmless *Bratkartoffel-Verhältnisse* [fried-potato relationships] with pretty young Ukrainians'.[22] The term 'fried-potato relationships' appears in the ego documents of other soldiers as well; it generally referred to relationships that offered external comforts without involving a serious commitment. An emphasis is often placed on the innocence of these encounters; the soldiers write about '*Backfische*' (female teenagers) and 'virginal' girls, with sexuality playing almost no role in their accounts. Only in some cases do the men mention 'shy' kisses or a fleeting touch. The context for all of this – the military combat, the women's family environment and potential male rivals – is left out.

However, a diary entry from Ernst Günther K., a soldier with the 170th Division, shows that the men were certainly aware that the women's perspective on such 'harmless' encounters could be very different. On 1 January 1942 he noted:

> One young girl has a picture of a German soldier, and the cheeky little thing declares proudly that he's her 'monch' [husband]. He's going to come back from Sevastopol and take her to Germany with him and then they'll get married. Really! she insists. And the woman looks great and clean! Well then, good luck – we naturally don't believe it, this fine fellow had a quick fiddle, made promises and was gone.[23]

K. draws attention to the woman's naïvety by leaving no doubt that the solider lured her with false promises. The men often seem to have viewed the women as gullible, silly or contradictory. A former medic from Austria recalled how a young woman from Odessa with whom he had become acquainted showed him a picture of a German non-commissioned officer. There was a dedication on the back to 'My dear . . .'. When he asked her about it, she told him of 'her love for this man. I couldn't understand it, because the girl actually wanted to fight as a partisan in a women's company'.[24] The same veteran also explained how a few officers stationed in Ukraine had brought along French wines and 'lingerie' which they 'gave to the Ukrainian girls as gifts'. While he and his comrades were risking their lives as infantrymen, he said, these officers 'probably would have liked the war to go on even longer'[25] – another hint at the rivalries mentioned earlier.

Some ego documents reveal that the men tried to create a kind of counter-world to their everyday soldierly life through imagined or real romantic encounters. This is how Claus Hansmann expressed it in his diary:

> Over the wretched, empty furrows that extend from our miserable hut treads now the deathly pale sheen of the moon. The feeling of apprehension, the many thoughts and burdens desert me, and almost cheerfully the fantasy of life bears a fruit that perhaps will never mature. First there are only the eyes, inscrutable, then hesitantly, tentatively the picture forms for me . . . Shyly and furtively your image laughs . . . The taste of your kisses presses on my lips . . . My arms yearn for you . . . Never before has your expression had such power over me and your caress such sweetness . . . The blue dreams of your eyes are so enigmatic, they are the last that remains with me when you disappear in the fog.[26]

Hansmann referred to his wishful thinking as a 'fantasy of life'. It seems to have been an antithesis to his strenuous, desolate and oppressive everyday life, in which he was repeatedly confronted with the possibility of his own death.[27] Similar images are found in *Feldpost* letters sent to girlfriends, fiancées and wives back home, which deal with everyday family life and sexual desire, but also infidelity and fears of loss.[28]

Martin Humburg has shown that the soldiers were often driven by the thought that they were risking their lives in foreign lands for their loved ones back home. This meant that their girlfriends and wives in Germany continued to be their emotional and mental point of reference. In light of this 'ideationally inflated concept of love', sexual adventures could be 'considered peripheral'.[29] It seems that some men coped with their fears and desires by being unfaithful themselves and having 'a girlfriend in every village', as former Wehrmacht soldier Otto Pauls put it.[30] Others created a 'parallel world' in the occupied territories, one which was kept carefully separated from the world back home. Jewish survivor Sheli Lagin, who worked in a canteen kitchen in the ghetto in Šiauliai (Lithuania), recalled how she frequently had to iron the dress uniform of one of the German cooks so he would look nice during his evening visits to his Lithuanian 'wife', as he put it. The man had an actual wife and two children back in Germany. When Lagin asked him how he reconciled this double life, he mocked her for being naïve. As he portrayed it, one thing had nothing to do with the other.[31]

The soldiers may have wanted to separate war and violence from flirtation, romance and love, and many diaries and letters testify to their attempts to do so.[32] But it was impossible to block out the war and occupation entirely, as this situation actually shaped both the genesis and development of these encounters. A diary entry by the sailor Karl Heinz L. shows just how closely flirtation could sit alongside violence. Shortly after invading Latvia, the Germans began carrying out daily shootings in the port city of Libau (Liepāja). Describing the evening of 15 July 1941, Karl Heinz L. writes:

> We horse around in the water and try to score with the little Latvian chicks. But all good things must end, and we all have to be back on board at 8 o'clock. We're strolling back when, not far from the beach, we come upon a lot of people. [. . .] We've come upon the place where so and so many snipers are shot every evening. [. . .] Soldiers are standing around, I guess around 600 to 800 men, satisfying their gruesome curiosity.[33]

This diary is one of the few autobiographical accounts that makes any mention of shootings. The author is clearly somewhat repulsed by the violence and distances himself from the 'gruesome curiosity' of the soldiers standing around, a distance that is further emphasised by his distinctly harmless depiction of trying to 'score' with the girls on the beach.

The soldier Herbert K. viewed the situation very differently. Manfred Oldenburg's study of the Wehrmacht's occupation policy in Crimea cites a Feldpost letter from NCO Herbert K. of the 72nd Division, who wrote on 30 July 1942 during his assignment in Sevastopol:

> Lately we've always been staying in one place and have plenty of opportunities to chat with girls above all. Many of my comrades take full advantage of this. But in this matter I have my principles. They are Russians and therefore our enemies. So keep your distance. Dear comrades died at their hands just a few weeks ago. Many a soldier has fallen victim to the treacherous attacks of partisans in this very region.[34]

From Herbert K.'s perspective, a soldier should never lose sight of the combat situation – for reasons of both military security and morality. 'Racial' objections to contact with civilians categorised as 'ethnically alien' or 'racially alien', by contrast, rarely play a role in the ego documents of soldiers. This may have to do with the fact that the criteria for 'racial evaluation' were often unclear, and there was no definitive answer to the question of how certain 'ethnic groups' should be categorised.[35] If the woman that a man was involved with was not Jewish, the man might well have believed or pretended that he was not violating the Nazis' 'race laws'. This belief was reflected in the fairly large number of marriage applications that were submitted, as we will see. But even if a man knew he was violating Nazi racial ideology – like Willi Schulz, a guard in the Minsk ghetto who fell in love with Ilse Stein, a Jewish German woman, and fled with her and her family right before they were to be murdered – it did not necessarily mean that the man had consciously rejected his National Socialist convictions.[36]

For many soldiers, such bonds may also have been influenced by the assumption – based on the specific situation in 'the East', the proximity to the front line and the lack of respectful forms of interaction with the local population – that they were allowed to do things in the occupied territories that would have been punishable offences within the borders of the Reich.[37] Soldiers could have such close personal contact or ties with local women that they would try to help the women or sometimes even their entire families. For example, the area representative for the general commissioner in Brest-Litovsk complained at the end of April 1944 that German employees were helping local families leave the city.[38] In some fields of work, 'protective relationships' such as this were fairly commonplace, as illustrated by the activity report of the German labour office in Brest-Litovsk for the years 1941 to 1944. With respect to locals working for the Wehrmacht, the report said:

> Major difficulties always arose when it came to acquiring workers for labour in Germany or making cuts in overstaffed enterprises on the basis of company audits. In the offices of the Wehrmacht in particular, protectionism [*Protektionswesen*] was especially strong, and it was necessary to repeatedly counter the efforts of soldiers, officials and officers to claim certain female workers for themselves.[39]

This form of 'protectionism' clarifies the power structure that is likely to have shaped many relationships. The German men functioned as protectors, and the women were dependent on them for protection. However, the labour office report also makes it clear that the influence of ordinary soldiers and officers alike could be limited in this situation.

Conversely, a few soldiers sought the protection of their girlfriends. Various military files reveal that deserters hid amongst civilians who looked after them. For example, a military police station reported in February 1942 that 'deserters' were living with their 'Crimean lovers', leading to the development of 'quasi-marital relations'.[40] Secret Field Police Group 647 also noted in its activity reports that deserters were hiding with unmarried women.[41] This was extremely risky for the civilian population. In August 1942, Secret Field Police Group 720 shot a Ukrainian woman 'because she had enticed a German soldier to desert and sheltered him for several weeks'.[42]

The Women's Desire for New Experiences

The motives that prompted women from the German-occupied territories of the USSR to engage in affairs or relationships with German soldiers have generally been a matter of cautious speculation to date. Very few women have ever spoken publicly about it. This has to do in part with the tremendous heterogeneity of the countries referred to collectively as 'occupied Eastern territories' by the Nazis. In areas that had resisted incorporation into the USSR, involvement with German men was sometimes condoned because the population viewed Wehrmacht soldiers as allies in the 'fight against Bolshevism' (at least until they realised how brutal and repressive the German occupation was). But in areas that opposed the German occupying forces, women who made such a decision were consciously and inevitably pitting themselves against their environment. These different societal views have had repercussions to this day. With this in mind, the following deliberations should be considered merely an initial approach to the subject.

Numerous women from the former Soviet Union stress in their accounts that the Germans were different than the men they had known previously. They mention the 'allure of the foreigner', which attracted and interested them. Aija, who was sixteen at the time and lived at the edge of a German airstrip, describes the fighter pilots she saw there. She says the officers were very young, fun-loving, polite and dashing.[43] Zita Vidrinskiene, a Lithuanian woman interviewed by Hartmut Kaminski, explains that her family had contact with Germans even before the start of the war because her grandfather had fought on the German side in World War I. She recalls how well-groomed the German men were:

> When the Germans visited my grandfather, my mother appreciated the fact that they looked very attractive, tidy, they were elegantly dressed and perfumed. And they always had chocolate to give to the girls. So the women liked these men a lot, and maybe that was the reason our Lithuanian woman loved the Germans so much.[44]

With their appearance, their clothing, their scent and their gifts, their vitality and their politeness, these men embodied a world that lay beyond everyday wartime life – and beyond what many women, especially those in the countryside, had known in their lives prior to the war as well. They promised a secure existence within orderly, prosperous and modern structures. This was particularly true for women in regions such as the Baltic states, where there was often a deep affinity for Germany, and where contested power relations had resulted in decades of insecurity. Soviet troops had invaded Latvia, Estonia and Lithuania in the spring of 1940 to annex the territories that had, until then, remained independent with German support. When German soldiers arrived in the summer of 1941, they were initially welcomed as 'liberators' and glorious victors who sparked the hope of new experiences and a better life amongst many people.

Furthermore, the war posed entirely new challenges for the female population. Most men were gone, either serving in the Red Army, fighting with the partisans or being held in German prisoner-of-war camps. Additionally, nearly one million men had sided with the new occupiers and were fighting alongside the Germans against the Soviets.[45] The women often did not know whether their partners or male relatives were even still alive, so they had to take their subsistence into their own hands.[46] They might therefore take up with a German soldier in an attempt to fight their fears and ensure their food supply and protection. In a few cases that have come to light in memoirs published since the early 1990s, Jewish women also forged relationships with German soldiers or their collaborators for this reason. Some of them hid their origins from their non-Jewish partners. The Polish woman Zofia Jasinska, for instance, speaks of the feeling of superiority she felt towards her partner because she was able to keep her secret.[47] Other women were knowingly protected by their partners, or at least not betrayed, including Fanya Gottesfeld Heller, who established a relationship with a Ukrainian policeman, a Nazi collaborator, and writes in her memoirs about the arguments she had with him.[48]

Besides sheer survival, women may have been prompted to engage in relationships in an attempt to achieve a certain degree of agency and autonomy in the midst of the war and desolation. In an environment where there were almost no men, heterosexual women and girls who entered relationships with enemy soldiers would at least have the opportunity to satisfy their desires for male companionship, intimacy, tenderness and sexual experiences. And if they kept their liaison secret, they could achieve this without their family or social circle finding out about it.[49] The constant fear of sexual violence may also have led some women to take action themselves and flirt with the enemy in an attempt to counter their own feelings of powerlessness.

While some women maintained their relationships in secret, others were decidedly open about them. In the first months of the occupation, a relationship with a victorious German could give a local woman a certain position of power or apparent autarchy. In Hartmut Kaminski's film *Liebe im Vernichtungskrieg* (Love in the War of Annihilation), a witness recalls that all the girls in her circle had envied a particular woman because she entered a relationship with a handsome German from the Organisation Todt.[50] Research into such relationships in Norway has shown that some young women savoured this feeling of power so much that if relatives or acquaintances criticised their behaviour, the women would threaten to denounce them to their German boyfriends.[51] Further research is required into whether such situations also occurred in the countries of the former Soviet Union.

This potential acquisition of power was associated with significant risks, however. The soldiers with whom the women were involved had been brutalised by combat, and the women faced the possibility of becoming the object of their aggression. Moreover, the German soldiers and local women often did not even speak the same language, or they spoke it only rudimentarily. They could not make themselves entirely understood, so their communication was frequently plagued by misunderstandings. Furthermore, the women were forming relationships with men whose near future was completely uncertain. A soldier could be re-stationed from one day to the next, even if he and his partner actually desired a long-term relationship; this happened to a high-ranking German NCO and a Ukrainian woman, according to one former Wehrmacht soldier.[52] Soldiers could also wind up staying in the same place longer than expected, which could be just as unpleasant or even frightening for a woman who had only wanted a brief dalliance as the prospect of suddenly being alone again.

More serious still were the conflicts of loyalty. Even if the people in a woman's environment generally viewed the Germans as 'liberators from the Bolshevists', and even her family explicitly approved of her relationship with a German – perhaps because her father or brother was fighting alongside the Germans against the Red Army – the woman's friends or neighbours might judge the situation very differently. And if a woman in an environment unsympathetic to the Germans decided to pursue a sexual relationship with the enemy, she would either have to maintain a high level of secrecy or she would face accusations of collaboration, which could go hand in hand with conflicts, insults and a rupture in her social environment.[53]

Rolf-Dieter Müller quotes a young Belarusian woman named Galina who was active in the resistance against the Germans. In the course of this activity, she met with young German men:

> The Germans, these young soldiers, often visited us. There were three of us girls: me, Luba and Ira. A phonograph, dances – it was just fun. The war raged around us, but there was still an opportunity here to amuse yourself a bit, to relax. It was just purely human.[54]

Galina's task during these encounters was actually to spy on the soldiers. Whether she also had sexual contact with a German remains unaddressed in her account. Regardless of this, the desire expressed here to 'amuse' oneself and 'relax' was probably a decisive motivation for many women. Falling in love could fulfil the need for a normality that was sorely missed in the exceptional situation of the war.[55]

Galina, the resistance fighter, found herself in a moral dilemma with her 'purely human' longing for dance, music and distraction. It was not for nothing that she tried to justify her behaviour after the fact – because her desire for the 'normal' amusements of a girl in peacetime was considered anything but harmless in wartime. When a woman chose to meet with a German soldier or dance with him, she was making a political statement. In this moment, before the eyes of her community, she was forming a connection with the occupying power that was subjugating the local population, shooting Jews on a massive scale and decimating entire tracts of lands.

Partisans and Red Army soldiers also took notice of the local women who flirted or had relations with enemy soldiers. Vladimir Panasiuk, a former partisan from Belarus, recalls a German garrison:

> Every German soldier and every officer had a girl they had a fling with. [. . .] And our Russian girls were invited to the evening dances. There were German officers and soldiers there too, obviously, and they danced with our girls. You see, the front is the front. The front is horrible. But here everything was like peacetime. No one felt the war here. There were soldiers who were friendly, who even gave out pralines and chocolate.[56]

It is with a certain matter-of-factness that Panasiuk describes how these soldiers, like soldiers in every war, got involved with local women. He even expresses some understanding for the women. But such understanding was not a given. In more than a few cases, a woman whose relationship with a German became public knowledge could face discrimination, physical assault or even death.[57] For example, another resistance fighter describes how three partisans came upon a German man with a Russian girl.[58] They took both of them prisoner and murdered not only the enemy German but also the woman. In the eyes of the partisans, the Russian woman had betrayed her objectives. Intimacy with a German soldier, a representative of the brutal Nazi regime, was seen as an act of personal weakness and national treachery – because in wartime especially, it was considered the responsibility of women to ensure stability at home, not least through virtuousness and respectability.[59]

There are hints in the German files that the Soviet secret service (the NKVD) also took retributive action against women. In 1943, the Red Army drove the Wehrmacht out of Kharkiv, but just two months later the Germans briefly recaptured the city. The reports covering their 'second arrival' mention that women who had previously been impregnated by

Germans had been shot as collaborators, presumably by the NKVD.[60] Ole Ligeikaite, a Lithuanian woman, also recalled that after the victory of the Red Army, many women were first interrogated and then either shot or deported to Siberia.[61] It has not yet been possible to determine whether or to what extent these reports reflect reality.[62] Furthermore, the comments of a former Wehrmacht soldier indicate that such supposed or actual measures were occasionally mentioned by Germans at the time to emphasise the crimes of the partisans and justify their own behaviour. This former soldier said that the partisans had not been defending themselves, they had been fighting illegally and committing crimes that should have been 'punished according to the law of war': 'It's just not right for a Ukrainian girl to be killed by the partisans just because she was seen on the street with a German soldier'.[63]

A few witnesses suggest that, right before and after the end of the war, it could be safer for some women to go into hiding, especially if they were expecting or had already given birth to a child fathered by a German.[64] The accounts of the few women from Estonia, Latvia and Ukraine who are willing to talk about this today seem to have been heavily shaped by Cold War history since 1945. For example, Meile Motuziene, the daughter of a Lithuanian woman and German man, still considers it 'the *worst* punishment' that her mother was discriminated against as a collaborator in the Stalinist era, even though she had simply fallen in love.[65] Another interviewee in Hartmut Kaminski's documentary film says that the object of a woman's affections had been a private matter for the women themselves, one that had nothing to do with political or national conflicts. These women firmly reject the accusation of collaboration, arguing that their mothers had not fallen in love with a German soldier, an enemy of their country or even a Nazi, but just a man. They say that feelings towards one's fatherland had no bearing on these private love affairs.[66]

In the first book published in German about women who had relationships with German soldiers in the occupied countries, the author Ebba Drolshagen argues that it is important to take the perspective of these women and their children seriously. Drolshagen believes there is some justification for both the attitude of the women, who say that wartime love affairs are a private matter, and that of the critics, who say that wartime love affairs are political. The two perspectives 'are like a tilt card where the viewer can only ever see one of two possible images, never both at once'.[67] This view is not shared by Danish historian Annette Warring, who has studied relationships between Danish women and German men. Warring says that while the women's motives may have been private, as soon as a woman appeared publicly with an occupying soldier, her relationship inevitably became a political factor. From this moment on, she was 'both a private individual and a fraternising woman'.[68] Future studies will have to determine whether and to what extent the accounts of women from the Soviet Union differ in specific ways from those of women in northern and western Europe.

Regulation by the Wehrmacht

Relationships between German soldiers and non-German women were often publicly apparent, which posed problems for many troop leaders. In the spring of 1942, eight months after Germany invaded the Soviet Union, Lieutenant Helmut D. wrote a letter describing a dilemma that repeatedly confronted him:

> The relationship with the civilian population is good. But I've impressed upon my soldiers that they're our enemies, and I've even sent a few home after seeing them in 'improper' situations with girls. They say they were just flirting with the girls and they give me a very funny look. But you have to put the brakes on. The soldier has been away from home for a long time, away from his wife or girlfriend, and now he's looking for some affection. And it's springtime to boot, which also has an effect.[69]

Helmut D. certainly sympathised with his subordinates' desire for 'some affection', but he felt required to intervene nonetheless. The Wehrmacht leadership believed that intimate contact with the civilian population, like sexual violence and sexual bartering, was harmful to Germany's military policy and should therefore be prevented. Along with the risks to health and 'racial policy' – namely, the spread of sexually transmitted diseases and the fathering of children considered 'undesirable'[70] – consensual relationships were problematic from a psychological viewpoint. The OKW and OKH feared that a man who became intimately acquainted with a local woman would be less reliable, dissociate himself from his comrades, no longer view the local population as the enemy and ultimately lose sight of the objectives of the war. They also thought that intimate relations could plunge soldiers into emotional conflicts. Experience had shown that some men felt pressured, desperate and powerless when there were misunderstandings or fights with their new girlfriends, or when their sexual experiences in the occupied territories came into conflict with their love life back home.

But many soldiers felt harassed by commanders wanting to dictate to them what they should or should not do when they were off duty.[71] Unlike the OKW and OKH, the soldiers themselves considered 'flirting' with local women to be an entirely apolitical act and thus their own private affair. Helmut D. was not the only officer who found it difficult in this situation to convince his men otherwise.[72] According to a headquarters order in Rear Army Area 585 from 6 February 1942:

> The number of cases is multiplying in which German Wehrmacht members have been observed consorting with Russian female individuals (consorting in houses, accompaniment on the street, even arm in arm). Aside from the indignity of consorting with Russian women, the German soldier cannot know whether the male relatives of these persons are pitted against us in battle on the side of the Red Army, meaning that they might be killing our comrades, while here they are consorting with the female members of these families – often in all too intimate a manner. The German soldier can also easily fail to see that this is directly promoting and supporting enemy espionage.[73]

The message to the soldiers was clear: relations with local women could never be dismissed as a private matter because they were relevant to various aspects of military and occupation policy. The men were said to be gambling with the reputation of the Wehrmacht, blurring 'racial' boundaries and running the risk of being pumped for information. The Wehrmacht leadership therefore urged soldiers to exercise the 'greatest caution' in dealing with the local population. Leaflets were circulated to spread threatening images of the enemy and undermine any 'sympathy or softness towards the local population'. General Hoth of the 17th Army called upon soldiers to be vigilant 'if the population that once tolerated the Bolshevist yoke now wants to reel us in with friendliness and submissiveness'.[74] To stoke the soldiers' mistrust and lower their inhibitions towards killing women in addition to men, the OKW conjured up the image of the female Russian spy who would exploit the good nature of German soldiers.[75] According to a 12th Infantry order, these women were 'mostly Jewish females . . . whose Jewish origin cannot be seen'.[76]

Ordinary soldiers were clearly only marginally deterred by such scenarios. In any case, the large number of rules of conduct issued in regions where German men were in direct contact with local women reveal that the Wehrmacht faced a serious military problem. Martin Dean interprets the repeated warnings and prohibitions relating to alcohol consumption and contact with local women as 'a good indication of what was really going on'.[77] In March 1942, for example, the Wirtschaftsstab Ost reminded its soldiers that female labourers were to be treated with the 'utmost restraint': 'Communal drinking, intimately approaching local women and girls, dancing with them and giving them courtesy rides in official vehicles are prohibited under all circumstances'.[78] The letters and diaries of soldiers also mention that soldiers sometimes drove with local women in military vehicles. The women were thus granted a privilege that was generally denied to ordinary infantrymen.[79] The order issued by *Wirtschaftsstab Ost* also makes it clear that the aim was not just to prevent *sexual* encounters; instead, there was to be no public acknowledgement of the enemy civilian population whatsoever. Further research is needed to determine the extent to which violations of these prohibitions resulted in consequences such as disciplinary measures. The civilian occupation authorities, and particularly German labour offices, were additionally troubled by the fact that soldiers were carrying letters back and forth between their lovers and the women's relatives who were in Germany as 'Eastern workers'. Because information about the brutal working conditions in Germany could reach the occupied territories through these letters, military superiors feared that it would become more difficult in the future to attract volunteers to work in the Reich.[80]

Housing soldiers with the local population was believed to pose a major military risk by the OKW, as can be seen in a decree from 15 September 1942:

> According to the reports received, quartering soldiers with the civilian population in the occupied Eastern territories has led to close contact and sometimes permanent relationships between German soldiers and local women. [...] These occurrences, which cannot be tolerated, are to be countered through orders and strict supervision. [...]
>
> Furthermore, territorial commanders are to prohibit the long-term quartering of German Wehrmacht members with native inhabitants. All Wehrmacht members, incl. officers, are to be housed in closed quarters without exception. If houses occupied by the civilian population are needed for accommodations, the occupants are to be evicted. Local residents are to be reaccommodated or expelled indiscriminately.[81]

It is clear from this that the control measures were not directed solely at the soldiers. To preserve the desired distance between the troops and the local population, the Wehrmacht did not hesitate to destroy the basis of existence of the women and men whose houses they seized. For example, the *Grossdeutschland* division of the Wehrmacht expelled many locals from their homes in Russia with the justification that it wanted to solve the problem of 'fraternisation'.[82]

Despite everything, the army leadership did not take a general ban on sexual encounters with non-German women in consideration. Instead, it banked on education. On 12 September 1942, the OKH responded to the reports and orders from various regions by issuing the following decree on 'Intercourse by German soldiers with the civilian population in the occupied Eastern territories':

> A prohibition on sexual intercourse between soldiers and the female population of the occupied territories will not effectively remedy the situation. In permanently occupied garrisons, it would be advisable to arrange for protective measures under the supervision of troop doctors.
>
> Instead, it is the task of enlightenment and education to make it clear to the soldiers how they can promote the prestige of the Reich and the Wehrmacht, which they represent, vis-à-vis the population in the Ostraum, and which disadvantages and dangers could arise in the event of non-compliance with this baseline.[83]

Much like General von Brauchitsch, who had warned two years earlier that soldiers had to satisfy their 'sexual tensions and needs',[84] OKW commander Wilhelm Keitel (who signed this decree) clearly felt that a prohibition was neither suitable nor feasible. In addition to 'sanitation stations' and military brothels, which are referred to here euphemistically as 'protective measures under the supervision of troop doctors', Keitel advised that talking to the soldiers personally was the most important way of giving the men an insight into the bigger picture so they would exercise self-discipline and restraint.

But this 'enlightenment and education' turned out to be difficult, as mentioned earlier. The men distanced themselves from the issue by making suggestive jokes and teasing remarks, there was never much time for proper troop briefings, and medical officers and troop doctors were often not particularly eager to put themselves in embarrassing situations. Nonetheless, the latter were explicitly called upon when it came to helping soldiers who found themselves facing psychological conflict on account of their relationships with local women. In Norway, the Wehrmacht leadership had to deal with several cases of soldiers committing suicide because they felt hopelessly trapped between their family in Germany and their girlfriend in the occupied territory.[85] In his 'Briefing on the prevention of suicide' dated 6 October 1942, the Inspector of the *Luftwaffe* Medical Service instructed troop doctors to pay special attention to the psychological problems of married or engaged soldiers:

> Liaisons involving married or engaged soldiers are to be taken especially seriously, particularly when such relations have consequences, such as if pregnancies occur or conflicts arise with the women's husbands or boyfriends. The number of cases in which soldiers see no way out of these difficulties is exceptionally high, so the utmost vigilance is required. In 19.4 per cent of cases of suicide in the Luftwaffe, which were handled by L.In. 14 [the Luftwaffe Medical Inspectorate], romantic and marital conflicts proved to be the main cause [. . .]. Sensible encouragement and masculine-comradely understanding as well as contact with the women back home, with the agreement of everyone involved, can prevent many an irrational act. The prerequisite here is a thorough knowledge of the soldier's personality. If such men are sent on leave, the troop doctor should intervene in a skilful and tactful way to prevent adverse reactions during the leave, which are not at all infrequent. A soldier who can be confident that the medical officer is not only his superior but also his understanding medical friend will be able to find his way out of his difficult and seemingly desperate situation as long as he possesses the necessary character traits.[86]

The soldier's sex life thus became the troop doctor's field of work. The doctor was expected to take on the role of a paternal friend and even mediate between spouses if necessary – another indication that the Wehrmacht considered the most private aspects of a soldier's life to be a military matter. The bond with family and friends back home, which was a key motivator for many soldiers in combat, was to remain as untroubled as possible. The same applied to the often long-awaited home leave, the purpose of which was to enable soldiers to relax and revive, and to remind them of who they were fighting for and why.[87] It was also important to the regime that soldiers sired offspring during their home leave,[88] specifically with women who – unlike the local women in the occupied territories – were 'racially desirable' from the Nazis' point of view and thus supposedly destined to bear such children. Relationship crises, arguments and jealousy threatened to undermine these goals, which is why troop doctors were instructed to defuse such situations with sensitivity and tact.

As these examples demonstrate, the problem confronting the Wehrmacht when German men engaged in consensual relations with local women was that the men evaded the grasp of the military. They were breaching discipline (by using military vehicles improperly, for instance), forgetting their role as representatives of the occupying forces and running the risk of weakening their combat readiness due to personal difficulties, lovesickness, feelings of guilt and conflicts of loyalty. An additional complicating factor was that members of the German civilian administration were allowed to send for their wives and children, but members of the German military were not. This repeatedly led to discontent and conflict.[89]

To provide a distraction for the soldiers and give them opportunities to meet German women within the framework of their male world, the Wehrmacht arranged performances by mixed-sex theatre ensembles and music groups from the Reich as part of its troop entertainment service. And, in fact, the memory of 'pretty girls who liked to celebrate with us after their shows' plays a role in many military memoirs.[90] However, there was some debate about the external impact of these evenings. Unit leaders and troop doctors complained that the women did not always conduct themselves in a manner appropriate to their position and sometimes acted like 'prostitutes' ('*Dirnen*'), so the men risked losing respect for 'honourable women'. They said this also gave the local population the wrong impression of 'the German woman', something that ultimately damaged the 'reputation of the German people abroad'. Instead of keeping the soldiers away from local women, these cabaret and theatre groups were apparently achieving the opposite: After their performances, the men were more eager than ever to turn to local women.[91] Discussions such as this make it clear that, in the opinion of many military commanders, 'masculine nature' was simply uncontrollable.

SS Directives

On 19 April 1939, Reichsführer-SS and Chief of the German Police Heinrich Himmler issued a 'Prohibition against sexual intercourse between members of the SS and police with women of a different race'. This initially pertained mainly to sexual contact with Polish and Czech women within the borders of the Reich, but it eventually applied to the occupied territories as well.[92] After the invasion of Poland, however, a growing number of officials were of the opinion that 'a certain loosening [of the rules] would better suit the actual situation', as the Head of the SS Legal Office put it on 12 December 1940.[93] He recommended that men only be prosecuted if their behaviour was 'damaging to the SS' – 'e.g., if an SS leader takes a Polish woman as a long-term lover'. Himmler explicitly opposed such a position and insisted that every single violation was to be legally punished.[94] In his view, it was 'irrelevant whether the people involved are engaged in a love affair or only having casual sexual intercourse one or more times without any sort of emotional bond'. Only in special cases would Himmler countenance milder disciplinary measures – if, for instance, a 'very young ethnic German who grew up in Poland and, as a result of his very brief membership in the SS or police, has not yet learned to maintain the necessary distance from the Polish population and has, on occasion, had sexual intercourse with a Polish woman'.[95] At the end of 1941, Himmler reiterated that the ban also applied to the occupied territories of the Soviet Union, and every violation was to be reported to him personally for a ruling.[96] Even non-German 'Germanic' SS volunteers were expected to submit to this rule, although they would only face legal punishment in the event of repeat offences.[97]

In practice, the sexual encounters of SS men were handled much less rigidly. The Chief of the Security Police and SD claimed in the spring of 1942 that it was difficult for the men because 'the Russian girl' viewed the German soldier as 'the "ideal" of a man' and therefore desired 'sexual intercourse regardless of the question of remuneration'. As a consequence, he noted, it would not always be possible for German men to refuse the countless offers.[98] Some letters of complaint bemoaned the fact that SS men strolled around in public with their 'Russian relations', but as long as no one was mentioned by name, the RF-SS Personal Staff would forgo further investigation.[99] Some men used actual or suspected relationships with local woman to denounce hated comrades or rivals.[100] But even when the RF-SS Personal Staff did pursue a particular case and find evidence, this did not necessarily mean the man in question would be brought before a court.[101]

Over the course of time, Himmler seems to have relaxed his position on this issue. In the summer of 1942, as mentioned, he declared that the ban did not apply to visits to prostitutes monitored by the military.[102] And in a speech about the future of the German occupation of Eastern Europe and Russia on 16 September 1942, he said that 'undesirable sexual intercourse' was to be 'avoided as much as possible!'. With this qualifier – 'as much as possible' – he was conceding that it was impossible to completely control the sexual desires of his SS men. In practice, therefore, he backed down from his strict prohibition against all sexual intercourse with women of a 'different race'. Instead, he appealed directly to the men's 'racial awareness': members of the SS and police were only supposed to have sexual contact with a woman if they could answer for her as a potential mother 'before Germany, before their own blood and before their future child'.[103]

But the authorities did not want to leave this assessment to the SS men on the ground. Referring to the original prohibition of 1939, Dr Klahre from the court of the 1st SS Infantry Brigade asked Himmler at the end of November 1941 whether the 'sex ban' also applied to intercourse with Ukrainian women:

> With regard to Ukrainian women this is likely to be doubtful considering the special position of the Ukrainians and their recruitment in the fight against Bolshevism. As we know here, the general view among the Waffen-SS and police units stationed in the General Government prior to the war with Russia was that sexual intercourse with women of Ukrainian ethnicity [*Volkstumszugehörigkeit*] was permitted.[104]

It is clear here that the characteristics for judging who was of a 'different race' ('*andersrassig*') were highly debatable.[105] Himmler himself admitted in September 1942 that it was 'a matter of pure chance' whether 'the girl a soldier gets attached to is racially valuable or unsuitable'. At issue here was not just the external evaluation of the women in question, but also their health, their 'character' and their 'mental' and political classification.[106] Klahre additionally made an argument for how the members of the SS and police in the occupied territories were interpreting the law. Since the men in the General Government had assumed that sexual contact with Ukrainian women was allowed, they believed they same law applied to other regions. Therefore, if they had been operating under a mistake of law at the time, they could not be summarily sentenced by an SS court. Klahre's arguments were met with little understanding, however. On 28 December 1941, the SS judge for the RF-SS stated with certainty that 'even Ukrainian women are covered by the term "women of a different race"'.[107] Four weeks later, the head of the SS Court Main Office elaborated on this, saying that the order covering 'sexual intercourse by members of the SS and police with women of a "different race"' applied only to 'the occupied Russian territories'.[108] Depending on the territory, therefore, sexual contact with Ukrainian women could be judged in different ways – and this also applied to sexual relations with Ukrainian 'Eastern workers' within the borders of the Reich.[109]

For the men in the occupied territories, such debates are unlikely to have played a significant role. At a conference of presiding judges from the SS and police courts in Poland and the 'occupied Eastern territories' in May 1943, the participants estimated that at least 50 per cent of all members of the SS and police had violated the prohibition against 'sexual intercourse with women of a different race'. They ultimately agreed to suggest to Himmler that the prohibition should be eased until further notice, as it did not align with reality.[110]

At the end of July 1943, SS-*Obergruppenführer* Gottlob Berger took yet another stab at differentiation. In a letter to Himmler, he tried to define an approach for dealing with Estonian, Latvian and Lithuanian women within the borders of the Reich and thus pave the way for future policies in the occupied territories:

> Estonian and Latvian women who enter the Reich are treated just like women from the East. They must sign a document confirming that they will not have sexual intercourse and so on with a German. But these are very often wives, siblings or fiancées of SS members who suffered greatly under the Bolshevists and want to work voluntarily. I ask that Estonian and Latvian women be excluded from the usual regulations relating to women from the East.[111]

In his appeal, Berger referred to the privileged position of the 'Baltic peoples' in the Nazis' plans for the future.[112] According to the logic of the Nazis' racial hygiene ideology, these people tended to be 'Nordic', 'racially desirable' and 'Germanisable'. This assessment was bolstered by the fact that the majority of the population of the Baltic states had welcomed the Wehrmacht as an army of liberation in 1941.[113] Within this classification, however, the Nazis made further distinctions. Alfred Rosenberg, Reich Minister for the Occupied Eastern Territories, had stated on 2 April 1941, even before the start of the war against the Soviet Union, that the Estonian population should be considered the elite amongst the 'Baltic peoples'. Latvia, by contrast, was said to have been relatively heavily infiltrated by 'the Russian', while Lithuanian society was additionally under 'Jewish pressure'.[114] In accordance with this, Berger took the Lithuanians out of his proposal; only Estonian and Latvian women were to be allowed more freedom of movement in Germany. Himmler approved Berger's recommendation in September 1943 and revoked the 'Prohibition against sexual intercourse with Estonians and Latvians' in the Reich. He explicitly excluded Lithuanian women from this regulation because, as he claimed, the Lithuanians were 'a people' who 'behaves so badly and is of such poor racial value that a revocation is neither warranted nor justified'.[115]

Word of Himmler's decision was received by the RKO as well. It was expected that the ban would be lifted in the occupied territory, too, and that even the prohibition against SS men marrying Estonian and Latvian women would be rescinded.[116] But no such measures were introduced before the end of the war. In fact, such an exception would have caused additional difficulties for the staff of the SS and police judiciary, as illustrated by a comparable case from Croatia. According to the regulations of the RF-SS, 'sexual intercourse by members of the SS and police with Croatian women' was not fundamentally prohibited. But at the end of 1944, SS-*Sturmbannführer* Graf von Korff complained that many SS men were having sexual contact with Croatian women who were 'racially inferior'. He called for the men in question to be punished.[117] Horst Bender, the legal advisor to the RF-SS, responded by declaring that 'racially inferior' was not a category that lent itself to criminal prosecution because it could be 'neither defined' nor 'left to the discretion of the individual man':

> [The] question of whether someone is racially valuable or not [will be] answered differently by every average soldier [...], meaning that, in most cases, even if racial inferiority exists objectively, it will hardly be possible to prove any subjective fault on the part of the culprit.[118]

It is apparent from this that the criteria for 'racial evaluation' could quickly reach their limit. Himmler's repeated demand that members of the SS and police be guided by their 'racial awareness' in their sexual encounters in the occupied territories was therefore primarily a plea. The threat of punishment served mainly to keep the men in line and seems to have rarely been put into action.

Negotiations Regarding Marriage Applications

Different considerations played a role for the civilian occupation authorities when it came to evaluating consensual relations between their subordinates and the civilian population. Ludwig Runte from the RMbO complained in November 1941 that 'the formation of romantic attachments between Germans working in the occupied Eastern territories and local girls' was not appropriate to the 'attitude the German man is supposed to take towards the country's native inhabitants'.[119] But unlike the Wehrmacht, SS and police, the civilian administration was also thinking of the importance of such relationships to Germany's long-term occupation policy.

In March 1942, Dr Ernst Wegner and Friedrich Trampedach from the RKO stated that 'the local female population of the Baltic general districts' had been 'exceptionally accommodating towards German soldiers since the day of liberation'. A post hoc 'prohibition against extramarital sexual intercourse between Germans and natives in the Ostland' would therefore be pointless. Moreover, it would be a blow to the self-confidence and sense of honour of the 'Baltic peoples'. To ensure a successful occupation policy, they argued, it was absolutely essential not to make these 'German-friendly peoples' feel declassed, otherwise they would turn their backs and be less 'willing to collaborate'.[120] In this respect, the RKO employees were explicitly calling for such relationships to be tolerated and even legalised if necessary.

The RMbO in Berlin, however, feared that this kind of occupation strategy would give German men the impression that sexual contact with 'ethnically alien' women was not only condoned but actually encouraged – and this was something to be emphatically opposed. On 27 July 1942, Ludwig Runte from the RMbO sent instructions to this effect to the RKO:

> I ask [...] in consultation with the offices involved, particularly with the General Postal Commissioner and the Main Railway Directorate Nord and Mitte, that it be ensured that all Germans employed there be instructed at once in a suitable manner of the necessity of maintaining distance from the female population of the Ostland. It must be emphasised above all that intimate relations with local girls are not in keeping with the status of the Germans in the occupied Eastern territories, and furthermore, that children from such liaisons are racially undesirable and no authorisation for marriage can be expected in such cases.[121]

The RMbO was banking on a form of education similar to that found in the military. Postal service and railway employees were expected to attend courses where they, like the soldiers, would be reminded of their responsibility with regard to sexual encounters. The RMbO also felt it necessary to impress upon these employees that they could not count on receiving permission to marry and start a family. All the same, the historical sources generally give the impression that sexual relations between German civilian employees and local women were largely tolerated. The way such relations were handled probably depended on the convictions of the respective employee's superior. For example, Erich Selle, who worked for the Main Food and Agriculture Department of the RMbO, submitted a claim in the summer of 1944 for the reimbursement of treatment expenses after an accident. The personnel department of the general commissioner for White Ruthenia (now Belarus) noted on 11 October 1944 that it was rejecting the application. The department said that Selle had not stopped working due to an accident, he had actually been dismissed for having 'a forbidden relationship with a White Ruthenian'.[122]

The differing interests of the military and civilian authorities are particularly apparent in their respective approaches to marriage applications. The German occupation authorities intervened in individual cases when German men applied to marry non-German women from the occupied territory, but they were also concerned with marriage policy in general. Their approach was based on the marriage legislation that applied within the borders of the Reich. In the territory of 'White Ruthenia', for example, 'marriages between non-Jews and Jews' were fundamentally prohibited, while all other marriages between members of different population groups required the authorisation of the responsible regional commissioner.[123] Marriages in which no Germans were involved were also supposed to be subject to German regulations, because even in these relationships the 'ethnic contrasts' ('*Volkstumsgegensätze*') would have grave consequences, as the SS and Police Leader of Brest-Litovsk put it.[124] In many regions in 1942, RMbO officials compiled 'village reports' which meticulously recorded all of the constellations for 'mixed marriages'.[125] In the RKO, several 'incomers' from Russia and a few prisoners of war requested permission to marry local women, but both the German civilian authorities and the Wehrmacht refused them.[126]

But the authorities were most concerned with marriages involving a person who was considered a 'Reich German' or 'ethnic German'. As early as the autumn of 1941, Ludwig Runte from the RMbO anticipated that German men would starting 'thinking about marriage' in the near future. The only possible response to such plans, as he saw it, was for 'marriages between Germans and members of a different ethnic group [*Volkstum*]' to be 'fundamentally prohibited'. According to Runte, a ban was the only way to prevent the spread of sexually transmitted diseases and the conception of children 'who, as crossbreeds [*Mischlinge*] of German and foreign ethnicity, are undesirable from a racial policy perspective'. He said there could potentially be exceptions in Estonia and, to a lesser extent, in Latvia and Lithuania.[127] But it was important not to act rashly and approve marriages thoughtlessly. The RMbO therefore instructed the local registry offices to reject applications from the Baltic countries until further notice.[128] According to paragraph 8 of the 'Regulation on the Application of German Law to German Citizens in the Occupied Eastern Territories' from 27 April 1942, marriages between 'Reich Germans and the native population' were explicitly forbidden, with the exception of individual cases that were to be carefully reviewed.[129]

But it soon became apparent that the civil servants and military officials in the occupied territories were dissatisfied with these categorical prohibitions issued by the Reich authorities. While politicians in Berlin were still hammering out regulations, the first German men in Estonia and Latvia were already submitting applications for the 'racial evaluation of their fiancées'. The Wehrmacht, which did not want to affront its soldiers, did not initially voice any general objections to the legalisation of such relationships. In Estonia, the High Command of Army Group North ruled on 30 July 1942 that 'individual applications for granting permission to marry Estonian women' could be submitted and would be given sympathetic consideration following a positive 'racial' and political evaluation of the women in question.[130] This decision was explicitly based on the provisions that had been established in early 1942 regarding marriage between Wehrmacht members and Dutch, Norwegian, Danish and Swedish women, which read as follows: 'The Führer has decided that [...], for the duration of the special deployment of the Wehrmacht, there is no objection in principle to marriages between Wehrmacht members and racially related persons from neighbouring Germanic states'.[131] Three weeks after the ruling of the High Command of Army Group North, Security Division 207 in Dorpat[132] (now Tartu, Estonia) issued a daily order which offered its men stationed in the rear area the opportunity to submit applications for marriage to Estonian women.[133]

The civil servants of the RKO also felt it was imperative to allow such marriages. Their arguments, however, stemmed primarily from their view of the local population. In March 1942, Trampedach, head of the Political Affairs department of the RKO, wrote to the RMbO in an attempt to explain the importance of marriages to Germany's occupation policy:

> The prohibition against registry offices contracting marriages involving Reich Germans had already provoked hefty agitation [amongst the local population; R. M.], which was placated by the announcement that it was only a temporary measure until the observance of German marital law, and particularly marital health regulations, had been ensured in the Ostland.
>
> This agitation of the Baltic peoples, arising from the feeling that they are being equated with Poles and Jews, must be avoided at all costs because it spoils the opportunity to lead these peoples towards the German *Volk*'.[134]

Trampedach's comments illustrate that the authorities in the occupied territories were guided by different requirements than the ministries in the Reich. In the conflict between specific marriage requests and the general ban imposed by Berlin, local officials mollified the applicants and their families by holding out the prospect of new options in the near future.[135] Trampedach attributed a particular 'racial pride' to the 'Baltic peoples', which supposedly made them want to distinguish themselves from Poles and Jews.[136] He claimed that non-Jewish Estonians, Latvians and Lithuanians had developed an understanding of 'racial' hierarchies, so it was important to win them over as allies and 'lead' them 'towards the German *Volk*'.[137]

Similar arguments were put forward by the regional commissioner in Mitau[138] (now Jelgava in Latvia), SA-*Standartenführer* von Medem. He felt that German-Latvian marriages should be approved because the 'racially desirable' Latvians shared the view of the occupying power that 'racial hygiene measures' were necessary for ruling out 'undesirable elements' when it came to marriage. Offending the Latvians with a general marriage ban would not only lessen their willingness to collaborate, according to von Medem, it would also make them question their understanding of 'the German' and the honour of the German man:

> Latvian girls, trusting in the word of a German soldier, have given themselves to him, and their parents, trusting in the word of a German soldier, have even permitted this intimate intercourse. The German soldier cannot now go back on his word.[139]

Von Medem conjured up an idealised image of romantic trust and a sense of duty on the part of everyone involved. He claimed that local women and girls had succumbed to the advances of German soldiers in the belief that they would lead to long-term, legal relationships. German soldiers, in turn, had courted these women with serious intentions, perhaps so they could marry into a farming family and start a new life in Latvia after the war. And even the parents of these women, 'trusting in the word of a German soldier', had approved such liaisons. From this perspective, the general marriage ban seemed to have been implemented solely to compromise all of the involved parties and cause rifts that would be almost impossible to heal – especially if children were expected.[140] In the end, von Medem said, the marriage ban would result in the self-inflicted collapse of the successful and promising German settlement and occupation of Latvia. Many Germans who were familiar with the region appear to have shared these fears, including the 'ethnic German' interpreter Anatol Herlitz. 'They say the German man may not marry a decent Russian girl, for instance', he complained, 'but he can amuse himself with Russian whores in front of the entire population'. Herlitz believed this discredited the Germans in the eyes of the local population and seriously challenged their occupation policy.[141]

In addition to concerns about the reputation of the occupying power, officials asserted that there were military risks. Both von Medem and the general commissioner in Riga believed it was problematic to discriminate against the sisters of men serving as 'foreign volunteers' in the Wehrmacht and SS by refusing them permission to marry a German. They worried that this would impact the self-perception of the 'foreign volunteers' and ultimately impair their combat readiness. As long as German men exhibited a willingness to marry Soviet women, so the logic went, Soviet men had an opportunity to view the Germans as brothers. But the moment German men 'conquered' these women without marrying them, they implicitly declared the Soviet men to be vanquished opponents who had failed to look after their women. This was thought to make successful collaboration impossible.[142] The 'current prohibition against contracting marriages between German citizens and members of non-German ethnic groups' was 'no longer politically justifiable' according to the general commissioner in Riga in May 1942.[143]

The regional commissioner in Mitau worried that the German labour market, too, would suffer under the marriage ban. The Reich Labour Service had started employing Latvian men as volunteers in the Reich in the spring of 1942, and it was about to begin recruiting Latvian women as well. It was thought that if these women were fundamentally forbidden from marrying a German, it would be difficult to convince them to work in the Reich. This would be particularly regrettable because the 'especially racially good elements' of the young female population were said to be interested in supporting the Nazis and serving as workers in the Reich.[144] This viewpoint was contested, however. The Nazis' 'racial experts' tended to assume that most of the women from the 'occupied Eastern territories' who got involved with Germans were 'racially inferior'.[145] Their readiness to 'flirt with' foreign men made them appear suspicious and frivolous. Following this logic, the defining factors in the 'racial evaluation' of women were based on patriarchal gender concepts concerning respectable and 'immoral' behaviour. While a willingness to collaborate could be seen as a measure of 'racial desirability' amongst the local men, a similar friendliness towards Germans exhibited by the local women became dubious as soon as sexuality played a role.

Evaluation Criteria: 'Race' and 'Ethnicity'
The objections to the marriage ban in Riga and Mitau were initially successful. In early June 1942, Ludwig Runte from the RMbO formulated a proposal 'for implementing and supplementing the regulation on the application of German law to German citizens in the occupied Eastern territories', an indication that the ministry had clearly changed course. This proposal called for marriages to be fundamentally allowed in the RKO as long as both partners underwent a racial examination and were found to be 'desirable'. The respective general commissioner was responsible for judging each case. If he determined 'that there are no objections to the planned nuptials', then the marriage could take place. In cases of doubt, Himmler was to be consulted in his role as Reich Commissioner for the Consolidation of the Ethnic German Nation. The RMbO was pursuing two goals here: it wanted to keep the local population on its side while simultaneously preventing German men from marrying 'racially undesirable' women.[146]

It was clear to the responsible civil servants, however, that there were no generally applicable, objective criteria for 'racially evaluating' the population in the RKO. To provide guidance to the offices in Estonia, Latvia and Lithuania, the RMbO drew up guidelines that were sent out on 13 July 1942 in the context of a new proposal concerning 'marriages between German citizens of the Reich and members of a different ethnicity in the territories of the Reich Commissariat Ostland'. According to this proposal, German citizens were fundamentally forbidden from marrying people classified as Jews or 'half-Jews'. Marriage to members of the thirteen other 'alien ethnic groups' in the RKO identified by the RMbO – 'Lithuanians, Latvians, Latgalians, Livonians, Estonians, Ingrians, Izhorians, Votes, Setos, Russians, Ukrainians, White Russians and Poles' – would be possible in principle as long as 'they themselves and [. . .] their kinship group predominantly have the traits of the Nordic-Phalian race and [. . .] can thus be viewed as hailing from the same stock [*stammesgleich*]'.[147]

To determine whether a person had these 'racial traits', the officials would review their 'racial appearance' as well as their character and capabilities, and they would also investigate the individual's parents and grandparents. The RMbO sent out this proposal together with an examination form that the non-German part of the couple – usually the woman – was supposed to fill out with information about her medical, 'racial' and family background. The applicant was to be asked explicit questions about her political stance and her 'kinship group' ('*Sippe*'), her willingness to send her future children to a German school (both parents were expected to provide written confirmation of this), and her intention to either learn German or improve her existing knowledge of the language.[148] This written information was to be submitted together with three photographs, one taken from the front and two in profile.

While Friedrich Trampedach, head of the Political Affairs department of the RKO, approved the proposal, Wilhelm Burmeister, the senior department head and deputy general commissioner, flatly rejected it.[149] Burmeister argued that focusing so intensively on the 'racial evaluation' of the female applicants would only lead to 'individualistic and thus un-National-Socialist' judgements. To establish a fixed policy instead of having to judge each case individually, he said that 'ethnic membership' ('*Volkszugehörigkeit*') should be the defining factor; only once this had been determined could the 'racial suitability' ('*rassische Eignung*') of the applicants be taken into consideration. Burmeister offered the following comparison for explanation:

> Marriages between East Frisians and Tiroleans – that is, between Germans – are generally more likely to be marriages between people who are racially far apart than, say, marriages between Saxons and Latvians. Nonetheless, there is no question that the former should be approved, while the latter are to be accepted with the utmost caution, not because there are racial differences, but because there are ethnic differences [*Volkstumsverschiedenheiten*], and ethnicity [*Volkstum*], not race, is the decisive factor in the lives of peoples [*Völkerleben*].[150]

Burmeister assumed that 'ethnicity' and 'race' were two hierarchically differentiated categories: '*Volkstum*' or 'ethnicity' was the fundamental, permanent category, while 'racial traits', such as those exhibited by northern and southern Germans, were changeable and dependent on external conditions. In his opinion, the '*Volk*' was an extant factor, 'while the races, even in prehistory not to mention the present, do not exist purely and never have'.[151] Applying this thinking to the situation in the RKO, Dr Werner Essen said:

> Marriages between members of the German people and members of the native peoples in the Ostland should only be taken into consideration with Estonians, Latvians (including Livonians) and Lithuanians, and specifically, marriages with Estonians should be approved generously, with Latvians reticently, and with Lithuanians after the most detailed review in line with the proposal.[152]

It is apparent from this that an individual's 'ethnicity' as well as their 'racial' classification could be interpreted differently depending on the perspective. This not only highlights the delusional thinking behind the underlying ideology, it also shows that the people involved were using these categories to find a supposedly rational, strategic response to an ambiguous situation.[153]

At the start of 1943, the RMbO tried to press ahead with the decision-making process at an inter-ministerial meeting. While the 6th Army was on the brink of defeat in Stalingrad, several representatives of the Reich's highest authorities – including officials representing the Reich Ministry of the Interior, the Reich Commissioner for the Consolidation of the Ethnic German Nation, the Reichsführer-SS and Chief of the German Police, the Reich Security Main Office (RSHA), the Reich Minister of Justice and the Party Chancellery – met at the RMbO in Berlin with members of the OKW and the relevant departments of the RMbO and RKO. To begin with, senior civil servant Willi Eckelberg from the Ministry of the Interior declared that the entire discussion would become superfluous in the near future, as Hitler was going to adopt a proposal drawn up before the start of the war for a 'general prohibition on marriage between Germans and foreigners'. Since many German men had died in the war, Eckelberg said, it was the duty of every German man to marry a German woman so she would not remain alone and childless.[154] This clear line on population policy made sense, he claimed, not least because experience had shown that, even in 'Nordic countries' such as Norway and Denmark, German men would 'not marry the racially valuable girl'. His explanation for this was that soldiers who had not been home for a long time had 'unfortunately lost the right view of things'. Furthermore, he noted, one positive side-effect of the general ban for all occupied territories was that the 'Baltic peoples' could no longer consider themselves declassed. After all, from now on they would be treated the same way as 'the Germanic peoples who are closer to us and the peoples of allied states'.[155]

The other participants at the meeting doubted that Hitler would actually opt for a general marriage ban, however. Disregarding Eckelberg's comments, they used the meeting to come to an arrangement on potential regulations and exceptions. In principle, everyone agreed that it would have to be possible for a German man to marry an Estonian, Latvian or Lithuanian woman who was judged to be 'racially desirable'. The foremost issue here was to ensure that a pregnant woman could safely give birth to her 'racially valuable offspring' and raise them in keeping with their 'German ethnicity'. By contrast, a German-Estonian marriage that produced no children – as district court judge Dr Erhard Wetzel from the RKO put it – was 'of no value' to Germany.[156]

The main point of contention turned out to be how the prohibition should be formulated. The representatives of the Ministry of the Interior, RSHA and Party Chancellery argued that under no circumstances should it be made public that marriages between Germans and foreigners were fundamentally possible because otherwise

> the Germans deployed in the Ostland, especially soldiers, would believe that they could readily receive such an authorisation and they would not exercise the necessary restraint in their effort to marry ethnically alien women.[157]

The responsible civil servants in Berlin were therefore concerned first and foremost with the preventive disciplining of each man. They thought that if a man believed it was illegal to establish a family in the Baltic countries, he would conduct himself accordingly from the start. The officials said the ban could always be suspended in exceptional cases. The representatives of the RKO firmly opposed this view. In their opinion, the men in the occupied territory would not be held back by such a ban and would engage in sexual contact in any case. It was the task of the German administration, therefore, to deal with this situation responsibly and avoid occupation policy problems. They said these problems would arise if the local population were led to believe that such relationships could not be legalised, because the Germans would be discrediting themselves. The representatives of the OKW shared this view, but they assured the others that the enlightenment and education of the men in the Wehrmacht was already under way.[158] The meeting ended inconclusively.

The existing records do not reveal whether the discussion continued amongst the Wehrmacht leadership. But a few months later, the OKH published a training text which included a fictitious Feldpost letter with the heading 'Between Men'. In this letter, a certain Oskar wrote to his comrade Arthur, whose non-German girlfriend was expecting a child:

> I also bridle at the notion that you believe, with the usual good nature of the German, that you must now get married. It is regrettable that German decency, on the one hand, but also a certain occasional sexual dependency, on the other, cause such a significant complication. You yourself admit that the best nationally minded girls of other peoples only rarely marry a foreigner. I cannot imagine that you welcome the fact that it is the more inferior representatives who should then be married by Germans. Aside from this, there is certainly no shortage of German women. [. . .] Your reference to the developing European community also simply shocked me. It shows me that you still

have no idea of what this cultural, economic and military cooperation actually entails. It is a tremendous community of fate [*Schicksalsgemeinschaft*], but one that derives its power and cultural strength from the fact that the unity and simultaneous diversity of our continent lies in the particularity of the cultured peoples [*Kulturvölker*] inhabiting Europe. Any destruction of this racial-ethnic [*rassisch-völkisch*] classification honestly represents an irrevocable loss for the cultural strength of our continent and would always happen solely at the expense of the German people.[159]

Because this fictional soldier was addressed directly – not by his superior but by a comrade, someone on his level, so to speak – potential readers were first encouraged to have some sympathy for sexual adventures and the specific problems in the occupied territory. Against this backdrop, the writer's firm rejection of matrimony was all the more weighty. It is interesting to note that the fictional Oskar first casts doubt on his friend's choice of woman. Even if Arthur had chosen a 'racially valuable girl' (which would have been an exception, according to the author), he was not supposed to marry her – not just because a German woman would then be left without a husband, but because any mixing of 'cultured peoples' was undesirable in the interest of the concept of Europe. Many soldiers obviously interpreted the 'developing European community' quite differently. Oskar therefore clarifies what is meant by 'cooperation' and stresses that the intended differentiation must be self-evident even to a non-German woman if she considers herself part of a 'cultured people'.[160] This letter shows that the OKH was trying to influence its soldiers' views on marriage without calling their emotions into question.

Room to Manoeuvre
Since no decree from Hitler was forthcoming regarding marriage between Germans and foreigners, the situation remained murky for the German administration in the occupied territories. On 5 February 1943, the RKO circulated an internal memo announcing that standardised regulations were not expected until a later date. For the time being, however, marriages were to be prevented. Exceptions were only possible in isolated cases – with the involvement of the RMbO – if an official had the impression that a rejection would be taken exceptionally hard.[161] With this temporary solution, which would remain in place until the end of the war, the Reich ministries were continuing a practice that had been characteristic of marriage policy in the Soviet Union since the start of the German occupation. Ultimately, it was left to the discretion of the

officials involved whether they would support, encourage or deter applicants, and whether they would accept or reject petitions for marriage.

In the Wehrmacht, it was generally the responsibility of the unit leaders to grant soldiers permission to marry. To make their evaluation, they required that soldiers submit the examination results for the woman in question. Women living within the borders of the Reich were usually examined by their local health officer, and the patient was given a report that her boyfriend could submit to the Wehrmacht. From the end of 1941, it was sufficient for Wehrmacht soldiers to submit a medical *Eheunbedenklichkeitsbescheinigung* (marriage eligibility certificate) without any more detailed findings. After the responsible unit leader had evaluated all of the documents, he would inform the soldier of his decision. If the decision was positive, the soldier could give notice of his intention to marry at the registry office.[162]

There was no such rule in the occupied territories of the Soviet Union, but most soldiers assumed that here, too, the women would have to contact the responsible public health officer. In some cases, it seems that the respective troop doctor was consulted as well. In mid-1944, however, the head of the Luftwaffe Medical Service explicitly stated that troop doctors in the RKO were not authorised to 'examine and certify the marriageability of women of alien ethnicity wanting to marry German Wehrmacht members'. He referred all applicants to the public health officers of the RKO instead, which shows that the civilian authorities were ultimately able to assert their authority here.[163]

The responsible public health officers handled such applications as they saw fit. In the first months of the occupation in particular, some had no doubt that Germans were permitted to marry local women; after all, much of the civilian population had proved to be friendly, loyal and willing to the collaborate with the Germans.[164] For example, the public health officer working for the general commissioner in Reval[165] (now Tallinn in Estonia) issued a number of marriage eligibility certificates in the first half of 1942 for Estonian women who wanted to marry German soldiers. Before issuing the certificates he thoroughly examined the women, took urine, stool and blood samples, and asked about their family medical history and history of mental health. He also enquired about the female applicants' past sexual experiences and looked for signs of sexually transmitted diseases. The doctor recorded his findings on a pre-printed questionnaire. After the exam, the doctor was required to submit a written opinion on whether he felt the woman was suitable for marriage or not. In the case of a certain Dr Hille, the RMbO later complained that, based on his assessments, at least three marriages had taken place which violated the 'Regulation on the Application of German Law to German Citizens in the Occupied Eastern Territories'. When the RKO demanded a statement from Hille, the doctor denied any responsibility. He said he had merely conducted the medical exams – it was up to the Wehrmacht alone to reject unsuitable marriages.[166]

Other doctors categorically refused to examine local women for their 'suitability for marriage', despite earnest pleas on the part of the applicants. On 15 December 1942, for example, Dr Harry Marnitz, the public health officer for the regional commissioner in Riga, received a handwritten letter from *Obergefreiter* Paul Z. asking the doctor to examine his fiancée:

> Please excuse my forwardness, but my fiancée, born in Riga, now living at Pleskauer Str. No. 135, Flat 35, whom I intend to marry, requires a health certificate from a German doctor if we are to wed. As I already have all of the other papers, I am asking you on behalf of my fiancée, who has already been rejected a few times and is now afraid to try again, whether you could please examine her and help us find happiness. If you are able to fulfil my request, you can reach my fiancée at the address given above.[167]

The tone of the letter makes it clear that Paul Z. viewed the doctor as an authority who held the soldier's fate in his hands. His reference to his fiancée's fear of not being admitted to an examination or of receiving a negative result hints at how stressful it could be for the women to have to deal with the authorities in this way. In his response to the petition a few weeks later, Dr Marnitz confirmed the position of power that had been attributed to him. Referring to paragraph 8 of the regulation from April 1942, he stated that 'marriage between Reich Germans and members of the occupied Eastern territories' was forbidden and he was therefore not authorised to conduct the requested medical exam. He expanded upon his decision with a personal remark, saying that he 'welcome[d] the prohibition of the minister for the East' because it was 'the duty of every young German' to 'give his children a German mother and grant marital bliss to a German girl, not an ethnically alien one'.[168] Elsewhere he noted that potential exceptions to the ban were not his area of expertise but were subject to the jurisdiction of the administrative and legal departments of the RKO.[169]

Even when a woman could submit a certificate of approval for naturalisation, Marnitz refused to carry out a medical exam. On 6 August 1943, the doctor received a letter from sergeant Bruno Kleindienst, who asked him to examine his girlfriend:

My fiancée was already rejected two times, even though the second time she presented an official certificate from the SS in Riga worded as follows:

Frau Lilly Wiksne is hereby certified upon application that she has been approved for naturalisation by the Central Immigration Office in Litzmannstadt and has already been funnelled through.

The naturalisation papers are currently in Litzmannstadt. Frau W. is de facto a German Reich citizen without being in possession of a German passport.

As I will soon be dispatched to my unit on the front, I ask you, Herr Doktor, to please settle this matter quickly and conduct the marriage suitability examination for my fiancée.[170]

Kleindienst appealed to Marnitz as both a doctor and a man. The soldier said that he was fighting for Germany and was therefore under time pressure and wanted to get his family arrangements in order before facing the risk of dying for the fatherland. Dr Marnitz could not be convinced to change his mind, however. He informed Kleindienst that he could only examine the woman if he was presented with the actual naturalisation certificate or with 'Reich German' identity papers that showed 'that your fiancée has been naturalised'.[171]

When other Nazi officials asked Marnitz to examine local women, however, he would agree and sometimes even declare the patient to be 'suitable for marriage'.[172] Marnitz also proved much more amenable when it came to German women who had been born in the Reich and were working in Riga as Reich Railway assistants or postal employees, for example. In these cases, he would issue marriage eligibility certificates even without performing a detailed examination.[173] The 'ethnic German' woman Senta D., born in Libau (Liepāja) in Latvia in 1890, also received a certificate of 'marriage suitability' even though she admitted to having had two abortions.[174] Other people sometimes concealed aspects of their medical history in order to be approved for marriage. For example, Hans-Joachim G., a teacher from Berlin, requested that Marnitz examine his girlfriend. He did not mention that he himself had been dismissed from the Wehrmacht in 1941 with a diagnosis of 'circular insanity'. By the time the responsible health authority in the Reich had initiated an investigation and Dr Marnitz found out about it, the marriage had already taken place and the couple had moved to an 'unknown address'.[175]

Even if a couple overcame the marriage authorisation hurdle, they could not be certain that the positive decision would hold. Marriage eligibility certificates expired three months after they were issued, so if a couple did not marry in this period, they would have to be examined all over again.[176] Furthermore, the Nazi authorities sometimes revoked the authorisation after the marriage had already taken place. Franz Gaueris, a 'Reich German' civilian employee, married a Lithuanian woman named Marja Mockute in mid-1943 in the Roman Catholic church in Tauroggen[177] (now Tauragė) in Lithuania. The RMbO became aware of the case and decided that the marriage violated the 'Regulation on the Application of German Law to German Citizens in the Occupied Eastern Territories' and was therefore 'annulled without the need for a special certificate of annulment'. In January 1944, the regional commissioner in Schaulen (now Šiauliai) expelled Franz Gaueris from the General District of Lithuania.[178] Gaueris subsequently travelled to the Reich and joined the Wehrmacht with the intention of spending his leave in April with his former wife. However, cooperation between the civilian and military authorities thwarted his plan. Before he could take leave, the general commissioner in Kaunas asked the responsible commander for monitoring leave in the Wehrmacht not to issue Gaueris with a permit to remain in Lithuania.[179]

This clearly shows how ambiguous the legal situation could be in the RKO and the degree to which the people affected were at the mercy of chance and the goodwill of the responsible authorities. Because of this, several couples tried to circumvent the occupation authorities altogether. They thought they would be more successful having their marriage approved in the Reich, in the German soldier's place of residence.[180] For example, in early 1943, the Estonian woman Linde Karik applied for an exit permit from the general commissioner in Reval (Tallinn). She travelled to Belzig in Brandenburg not long after, where she took a job as an office clerk and submitted an application to the Racial Policy Office of the Nazi Party asking for permission to marry a German Wehrmacht soldier named Lauterbacher. Her petition was turned town. In a letter of complaint to the RMbO, Dr Walter Gross, who was head of the Racial Policy Office, declared that Karik was 'not an especially desirable type, racially speaking', and he criticised the fact that the Estonian woman had been granted a permit to enter the Reich in the first place.[181] The general commissioner in Reval was ultimately ordered in November 1943 to ensure that 'no certificates of passage are issued in similar cases'.[182] This was the only warning that was sent, however; the other general commissioners were not notified by the RKO. The authorities apparently had no interest in establishing clear guidelines because otherwise they would lose the ability to make case-by-case decisions.[183]

Rhetoric of Defeat

From the start of 1944, hardly any marriage authorisation applications were submitted, or at least not many were recorded. As the war in the east dragged on, those who still held fast to the regime's goals took an increasingly dim view of consensual relations in particular. The sympathy for the sexual and emotional needs of the soldiers that had dominated the Nazis' policies at the start of the occupation began to give way to the search for someone to blame for Germany's looming defeat. 'They cart their Russian prostitutes with them and sell their weapons', as Joseph Goebbels complained on 31 March 1944, referring to the soldiers in the rear echelon.[184] The soldiers' sexual activity – a symbol of virility and fighting power during the successful conquest – now represented the erosion of the troops.

Gerhard Eschenhagen, who spent two years working for the Nazi press management office in Belarus and Ukraine, similarly blamed the failure of the occupation on a 'lack of discipline' amongst German civilian employees. In August 1944 he wrote:

> You have the widespread rear-echelon clan who could be characterised by two big W's: *Weibern und Wodka* [women and vodka]. [...] Or our undignified compatriots who display racial pride in a stupid and damaging way through coarse and disrespectful conduct towards the local population, but who do not think themselves too good for a little dalliance with a Slavic woman, which they try to keep secret from the Germans but which the locals know all about.[185]

The behaviour of the German men supposedly demonstrated that they were still 'not mature' enough to rule over 'other peoples'. If the Soviet Union were to be occupied again, Eschenhagen wrote curtly, the German authorities would have to pay much closer attention to their choice of personnel. Erich Koch, who served as a Nazi Party *Gauleiter* in East Prussia from 1928 to 1945 and was additionally Reich Commissioner of Ukraine from 1941 to 1944, focused more on the women as the underminers of the 'German fighting spirit'. On 7 August 1944, as around 200,000 soldiers from defeated Wehrmacht units were streaming towards East Prussia, he bemoaned that there were 'also Russian women [*Weiber*] amongst these rear services who are spoiled and pampered by German officers and troops. These women are either idlers and whores or agents of the Bolshevists.'[186]

An alleged lack of 'racial awareness' continued to play an especially important role when it came to the official assessment of consensual relations. The leader of Sonderkommando 7b of the Security Police and the SD in the 4th Army reported in early 1945 that he had often seen German men 'express undignified sentimental babble in letters to ethnically alien women (Russians, Poles)'. In his view, the fact that the men were fixating on women of 'alien stock' (*'fremdstämmig'*) was evidence that not only had they been militarily defeated, they had failed as German men, too.[187]

It was, specifically, the emotional bond that some men developed with women from the occupied Soviet territories that caused considerable uncertainty amongst the responsible military and administrative officials throughout the war and occupation – because it demonstrated that the racial policy goals of the regime and the ideas held by individuals were in no way congruent. The children born of sexual encounters between German men and local women were therefore particularly problematic, as they were visible proof of the lack of 'racial awareness' amongst the men and ultimately symbolised the ambiguity of Germany's occupation policy objectives.

Notes

1. Lejeune, 'How Do Diaries End?', p. 106.
2. Jürgen W., 'Tagebuch in Russland', HIS-Arch, NS-O 22, box 4.
3. Gerlach, *Kalkulierte Morde*, p. 123.
4. Drolshagen, *Nicht ungeschoren davonkommen*; Kaminski, *Liebe im Vernichtungskrieg*, documentary film; Müller, 'Liebe im Vernichtungskrieg'.
5. Müller, 'Liebe im Vernichtungskrieg', p. 122.
6. Dostal, *Penal Battalion*, television series. Also see Skvorcova, 'Das Bild der deutschen Armee', p. 173.
7. See, e.g., Virgili, *Shorn Women*; Warring, 'War, Cultural Loyalty and Gender'; Müller, 'Liebe im Vernichtungskrieg'; Kaminski, *Liebe im Vernichtungskrieg*, documentary film; Drolshagen, *Nicht ungeschoren davonkommen*.
8. See in particular Kaminski, *Liebe im Vernichtungskrieg*, documentary film; Müller, 'Liebe im Vernichtungskrieg'.
9. Langhamer, 'Love and Courtship in Mid-Twentieth-Century England', p. 173.
10. For a differentiated study of the development of a German–Jewish romantic relationship under the Nazis which oscillated between love, dependency, prostitution, gratitude and blackmail, see Meyer, 'Grenzüberschreitungen'.
11. Jahn, 'Vorwort', pp. 9f.
12. Schmiegelt, '"Macht Euch um mich keine Sorgen ... "', p. 29; Jahn and Schmiegelt (eds), *Foto-Feldpost*, p. 109.
13. 'Oberbefehlshaber der 11. Armee, Generaloberst von Manstein, Befehl', 20.11.1941, published in *Trial of the Major War Criminals*, vol. 20, p. 643, and in Ueberschär and Wette (eds), *'Unternehmen Barbarossa'*, p. 246. Also

see 'Richtlinien für das Verhalten der Truppen in Russland', 19.5.1941, BA-MA, RW 4/v.524, published in Ueberschär and Wette (eds), *'Unternehmen Barbarossa'*, p. 312.
14. *Völkischer Beobachter*, 20.7.1941, p. 8. Also see ibid. 13.8.1941, p. 3.
15. See, e.g., Lieutenant Joachim H., letter, 25.10.1941, BfZ, Sterz Collection; Hans Albert Giese, letter, 19.12.1941, published in Elmshäuser and Lokers (eds), 'Man muss hier nur hart sein', p. 166. In many Feldpost letters, the men describe the alleged lack of hygiene and the primitiveness of the population, especially the women. See, e.g., Latzel, *Deutsche Soldaten*, p. 179; Müller, *Deutsche Soldaten*, pp. 179ff.
16. Regarding the first comments made about 'Asiatic peoples' in Feldpost letters, see Müller, *Deutsche Soldaten*, pp. 200ff.
17. Jürgen W., 'Tagebuch in Russland', HIS-Arch, NS-O 22, box 4.
18. Claas, *Ein Heeresrichter im Russlandkrieg*, p. 32. In July 1943, after a concert in Kharkiv, Meier-Brennecke wrote to his wife: 'One of the three singers sat at my table, very pleasant and modest, absolutely looks like a German' (ibid. p. 83).
19. Quoted in Vegesack, *Als Dolmetscher im Osten*, p. 27.
20. The Crimean Autonomous Soviet Socialist Republic of the Russian Soviet Federative Socialist Republic was declared in 1921. The republic initially promoted the language and culture of the Crimean Tatars, including Sunni Islam. This changed under Stalin when many Crimean Tatars were murdered. By the end of the 1930s, less than a quarter of the Crimean population was Tatar (Kappeler, *The Russian Empire*, pp. 44ff., 360, 380ff.). The Tatars first welcomed the Germans as 'liberators', but their attitude soon changed in the face of the occupiers' brutality. Around 15,000 to 20,000 men collaborated with the Germans, while the same number fought with the Red Army and the partisans (Kreindler, 'The Soviet Deportation of Nationalities', p. 391).
21. Quoted in Claas, *Ein Heeresrichter im Russlandkrieg*, p. 147, also published in Müller, 'Liebe im Vernichtungskrieg', p. 248.
22. Hahl, *Mit 'Westland' im Osten*, pp. 75, 141.
23. Diary of soldier Ernst Günther K. (23.3.1941–27.4.1942), BfZ, Sterz Collection, p. 30, also quoted in Oldenburg, *Ideologie und militärisches Kalkül*, p. 118.
24. Quoted in Beckermann, *Jenseits des Krieges*, p. 107.
25. Quoted in ibid. p. 112.
26. Hansmann, *Vorüber – nicht vorbei*, pp. 64f., also quoted in Fritz, *Frontsoldaten*, p. 78.
27. Also see the correspondence between non-commissioned officer Gerhard H. and his Ukrainian lover Helene H., to whom he continued to write for months after his unit had pulled out of Vinnitsa, 1943, USHMM, RG-31.011M, reel 1, 1312c/1c/8.
28. See Knoch, *Kriegsalltag*, pp. 227, 246; Jureit, 'Zwischen Ehe und Männerbund', pp. 66ff., 70f.; Marszolek, '"Ich möchte Dich zu gerne mal in Uniform sehen"', p. 51; Latzel, 'Die Zumutungen des Krieges', pp. 213f.; Reulecke and Kohut, '"Sterben wie eine Ratte"', pp. 188f. For an example of written allusions to

the desire for sex in letters to wives, see Claas, *Heeresrichter im Russlandkrieg*, pp. 82, 97.
29. Humburg, *Das Gesicht des Krieges*, pp. 1173f., also quoted in Vossler, *Propaganda in die eigene Truppe*, p. 341.
30. Kaminski, *Liebe im Vernichtungskrieg*, documentary film.
31. Sheli Lagin, *Under Soviet Rule and in Ghetto Shavli*, personal recollections, 1996, USHMM, DS 135 L 53 L 345.
32. See, e.g., Reese, *A Stranger to Myself*; Sajer, *The Forgotten Soldier*; Hansmann, *Vorüber – nicht vorbei*.
33. Diary of Karl Heinz L., quoted in Haase, '" . . . eine Sportveranstaltung, wenn auch etwas besonderer Art . . ."', p. 207f., also quoted in Vestermanis, 'Local Headquarters Liepaja', p. 230.
34. 'Unteroffizier Herbert K., 13. Kp./Inf.Rgt. 105 (72 ID)', letter, 30.7.1942, BfZ, Sterz Collection, quoted in Oldenburg, *Ideologie und militärisches Kalkül*, p. 118.
35. Regarding these 'ethnic' and 'racial' hierarchies, see Wolf, *Ideologie und Herrschaftsrationalität*.
36. Winter, 'Hauptmann Willi Schulz', pp. 122ff. Regarding the 'exceptional case' ('*Ausnahmefall*') that men could experience without rejecting their National Socialist convictions, also see Benz, Kwiet and Matthäus (eds), *Einsatz*, p. 163.
37. See, e.g., Vegesack, *Als Dolmetscher im Osten*, p. 40.
38. 'Gebietskommissar Brest-Litowsk, Ortsbeauftragter Brest-Litowsk, Schreiben an den Gebietskommissar Brest-Litowsk, betr.: Lagebericht Oktober 1943', 23.10.1943, BArch, R 94/8, unpaginated, p. 11 of the document. Also see 'Ortsbeauftragter Brest-Litowsk, Lagebericht, Streng vertraulich!!', 27.5.1944, BArch, R 94/8, unpaginated.
39. 'Tätigkeitsbericht des Arbeitsamtes Brest-Litowsk für die Jahre 1941–1944', 24.8.1944, BArch, R 93/14, P. 1, unpaginated. This was not an isolated case; see, e.g., Lower, *Nazi Empire-Building*, p. 111.
40. 'Stabsoffizier der Feldgendarmerie, Schreiben an AOK 11/O.Qu', 5.2.1942, BA-MA, RH 20-11/407.
41. 'Geheime Feldpolizei 647, Tätigkeitsbericht für den Monat Juni 1942', 26.6.1942, BA-MA, RH 20-11/337; 'Geheime Feldpolizei 647, Tätigkeitsbericht für den Monat August 1942', 25.8.1942, BA-MA, RH 20-11/337. Regarding similar cases in northern and western European countries, see, e.g., Bargheer, 'Subjektive Erzählung, objektive Akten?', pp. 54f.
42. 'Geheime Feldpolizei 720, Tätigkeitsbericht für den Monat August 1942', 25.8.1942, BA-MA, RH 20-11/337. Also see Oldenburg, *Ideologie und militärisches Kalkül*, p. 316; Büttner, '"Der ganze Krieg ist ja Wahnsinn"'.
43. Müller, 'Liebe im Vernichtungskrieg'. Also see Ole Ligeikaite in Kaminski, *Liebe im Vernichtungskrieg*, documentary film.
44. Kaminski, *Liebe im Vernichtungskrieg*, documentary film, also quoted in Müller, 'Liebe im Vernichtungskrieg', p. 242.
45. Regarding foreign volunteers in the Wehrmacht and SS, see Müller, *The Unknown Eastern Front*.

46. Drolshagen, *Nicht ungeschoren davonkommen*; Kaminski, *Liebe im Vernichtungskrieg*, documentary film; Müller, 'Liebe im Vernichtungskrieg'.
47. Jasinska, *Der Krieg, die Liebe und das Leben*. The Jewish Austrian woman Edith Hahn Beer assumed a false identity and lived in Vienna, within the borders of the Reich, as the wife of a Wehrmacht officer. She believes that stories such as hers also took place elsewhere in the Reich and the occupied territories (Hahn Beer, *The Nazi Officer's Wife*).
48. Gottesfeld Heller, *Strange and Unexpected Love*. Her story as well as other cases have recently been explored in detail by Katya Gusarov, 'Sexual Barter and Jewish Women's Efforts to Save Their Lives'.
49. Drolshagen, *Nicht ungeschoren davonkommen*.
50. Kaminski, *Liebe im Vernichtungskrieg*, documentary film.
51. Drolshagen, *Nicht ungeschoren davonkommen*, pp. 124f. In a personal conversation, Ebba Drohlshagen recounted a case in which a woman denounced a former friend who was in competition with her. This is a difficult subject to address, however.
52. Beckermann, *Jenseits des Krieges*, p. 112.
53. Kaminski, *Liebe im Vernichtungskrieg*, documentary film.
54. Ibid. also quoted in Müller, 'Liebe im Vernichtungskrieg', p. 251.
55. Other first-hand accounts, too, discuss the desire for normality, such as the opportunity to fall in love. However, some witnesses insist that it was absolutely impossible to pursue this desire against the backdrop of war and mass murder; see, e.g., Schulman, *A Partisan's Memoir*, p. 148.
56. Kaminski, *Liebe im Vernichtungskrieg*, documentary film.
57. See the various statements from eyewitnesses in Kaminski, *Liebe im Vernichtungskrieg*, documentary film.
58. Quoted in Müller, 'Liebe im Vernichtungskrieg', p. 247.
59. See, e.g., Lenz, *Haushaltspflicht und Widerstand*; Yuval-Davis, *Gender and Nation*, p. 111.
60. 'Stimmungsbericht über Charkow', September 1943, quoted Kaminski, *Liebe im Vernichtungskrieg*, documentary film.
61. Kaminski, *Liebe im Vernichtungskrieg*, documentary film.
62. According to Pavel Polian (Moscow), there are no references to such retributive measures in the records of the NKVD.
63. Quoted in Beckermann, *Jenseits des Krieges*, pp. 125f.
64. Kaminski, *Liebe im Vernichtungskrieg*, documentary film, also quoted in Müller, 'Liebe im Vernichtungskrieg', p. 247.
65. Kaminski, *Liebe im Vernichtungskrieg*, documentary film, also quoted in Müller, 'Liebe im Vernichtungskrieg', p. 243.
66. Kaminski, *Liebe im Vernichtungskrieg*, documentary film. It would be interesting to research the extent to which women who talk about their war experiences now continue to give expression to the social expectation that they were naïve girls who were seduced. Claudia Lenz has shown that some Norwegian women position themselves in this way to avoid touching on the myth that

their country had been firmly opposed to the Nazis; see Lenz, *Haushaltspflicht und Widerstand*.
67. Drolshagen, *Nicht ungeschoren davonkommen*, p. 75.
68. Warring, 'War, Cultural Loyalty and Gender', pp. 45f.
69. 'Leutnant Helmut D., 2. Kp./Geb.Jäg.Rgt. 13 (4. Geb.Div.)', BfZ, Sterz Collection, also quoted in Oldenburg, *Ideologie und militärisches Kalkül*, p. 245. The 4th Mountain Division ('4. Geb.Div.') was under the command of the 1st Panzer Army from January to the end of May 1942.
70. See, e.g., 'OKW, gez. Keitel, Erlass, betr.: Unerwünschter Verkehr deutscher Soldaten mit Einwohnern in den besetzten Ostgebieten', 15.9.1942, copy, BArch, NS 19/1691, p. 1.
71. Müller, *Deutsche Soldaten*.
72. The difficulties that superiors faced in attempting to resolve such conflicts were also addressed by a military doctor in the journal *Medizinische Welt* in 1944; see Rost, 'Sexuelle probleme', p. 7.
73. 'Rückw. Armeegebiet 585, Abt. Qu., Kommandanturbefehl Nr. 5', 6.2.1942, NARA, RG-242 501/65, pp. 334–8, here p. 334.
74. See, e.g., 'Oberbefehlshaber der 17. Armee, gez. Hoth, Befehl über das Verhalten der deutschen Soldaten im Ostraum', 17.11.1941, BA-MA, RH 20/17-44, also published in Ueberschär and Wette (eds), *'Unternehmen Barbarossa'*, p. 342.
75. Bartov, *The Eastern Front*, p. 127.
76. Order of the 12th Infantry, quoted in Bartov, *Hitler's Army*, p. 94.
77. Dean, *Collaboration in the Holocaust*, p. 109.
78. 'Wirtschaftsstab Ost, Besondere Anordnungen Nr. 61', 5.3.1942, BA-MA, RW 31/141, quoted in Müller, 'Liebe im Vernichtungskrieg', p. 246.
79. Jürgen W., 'Tagebuch in Russland', HIS-Arch, NS-O 22, box 5.
80. Lower, *Nazi Empire-Building*, p. 111.
81. 'OKW, Erlass betr.: Unerwünschter Verkehr deutscher Soldaten mit Einwohnern in den besetzten Ostgebieten, gez. Keitel', 15.9.1942, BArch, NS 19/1691, p. 1, and BArch, NS 19/1971, p. 1. At the end of January 1943, the OKW expanded this decree to cover the General Government as well ('SS-Führungshauptamt, betr.: Unerwünschter Verkehr deutscher Soldaten mit Einwohnern in den besetzten Gebieten', 28.1.1943, BArch, NS 19/1691, pp. 2f.).
82. Bartov, *The Eastern Front*, pp. 126ff.
83. 'OKH, General Keitel, betr.: Verkehr des deutschen Soldaten mit der Zivilbevölkerung in den besetzten Ostgebieten', 12.9.1942, BA-MA, H 20/825.
84. See 'Oberkommando des Heeres, von Brauchitsch', 31.7.1940, BA-MA, RH 53-7/v. 233a/167; 'Anl. 1 zu OKH, 6.9.1941, betr.: Selbstzucht', BA-MA, H 20/825. Also see the detailed analysis in Chapter 2.
85. Olsen, *Vater: Deutscher*, pp. 25f., 123.
86. 'Inspekteur des Sanitätswesens der Luftwaffe, Anweisung für Truppenärzte über Verhütung von Selbstmord', Berlin, 6.10.1942, NARA, RG-242 78/192, pp. 6135832–7, here p. 6135834.
87. Sven Oliver Müller's study of the Feldpost letters of German soldiers shows

that many soldiers really did write to their mothers, wives and girlfriends that they were fighting particularly so that German women were protected from the 'Bolshevist hordes'; see Müller, *Deutsche Soldaten*, pp. 163ff.
88. Czarnowski, *Das kontrollierte Paar*.
89. For example, the Wehrmacht Patrol Service in the Ostland administrative district reported in January 1944 that 'there is just as little understanding for the fact that civil servants in Ostland often drive their wives in cars, while Germans who are soldiers are not even permitted to send for their wives' ('Wehrmachtsbefehlshaber Ostland, Kommandeur Wehrmachtsstreifendienst ['Aufgabengebiet General z. b.V.'], Bericht Nr. 8, umfassend die Zeit vom 5.6.1943 bis 10.1.1944', Riga, 11.1.1944, BA-MA, RW 41/57, unpaginated, p. 8 of the document). Regarding the granting of residence permits for wives and children, see 'Reichskommissar für das Ostland, Akten zur Aufenthaltsgenehmigung für Reichsdeutsche im Ostland', 1944, BArch, R 92/10032, passim.
90. See Hahl, *Mit 'Westland' im Osten*, p. 142.
91. Vossler, *Propaganda in die eigene Truppe*, pp. 342ff.
92. 'Sammelerlass Nr. 10/5, betr.: Geschlechtsverkehr von Angehörigen der SS und Polizei mit anders rassigen Frauen', copy in BArch, NS 19/3872.
93. 'Chef des Rechtsamtes, Schreiben an den SS-Richter beim RF-SS, SS-Sturmbannführer Bender, betr.: Verhalten von SS-Angehörigen gegenüber Polinnen', 12.12.1940, BArch, NS 7/265, p. 1.
94. In a circular, Himmler described the case of a *Scharführer* (squad leader) in the General SS who had 'indiscriminately engaged in sexual intercourse with Polish women throughout the year 1940' and later infected both his wife and another 'ethnic German girl' with syphilis. Himmler said he 'dishonourably discharged' the man from the SS and sent him to a concentration camp ('RF-SS und Chef der deutschen Polizei, betr.: Geschlechtsverkehr mit Polinnen', 21.6.1941, BArch, NS 7/265, p. 5).
95. 'RF-SS, Schreiben an den Höheren SS- und Polizeiführer Ost, SS-Obergruppenführer Krüger', Krakow, 30.6.1942, BArch, NS 19/1913, pp. 3f.
96. See, e.g., 'SS-Richter beim RF-SS und Chef der Deutschen Polizei, Schreiben an das Hauptamt SS-Gericht, betr.: Geschlechtsverkehr von Angehörigen der SS und Polizei mit Frauen einer anders rassigen Bevölkerung', 12.11.1941, BArch, NS 7/265, p. 21; 'RF-SS, Hauptamt SS-Gericht, Geheimer Erlass, betr.: Geschlechtsverkehr von Angehörigen der SS und Polizei mit andersrassigen Frauen', 9.12.1941, BArch, NS 19/3872, p. 27; 'RF-SS und Chef der Deutschen Polizei, Schreiben an den Höheren SS- und Polizeiführer Ost, SS-Obergruppenführer Krüger, Krakau, betr.: Geschlechtsverkehr von Angehörigen der SS und Polizei mit Frauen einer andersrassigen Bevölkerung', 30.6.1942, BArch, NS 19/1913, pp. 3f.
97. 'SS-Richter beim RF-SS, Schreiben an den Kommandeur der SS-Freiwilligen-Standarte "Nordwest"', 25.10.1941, BArch, NS 7/265, p. 8.
98. 'Chef der Sicherheitspolizei und des SD, Kommandostab, Meldungen aus den

besetzten Gebieten der UdSSR', 25.2.1942, USHMM, RG-31.002M, reel 11, 3676/4/105, p. 14. The notion that the Russian population looked up to the Germans, their culture and their love of order appears in numerous ego documents as well. See, e.g., 'Sof. (Z) Anatol Herlitz, Dolmetscher der Ersten Kompanie 16, Die Verwaltungsprobleme im Osten', 13.9.1943, BArch, R 93/6, fol 1, unpaginated.
99. See, e.g., 'Fritz Kranefuss, Schreiben an SS-Obersturmbannführer Rudolf Brandt, Persönlicher Stab RF-SS', 16.9.1943, BArch, NS 19/2220, pp. 170, 173.
100. See, e.g. 'Reichsführer-SS und Chef der Deutschen Polizei, gez. SS-Obersturmbannführer Eduard Strauch, Schreiben an den Chef der Bandenkampfverbände, SS-Obergruppenführer und General der Polizei, Erich von dem Bach, betr.: Generalkommissar für Weissruthenien, Gauleiter Kube', 25.7.1943, published in 'Aus den Akten', p. 83.
101. See, e.g., the investigation against SS-*Standartenführer* Fegelein for 'sexual intercourse with a Polish woman', BArch, NS 19/3878, pp. 1–16.
102. 'RF-SS, Schreiben an den Höheren SS- und Polizeiführer Ost, SS-Obergruppenführer Krüger', Krakow, 30.6.1942, BArch, NS 19/1913, pp. 3f.
103. 'RF-SS Himmler, Rede auf der SS- und Polizeiführer-Tagung in der Feldkommandostelle Hegewald bei Shitomir', 16.9.1942, BArch, NS 19/4009, pp. 78–127, here p. 125.
104. 'Gericht der 1. SS-Inf.-Brig. (mot), gez. Dr. Klahre, Schreiben an das Hauptamt SS-Gericht, Rechtsamt, betr.: 1. Geschlechtsverkehr mit Ukrainerinnen und Russinnen', 24.11.1941, BArch, NS 7/265, pp. 26f.
105. See Heinemann, *'Rasse, Siedlung, deutsches Blut'*, pp. 476f.; Wolf, *Ideologie und Herrschaftsrationalität*.
106. 'RF-SS, Himmler, Rede auf der SS- und Polizeiführer-Tagung in der Feldkommandostelle Hegewald bei Shitomir', 19.9.1942, BArch, NS 19/4009, pp. 78–127, here p. 125.
107. 'SS-Richter beim RF-SS und Chef der Deutschen Polizei, Schreiben an das Hauptamt SS-Gericht, betr.: Geschlechtsverkehr mit Ukrainerinnen', 28.12.1941, BArch, NS 7/265, p. 28.
108. 'RF-SS, Hauptamt SS-Gericht, Erlass, Verteiler A und B, betr.: Geschlechtsverkehr von Angehörigen der SS und Polizei mit andersrassigen Frauen', 20.1.1942, BArch, NS 19/3872, p. 26.
109. Gender-specific constellations also played a major role in the Reich. If a German man had a relationship with a female Ukrainian forced worker, this was more likely to be tolerated than if a German woman had a similar relationship with a non-German man; see Czarnowski, 'Zwischen Germanisierung und Vernichtung'; Kundrus, 'Forbidden Company'.
110. 'Richtertagung in München am 7.5.1943, Bericht und Vermerk zu diversen Besprechungspunkten', BArch, NS 7/13, pp. 1–21, pp. 7ff. Regarding sexual encounters between SS members and local women, see Angrick, *Besatzungspolitik und Massenmord*, pp. 359, 450; Mallmann, Riess and Pyta (eds), *Deutscher Osten*, p. 93; Wilhelm, 'Die Einsatzgruppe A', p. 480.

111. 'SS-Obergruppenführer Berger an den Reichsführer-SS, Aktenvermerk zu einer Besprechung im Reichsostministerium', 14.7.1943, BArch, NS 19/382, pp. 137–9, here p. 138. Also see 'Persönlicher Stab Reichsführer-SS, Schreiben an den Chef der Sicherheitspolizei und des SD, Feldkommandostelle', 20.8.1943, BArch, NS 19/382, p. 133; 'Cher der Sicherheitspolizei und des SD, gez. SS-Obergruppenführer Dr. Kaltenbrunner, Telegramm an den Reichsführer-SS und Chef des deutschen Polizei, betr.: Arbeitskräfte aus den Baltenländern', here: 'Verbot des Geschlechtsverkehrs', BArch, NS 18/382, pp. 131–3.
112. See Hiden and Salmon, *The Baltic Nations*, p. 117.
113. See the Nazi collection of travel reports and country profiles published by the RKO: Zimmermann (ed.), *Auf Informationsfahrt im Ostland*.
114. Rosenberg, unsigned memorandum no. 1, 2 April 1941, published in *Trial of the Major War Criminals*, vol. 26, p. 547, Document 1017 PS.
115. 'RF-SS, Schreiben an den Chef der Sicherheitspolizei und des SD, Feldkommandostelle', 8.9.1943, BArch, NS 19/382, p. 129. Also see 'Persönlicher Stab RF-SS, Schreiben an SS-Obergruppenführer Berger, Feldkommandostelle', 20.8.1943, BArch, NS 19/382, p. 134.
116. 'RKO, Schreiben an den Reichskommissar in Reval, betr.: Rassenpolitische Beurteilung estnischer Bräute von Angehörigen der Waffen-SS', 1.9.1943, BArch, R90/460, pp. 212f.
117. 'Graf von Korff, Schreiben an SS-Oberführer Bender', 28.12.1944, BArch, NS 7/265, p. 30.
118. 'SS-Richter beim RF-SS, Bender, Schreiben an Graf von Korff', 29.1.1945, BArch, NS 7/265, p. 33.
119. 'RMbO, gez. Dr Runte, Schreiben an den RKO betr.: den aussereehelichen Verkehr zwischen Deutschen und Angehoerigen eines fremden Volkstums', 24.11.1941, BArch, R 90/460, pp. 170f., here p. 170.
120. 'RKO, gez. Wegner und Trampedach, Schreiben an den RMbO, betr.: Aussereehelicher Verkehr Deutscher mit Angehoerigen fremden Volkstums', March 1942, BArch, R 90/460, pp. 167–9, here pp. 168f.
121. 'RMbO, Dr. Runte, Schreiben an den RKO, betr.: Aussereehelicher Verkehr zwischen Deutschen und Angehörigen eines fremden Volkstums', 27.7.1942, BArch, R 90/460, p. 166.
122. 'Generalkommissar für Weissruthenien, Personalabteilung, Aktenvermerk!', 11.10.1944, BArch, R 93/4, fol 1, unpaginated.
123. 'Generalkommissar für Weissruthenien, Entwurf einer Verordnung über das Eherecht im Generalbezirk Weissruthenien', 5.8.1941, BArch, R 93/21, pp. 428–35. Regarding the discussion and scope of this policy, see, e.g., 'Generalkommissar für Weissruthenien, Schreiben an die Abteilung Gesundheitswesen und Volkspflege, betr.: Eherechtliche Fragen', 6.7.1942, BArch, R 93/21, pp. 422–5; 'Generalkommissar für Weissruthenien, Abteilung Gesundheitswesen und Volkspflege, Schreiben an die Abteilung 2d, betr.: Eherechtliche Fragen', 17.7.1942, BArch, R 93/21, p. 426; 'Generalkommissar

in Minsk, Abt. II Verw., Lagebericht', 15.10.1942, BArch, R 93/3, pp. 2–44, here p. 10.
124. 'SS- und Polizeiführer in Brest-Litowsk, Lagebericht für die Zeit vom 16. Februar bis 15. März 1942', 15.3.1942, BArch, R 94/6, unpaginated.
125. See the respective reports and correspondence from the Reich Commissariat Ukraine, USHMM, RG-31.002M, reel 11, 3676/4/4, and RG 31.002M, reel 11, 3676/4/10.
126. 'OKW, im Auftrag gez. Breyer, Schreiben an das M-Stammlager 340, betr.: Eheschliessung zwischen Kriegsgefangenen und der einheimischen Bevölkerung', 25.11.1942, BArch, R 90/460, p. 181; 'RMbO, Schreiben an den RKO, betr.: Eheschliessung sowjetischer Kriegsgefangener mit Estinnen, Lettinnen und Litauerinnen', 8.3.1943, BArch, R 90/460, P. 179; 'RMbO, im Auftrag Leibbrandt, Schreiben an den RKO, betr.: Eheschliessung zwischen einem Protektoratsangehörigen und einer Lettin', 31.5.1943, BArch, R 90/460, p. 182; 'Generaldirektor des Innern, Anordnung über das Verbot der Eheschliessung mit Zuzüglern v. 10. 9. 1943', copy of translation, BArch, R 90/460, p. 184; sent with 'Anschreiben vom Generalkommissar in Riga, Schreiben an den RKO, betr.: Eheschliessung von Zuzüglern mit Einwohnern des Generalbezirks Lettland', 13.9.1943, Ibid.; 'RKO, Abt. I Pol., Trampedach, Schreiben an die Abt II Verw, betr.: Verbot der Eheschliessung mit Zuzüglern', 8.1.1944, BArch, R 90/460, p. 215.
127. 'RMbO, gez. Dr. Runte, Schreiben an den RKO, betr.: den ausserehelichen Verkehr zwischen Deutschen und Angehoerigen eines fremden Volkstums', 24.11.1941, BArch, R 90/460, pp. 170f., here p. 170.
128. 'RKO, gez. Wegner und Trampedach, Schreiben an den RMbO, betr.: Aussereheliche Verkehr Deutscher mit Angehoerigen fremden Volkstums', March 1942, BArch, R 90/460, pp. 167–9, here pp. 168f.
129. RGBl. 1942, vol. 1, p. 255.
130. 'OK Heeresgruppe Nord, gez. Henn, Schreiben an den Befehlshaber Heeresgruppe Nord, betr.: Heirat mit Estinnen', 5.8.1942, BArch, R 90/460, p. 211; 'Kommandierender General der Sicherungstruppen u. Befehlshaber im Heeresgebiet Nord, gez. Rübesamen, Schreiben an den RKO, betr.: Heirat mit Estinnen', 23.2.1943, BArch, R 90/460, p. 210.
131. 'OKW, Keitel, Allgemeine Heeresmitteilung, Nr. 187, Heirat von Wehrmachtsangehörigen mit Holländerinnen, Norwegerinnen, Däninnen und Schwedinnen', 26.1.1942, copy, BArch, R 90/460, pp. 205f.; 'OKW, Keitel, Allgemeine Heeresmitteilung, Nr. 288, Heirat von Wehrmachtsangehörigen mit Holländerinnen, Norwegerinnen, Däninnen und Schwedinnen', 2.3.1942, copy, BArch, R 90/460, p. 205.
132. City in southeastern Estonia which was occupied by German troops on 11 July 1941. By 28 July 1941, German military police units had already ensconced themselves in the city; see Birn, *Die Sicherheitspolizei in Estland*, p. 14.
133. 'Sicherungsdivision 207 Abt. 2a, Tagesbefehl Nr. 47', 18.8.1942, copy, BArch, R 90/460, p. 207.

134. 'RKO, gez. Wegner and Trampedach, Schreiben an den RMbO, betr.: Ausserehelicher Verkehr Deutscher mit Angehoerigen fremden Volkstums', March 1942, BArch, R 90/460, pp. 167–9, here pp. 168f.
135. 'RMbO, Bericht über die am 28. Januar 1943 vormittags 10 Uhr stattgefundene Sitzung, betr.: Eheschliessung von deutschen Staatsangehörigen mit Angehörigen eines fremden Volkstums im Gebiet des Reichskommissariats Ostland', 1.2.1943, BArch, R 90/460, pp. 188-197, here p. 191.
136. The extent to which this points to real forms of racism and antisemitism in Estonia, Latvia and Lithuania remains unclear.
137. A similar argument can be found in 'RKO, Lohse, Rede an die verwundeten Kameraden, Offiziere und Soldaten der deutschen Wehrmacht', 23.2.1942, BArch, R 90/19, unpaginated.
138. City south of Riga that was occupied by the Germans in July 1941.
139. 'Gebietskommissar in Mitau, Schreiben an den Generalkommissar in Riga', 21.5.1942, BArch, R 90/460, p. 165. Regarding the topos of Latvian 'racial' and national pride, also see 'Generalinspekteur der lettischen SS-Freiwilligen-Legion, SS-Gruppenführer und Generalleutnant der Waffen-SS, Bangerskis, Schreiben an den RMbO, Alfred Rosenberg', 6.3.1944, BArch, R 90/460, pp. 126–9.
140. Both arguments – that the 'honour of the German man and soldier requires him to stick to his word' and that a general marriage ban would be taken as a 'serious insult' – were also made by German civil servants and Norwegian National Socialists in the discussion of Norwegian–German marriages; see Olsen, *Vater: Deutscher*, pp. 132ff.
141. 'Sof. [Z] Anatol Herlitz, Dolm.Ers.Komp. 16, Die Verwaltungsprobleme im Osten', 13.9.1943, BArch, R 93/6, fol 1, unpaginated.
142. 'Gebietskommissar in Mitau, Schreiben an den Generalkommissar in Riga', 21.5.1942, BArch, R 90/460, p. 165; 'Generalkommissar in Riga, Schreiben aus Mitau als Abschrift weitergesandt an den RKO, betr.: Eheschliessung zwischen deutschen Staatsangehoerigen und Angehoerigen nichtdeutschen Volkstums', 28.5.1942, BArch, R 90/460, p. 164. The growing reticence of the local men after their initial loyalty was also noted by Gerdes, 'Männer im Ostland' (1943).
143. 'Generalkommissar in Riga, Schreiben aus Mitau als Abschrift weitergesandt an den RKO, betr.: Eheschliessung zwischen deutschen Staatsangehoerigen und Angehoerigen nichtdeutschen Volkstums', 28. 5. 1942, BArch, R 90/460, P. 164.
144. 'Gebietskommissar in Mitau, Schreiben an den Generalkommissar in Riga', 21.5.1942, BArch, R 90/460, p. 165; also see Müller, 'Liebe im Vernichtungskrieg', p. 250.
145. See, e.g., 'RF-SS, Himmler, Rede auf der SS- und Polizeiführer-Tagung in der Feldkommandostelle Hegewald bei Shitomir', 16.9.1942, BArch, NS 19/4009, pp. 78–127, here p. 92, also published in Jacobsen and Jochmann (eds), *Ausgewählte Dokumente zur Geschichte des Nationalsozialismus 1933–1945*; 'RF-

SS, Himmler, Niederschrift über Besprechung mit dem Führer zur Heirat von Wehrmachtsangehörigen mit Angehörigen der artverwandten germanischen Völker', 17.6.1943, BArch, NS 19/2706, p. 1.

146. If the general commissioner prohibited a marriage, the legal status of any potential children was to be determined on the basis of paragraph 129 of the Marriage Act ('Entwurf zur Durchführung und Ergänzung der Verordnung über die Anwendung deutschen Rechts auf deutsche Staatsangehörige in den besetzten Ostgebieten', 3.6.1942, BArch, R 90/460, pp. 133-6).

147. 'RMbO, Schreiben an den RKO, Entwurf, betr.: Eheschliessungen von deutschen Reichsangehörigen mit Angehörigen eines anderen Volkstums im Gebiete des Reichskommissariats Ostland', BArch, R 90/460, pp. 139-50, here p. 140, and BArch, R90/136, unpaginated.

148. Ibid.

149. 'RKO, Hauptabteilungsleiter II, Ministerialrat Burmeister, Vermerk an Hauptabteilungsleiter Pröhl', 15.2.1943, BArch, R 90/136, unpaginated.

150. 'RKO, Hauptabteilungsleiter II, Burmeister, Stellungnahme zu dem Vermerk des Abteilungsleiters I Politik, Regierungsrat Trampedach, vom 15. Februar 1943, und des rassepolitischen Referenten Regierungsrat Dr. Steininger vom 15.3.1943 zur Frage der Eheschliessung zwischen Deutschen und Angehörigen der ehemals baltischen Staaten', 19.3.1943, BArch, R 90/136, unpaginated. Burmeister was referring to Karl C. von Loesch and his theories of ethnicity; see Loesch, 'Völker im Wandel der Zeiten', undated (1943). A copy of the print proofs can be found in BArch, R 90/460, pp. 239-43.

151. 'RKO, Hauptabteilungsleiter II, Burmeister, Schreiben an Herrn Regierungsrat Trampedach, betr.: Eheschliessung zwischen Deutschen und Angehörigen der ehemaligen Baltischen Staaten', 3.5.1943, BArch, R 90/136, unpaginated. Regarding conflicts about the weighting of 'race' and 'ethnicity', also see Wolf, *Ideologie und Herrschaftsrationalität*.

152. 'RKO, Ministerialrat Dr. Essen, Schreiben an den RMbO, betr.: Eheschliessungen von deutschen Staatsangehörigen mit Angehörigen eines nichtdeutschen Volkstums im Reichskommissariat Ostland', 7.7.1942, BArch, R 90/460, pp. 151-6, here p. 153, and BArch, R90/136, unpaginated.

153. The extent to which forms of racism appear throughout history not as fixed ideologies but as flexible constructs that can be changed and adapted to fit specific situations is demonstrated by Stoler, 'Racial Histories and Their Regimes of Truth', and Goldberg, *Racist Culture*, amongst others.

154. Dr Kinkelin from the RMbO concluded that, on account of the 'surplus of women' in Germany, they should welcome the idea of 'racially desirable foreigners marrying German women'. No one else backed this position, however; see 'RMbO, Bericht über die am 28. Januar 1943 vormittags 10 Uhr stattgefundene Sitzung, betr.: Eheschliessung von deutschen Staatsangehörigen mit Angehörigen eines fremden Volkstums im Gebiet des Reichskommissariats Ostland', 1.2.1943, BArch, R 90/460, pp. 188-97, here p. 193.

155. Ibid. p. 189. Also see 'RKO, gez. Trampedach, Vermerk, betr.: Sitzung im

RMbO über Eheschliessungen mit Angehörigen baltischer Völker am 28. Januar 1943', 15.2.1943, BArch, R 90/460, pp. 175–8.
156. 'RMbO, Bericht über die am 28. Januar 1943 vormittags 10 Uhr stattgefundene Sitzung, betr.: Eheschliessung von deutschen Staatsangehörigen mit Angehörigen eines fremden Volkstums im Gebiet des Reichskommissariats Ostland', 1.2.1943, BArch, R 90/460, pp. 188–97, here p. 195.
157. 'RKO, gez. Trampedach, Vermerk, betr.: Sitzung im RMbO über Eheschliessungen mit Angehörigen baltischer Völker am 28. Januar 1943', 15.2.1943, BArch, R 90/460, pp. 175–8, here p. 176; 'RMbO, Bericht über die am 28. Januar 1943 vormittags 10 Uhr stattgefundene Sitzung, betr.: Eheschliessung von deutschen Staatsangehörigen mit Angehörigen eines fremden Volkstums im Gebiet des Reichskommissariats Ostland', 1.2.1943, BArch, R 90/460, pp. 188–97, here pp. 189f.
158. 'RKO, gez. Trampedach, Vermerk, betr.: Sitzung im RMbO über Eheschliessungen mit Angehörigen baltischer Völker am 28. Januar 1943', 15.2.1943, BArch, R 90/460, pp. 175–8, here p. 176; 'RMbO, Bericht über die am 28. Januar 1943 vormittags 10 Uhr stattgefundene Sitzung, betr.: Eheschliessungen von deutschen Staatsangehörigen mit Angehörigen eines fremden Volkstums im Gebiet des Reichskommissariats Ostland', 1.2.1943, BArch, R 90/460, pp. 188–97, here p. 190.
159. Excerpt from 'Der Schulungsbrief', frontline edition, 5th issue, 1943, BArch, R 90/136, unpaginated.
160. Eckelberg put forward a similar argument at the interministerial meeting. He used the example of Italy (still allied with Germany at the time), which had, of its own accord, introduced regulations regarding marriage between Italian women and German men. Eckelberg said that surely all 'cultured nations' must have an interest in this ('RKO, gez. Trampedach, Vermerk, betr.: Sitzung im RMbO über Eheschliessungen mit Angehörigen baltischer Völker am 28. Januar 1943', 15.2.1943, BArch, R 90/460, pp. 175–8, here pp. 175f.).
161. RKO, note, 5.2.1943, BArch, R 90/460, p. 173.
162. Regarding the general marriage regulations applicable to Wehrmacht members, see Czarnowski, *Das kontrollierte Paar*.
163. 'Chef des Sanitätswesens der Luftwaffe, gez. Schröder, Anweisung für Truppenärzte, Einzelanordnung Nr. 10', 14.7.1944, NARA, RG 242/T 78/R 192, pp. 6135744–53, here p. 6135748.
164. This assessement changed over the course of 1943, however; see *Auf Informationsfahrt im Ostland*.
165. Battles raged for many weeks before the port city now known as Tallinn was taken by the Germans on 28 August 1941. Many Estonian Jews lived there; most of them were able to escape, but those who remained were deported to camps and murdered. The Red Army liberated the city on 22 September 1944; see Birn, *Die Sicherheitspolizei in Estland*, pp. 14f.
166. 'Generalkommissar in Reval, Schreiben an den RKO, Abt. Gesundheits- und Volkspflege, betr.: Untersuchung estnischer Frauen auf Tauglichkeit für die Ehe

mit reichsdeutschen Wehrmachtsangehörigen', 24.8.1942, BArch, R 90/460, pp. 201ff. Regarding the importance of a woman's sexual history in these 'racial evaluations', see Bergen, 'Sex, Blood, and Vulnerability', p. 115.
167. Paul Z., Hamburg, handwritten letter to the public health officer for the general commissioner in Riga, Dr Marnitz, 15.12.1942, BArch, R 92/10035, unpaginated.
168. 'Amtsarzt, gez. Dr. Marnitz, Schreiben an den Obergefreiten P.Z., Feldpostnummer L.34479, betr.: Amtsärztliche Untersuchung ihrer Braut', 8.1.1943, BArch, R 92/10035, unpaginated.
169. 'Amtsarzt beim Generalkommissar in Riga, gez. Dr. Marnitz, Schreiben an die Abteilung II Verwaltung und die Abteilung II Recht, betr.: Anna Klopstock', 10.4.1943, BArch, R 92/10035, unpaginated; 'Amtsarzt beim Generalkommissar in Riga, gez. Dr. Marnitz, Schreiben an Erich Lambert, Leslau/Weichsel, betr.: Ehefähigkeitszeugnis', 11.6.1943, BArch, R 92/10035, unpaginated.
170. 'Feldwebel Bruno Kleindienst, Lgpa Königsberg, Schreiben an Herrn Dr Marnitz', 6.8.1943, BArch, R 92/10035, unpaginated.
171. 'Amtsarzt, gez. Dr. Marnitz, Schreiben an Feldwebel Bruno Kleindienst', 17.8.1943, BArch, R 92/10035, unpaginated.
172. 'Deutscher Standesbeamter in Riga, Schreiben an den Amtsarzt beim Generalkommissar in Riga, betr.: Amtsärztliche Untersuchung auf Ehetauglichkeit der Margarete H. geb. am 6.10.1913, wohnhaft Riga [...]', 19.11.1943, BArch, R 92/10035, unpaginated; 'SS-Führer im RuS Wesen, Schreiben an Dr. Marnitz, Bitte um ärztliche Untersuchung zwecks Heirat', 11.11.1943, BArch, R 92/10035, unpaginated; 'Prüfungsbogen für Eheeignung, Hermine P., geb. 31.1.1921 in Lettland, wohnhaft in Riga', Riga, 16.11.1943, BArch, R 92/10035, unpaginated.
173. 'Staatliches Gesundheitsamt Dresden-Land, Ergänzungsfragebogen zum Antrag auf Ausstellung einer Eheunbedenklichkeitsbescheinigung Hildegard S., April 1943', BArch, R 92/10035, unpaginated. Also see 'Prüfungsbogen für Eheeignung Margarete P.', 1.3.1943, BArch, R 92/10035, unpaginated; 'Generalkommissar in Riga, Amtsarzt, Eheunbedenklichkeitsbescheinigung Ruth Sch.', 19.3.1943, BArch, R 92/10035, unpaginated; 'Generalkommissar in Riga, Amtsarzt, Eheunbedenklichkeitsbescheinigung Elsa M.', 30.6.1943, BArch, R 92/10035, unpaginated; 'Antrag auf Ausstellung einer Eheunbedenklichkeitsbescheinigung, Elisabeth H.', 23.7.1943, BArch, R 92/10035, unpaginated.
174. 'Prüfungsbogen für Eheeignung Senta D.', 15.3.1943, BArch, R 92/10035, unpaginated.
175. 'Gesundheitsamt Prenzlauer Berg, Schreiben an den Amtsarzt in Riga', 24.9.1943, BArch, R 92/10035, unpaginated; 'Standortarzt Schwerin/Warthe, Abschrift, Schreiben an das Gesundheitsamt Prenzlauer Berg, betr.: Entlassung des O.Schtz Hans-Joachim G.', 21.11.1941, BArch, R 92/10035, unpaginated; 'Amtsarzt, gez. Dr. Marnitz, Schreiben an den Gebietskommissar Riga-Stadt,

betr.: Eheunbedenklichkeitsbescheinigung des Studienrats Hans Joachim G.', 12.10.1943; BArch, R 92/10035, unpaginated; 'deutscher Standesbeamter in Riga, Schreiben an den Generalkommissar in Riga, Gesundheitsamt, betr.: Eheunbedenklichkeitsbescheinigung des Studienrats Hans Joachim G.', 27.10.1943; 'Gebietskommissar Riga, Abt. Gesundheit und Volkspflege, Schreiben an das Gesundheitsamt Prenzlauer Berg', 2.11.1943, BArch, R 92/10035, unpaginated.

176. See, e.g., 'Generalkommissar in Riga, Amtsarzt, Eheunbedenklichkeitsbescheinigung Elsa M.', 30.6.1943, BArch, R 92/10035, unpaginated; 'Generalkommissar in Riga, Amtsarzt, Eheunbedenklichkeitsbescheinigung Ruth Sch.', 19.3.1943, BArch, R 92/10035, unpaginated. In individual cases, the certificate could be renewed by the doctor ('Generalkommissar in Riga, Amtsarzt, Eheunbedenklichkeitsbescheinigung Johanna H.', 7.5.1943, BArch, R 92/10035, unpaginated).

177. This city in southwestern Lithuania was occupied by the Wehrmacht on 22 June 1941, the day Germany invaded the Soviet Union.

178. 'RKO, Schreiben an den Herrn Generalkommissar in Kauen, betr.: Eheschliessung zwischen Reichsdeutschen und Angehörigen der ehemals baltischen Staaten', undated (January 1944), BArch, R 90/460, p. 221.

179. 'Generalkommissar in Kauen, Schreiben an den RKO, betr.: Eheschliessung zwischen Reichsdeutschen und Angehörigen der ehemals baltischen Freistaaten', 29.3.1944, BArch, R 90/460, p. 222.

180. The general commissioner in Reval (Tallinn) disovered that this was common practice ('Schreiben an RKO, betr.: Untersuchung estnischer Frauen auf Tauglichkeit für die Ehe mit reichsdeutschen Wehrmachtsangehörigen', 24.8.1942, BArch, R 90/460, pp. 201ff., here p. 202).

181. 'Reichsleitung der NSDAP, Rassenpolitisches Amt, Schreiben an das RMbO', 30.7.1943, BArch, R 90/460, p. 217.

182. 'RKO, gez. Trampedach, Schreiben an den Generalkommissar in Reval, betr.: Ausreisegenehmigungen für eine Estin zum Zwecke der Eheschliessung mit einem Reichsdeutschen', 26.11.1943, BArch, R 90/460, p. 218.

183. The Nazis' approach to marriage in Poland was similarly flexible; see Kundrus, 'Regime der Differenz', esp. pp. 117ff.

184. Goebbels, *Die Tagebücher*, vol. 11, p. 587, also quoted in Müller, 'Liebe im Vernichtungskrieg', p. 262.

185. Gerhard Eschenhagen, 'Drei Jahre Prüfung im Osten: Gedanken zum deutschen Zivil-Einsatz in den besetzten Ostgebieten', 20.8.1944, BArch, R 93/6, fol 1, unpaginated.

186. 'Gauleiter Koch, Fernschreiben an Bormann', 7.8.1944, BA-MA, RH 19 II/203, also quoted in Müller, 'Liebe im Vernichtungskrieg', p. 263.

187. 'Sonderkommando 7b, Tagesmeldung an den OB der 4. Armee', 15.1.1945, BA-MA, RH 20-4/623, also quoted in Müller, 'Liebe im Vernichtungskrieg', p. 263.

Private Photographs by Wehrmacht Soldiers, Part 2

Selection and research by Petra Bopp

The soldiers also photographed local women going about their everyday lives – doing household chores, working in the field, going to church and chatting.
   Many of these photographs are either candid snapshots or posed pictures of younger women.

Fig. 19 Heinrich Kleemeyer, album, Soviet Union, 1942–3

Fig. 20 Johannes Gravemeyer, bundle of photographs, Ukraine, 1942

Fig. 21 Karl Hellbusch, bundle of photographs, Soviet Union, between 1941 and 1943

Private Photographs by Wehrmacht Soldiers, Part 2 / 247

Fig. 22 Heribert Osburg, album, Soviet Union, 1943–4

Fig. 23 Heinrich Hindersmann, bundle of photographs, 'Lithuania, 28.6.1941'

Fig. 24 Heinrich Kleemeyer, album, Soviet Union, 1942–3

Fig. 25 Gisbert Witte, bundle of photographs, Soviet Union, 1941

Fig. 26 Heinrich Hindersmann, bundle of photographs, '35°–40° cold' (Volga), Soviet Union, 1941

Fig. 27 Hermann Jaspers, album, Soviet Union, undated

Some photos show everyday encounters between soldiers and local women in villages and in the private sphere of the home.

Fig. 28 Willi Rose, bundle of photographs, 'From Donets to Don 1942'

Fig. 29 Helmut Severin, album, '12. X. 41, Suatschkiwka b. Poltawa', Ukraine

Fig. 30 Hans-Georg Schulz, album II, Ukraine, 1942

Fig. 31 Willi Rose, bundle of photographs, Ukraine, 1942

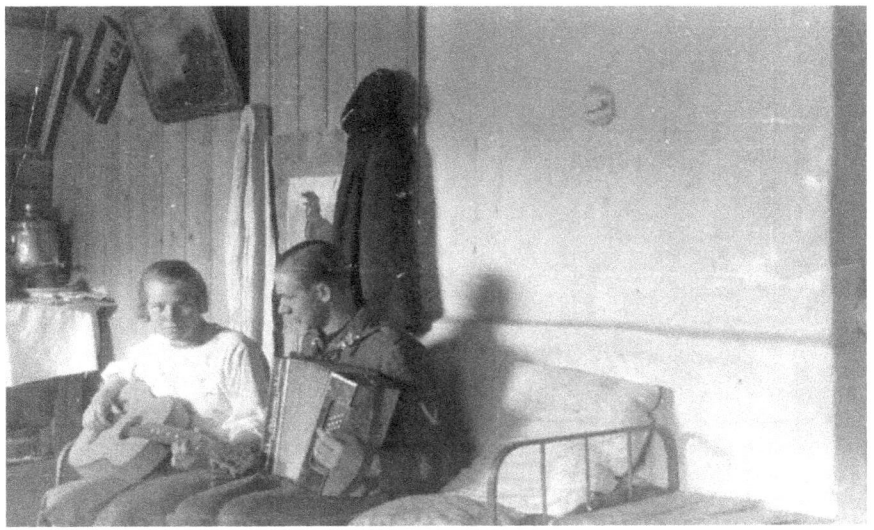

Fig. 32 Gisbert Witte, bundle of photographs, 'Quarters (Toni), Bukowa-Malwotitz', Soviet Union, 1941

Fig. 33 Heinrich Kleemeyer, album, Soviet Union, 1942–3

Fig. 34 Heinrich Hindersmann, bundle of photographs, Soviet Union, 1941

Fig. 35 Heinrich Hindersmann, bundle of photographs, 'The Soviet paradise', Soviet Union, 1941

Fig. 36 Willi Rose, bundle of photographs, Soviet Union, undated

CHAPTER 5

Occupation Children

On 21 May 1942, barely a year after German troops had invaded the Soviet Union, SS-*Oberführer* Walther-Eberhard Freiherr von Medem, the regional commissioner of Mitau (now Jelgava in Latvia), warned that the 'general military ban on marriage with Latvian women' would have serious consequences for the children of German men and Latvian women:

> The expected child [. . .], who in himself represents a welcome addition to the policy of Germanisation, will be discriminated against as if he were a Negro bastard [*Negerbastard*]. Since he cannot be legitimised on the German side despite his element of German blood, he will be rejected all the more on the Latvian side and his share of German blood will actually become a shame that attaches itself to him for life.[1]

Von Medem himself had grown up in Latvia as a Baltic German.[2] His brash comparison between Wehrmacht children in Latvia and the non-marital children of German colonists in Africa,[3] or the children of white German women and French colonial soldiers who were born during the occupation of the Rhineland and referred to as 'Rhineland bastards',[4] reveals the constructed nature of racist categories. Von Medem swaps the roles here: he puts the supposedly 'racially aware' white German occupying soldiers in the place of the Black soldiers accused of being *'triebhaft'* or 'libidinous'.[5] He was thus suggesting that the children of German men would face the same fate as the children of French colonial soldiers in Germany, who not only experienced social discrimination but were also politically persecuted and had been forcibly sterilised in the context of a secret Gestapo initiative in 1937.[6] With this argument, von Medem was also implying that the Nazis' concepts of race would have only a limited impact, and that other societies possibly did not share the exaggerated self-image of the 'Aryan master race' and had developed similar exclusion mechanisms of their own based on their respective 'racial awareness'.[7] While von Medem was actually using the comparison between Wehrmacht children and '*Negerbastarden*' to convince the German authorities of the need for cooperation with the Latvians, he was simultaneously relativising the Nazis' claim to the absolute truth of their racial ideology.

There is no record of the response to von Medem's letter. But the state's approach to the children of Wehrmacht soldiers was a topic that the civilian occupation authorities and Wehrmacht alike had been forced to grapple with all over German-occupied Europe ever since the start of the war. To demonstrate Germany's willingness to cooperate with local communities and establish a peaceful occupation regime, the OKW suggested in early 1941 that these children and their mothers – at least in a few northern and western European countries, namely, Norway, the Netherlands, Belgium, France and Britain's Channel Islands – should be given the opportunity to request child support from the fathers and have maintenance disputes handled by Wehrmacht courts.[8] Hitler adopted this plan but decided to apply it only to Norway and the Netherlands, saying that Nazi Germany had 'no racial policy interest' in France.[9] One year later, on 28 July 1942, Hitler announced his 'Regulation on Supporting the Children of German Wehrmacht Members in the Occupied Territories in Norway and the Netherlands', the aim of which was the 'preservation and promotion of racially valuable Germanic genetic material'.[10] The measures included covering the costs of childbirth, maintenance payments, benefits such as cots, housing for the mothers and children, and arranging jobs for the mothers.[11] To ensure that the mothers and children were looked after, the *Lebensborn* initiative and the National Socialist People's Welfare organisation (NSV) expanded their activities in the occupied territories.[12]

In contrast to the clear support offered to pregnant women in northern and northwestern Europe, the Nazis' view of the non-marital children of German occupying soldiers in the Soviet Union was shaped by different ideological premises. To begin with, the Nazi authorities assumed that most of these children sired there would be 'racially undesirable'.[13] Nonetheless, from the end of 1942 they began to take an interest in these children, debating the question of which of them could be 'Germanised' and which could not. Opinions on this were divided, particularly with respect to the different population groups in the Baltic countries.[14] When von Medem claimed that the children of German men and Latvian women represented a 'welcome addition to the policy of Germanisation', he was entering a hotly contested field characterised by disputes over authority. This chapter deals with how these conflicts played out and which attitudes, interests and contradictions shaped the respective arguments. I will initially focus on the demographic and 'ethnic policy' hopes and fears that the Nazi authorities associated with the Wehrmacht children. What importance did the authorities ascribe to these children in terms of Germany's future war and occupation policy? I will then look at the concrete measures implemented to register and control the children. What form did these measures take, and how did they differ from the approach in other occupied territories?

Population Policy Strategies

On 8 September 1942, *Generaloberst* Rudolf Schmidt, commander of the 2nd Panzer Division, presented Hitler with a hand-out in which he estimated that around one and a half million *Soldatenkinder* (soldiers' children) were likely to be born each year 'in the East'. Schmidt's estimate was based on a very simple extrapolation: around six million German men were stationed in the occupied territories of the Soviet Union. Half of them were said to be having sexual intercourse with local women, and in half of these cases, according to Schmidt, the encounters were 'not without consequences'. Simplifying the calculation further, Schmidt assumed that 750,000 'half-German' girls and 750,000 'half-German' boys would be born each year.[15]

Schmidt's hand-out is evidence that a high-ranking Wehrmacht officer could say to Hitler, without being challenged, that half of all German men on the front and in the occupied territories of Poland and the Soviet Union were having sexual intercourse with local women.[16] This is all the more remarkable because Schmidt did not say this in order to suggest prohibitions or regulation measures. Instead, he used completely baseless figures to calculate that a German man would father a child in one out of every two instances of sexual contact. This reflected the Nazis' fantasies of the omnipotent warrior as well as an ignorance of the women's perspective – since Schmidt did not take into account that these women often did not want to bear such children and that they knew about contraception and abortion.[17]

Despite his clearly dubious extrapolations, further steps were taken immediately after Schmidt's meeting with Hitler. The following note can be found in the reference file of Major Hans von Payr zu Enn und Caldiff from the OKW: 'The Führer fully agreed with [Schmidt's] report'.[18] And just one week later, Himmler – in his role as Reich Commissioner for the Consolidation of the Ethnic German Nation – met with Otto Hoffmann, head of Race and Settlement Main Office (RuSHA), and Erich Hilgenfeldt, head of the NSV, to discuss what should be done about the children who had already been born and those who were expected.[19] On 16 September 1942, Himmler announced the following at a meeting of SS and Police Leaders:

> I come now to an issue that will keep you very occupied in the future. The Führer, alerted by several reports, has addressed the issue that around 1 to 1 1/2 million children have been sired by German soldiers in Russia. It might be somewhat less, but it is certain to be many 100,000s or nearly 1 million.[20]

Himmler thus corroborated Schmidt's estimate with the unprovable claim that multiple reports had been submitted to Hitler confirming these figures. Other officials were far more cautious, however. The previously mentioned Major Hans von Payr zu Enn und Caldiff had expressed doubts in his summary of Schmidt's hand-out: 'An army high commander on the Eastern Front estimates that there are 6 million soldiers in the East and that 3 million of them are liaising with Russian women (based on my observations, this percentage is much too high)'.[21] Objections were soon voiced in the RMbO as well. Following an internal exchange of letters with the RKO at the start of 1943, Reich Minister Alfred Rosenberg – who was involved in an ongoing power struggle with Himmler – said it was 'improbable' that the births of 'illegitimate children of Reich Germans [. . .] would reach the numbers that [. . .] have been assumed'.[22] In the occupied territories, too, officials expected the number of children to be smaller and to actually decline over time. Himmler's liaison at the RMbO, SS-*Obergruppenführer* Gottlob Berger, summarised the estimates of the German regional commissioners in Belarus, Ukraine and the Baltic States in November 1943 and declared that the numbers were much lower than expected, but they were also 'exceptionally imprecise' because locating the children was extremely difficult or even impossible in some countries.[23]

Himmler's claim that there would be 'many 100,000s or nearly 1 million' children was therefore without any statistical foundation and testified first and foremost to the fact that he wanted to open up a new field of ethnic policy. While Schmidt justified the German interest in the Wehrmacht children born in the Soviet Union by saying that they were a 'valuable replacement for the lack of births due to the war',[24] Himmler initially argued from a negative standpoint. He said Germany had to ensure access to these children so that their mothers' societies of origin would not be significantly strengthened by the addition of hundreds of thousands of children fathered by German men. In different ways, both Himmler and Schmidt were harking back to a traditional wartime numbers game, namely, calculating a nation's own birth rate and that of its enemy and offsetting one against the other. Neither went so far as to explicitly encourage the conception of children between German men and local women in the Soviet Union, and both of them, like OKW head Wilhelm Keitel, considered the siring of such children 'in the East' to be 'undesirable' in itself.[25] But they also both suspected that, despite every effort, it would ultimately be impossible to prevent such births, so they intended to take this new reality into account in their plans for the future.

Balancing the Birth Rate
Long before the Wehrmacht invaded Poland and the Soviet Union, statisticians had compared the birth rate in Germany with that in England, France, Italy and Poland.[26] They found that, between 1928 and 1933, the birth rate had fallen in all of these countries, but it had declined the most in Germany. This led to fierce debates about the potential 'death of the people' ('*Volkstod*').[27] Friedrich Burgdörfer, the leading demographer of the time, believed that one of the main reasons for the 'adverse balance' of Germany's birth rate was the 'long-distance effect' of World War I, which had led to a 'deliberate minimisation' of family size and a 'profound change in the attitude to life'.[28] The noticeable increase in the birth rate in 1933 and 1934 was therefore celebrated as an 'unsurpassed population policy success' and the 'effect of the unique trust in the Führer that animates the German people'.[29] The triumph was short-lived, however; in 1937 the birth rate collapsed again, and it declined further after the start of the war against Poland.[30]

In June 1935, Himmler distributed a paper to all SS leaders entitled 'Birth Rate Decline: An Exhortation to the German People', which essentially stated that siring 'children of good blood' was the duty of every SS man.[31] Half a year later, in December 1935, the SS established its *Lebensborn* organisation, one of the aims of which was to promote the birth of children with a 'Nordic hereditary disposition'.[32] In a speech to his SS Group Leaders on 18 February 1937, Himmler emphasised how important it was for Germany to have a wealth of children compared to its enemies:

> A people that has very many children has the entitlement to world power and world domination. [...] A people of a good race [*gutrassig*] that has very few children has a ticket straight to the grave, to irrelevance in 50 or 100 years, to burial in 200 or 500 years.[33]

From this perspective, the realisation of the Nazis' dream of a 'Thousand Year Reich' was tied primarily to demographic conditions. Only through an abundance of children could the German *Volk* create the biological foundation for world domination and implement the Nazis' policy of domination in perpetuity; an ongoing shortage of children, by contrast, would mean the downfall of the Reich. This clearly reveals how much anxiety was attached to the thought that, on account of insufficient population growth, Germany might disappear from the global political stage and ultimately forfeit the existence of the *Volk* and the state, not to mention the 'Thousand Year Reich'.

When the war started, the need to boost the birth rate in the interest of population policy became increasingly urgent. In 1940, Hitler declared that a successful end to the war would 'confront the German *Volk* with tasks that it can only fulfil by increasing its population size'.[34] In the interests of this goal, abortions by 'Aryan' women were severely punished, home leave and opportunities for soldiers' wives to visit them at the front were encouraged to promote births, proxy marriages were simplified and posthumous marriages were allowed. Nazi officials also strove to improve the status and financial support of single mothers and children born out of wedlock.[35]

After the start of the war against the Soviet Union, Himmler encouraged every SS man to sire at least four children, since having only two children would 'mean the extinction of the people'.[36] To this end, he was even prepared to make compromises 'between the necessary quantity and the best possible quality'.[37] 'The most important thing I can and want to achieve', he wrote to SS-*Obergruppenführer* von Woyrsch in 1943, 'is for every SS man to have a child before he falls. If this makes the number of children larger overall, then – in breeding terms – I will take misbreeding [*Fehlzüchtungen*] into account'.[38] Other Nazi officials also tried to raise the birth rate. For example, at the prompting of the Reich Ministry of Justice, maternity protection laws were expanded in June 1943 to cover Danish, Dutch, Norwegian, Romanian, Swedish and Swiss women living the Reich.[39]

The Nazis additionally outlined extensive population policy plans for all occupied countries as part of their 'racial reordering of Europe'. They placed their greatest hopes in Norway, where the population was judged to be 'Nordic' according to Nazi racial doctrine; the SS even considered sending pregnant Norwegian women to southern Germany to 'Nordicise' the population there.[40] But in Norway, too, the birth rate had dropped dramatically in the preceding years. The SS publication *Schwert und Wiege* (Sword and Cradle) from 1943 attributed this to a misguided liberalism which had led 'the Norwegian, in his morbid fear of being considered backward' to follow leftist reformers and Jewish doctors, resulting in the degeneration of morality as regards sexuality and marriage, the increased use of contraceptives and the 'propagation of abortion with impunity following the Soviet model'. As a consequence, Norwegians were said to lack 'any sense of duty towards [their] people and the Germanic race'. While the 'Norwegian mind-set' was thus dismissed as being incomprehensible, the Nazis considered the 'racial values and hereditary health of the Norwegian people' to be at least as good as that of the Germans. They therefore believed it was necessary to heighten the Norwegians' awareness of 'the importance of race' so they would once again conceive of themselves as a 'Nordic people' and would fight together with the Germans.[41]

The German occupation authorities hoped to be able to increase the birth rate in Norway in two ways. First, they wanted to teach the Norwegians a sense of 'racial awareness' and 'Nordic pride' in order to encourage them to have more Norwegian children. In 1941, SS-*Obergruppenführer* Wilhelm Rediess, the general of the German police in Norway, drew up a three-year plan specifically for this purpose.[42] Second, the German occupiers themselves were supposed to sire offspring with Norwegian women. Rediess informed Himmler on 5 December 1940 that the signs pointed to a significant rise in births from the non-marital children of members of the Wehrmacht, SS and police. Himmler responded that he would welcome 'every child [. . .] we get from there'.[43] The *Lebensborn* branch in Norway, which was established in the spring of 1941, subsequently concerned itself first and foremost with Wehrmacht children and their mothers.

With respect to Eastern Europe and Russia, the Nazis' population policy was completely different. Although the SS did establish a *Lebensborn* department in Poland with the aim of acquiring children with 'valuable genetic material' for Germany, the population as a whole did not fall into this category in the opinion of the Nazis' race theorists. According to '*Ostforscher*' ('Eastern researcher') Erich Keyser, one reason for this was an increase in 'ethnically mixed marriages' in the nineteenth century, which had taken place in cases of 'identical denomination' but 'without the previously customary consideration given to differences in blood', leading to the 'racial inferiority' of the offspring. Keyser also blamed the situation on the expulsion of Germans from 'the countries of the East' after the end of World War I, which had allowed the 'Slavic flood' to spread, as he said.[44] Demographers at international conferences in the mid-1930s generally claimed to see a threat of 'overpopulation' in Eastern Europe, especially Poland.[45] Other Nazi 'Eastern researchers' such as Theodor Oberländer and Anton Reithinger blamed 'overpopulation pressure' for the allegedly untenable social and economic conditions in Poland and Russia.[46] As Götz Aly and Susanne Heim show, these images of 'Polish overpopulation' and 'German underpopulation' had increasingly come to be associated with the 'Jewish question' even before the invasion of Poland. For example, in his book *Das Judentum im osteuropäischen Raum* (Jews in Eastern Europe) from 1938, Peter-Heinz Seraphim complained of a 'Jewish birth surplus'.[47] All of this shaped the Nazis' view of Eastern Europe and stoked German fears of being overrun by 'vast uncivilised masses'.[48]

The war against the Soviet Union exacerbated this situation from Germany's perspective because birth rates in the Reich continued to fall.[49] Based on experiences after World War I, Reich Health Leader Leonardo Conti mostly feared the 'gaps [. . .] in the body of the people caused by the war' – the 'loss of men' and the associated 'surplus of women'.[50] The prediction that the steadily dropping birth rate in Germany would be countered by a tremendous surplus of births amongst the 'peoples in the East' became an increasingly pressing issue. In contrast to other occupied territories, local women in the Soviet Union were not forbidden from terminating their pregnancies; in fact, the German authorities were supposed to encourage it.[51]

Reichsleiter Martin Bormann spoke of 'Slavic birth pressure'[52] as early as July 1942 and commented in January 1944 after a discussion with Hitler:

> I urgently referred multiple times before to the situation that will exist after the end of this war: We must keep in mind the map of peoples in Europe and Asia from the years 1850, 1870 and 1900 and 1945: The Asiatic peoples are multiplying at a much faster pace than the Nordic peoples [. . .]. If this ratio were to stay the same, then it would be of no use whatsoever to our Nordic peoples if we win this war, because in a hundred years at the latest they will have been crushed by the vast Asiatic mass of people.[53]

Like Himmler and Hitler, Bormann considered population numbers to be the decisive weapon in the fight against 'Asia', a term he used here – very much in the style of the time[54] – as a synonym for the Soviet Union. While the people in Poland and the 'occupied Eastern territories' were often outwardly indistinguishable from Germans, there was no doubt in his mind that 'the Asiatic' was different. Bormann's word choice once again emphasised the threat that the regime thought it was facing: that of an alien, uncivilised 'mass of people' which was multiplying unchecked and would inevitably 'crush' the 'Nordic peoples'.

A notice published in the SS newspaper *Das Schwarze Korps* on 25 March 1943 reveals the fruits born of this fear of superior numbers.[55] Under the sub-heading 'If the soul were to die . . .', the author reported that Stalin had ordered the compulsory impregnation of 'all Soviet Russian women' for whom 'fertilisation [was] no longer possible due to the death or absence of the husband': 'The regulation is based on the tremendous losses of men in the Soviet Union and the decline in birth rates expected as a result'. The author went on to say that a certain 'soullessness of the Russians' was apparent in that, after birth, these children were to be 'taken from the mothers and housed in state homes'.[56] Nazi officials happened to be flirting with similar ideas at the time,[57] but this was not mentioned in the notice.[58]

Interestingly, the fact that German soldiers, through their 'lack of discipline', were contributing to the rise in the enemy's birth rate and thus strengthening their opponent was barely addressed. This was apparently viewed as an unavoidable reality of war. Instead, Nazi officials focused on whether and how they could get hold of the children who had acquired their mother's nationality according to the law.

Control Measures

A year before the children of German men in the occupied Soviet territories became an item on Himmler's political agenda, they had already attracted the attention of the RMbO and RKO. Though officials were divided in their opinion of the 'racial value' of the children,[59] both sides agreed that they had to look reality in the eye and clarify the 'legal and ethnic [*volkstumsmässig*] position of the children'.[60] But no children had been born by this point, so the discussion developed haltingly. When the previously mentioned 'Regulation on Supporting the Children of German Wehrmacht Members in Norway and the Netherlands' was published in the Reich Law Gazette at the end of July 1942,[61] Ludwig Runte from the RMbO raised the question of whether there was a need for a standardised approach to dealing with the children in the 'occupied Eastern territories' as well, or at least in the Baltic countries. In his opinion, this would depend first and foremost on the number of 'cases to come into consideration'.⁶²

While the officials in the RMbO and RKO grappled with the issue of a regulated approach, the Reich Chancellery began to hammer out a 'Führer Decree on Supporting the Illegitimate Children of Reich Germans from the Occupied Eastern Territories'. In December 1942, Hans Heinrich Lammers, Reich Minister and Head of the Reich Chancellery, sent the first draft of this decree to all of the authorities involved.⁶³ This was followed by months of consultation between the various departments in the RKO and RMbO. Reich Minister Rosenberg argued for only registering the children to begin with and postponing all questions of 'racial selection' and child support until after the war was over. Since Rosenberg was expecting much lower numbers of children than Himmler and the Reich Chancellery, he saw no reason to claim the children for Germany and cause turmoil in their local families.⁶⁴ Friedrich Trampedach, head of the Political Affairs department in the RKO, argued the opposite, saying that it was necessary to clearly indicate 'German interest' in the children early on by providing material support to mother and child even before the birth. He believed this was the only way to guarantee the children would grow up healthy.⁶⁵

The final version of the decree that Hitler presented to senior Reich officials in October 1943 showed no concern for the local population 'in the East', nor did it make any provisions for supporting the mothers. First and foremost, it was a proclamation of German interest in the children:

Decree of the Führer
on supporting the illegitimate children of Germans in the occupied Eastern territories from 11 October 1943

I.

Children who are born illegitimately to native women in the occupied Eastern territories and whose sires are German will be identified and listed by the regional commissioners in the countryside, by SS and Police Leaders in the cities.

In the territories not under civilian administration, this identification and listing will be carried out by the offices of the SS and police as well as the Wehrmacht.

The offices carrying out this registration shall forward their completed lists through their superior authorities to the Reichsführer-SS, in his role as Reich Commissioner for the Consolidation of the Ethnic German Nation, or to the office appointed by him.

II.

The Reich will take responsibility for the welfare of the registered children if they are racially valuable.

This selection will be made by the Reichsführer-SS, in his role as Reich Commissioner for the Consolidation of the Ethnic German Nation, in cooperation with the NSV. Furthermore, the Reichsführer-SS will prescribe measures for the further upbringing of the children in consultation with the NSV. In territories under the control of the civilian administration, the Reich Minister for the Occupied Eastern Territories shall be involved in both cases.

III.

Further details will be arranged by mutual agreement between the Reich Minister for the Occupied Eastern Territories, the Reichsführer-SS in his role as Reich Commissioner for the Consolidation of the Ethnic German Nation and Chief of the German Police, the Head of the Wehrmacht High Command and the leader of the Party Chancellery.

IV.

All costs arising from the measures above will be born by the Reich after further agreement between the Reich Minister of Finance, the Reich Minister for the Occupied Eastern Territories and the Reich Treasurer of the Nazi Party.

Führer Headquarters, 11 October 1943

> Der Führer
> signed Adolf Hitler
>
> Reich Minister and Head of the Reich Chancellery
> signed Dr Lammers[66]

With this decree, Hitler declared that policies for dealing with occupation children were the responsibility of Himmler, who was to be involved in all issues pertaining to the children in his role as Reich Commissioner for the Consolidation of the Ethnic German Nation. The first main task of everyone involved was to track down the children. To press ahead with locating the children and discussing their legal status and upbringing, SA-*Gruppenführer* Wilhelm von Allwörden, who was head of the Economic Affairs department of the RMbO, presented a written draft of a 'Regulation on the Implementing Provisions for the Führer's Decree' at the end of November 1943.[67] In the months that followed, employees of the RMbO, RKO, RKF, Reich Ministry of the Interior and OKW discussed the specific form of the provisions.

Registration

In view of the widely diverging estimates regarding the number of children, the officials first needed to conduct as thorough a registration process as possible. But the measures intended for this proved to be difficult to implement. For example, in the early phase of the German occupation of Estonia and Latvia, some couples applied for marriage permits on the basis of an existing pregnancy, but looking at the history of the occupation as a whole, this was the exception. In many more cases, neither the German men nor the local women had any interest in giving the German authorities an insight into their sexual encounters.

There were many reasons for the women to want to conceal a pregnancy. If the sexual contact had been fleeting or violent, a woman might not know anything about the man who impregnated her, and she might try to repress the memory of the event as much as possible or even fear that she would be branded a 'German's whore', traitor or collaborator. As explained in the preceding chapter, such an accusation could lead to social exclusion, severe punishment or even death. Some women tried to terminate their pregnancy, even though this was often difficult and expensive, as illustrated by a letter from the Wehrmacht judge Hans Meier-Brennecke to his wife. A Ukrainian woman named Olga, who worked as a cleaner in his office, had admitted to him that she was pregnant:

> Since her only possessions are the clothes on her back, it is a mystery to us how this Ukrainian-German *Mischling* (a soldier in Poltava was the culprit) is supposed to grow up and exist. She should have an abortion, but the Ukrainian doctor demanded 1,000 RM!'[68]

The fact that Meiner-Brennecke took an abortion into consideration but did not advise the woman to report to the German authorities raises the question of the extent to which the men in the occupied territories even knew that the regime was interested in such children.

Other women opted to give birth to their children but then either give them away or pass them off as the offspring of another man. For example, a woman named Tatjana Kosoris reported that her mother and grandmother placed her out in the garden right after she was born. Only after the neighbours found her there did her mother and grandmother take her in as a supposed foundling. In this way, the two women hoped to avoid discrimination against mother and child.[69] Reich Minister Rosenberg assumed that married women in particular, whose husbands – soldiers, partisans or forced labourers – had not been living at home at the time of the conception would take drastic measures to avoid 'family unrest'.[70] Women who were in love with the father of their child might also prefer to keep his identity secret, not least because otherwise they would attract the attention of the German authorities and be subjected to a variety of examinations and control measures.

In general, registration offered a number of disadvantages to the women and few if any advantages. While the majority of pregnant women in Norway and the Netherlands received material and social support from the German authorities – such as jobs, children's clothing, housing and obstetric care in a *Lebensborn* home or a hospital with German nurses – no comparable options existed in the occupied countries of the Soviet Union.[71] Although the RKO had suggested introducing similar support measures for local women 'in the East',[72] and a handwritten note from Himmler from September 1942 mentioned 'monthly payment for the mother',[73] nothing of this sort was put into practice. A few women were apparently accepted into NSV homes,[74] but their number is likely to have been very small. Another attempt by Himmler in July 1944 to entice women to register by promising them clothing and prams also ran aground; at the time, in the middle of the Wehrmacht's rearguard action, the occupying power would hardly have been in a position to provide such benefits.[75]

The German men often had just as little reason to report the pregnancy of a woman with whom they had had sexual contact. Many of them probably never even found out about the pregnancy. Even if the relationship had been consensual or romantic, the father might be transferred to a different part of the front before the woman realised she was pregnant. If the man did find out but had a wife or fiancée back in Germany (and wanted to keep it that way), it made sense for him to hide his sexual infidelity. Other men might have feared punishment for sexually transgressing 'racial' boundaries. As mentioned earlier, it was relatively uncommon for this to result in severe sanctions, but a child who was a symbol and evidence of such a transgression could make a man especially vulnerable.[76] Overall, the reality in the occupied territories of the Soviet Union soon made it clear that Himmler's handwritten note of 17 September 1942, which said that the children should be registered by 'military superiors',[77] would be much more difficult to implement than initially expected.

The authorities seem to have been all the more eager to determine who should be responsible for registering the children and how the process could be set in motion. Himmler wanted to assign the task to his SS and Police Leaders. Rosenberg, by contrast, argued that the registration of the children could only be carried out by lower-level authorities – meaning the regional commissioners – because they alone could win the trust of the women, and it was important to carry out the registration in a way that avoided any 'disgruntlement amongst the population in the occupied Eastern territories'.[78] The RKO agreed with Rosenberg's argument and additionally wanted to coordinate the registration process with the administrative procedures that were already in place in the youth welfare offices.[79] The Führer's decree of 11 October 1943 resolved this debate by means of a compromise: the respective regional commissioners would be responsible for the occupation children in rural areas, while the SS and Police Leaders would be responsible in the cities. In the territories not under civilian administration, the registration would be handled by the offices of the SS and police as well as the Wehrmacht. The resulting data was to be forwarded directly to Himmler in his role as RKF or to the offices specified by him.[80]

How the data was supposed to be collected had not yet been determined, however. In Norway, officials had tried to completely bypass the local authorities by forcing the women in question to contact the German offices directly,[81] but this approach had been judged inadequate by various parties. It was generally assumed that effective control was impossible without the cooperation of the local authorities.[82] In April 1944, the RKO finally specified three technically feasible registration methods: first, local registrars could notify the regional commissioners or SS and Police Leaders; second, the 'German sires [*Erzeuger*]' could notify the Wehrmacht units, Wehrmacht retinue or civilian administration; or third, the local women and German men could notify the officials who processed marriage applications, as these were sometimes submitted on the basis of a pregnancy.[83]

Since everyone involved assumed that only a fraction of the actual pregnancies would be reported if registration were voluntary, the subsequent discussions revolved around how German officials might cooperate with the local authorities. The RKO had already suggested in January 1943 that local registrars should be required to notify the youth welfare office – that is, the respective general commissariat – whenever a birth involving a 'illegitimate Reich German sire' was entered in the register of births.[84] The Nazi officials knew that even this method would not lead to the registration of all children, since many children would be born to married women who would enter their husband's name instead of that of the biological father in the birth register. Despite this limitation, however, this method was deemed the most promising.[85]

But in Estonia, Latvia, Lithuania and Ukraine, for example, there were no provisions for entering the name of an 'illegitimate sire' in the register of births.[86] Burmeister from the RKO therefore suggested intervening in the operations of local registrars and making it generally compulsory for the 'illegitimate mother' to 'name the illegitimate sire when registering the child with the registrar'.[87] Since this procedure would have deeply impacted local family policy,[88] no agreement was reached on it. In July 1944, after the war situation had turned and the Germans were being forced to retreat ever further, Himmler ultimately decided against such a regulation in his role as RKF. He said it was 'already apparent that the Latvians and Estonians are making efforts to acquire the illegitimate children of Germans for the Latvian and Estonian people [*Volkstum*]'.[89] In light of this, he felt it was important not to make the regional authorities aware of the fact that the Germans were also interested in the children – especially as it was thought that 'the Bolshevists' would 'specifically search for and abduct German *Soldatenkinder* in the territories they now occupy' in order to 'use them against the German people'.[90] He said the registration should therefore be restricted to the 'territories still in German hands', primarily the RKO, and should be conducted 'in a quiet way without involving the country's local authorities as far as possible'.[91] In mid-1944, therefore, Himmler pragmatically called off any further efforts to devise a formal procedure and instead argued for taking as many children as possible 'as unobtrusively as possible'.[92]

While the authorities were still debating their precise approach without reaching any conclusions, the 4th Army in Army Area Centre had already started registering children. From the summer of 1943, some raion headquarters began enclosing an attachment with the subject 'Registration of illegitimate children of Reich Germans' with their monthly situation reports.[93] The authors of these reports were required to list the child's name and date of birth, the mother's name and place of residence, and the father's name and location.[94] In most of these reports, however, the subject lines were followed only by 'nil return' or 'nothing to report'.[95]

But there were exceptions. The 'Situation report for the Smolensk Raion for the period from 15 July to 15 August 1943' said 'the number of illegitimate children of Reich Germans was determined to be 13',[96] though no further details were given about these children. By contrast, the situation report for the 'District of Smolensk City', also from August 1943, included a table listing twelve children with their forenames and birth dates. The table also provided information about the 'mother's forename and surname', the 'address of the mother and child in Smolensk', the 'father's name' (that is, name of the mother's father) and the 'mother's ethnicity' ('*Volkstumszugehörigkeit*'). For '*Volkstumszugehörigkeit*', all of the mothers were reported as being 'Russian'. There was one final comment beneath the table: 'The names of the sires have not yet been determined'.[97] It is unclear whether the fathers were actually Germans or whether the list is simply an excerpt from the local register of births recording children born out of wedlock.

'Attachment 2 to the monthly situation report of Raion Headquarters I/302 Karoynowo for the month of July', dated 15 August 1943, is the only document evaluated in the context of this study that includes more detailed information about one of the 'sires'. The mother of the child in question named non-commissioned officer Anton E. as the father. She did not know his Feldpost number or home address, but she provided the address of a comrade from his unit, Fritz F. As 'evidence for the paternity of the German Wehrmacht member', the woman attached a photograph that Anton E. had sent to Smolensk two weeks earlier.[98] This illustrates just how insubstantial the information gathered by the Wehrmacht actually was. It would have taken considerable effort to identify the biological fathers of these children, if it were possible at all.

Army Group Centre had registered a total of around 70 children by April 1944.[99] This low figure confirms the assumption of the regional commissioners, RKO and RMbO that the number of children would not be nearly as large as predicted by Schmidt and Himmler in September 1942. Gottlob Berger, head of the SS Leadership Office, also had to concede this on 17 November 1943. He said the number of 'illegitimate children of Reich Germans' in the general commissariats of Estonia, Latvia and Lithuania was likely to be 1,000 to 2,000, but he did not rule out the possibility that 'the number would be several times higher with accurate registration'.[100] But this 'accurate registration' never took place. The general commissioner in Riga declared in his situation report of 29 April 1944 that the total number of non-marital children amounted to around 3,000 annually and had 'not risen significantly' since the German troops arrived. Even if it were assumed that some of these children – just like some of the children born in wedlock – were the offspring of German soldiers, the figures were nowhere near the initial estimates.[101]

Locating 'Shares of German Blood'
'Racial evaluation' was the central factor in determining whether children should ultimately belong to their father's native country. On 9 October 1942, barely four weeks after Wehrmacht children in the Soviet

Union became an item on Himmler's political agenda, Reich Minister Rosenberg brought up the topic as well and outlined the dilemma:

> As fundamentally undesirable as it is for Germans to engage in extramarital sexual relations with ethnically alien women, it is also important to prevent a flow of German blood into the alien peoples of the East through the children sired illegitimately by Germans while the German *Volkstum* [ethnicity] loses valuable strength at the same time.[102]

In his view, the notion that the blood of German men flowed through the veins of these children is what established their connection to Germany. As Christina von Braun has shown, images of blood serve as a 'symbol of the cohesion of a community' in many religions and cultures. Blood stands for an unbreakable bond that links and unifies different members of a group.[103] It was in keeping with this that Rosenberg used the metaphor of blood to give a sheen of reality to the dream of the 'Aryan *Volkskörper*' – imagined to be the unified physical, mental and spiritual body of the people.[104] The 'purification of the blood community' thus became a story of salvation[105] as well as the basis of a 'healthy *Volkskörper*' and an invincible community.

Rosenberg's talk of a 'flow of German blood' that would be introduced to the 'peoples in the East' through the children of German men also picked up on the dynamic element of this image, namely, that blood could be 'lost' or gained. The concept of blood as something like a spiritual substance that had to be protected and potentiated was a permanent aspect of the Nazis' Germanisation policies in the occupied Polish and Soviet territories. Himmler was operating on the basis of this notion when, with respect to various 'Germanisation measures' – not least the abduction of 'racially good' children[106] – he postulated in September 1942: 'Amongst all the peoples we have before us, everything in this mishmash – be it Pole, Ukrainian, White Russian, etc. – which has good blood in this giant organism, if I take the people to be a complete organism, every distilled pure drop of blood will be taken over or, if it can no longer be carried over, it will be extinguished.'[107]

'Blood', as this passage shows, was considered a resource that could and should be viewed in isolation from the people who carried it. Moreover, '*Rassenmischlinge*' or 'racial mongrels' – including occupation children – were thought to carry both 'good' and 'bad' blood in their bodies. In the context of the Nazis' ethnic and racial policies, these supposed components were referred to as different '*Blutsteile*' or '*Blutsanteile*' ('portions' or 'shares' of blood). Depending on their quantitative and qualitative strength, certain shares of blood were said to be dominant or subordinate. But even the subordinate shares, according to Himmler, would continue to exist and be passed on:

> Even the child that springs from the liaison of a German man with a racially poor Russian woman is an improvement for the Russians; because we do not know what will suddenly come out of this blood in the third, fourth, sixth and even later generations if it once again encounters a portion of blood of the same kind.[108]

The fact that Himmler thought 'shares' of German blood would have any significant impact after multiple generations shows just how delusional his racial ideology was. Furthermore, the definition of who had 'blood of the same kind' ('*gleichgeartetes Blut*') in their veins was subject to change and – particularly in the case of so-called '*Rassenmischlinge*' – was often a matter of debate. After the Wehrmacht invaded Poland and the Soviet Union, Nazi administrators therefore found it necessary to define the fundamental concepts of Nazi racial theory more precisely in order to better control and regulate the increased contact with individuals classified as 'Slavic'. This applied to encounters in the occupied territories as well as interactions with male and female 'Eastern workers'.[109]

Up until this point, a distinction had only been made between '*artfremdes Blut*' ('racially alien blood') and '*artverwandtes Blut*' ('racially related blood'). The people considered 'racially alien' were Jews, first and foremost, but also Sinti, Roma and Black people, while 'racially related' applied to 'the blood of all peoples who are settled cohesively in Europe',[110] including 'Russians as well as [...] Norwegians'.[111] At the end of 1941, the Main Staff Office of the RKF made an attempt to clarify the key concept of 'racially related blood'. The Reich Security Main Office and the Race and Settlement Main Office supported this course of action, and a few months later, on 23 March 1942, the RKF published a new conceptual formulation: 'racially related peoples' ('*artverwandte Völker*') would now be differentiated according to whether their blood was 'Germanic' ('*stammesgleich*' or 'from the same stock') or 'non-Germanic' ('*nichtstammesgleich*' or 'not from the same stock').[112] Russians were now categorised as 'not from the same stock', while Norwegians were considered to be 'from the same stock'.

This new definition of March 1942 was explicitly intended to prevent the sexual transgression of 'racial' boundaries and siring of '*Mischlingskinder*' or 'mixed-blood children'. Himmler had declared that 'the danger of race-mixing threatens the German *Volk* not only on account of some alien race or other, but through a mixing with the blood of peoples not of the same stock in Europe, above all with Slavdom'.[113] As far back as 1924, Hitler had claimed in *Mein Kampf* that 'racial mixture' led to the degeneration and infertility of the 'higher race'.[114] From a scientific perspective, the concept of races as separate species that could not bear offspring together had been debunked by the end of the nineteenth century at the latest. Despite this, the belief that '*Mischlinge*' or people with 'mixed blood' were often infertile and susceptible to disease continued to be fostered.[115] Individuals defined as '*Mischlinge*' could still contribute to 'desirable population growth', however. This was most apparent in the new definition formulated by the Main Staff Office of the RKF, which attributed a special status to 're-Germanisable members of non-Germanic peoples'. People with 'portions of blood of the same stock' could therefore be assimilated even if they belonged to a 'people not of the same stock'.[116] It was in the context of this 'Germanisation policy' that the usefulness of the category of 'blood' was most apparent. 'Shares of blood' ultimately could not be measured – despite a good deal of research in this area[117] – but under certain conditions they could always been claimed or denied.

The idea of the 'supremacy of Germanic blood' also shaped the approach to dealing with Wehrmacht children from the Soviet Union. Nazi officials wanted to identify them and then isolate their 'German shares of blood' and make them 'usable for the *Volksgemeinschaft*'[118] so the children would not turn against Germany at some point. Himmler had said that, in the hands of the enemy, these children could become a particular danger because, as bearers of their fathers' 'German shares of blood', they possessed a 'racially identical soul' and a special knowledge of 'Germandom'.[119] If, however, it were possible to win over the 'racially valuable' children amongst them for the benefit of the 'German *Volksgemeinschaft*', it was thought that the children could be of use for Germany's future consolidation of power 'in the East'.[120]

Himmler and others planned to sift out the 'racially desirable' occupation children while they were still young and malleable. Himmler's idea was to bring the children to Germany and socialise them in a German environment before they had been 'incited by the alien ethnic group [*Volkstum*]'. They were to be raised as Germans in children's homes or foster families until they were old enough to undergo a final Nazi racial examination. It was still too early to implement such ideas, however. This racial examination was supposed to cover physical criteria as well as cultural and social adaptive performance, but the children themselves were still infants whose physical attributes and, above all, 'character' traits could not yet be judged. The responsible officials therefore faced considerable uncertainty when it came to selecting the children.

Himmler and Hitler generally suspected that 'undesirable' children would be easier to identify than 'racially good' ones:

> The local offices consistently report that only the more inferior lot of ethnically alien mothers is prepared to place their children in the care of others. In general, it is not exactly the best of the ethnically alien women who have children by German soldiers, and yet another negative selection takes place in that it is the less characterful amongst them who admit to the birth of a child by a German soldier, and only the more inferior lot of these, in turn, is prepared to give the child to a German foster family.[121]

A non-German woman who chose to have a child with a German (that is, a foreigner) was automatically viewed suspiciously by the Nazis' race ideologists; this applied to women who were considered to be 'of alien stock' ('*fremdstämmig*') as well as to those classified as 'Germanic'.[122] Since women were defined and judged primarily on the basis of their function as mothers, a woman who was willing to give away her child could not be a good mother. As a consequence, she was considered 'racially inferior' because she deviated from the ideal concept of femininity. This 'racial' evaluation of the mother, which was based on gender-specific assumptions, also influenced how her child would be judged.

The discussion of 'negative selection' also brought up the notion of 'adverse selection', which was common in eugenics. The thinking behind this was that modern medicine and social reforms had disrupted the process of 'natural selection' and turned it into its exact opposite. It was now the 'inferior' specimens that would survive and multiply disproportionately because they engaged in 'nearly animalistic' copulation and 'unrestrained reproduction'.[123] 'Racially desirable' children, by contrast, were thought to be much more difficult to get hold of because even though their mothers were from an 'alien ethnic group', these women – unlike the 'inferior' women – felt a bond with their environment and demonstrated traits such as loyalty, strength of will, honour and pride.[124] A 'racially desirable' woman who was expecting a child fathered by a German would thus presumably not be willing either to give away her child or leave her social environment and move to Germany.[125]

The ambiguity surrounding these children and the fears associated with them – namely, that 'racially good' children would remain in their 'alien ethnic group' while 'inferior' ones threatened to infiltrate the German *Volk* – were a source of concern for the responsible officials. On 18 September 1942, Hans von Payr zu Enn und Caldiff from the War Economy and Armaments Office of the Wehrmacht High Command suggested the following method of identifying occupation children:

> Following the convention of designating Jews as 'Israel' and 'Sarah', the illegitimate children under discussion here should be given the names 'Friedrich' or 'Luise' in addition to their Russian forenames. Head of OKW forwarded procedure to WFSt. [Wehrmacht leadership staff] with the comment 'A new area of work!'.[126]

The outwardly unidentifiable occupation children would thus have been visibly marked. The analogy to the mandatory identification of Jews indicates that the officials wanted to assign these children to their own place in the 'racial pyramid', as they were thought to cross 'racial' boundaries and belong both to German society and to the country of their mothers.[127] While this would have stigmatised the Wehrmacht children, the suggestion also reveals the Nazis' fascination with the children. The OKW was not discussing whether to give the children random German names; by suggesting that they be named 'Friedrich' and 'Luise', the military was harking back to King Friedrich Wilhelm III of Prussia and his wife, Queen Luise, both of whom were considered the epitome of Prussian virtue. Luise in particular had given rise to a veritable cult even during her lifetime, and her glorification as a kind of Prussian Madonna persisted into the Weimar era, especially in German nationalist and monarchist circles.[128] One might therefore wonder whether the suggestion was a concession by the OKW to German soldiers, who feared their offspring could fall victim to the Nazis' extermination policies.

In the end, the proposed plan was not discussed any further. In reality, the civilian occupation authorities, including Reich Minister Rosenberg, tended to want to conceal the children's German 'share of blood' in order to avoid causing unrest in the local societies in the occupied territories. For instance, the RMbO suggested avoiding German forenames for Estonian-German children.[129] In retrospect, this latter measure seems especially remarkable because German forenames were already very common in some regions – at least in Estonia and Latvia, which were widely multi-lingual – and such names were not a direct indication that a child had a German father.[130]

The closer Germany moved towards military defeat, the more obvious it became that the initially high estimates concerning the number of children and their importance to Nazi Germany had been an exaggerated fantasy. On 4 July 1944, Himmler noted that the number of non-marital children of German men who had been registered by the NSV in Estonia, Latvia, Lithuania and Belarus amounted to fewer than 500, with less an third of them – around 150 – expected to be 'valuable or usable'.[131] Though Himmler could assume that the actual number of children was far higher than the number registered, the issue had clearly proven to be politically marginal.

However, this did not dissuade Himmler from wanting to acquire the children for the 'German *Volksgemeinschaft*'. As late as July 1944 he met with Otto Ziegenbein, a Nazi Party district leader, and Walter Leiter, head of the welfare department of the RKO, to discuss further measures.[132] And Himmler was not the only one still making plans for the children in mid-1944. One month earlier, in June 1944, General Georg von Unold, Supreme Quartermaster of Army Group Central, suggested the following:

> In the course of the war, around 500,000 children have been born in the occupied Eastern territories who are of 50% German descent. From the aspect of 'biological warfare', the question is whether and when these children should be transferred to Germany. O.Qu. [*Oberquartiermeister*; R. M.] suggests bringing Russian children under 10 years of age to the Reich and starting with a transport of 10–20,000 children 8–10 years old.[133]

Only 500 children had been registered by this point, but von Unold was still blustering about half a million. His proposal bore little relation to reality. Instead, it illustrates the fantasies of power and potency that some Nazis still harboured even as – or perhaps precisely because – they were confronted with military defeat. The degree to which the children were repeatedly used over the years as a surface for projecting racist visions of the future can also be seen in the many initiatives and attempts made by various Nazi authorities to get a handle on the alleged problem.

'Racial Selection'
The issue of 'racial' evaluation was debated at length, nonetheless. For the authorities involved, there were three main questions: when should 'racial selection' take place, which criteria should be applied, and who should carry out the evaluation? The first draft of the Führer's decree of December 1942 called for registering the children as quickly as possible but delaying the 'racial selection' until a later date.[134] Burmeister from the RKO thought this was counterproductive:

The planned regulation would not achieve its intended purpose if the upbringing of the illegitimate child were left to the child's mother who, as mentioned, is even the legal representative of the child. Contrary to the view taken in the decree, therefore, it will be necessary to make the racial selection as early as possible, which can happen by assessing the parents.[135]

From Burmeister's perspective, early classification was necessary for quickly separating the children from their mothers, or at least ensuring control over the mothers. But since the logic behind the Nazis' 'racial hygiene' programme deemed that children could only be 'racially' evaluated after their hair colour, eye colour, head shape, physique and 'character' had developed – meaning that they had to have at least matured into young adults – Burmeister suggested assessing the children's parents instead.[136]

Reich Minister Rosenberg agreed with this argument and even expanded upon it by insisting that the 'racial selection' should apply not only to the child and its parents, but also to their '*Sippen*' or 'kinship groups'. The 'racial appearance', capabilities and 'attitude' of these individuals were to be repeatedly reviewed until the child came of age. Rosenberg based this proposal on what was known as the '*Sippenfragebogen*' or 'kinship questionnaire', which public health officers also gave to couples applying for marriage loans.[137] The 'kinship questionnaire' covered the education, health and family status of the applicants as well as that of the parents and siblings of both partners.[138] Rosenberg additionally wanted all family members to undergo a 'hereditary health examination'. But even while this plan was being worked out, Rosenberg qualified his argument by admitting that such extensive measures would not be possible during the war on account of a shortage of personnel and finances. 'Due to the technical difficulties', he said, the same applied to the welfare and education measures set out in the Führer's decree. The only realistic plan at the time, according to Rosenberg, was to record the number of children and where they lived.[139]

Rosenberg's ideal of 'racial selection' reveals the fundamental weakness of the Nazis' mania for control and regulation. Nazi officials knew there was no absolutely certain process for selecting the children. The benchmarks for 'racial evaluation' varied from place to place and depended on the phase of the war and the level of knowledge and norms of the individuals responsible.[140] Rosenberg's sprawling plan also prompts the question of whether he brought it into play mainly to relativise the approaches proposed by others – especially Himmler – and cast doubt on their feasibility. Rosenberg not only thought that

Himmler's figures were totally overblown, he had different ideas about how to deal with the local population, at least in the Baltics. In his view, there was absolutely no need to remove occupation children from these societies because he harboured visions of the collective 'Germanisation of entire peoples', particularly the Estonians and Latvians, whom he considered '*artverwandt*' or 'racially related'.[141]

Himmler, by contrast, wanted to assemble the children and their mothers in 'registration homes' under the authority of the NSV, where they would be 'racially' examined by employees of the Race and Settlement Main Office.[142] The findings from these examinations regarding the 'attitude of the mothers and the state of the children' were to be forwarded to the Higher SS and Police Leaders, who were ultimately responsible for deciding on each child's future. If the evaluation was positive, mother and child were to be 'Germanised' and 'transferred to the Reich'. If it became apparent over time that some of the children selected in this way were developing negatively, Himmler said they would be summarily sent back to where they had come from.[143]

Since Hitler's decree of 11 October 1943 had made Himmler the main official responsible for the registration and selection of the children, the civilian administrative authorities in the occupied territories faced the threat of being excluded from the process entirely.[144] The RKO therefore tried to play on the importance of the regional commissioners who decided on the 'racial suitability' and 'hereditary health' of women in Norway and the Netherlands. As this arrangement was said to have produced only positive results thus far, the RKO argued that it made sense to assign this responsibility to the regional commissioners in the 'occupied Eastern territories' as well. They could then promptly inform the NSV of the findings in each case.[145]

From mid-1944, the 'racial review' of the children began to play a diminishing role, at least for the politicians in Berlin. Himmler had already made it clear that he wanted to bring as many children as possible to Germany, even though he now assumed the majority of them would be 'racially undesirable'.[146] Kinkelin from the RMbO put forward a very similar argument in July 1944; he said that, while every child needed to be assessed, the aim at this point in the war could not be to measure the children against the conventional criteria for evaluating 'ethnic aliens':

> When it comes to the question of dealing with the illegitimate children of Germans [. . .] such strict standards do not need to be applied because in these cases, after all, we are dealing with the child of a German [. . .], so it has half

an element of German blood. The child is therefore not as alien to us as the mother of an alien ethnicity [*Volkstum*]. Because there is also German blood in the child, more lenient standards can be applied. It is sufficient for the children in question to be racially acceptable [*tragbar*], i.e., that they at least correspond to the average of the German people.[147]

Kinkelin advocated transferring the children directly to Germany if they passed an initial physical evaluation. The evaluation of the mothers played hardly any role in his plan, as these women were supposed to remain in the Soviet Union unless they were explicitly 'racially desirable'.[148] Himmler did not think this was practicable, but he also argued against any comprehensive evaluation of the mothers. Unless they were 'decidedly inferior', he thought it was better to influence them so they would decide 'voluntarily and for reasons of their personal safety and that of the children to be included in the return operation [*Rückführungsaktion*]'.[149] Himmler's use of the phrase 'decidedly inferior' and Kinkelin's category of 'racially acceptable' illustrate the degree to which the Nazis' ideological standards and demands had changed over the course of the war. While they had initially only wanted to claim 'racially valuable' children for Germany, now the fact that a child had a German father was enough for the child to be considered 'racially acceptable' and deported to Germany.

Identifying the Fathers
It was consequently of critical importance to the German authorities to establish a child's paternity. Having a German father – whether he was a member of the Wehrmacht, SS, police, civilian administration or working in another role in the 'occupied Eastern territories'[150] – was what made the child a 'bearer of German blood' and thus potentially 'racially valuable'. Incidentally, the correspondence relating to the Führer's decree reveals that not only 'Reich Germans' but also 'ethnic Germans' could be recognised as German fathers.[151]

Proving paternity was extremely difficult for the authorities, however. In an age before DNA tests, the only thing to do in case of doubt was check whether the father and child had the same blood type. If the result was positive, the man in question could potentially be the father of the child, but nothing more specific could be determined; only if the result was negative could paternity be ruled out definitively.[152] 'In many cases', Himmler admitted in September 1942 to his SS and Police Leaders, 'we will not be able to identify the father at all'.[153] The German authorities placed very little trust in the statements of the mothers. Whether they believed a woman and how they handled her case would ultimately depend on how the local officials judged 'her personality, her character and her way of living'.[154]

In Norway, the question of the women's credibility had already led to disputes over authority. While the Wehrmacht usually placed its faith in the word of its soldiers (either actually or for reasons of military strategy), the SS was inclined to trust the statements of the women in many cases.[155] That said, a Norwegian woman who was likely to be carrying the child of a German would in any case be protected by the German authorities, even if she could not provide any information about the father.[156] The same did not apply in the occupied territories of the Soviet Union. In 'the East', a woman's statement was most likely to be considered reliable if a German man had submitted an application to marry her.[157] But even then, the responsible officials would not rule out the possibility that the woman was trying to exploit the good nature of the German man and 'foist' a child on him. Himmler's fears went even further than this. In the previously mentioned discussion about reporting requirements for registrars, he raised the prospect of enemy organisations attempting to weaken the 'German people' with 'racially undesirable' infants. 'If it becomes apparent in a clumsy way that the German soldiers are wanting to acquire children for Germandom [*Deutschtum*]', he claimed, it could be expected that 'a disguised or open counter-organisation of Latvians and Estonians' was involved.[158] Himmler turned the definition of the children's biological origin into an aspect and method of warfare. His use of the term 'counter-organisation' reveals the scope of his fears regarding 'racial' competition and the espionage associated with it.

According to the RKO, however, cases could also be expected in which the German father acknowledged paternity but the mother disputed it.[159] The RMbO therefore warned in October 1942 that, if there were any doubts, the child's father should be 'identified by means of a special procedure'.[160] The war ended before this procedure was clarified, however. Experiences in Norway had shown that the search for the fathers could fail at the first hurdle, namely, determining the identity and location of the men in question. The women often only knew the men's forenames, but not their Feldpost number or where they had been re-stationed. Confusion concerning the spelling of names further complicated matters.[161] If the authorities found the man despite all of this, he would often not be willing to acknowledge paternity.[162] Another complicating factor was that the Wehrmacht insisted on not placing undo pressure on 'its' men in such cases in order to avoid causing them psychological distress and thus impacting their fighting power – especially if they were engaged or married to a woman back in Germany.[163] Paternity could only be determined in about one third of all the cases handled by *Lebensborn* in Norway – and the men in question had often already been killed or listed as missing.[164]

In the 'occupied Eastern territories', the authorities anticipated even greater difficulties – first, because the war and occupation situation was much more unstable and unclear than in northern and western Europe, and second, because the encounters between German men and local women and their environment were less distinct and binding than in other occupied countries. When the authorities managed to track down a potential father, he was first supposed to be questioned and have his blood type tested. This could be complicated, as illustrated by the case of Ursula Sch. She had gone to Germany to join the Labour Service in early 1943, and in August of the same year she contacted the German court in Riga to have the paternity of her child confirmed. The court asked the public health officer working for the regional commissioner in Riga to perform a blood test; the health officer passed this request on to the University Institute for Forensic Medicine and Criminology in Königsberg (now Kaliningrad), which, in turn, contacted the Wehrmacht unit of the alleged father and demanded that a blood test be carried out following a very precise procedure: the sample was to be packed in cellulose for protection, and if the outside temperature was high, the sample was not supposed to be sent off unless it was certain that it would not be spoiled during the transport. In the end, the sample never reached the institute because the man in question was said to be untraceable.[165] The same applied to a man who had apparently joined the Wehrmacht or SS since his time working as a civilian in Riga.[166] The local situation was therefore often to blame for the failed attempts of the Nazi authorities to clearly identify the fathers of the children.

The RMbO wanted to make it as simple as possible for men, especially 'Reich Germans', to acknowledge their paternity. After a meeting on 30 October 1943, the responsible officials suggested that either local administrative authorities or any Wehrmacht, police, Reich Labour Service or Organisation Todt office should be authorised to handle this procedure.[167] The OKW argued against this, however, pointing out the shortage of personnel. Wehrmacht officials said it was completely out of the question to make troop leaders responsible for certifying acknowledgements of paternity, not least because they did not have the necessary legal knowledge as regards the prerequisites and consequences of the procedure. If anyone in the Wehrmacht could be responsible for this, it would have to be the judges.[168] Ultimately, no binding procedure was defined before the end of the war.

The question of when the courts should get involved also remained unanswered. The lines of conflict were different in this debate, however. If the authorities could not clarify whether the man named by the mother was actually the father of the child, the case was usually brought before a German court; this was the process in Norway and the Netherlands, for example.[169] The RMbO wanted to adopt this procedure for the 'occupied Eastern territories' as well,[170] and the Wehrmacht also argued for calling on German courts in disputes.[171] In March 1943, however, the Reich Ministry of Justice came to a different decision regarding the non-marital children of Polish women: the ministry said a German court had to be consulted in *every* case when it came to determining paternity, even if the German father had submitted an acknowledgement of paternity.[172]

The fact that all these issues remained unresolved probably had to do with the above-mentioned difficulties in tracking down the men and the vanishingly small number of actual acknowledgements of paternity. Paternity was generally only acknowledged voluntarily when the man in question planned to marry the mother – not least because the men feared that, by acknowledging paternity otherwise, they would be forced to make maintenance payments. This was not of immediate concern in the cases discussed here since the Führer's decree had exempted the fathers from maintenance obligations until further notice and made the Reich responsible for all costs pertaining to the examination and upbringing of the children.[173] This regulation only applied during the war, however; it was unclear whether the fathers would be required to make payments at a later date.[174] Since regular paternity proceedings in court usually revolved around maintenance payments, but this was initially irrelevant to the cases discussed here, the RKO additionally proposed forgoing the usual 'procedural evidence (oath, acknowledgement)' when it came to determining paternity in contested cases and instead using 'genetic assessments' (*'erbbiologische Gutachten'*).[175] But this also did not result in a clearly definable procedure. The RKO helplessly summarised the discussion in April 1944 by saying that children should only be supported if it were at least 'very probable' that the father was a 'Reich German'.[176] Even if the plan devised by Himmler and Kinkelin in the summer of 1944 to take as many children as possible back to the Reich during the rearguard action had been implemented, it would have been impossible to identify their biological fathers.

Status of Mother and Child
The status of the mothers posed entirely different problems for the Nazi authorities. According to the law of both Germany and the other countries, children in the 'occupied Eastern territories' belonged to their mothers. The Reich Ministry of Justice had not changed the fundamental provisions of the German Civil Code of 1896, according to which a non-marital child acquired its mother's citizenship upon birth.[177] The biological father was not permitted to make any decisions about the child's life, even if he acknowledged the child's paternity and made maintenance payments, or if he and the mother were living together without a marriage certificate and he effectively took on the role of father. At the end of the 1930s, the Academy for German Law had tried to have 'parental authority' transferred to the father as well in special cases and to modify the 'illegitimacy law' to make a sharper distinction between 'racially valuable' and 'worthless' ['*wertlose*'] children.[178] But these reforms were rejected by Hitler in 1940 with the justification that they would amount to a law 'for the deprivation of the illegitimate mother's rights'.[179] In Estonia, Latvia, Lithuania and Ukraine, too, it was a fundamental principle that guardianship of a non-marital child was automatically granted to the mother.[180] As mentioned, the biological father was not even recorded in the register of births in these countries. If the German authorities wanted to take custody of the occupation children they considered 'racially desirable', they either had to get the mother's approval, change the legal situation or bypass the law altogether – since the Führer's decree specifically called for registering those children who were born 'born illegitimately to native women in the occupied Eastern territories and whose sires are German'.[181]

This spawned a discusson of the term '*unehelich*', meaning 'non-marital'. The term was generally used to describe the children of unmarried women.[182] But representatives of the RMbO and RKO assumed that German men were fathering children not only with single women, but with married ones as well. Though married women often lived as 'single women' during the war, officially their family status was clear.[183] RMbO officials even suspected that more married than unmarried women were having children by German men.[184] Since even the children of married mothers were supposed to be subject to the provisions of the Führer's decree, some of the responsible officials began applying the category of '*unehelich*' not to the status of the mothers, as was usual, but rather to that of the children. An occupation child was to be considered '*unehelich*' if the biological father was not married to the mother. This concept was restricted exclusively to occupation children, however.

Reich Minister Rosenberg argued against this interpretation in November 1943. After all, he said, the children had to be considered

> born in wedlock [*ehelich*] even according to the law applicable to the native population. The intention cannot be to cause unrest in the ethnically alien families by registering such children. [...] In accordance with this, such a child can [only] be registered if the husband, by contesting the child's legitimacy, has expressed that he does not view the child as part of his family.[185]

Rosenberg's comments shine a light on the competing interests in the 'occupied Eastern territories'. While Himmler and others viewed the territories and their populations primarily as a reservoir that the 'German people's community' could ruthlessly exploit for its own benefit, the representatives of the RMbO and RKO wanted to establish a stable occupation regime at least. To this end, it was necessary to ensure that the local population was willing to collaborate. As in the case of marriage authorisation, it was important to the civilian administration not to intervene all too obviously in the personal matters of the civilian population and to avoid obvious humiliations. Bearing the child of a 'Reich German' often had serious social consequences for the woman in question. As mentioned earlier, the regional commissioner in Riga had even compared these children with 'Negro bastards' to emphasise the potential discrimination faced by mother and child.[186] If the mother was married to a local on top of this, the forced disclosure of the sire's identity was even more likely to lead to her exclusion and thus the long-term disruption of family structures. The RMbO therefore only wanted to review the 'non-marital' status of a child and follow the further regulations regarding the child's registration and support if the mother had voluntarily reported the child to the authorities.[187] In November 1943, therefore, the RMbO drafted a 'Regulation on Supporting the Illegitimate Children of Germans in the Occupied Eastern Territories' to modify the provisions in the Führer's decree and sent it to the Party Chancellery and the RF-SS.[188] Rosenberg had thus asserted himself in the RMbO and RKO, but no agreement was reached on the final guidelines before the end of the war.

There was also disagreement concerning the guardianship of the children and the corresponding plans for looking after them. On 16 September 1942, Erich Hilgenfeldt, head of the NSV, noted that Martin Bormann, head of the Party Chancellery, had tasked him with carrying out the Führer's order to bring the occupation children who met the 'racial requirements' to Germany and arrange for their care in NSV homes.[189] But the RMbO and civilian occupation authorities were working under different assumptions at the same time; they thought the children would be registered and supervised by the German authorities but would continue to live with their mothers. A well-developed child, Friedrich Trampedach of the RKO declared in the spring of 1944,

> can stay with the mother if it is assured that it 1. will learn the German language, that it 2. will be admitted to a German kindergarten and that it 3. will attend a German school. If these prerequisites for raising the child as a German are not in place, the child can be taken from the mother and housed in a German reform home.[190]

Language acquisition was generally a key factor in the Nazis' 'Germanisation policy'. 'The Germanisable individual [*Eindeutschungsfähiger*] will only find his way to the German people's community if he can consider himself a member of the German language community'.[191] Trampedach went on to suggest that the mother's 'social suitability' should be checked and that, at least in cases of doubt, the women should be employed by the NSV for three months so their behaviour could be observed:

> It is important that the child's mother is assigned an activity that does not run counter to her previous professional activity. Furthermore, from a medical point of view, it is not feasible for the evaluation by means of a labour assignment to be carried out during the last three months of pregnancy or during the nursing period, as this would be too much of a psychological strain on the child's mother and could easily lead to a misjudgement due to psychological changes during the time mentioned.[192]

If the evaluation were positive, Trampedach said that consideration should be given to 'Germanising' the women – a view that others opposed.[193] Trampedach's remarks make it clear that a few of the responsible officials combined their 'racial' goals and population policy aims with welfare impulses, even 'in the East'. Trampedach apparently wanted to deliberately include the women in the plans for their children, particularly since he, unlike Himmler and Hitler, reckoned that most of the women would be 'racially valuable' and 'socially suitable'.[194] In April 1943, he mentioned the special legal status and extensive support provided to the mothers of Wehrmacht children in Norway and suggested that the Führer's decree should stipulate that the German authorities would cover childbirth costs and expenses for housing the mothers in clinics and homes in the 'occupied Eastern territories' if necessary,[195] not least because the RKO was aware of a number of 'Reich German' and 'ethnic German' women who had experienced premature delivery or miscarriages due primarily to a lack of medical care.[196] However, General of the Waffen-SS Gottlob Berger from the RMbO feared that the de facto equivalence of 'ethnically alien' women and German mothers would cause new problems, and he proposed that women should generally give birth at home. If a home birth was not possible 'because the relatives are causing problems, for example', then the woman should be tended to in one of her country's own hospitals. Only in absolutely exceptional cases should these women be admitted to a German facility, he said, and even then it was critical to ensure that they were 'kept separate from German women'.[197] A clear regulation on this was never established in the end.

The respective general commissioner was to be responsible for arranging the children's care.[198] And, in fact, the RKO reported in April 1943 that 'various applications for support have been submitted by locals, and guardianships have been requested from the youth offices of the general commissioners'.[199] The RKO wanted to transfer the responsibilities of the guardianship courts (organising maintenance payments and child care, and so on) to the German courts.[200]

German law was to apply to a child for as long as he or she were considered 'racially valuable'. If the child did not develop satisfactorily, the German court was authorised to hand over the proceedings to the respective country's own administration at any time. It is clear from this that the children's legal status was to be provisional. But the individuals involved did not find this procedure entirely unproblematic. For example, Wilhelm von Allwörden from the RMbO suggested to Himmler that comprehensive and complicated legal safeguards should be put in place to make it impossible for the mothers to raise any objections.[201] Whether or how Himmler responded to this suggestion is not known.

In the end, all of these plans, drafts and implementing provisions, along with the long-winded correspondence of the authorities involved, wound up as wastepaper. When the Reich Ministry of Justice intervened in December 1943 – because providing support to children within the Reich would fall under its jurisdiction – von Allwörden responded by saying that there were 'no plans for the time being' for 'supporting the children within the territory of the Reich'.[202] In June 1944, Himmler ended the discussion once and for all, saying that at the time of the Führer's decree in October 1943, no one could have known that the 'front in the East' would be 'largely taken back'. Now was not the time to develop a standardised procedure, he declared; instead, it was important to concentrate on registering as many children as possible and bringing them to the Reich.[203]

There is no way to determine the extent to which such measures were actually implemented. In the files of the NSV, not a single example has yet been found of a child having been taken to an NSV home during the Nazis' deportation and Germanisation plans for 'racially desirable' occupation children. After the end of the war, the United Nations Relief and Rehabilitation Administration attempted to determine the origin of unaccompanied stateless children and return them to their families. The organisation's records reveal that many very young children from Eastern Europe and Russia had been taken to Germany by German troops in the last months of the war, but in many cases it is not possible to say who their parents were.[204]

One exception is the case of Rosalinde T., who was one year old when the war ended. Her mother, Maria, had met the Wehrmacht soldier Martin A. in her Ukrainian hometown in 1943. When Maria became pregnant, he promised to marry her, and during the Wehrmacht's retreat in 1944 he took her to Germany on a military transport. But the couple's plans for the future collapsed when Martin A.'s mother refused to accept the Ukrainian woman as her daughter-in-law. The young woman subsequently left her boyfriend and began working as a translator for the Red Army. Fearing discrimination, Maria T. ultimately gave her daughter Rosalinde to a German foster family.[205] Another exception was the Latvian woman B. T., who fled from Riga to the west in early 1945 after her German boyfriend was killed in the Soviet Union. Once she arrived in Germany, she put their son Andre into foster care. She later married an American soldier and moved to the USA.[206] Examples such as these only hint at the varied and convoluted experiences of children and their mothers at the end of the war and in the post-war period. It will be up to future researchers to show how the children of German soldiers and women from the Soviet Union grew up and coped with their past.

Notes

1. 'Gebietskommissar Mitau, Schreiben an den Generalkommissar Riga', 21.5.1942, BArch, R 90/460, p. 165.
2. I would like to thank Peter Klein for information about von Medem's personal background.
3. See, e.g., Kundrus, *Moderne Imperialisten*.
4. See Koller, '"*Von Wilden aller Rassen niedergemetzelt*"', p. 248.

5. The *'Schwarze Schmach'* ('Black Shame') propaganda campaign, which was directed against French colonial soldiers stationed in the Rhineland, conjured up images of sexually overpowering Black men who sought to weaken German society by means of sexually transmitted diseases, particularly syphilis. The colonial soldiers were viewed as a 'moral and racial threat'; see, e.g., Koller, 'Die "Schwarze Schmach"', pp. 159f.; Mass, *Weisse Helden, schwarze Krieger*, pp. 206ff.
6. Pommerin, *Sterilisierung der Rheinlandbastarde*. Christian Koller has shown that, shortly after the Nazis took power, a number of books were published with the intention of evoking memories of the occupation of the Rhineland and highlighting the supposed brutality of the French colonial troops (Koller, '"*Von Wilden aller Rassen niedergemetzelt*"', p. 347).
7. Björn Felder has shown that thinking in categories of 'race' and 'hereditary hygiene' and the idea of eugenics were not actually imported to Latvia by the Nazis; see Felder, *Lettland im Zweiten Weltkrieg*, pp. 277ff.
8. 'Chef des OKW, Schreiben an die Reichskanzlei', 13.1.1941, BArch, R 43II/1520a, p. 149.
9. Note, 'Der Führer hat entschieden', 27.6.1941, BArch, R 43II/1520a, p. 160.
10. RGBl., 1942, vol 1., para. 1, p. 488.
11. Olsen, *Vater: Deutscher*; Diederichs, 'Stigma and Silence'.
12. This led to major disputes about authority; see Lilienthal, *Der 'Lebensborn e.V.'*, pp. 166ff.
13. One exception were the children of so-called 'ethnic German' mothers. Regarding the Nazi categories of 'ethnic German' and 'Reich German', see, e.g., Bergen, 'Sex, Blood, and Vulnerability'.
14. See, e.g., Heinemann, *'Rasse, Siedlung, deutsches Blut'*, pp. 474ff.
15. Schmidt's original hand-out has not been found, but its content is documented extensively in 'Persönliche Handakte Major Hans von Payr zu Enn und Caldiff, Oberkommando der Wehrmacht/Wehrwirtschafts- und Rüstungsamt, Notiz, 18. 9. 1942, betr.: Vorsorgliche Erfassung von zusätzlichen Arbeitskräften', BA-MA, RW 19/473. Also see Drolshagen, *Wehrmachtskinder*, p. 293; Beck, *Wehrmacht und sexuelle Gewalt*, p. 212; Heinemann, *'Rasse, Siedlung, deutsches Blut'*, p. 528; Müller, 'Liebe im Vernichtungskrieg'; Gerlach, *Kalkulierte Morde*, p. 1080; Johr and Sander, *BeFreier und Befreite*, p. 69. Schmidt's hand-out is also mentioned in other Nazi records; see, e.g., 'RMbO, Berger, Schreiben an den Reichsminister und Chef der Reichskanzlei, betr.: Uneheliche Kinder von Reichsdeutschen in den besetzten Ostgebieten', 17.11.1943, copy, BArch, R 6/383, p. 41; microfilm copy BA-MA, FPF-01/7840.
16. In Norway, too, Nazi officials seemed to consider it self-evident that German soldiers would sire children in the occupied country; see Olsen, *Vater: Deutscher*, p. 19.
17. Regarding the contraception methods and pregnancy termination procedures of the time, see Jütte, *Contraception*, pp. 199ff.; Bergmann, *Die verhütete Sexualität*, pp. 171ff.

18. 'Persönliche Handakte Major Hans von Payr zu Enn und Caldiff, Oberkommando der Wehrmacht/Wehrwirtschafts- und Rüstungsamt, Notiz, 18. 9. 1942, betr.: Vorsorgliche Erfassung von zusätzlichen Arbeitskräften', BA-MA, RW 19/473.
19. These discussions took place on 13 and 14 September 1942 in Himmler's field headquarters in Ukraine, near Vinnitsa (Himmler, *Der Dienstkalender*, pp. 548ff.; also quoted in Heinemann, *'Rasse, Siedlung, deutsches Blut'*, p. 529).
20. 'RF-SS, Himmler, Rede auf der SS- und Polizeiführer-Tagung in der Feldkommandostelle Hegewald bei Shitomir', 16.9.1942, BArch, NS 19/4009, pp. 78–127, here p. 88; also published in Jacobsen and Jochmann (eds), *Ausgewählte Dokumente zur Geschichte des Nationalsozialismus 1933–1945*. Also see Himmler's handwritten notes, 'Vortrag beim Führer', 22.9.1942, BArch, NS 19/1447, pp. 78–88, here p. 86; Lilienthal, *'Der Lebensborn e.V.'*, p. 204.
21. 'Persönliche Handakte Major Hans von Payr zu Enn und Caldiff, Oberkommando der Wehrmacht/Wehrwirtschafts- und Rüstungsamt, Notiz, 18. 9. 1942, betr.: Vorsorgliche Erfassung von zusätzlichen Arbeitskräften', BA-MA, RW 19/473.
22. 'RKO, Burmeister, Schreiben an den RMbO, betr.: Behandlung der von deutschen Staatsangehörigen in den besetzten Ostgebieten mit einheimischen Frauen erzeugten unehelichen Kinder', 25.1.1943, BArch, R 90/460, pp. 254–7; 'RMbO, Rosenberg, Schreiben an den Reichsminister und Chef der Reichskanzlei, betr.: Entwurf eines Führererlasses über die Betreuung der unehelichen Kinder von Reichsdeutschen aus den besetzten Ostgebieten', 19.2.1943, BArch, R 6/383, p. 2.
23. 'RMbO, Berger, Schreiben an den Reichsminister und Chef der Reichskanzlei, betr.: Uneheliche Kinder von Reichsdeutschen in den besetzten Ostgebieten', 17.11.1943, copy, BArch, R 6/383, p. 41. Also see 'Generalkommissar in Riga, Lagebericht vom 29. April 1944', duplicate excerpts in BArch, R 6/383, pp. 113f., 116f.
24. 'Persönliche Handakte Major Hans von Payr zu Enn und Caldiff, Oberkommando der Wehrmacht/Wehrwirtschafts- und Rüstungsamt, Notiz, 18. 9. 1942, betr.: Vorsorgliche Erfassung von zusätzlichen Arbeitskräften', 18.9.1942, BA-MA, RW 19/473.
25. See 'OKW, gez. Keitel, Erlass, betr.: Unerwünschter Verkehr deutscher Soldaten mit Einwohnern in den besetzten Ostgebieten', 15.9.1942, copy, BArch, NS 19/1691, p. 1.
26. Since the 1870s, statisticians in Germany and other industrialised countries had recorded declining numbers of children born in wedlock; see Dienel, *Kinderzahl und Staatsräson*, pp. 32ff.; Bergmann, *Die verhütete Sexualität*, pp. 23ff.; Bergmann, 'Von der "unbefleckten Empfängnis"'; Jütte, *Contraception*, pp. 106ff. Shortly before the start of World War I, Carl Ballod, the demographer of the Prussian State Office of Statistics, said that this heralded the 'death of the race'; politicians, political scientists, economists, doctors and representatives of the socialist workers' movement all worried about the state's ability

to wage war, the potential of the German workforce, and Germany's morality (Bergmann, *Die verhütete Sexualität*, pp. 23ff.).
27. Korherr, *Geburtenrückgang* (1935), p. 32; Burgdörfer, *Volks- und Wehrkraft* (1936), pp. 17–20, 126f.; 'SS-Untersturmführer Wangemann, Entwurf für die bevölkerungspolitische Schrift an die SS-Führer, Die Wehrmächtigkeit der Völker: ein Bevölkerungsproblem', 1938, BArch, NS 19/3964, pp. 3–30, here pp. 5ff. Also see Czarnowski, 'Frauen als Mütter der "Rasse"', p. 58. People in Italy and France were also alarmed by falling birth rates, and the Nazis' policy of 'racial selection' found many adherents. However, German population policy differed significantly from that of other European countries in its racist radicalism; see Quine, *Population Politics in Twentieth-Century Europe*, pp. 9ff.; Riddle, *Contraception and Abortion*, pp. 216ff.; Jütte, *Contraception*, pp. 106ff., 174ff. Regarding efforts since the nineteenth century to regulate Europe's population in terms of 'race' and numbers, see Foucault, '*Society Must Be Defended*', pp. 239–63.
28. Burgdörfer, *Volks- und Wehrkraft* (1936), pp. 17, 126; Burgdörfer, *Volk ohne Jugend* (1935), p. 81. Doctors and politicians feared that men might have been made impotent by their experiences in the trenches and become anti-social in a family context. Regarding the far-reaching discussion of the reasons for the decline in births, see Bock, *Zwangssterilisation*, p. 31.
29. Burgdörfer, *Kinder des Vertrauens* (1942), p. 6. Also see Korherr, *Geburtenrückgang* (1935), p. 44.
30. Bock, *Zwangssterilisation im Nationalsozialismus*, pp. 142–6.
31. 'RF-SS, Rundbrief an alle SS-Führer', 4.6.1935, BArch, NS 19/ 3973, p. 1. Also see 'RF-SS, Himmler, Rundbrief an alle SS-Führer', 13.9.1936, BArch, former Schumacher 433 collection, quoted in Lilienthal, *Der 'Lebensborn e.V.'*, p. 44, note 19. The success of these repeated appeals was modest, however; on average, only 1.52 children per SS man were born until 1937, but at least twice that number had been expected ('Abteilung Statistik im SS-Personalamt, Nachtrag für die bevölkerungspolitische Schrift an die SS-Führer' 1.12.1937, BArch, NS/3965, pp. 1–17, here pp. 5 and 8).
32. Regarding the foundation of the organisation, see Lilienthal, *Der 'Lebensborn e.V.'*, pp. 40ff.
33. Himmler's speech to the SS Group Leaders on 18 February 1937, published in Himmler, *Geheimreden*, p. 94, also quoted in Lilienthal, *Der 'Lebensborn e.V.'*, p. 25.
34. Adolf Hitler, 15 November 1940, quoted in Kurt Daluege, 'Familiennachwuchs des Führerkorps der Ordnungspolizei', undated, BArch, NS 19/2756, pp. 2–5, here p. 3.
35. See, e.g., Bock, *Zwangssterilisation*, pp. 126ff.; Kundrus, *Kriegerfrauen*, pp. 357–63; Schwarz, *Eine Frau an seiner Seite*, pp. 187–99.
36. Kurt Daluege, 'Familiennachwuchs des Führerkorps der Ordnungspolizei', undated (October 1942), BArch, NS 19/2756, pp. 2–5, here p. 5.
37. This formulation can be found in a letter from Himmler which addressed the

selection criteria for SS members (letter to SS-*Obergruppenführer* Eicke, 30 April 1942, published in *Reichsführer!*, document number 107, pp. 116f.).
38. 'RF-SS, Himmler, Schreiben an SS-Obergruppenführer von Woyrsch', 22.3.1943, BArch, NS 2/240, pp. 1f., also quoted at length in Lilienthal, '*Lebensborn e.V.*', p. 94.
39. 'Anwendung des Mutterschutzgesetzes auf Ausländerinnen', *Reichshaushalts- und Besoldungsblatt*, no. 13, 14.7.1943, section 4243, BA-MA, R 16/135, unpaginated. The law had been passed in this form on 17 May 1942 (RGBl., 1942, vol. 1, p. 324).
40. See Lilienthal, *Der 'Lebensborn e.V.'*, p. 170; Olsen, *Vater: Deutscher*; Lenz, *Haushaltspflicht und Widerstand*.
41. Rediess (ed.), *Schwert und Wiege* (1943), pp. 8f., 14ff. I would like to thank Kåre Olsen from the Riksarkiv in Oslo for providing a copy of this volume. Also see Olsen, *Vater: Deutscher*, pp. 18f.
42. Olsen, *Vater: Deutscher*, p. 30.
43. Quoted in Lilienthal, *Der 'Lebensborn e.V.'*, p. 170.
44. Keyser, 'Die Erforschung der Bevölkerungsgeschichte des deutschen Ostens' (1942), pp. 94, 100.
45. See Aly and Heim, *Architects of Annihilation*, pp. 41ff.
46. Oberländer, *Die agrarische Überbevölkerung Polens* (1935), p. 116; Reithinger, 'Das europäische Bevölkerungsproblem' (1934), p. 23.
47. Seraphim, *Das Judentum im osteuropäischen Raum* (1938); Seraphim, *Das Judentum* (1942), pp. 46ff. Also see Aly and Heim, *Architects of Annihilation*, pp. 54ff.
48. See, e.g., the statistics published in an SS paper in 1938 which claimed that the number of Polish 'men fit for military service' ('*wehrfähige Mannschaft*') would grow to three million between 1930 and 1960, while Germany's number would fall by 700,000 ('Entwurf für die bevölkerungspolitische Schrift an die SS-Führer, Die Wehrmächtigkeit der Völker: ein Bevölkerungsproblem', 1938, BArch, NS 19/3964, pp. 3–30, here pp. 7f.).
49. 'Reichsgesundheitsführer Conti, Rede in der Aula der Friedrich-Wilhelm-Universität in Berlin bei der Gründung einer Reichsarbeitsgemeinschaft für Arbeits- und Leistungsmedizin', 21.2.1943, published in *Ziel und Weg: Zeitschrift des Nationalsozialistischen Deutschen Ärzte-Bundes*, March 1943, issue 3, pp. 57–61, here p. 60, BArch, NS 19/1590, pp. 94ff., here p. 96.
50. 'Leonardo Conti, Schreiben an den Reichsführer-SS, betr.: Frauenüberschuss nach diesem Kriege', Berlin, 10.2.1944, BArch, NS 19/55, pp. 3f.; 'Prof. Dr. F. Reichert, Der Frauenüberschuss nach dem Kriege, ein Informationsdienst des Hauptamtes für Volksgesundheit der NSDAP, 3. Jg., Folge 1–3, Januar bis März 1944', p. 44, copy, BArch, NS 19/55, p. 14.
51. Hitler, *Monologe im Führerhauptquartier*, pp. 199f.
52. See Martin Bormann, letter to Alfred Rosenberg concerning 'Äusserungen Hitlers', 23.7.1942, quoted in Dallin, *German Rule in Russia*, p. 457; also see Gerlach, *Kalkulierte Morde*, p. 1075, note 106; Heiber, 'Der Generalplan Ost',

pp. 315, 318. Also see the statements of various Nazi politicians regarding the 'Bormann letter' of 23 July 1942 concerning German policy in the occupied Eastern territories, BArch, R 6/85, pp. 16ff.
53. 'Martin Bormann, Vermerk zur Sicherung der Zukunft des Deutschen Volkes, Führerhauptquartier', 29.1.1944, BArch, NS 19/3289, pp. 2–12, here p. 2, also published in Jacobsen and Jochmann (eds), *Ausgewählte Dokumente*, vol. 1, unpaginated. Also see Martin Bormann, note, 10.3.1944, BArch, NS 19/3289, pp. 23–26, here p. 23.
54. Regarding the conflict with 'Asia', see, e.g., Longerich, *Heinrich Himmler*, pp. 261–5. This linguistic convention became deeply rooted and was customary even after the end of the war. For example, in March 1946, Konrad Adenauer wrote to Wilhelm Sollmann, a social democrat who had emigrated to the USA, saying that 'Asia stands on the Elbe. [...] Only an economically and spiritually healthy Western Europe, an essential component of which is the part of Germany not occupied by Russia, can stop the further advance of Asia in terms of spirit and power' (quoted in Loth, *Der Weg nach Europa*, p. 42).
55. Regarding the history of this weekly newspaper, see Zeck, *Das Schwarze Korps*, especially pp. 89–149.
56. 'Das Ende des Lebens. Wenn die Seele stürbe . . .', in *Das Schwarze Korps*, vol. 9, issue 12, 25.3.1943, p. 4, copy of the article in BArch, NS 19/160, unpaginated.
57. See, e.g., Lilienthal, *Der 'Lebensborn e.V.'*.
58. Himmler immediately contacted *Das Schwarze Korps* to enquire about 'further documents concerning compulsory impregnation in Russia' ('SS-Obersturmbannführer Brandt, Fernschreiben an SS-Hauptsturmführer Meine, Persönlicher Stab RF-SS', 26.3.1943, BArch, NS 19/160, p. 5). After some back and forth, the office of the Chief of the Security Police and the SD was forced to acknowledge that, 'based on the findings thus far', the report had to be considered 'a free invention' (see the subsequent correspondence, ibid. pp. 6–14, especially 'Chef der Sicherheitspolizei und des SD, Schreiben an den Reichsführer-SS und Chef der Deutschen Polizei, betr.: Zwangsweise Schwangerschaft in der Sowjetunion', 17.7.1943, BArch, NS 19/160, p. 13).
59. Some considered them 'undesirable'; see 'RMbO, gez. Dr. Runte, Schreiben an den RKO, betr.: den ausserehelichen Verkehr zwischen Deutschen und Angehoerigen eines fremden Volkstums', 24.11.1941, BArch, R 90/460, pp. 170f., here p. 170; 'RKO, gez. Wegner und Trampedach, Schreiben an den RMbO, betr.: Aussereheliche Verkehr Deutscher mit Angehoerigen fremden Volkstums', March 1942, BArch, R 90/460, pp. 167ff., here p. 169. For an opposing view, see 'Gebietskommissar in Mitau, Schreiben an den Generalkommissar in Riga', 21.5.1942, BArch, R 90/460, p. 165.
60. 'RKO, gez. Wegner und Trampedach, Schreiben an den RMbO, betr.: Aussereheliche Verkehr Deutscher mit Angehoerigen fremden Volkstums', March 1942, BArch, R 90/460, pp. 167ff., here pp. 168f.
61. 'Verordnung über die Betreuung von Kindern deutscher Wehrmachtsangehöriger in den besetzten Gebieten vom 28. Juli 1942, gez. Führer Adolf Hitler, Chef

des OKW Keitel, Reichsminister und Chef der Reichskanzlei Lammers', RGBl., 1942, vol. 1, p. 488. Copies of this decree can be found in various RKO and RMbO files; see 'Auszug aus dem Reichsgesetzblatt, Teil I, ausgegeben zu Berlin', 7.8.1942, BArch, R 90/460, pp. 224ff.

62. 'RMbO, gez. im Auftrag Dr. Runte, Schreiben an den RKO und den RKU, betr.: Behandlung der von deutschen Staatsangehörigen in den besetzten Ostgebieten mit einheimischen Frauen erzeugten unehelichen Kinder', 9.10.1942, BArch, R 90/460, pp. 235f.

63. See, e.g., 'RMbO, Fernschreiben an den Reichskommissar Riga, betr.: Betreuung der unehelichen Kinder von Reichsdeutschen aus den besetzten Ostgebieten', 29.12.1942, BArch, R 90/460, pp. 245f., 247– 247a.

64. 'RMbO, Rosenberg, Schreiben an den Herrn Reichsminister und Chef der Reichskanzlei, betr.: Entwurf eines Führererlasses über die Betreuung der unehelichen Kinder von Reichsdeutschen aus den besetzten Ostgebieten', 19.2.1943, BArch, R 90/40, pp. 258f., also found in R 6/383, p. 2.

65. 'RKO, gez. Trampedach, Schreiben an den RMbO, betr.: Entwurf eines Führererlasses über die Betreuung der unehelichen Kinder von Reichsdeutschen aus den besetzten Ostgebieten', 27.4.1943, BArch, R 90/460, p. 261.

66. 'Erlass des Führers über die Betreuung der unehelichen Kinder von Deutschen in den besetzten Ostgebieten', 11.10.1943, certified copy, BArch, R 6/ 383, p. 32.

67. 'RMbO, gez. Allwörden, Schreiben an den RF-SS und RKF, den Leiter der Parteikanzlei und den Chef OKW, betr.: Durchführung des Führererlasses über die Betreuung der unehelichen Kinder von Deutschen in den besetzten Ostgebieten', 20.11.1943, BArch, R 6/383, pp. 43–48, 49–53.

68. Claas, *Ein Heeresrichter im Russlandkrieg*, pp. 91f. For correspondence about abortions, see, e.g., 'Stadtkommissar der Hauptstadt Minsk, Schreiben an den Generalkommissar für Weissruthenien, betr.: Abtreibung', 2.6.1942, BArch, R 93/21, p. 446; 'Stadtkommissar der Hauptstadt Minsk, Schreiben an den leitenden Arzt beim Generalkommissariat, Herrn Doktor Weber', 2.11.1942, BArch, R 93/21, p. 447; 'Dr. Krainow, Schreiben an den leitenden Arzt beim Generalkommissar für Weissruthenien, Dr. Weber, Anzeige gegen die Ärztin Kowalewskaja', 13.3.1943, BArch, R 93/21, pp. 448f.; 'Angestellte des Krankenhauses', file, undated, BArch, R 93/21, p. 450; 'schriftliche Erklärung der Ärztin Kowalewskaja', 18.3.1942, BArch, R 93/21, p. 451; 'Generalkommissar für Weissruthenien, Abteilung Gesundheit und Volkspflege, gez. Dr. Weber, Schreiben an die Staatsanwaltschaft', 29.3.1943, BArch, R 93/21, p. 452.

69. Kaminski, *Liebe im Vernichtungskrieg*, documentary film.

70. 'RMbO, Rosenberg, Schreiben an den Herrn Reichsminister und Chef der Reichskanzlei, betr.: Entwurf eines Führererlasses über die Betreuung der unehelichen Kinder von Reichsdeutschen aus den besetzten Ostgebieten', 19.2.1943, BArch, R 90/40, pp. 258f., also found in R 6/383, p. 2.

71. 'Verordnung über die Betreuung von Kindern deutscher Wehrmachtsangehöriger in den besetzten Gebieten vom 28.7.1942, gez. Führer Adolf Hitler, Chef des

OKW Keitel, Reichsminister und Chef der Reichskanzlei Lammers', RGBl., 1942, vol. 1, p. 488. Kåre Olsen suspects that such incentives in Norway also prompted women to report to the authorities when they otherwise would not have done so (Olsen, *Vater: Deutscher*, p. 73).
72. 'RKO, gez. Trampedach, Schreiben an den RMbO, betr.: Entwurf eines Führererlasses über die Betreuung der unehelichen Kinder von Reichsdeutschen aus den besetzten Ostgebieten', 27.4.1943, BArch, R 90/460, p. 261.
73. Copy of the document published in Johr and Sander, *BeFreier und Befreite*, p. 70.
74. 'RKO, Abt. II Verw., gez. Gentz, Vermerk, betr.: Behandlung der von deutschen Staatsangehörigen in den besetzten Ostgebieten mit einheimischen Frauen erzeugten unehelichen Kinder', 19.11.1942, BArch, R 90/46, p. 231; 'RKO, Berichterstatter Landgerichtsrat Gräser, gez. Burmeister, Schreiben an den RMbO, betr.: Behandlung der von deutschen Staatsangehörigen in den besetzten Ostgebieten mit einheimischen Frauen erzeugten unehelichen Kinder', 25.1.1943, BArch, R 90/460, pp. 254ff.
75. 'RKF, Himmler, Vermerk, betr.: Erfassung von unehelichen Kindern in den besetzten Ostgebieten', 4.7.1944, BArch, R 6/383, pp. 127f.
76. For example, Himmler was of the opinion that a sexual transgression had to be judged on the basis of its 'result', meaning the 'racial value' of the child ('RF-SS, Himmler, Rede auf der SS- und Polizeiführer-Tagung in der Feldkommandostelle Hegewald bei Shitomir', 16.9.1942, BArch, NS 19/4009, pp. 78–127, here p. 125).
77. Published in Johr and Sander, *BeFreier und Befreite*, p. 70.
78. 'RMbO, Rosenberg an den Reichsminister und Chef der Reichskanzlei, betr.: Entwurf eines Führererlasses über die Betreuung der unehelichen Kinder von Reichsdeutschen aus den besetzten Ostgebieten', 19.2.1943, BArch, R 6/383, p. 2.
79. 'RKO, Abt. Gesundheit und Volkspflege, Schreiben an RKO, Abteilung II Politik, betr.: Entwurf eines Führererlasses über die Betreuung unehelicher Kinder von Reichsdeutschen in den besetzten Ostgebieten', 9.4.1943, BArch, 90/460, p. 260.
80. Certified copy of 'Rk. 851 D g, Erlass des Führers über die Betreuung der unehelichen Kinder von Deutschen in den besetzten Ostgebieten vom 11.10.1943', BArch, R 6/383, p. 32. For a more detailed justification of this allocation of responsibility, see 'RMbO, Führungsstab Politik, Vermerk für den Leiter der Führungsgruppe Deutschtum, SS-Brigadeführer Dr. Kinkelin, betr.: Durchführungsbestimmungen zum Führererlass über die Betreuung der unehelichen Kinder von Deutschen in den besetzten Ostgebieten, Besprechung bei II 5 am 29.10.1943', 30.10.1943, BArch, R 6/383, pp. 38f.
81. This was because the Norwegian authorities had tried to get around or slow down the German process (Olsen, *Vater: Deutscher*, pp. 24ff.). Regarding the approach of the German occupation authorities in the Netherlands and France, see, e.g., Lilienthal, *Der 'Lebensborn e.V.'*, pp. 163f., 182ff.

82. Olsen, *Vater: Deutscher*.
83. 'RKO an den RMbO, betr.: Führererlass über die Betreuung der unehelichen Kinder von Reichsdeutschen in den besetzten Ostgebieten', 17.4.1944, BArch, R 6/383, pp. 92ff. This letter makes it clear that the Reich Commissioner felt he had been overlooked, because in Section III of the Führer's decree, which specified the individuals responsible for defining the 'further details', he had not been taken into consideration.
84. 'RKO, Burmeister, Schreiben an den RMbO, betr.: Behandlung der von deutschen Staatsangehörigen in den besetzten Ostgebieten mit einheimischen Frauen erzeugten unehelichen Kinder', 25.1.1943, BArch, R 90/460, pp. 254–7. Also see 'Gebietskommissar Riga-Stadt an den Generalkomissar Riga', 18.3.1943, BArch, Berlin R 92/579, unpaginated.
85. 'RMbO, Führungsstab Politik, Vermerk für den Leiter der Führungsgruppe Deutschtum, SS-Brigadeführer Dr. Kinkelin, betr.: Durchführungsbestimmungen zum Führererlass über die Betreuung der unehelichen Kinder von Deutschen in den besetzten Ostgebieten, Besprechung bei II 5 am 29.10.1943', 30.10.1943, BArch, R 6/383, pp. 38f.
86. The RKO had complained about this back in December 1942 ('RKO, gez. im Auftrag Richter, Schreiben an die Abteilung II Verw., betr.: Behandlung der von deutschen Staatsangehörigen in den besetzten Ostgebieten mit einheimischen Frauen erzeugten unehelichen Kinder', 28.12.1942, BArch, R 90/46, p. 234).
87. 'RKO, Burmeister, Schreiben an den RMbO, betr.: Behandlung der von deutschen Staatsangehörigen in den besetzten Ostgebieten mit einheimischen Frauen erzeugten unehelichen Kinder', 25.1.1943, BArch, R 90/460, pp. 254–7.
88. 'Dr. Kinkelin an die Abteilung II 5, betr.: Verordnung über die Betreuung der unehelichen Kinder von Reichsdeutschen mit einheimischen Frauen in den besetzten Ostgebieten, geheim', 10.2.1944, BArch, R 6/383, p. 72.
89. 'Vermerk des RKF, Stabshauptamt', 4.7.1944, BArch, R 6/383, pp. 127f., here p. 127.
90. Ibid, p. 128.
91. Ibid. p. 127.
92. 'RKF, gez. im Auftrag De Vries, Schreiben an den RMbO, betr.: Betreuung unehelicher Kinder von Deutschen in den besetzten Ostgebieten', 17.6.1944, BArch, R 6/383, pp. 104f.
93. This '*Anlage 2*' (attachment 2), as it was known, was one of ten to twelve attachments on various topics that were reported on monthly.
94. BA-MA, WF 03/14396, pp. 1108–21, here p. 1115.
95. BA-MA, RH 23/155, p. 33, p. 49, p. 58, p. 71, p. 80, p. 91, p. 104, pp. 111 and 122; on microfilm: BA-MA, WF 03/14396, p. 1115, p. 1129, p. 1141, p. 1150, p. 1161, p. 1174, p. 1181, p. 1194, pp. 1205 and 1218.
96. BA-MA, WF 03/14396, pp. 1108–21, here p. 1115.
97. Ibid. pp. 1091–1109, here p. 1096.
98. Ibid. pp. 1156–76, here p. 1161. It would be interesting to conduct a more in-depth investigation of the 'excerpts from the register of births' that regional

commissioners drew up in some areas in an attempt to evaluate the 'genetic material' ('*Erbmaterial*') of the local population. Some of the children were given forenames such as Adolf or Eduard. See, e.g., the documents for the 'Bezirk Mitau', BArch, R 91/145, unpaginated; 'Riga-Stadt', BArch, R 92/579, unpaginated.
 99. 'OKW, Schreiben an den RMbO, betr.: Betreuung der unehelichen Kinder von Deutschen in den besetzten Ostgebieten', 22.5.1944, BArch, R 6/383, pp. 95–8.
100. 'RMbO, Berger, Schreiben an den Reichsminister und Chef der Reichskanzlei, betr.: Uneheliche Kinder von Reichsdeutschen in den besetzten Ostgebieten', 17. 11. 1943, BArch, R 6/383, P. 41. Also see Gerlach, *Kalkulierte Morde*, p. 1081.
101. Copy of excerpts from the situation report of the general commissioner in Riga from 29 April 1944 – 'Tgb.Nr. 2812/44g, als Anlage bei RMbO, P2, Kinkelin, Schreiben an RMbO, Abt. II/5, betr.: Führererlass vom 11. Okt. 1943', 5.7.1944, BArch, R 6/383, pp. 112ff.
102. 'RMbO, Schreiben an den RKO, betr.: Behandlung der von den deutschen Staatsangehörigen in den besetzten Ostgebieten mit einheimischen Frauen erzeugten unehelichen Kinder', Riga, 9.10.1942, BArch, MA R 90/380. It is interesting that Rosenberg talks about Germans here, not 'Reich Germans'. As a 'Baltic German', he had made it his mission to have so-called 'ethnic Germans' in the occupied territories of the Soviet Union integrated into the Nazis' political programmes on the same level as 'Reich Germans' (Essner, *Die 'Nürnberger Gesetze'*). The fact that, in contrast to others, he spoke specifically about 'extramarital sexual relations' also indicates that he believed marital relations between Germans and 'ethnic aliens' in the 'occupied Eastern territories' should not only be possible, after careful review, but were actually desirable.
103. These images usually lead to the idea of a common origin, or descent from a historical or mythical *ur*-figure. The acceptance of a new member into the community is sealed by rites that emphasise the mingling and unification of the blood, such as in blood brotherhoods; see von Braun, 'Viertes bild', p. 80. According to von Braun, the concept of the whole body as the community body ('*Gemeinschaftskörper*') took on secular traits with the racist notions of the '*Volkskörper*' or 'body of the people' (ibid. p. 94). In contrast to this, Claus Ekkehard Bärsch stresses the religious dimension of the Nazis' racial ideology (Bärsch, *Die politische Religion des Nationalsozialismus*, pp. 267ff.).
104. Rosenberg illustrated this connection when he wrote 'Race and I, blood and soul are most closely connected'; quoted in Bärsch, *Die politische Religion des Nationalsozialismus*, p. 266.
105. Rosenberg, *The Myth of the 20th Century*, p. 66.
106. Even shortly before the Wehrmacht invaded Poland, the Racial Policy Office of the Nazi Party was developing measures for the 'special treatment of racially valuable children'. Half a year later, Himmler announced his plans for the

abduction and 'Germanisation' of 'racially good children of alien ethnicity'. From 1940, SS members abducted tens of thousands of children from Poland, Czechoslovakia, the Baltic countries, Belarus, Ukraine and Slovenia. In 'Order 67/I' from 19 February 1942, Himmler circulated the idea that the Poles had 'formerly systematically taken all orphans born of ethnic German parents and placed them as "foundlings" in Polish orphanages or with Polish foster parents', meaning that the children should fundamentally be considered German in any case. See Hrabar et al., *Kinder im Krieg*, p. 183; Heinemann, *'Rasse, Siedlung, deutsches Blut'*, p. 508; Harvey, *Women and the Nazi East*, p. 191; Lilienthal, *Der 'Lebensborn e.V.'*, pp. 196 ff.

107. 'RF-SS Himmler, Rede auf der SS- und Polizeiführer-Tagung in der Feldkommandostelle Hegewald bei Shitomir', 16.9.1942, BArch, NS 19/4009, pp. 78–127, here p. 84.
108. Ibid.
109. Regarding the hierarchies of forced labourers in the Reich, see 'RKF, Chef des Stabshauptamtes, Vorg.: Änderung des Begriffes "artverwandtes Blut"', Berlin, 11.12.1941, BArch, NS 19/3680, p. 4. Also see Heinemann, *'Rasse, Siedlung, deutsches Blut'*, pp. 474ff.
110. 'RF-SS, gez. Himmler, geheime Anordnung Nr. 79/I, Änderung des Begriffes "artverwandtes Blut", Führerhauptquartier', 23.3.1942, BArch, NS 19/3680, pp. 10f., here p. 10.
111. 'RKF, Chef des Stabshauptamtes, Vorg.: Änderung des Begriffes "artverwandtes Blut"', Berlin, 11.12.1941, BArch, NS 19/3680, p. 4.
112. 'RF-SS, gez. Himmler, geheime Anordnung Nr. 79/I, Änderung des Begriffes "artverwandtes Blut", Führerhauptquartier', 23.3.1942, BArch, NS 19/3680, pp. 10f., here p. 11.
113. Secret order no. 79/I of the RF-SS, signed by Himmler, from 23 March 1942 regarding the change in the term 'racially related blood'. Preparations for this order had been under way since the end of 1941. See the respective correspondence in BArch, NS 19/3680, pp. 4ff., 10f., also quoted in Heinemann, *'Rasse, Siedlung, deutsches Blut'*, p. 476.
114. Hitler, *Mein Kampf*, pp. 284ff.
115. Essner, *Die 'Nürnberger Gesetze'*, pp. 40ff.; Lacey, 'Driving the message home', p. 190.
116. Following the same logic, Himmler planned to draw up a 'comprehensive new blood protection law after the war', according to which 'Germanisable persons or kinship groups' amongst the 'non-Germanic peoples' were to be selected and 'incorporated into the German *Volkskörper*' (Essner, *Die 'Nürnberger Gesetze'*, pp. 421f.).
117. For example, experiments were conducted at the Robert Koch Institute and the Kaiser Wilhelm Institute in an attempt to prove that there were serological differences between the 'human races'; see Cottebrune, 'Blut und "Rasse"'; Schmuhl, *Grenzüberschreitungen*.
118. 'RF-SS, Himmler, Rede auf der SS- und Polizeiführer-Tagung in der

Feldkommandostelle Hegewald bei Shitomir', 16.9.1942, BArch, NS 19/4009, pp. 78–127, here p. 97.
119. 'Vermerk des RKF, Himmler, Stabshauptamt', 4.7.1944, BArch, R 6/383, pp. 127f.
120. In Norway, one of the declared goals of the Nazi administration was to use the children's bi-nationality, or their special position and knowledge, to establish 'German outposts' in the occupied territory; see 'Aktenvermerk, Besprechung betr. uneheliches Kind und Errichtung von Lebensborn-Heimen in Norwegen', 22.10.1940, BArch, Koblenz, R2/11470, also documented (with transcription errors) at <https://web.archive.org/web/20070927192253/http://www.nkbf.no/EnHvitbok/Aktenvermerk_221040.htm> (last accessed 29 May 2019). Kåre Olsen points out that the handwritten date of '22.10.1940' on this note must be wrong because the meeting did not take place until February 1941 (Olsen, *Vater: Deutscher*, p. 377, note 9). The fact that the meeting was held in February is also documented in Rediess (ed.), *Schwert und Wiege* (1943), p. 22.
121. 'RKF, gez. SS-Obersturmbannführer Dr. Stier, Schreiben an den RMbO', Berlin, 17.6.1944, BArch, R 6/383, pp. 104f.
122. Hitler went so far as to claim that 'in 90 % of cases' German men married 'the most inferior girls and women that you can imagine in a people' ('RF-SS, gez. Himmler, Niederschrift über Besprechung mit dem Führer zur Heirat von Wehrmachtsangehörigen mit Angehörigen der artverwandten germanischen Völker, Feld-Kommandostelle', 17.6.1943, BArch, NS 19/2706, p. 1).
123. Bock, *Zwangssterilisation*, pp. 28–33.
124. This logic also came into play in Himmler's belief that the children of murdered partisans in the USSR would be particularly 'worth Germanising'. He thought they would have a good disposition precisely because their parents had fought proudly and loyally for 'their people'. However, Himmler said everything depended on successful 're-education' – otherwise these 'racially good' children could easily turn against the Germans. See, e.g., Heinemann, 'Rasse, Siedlung, deutsches Blut'.
125. 'RKF, gez. SS-Obersturmbannführer Dr. Stier, Schreiben an den RMbO', Berlin, 17.6.1944, BArch, R 6/383, pp. 104f.
126. 'Persönliche Handakte Major Hans von Payr zu Enn und Caldiff, Oberkommando der Wehrmacht/Wehrwirtschafts- und Rüstungsamt, Notiz, 18.9.1942, betr.: Vorsorgliche Erfassung von zusätzlichen Arbeitskräften', BA-MA, RW 19/473.
127. This plan is especially remarkable considering that the Polish and Ukrainian children who were abducted and 'Germanised' from 1942 by order of Himmler were deliberately not outwardly identified in any way. It was thought that the prerequisite for 'successful ethnic [*volkliche*] re-education' in these cases was to sever all ties between the children and their previous environment and make them forget that they had not been born in Germany. Their names were 'Germanised' and they were issued with falsified German birth certificates; see Lilienthal, *Der 'Lebensborn e.V.'*, pp. 212f.; Hrabar et al., *Kinder im*

Krieg, pp. 230f., 236f. This ultimately also made it impossible for the German authorities to trace the children's origins. The goal here was not to keep the children's development under control, but rather to fully assimilate the children.
128. See Demandt, *Luisenkult*.
129. 'RMbO an den RKO, Riga, betr.: Behandlung der von den deutschen Staatsangehörigen in den besetzten Ostgebieten mit einheimischen Frauen erzeugten unehelichen Kinder', 9.10.1942, BA-MA, R 90/380.
130. Lilienthal, *Der 'Lebensborn e.V.'*.
131. 'RKF, Stabshauptamt, geheimer Vermerk, betr.: Erfassung von unehelichen Kindern in den besetzten Ostgebieten', Berlin, 4.7.1944, copy, BArch, R 6/383, pp. 127f. Also see 'RKF, Stabshauptamt, Schreiben an den RMbO', Berlin, 31.7.1944, BArch, R 6/383, p. 125.
132. 'RKF, Himmler, geheimer Vermerk, betr.: Erfassung von unehelichen Kindern in den besetzten Ostgebieten', 4.7.1944, copy, BArch, R 6/383, pp. 127f.
133. 'Chef WiStab Ost, Reisebericht über die Dienstreise Chef WiStab Ost 17.–21.5.', 24.5.1944, BArch, MA F 43390, p. 624, also quoted in Gerlach, *Kalkulierte Morde*, p. 1081.
134. 'RMbO, Fernschreiben an den Reichskommissar Riga, betr.: Betreuung der unehelichen Kinder von Reichsdeutschen aus den besetzten Ostgebieten', 29.12.1942, BArch, R 90/460, pp. 245f., also pp. 247f.
135. 'RKO, Burmeister, Schreiben an den RMbO, betr.: Behandlung der von deutschen Staatsangehörigen in den besetzten Ostgebieten mit einheimischen Frauen erzeugten unehelichen Kinder', 25.1.1943, BArch, R 90/460, pp. 254–257.
136. Regarding the 'racial selection' of children and their mothers, also see Lilienthal, *Der 'Lebensborn e.V.'*, pp. 94ff., 212.
137. Regarding the marriage loan policy, see, e.g., Czarnowski, *Das kontrollierte Paar*, pp. 101ff.
138. See, e.g., the 'kinship questionnaires' of the public health officer in Riga, Dr Marnitz, in BArch, R 92/10035, passim.
139. 'RMbO, Rosenberg, Schreiben an den Reichsminister und Chef der Reichskanzlei, betr.: Entwurf eines Führererlasses über die Betreuung der unehelichen Kinder von Reichsdeutschen aus den besetzten Ostgebieten', 19.2.1943, BArch, R 90/460, pp. 258f., and BArch, R 6/383, p. 2.
140. See, e.g., Bergen, 'Sex, Blood, and Vulnerability', pp. 275ff.
141. See Essner, *Die 'Nürnberger Gesetze'*, pp. 344f.
142. 'Chef der RuSHA, SS-Gruppenführer Hofmann, Schreiben an das RSHA', 23.10.1942, BArch, NS 2/711, pp. 34f.
143. 'RKF, Himmler, Vermerk, betr.: Erfassung von unehelichen Kindern in den besetzten Ostgebieten', 4.7.1944, BArch, R 6/383, pp. 127f.
144. 'Erlass des Führers über die Betreuung der unehelichen Kinder von Deutschen in den besetzten Ostgebieten', 11.10.1943, certified copy, BArch, R 6/ 383, p. 32. Rivalry was also rife between Himmler as the RKF and Erich Hilgenfeldt,

who was the senior official responsible for *Lebensborn* e.V. and the head of the NSV; see Lilienthal, *Der 'Lebensborn e.V.'*, pp. 198ff.

145. 'RKO, gez. Trampedach, Berichterstatter Landesoberrat Dr. Steininger, Schreiben an den RMbO, betr.: Führererlass über die Betreuung der unehelichen Kinder von Reichsdeutschen in den besetzten Ostgebieten', 17.4.1944, BArch, R 90/460, pp. 269f. In Norway, the 'racial evaluation' results also influenced the amount of material support provided. The German authorities in Norway covered the costs of childbirth for all women who could prove that the child's father was German, but the 'racial assessment' of the mothers determined whether they would give birth in a *Lebensborn* home or a Norwegian hospital (Olsen, *Vater: Deutscher*, pp. 87ff.). Olsen points out, however, that this guideline was not always followed in practice (ibid. p. 91).

146. 'RKF, gez. im Auftrag De Vries, Schreiben an den RMbO, betr.: Betreuung unehelicher Kinder von Deutschen in den besetzten Ostgebieten', 17.6.1944, BArch, R 6/383, pp. 104f.

147. 'RMbO, P 2, Kinkelin, Schreiben an den RKO, betr.: Betreuung der unehelichen Kinder von Reichsdeutschen mit einheimischen Frauen', 6.7.1944, BArch, R 6/383, p. 118.

148. Ibid. pp. 110f.

149. 'RKF, gez. im Auftrag De Vries, Schreiben an den RMbO, betr.: Betreuung unehelicher Kinder von Deutschen in den besetzten Ostgebieten', 17.6.1944, BArch, R 6/383, pp. 104f.

150. 'RMbO, Rosenberg, Schreiben an den Herrn Reichsminister und Chef der Reichskanzlei, betr.: Entwurf eines Führererlasses über die Betreuung der unehelichen Kinder von Reichsdeutschen aus den besetzten Ostgebieten', 19.2.1943, BArch, R 90/460, pp. 258f., also found in R 6/383, p. 2.

151. Compared to earlier drafts, the final, published version of the decree was deliberately formulated in a non-specific way. The decree applied to 'children who are born illegitimately to native women in the occupied Eastern territories, and whose sires are Germans' ('Erlass des Führers über die Betreuung der unehelichen Kinder von Deutschen in den besetzten Ostgebieten', 11.10.1943, certified copy, BArch, R 6/383, p. 32).

152. Kåre Olsen points out that this test could place so much psychological pressure on the men that they would simply give in and admit to paternity in the end (Olsen, *Vater: Deutscher*, p. 120).

153. 'RF-SS, Himmler, Rede am 16.9.1942 auf der SS- und Polizeiführer-Tagung in der Feldkommandostelle Hegewald bei Shitomir', BArch, NS 19/4009, pp. 78–127, here p. 91.

154. 'RKO, gez. Trampedach, Schreiben an den RMbO, betr.: Entwurf eines Führererlasses über die Betreuung der unehelichen Kinder von Reichsdeutschen aus den besetzten Ostgebieten', 27.4.1943, BArch, R 90/460, p. 261.

155. Olsen, *Vater: Deutscher*, pp. 124ff.

156. Ibid. pp. 127f.

157. 'RKO an den RMbO, betr.: Führererlass über die Betreuung der unehelichen

Kinder von Reichsdeutschen in den besetzten Ostgebieten', 17.4.1944, BArch, R 6/383, pp. 92ff.
158. 'Vermerk des RKF, Himmler, Stabshauptamt', 4.7.1944, BArch, R 6/383, pp. 127f.
159. 'RKO, Berichterstatter Landgerichtsrat Gräser, gez. Burmeister, Schreiben an den RMbO, betr.: Behandlung der von deutschen Staatsangehörigen in den besetzten Ostgebieten mit einheimischen Frauen erzeugten unehelichen Kinder', 25.1.1943, BArch, R 90/460, pp. 254-7.
160. 'RMbO, gez. im Auftrag Dr. Runte, Schreiben an den RKO und den RKU, betr.: Behandlung der von deutschen Staatsangehörigen in den besetzten Ostgebieten mit einheimischen Frauen erzeugten unehelichen Kinder', 9.10.1942, BArch, R 90/460, pp. 235f.
161. Olsen, *Vater: Deutscher*, pp. 118ff.
162. Ibid. p. 51.
163. Ibid. pp. 25f., 123.
164. Ibid. pp. 126, 130f. In the case of non-marital children, the paternity of fallen or missing soldiers had to be confirmed before a court in the Reich, even if the deceased had acknowledged his paternity multiple times, both orally and in writing (Boberach [ed.], 'Chef der Sicherheitspolizei und des SD', *Meldungen aus dem Reich*, Nr. 203 vom 17. 7. 1941', BArch, R 58/162, pp. 115-42, here pp. 133f.).
165. 'Universitätsinstitut für gerichtliche Medizin und Kriminalistik, Königsberg (Pr.), Schreiben an das Deutsche Krankenhaus in Riga, in Sachen D./J.', 15.2.1943, BArch, R 92/10035; 'Amtsarzt beim Generalkommissar in Riga, gez. Dr. Marnitz, Schreiben an das Institut für gerichtliche Medizin und Kriminalistik der Universität München, betr.: Blutgruppenuntersuchung der Kindesmutter Ursula Sch.', 4.8.1943, BArch, R 92/10035, unpaginated.
166. See, e.g., 'Amtsarzt beim Generalkommissar in Riga, Schreiben an das Universitätsinstitut für gerichtliche Medizin und Kriminalistik, Königsberg (Pr.), betr.: Blutuntersuchung betr. Feststellung der Vaterschaft Jan M.', 7.9.1943, BArch, R 92/10035, unpaginated.
167. 'Vermerk für den Leiter der Führungsgruppe Deutschtum, Dr. Kinkelin, betr.: Durchführungsbestimmungen zum Führererlass über die Betreuung der unehelichen Kinder von Deutschen in den besetzten Ostgebieten, Bezug: Besprechung bei II 5 am 29.10.1943', 30.10.1943, BArch, R 6/383, pp. 38f., here p. 38. The RKO confirmed this regulation in April 1944 ('RKO, gez. Trampedach, Berichterstatter Landesoberrat Dr. Steininger, Schreiben an den RMbO, betr.: Führererlass über die Betreuung der unehelichen Kinder von Reichsdeutschen in den besetzten Ostgebieten', 17.4.1944, BArch, R 90/460, pp. 269f.).
168. 'OKW, Schreiben an den RMbO, betr.: Betreuung der unehelichen Kinder von Deutschen in den besetzten Ostgebieten', 22.5.1944, BArch, R 6/383, pp. 95-8.
169. Olsen, *Vater: Deutscher*, pp. 121ff.

170. See, e.g., 'RMbO, gez. im Auftrag Dr. Runte, Schreiben an den RKO und den RKU, betr.: Behandlung der von deutschen Staatsangehörigen in den besetzten Ostgebieten mit einheimischen Frauen erzeugten unehelichen Kinder', 9.10.1942, BArch, R 90/460, pp. 235f.
171. Quoted in 'RKO, Berichterstatter Landgerichtsrat Gräser, gez. Burmeister, Schreiben an den RMbO, betr. Behandlung der von deutschen Staatsangehörigen in den besetzten Ostgebieten mit einheimischen Frauen erzeugten unehelichen Kinder', 25.1.1943, BArch, R 90/460, pp. 254–7.
172. To ensure that the information provided by everyone involved was true, the Security Police were also supposed to be involved in every case ('Aktenvermerk über die Besprechung im Reichs-Justiz-Ministerium am 10.3.1943, betr.: Behandlung von Unterhaltsklagen unehelicher Kinder polnischen Volkstums gegen ihre Erzeuger', BArch, NS 47/34, unpaginated).
173. 'Erlass des Führers über die Betreuung der unehelichen Kinder von Deutschen in den besetzten Ostgebieten', 11.10.1943, certified copy, BArch, R 6/383, p. 32. The fact that this cost coverage was approved without further negotiation is all the more remarkable because the refusal of financial child benefits for '*Mischlingskinder 2. Grades*' ('2nd-degree mixed-blood children') in the Reich had not been formalised until the end of 1942 (Meyer, '*Jüdische Mischlinge*', p. 177).
174. Regarding the discussions concerning guardianship with respect to maintenance payments, see the holdings in BArch, R 6/383, passim.
175. 'RKO, Berichterstatter Landgerichtsrat Gräser, gez. Burmeister, Schreiben an den RMbO, betr.: Behandlung der von deutschen Staatsangehörigen in den besetzten Ostgebieten mit einheimischen Frauen erzeugten unehelichen Kinder', 25.1.1943, BArch, R 90/460, pp. 254–7.
176. 'RKO, gez. Trampedach, Berichterstatter Landesoberrat Dr. Steininger, Schreiben an den RMbO, betr.: Führererlass über die Betreuung der unehelichen Kinder von Reichsdeutschen in den besetzten Ostgebieten', 17.4.1944, BArch, R 90/460, pp. 269f.
177. Regarding legal developments between 1900 and 1970 see Buske, *Fräulein Mutter und ihr Bastard*, pp. 75ff., 148ff.
178. Ibid. pp. 149ff.
179. Quoted in ibid. pp. 160ff.
180. At least, this was the conclusion reached by the Nazi authorities after they had familiarised themselves with the matter; see, e.g., 'RKO, gez. im Auftrag Richter, Schreiben an die Abteilung II Verw., betr.: Behandlung der von deutschen Staatsangehörigen in den besetzten Ostgebieten mit einheimischen Frauen erzeugten unehelichen Kinder', 28.12.1942, BArch, R 90/46, p. 234; 'RKO, Berichterstatter Landgerichtsrat Gräser, gez. Burmeister, Schreiben an den RMbO, betr.: Behandlung der von deutschen Staatsangehörigen in den besetzten Ostgebieten mit einheimischen Frauen erzeugten unehelichen Kinder', 25.1.1943, BArch, R 90/460, pp. 254–7; 'RMbO an den RF-SS, betr.: Durchführung des Führererlasses über die Betreuung der unehelichen Kinder

von Deutschen in den besetzten Ostgebieten', 20.11.1943, BArch, R 6/383, pp. 43ff., here p. 44.
181. 'Erlass des Führers über die Betreuung der unehelichen Kinder von Reichsdeutschen in den besetzten Ostgebieten', copy by Dr Kinkelin from 11.8.1943, BArch, R 6/383, p. 16.
182. Buske, *Fräulein Mutter und ihr Bastard*.
183. 'RMbO, Führungsstab Politik, Vermerk für den Leiter der Führungsgruppe Deutschtum, Dr. Kinkelin, betr.: Durchführungsbestimmungen zum Führererlass über die Betreuung der unehelichen Kinder von Deutschen in den besetzten Ostgebieten, Bezug: Besprechung bei II 5 am 29.10.1943', 30.10.1943, BArch, R 6/383, pp. 38f., here p. 39.
184. 'RMbO, Führungsstab Politik, Vermerk für den Leiter der Führungsgruppe Deutschtum, Dr. Kinkelin, betr.: Durchführungsbestimmungen zum Führererlass über die Betreuung der unehelichen Kinder von Deutschen in den besetzten Ostgebieten, Bezug: Besprechung bei II 5 am 29.10.1943', 30.10.1943, BArch, R 6/383, pp. 38f., here p. 39.
185. 'RMbO, Schreiben an den RF-SS, betr.: Durchführung des Führererlasses über die Betreuung der unehelichen Kinder von Deutschen in den besetzten Ostgebieten', 20.11.1943, BArch, R 6/383, pp. 43ff., here p. 44.
186. 'Gebietskommissar in Mitau, Schreiben an den Generalkommisar in Riga', 21.5.1942, BArch, R 90/460, p. 165.
187. 'RMbO, gez. im Auftrag Dr. Runte, Schreiben an den RKO und den RKU, betr.: Behandlung der von deutschen Staatsangehörigen in den besetzten Ostgebieten mit einheimischen Frauen erzeugten unehelichen Kinder', 9.10.1942, BArch, R 90/460, pp. 235f.
188. 'Entwurf einer Verordnung über die Betreuung der unehelichen Kinder von Deutschen in den besetzten Ostgebieten', signed by Allwörden, 23.11.1943, BArch, R 6/383, pp. 46ff., here p. 47.
189. 'NSV, Hilgenfeldt, Schreiben an Bormann', 16.9.1942, BArch, NS 119/2427. The NSV was also supposed to cover the costs until the right of recourse had been decided in favour of the guardian or the father ('RKO, Abt. II Verw., gez. Gentz, Vemerk, betr.: Behandlung der von deutschen Staatsangehörigen in den besetzten Ostgebieten mit einheimischen Frauen erzeugten unehelichen Kinder', 19.11.1942, BArch, R 90/46, p. 231).
190. 'RKO, gez. Trampedach, Berichterstatter Landesoberrat Dr. Steininger, Schreiben an den RMbO, betr.: Führererlass über die Betreuung der unehelichen Kinder von Reichsdeutschen in den besetzten Ostgebieten, 17.4.1944, BArch, R 90/460, pp. 269f.
191. 'RMbO, Abt. III B 4, Bericht über den Verlauf der Eindeutschung von rassisch wertvollen Fremdstämmigen', undated (December 1942), BArch, NS 19/1780, pp. 3–13, here p. 5. However, it was difficult to acquire the German language in the 'occupied Eastern territories' on account of access restrictions and a shortage of personnel and teaching materials (see, e.g., 'Generalkommissar für Wolhynien und Podolien, Lagebericht', Luzk [Lutsk], 1.11.1942, BArch,

R 6/687, pp. 8, 11; 'Gebietskommissar in Brest-Litowsk, Schreiben an den Generalkommissar für Wolhynien und Podolien, betr.: Lagebericht für die Monate Juli/August 1943', 21.8.1943, BArch, R 94/8, p. 3).

192. 'RKO, gez. Trampedach, Berichterstatter Landesoberrat Dr. Steininger, Schreiben an den RMbO, betr.: Führererlass über die Betreuung der unehelichen Kinder von Reichsdeutschen in den besetzten Ostgebieten', 17.4.1944, BArch, R 90/460, p. 269.

193. For example, SS-*Hauptsturmführer* Dr Franz Grohmann believed women of 'alien stock' (*'fremdstämmig'*) would be 'bad German mothers' on account of their 'different racial structure' ('SS-Hauptsturmführer Grohmann, Schreiben an die Pflegestelle der 112. SS-Standarte, betr.: SS-Ehetauglichkeit der Polin Regina M.', 8.4.1942, BArch, NS 48/24, unpaginated).

194. 'RKO, gez. Trampedach, Berichterstatter Landesoberrat Dr. Steininger, Schreiben an den RMbO, betr.: Führererlass über die Betreuung der unehelichen Kinder von Reichsdeutschen in den besetzten Ostgebieten', 17.4.1944, BArch, R 90/460, p. 269.

195. 'RKO, gez. Trampedach, Schreiben an den RMbO, betr.: Entwurf eines Führererlasses über die Betreuung der unehelichen Kinder von Reichsdeutschen aus den besetzten Ostgebieten', 27.4.1943, BArch, R 90/460, p. 261.

196. See 'Anzeigen einer Unterbrechung der Schwangerschaft, einer Fehlgeburt (Fruchtabgang) oder Frühgeburt vor Vollendung der 32. Schwangerschaftswoche beim Amtsarzt beim Generalkommissar in Riga, Dr. Marnitz', 1942/43, collected in BArch, R 92/10035. If a woman was suspected of having deliberately caused a premature delivery, miscarriage or stillbirth, an investigation would be initiated; see 'Deutsche Klinik Riga, Anzeige einer Fehlgeburt, Jadwiga B.', 2.9.1943, BArch, R 92/10035, unpaginated; 'Amtsarzt beim Generalkommissar in Riga, Schreiben an den Gebietskommissar Riga-Stadt, betr.: Verdachtsmeldung auf Herbeiführen einer Fehlgeburt durch strafbaren Eingriff', 6.9.1943, BArch, R 92/10035, unpaginated; 'Gesundheitsamt Riga, gez. Dr. Carlile, Schreiben an die Staatsanwaltschaft des Deutschen Gerichts, im Hause, betr.: Ermittlungsverfahren Hedwig B.', 11.11.1943, BArch, R 92/10035, p. 23.

197. 'Berger an den RKO vom 17.11.1943, betr.: Entwurf des Führererlasses über die Betreuung der unehelichen Kinder von Reichsdeutschen in den besetzten Ostgebieten', BArch, R 6/383, p. 42. We know of two cases in which women expecting the child of an SS member were allowed to give birth in one of the *Lebensborn* homes in Poland with Himmler's personal authorisation; regarding the admission of a Ukrainian woman, see 'Pers. Stab RF-SS, Schreiben an den HSSPF Ost in Krakau, SS-Obergruppenführer Krüger', 8.1.1943, BArch, NS 19/165. Lilienthal also mentions the admission of a Polish woman (Lilienthal, *Der 'Lebensborn e.V.'*, p. 93, note 167).

198. 'RMbO, gez. im Auftrag Dr. Runte, Schreiben an den RKO und den RKU, betr.: Behandlung der von deutschen Staatsangehörigen in den besetzten Ostgebieten mit einheimischen Frauen erzeugten unehelichen Kinder',

9.10.1942, BArch, R 90/460, pp. 235f.; 'RKO, Vermerk, Jugendämter für deutsche Kinder', 19.10.1942, BArch, R 90/460, p. 230; 'RKO, Abt. II Verw., gez. Gentz, Vermerk, betr.: Behandlung der von deutschen Staatsangehörigen in den besetzten Ostgebieten mit einheimischen Frauen erzeugten unehelichen Kinder', 19.11.1942, BArch, R 90/46, p. 231

199. 'RKO, Abt. Gesundheit und Volkspflege, Schreiben an RKO, Abteilung II Politik, betr.: Entwurf eines Führererlasses über die Betreuung unehelicher Kinder von Reichsdeutschen in den besetzten Ostgebieten', 9.4.1943, BArch, R 90/460, p. 260.

200. Regarding the history of guardianship, see Buske, *Fräulein Mutter und ihr Bastard*, pp. 53ff. The draft of the implementing provisions for the Führer's decree, which the RMbO sent out on 20 November 1943, followed these suggestions from the RKO ('RMbO, gez. von Allwörden, Schreiben an den RF-SS und RKF, den Leiter der Parteikanzlei und den Chef OKW, betr.: Durchführung des Führererlasses über die Betreuung der unehelichen Kinder von Deutschen in den besetzten Ostgebieten', 20.11.1943, BArch, R 6/383, pp. 43–8, 49–53).

201. 'RMbO, Schreiben an den RF-SS, 20.11.1943, betr.: Durchführung des Führererlasses über die Betreuung von unehelichen Kindern von Deutschen in den besetzten Ostgebieten', BArch, R 6/383, pp. 43ff., here p. 44.

202. 'RMbO, gez. von Allwörden, Schreiben an den Reichsminister der Justiz, betr.: Betreuung der unehelichen Kinder von Deutschen in den besetzten Ostgebieten', 16.12.1943, BArch, R 6/383, p. 57; Reichsminister der Justiz, Schreiben an den RMbO, betr.: Betreuung der unehelichen Kinder von Deutschen in den besetzten Ostgebieten', 6.12.1943, BArch, R 6/383, p. 55.

203. 'RKF, gez. im Auftrag De Vries, Schreiben an den RMbO, betr.: Betreuung unehelicher Kinder von Deutschen in den besetzten Ostgebieten', 17.6.1944, BArch, R 6/383, pp. 104f.

204. Holdings of the US High Commissioner for Germany, Bavaria Land Commissioner, Pol. Affairs Div., Displaced Populations, Br., 1946–1951, Children's Resettlement Case Files, NARA, RG-466, 250/72/12–13.

205. Case file for Linde (Rosalinde) T., 1947, NARA, RG-466, 250/72/12–13/7–2, 198, box 11.

206. Case file for Andre T., 1948, NARA, RG-466, 250/72/12–13/7–2, 198, box 11.

CHAPTER 6

Concluding Remarks: Gender, Sexuality and Violence in the War and Post-War Period

In his daily order of 14 April 1945, Hitler exhorted the soldiers engaged in rearguard action on the Eastern Front not to contemplate desertion but to 'stand their ground':

> You soldiers from the East already know to a large extent the fate that lies in store above all for German women, girls and children.
> While the old men and children will be murdered, women and girls will be debased as barracks whores. The rest will march to Siberia [. . .].[1]

In the last months of the war, acts of sexual violence against German women and girls were regularly evoked to encourage the men at the front to persevere. In weekly newsreels and on posters and flyers, the propaganda department of the Nazi Party depicted German women as future victims of the 'bestial hordes'.[2] And in letters to their wives, girlfriends and mothers, Wehrmacht soldiers themselves declared that they had to remain strong to protect the people back home from the 'Bolshevists' who would do 'what they want' with the women.[3] It was not just racist thinking or propaganda that stoked such fears amongst the soldiers. Many men had seen or heard about Soviet soldiers committing acts of sexual violence against women as they advanced west – acts that were often indiscriminately directed against all women, regardless of whether they were on the side of the enemy or the allies.[4] In the course of this book, it has become clear that the majority of the men fundamentally viewed this as a 'normal' and practically unavoidable aspect of war. Additionally, men may have feared that German women would be sexually assaulted as revenge for the crimes they themselves had committed in the Soviet Union.[5]

Today it is almost impossible to determine the extent of the acts of sexual violence committed by members of the Wehrmacht, SS and police in the Soviet Union during the war, occupation and 'Final Solution'. But the book at hand has shown that violent sexual crimes were not an exception. German soldiers forced women and girls (as well as boys and men) to undress, they subjected them to sexual torture and they committed rapes, both individually and in groups. In addition to these violent acts, other types of sexual encounters took place between the occupiers and the occupied. For some men, visiting 'secret' prostitutes and military brothels was a normal part of soldierly life. In view of the catastrophic food situation during the war, it was often possible for members of the Wehrmacht and SS to offer food or other vital goods in exchange for sexual satisfaction. Some of the men who were stationed for weeks or months in the same location also engaged in longer-term intimate relationships. In Estonia and Latvia in particular, German soldiers even petitioned the Nazi authorities for permission to marry.

The military and political elites tolerated these heterosexual practices because it was generally assumed that they strengthened the soldiers' fighting power. This code, and the image of soldierly masculinity upon which it was based, was widely enshrined in European culture. However, it could collide with the principles of '*Manneszucht*' and military discipline as promoted by the Wehrmacht especially. It could also conflict with German racial ideology, according to which the populations in Eastern Europe and Russia were largely considered 'racially inferior' – although many different and in no way consistent 'racial' classifications were applied here.

Preparing soldiers for combat generally involves unleashing their 'individual potential for violence' (Ulrich Bröckling) while simultaneously attempting to keep it under control.[6] To this end, armies employ the maximum possible number of disciplinary techniques, and transgressions are punished more harshly than elsewhere. But armies also offer compensation in return for the subjugation they demand. As Jan Philipp Reemtsma put it, the order 'You shall!' is accompanied by the concession 'You may!'.[7] Soldiers are not only prohibited from doing more things than other people, they are also – at least during wartime – allowed to do more things. In the Nazis' war of annihilation, acts of sexual violence were among the deeds that, while not legal, were nonetheless allowed. Though some cases of rape were tried before Wehrmacht courts and the perpetrators were sentenced, this applied only to a relatively small proportion of all acts of sexual violence. By rarely intervening and applying disciplinary measures in a lax way, troop leaders opened up spaces of opportunity for the soldiers in which sexual violence would tend to be viewed as a normal aspect of wartime life.

The commanders reckoned that their men would commit sexual violence, and this knowledge was at least implicitly part of their operational, tactical and strategic considerations. As my close reading of the Military Jurisdiction Decree in Chapter 2 shows, it was by no means their intention to allow the men to rape at will. Troop leaders tacitly approved, incited, disapproved of or punished sexual violence by their men depending on the conditions and interests in the respective military situation (the latter included ensuring the soldiers' loyalty or effectively hurting the enemy).

The ego documents of soldiers show that many men believed they had total power of control over the 'women of the enemy'. They wilfully interpreted military instructions, such as guidelines for conducting searches, in a way that aligned with their own interests. As the wartime situation became increasingly mundane for some of the men – with the soldiers experiencing boredom, fear and depression – verbal, voyeuristic and physical sexual assaults could give individuals or groups the chance to release psychological pressure and affirm their own position of power. The brutality of many acts of sexual violence, and the mutual goading that occurred in group situations, reveal that the loss of boundaries could be situational; some men probably experienced sexuality in a way they had never imagined before.

When it came to prostitution policies, too, the foremost aim of the Wehrmacht and SS was not to strictly prevent their men from engaging in sexual activities. Although 'secret' prostitution was repeatedly prohibited shortly after the start of the invasion in the summer of 1941, and women suspected of engaging in sexual bartering or professional prostitution were deliberately prosecuted, the OKH, OKW and RF-SS simultaneously presumed that such measures would not deter the men from seeking out prostitutes. To control and protect the soldiers and members of the SS and police, therefore, the medical services of both organisations established an extensive system of support that revolved around medical and 'racial policy' briefings for individual soldiers as well as hygienic preventative and follow-up measures. The OKH also instructed the medical service to set up brothels run by the Wehrmacht itself, which were meant to ensure medical control over the women (some of whom were sexually enslaved) and their clients.

Structurally, this dual strategy of curbing 'secret prostitution' while simultaneously providing monitored sexual services resembled the prostitution policy that had prevailed in Germany since the start of the twentieth century, when the authorities began registering street prostitutes in big cities and requiring them to undergo regular examinations.[8] The Society for Combatting Venereal Diseases was of the opinion that 'dirty' prostitution should be prevented and 'clean' prostitution encouraged. This view was widely accepted not only in Germany but also other countries, including England and France, and it had led to the establishment of brothels for officers on all sides even in World War I.[9] For young men in particular, this offered relatively uncomplicated and risk-free access to sexual experiences. To use Foucault's terminology, the Nazis' prostitution policies were not solely repressive for the men; in fact, they produced new forms of heterosexual encounters. Military commanders used the idealised image of the virile, combat-ready soldier to legitimise the creation of Wehrmacht brothels, and this same image was repeatedly reconfirmed and regenerated through the operation of the brothels.

The brothels run by the Wehrmacht also bound soldiers to the system. They were a reward for the soldiers' loyalty and participation in the war, as they demonstrated to the men that their superiors sympathised with their needs and would spare no effort to provide them opportunities for safe and affordable sexual contact. This conveyed to the soldiers that they shared in Germany's victory and that their association with the occupying power offered private advantages. However, this policy contradicted the Nazis' ideological primacy of the 'purity of the German *Volkskörper*'. For this reason, some of the Wehrmacht's prostitution measures were quite controversial. A few officers feared that by setting up 'sanitation stations' and failing to seriously punish soldiers who violated the rules, recruits might believe they had carte blanche to pursue their sexual desires unimpeded at any time. The establishment of Wehrmacht brothels was also a topic of fierce debate until the end of the war. A number of military officials complained that such public establishments did nothing to prevent the spread of sexually transmitted diseases and they harmed the reputation of the Wehrmacht to boot. Another argument was that if an entire generation of young German men had their first sexual experiences in a brothel, this might normalise sexual practices that should otherwise be considered 'abnormal' and thus do lasting harm to the sex lives of German couples.

While such debates focused on the reputation and dissoluteness of German men, there was usually remarkably little discussion of the sexual transgression of 'racial' boundaries. No issue was made of the fact that German men were visiting prostitutes considered 'ethnically alien' according to the Nazis' racial ideology. Only Jewish women were ruled out of serving in the brothels, at least officially. One reason for the 'racial policy tolerance' that applied to both commercial sexual transactions and rape was that these forms of sexuality were viewed as a short-term satisfaction without any emotional ties or urge to procreate.

By contrast, the OKH, OKW and RF-SS certainly considered longer-lasting intimate relations with 'ethnically alien' women to be a threat to the 'German people's community'. Such relationships were seen as proof of a lack of 'racial awareness' amongst German men and a long-term danger to the substance of the 'German master race'. All the same, even these longer-lasting consensual relations were not fundamentally prohibited. Instead, the Wehrmacht tried to help its soldiers develop an understanding of the situation and teach them to forgo such relationships. The SS, in turn, had prohibited all sexual contact early on, including consensual relations, but it only sporadically punished men who violated this ban.

From the end of 1941, German Wehrmacht soldiers and SS men in Estonia, Latvia and Lithuania began to apply for permission to marry local women. Some couples were even expecting children. The RMbO initially issued a far-reaching marriage ban in April 1942, but the responsible officials in the RKO objected to it. The discussion that arose from this lasted until the end of the war. The representatives of the Reich Chancellery and the Nazi Party in Berlin declared that marriages between German men and foreign women should be generally prohibited. They argued that this was even more necessary considering the shortage of men due to the war, because 'Aryan' German women without suitable partners would not be able to bear 'racially valuable' children. The duty of 'the German man', therefore, was to give preference to a German woman. The military commanders in the occupied territories were ambivalent towards such marriages. On the one hand, they feared that the soldiers would be distracted from the goals of the war and become entangled in emotional conflicts, but on the other hand, they had no interest in denying the men their requests and thus fomenting resentment and risking military disobedience. The representatives of the OKW therefore argued against a strict prohibition on marriage. Some of the civilian occupation authorities went even further. They felt it was virtually necessary to promote ties between German men and local women if Germany wanted to form a good relationship with the local population in the long run and establish a stable occupation regime. In the absence of standardised regulations, the officials often made decisions on a case-by-case basis.

Viewed as a whole, the sexual policy strategies of the Wehrmacht, SS, civilian and military administration were based on different notions of gender, sexuality, race and violence, which could also change depending on the region, the war situation and the respective interests of the authorities involved. The development and implementation of general directives for dealing with rape, sexual transactions and consensual relations, in turn, depended largely on the mid-level officials: the civil servants working for the occupation authorities who formulated the implementing provisions, and the officers who were responsible for leading the troops as well as planning, carrying out and, in particular, controlling military operations.

In her analysis of sexual violence in military conflicts, Elisabeth Jean Wood describes armed groups as 'complex organisations that (in a particular setting, with more or less success) define opportunities, enforce specific norms, shape particular incentive structures, embrace some strategies and condemn others'.[10] But what ultimately happens on the ground cannot be understood by taking a one-sided, top-down approach. To comprehend the variation in forms of sexual violence during war, Wood suggests examining four groups and their relationships with one another: the military leadership, its hierarchy, the small unit and the individual soldier.[11] Following Wood's model, I would suggest that, in future, this analysis of the institutional levels and their mediation should be applied to the entire spectrum of sexual politics in war, including those relating to sexual transactions and consensual relations. This would take account of the gender and sexuality concepts of the respective actors as well as the range of sexual practices in question, the negotiations within the troops and the situational factors that came into play.

In the case examined here, for example, it is apparent that the conflicting notions of 'race' and 'racial purity' of the officials involved were a source of irritation, but they did not negatively impact Germany's occupation policy as such. Instead, the complex interplay of official orders, individual decisions and targeted rule modifications enabled the Nazi regime to continually spread its racial ideology while still reacting flexibly on a local level and thus assuring the individual soldier that the system was there for him.

A very similar flexibility is apparent in the Nazis' approach to the children of German soldiers and local women. Occupation children are a phenomenon to be found in nearly every war and every period of occupation. In the occupied societies, such children are often viewed as a disgrace and symbol of defeat, and they face the fears and ostracisation of those around them. In the context of the study at hand, the main question was how the occupying power dealt with the children.

It is apparent that the Wehrmacht children were a surface upon which both fantasies of victory and fears of defeat could be projected. When the German authorities discussed what to do about these children, their deliberations were not shaped by specific inquiries or individual cases but rather by wishful thinking and threat scenarios. Some of the individuals involved became downright paranoid, believing that the children posed a totally exaggerated threat; others considered them to be an equally exaggerated opportunity. In this way, the actors created a new field of action in which they could ultimately emphasise their own importance. In the end, they were generally in agreement that 'well-developed' children should be acquired for Germany despite their status as '*Mischlinge*'. But this plan was apparently only implemented in a few isolated cases.

A good deal of research to date has focused on the relationship between the Nazi state and mothers or motherhood. But the approach to dealing with the children of German soldiers in the occupied territories makes it clear that the fatherhood of 'Aryan' men was also considered a matter of state under National Socialism. Nazi institutions wanted access to the children sired by German men, even if it went against the will of the men themselves. These men were expected to relinquish their paternal responsibility to the state. Senior Reich officials were prepared to take on the role of provider and (at least temporarily) ensure a financially and socially secure upbringing for 'racially desirable' children. As Himmler imagined it, this model of biological fatherhood without the obligation to accept paternal responsibility would be applied to the entire German population after the war was over.[12] In his vision for the future, male potency and 'virility' would be unleashed to enable the optimised and efficient reproduction of 'the German people'. Himmler was therefore interested in the 'naturalisation' ('*Vernatürlichung*') of the men, so to speak, meaning that their biological functions were to be given priority, while their social functions as fathers and paterfamilias were to be transferred to state authorities. This would replace the models of masculinity that are constituted in heterosexual couples and families; masculinity would instead be shaped primarily in the male society of the military, from which soldierly men would emerge to encounter and impregnate women. In this effort to dissolve bourgeois family structures,[13] even women were allowed to engage in polygamy – not as an act of sexual autonomy, however, but rather with the goal of promoting the birth of 'Aryan' offspring. This concept was based on a totalitarian model of socialisation that sought to subordinate all aspects of private life to the goals of the state. But the speed at which state fantasies of omnipotence could reach their limit when it came to sexuality is clear from this study. Many soldiers exploited the leeway and opportunities they were offered by the state and its institutions, and they disregarded or undermined prohibitions and measures that ran counter to their interests.

After the end of the war, most men chose to keep silent about their sexual experiences. In the first post-war years, therefore, the sexuality of German women became the focus of private and public interest. Rapes by Red Army soldiers were a topic of discussion, as was the fact that some women had engaged in relationships with Allied soldiers or prisoners of war.[14] These women were repeatedly accused of having betrayed the men: 'Did the German woman fail?' asked *Stern* magazine in 1948.[15] The subsequent debate occasionally addressed the sexual experiences of German men as well – for example, a reader wrote to *Stern* calling for more sympathy for the women because the men had been guilty of sexual breaches as well, after all: 'Dear war comrades, have you forgotten so soon how in Smolensk, Odessa, and Simferopol you went into the Russian houses? That in the retreat in the final years in the East, Russian women had to come along with your battalion . . .'[16] But such concessions did not impact the prevailing social interpretation of the situation. At the end of the 1940s, as Elizabeth Heineman has shown, the fraternisation of German women with Allied soldiers became a powerful metaphor for the downfall of Germany and betrayal of German men.[17] In the context of this shifted moral debate – which focused on the sexual conduct of German women instead of on war crimes and the Holocaust[18] – the soldiers who returned home were depicted as 'desexualised' men who had fallen victim to flighty, disloyal women.

Many men did experience depression, impotence and other sexual problems after they returned home from the war. At medical conferences in West Germany in the 1950s, the men's psychological and physical symptoms were even interpreted as an expression of 'defective' masculinity.[19] A very different picture was painted in the memoirs and articles that began to be published at the time. Glossy magazines increasingly depicted the Wehrmacht soldier as an attractive, daring man – looking amiably at the camera, unshaven, his collar unbuttoned, his hair mussed and a cigarette in the corner of his mouth. This 'rakish romanticisation of the war hero', according to Habbo Knoch, was 'the commercial response to the German "crisis of masculinity" in the post-war period'.[20]

According to this image, which was also found in literature,[21] the Wehrmacht soldier had fought against Bolshevism in keeping with the anti-communism of the time and had simply been misused for the Nazi cause. In this context, the crimes committed in the Soviet Union were almost exclusively passed off as the deeds of the SS.[22] In German-language publications, acts of sexual violence and other crimes were sometimes deliberately erased. Erich Maria Remarque's novel *Zeit zu leben und Zeit zu sterben* – which was published in New York in 1954 as *A Time to Love and a Time to Die* and tells the story of the private Ernst Graeber, whose unit was stationed on the Eastern Front in 1943 – was heavily rewritten for the German edition that appeared three months after the English translation. A reference to women being raped prior to their execution was edited out, as were several passages about the mass murder of Jewish women and men.[23] The war memoirs of the Wehrmacht soldier Guy Sajer, which were published in French in 1967, were also edited for the first German version to remove all passages referring to sexual violence.[24]

While references to sexual experiences were cautious and reserved in depictions such as Sajer's, they were often specially highlighted in the *Landserromane* or war novels of the 1970s.[25] For example, *Der kleine Quast* (published in English as *If This Be Glory*) by Hasso G. Stachow, who was stationed in Russia with the Wehrmacht, recounts the experiences of the infantryman Herbert Quast. The novel describes the German defeat at Stalingrad, after which Quast continues to fight, not out of 'loyalty to the Führer' but for comradeship. 'The men gradually get soused,' Quast the first-person narrator says, 'and indulge in tales of their exploits with women. Everyone views himself as a hero no woman can resist.' In reality, however, the men have to resort to 'prostitutes' and the 'charity of women'. Quast explains the common soldier's philosophy of life and death: 'Take what you can today. Tomorrow you'll be dead or mutilated.' The men in the novel use this motto to justify all kinds of 'smut'.[26] The reader learns of Quast's numerous sexual adventures in great detail; he kisses a young Russian partisan, meets with a prostitute and flirts with an Estonian woman named Lena. Sexual violence has no place here, however.[27]

A more detailed future analysis of magazines, novels and memoirs could provide insights into the importance attributed to the soldiers' (real and fictitious) sexual experiences after the war and the concepts of masculinity that emerged from them. The photo album of an anonymous solider suggests just how normal and positively tinged the image of the virile soldier was – and likely still is – for many combatants. One page of the album, which shows the soldier's quarters in Iași in northern Romania on the border with Russia, includes a photograph at

Fig. 37 Anonymous album, 'Brothel (only for German Wehrmacht), Iasi 21.8.–28.9.41', Iasi, Romania, 1941

the bottom right of a boy exiting a shop. The subject of the photo is not immediately evident, so the shop pictured could be almost anything: a salon, a bakery, a tailor's shop. Only the caption written to the right of the picture indicates what is hidden behind the shutters: 'Brothel (only for German Wehrmacht), 1st target date [*Stichtag*] 27.8.41 (25 years!)'. It is impossible to know whether the solider pasted this photo into his album during the war or only afterwards.[28] It can be assumed, however, that the 'target date' or '*Stichtag*' (which derives from the German verb *stechen*, to thrust or stab, and therefore has a dual meaning) was not a reference to the opening of the brothel; instead, it probably marked the soldier's first time visiting a brothel – presumably on his twenty-fifth birthday.

At first glance, the documentation of sexual encounters after the end of the war may appear to be a purely private matter for the men involved. But upon closer examination, it is clear that this documentation also marks a boundary between the private and the public. Sexual encounters in wartime and the recounting of such experiences afterwards do not take place in a social vacuum. They have specific meanings for the individuals involved and their respective social environments, and they reveal the entanglement of war, gender concepts and sexuality. 'Practices during the so-called exceptional situation [*Ausnahmezustand*] of war', Gaby Zipfel writes, 'are inscribed in the experience and action potential of a society and passed on from one generation to the next'.[29] What this means for German society in the post-war period and today is a subject for future investigation.

Notes

1. Quoted in Engert, *Soldaten für Hitler*, p. 114.
2. See, e.g., *Deutsche Wochenschau*, 755/19, December 1944, quoted in Johr and Sander, *BeFreier und Befreite*, p. 131. Also see Grossmann, 'A Question of Silence', pp. 50f., 59.
3. Quoted in Müller, *Deutsche Soldaten*, p. 163. The men were associating a sexual threat with a 'racial' threat here; very much in keeping with traditional racist fantasies, they imagined that 'the Mongol' or 'the Jew' had always been more potent and virile than European men (ibid. pp. 164ff.).
4. The acts of sexual violence committed by members of the Red Army have been researched relatively extensively; see, e.g., Burds, 'Sexual Violence'; Mark, 'Remembering Rape'; Pető, 'Stimmen des Schweigens'; Withuis, 'Die verlorene Unschuld des Gedächtnisses'; Grossmann, 'A Question of Silence'; Heineman, 'The Hour of the Woman'; Eifler, 'Nachkrieg und weibliche Verletzbarkeit'; Naimark, *The Russians in Germany*; Beevor, *Berlin: The Downfall*; Mühlhäuser, 'Vergewaltigungen in Deutschland 1945'; Bos, 'Feminist Interpretations of Wartime Rape'.
5. Regarding fears of revenge in general, see, e.g., Müller, *Deutsche Soldaten*, p. 223.
6. Bröckling, *Disziplin*, p. 10.
7. Reemtsma, 'Die Wiederkehr der Hobbesschen Frage', p. 51.
8. Roos, 'Backlash Against Prostitutes' Rights'; Freund-Widder, *Frauen unter Kontrolle*.
9. Ibid. pp. 27ff.; Sigusch, *Geschichte der Sexualwissenschaft*, pp. 247ff.
10. Wood, 'Sexual Violence During War', pp. 343f.
11. Ibid, p. 344.
12. 'Geheimer Vermerk von Bormann für SS-Hauptsturmführer Meine vom 29.1.1944, betr.: Sicherung der Zukunft des deutschen Volkes', BArch NS 19/3289, pp. 1–11, here pp. 3ff.; cf. also pp. 21ff.
13. Churches and other institutions consequently opposed these concepts; see, e.g., 'Chef der Sicherheitspolizei und des SD, AMT III, Boberach (ed.), *Meldungen aus dem Reich*, Nr. 202 vom 14.7.1941', BArch R 58/162, pp. 86–120, here p. 109.
14. Heineman, *What Difference Does a Husband Make?*, pp. 96ff.
15. Excerpts from this discussion have been documented by Boyer and Woller, '"Hat die deutsche Frau versagt?"', pp. 33ff.
16. Quoted in ibid. p. 36, and Herzog, *Sex After Fascism*, p. 60. Regarding the same argument in other contexts, also see Biess, 'Men of Reconstruction' p. 344f.; Schneider, '"Einigkeit im Unglück"?', p. 217; and Meyer and Schulze, *Von Liebe sprach damals keiner*, p. 135.
17. Heineman, 'The Hour of the Woman', pp. 380ff. The situation in the areas around US military bases in the 1950s is discussed by Höhn, *GIs and Fräuleins*, pp. 126ff.
18. Herzog, *Sex After Fascism*, pp. 72ff.
19. See Goltermann, 'Die Beherrschung der Männlichkeit', pp. 14f.; Biess, 'Men

of Reconstruction', pp. 339f., 345. Frank Biess has shown that West German psychiatrists ascribed some of the same physical and psychological 'deficiencies' to the soldiers returning home as they did to victims of the Nazis. East German society, by contrast, almost entirely ignored the physical, psychological and sexual constitution of the returning men (Biess, 'Men of Reconstruction', pp. 340f.).

20. Knoch, *Die Tat als Bild*, p. 451.
21. Amberger, *Männer*.
22. Naumann, 'Die "saubere" Wehrmacht'.
23. Heer, *Tote Zonen*, p. 276. In the current German edition of the book, these passages have been restored (Remarque, *Zeit zu leben und Zeit zu sterben* [1998], pp. 177f., 371f.).
24. Sajer, the son of a French father and German mother, had initially joined the Wehrmacht with enthusiasm during the German occupation of Alsace (Sajer, *Le soldat oublié*; Sajer, *Denn dieser Tage Qual war gross*). These passages do appear in the English translation (Sajer, *Forgotten Soldier*) and in the new German translation (Sajer, *Der vergessene Soldat*).
25. Kühne, *Kameradschaft*, p. 249; also see Kühne, *The Rise and Fall of Comradeship*, pp. 262f.
26. Stachow, *Der kleine Quast*, pp. 146f.
27. Ibid. pp. 52, 64, 102, 114, 116f., 131f., 146f., 159f., 227, 234f.
28. Regarding German soldiers collecting photos, pasting them into albums and captioning them, see Bopp, *Fremde im Visier*.
29. Zipfel, 'Ausnahmezustand Krieg?', p. 74.

CHAPTER 7

Epilogue: What Can We Learn from the Nazi Case?

In recent years, we have seen a remarkable societal willingness to engage critically with sexual violence in armed conflicts, its victims and perpetrators. Since the early 1990s – with the end of the Cold War, the growing interest in human rights work in the new world order, the wars in Yugoslavia, and the war and genocide in Rwanda – sexual violence in armed conflict has attracted growing public attention. This form of violence is now a highly visible and contested subject in international criminal law, transitional and post-war justice, international peace and security politics as well as media coverage and academic research.[1]

Following the current debates in the US and Western Europe, one could easily get the impression that sexual violence primarily occurs in the warfare of irregular actors, such as terror groups, rebels or private armies. Sexual violence is described as a problem that arises when order collapses and chaos and savagery seem to reign. In such scenarios, sexual violence often appears to be an expression of particularly cruel, uncivilised behaviour, 'a deviation from the norm with women as "natural victims"'.[2] In some cases, the focus is also increasingly placed on men and boys as victims of sexual violence, a situation often regarded as even more humiliating and inhumane.[3] As an overall response, measures to prevent sexual violence – including policies and legal interventions – seem to focus on restoring order and protecting the groups of women (and sometimes men) who are identified as victims.

The historical example of World War II, however, suggests that the reality of who perpetrates sexual violence when, where and against whom is more complicated. On the one hand, the growing body of work in this field demonstrates that military actors on all sides perpetrated sexual violence against 'enemy women': the aggressor armies of

Germany and Japan as well as their collaborators, but also partisans and other resistance groups, along with soldiers from the allied armies of the Soviet Union, the United States, Great Britain and France.[4] What is more, we know of cases of sexual violence perpetrated against allies, such as when Soviet soldiers raped female victims of Nazi persecution in Poland or US soldiers raped local women in Britain or France.[5] In-group sexual violence has also recently become a subject of research, one example being the sexual exploitation of female prisoners by male prisoners in camps and ghettoes during the Holocaust.[6] The grey zones between sexual violence, coercion, bartering, prostitution and consensual encounters further complicate the picture. Overall, practices of sexual violence and exploitation were pervasive throughout various geographical and cultural spaces, in different stages of the war, during combat, in times of occupation as well as in practices of genocide.

On the other hand, the ubiquity of these forms of violence in World War II does not mean that the phenomenon can solely be understood in a universal manner. A deep study of historical scenarios reveals that the perpetration of sexual violence varied, as did its forms, patterns and frequencies, the experiences of the victims and perpetrators, and the ways in which this form of violence was (and is) understood, communicated and responded to. For example, the sources suggest that the behaviour of US and British soldiers was often more brutal in the Asian than the European theatre of war, a context permeated by colonial legacies and the fear of the Exotic Other.[7] The way the different constellations of sexual violence are broached or silenced, remembered or forgotten, depends on the respective socio-political constellations during the war and in the post-war decades until today.[8]

This book hopes to deepen our understanding of the factors that facilitate and shape but also curtail sexual violence. It also aims to broaden the debate and ask more generally how sex, violence and war intersect, even in non-violent sexual encounters.

Racist 'Pollution Taboos'

The observation that the perpetration of sexual violence varies and the question of how we can explain these variations has been a long-standing subject of feminist research.[9] More recently, the subject has been investigated in comparative political science research. Elisabeth Jean Wood has started to explore the issue by asking 'When is wartime rape rare?' and she finds the answer to this question primarily in the organisation of armed groups. Where little sexual violence occurs, she argues, leaders manage to keep their men from perpetrating this form of violence through strong disciplinary mechanisms and/or ideological indoctrination.

Commanders, Wood observes, can prevent sexual violence if they choose to do so; it is thus important to understand when and why they might make that decision. Looking at research on different empirical cases, she establishes that commanders introduce measures to prohibit sexual violence when they determine that the perpetration is counterproductive to their interests (for example, when a military unit depends on the collaboration of the local population). The subordinate soldiers, in turn, are more likely to obey such rules when they take the form of internalised cultural or institutional norms. This can be observed in 'pollution taboos', for example, 'whereby sexual violence with civilians associated with the enemy is perceived as polluting the perpetrator'.[10] One case that Wood cites for her hypothesis is the allegedly small amount of sexual violence perpetrated in Nazi concentration and labour camps.[11]

Wood puts her finger on a crucial question, namely, if and how ideological factors affect the ways armed men act regarding sexuality and sexual violence. The Nazi war and genocide is a promising case for exploring this question, since the Nazi idea of power was so deeply intertwined with the fantasy of the superiority of the Aryan race and the fear that this superiority could be soiled and destroyed by sexual intercourse with 'inferior' people. Yet a close examination of the historical sources suggests that the reality of war and genocide confronts us with a complex and ambivalent scenario. Germans soldiers and SS men did not 'simply accept propagandists' insistence that Jews were unthinkable as sexual partners'.[12] And even when they did, this did not necessarily prevent them from perpetrating sexual violence. As we have seen in the course of this book, the men did perpetrate sexual violence, including penile rape and sexual enslavement, against women and girls regarded as 'racially inferior' (*fremdvölkisch*) or 'of alien races' (*artfremd*). In other cases, men even developed romantic feelings for such women. The frequency of such acts, however, seems to have varied depending on the material conditions and the morale of the German Wehrmacht and SS at different times, in different territories (within the Reich and beyond its borders) and in different locations during the war (combat, front lines and occupation zones) and the genocide (ghettoes; labour, concentration and extermination camps; and execution sites).

Since I believe this point is central for understanding sexual violence by Nazi perpetrators, allow me to make a short detour and address

Wood's hypothesis that sexual violence was rare in concentration and extermination camps before I return to the war zone. To begin with, we can note that descriptions of penile rape by SS guards in concentration and extermination camps are, indeed, relatively rare. Whether rape was, in fact, infrequent or whether the small number of accounts indicates that both women and men concealed such experiences is still a matter of debate among scholars.[13] In various theatres of war and armed conflict, perpetrators have been known to commit penile rape in privacy, meaning in secluded spaces with no spectators.[14] Since many female prisoners in the concentration camps were killed, we ultimately cannot know how common such practices might have been.

Na'ama Shik has posed the hypothesis that penile rape by guards in concentration camps was rare because the prisoners' shorn hair, dirty clothing and poor physical condition would make them unthinkable as (sexual) Others for German men.[15] Similarly, Doris Bergen has hypothesised that SS men did not rape Jewish women because they designated and treated Jews as subhuman and felt that sexual intercourse with Jewish women would be 'comparable to having sex with animals or corpses'. She continues, 'here a terrible paradox seems to have come into play: rape is something one only does to fellow human beings'.[16] Scholars who have examined other genocides, however, make the opposing argument, proposing that genocidaires rape their victims specifically *because* they hate and fear them as subhumans.

Another explanation for the potentially limited sexual abuse of Jewish women in concentration camps might be found in the organised and industrialised nature of the spaces that created an atmosphere of social surveillance among the guards, in which they could not easily transgress racial borders.[17] Here, the question of time seems to be crucial. In the early years of National Socialism in particular, the monitoring and condemnation of sexual encounters was a critical tool for dividing society into those who belonged to the 'people's community' and those who did not.[18] After the Nuremberg laws introduced the criminal offence of 'race defilement' in September 1935, the Nazi authorities were able to resort to long-established mechanisms for the sexual surveillance and denunciation of women, non-Germans and dissenters.[19] In this societal context, SS guards in concentration camps were likely to internalise the ban on penile intercourse with people regarded as 'inferior' – not merely as an organisational norm enforced within the SS, but rather as a societal framework and a marker of identity and belonging to the German '*Volksgemeinschaft*'. However, after the first years of the war, when the German armed forces began to experience defeats (like Stalingrad in the winter of 1942–43), concentration camp guards often vented their frustrations openly against prisoners, and the trespassing of Nazi rules became increasingly normalised.

But even if penile rape might have been rare in concentration and extermination camps, other forms of sexual violence were remarkably pervasive and part of the institutionalised violence that characterised the genocide of the Jews, Sinti and Roma, and people with disabilities. Indeed, sexual violence in the form of enforced disrobement, unwanted genital touching, genital beating, rape with fingers or objects, sexual torture, medical experiments on the sexual organs or forced sterilisation were not considered to be race defilement.[20] These acts were perpetrated by both male and female SS guards[21] and directed against both female and male prisoners (even though the meanings of such actions were different for women and men).[22] Testimonies indicate that such acts affected the prisoners in particular ways, violating their intimacy and their capacity for reproduction. Ultimately, sexual violence appears to have been an effective means of shaming prisoners and destroying the bonds between them. Elisa von Joeden-Forgey has coined the term 'life force atrocities' to refer to ritualised forms of violence that target the family and the reproduction of human life: the bearing of children, the organisation of social, cultural, emotional and spiritual life, and so on. In her thinking, the life force of a group is organised primarily through the social institution of the family. To attack and destroy family structures and their norms and values thus constitutes 'one way that perpetrators express genocidal rage'.[23]

Following this line of reasoning, sexual violence in Nazi concentration and extermination camps can be seen as a practice by which the perpetrators attempted to annihilate prisoners as social beings before killing them.[24] If we take this into account, a narrow focus on penile rape (and the uncertainty as to how pervasive it was) risks trivialising and obliterating the dynamics of sexual violence in the enclosed spaces of the camps.

In the war zone in the Soviet Union, penile rape seems to have been more pervasive, depending on the territory and time. How can we understand this? To begin with, it should be noted that the laws prohibiting racial transgression no longer had the same relevance when the Germans invaded the Soviet Union in the summer of 1941. Eight years after the Nazis came to power and two years after the beginning of the war, the societal exclusion of Jews, Sinti and Roma people, and people with disabilities had already been clearly established. In the following months, the persecution measures intensified rapidly. After deciding on the implementation of the so-called 'Final Solution to the Jewish Question' at the Wannsee Conference on 20 January 1942, all previously prevailing concerns about persecution and violence against Jews were finally dismissed as a sign of weakness. In accordance with this, the disciplining and prosecution of racial transgressions was no longer directly relevant to the far-advanced policy of racial exclusion, particularly during the war and genocide in the 'occupied Eastern territories'.[25] All Jews were doomed to be annihilated, so things could be done to them that were unimaginable before.

Furthermore, we have to take into account that there is a difference between military operations, violence and mass killings in the vast territory and different social situations at the front on the one hand, and overseeing prisoners, perpetrating violence and killings in the enclosed spaces of camps on the other. The bodily conditions and the spaces for interpretation and action of the actors varied.

As Gaby Zipfel notes, the war zone is 'marked by extreme bodily reactions, by killing and dying, suffering and enjoyment, panic and triumph'; it is a situation in which 'emotions, bodily sensations and affects take centre stage'.[26] In this context, Wehrmacht soldiers, SS members and policemen, as well as their respective leaders, acted and reacted in complex and contradictory ways that were by no means congruent with the Nazis' racist pollution taboos.

The military commanders knew that they had only limited control over the physical actions of their men, but they had little interest in strictly condemning and prosecuting sexual violence against women, including Jewish women. While the Wehrmacht and the SS issued a variety of bans to curb sexual violence and sexual contact with women and girls deemed 'racially inferior' or 'of alien races', they did not enforce them vigorously or consistently.

In this atmosphere of tacit agreement, German men in uniform took advantage of the opportunities for sexual activity according to their individual preferences as well as to the habitual practices within their units. Their degree of commitment to Nazi ideology did not necessarily have a direct influence on their actions. Even soldiers and SS men who were enthusiastic Nazis could breach the racial laws by raping Jewish women without assuming that their behaviour contradicted Nazi aims. In the male-dominated society at the front, specifically male warrior standards were created that emphasised the capacity to overstep rules and overcome doubts as a masculine strength.[27] Here, too, particular forms of sexual violence (those that did not violate Nazi racial laws in the first place, such as enforced undressing or body searches) were part of the organised and institutionalised military and genocidal violence during the war and in the killing fields.

It is clear that we must be cautious in assuming that ideological beliefs simply prevent men from committing rape. Where ideology is negotiated, reproduced and produced, the actions chosen by different individuals are never merely coherent and purposeful.[28] The sexual sphere, in particular, is characterised by emotions and affects that seem to influence the actions of the individual men in often uncontrolled ways. This is not to suggest that ideological restrictions such as racist pollution taboos do not play a role. Rather, we need to examine the conditions in certain spaces and the dynamics that unfold between perpetrators, victims and bystanders to understand which effects ideological norms and laws have on the understanding and behaviour of soldiers and genocidaires.

Conflicting Military Interests

Neither the Wehrmacht nor the SS leadership in the Soviet Union had a decisive interest in preventing sexual activity, including sexual violence against Jewish and non-Jewish women and girls. In the Wehrmacht in particular, commanders experienced a conflict of interest. On the one hand, they associated their soldiers' sexual activity with a specific set of risks, including the spread of sexually transmitted diseases, the loss of the army's reputation, the incitement of resistance amongst occupied populations and the potential birth of 'racially mixed bastards'. On the other hand, they had little interest in banning and punishing the sexual activities of their men. The commanders understood sexuality to be a form of consolation for the men that compensated them for the hardships of war and secured their loyalty to the army. Moreover, it was common knowledge amongst the commanders that sexual violence was a particularly effective means of destroying bonds and spreading insecurity in enemy societies. As a result, the Wehrmacht's sexual policies were ambivalent and often contradictory; though there were clear laws and orders against sexual violence and other forms of sexual activity, they were seldom enforced. Overall, the Wehrmacht displayed a benevolent understanding for the 'sexual needs' of its men and facilitated opportunities for sexual encounters, including rape.

That sexual regulations and policies were largely conflicting does not seem to be a particular characteristic of the Nazi war in the Soviet Union. We also see this tendency in the Allied armies of World War II and many armies today. The question is how we can understand the ways in which military leaders deal with this dilemma. In her more recent work, Wood reflects on the largely ambivalent character of military sexual politics: 'Many organizations appear to formally prohibit sexual violence but do not build the institutions or exert the will to effectively do so – with the result that rape, if it emerges, is neither ordered nor punished but is tolerated'.[29]

Wood grasps this toleration of rape by distinguishing between 'opportunistic rape' (rape perpetrated for private reasons), 'strategic rape' (rape purposefully adopted in pursuit of an organisation's objectives) and 'rape as a practice' (rape as a product of social interactions, such as the combatant's desire to conform to the behaviour of others in the unit). If rape is punished by the chain of command, Wood argues, it is clearly regarded as opportunistic and thus private and contrary to military aims. By contrast, rape can become a matter of military strategy:

> as a form of sexual torture of political prisoners, the public rape of members of particular groups as they are 'cleansed' from an area, as a form of collective punishment (usually in the context of orders to terrorize civilians), or as a signal of the organization's resolve.

In some settings, furthermore, rape can become 'an institutionalized form of compensation or reward, as when combatants are rewarded for exemplary service with civilians to victimize (or sex slaves, or wives in forced marriage)'.[30]

Between these distinct poles – with the punishment of rape on one end and the promotion of rape on the other – Wood identifies 'rape as a practice'. In this case, commanders largely tolerate such behaviour because to punish it would present serious challenges to their military goals:

> It may require the disciplining or dismissal of otherwise effective subordinates; it may divert scarce resources to an issue seen as unimportant; it may lessen the respect of subordinates for their superiors ... and thereby undermine vertical cohesion; or it may simply be too much trouble.[31]

Other recent scholarship comes to similar conclusions. Amelia Hoover Green argues that 'most commanders, given the reputational costs of rape, would rather avoid it. They may not particularly *care* about sexual violence, but they understand (as American officers did in Vietnam) that the optics are bad'.[32] Both Wood and Hoover Green's depictions indicate that a majority of commanders think it is just too much trouble to try to control and prohibit rape. If this observation reflects the reality, however, we must probe the particular character of this form of violence. Why can senior commanders simply 'tolerate' practices of sexual violence over long periods of time? Would this also be possible with other forms of violence, such as beating or killing? And if not, how can we grasp the specificity of sexual violence?

The sources I examined in this book suggest that one specificity of sexual violence is the lack of a clear military (or, for that matter, societal) agreement that this form of violence constitutes a wrongdoing, let alone a crime. Historical studies from different theatres of war and armed conflicts in the nineteenth and twentieth centuries have demonstrated that military courts generally only indict and pass sentences on sexual violence with specific dynamics and constellations, without necessarily conceding the criminal nature of acts of sexual violence. For example, the 1863 Lieber Code (the military code for the US Union Army) codified rape in women-specific terms as a crime against property, troop discipline and family honour. The number of cases that ended up in court was limited and, as Crystal Feimster observes, they were at least in part 'about discipline, and enforcing a code of conduct'.[33] Similarly, Birgit Beck found that the Wehrmacht only prosecuted sexual assaults (*'Notzucht'*) during World War II when it feared grave disciplinary problems or serious harm to the reputation of the forces. Beck's work shows that a soldier's prosecution did not involve acknowledging the harm suffered by the victims. Rape was usually tried in line with the strategic calculations of the military command. Cases were only brought before a military court once the Wehrmacht had begun to establish a longer-term occupation regime that required collaboration with large segments of the local population, because the military authorities needed to restrain and discipline their men to ensure this cooperation. In accordance with this, sentences were passed on the Western Front and at the start of the occupation of Poland in 1939–40, but as the war on the Eastern Front grew more brutal – and especially after the invasion of the Soviet Union on 22 June 1941 – the military rarely exercised its jurisdiction over rape anymore.[34]

One might argue that this is not all that different from the way militaries handle other forms of violence, such as looting. Indeed, looting, like rape, is codified as a crime in military law and codes of conduct. Nonetheless, in certain time periods and within certain limits, soldiers are granted the liberty to loot. For a long time, in fact, both looting and rape were treated as property crimes and 'normal' by-products of warfare. However, while an 'international prohibition regime' against looting was established with relatively little controversy in the late nineteenth century, Tuba Inal notes that similar steps were taken against rape only at the end of the twentieth century. She suspects that the main reason for this long-lasting toleration of rape was that 'states did not believe they could prevent rape in war because they believed rape in war was inevitable'.[35]

Underlying Inal's observation that states did not believe they could prevent wartime rape is the belief that the frictions of the battlefield and sexual excitement are inextricably linked. In April 1942, Hitler asserted that 'If the German man as a soldier is to be ready to die unconditionally he must have the freedom to love unconditionally'.[36] This comment reveals an understanding prevalent in modern thinking, namely, that combat and sex are *the* quintessential existential experiences of human – or, more precisely, male – existence. In fact, the idea that male virility is an affirmation of male vitality can be found in different regions of the world. According to David Tombs, 'one of the most significant ways that a man can define himself as victor not victim is through his sexual identity as an active and powerful man'.[37] And affirming one's non-victim status becomes all the more important in wartime.

This does not mean that all soldiers are sexually active and aim to fulfil the ideal of the virile man. But even men who refuse to engage in sexual bragging or brothel visits, for example, contribute to bringing the culturally shared and socially accepted hegemonic ideal of the virile man to the fore. By tolerating this kind of behaviour (with sympathy, more or less) they are not merely observers, but they accept, affirm and support the paradigm. Ultimately, we find a tacit agreement in many military formations that condone and indeed accept the male soldiers' sexual advances towards women as a natural part of military life. It is this understanding, I believe, that lies at the core of the ambiguity of military politics and policies on sexual violence.

Sexual Violence and Sexuality

Men do not necessarily perceive acts of sexual violence against women to be serious crimes. Moreover, male combatants are sometimes not even aware that their actions constitute violence and thus wrongdoing. In September 1940, for example, two Wehrmacht soldiers forced two Jewish women, aged seventeen and eighteen, to leave their home at gunpoint and go to a Polish cemetery. The soldiers raped one of the women. The other woman was menstruating, so they let her go but 'offered' to pay her five zloty if she came back the following week to have sex with them.³⁸ While the women must have experienced this encounter as violent, the men could view it as somehow consensual, as something the women could agree to, at least in exchange for money.

Why and how this divergence of perspectives works needs to be explored in future research. Gaby Zipfel has suggested one possible point of departure for such an analysis by highlighting the need to assess the ways in which sexual violence in modern times aims not only to inflict pain, but also to exploit the sexual sensations of the victim. A sexually violent act thus also represents an attack on the libido:

> A person beaten up in the street may not reckon with the empathy of those present, may even experience blame for allegedly contributing to the violence through some form of provocation, but she/he can assume that her/his experience of violently inflicted physical pain is unequivocally considered an unwanted, negative experience. Victims of sexual violence, by contrast, are often denied a clear assessment in this sense. This is because this kind of attack targets a body that is not only sensitive to pain, but also able to take pleasure. Sexual violence subjects the body of the victim to pain and at the same time seizes its libidinal sensibility.³⁹

These implicit or explicit insinuations that the victim 'reacts ambiguously to the attack' arise because of the possibility of sexual arousal as a condition of the body. Thus 'a possible agreement between the perpetrator and the victim' is implied ('she asked for it'), and the victim is denied empathy and a clear classification of this form of violence as wrongdoing.⁴⁰

If we take this into account, we also come to a better understanding of why most women and girls kept silent about their experience of sexual violence during World War II. As the sources in this book reveal, women often found themselves confronted with insinuations of collaboration and prostitution. Only when an act of sexual violence was accompanied by excessive brutality and/or when the perpetrator killed the victim during or after the sexual attack could 'the previously questioned unambiguity [. . .] cynically be established as proven' – not least because now the sexuality expressed in the act of violence practiced by the perpetrator and visited on the victim could 'be marginalized'.⁴¹

It might be precisely this ambiguity surrounding rape (directed against the body as subject to pain as well as to arousal and lust) that makes this form of violence such an effective means of warfare. The alleged complicity of the victim suggests that the responsibility for the attack does not lie solely with the perpetrator, and that the victim contributed to her violation. This, in turn, seems to cause the victim's community to view her with suspicion, distrust and contempt. These negative responses may even rebound on and attach to the community itself, particularly the men in the community since they allowed the act to happen. As a result, the rape victim's collective can be seriously shaken, torn apart and destroyed.

As we have seen in different theatres of armed conflict, victims of sexual violence often report struggling with feelings of defilement and shame. How such feelings are generated and what they mean has yet to be explored in detail. Bülent Diken and Carsten Bagge Laustsen argue that such feelings are connected to the social construction of rape victims as abject. The abject person, they explain, is seen as a threat to the normal social order because she is defined as polluted (and feels herself to be polluted) and is thus no longer able to be part of the normal order. An abject person symbolises not just the other, a subject outside of one's own community; an abject person also denotes indistinctness and formlessness and thus a threat within the community.[42] If we follow this argument, wartime rape is an attempt to devalue women, thereby harming the whole community.[43]

This resonates with an earlier feminist observation that wartime rape is ultimately directed at men who are understood to be protectors of women and the community. Consequently, sexual violence uses women's bodies to transport a message from men to men, namely, that the men in the victim's collective are no longer able to protect 'their' women.[44] This observation also explains why sexual violence can become such an obsessive topic in war propaganda. As Elizabeth Heinemann has argued, representations of sexual violence in war 'do not simply occur after the fact: rather, they are often part of the conflict itself.'[45] Indeed, public stories about enemy rape in times of war are largely meant to mobilise hatred against the enemy and to enlist active support for the war effort.

In a somewhat contradictory figure, sexual violence appears, on the one hand, to be a particularly cruel crime that reveals the alleged inhumanity of the enemy and, on the other hand, to be normal male behaviour, known and knowable, a seemingly natural by-product of war. In both cases, the experiences and voices of the victims of this form of violence remain unheard. They are regularly not authorised to talk about their experiences, at least not in public. Even women who are ready to share their experiences find themselves hindered by people suggesting it would be too shameful for them.[46] As a consequence, sexual violence is largely mythologised, since there are almost no thick descriptions of who does what to whom when sexual violence occurs. Ultimately, this plays into the hands of the perpetrators who have little difficulty concealing their crimes.

Soldiers' Corporeality

Those who go to war experience a loss of complete control. No matter how hard they try to imagine themselves invincible, ultimately they know that they are vulnerable and might die at any moment.[47] In this situation, 'emotions such as the fear of injury, pain and death, but also anger or hatred, can feel overpowering. Contradictory affects and emotions, such as simultaneous anger and anxiety, also have an effect on their personality'.[48]

Men learn that their bodies can react to combat in uncontrolled ways, and they 'fear what their bodies might reveal.'[49] German army doctors in World War II observed that the men would sometimes experience uncontrolled trembling. Alcohol and drugs were handy measures for trying to deal with fear and psychological and physiological effects.[50] Uncontrolled bodily reactions could also be connected to sexuality. After World War I, for example, German military doctors noted that experiences on the battlefield and in the trenches could cause impotence.[51] Furthermore, German, British and American soldiers alike described experiencing arousal and orgasm while perpetrating violence or killing during World War II, as Joanna Bourke has demonstrated.[52]

Military commanders know that war is a bodily practice and a test for the body, and they are aware that they must take into account the physical and psychological frictions that men experience during battle. 'Ultimately, the battlefield is a place of extreme affects – from the stupor of agony to the furore of battle-frenzy – that inhibit or disinhibit actions and change their direction', according to Ulrich Bröckling. He concludes that a military command thus needs to deal with the soldiers' 'radicalized experience of contingency'.[53]

Men in state armies are therefore trained to deal with their bodily sensations, emotions and affects. This involves efforts to establish action routines for soldiers that they can fall back on when exposed to great emotional stress (how men in non-state armed groups are trained has yet to be investigated more systematically). As Frank Barrett has shown, such training is largely based on misogynist ideas of what it means to be the ideal warrior, independent of women, family and civilian morale. Following this logic, femininity represents weakness, subordination, emotionalism, dependency and disloyalty.[54]

At the same time, however, the soldier cannot merely reject the traits regarded as feminine; he must also embody them.[55] In the military institution, he must submit, obey and endure violence. To survive, he is dependent on his comrades as well as his troop leader. He is also faced with loyalty conflicts and disloyalties between superiors and comrades. Within small military units – away from family and friends – some men also take caring and nurturing positions that would be coded as female in civil society, as Thomas Kühne has shown with respect to Wehrmacht soldiers.[56]

This conflation of the dominant and the submissive becomes a source of confusion. As Aaron Belkin observed regarding US servicemen in the twentieth century:

> Ambiguity around what constitutes the symbolic order/meaning of masculinity has been a tool that tightened the screw of military discipline by making it impossible for soldiers to know whether or not they are masculine, whether or not they are on the right side of the line. [. . .] Unable to embody subject positions which are coded as oppositional yet indistinguishable, and unable to ascertain the difference between what they are supposed to idealize and that which they must disavow, they have found that surrender to authority is the most viable option.[57]

Ultimately, Belkin argues, this institutionally constructed and highly confusing split between dominant and subordinate position, which the soldiers cannot resolve, forces men to resort to conformity and compliance. This conflating of the masculine and unmasculine creates a confusion that serves as a form of discipline for military leaders.

Belkin cites the example of US Marines who cleaned their penises with wire brushes during combat operations in the South Pacific during World War II, remarking that 'it is hard to say [. . .] whether [they] were emasculating themselves in an act of genital mutilation, or fortifying themselves in a hyper-masculine genital purification rite that echoed the cleaning of a weapon'.[58] Similar ambiguous messages can also be found in the practices and rites of the Wehrmacht and SS, such as the 'prick parade' (*Schwanzappell*) cited in Chapter 3. Military commanders work with these kinds of insecurities to keep their men under control. The men try to fulfil masculine ideals but can never be sure that they will succeed; they must always fear not living up to expectations.[59]

In this scenario, sexual activities and the perpetration of sexual violence seem to occupy specific positions. On the one hand, soldiers can experience their virility as a demonstration and affirmation of individual power, superiority and invincibility.⁶⁰ Zipfel, drawing on Judith Butler's work on precarity, has recently described such feelings of power and invincibility in connection with the dynamics between perpetrator and victim. The perpetrator knows that he is vulnerable because vulnerability is a human condition. By exposing the vulnerability of the victim, however, a perpetrator can 'relocate his vulnerability onto the other' and create the illusion of being invincible.⁶¹

On the other hand, the act of sexual violence also reveals the perpetrator's insecurity, his dependence on others: 'The ability to feel lustful desire is predicated on the experience of being desired. If this sense of being desired . . . is absent, then sexual desire can be experienced as a threat, as subjugation to another.'⁶² What becomes clear is that desire, insecurity, hostility and aggression are closely connected. And the perpetrator can hardly hide his insecurity from the victim; instead, he is exposed to her.⁶³ This might partially explain why perpetrators often kill their victims after the act.⁶⁴

That violence and sexuality as bodily affects, practices and experiences are deeply intertwined is an intrinsic part of military knowledge. The anticipation of sexual violence and sympathetic understanding for the offenders was commonly found in the Wehrmacht High Command as well. As I have discussed in more detail in Chapter 2, Commander-in-Chief of the Army Walther von Brauchitsch disseminated rules of action entitled '*Selbstzucht*' ('self-discipline') to the troop leaders on the Eastern Front in September 1941:

> As the dispositions of the men are diverse, it is inevitable that tensions and needs will arise now and then in the sexual realm, to which we cannot and must not turn a blind eye. Prohibiting sexual activity [. . .] will not solve the problem in any case.

Sources like this reveal that we must discuss the ways in which military commanders do more than simply tolerate the practices of sexual violence by their men, regarding them as being unimportant. How can we grasp and describe the fact that they harbour tacit assumptions about this form of violence and try to manage potential risks and benefits?

Sexual Violence as a Weapon

The case of Nazi soldiers in the Soviet Union also forces us to take a more nuanced view of the concept of sexual violence as a weapon of war because it demonstrates that sexual violence often might not be a strategy in the traditional military understanding of the word – that is, part of a communicated plan – but it can still be part of a military command's operational thinking.

We must assume that individual soldiers mostly perpetrated sexual violence on their own terms when the opportunity arose. But the military commanders of the Wehrmacht and SS tolerated, accepted, and thus facilitated (and sometimes even instigated) this behaviour because it corresponded with their interests. In fact, the men were by no means permitted to rape as they wished. If a case was considered to be harmful to the military operation, a perpetrator could be (and sometimes was) disciplined and punished.

Permitting sexual violence within the larger campaign of the war of annihilation served different functions: (1) it fostered cohesion in the small units and loyalty towards superiors, (2) it degraded local women and destroyed social ties in the victims' community and (3) it became a way to dehumanise Jews and produce a distancing effect towards them that facilitated genocidal killings.

If the scenarios outlined so far reflect reality, then we must revisit our theories of how sexual violence becomes part of a military's operational thinking.[65] How can we grasp the entanglement between individual actions, social norms and command considerations? In order to pursue this question, I would like to suggest that we rethink the common understanding of sexual violence as a form of military strategy and tactics in ways that stretch the usage of these terms common in military parlance.

Classic military theory distinguishes between strategy and tactics. Even though the working definitions of these terms vary over time and according to the form of an armed conflict, their overall interpretation and relationship to each other remain essentially the same. Strategy is generally defined as the comprehensive planning, coordination, and application of military means (and often also civilian resources) to meet political objectives. On the operational level, strategy helps to map out and organise the key battles that an army command has identified as necessary to meet its general military goals. Tactics, by contrast, are more short-term decisions during military operations – decisions concerning the movement of troops or the choice of weapons, for example – that are necessary to win a battle. In military logic, tactics aim at the successful realisation of operational goals, and operational planning (strategy) aims at the successful fulfilment of a campaign and thus the attainment of the political objective of the war.[66]

This hierarchical model of military planning and decision fails, however, to represent what every man and woman who has participated in a military mission knows: that no soldier merely follows orders. In the reality of the battlefield and in zones of occupation, soldiers evaluate orders according to their position and scope of interpretation and action (*Handlungsräume*) and make situationally dependent decisions. The soldiers' role as representatives of the military institution, the visual power of their uniforms, as well as their place in the military hierarchy even allow them to enact power in ways that would be unthinkable for a civilian. The military command is fully aware that when soldiers make decisions and perpetrate violence, the overall goal of winning the campaign recedes behind the need to evaluate the opportunities of the moment. As Ulrich Bröckling argues in his study of military discipline, military authorities must 'anticipate what eludes calculation'.[67] Only if a military command succeeds in predicting the actions of the men on the ground can it react quickly, remain in control, and sustain its power.[68] And, indeed, military commanders have to anticipate that their men will perpetrate sexual violence, taking its consequences into account whether they regard them as negative or positive for the war effort, depending on the respective circumstances.

When thinking about ways to integrate the agency of the soldier on the ground (the direct perpetrator of the sexual violence) into our discussion of rape as a weapon of war, I was particularly inspired by the work of Michel de Certeau, who posited that tactics are not necessarily subordinate to strategy but also opposed to it. Certeau's field of study was neither war nor the military. In *The Practice of Everyday Life* (1984) he attempted to explore the ways that individuals navigate the urban landscape, which he believed was created and structured by the interests of powerful institutions (for example, the state, banks, city planners). In order to investigate these social hierarchies, however, he borrowed from military theory and described strategic thinking as a practice of power that can be defined as 'the calculation (or manipulation) of power relationships'. Certeau argued that powerful institutions and structures strategise in order to claim, secure, and expand their space and purpose. An institution secures its independence and prepares its expansion through the deployment of a specific type of knowledge that is fuelled by the desire to maintain its place of power against an 'exteriority composed of targets or threats.'[69] In other words, a powerful institution utilises its knowledge to be and stay in control and to appropriate new space.

Having defined strategy in these terms, Certeau then insists that *tactics* are 'calculated actions' undertaken by nonpowerful subjects. Tactics, he suggests, are 'an art of the weak'. A tactic lacks a place to 'stockpile its winnings' or to secure an individual position: 'This nowhere gives a tactic mobility, to be sure, but a mobility that must accept the chance offerings of the moment, and seize on the wing the possibilities that offer themselves at any given moment.'[70] In this logic, the subject who does not have power and control (and who is aware of this powerlessness) uses his or her abilities to observe and evaluate his or her surroundings and makes (and corrects) decisions according to his or her own assessment of the situation. There is no long-term presumption about how things will turn out. Instead, the subject is ready to take advantage of unpredictable opportunities. As Stan Goff concludes,

> De Certeau understands tactics not as a subset of strategy, but as an adaptation to the environment, which has been created by the strategies of the powerful. This art of making-do is what de Certeau calls bricolage, a process that often implies cooperation as much as competition.[71]

If we follow Certeau's argument, strategies are efforts to secure a space against the 'erosion of time'. Indeed, the situation in which a strategy is devised is always changing. An institution must therefore be flexible, and leaders must recognise the changes and adapt to them in order not to lose control. Tactics, on the other hand, depend on a 'clever utilisation of time'; a subject must make use of opportunities in the moment in order to successfully navigate an environment that is structured by manifold power relations in order to survive within this system.[72] Reapplying Certeau's conception of strategy and tactics to the military in armed conflict, we have, on the one hand, the powerful military command that plans campaigns in order to secure and expand the military space and, on the other hand, the nonpowerful soldiers in the field, who operate 'on and with a terrain imposed on [them].' The soldiers take tactical advantage of opportunities; indeed, their operational success and, ultimately, their survival depend on such opportunities.

Of course, this reapplication is not without contradictions. For one thing, the individual soldier is also part of the military institution, identifies (more or less) with the institution's goals, and is identified with them (and thus with its power) by others. Second, for the soldier, the battlefield is a space structured by threats, and his decisions are also contingent upon psychological and physical frictions. Still, Certeau's model can help us to grasp that decisions made by the individual soldier are not necessarily motivated by strategic military aims and that the strategies of a command and the actions of the individual are never entirely congruent. What is more, the military command knows this and tries to make use of the frictions involved in the decisions of individual soldiers.[73]

If we think about it in this way, we must take into consideration that opportunistic rape might not merely be opportunistic. The individual soldier on the ground takes an opportunity (in accordance with his social values, his personal inclinations and the norms in his small unit) and commits an act of sexual violence, but the military command knows this and calculates with this knowledge, aiming to secure and expand the military space. And because rape is pervasive in many civil societies and there is little awareness that this form of violence constitutes a crime, soldiers on all levels of the military hierarchy can view sexual violence as a normal and acceptable behaviour that generally only becomes a crime when it harms the military operation.

Notes

1. Buss, 'Seeing Sexual Violence in Conflict and Post-Conflict Societies', Ní Aoláin, 'Gender Politics of Fact-Finding'; Gabriel, 'The Literature Database www.warandgender.net'.
2. Seifert, 'Vicissitudes of Gender', p. 262.
3. Zalewski, Drumond, Prügl and Stern (eds), *Sexual Violence against Men*.
4. See, e.g., Grossmann, 'A Question of Silence'; Heineman, 'The Hour of Women'; Naimark, *The Russians in Germany*; Burds, 'Sexual Violence in Europe'; Gebhard, *Als die Soldaten kamen*.
5. Withuis, 'Die verlorene Unschuld des Gedächtnisses'; Lilly, *Taken by Force*; Roberts, *What Soldiers Do*.
6. Goldenberg, 'Sex-Based Violence and the Politics and Ethics of Survival'; Hájková, 'Sexual Barter in Times of Genocide'; Waxman, *Women in the Holocaust*. Dorota Glowacka shows that boys and young men could also become victims of sexual violence by fellow prisoners (Glowacka, 'Sexual Violence Against Men and Boys During the Holocaust').
7. Tanaka, *Japan's Comfort Women*, pp. 110ff. See also my ongoing research project 'On All Fronts: Sexual Violence by British Soldiers in the European and the Asian Theatre of WWII'.
8. Bos, 'Sexual Violence'; Bos, 'Feminists Interpreting Wartime Rape'; Garraio, 'Hordes of Rapists'; Dahlke, '"Frau, komm!"'.
9. E.g. Brownmiller, *Against Our Will*, pp. 62f.; Arcel, 'Sexual Torture of Women as a Weapon of War'.
10. Wood, 'Armed Groups and Sexual Violence', pp. 141f.
11. Wood, 'Variation in Sexual Violence During War', p. 332.
12. Heineman, 'Sexuality and Nazism', 62.
13. See e.g., Shik, 'Sexual Abuse of Jewish Women'; Waxman, *Women in the Holocaust*; Sinnreich, 'The Rape of Jewish Women', p. 4.

14. Mischkowski, in Bergoffen, Bos, Bourke et al., 'Gaps and Traps', p. xxixff.; Combs, *Fact-Finding without Facts*.
15. Shik, 'Sexual Abuse of Jewish Women'.
16. Bergen, 'Sexual Violence in the Holocaust', p. 189.
17. Shik, 'Sexual Abuse of Jewish Women', p. 233.
18. Herzog, *Sex After Fascism*.
19. Szobar, 'Sexual Stories in the Nazi Courts of Law ', pp. 140–4.
20. Amesberger, Auer and Halbmayr, *Sexualisierte Gewalt*; Halbmayr, 'Sexualized Violence against Women during Nazi "Racial" Persecution'.
21. Mailänder, in Bergoffen, Bos, Bourke et al., 'Gaps and Traps', pp. xxxiff.
22. Flaschka, '"Only Pretty Women Were Raped"', pp. 86-8; Glowacka, 'Sexual Violence Against Men and Boys'. Furthermore, the SS enslaved non-Jewish female prisoners in 'special buildings' (*Sonderbauten*) for the use of a particular group of privileged male prisoners. They intended to boost the morale and working capacities of this particular group of prisoners by establishing these 'concentration camp brothels' (Sommer, 'Camp Brothels'). The extent to which SS guards themselves took advantage of this and raped the women in the special buildings is unknown (Mühlhäuser, 'Understanding Sexual Violence during the Holocaust').
23. Joeden-Forgey, 'The Devil in the Details', p. 6.
24. Mühlhäuser, 'Sexual Violence and the Holocaust', p. 114.
25. Mühlhäuser, 'Sex, Race, Violence, Volksgemeinschaft', p. 474.
26. Zipfel, 'What Do Bodies Tell?', p. 190.
27. Kühne, *Belonging and Genocide*.
28. Pendas, Roseman and Wetzell (eds), *Beyond the Racial State*.
29. Wood, 'Conflict-Related Sexual Violence and the Policy Implications of Recent Research', p. 469.
30. Ibid. p. 472.
31. Ibid. p. 473.
32. Hoover Green, *Commander's Dilemma*, p. 207.
33. Feimster, 'Rape and Justice in the Civil War', *New York Times*, 25 April 2013.
34. Beck, 'Sexual Violence and its Prosecution by Courts Martial of the Wehrmacht'.
35. Inal, *Looting and Rape in Wartime*, pp. 170–3.
36. Cited in Picker, *Hitlers Tischgespräche*, p. 332.
37. Tombs, 'Honor, Shame, and Conquest', p. 28.
38. Cited in Bergen, 'Sexual Violence in the Holocaust', p. 181; and Brownmiller, *Against Our Will*, p. 49.
39. Zipfel, 'Liberté, Egalité, Sexualité', p. 91.
40. Ibid.
41. Ibid.
42. Diken and Laustsen, 'Becoming Abject', p. 116–19.
43. Ibid. p. 117.
44. Seifert, 'War and Rape'.
45. Heineman, 'Introduction', p. 19.

46. Mischkowski and Mlinarevic, '... and that it does not happen to anyone anywhere in the world'.
47. Zipfel, 'What Do Bodies Tell?', p. 190ff.
48. Warburg, 'Paradoxe Anforderungen an soldatische Subjekte avancierter Streitkräfte im (Kriegs-)Einsatz', p. 260.
49. Seidler, 'Bodies, Masculinities and Complex Inheritances', p. 227; also cited in Zipfel, 'What Do Bodies Tell?', p. 196.
50. Steinkamp, *Zur Devianz-Problematik in der Wehrmacht*.
51. Crouthamel, 'Male Sexuality and Psychological Trauma', p. 61.
52. Bourke, *An Intimate History of Killing*, p. 150.
53. Bröckling, 'Schlachtfeldforschung', p. 189, cited in Zipfel, '"Let Us Have a Little Fun"', p. 40.
54. Barrett, 'Organizational Construction of Hegemonic Masculinity'.
55. Belkin, *Bring Me Men*.
56. Kühne, *Kameradschaft*; Kühne, *The Rise and Fall of Comradeship*.
57. Belkin, *Bring Me Men*, p. 34.
58. Ibid.
59. This observation is not limited to Western state armies but can also be found in other geographical territories and cultural spaces. See, e.g., Eriksson Baaz and Stern, 'Why Do Soldiers Rape?'.
60. Arcel, 'Sexual Torture of Women as a Weapon of War'.
61. Zipfel, 'What Do Bodies Tell?', p. 192.
62. Zipfel, 'What is Sexual About Sexual Violence?', p. 206.
63. If/how this applies to female perpetrators needs to be explored in future research.
64. Zipfel, '"Let Us Have a Little Fun"', p. 39.
65. The following passage is cited from Mühlhäuser, 'Reframing Sexual Violence as a Weapon and Strategy of War'. For a critical view on rape as a weapon of war and genocide, cf. Eriksson Baaz and Stern, *Sexual Violence as a Weapon of War?*; Buss, 'Making Sense of Genocide'.
66. Gray, *Modern Strategy*.
67. Bröckling, 'Schlachtfeldforschung', p. 190.
68. Bröckling, *Disziplin*.
69. De Certeau, *The Practice of Everyday Life*, p. 36.
70. Ibid. p. 37f.
71. Goff, 'The Tactics of Everyday Life', pp. 268f.
72. De Certeau, *The Practice of Everyday Life*, 38–39
73. Bröckling, 'Schlachtfeldforschung', pp. 189f.

BIBLIOGRAPHY

Archives

German Federal Archives, Berlin-Lichterfelde (BArch)
NS 2   SS Race and Settlement Main Office
NS 7   SS and Police Jurisdiction
NS 19 Reichsführer-SS Personal Staff
NS 31 SS Main Office, Medical Service
NS 33 SS Leadership Main Office, Medical Service
R 1   Reich Institute for the History of New Germany
R 6   Reich Ministry for the Occupied Eastern Territories
R 22   Reich Ministry of Justice
R 49   Reich Commissioner for the Consolidation of the Ethnic German Nation
R 55   Reich Ministry of Public Enlightenment and Propaganda
R 90   Reich Commissariat Ostland
R 92   General Commissioner in Riga
R 93   General Commissioner for White Ruthenia in Minsk
R 94   Reich Commissioner for Ukraine
R 187 Schumacher Collections

German Federal Archives/Military Archives, Freiburg (BA-MA)
FPF 01 Film collection, Reich Ministry for the Occupied Eastern Territories
H 20   Army Medical Inspectorate
RH 20   Army commands
RH 22   Commanders of rear army areas
RH 26   Infantry divisions
RH 53   Military district commands
RL 19   Luftwaffe Medical Service
RW 2   Head of the OKW

RW 19   OKW/War Economy and Armaments Office
RW 41   Territorial commanders in the Soviet Union

German Federal Archives, Central Records Office, Kornelimünster (BA-ZNS)
S1-411   Eastern collection, 'Sittlichkeit'

Institute of National Remembrance, Warsaw (IPN)
RSH 21   Reich Security Main Office

Library of Contemporary History, Stuttgart (BfZ)
Sterz Collection, Feldpost letters

United States Holocaust Memorial Museum, Washington DC (USHMM)
RG-02   Survivor Testimonies
RG-10.229   Jonathan Kempner collection 1933–45
RG-18.002M   Selected Records from the Latvian Central State Historical Archives
RG-20.015   Peter O. Vlcko Papers
RG-31.011M   Vinnitsa Oblast Archive
RG-31.002M   Selected Central Records of the Federal Security Service (FSB, formerly KGB) of the Russian Federation Relating to War Crimes Investigations and Trials in the Soviet Union
RG-50.030   Interviews with Survivors
RG-53.002M   Selected Records of the Belarus Central State Archive, Minsk
RG-53.004M   Selected Records from the Grodno Oblast Archive, Belarus
RG-53.006M   Mogilev Oblast Archive Records, 1941–45

United States National Archives & Records Administration, Washington DC (NARA)
RG-242   Records of Headquarters, German Army High Command
RG-466   US High Commissioner for Germany

Source Editions, Documentation and Edited Individual Documents

'Aus den Akten des Gauleiters Kube: Kommentierte Dokumentation', *Vierteljahrshefte für Zeitgeschichte*, 4(1), 1956, pp. 67–92.

Ayass, Wolfgang (ed.), *'Gemeinschaftsfremde': Quellen zur Verfolgung von 'Asozialen' 1933–1945 (Materialien aus dem Bundesarchiv, Bd. 5)* (Koblenz: Bundesarchiv, 1998).

Benz, Wolfgang, Konrad Kwiet and Jürgen Matthäus (eds), *Einsatz im 'Reichskommissariat Ostland': Dokumente zum Völkermord im Baltikum und in Weissrussland 1941–1944* (Berlin: Metropol, 1998).

Boberach, Heinz (ed.), *Meldungen aus dem Reich: Die geheimen Lageberichte des Sicherheitsdienstes der SS*, 17 volumes (Herrsching: Pawlak, 1984).

Fischer, Hubert (ed.), *Der deutsche Sanitätsdienst 1921–1945: Organisation, Dokumente und persönliche Erfahrungen*, 5 volumes (Osnabrück: Biblio Verlag, 1988).

Friedmann, Tuviah (ed.), *Die drei SS- und Polizeiführer im Ostland, die verantwortlich waren für die Ermordung der Juden im Ostland, 1941–1944: Dokumentensammlung* (Haifa: Institute of Documentation in Israel, 1998).
Gerdes, Reinhard, 'Männer im Ostland', in Walter Zimmermann (ed.), *Auf Informationsfahrt im Ostland* (Riga: 1944).
Hamburger Institut für Sozialforschung (ed.), *Vernichtungskrieg: Verbrechen der Wehrmacht 1941–1944*, exhibition catalogue (Hamburg: Hamburger Edition, 1996).
Hamburger Institut für Sozialforschung (ed.), *Verbrechen der Wehrmacht: Dimensionen des Vernichtungskrieges 1941–1944*, exhibition catalogue (Hamburg: Hamburger Edition, 2002).
Hamburger Institut für Sozialforschung (ed.), *Crimes of the Wehrmacht: Dimensions of a War of Annihilation 1941–1944*, exhibition outline, translated by Paula Bradish (Hamburg: Hamburger Edition, 2004).
Heiber, Helmut, 'Der Generalplan Ost', *Vierteljahrshefte für Zeitgeschichte*, 6(2), 1958, pp. 281–325.
Heiber, Helmut (ed.), *Hitler and His Generals: Military Conferences 1942–1945*, translated by Roland Winter, Krista Smith and Mary Beth Friedrich (New York: Enigma Books, 2003). [*Hitlers Lagebesprechungen*, 1962]
Himmler, Heinrich, *Der Dienstkalender Heinrich Himmlers 1941/42*, Peter Witte, Michael Wildt und Martina Voigt (eds) (Hamburg: Hans Christians Verlag, 1999).
Himmler, Heinrich, *Geheimreden 1933 bis 1945 und andere Ansprachen*, Bradley F. Smith and Agnes F. Petersen (eds) (Berlin: Propyläen, 1974).
Himmler, Heinrich, *Reichsführer! Briefe an und von Himmler*, Helmut Heiber (ed.) (Munich: dtv, 1970).
Hitler, Adolf, *Monologe im Führerhauptquartier 1941–1944: Die Aufzeichnungen Heinrich Heims*, Werner Jochmann (ed.) (Hamburg: A. Knaus, 1980).
Jacobsen, Hans-Adolf and Werner Jochmann (eds), *Ausgewählte Dokumente zur Geschichte des Nationalsozialismus 1933–1945*, 5 volumes (Bielefeld: Verlag Neue Gesellschaft, 1961).
Law Reports of Trials of War Criminals, Selected and prepared by United Nations War Crimes Commission, English Edition, 15 volumes (London: United Nations War Crimes Commission, 1947–9).
Müller, Norbert (ed.), *Deutsche Besatzungspolitik in der UdSSR 1941–1944: Dokumente* (Cologne: Pahl-Rugenstein, 1980).
Oberkommando des Heeres (ed.), *Heeresverordnungsblatt*, part B, vol. 10., Berlin 1943.
Plaut, Paul, 'Psychografie des Kriegers', *Zeitschrift für angewandte Psychologie*, supplement 21, 1920, pp. 1–123.
Reichsgesetzblatt (RGBl.), 1939, vol. 1; 1942, vol. 1 (Berlin: Reichsverlagsamt).
Reichsminister der Luftwaffe – Luftwaffenverwaltungsamt (ed.), *Luftwaffenverordnungsblatt*, vol. 15, 1943.
Rome Statute of the International Criminal Court, <https://www.icc-cpi.int/nr/rdonlyres/ea9aeff7-5752-4f84-be94-0a655eb30e16/0/rome_statute_english.pdf> (last accessed 13 February 2019).

Spiethoff, Bodo and Karl Zieler, 'Erklärung zur Frage der "naturgemässen" Behandlung der Syphilis', *Mitteilungen der Deutschen Gesellschaft zur Bekämpfung von Geschlechtskrankheiten*, vol. 1, 1942, pp. 1–3.

Trial of the Major War Criminals before the International Military Tribunal, Nuremberg, 14 November 1945–1 October 1946, Official Text in the English Language, 42 volumes (Nuremberg: International Military Tribunal, 1947–9).

Trials of War Criminals before the Nuremberg Military Tribunals under Control Council Law No. 10, Nuremberg, October 1946–April 1949, vol. XI: 'The High Command Case'/'The Hostage Case' (Washington, DC: United States Government Printing Office, 1950).

Wehrmachtsverbrechen: Dokumente aus sowjetischen Archiven, preface by Lew Besymenski, introduction by Gert Meyer (Cologne: PapyRossa, 1997).

The Women's International War Crimes Tribunal for the Trial of Japan's Military Sexual Slavery, Case No. PT-2000-1-T, Judgment, The Hague, 4 December 2001, <https://web.archive.org/web/20070807090835/http://www1.jca.apc.org/vaww-net-japan/english/womenstribunal2000/Judgement.pdf> (last accessed 12 February 2019).

Memoirs and Personal Accounts by Members of the Wehrmacht and SS

Böll, Heinrich, *Briefe aus dem Krieg 1939–1945*, 2 volumes, Jochen Schubert (ed.) (Cologne: Kiepenheuer & Witsch, 2001).

Buch, Wolfgang von, *Wir Kindersoldaten* (Berlin: Siedler, 1998).

Claas, Marlis, *Ein Heeresrichter im Russlandkrieg: Die Feldpostbriefe meines Vaters (1941–1945)* (Berlin: Frieling, 2003).

Elmshäuser, Konrad and Jan Lokers (eds), *'Man muss hier nur hart sein': Kriegsbriefe und Bilder einer Familie (1934–1945)* (Bremen: Edition Temmen, 1999).

Gercke, Fritz, *Nach Hause geschrieben: Aus dem Feldzug 1941 gegen Sowjet-Rußland* (Berlin: Erich Zander, n.d.).

Goebbels, Joseph, *Die Tagebücher von Joseph Goebbels, Teil 2: Diktate 1941–1945*, edited by Elke Fröhlich (Munich: K. G. Sauer: 1994).

Hahl, Fritz, *Mit 'Westland' im Osten: Ein Leben zwischen 1922 und 1945* (Reinsfeld: Munin, 2001).

Hansmann, Claus, *Vorüber – nicht vorbei: Russische Impressionen 1941–1943* (Frankfurt: Ullstein, 1989).

Hermand, Jost, *A Hitler Youth in Poland: The Nazis' Program for Evacuating Children during World War II*, translated by Margot Bettauer Dembo (Evanston: Northwestern University Press, 1997). [*Als Pimpf in Polen: Erweiterte Kinderlandverschickung 1940–1945*, 1993]

Lachenmaier, Fritz, *Zeitgeschichte wider den Zeitgeist: Alte Soldaten klagen die ganze Wahrheit ein* (Schwäbisch-Gmünd: self-published, 1997).

Maeger, Herbert, *Lost Honour, Betrayed Loyalty: The Memoir of a Waffen-SS Soldier on the Eastern Front*, translated by Geoffrey Brooks (London: Frontline Books, 2015). [*Verlorene Ehre, verratene Treue: Zeitzeugenbericht eines Soldaten*, 2002]

Manstein, Erich von, *Lost Victories: The War Memoirs of Hitler's Most Brilliant General*, edited and translated by Anthony G. Powell (St. Paul, MN: Zenith Press, 2004 [1958]). [*Verlorene Siege*, 1955]

Meiser, Anton, *Die Hölle von Tscherkassy: Ein Kriegstagebuch 1943–1944* (Schnellbach: Bulblies Siegfried, 2000).

Reese, Willi Peter, *A Stranger to Myself. The Inhumanity of War: Russia, 1941–1944*, translated by Michael Hoffmann, Stefan Schmitz (ed.) (New York: Farrar, Straus and Giroux, 2005). [*'Mir selber seltsam fremd': Die Unmenschlichkeit des Krieges, Russland 1941–1944*, 2003]

Remarque, Erich Maria, *A Time to Love and a Time to Die*, translated by Denver Lindley (New York: Random House, 2014 [1954]).

Remarque, Erich Maria, *Zeit zu leben und Zeit zu sterben* (Cologne: Kiepenheuer & Witsch, 1998 [1954]).

Rost, Joachim, 'Sexuelle Probleme im Felde', *Medizinische Welt* 18, 1944, pp. 7f.

Sajer, Guy, *Denn dieser Tage Qual war gross: Bericht eines vergessenen Soldaten*, translated by Wolfgang Libal (Vienna: Molden, 1969).

Sajer, Guy, *The Forgotten Soldier*, translated by Lily Emmet (New York: Harper & Row, 1971).

Sajer, Guy, *Der vergessene Soldat*, translated by Wolf Müller and Frederike Keller (Aachen: Helios, 2016).

Sajer, Guy, *Le soldat oublié* (Paris: Laffont, 1967).

Schmidt, Ilse, *Die Mitläuferin: Erinnerungen einer Wehrmachtsangehörigen* (Berlin: Aufau, 1999).

Schneider-Janessen, Karlheinz, *Arzt im Krieg: Wie deutsche und russische Ärzte den Zweiten Weltkrieg erlebten*, 2nd edition (Frankfurt: Lichtenwys, 1994).

Schönhuber, Franz, *Ich war dabei* (Munich: Langen Müller, 1981).

Stachow, Hasso G., *If This Be Glory*, translated by J. Maxwell Brownjohn (New York: Doubleday & Company, 1982).

Stachow, Hasso G., *Der kleine Quast* (Munich: Herbig, 2004 [1979]).

Thamm, Gerhardt B., *Boy Soldier: A German Teenager at the Nazi Twilight* (Jefferson, NC: McFarland & Company, 2000).

Trevor-Roper, Hugh (ed.), *Hitler's Table Talk 1941–1944: His Private Conversations*, translated by Norman Cameron and R. H. Stevens (New York: Enigma Books, 2000 [1953]).

Vegesack, Siegfried von, *Als Dolmetscher im Osten: Ein Erlebnisbericht aus den Jahren 1942–43* (Hanover: Harro von Hirschheydt, 1965).

Wellershoff, Dieter, *Der Ernstfall: Innenansichten des Krieges* (Cologne: Kiepenheuer & Witsch, 2006).

Memoirs and Personal Accounts of Victims and Survivors

Abramowitch, Maja, *To Forgive . . . But Not Forget: Maja's Story* (London: Vallentine Mitchell, 2002).

Abramowitsch, Ljuba Israeljewna and Hans-Heinrich Nolte, *Die Leere in Slonim* (Dortmund: Internationales Bildungs- und Begegnungswerk, 2005).

Anatoli, A. (pseudonym of Anatoly Kuznetsov), *Babi Yar: A Document in the Form of a Novel*, translated by David Floyd (New York: Farrar, Straus and Giroux). [*Babii Iar*, 1966]

Apenszlak, Jacob (ed.), *The Black Book of Polish Jewry: An Account of the Martyrdom of Polish Jewry Under the Nazi Occupation* (New York: American Federation for Polish Jews, 1943).

Berland Hyatt, Felicia, *Close Calls: Memoirs of a Survivor* (New York: Holocaust Library, 1991).

Bortniker (Averbuch), Maria, 'We Were in Distress All of the Time', in Boris Zabarko (ed.), *Holocaust in the Ukraine* (London: Vallentine Mitchell, 2005), pp. 23–25.

'Brest, Depositions and Documentary Testimony of the Residents of Brest; prepared for publication by Margarita Aliger', in Vasily Grossman and Ilya Ehrenburg (eds), *The Complete Black Book of Russian Jewry* (Piscataway, NJ: Transaction Publishers, 2003), pp. 176–84.

Brusch (Moschel), Yelisaveta, 'One Hundred and Six Members of Our Family Perished in the Ghetto, and Thirty-Eight at the Front', in Boris Zabarko (ed.), *Holocaust in the Ukraine* (London: Vallentine Mitchell, 2004), pp. 29–36.

Chernyakova, B., 'Liozno, prepared for publication by Vsevolod Ivanov', in Vasily Grossman and Ilya Ehrenburg (eds), *The Complete Black Book of Russian Jewry* (Piscataway, NJ: Transaction Publishers, 2003), pp. 187f.

Cohen, Dov and Jack Kagan, *Surviving the Holocaust with the Russian Jewish Partisans* (London: Vallentine Mitchell, 1998).

Cottam, Kazimiera J. (ed.), *Defending Leningrad: Women Behind Enemy Lines* (Nepean, Ontario: New Military Publishing, 1998).

Cottam, Kazimiera J. (ed.), *Women in Air War: The Eastern Front of World War II* (Nepean, Ontario: New Military Publishing, 1997).

Cottam, Kazimiera J. (ed.), *Women in War and Resistance: Selected Biographies of Soviet Women Soldiers* (Nepean, Ontario: New Military Publishing, 1998).

Demianova, Genia, *Comrade Genia: The Story of a Victim of German Bestiality in Russia Told by Herself* (London: Nicholson and Watson, 1941).

Desbois, Patrick, *The Holocaust by Bullets: A Priest's Journey to Uncover the Truth behind the Murder of 1.5 Million Jews*, translated by Catherine Spencer (New York: St. Martin's Press, 2008). [*Porteur des mémoires*, 2007]

'The diary of E. Yerushalmi of Siauliai (Shavli), prepared for publication by O. Savich', in Vasily Grossman and Ilya Ehrenburg (eds), *The Complete Black Book of Russian Jewry* (Piscataway, NJ: Transaction Publishers, 2003), pp. 294–314.

Epelfeld, Naum, 'May My Memory Keep Me from Forgetting', in Boris Zabarko (ed.), *Holocaust in the Ukraine* (London: Vallentine Mitchell, 2005), pp. 365–84.

'The Extermination of the Jews of Lvov, reported by I. Herts and Naftali Nakht; prepared for publication by R. Fraerman and R. Kovnator', in Vasily Grossman and Ilya Ehrenburg (eds), *The Complete Black Book of Russian Jewry* (Piscataway, NJ: Transaction Publishers, 2003), pp. 76–86.

Feld, Faina, 'The Town Was Invaded by Germans: That Was When it Became Scary', in Boris Zabarko (ed.), *Holocaust in the Ukraine* (London: Vallentine Mitchell, 2005), pp. 294–97.

'From the Deposition of Captain Salog, Police Regiment Commander', in Vasily Grossman and Ilya Ehrenburg (eds), *The Complete Black Book of Russian Jewry* (Piscataway, NJ: Transaction Publishers, 2003), pp. 567–74.

'From the Diary of Doctor Elena Buividaite-Kutorgene (June–December 1941), in Vasily Grossman and Ilya Ehrenburg (eds), *The Complete Black Book of Russian Jewry* (Piscataway, NJ: Transaction Publishers, 2003), pp. 335–68.

'From the Notebook of the Sculptor Elik Rivosh (Riga), prepared for publication by Vasily Grossman', in Vasily Grossman and Ilya Ehrenburg (eds), *The Complete Black Book of Russian Jewry* (Piscataway, NJ: Transaction Publishers, 2003), pp. 396–411.

Gekhtman, E. [Yefim], 'Riga', in Vasily Grossman and Ilya Ehrenburg (eds), *The Complete Black Book of Russian Jewry* (Piscataway, NJ: Transaction Publishers, 2003), pp. 379–96.

Gottesfeld Heller, Fanya, *Strange and Unexpected Love: A Teenage Girl's Holocaust Memoirs* (Hoboken, NJ: Ktav Publishing House, 1993).

Grossman, Vasily, 'The Minsk Ghetto', in Vasily Grossman and Ilya Ehrenburg (eds), *The Complete Black Book of Russian Jewry* (Piscataway, NJ: Transaction Publishers, 2003), pp. 109–38.

Grossman, Vasily, 'Treblinka', in Vasily Grossman and Ilya Ehrenburg (eds), *The Complete Black Book of Russian Jewry* (Piscataway, NJ: Transaction Publishers, 2003), pp. 462–83.

Grossman, Vasily and Ilya Ehrenburg (eds), *The Complete Black Book of Russian Jewry*, translated and edited by David Patterson (London: Routledge, 2017 [2002]). [*Chernaya kniga*, 1944]

Hahn Beer, Edith, *The Nazi Officer's Wife: How One Jewish Woman Survived the Holocaust*, with Susan Dworkin (New York: William Morrow, 1999).

'In Bialystock, prepared for publication by R. Kovnator', in Vasily Grossman and Ilya Ehrenburg (eds), *The Complete Black Book of Russian Jewry* (Piscataway, NJ: Transaction Publishers, 2003), pp. 197–203.

Inber, Vera, 'Odessa', in Vasily Grossman and Ilya Ehrenburg (eds), *The Complete Black Book of Russian Jewry* (Piscataway, NJ: Transaction Publishers, 2003), pp. 55–65.

Inciuriene, Joheved, 'Rettung und Widerstand in Kaunas', in Vincas Bartusevicius, Joachim Tauber, and Wolfram Wette (eds), *Holocaust in Litauen: Krieg, Judenmorde und Kollaboration im Jahre 1941* (Cologne: Böhlau, 2003), pp. 201–217.

Jasinska, Zofia, *Der Krieg, die Liebe und das Leben: Eine polnische Jüdin unter Deutschen* (Berlin: Aufbau, 1998).

Ka-Tzetnik 135633, *House of Dolls*, translated by Moshe M. Kohn (New York: Simon and Schuster, 955). [*Bet ha-bubot*, 1953]

'Kiev: Babi Yar, an Article Based on the Documentary Materials and Depositions from the People of Kiev, prepared for publication by Lev Ozerov', in Vasily Grossman and Ilya Ehrenburg (eds), *The Complete Black Book of Russian Jewry* (Piscataway, NJ: Transaction Publishers, 2003), pp. 3–12.

Klee, Ernst and Willi Dressen (eds), *'Gott mit uns': Der deutsche Vernichtungskrieg im Osten 1939–1945* (Frankfurt: Fischer, 1989).

Kohl, Paul, *'Ich wundere mich, dass ich noch lebe': Sowjetische Augenzeugen berichten* (Gütersloh: Gütersloher Verlagshaus G. Mohn, 1990).

Kohl, Paul, *Der Krieg der deutschen Wehrmacht und der Polizei 1941–1944: Sowjetische Überlebende berichten* (Frankfurt: Fischer, 1995).

Kozhina, Elena, *Through the Burning Steppe: A Wartime Memoir*, translated by Vadim Mahmoudov (New York: Riverhead Books, 2000).

Kruk, Herman, *The Last Days of the Jerusalem of Lithuania: Chronicles from the Vilna Ghetto and the Camps, 1939–1944* (New Haven: Yale University Press, 2002).

Laska, Vera (ed.), *Women in the Resistance and in the Holocaust: The Voices of Eyewitnesses* (Westport, CT: Praeger, 1983).

Lidin, Vladimir, 'Talnoe', in Vasily Grossman and Ilya Ehrenburg (eds), *The Complete Black Book of Russian Jewry* (Piscataway, NJ: Transaction Publishers, 2003), pp. 20f.

Lozansky Bogomolnaya, Rivka, *Wartime Experiences in Lithuania*, translated by Miriam Beckermann (London: Vallentine Mitchell, 2000).

Lustig, Arnošt, *Lovely Green Eyes: A Novel*, translated from the Czech by Ewald Osers (New York: Arcade Publishing, 2011).

Mackiewicz, Józef, 'Der Stützpunkt Ponary: Erzählung', *Dachauer Hefte*, 10(10), 1994, pp. 91–100.

Margolis, Rachel, *A Partisan from Vilna*, translated by F. Jackson Piotrow (Brighton, MA: Academic Studies Press, 2010). [*Nemnogo sveta vo mrake*, 2006]

Margolis, Rachel and Jim Tobias (eds), *Die geheimen Notizen des K. Sakowicz: Dokumente zur Judenvernichtung in Ponary 1941–1943*, translated by Elisabeth Nowak (Frankfurt: Fischer, 2005).

Michelson, Frida, *I Survived Rumbuli*, translated and edited by Wolf Goodman (New York: Holocaust Publications, 1979). [*IA perezhila Rumbulu*, 1973]

Pawlowicz, Sala, *I Will Survive*, with Kevin Klose (New York: Norton, 1962).

Picker, Henry (ed.), *Hitlers Tischgespräche im Führerhauptquartier. Entstehung, Struktur, Folgen des Nationalsozialismus*, 2nd edition (Berlin: Propyläen Verlag, [1951] 1997).

Pikman, Basya, 'The Story of Engineer Pikman from Mozyr, prepared for publication by Ilya Ehrenburg', in Vasily Grossman and Ilya Ehrenburg (eds), *The Complete Black Book of Russian Jewry* (Piscataway, NJ: Transaction Publishers, 2003), pp. 169–72.

'Ponary: The Story of Engineer Yu. Farber, *prepared for publication by R. Kovatnor*', in Vasily Grossman and Ilya Ehrenburg (eds), *The Complete Black Book of Russian Jewry* (Piscataway, NJ: Transaction Publishers, 2003), pp. 439–53.

Porudominskij, Wladimir (ed.), *Die Juden von Wilna: Die Aufzeichnungen des Grigorij Schur 1941–1944*, translated by Jochen Hellbeck (Munich: Deutscher Taschenbuch Verlag, 1999).

Press, Bernhard, *The Murder of the Jews in Latvia 1941–1945*, translated by Laimdota Mazzarins (Evanston, IL: Northwestern University Press, 2000). [*Judenmord in Lettland 1941–1945*, 1992]

Republic of Poland/Ministry of Foreign Affairs (ed.), *German Occupation of Poland: Extract of Note Addressed to the Allied and Neutral Powers* (New York: The Greystone Press, 1941).

Ringelblum, Emmanuel, *Ghetto Warschau: Tagebücher aus dem Chaos* (Stuttgart: Seewald, 1967). [*Notitsn fun Varshever geto*, 1952]

Schneider, Gertrude, *Journey into Terror: Story of the Riga Ghetto* (Westport, CT: Praeger Publishers, 2001).

Schulman, Faye, *A Partisan's Memoir: Woman of the Holocaust*, with the assistance of Sarah Silberstein Swartz (Toronto: Second Story Press, 1995).

Stabholz, Thaddeus, *Seven Hells*, translated by Jacques Grunblatt and Hilda R. Grunblatt (New York: Holocaust Library, 1990). [*Siedem piekieł*, 1947]

Streim, Alfred, *Sowjetische Gefangene in Hitlers Vernichtungskrieg: Berichte und Dokumente 1941–1945* (Heidelberg: C. F. Müller, 1982).

Sutzkever, Abraham, 'The Vilna Ghetto, translated from the Yiddish by M. Shambadal and B. Chernyak', in Vasily Grossman and Ilya Ehrenburg (eds), *The Complete Black Book of Russian Jewry* (Piscataway, NJ: Transaction Publishers, 2003), pp. 241–94.

Tory, Avraham, *Surviving the Holocaust: The Kovno Ghetto Diary*, Martin Gilbert (ed.), translated by Jerzy Michalowicz (Cambridge, MA: Harvard University Press, 1990). [*Geto yom-yom: yoman u-mismakhim mi-Geto Kovnah*, 1988]

Verbrechen und Strafe: Der Charkower Prozess über die von den deutsch-faschistischen Eindringlingen in der Stadt Charkow und Umgebung während der zeitweisen Okkupation verübten Greueltaten. Report on the trial before the military tribunal in Kharkiv, December 1943, s.l., s.n.

Wolff, Jeannette, *Sadismus oder Wahnsinn: Erlebnisse in den deutschen Konzentrationslagern im Osten* (Greiz in Thüringen: Ernst Bretfeld, 1947).

Zabarko, Boris (ed.), *Holocaust in the Ukraine*, translated by Marina Guba (London: Vallentine Mitchell, 2005). [*Zhivymi ostalis' tol'ko my: Svidetel'stva i dokumenty*, 1999]

Zvychaina, Olena, *Kharkiv*, translated by Jaroslaw Zurowsky, edited by Danny Evanishen (Summerland, BC: Ethnic Enterprises, 1996 [1947]).

Published Before 1945

Burgdörfer, Friedrich, *Kinder des Vertrauens: Bevölkerungspolitische Erfolge und Aufgaben im Grossdeutschen Reich* (Berlin: Eher, 1942).

Burgdörfer, Friedrich, *Volk ohne Jugend: Geburtenschwund und Überalterung des Deutschen Volkskörpers. Ein Problem der Volkswirtschaft, der Sozialpolitik, der nationalen Zukunft*, 3rd expanded edition (Heidelberg: Vowinckel, 1935).

Burgdörfer, Friedrich, *Volks- und Wehrkraft, Krieg und Rasse* (Berlin: Metzner, 1936).

Dringenberg, Otto, 'Untersuchungen an Hilfsschülern auf Lues connatalis', *Sozialhygiene der Geschlechtskrankheiten* 5, 1941, pp. 35f.

Finger, Ernst, *Der Krieg und die Bekämpfung der Geschlechtskrankheiten* (Vienna: Anzengruber Verlag, 1916).

Fischer, Willi, 'Zweites Sammelreferat über die bisher erschienenen Arbeiten über die Bekämpfung der Geschlechtskrankheiten in und nach dem Kriege', *Zeitschrift für Bekämpfung der Geschlechtskrankheiten*, 18(2/3), 1917, pp. 63–82.

Freund, Emanuel, *Wie bewahrt ihr euch vor Syphilis? Ein Mahnwort an junge Männer* (Graz, 1916).

Gesterding, Schwatlo, *Unteroffizierthemen: Ein Handbuch für den Unteroffizierunterricht*, 7th revised edition (Berlin: E.S. Mittler & Sohn, 1943).

Gottschalk, Hans, 'Die Syphilis in der amtlichen Todesursachenstatistik 1932–1938', *Sozialhygiene der Geschlechtskrankheiten* 5, 1942, pp. 33–6.

Hirschfeld, Magnus, *The Sexual History of the World War* (New York: Cadillac Publishing Co., 1941). [*Sittengeschichte des Weltkrieges*, 1930]

Hitler, Adolf, *Mein Kampf*, translated by Ralph Manheim (New York: Houghton Mifflin, 1999 [1943]). [*Mein Kampf*, 1924]

Jaeckel, Carl, 'Geschlechtskrankheiten', in Anton Waldmann and Wilhelm Hoffmann (eds), *Lehrbuch der Militärhygiene* (Berlin: Springer, 1936), pp. 574–85.

Jeannel, Julien, *Die Prostitution in den grossen Städten im neunzehnten Jahrhundert und die Vernichtung der venerischen Krankheiten*, translated from the French by Friedrich Wilhelm Müller (Erlangen: F. Enke, 1869). [*De la prostitution sans les grandes villes au dix-neuvième siècle et de l'extinction des maladies vénériennes*, 1868]

Keyser, Erich, 'Die Erforschung der Bevölkerungsgeschichte des deutschen Ostens', in Hermann Aubin et al. (eds), *Deutsche Ostforschung: Ergebnisse und Aufgaben seit dem Ersten Weltkrieg* (Leipzig: S. Hirzel, 1942), pp. 90–104.

Korherr, Richard, *Geburtenrückgang: Mahnruf an das Deutsche Volk. Mit einem Geleitwort von Reichsführer-SS Heinrich Himmler*, 3rd edition (Munich: Süddeutsche Monatshefte, 1935).

Löhe, Heinrich, 'Die Geschlechtskrankheiten', in Siegfried Handloser and Wilhelm Hoffmann (eds), *Wehrhygiene* (Berlin: Springer, 1944), pp. 150–61.

Lutz, Maria, 'Erbkrankheit oder angeborene Syphilis', *Sozialhygiene der Geschlechtskrankheiten* 5, 1942, p. 36.

Lutz, Maria, 'Über einen klinisch eindrucksvollen Fall von Lues connatalis', *Sozialhygiene der Geschlechtskrankheiten* 5, 1940, pp. 29–34.

Meyers Konversations-Lexikon, 4th edition (Leipzig: Bibliographisches Institut, 1887–9).

Meyers Lexikon, 8th edition (Leipzig: Bibliographisches Institut, 1936–42).

Oberländer, Theodor, *Die agrarische Überbevölkerung Polens* (Berlin: Volk und Reich Verlag, 1935).

Rediess, Wilhelm (ed.), *Schwert und Wiege* (*SS für ein Grossgermanien, III. Folge*) (Oslo: Aas & Wahls Boktrykkeri, 1943).

Reichskriegsministerium (ed.), *Wegweiser für den rassenhygienischen Unterricht* (Berlin, 1936).

Reithinger, Anton, 'Das europäische Bevölkerungsproblem', *Europäische Revue*, 10(9), 1934, p. 23.

Rosenberg, Alfred, *The Myth of the 20th Century: An Evaluation of the Spiritual-Intellectual Confrontations of our Age*, translated by James B. Whisker (Newport Beach, CA: Noontide Press, 1982). [*Der Mythus des zwanzigsten Jahrhunderts*, 1930]

Rost, Gustav, 'Die Verhütung der venerischen Krankheiten in der Kaiserlichen Marine', *Zeitschrift für Bekämpfung der Geschlechtskrankheiten*, 15(4), 1914, pp. 123–38.
Seraphim, Peter-Heinz, *Das Judentum im osteuropäischen Raum* (Essen: Essener Verlags-Anstalt, 1938).
Seraphim, Peter-Heinz, *Das Judentum: Seine Rolle und Bedeutung in Vergangenheit und Gegenwart* (Munich: Deutscher Volksverlag, 1942).
Sozialhygiene der Geschlechtskrankheiten, published by the Deutsche Gesellschaft zur Bekämpfung von Geschlechtskrankheiten im Reichsausschuss für Volksgesundheitsdienst e.V., 1935, vol. 1, to 1942, vol. 6.
Spiethoff, Bodo, 'Die Behandlung der konnatalen Syphilis', *Medizinische Welt* 42, 1941, pp. 1071–8.
Zeitschrift für Bekämpfung der Geschlechtskrankheiten, vol. 14, issue 1, 1914, to vol. 18, issue 10, 1918.
Zimmermann, Walter (ed.), *Auf Informationsfahrt im Ostland: Reiseeindrücke deutscher Schriftleiter* (Riga: Reichskommissariat Ostland, 1944).

Research Literature

Achinger, Christine, *Gespaltene Moderne: Gustav Freytags Soll und Haben – Nation, Geschlecht und Judenbild* (Würzburg: Königshausen & Neumann, 2007).
Adam, Birgit, *Die Strafe der Venus: Eine Kulturgeschichte der Geschlechtskrankheiten* (Munich: Orbis, 2001).
Alakus, Baris, Katharina Kniefacz and Robert Vorberg (eds), *Sex-Zwangsarbeit in nationalsozialistischen Konzentrationslagern* (Vienna: Mandelbaum, 2006).
Alison, Miranda, 'Wartime Sexual Violence: Women's Human Rights and Questions of Masculinity', *Review of International Studies 33*, 2007, pp. 75–90.
Alison, Miranda, Debra Bergoffen, Pascale Bos, Louise du Toit, Regina Mühlhäuser and Gaby Zipfel, '"My Plight is not Unique". Sexual violence in conflict zones: a roundtable discussion', *Eurozine*, 2 September 2009, pp. 1–18 ['"Meine Not ist nicht einzig". Sexuelle Gewalt in kriegerischen Konflikten: Ein Werkstattgespräch', 2009]
Aly, Götz and Michael Sontheimer, *Fromms: How Julius Fromm's Condom Empire Fell to the Nazis*, translated by Shelley Frisch (New York: Other Press, 2009). [*Fromms: Wie der jüdische Kondomfabrikant Julius F. unter die deutschen Räuber fiel*, 2007]
Aly, Götz and Susanne Heim, *Architects of Annihilation: Auschwitz and the Logic of Destruction*, translated by Allan Blunden (London: Weidenfeld & Nicolson, 2002). [*Vordenker der Vernichtung: Auschwitz und die deutschen Pläne für eine neue europäische Ordnung*, 2013 (1991)]
Amberger, Waltraud, *Männer, Krieger, Abenteurer: Der Entwurf des 'soldatischen Mannes' in Kriegsromanen über den Ersten und Zweiten Weltkrieg*, 2nd revised edition (Frankfurt: R.G. Fischer, 1987).
Amesberger, Helga, Katrin Auer and Brigitte Halbmayr, *Sexualisierte Gewalt: Weibliche Erfahrungen in NS-Konzentrationslagern* (Vienna: Mandelbaum, 2004).

Angrick, Andrej, *Besatzungspolitik und Massenmord: Die Einsatzgruppe D in der südlichen Sowjetunion 1941–1943* (Hamburg: Hamburger Edition, 2003).

Angrick, Andrej and Peter Klein, *The 'Final Solution' in Riga: Exploitation and Annihilation, 1941–1944*, translated by Ray Brandon (New York: Berghahn Books, 2009). [*Die 'Endlösung' in Riga: Ausbeutung und Vernichtung 1941–1944*, 2006]

Arad, Yitzhak, *The Holocaust in the Soviet Union* (Lincoln, NE: University of Nebraska Press, 2009).

Arcel, Libby Tata, 'Sexual Torture of Women as a Weapon of War: The Case of Bosnia-Herzegovina', in Libby Tata Arcel and Gorana Tocilj Simunkovic (eds), *War Violence, Trauma and the Coping Process: Armed Conflict in Europe and Survivor Response* (Zagreb: Nakladništvo Lumin, 1998), pp. 183–211.

Askin, Kelley Dawn, *War Crimes Against Women: Prosecution in International War Crimes Tribunals* (The Hague: Martinus Nijhoff, 1997).

Auerbach, Hellmuth, 'Die Einheit Dirlewanger', *Vierteljahreshefte für Zeitgeschichte*, 10(3), 1962, pp. 250–63.

Aussteller, Die (ed.), *Sex-Zwangsarbeit in NS-Konzentrationslagern*, exhibition catalogue, 2nd edition (Vienna: Verein zur Förderung von historischen und kunsthistorischen Ausstellungen, 2006).

Baer, Elizabeth R. and Myrna Goldenberg (eds), *Experience and Expression: Women, the Nazis, and the Holocaust* (Detroit: Wayne State University Press, 2003).

Baer, Elizabeth R. and Myrna Goldenberg, 'Introduction', in Elizabeth R. Baer and Myrna Goldenberg (eds), *Experience and Expression*, pp. xiii–xxxiii.

Bargheer, Margo, 'Subjektive Erzählung, objektive Akten? Zum Unbehagen bei der historischen Validierung eines Zeitzeugeninterviews am Beispiel des ehemaligen Wehrmachtsdeserteurs Heinz Schmidt', in Maren Büttner and Magnus Koch (eds), *Zwischen Gehorsam und Desertion* (Cologne: PapyRossa, 2003), pp. 49–77.

Barrett, Frank, 'The Organizational Construction of Hegemonic Masculinity: The Case of the US Navy', *Gender, Work and Organization*, 3(3), July 1996, 129–42.

Bärsch, Claus Ekkehard, *Die politische Religion des Nationalsozialismus* (Munich: Wilhelm Fink, 1998).

Bartov, Omer, *The Eastern Front, 1941–45: German Troops and the Barbarisation of Warfare* (Houndmills: Palgrave, 2001 [1985]).

Bartov, Omer, *Hitler's Army: Soldiers, Nazis, and War in the Third Reich* (New York: Oxford University Press, 1991).

Bartov, Omer, 'Kitsch and sadism in Ka-Tzetnik's other planet: Israeli youth imagine the Holocaust', *Jewish Social Studies*, 3(2), 1997, pp. 42–76.

Basham, Victoria M., 'Liberal Militarism as Insecurity, Desire and Ambivalence: Gender, Race and the Everyday Geopolitics of War', *Security Dialogue*, 49(1–2), 2018, pp. 32–43.

Bauer, Ingrid, '"Leiblicher Vater: Amerikaner (Neger)": Besatzungskinder österreichisch-afroamerikanischer Herkunft', in Helmuth A. Niederle, Ulrike Davis-Sulikowski and Thomas Fillitz (eds), *Früchte der Zeit: Afrika, Diaspora, Literatur und Migration* (Vienna: WUV Universitätsverlag, 2001), pp. 49–67.

Bauer, Yehuda, 'Jewish Baranowicze in the Holocaust', *Yad Vashem Studies*, 31, 2003, pp. 95–152.
Baumel, Judith Tydor, *Double Jeopardy: Gender and the Holocaust* (London: Vallentine Mitchell, 1998).
Baumel, Judith Tydor and Jacob J. Schacter, 'The Ninety-Three Bais Yaakov Girls of Cracow: History or Typology?', in Jacob J. Schacter (ed.), *Reverence, Righteousness and Rahamanut: Essays in Memory of Rabbi Dr. Leo Jung* (Northvale: Jason Aronson Inc., 1992), pp. 93–130.
Beck, Birgit, 'Sexual Violence and its Prosecution by Courts Martial of the Wehrmacht', in Roger Chickering, Stig Förster and Bernd Greiner (eds), *A World at Total War: Global Conflict and the Politics of Destruction, 1937–1945* (Cambridge, UK: Cambridge University Press, 2005), pp. 317–31.
Beck, Birgit, *Wehrmacht und sexuelle Gewalt: Sexualverbrechen vor deutschen Militärgerichten 1939–1945* (Paderborn: Schöningh, 2004).
Beckermann, Ruth, *East of War (Jenseits des Krieges)*, documentary film, Filmarchiv Austria, Vienna 1996.
Beckermann, Ruth, *Jenseits des Krieges: Ehemalige Wehrmachtssoldaten erinnern sich* (Vienna: Döcker, 1998).
Beckermann, Ruth and Constantin Wulff, 'Vom Mangel an Herzensbildung: Ein Gespräch', in Ruth Beckermann, *Jenseits des Krieges*, pp. 17–26.
Beevor, Antony, *Berlin: The Downfall 1945* (New York: Viking, 2002).
Belkin, Aaron, *Bring Me Men: Military Masculinity and the Benign Facade of American Empire, 1898–2001* (London: Hurst & Company, 2012).
Beorn, Waitman Wade, 'Bodily Conquests: Sexual Violence in the Nazi East', in Alex J. Kay, David Stahel (eds), *Mass-Violence in Nazi Occupied Europe* (Bloomington: Indiana University Press, 2018), pp. 195–215.
Berend, Ivan T., *Decades of Crisis: Central and Eastern Europe before World War II* (Berkeley: University of California Press, 1998).
Bergen, Doris L., 'Sexual Violence in the Holocaust: Unique or Typical?', in Dagmar Herzog (ed.), *Lessons and Legacies VII: The Holocaust in International Perspective* (Evanston, IL: Northwestern University Press, 2006), pp. 179–200.
Bergen, Doris L., 'Sex, Blood, and Vulnerability: Women Outsiders in German-Occupied Europe', in Robert Gellately and Nathan Stoltzfus (eds), *Social Outsiders in Nazi Germany* (Princeton: Princeton University Press, 2001), pp. 273–93.
Bergen, Doris L., 'The Volksdeutsche of Eastern Europe and the Collapse of the Nazi Empire, 1944–1945', in Alan E. Steinweis and Daniel E. Rogers (eds), *The Impact of Nazism: New Perspectives on the Third Reich and its Legacy* (Lincoln, NE: University of Nebraska Press, 2003), pp. 101–28.
Bergmann, Anna, *Die verhütete Sexualität: Die Anfänge der modernen Geburtenkontrolle* (Hamburg: Rasch und Röhring, 1992).
Bergmann, Anna, 'Von der "unbefleckten Empfängnis" zur "Rationalisierung des Geschlechtslebens": Gedanken zur Debatte um den Geburtenrückgang vor dem Ersten Weltkrieg', in Johanna Geyer-Kordesch and Annette Kuhn (eds),

Frauenkörper – Medizin – Sexualität: Auf dem Weg zu einer neuen Sexualmoral (Düsseldorf: Schwann, 1986), pp. 127–58.

Bergoffen, Debra, Pascale R. Bos, Joanna Bourke, Kirsten Campbell, Louise du Toit, Júlia Garraio, Elissa Mailänder, Gabriela Mischkowski, Regina Mühlhäuser, Fabrice Virgile and Gaby Zipfel, 'Gaps and Traps: The Politics of Generating Knowledge on Sexual Violence in Armed Conflict. A Conversation with Members of the SVAC Network', in Gaby Zipfel, Regina Mühlhäuser and Kirsten Campbell (eds), *In Plain Sight* (New Delhi: Zubaan, 2019), pp. xix–xlx.

Berkhoff, Karel, *Harvest of Despair: Life and Death in the Ukraine under Nazi Rule* (Cambridge, MA: Harvard University Press, 2004).

Bernstein, Fran, 'Prostitutes and Proletarians: The Labor Clinic as Revolutionary Laboratory in the 1920s', in William Husband (ed.), *The Human Tradition in Modern Russia* (Wilmington: Scholarly Resources Inc., 2000), pp. 113–28.

Bernstein, Laurie, *Sonia's Daughters: Prostitutes and their Regulation in Imperial Russia* (Berkeley: University of California Press, 1995).

Besl, Fritz, 'Eröffnungsrede', in Helga Embacher, Albert Lichtblau and Günther Sander (eds), *Umkämpfte Erinnerung: Die Wehrmachtsausstellung in Salzburg* (Salzburg: Residenz, 1999).

Biess, Frank, 'Men of Reconstruction – The Reconstruction of Men: Returning POWs in East and West Germany, 1945–1952', translated by Elizabeth Berdeck, in Karin Hagemann and Stefanie Schüler-Springorum (eds), *Home/Front* (Oxford: Berg Publishers, 2002), pp. 335–51.

Binner, Jens, 'Die Repatriierung und das Leben in der Sowjetunion', in Hans Heinrich Nolte (ed.), *Häftlinge aus der UdSSR in Bergen-Belsen: Dokumentation der Erinnerungen* (Frankfurt: Peter Lang, 2001), pp. 205–25.

Birn, Ruth Bettina, *Die Sicherheitspolizei in Estland 1941–1944: Eine Studie zur Kollaboration im Osten* (Paderborn: Schöningh, 2006).

Bischl, Kerstin, *Frontbeziehungen: Geschlechterverhältnisse und Gewaltdynamiken in der Roten Armee 1941–1945* (Hamburg: Hamburger Edition, 2019).

Bock, Gisela, *Zwangssterilisation im Nationalsozialismus: Studien zur Rassenpolitik und Frauenpolitik* (Opladen: Westdeutscher Verlag, 1986).

Boesten, Jelke, 'Of Exceptions and Continuities: Theory and Methodology in Research on Conflict-Related Sexual Violence', in *International Feminist Journal of Politics*, 19(4), 2017, pp. 506–19.

Boesten, Jelke, 'Revisiting Methodologies and Approaches in Researching Sexual Violence in Conflict', *Social Politics*, 25(4), 2018, pp. 457–68.

Boesten, Jelke and Marsha Henry (eds), *Revisiting Methods and Approaches in Researching Sexual Violence in Conflict.* Special Issue Social Politics: International Studies in Gender, State and Society, 25(4), 2018.

Boll, Bernd and Hans Safrian, 'On the Way to Stalingrad: The 6th Army in 1941–42', in Hannes Heer and Klaus Naumann (eds), *War of Extermination* (London: Berghahn, 2004), pp. 237–71.

Bopp, Petra, *Fremde im Visier: Fotoalben aus dem Zweiten Weltkrieg* (Bielefeld: Kerber 2009).

Bopp, Petra, 'Images of Violence in Wehrmacht Soldiers' Private Photo Albums', in Jürgen Martschukat and Silvan Niedermeier (eds), *Violence and Visibility in Modern History* (New York: Palgrave Macmillan, 2013), pp. 181–97.

Bopp, Petra, 'Wo sind die Augenzeugen, wo ihre Fotos?', in Hamburger Institut (ed.), *Eine Ausstellung* (Hamburg: Hamburger Edition, 1999), pp. 198–229.

Bordjugov, Gennadij, 'Terror der Wehrmacht gegenüber der Zivilbevölkerung', in Gabriele Gorzka and Knut Stang (eds), *Der Vernichtungskrieg im Osten: Verbrechen der Wehrmacht in der Sowjetunion aus Sicht russischer Historiker* (Kassel: Kassel University Press, 1999), pp. 53–68.

Borenstein, Eliot, 'Selling Russia: Prostitution, Masculinity, and Metaphors of Nationalism After Perestroika', in Helena Goscilo and Andrea Lanoux (eds), *Gender and National Identity in Twentieth Century Russian Culture* (DeKalb, IL: Northern Illinois University Press, 2006), pp. 244–78.

Borgersrud, Lars, 'Meant to be Deported', in Kjersti Ericsson and Eva Simonsen (eds), *Children of World War II* (Oxford: Berg, 2005), pp. 71–92.

Borodziej, Włodzimierz, *Der Warschauer Aufstand 1944* (Frankfurt: Fischer-Taschenbuch, 2004).

Bos, Pascale Rachel, 'Feminist Interpretations of Wartime Rape: Berlin 1945, Yugoslavia 1992–1993', in Insa Eschebach and Regina Mühlhäuser (eds), *Krieg und Geschlecht* (Berlin: Metropol, 2008), pp. 103–23. ['*Feministische Deutungen sexueller Gewalt im Krieg: Berlin 1945, Jugoslawien 1992–1993*']

Bos, Pascale Rachel, 'Sexual Violence in Ka-Tzetnik's House of Dolls', in Annette Timm (ed.), *Holocaust History and the Readings of Ka-Tzetnik* (London: Bloomsbury, 2018), pp. 105–38.

Bos, Pascale Rachel, 'Women and the Holocaust: Analyzing Gender Difference', in Elizabeth R. Baer and Myrna Goldenberg (eds), *Experience and Expression* (Detroit: Wayne State University Press, 2003), pp. 23–50.

Bourke, Joanna, *An Intimate History of Killing: Face-to-Face Killing in Twentieth-Century Warfare* (New York: Basic Books, 1999).

Bourke, Joanna, *Rape: A History from 1860 to the Present* (London: Virago, 2007).

Boyer, Christoph and Hans Woller, '"Hat die deutsche Frau versagt?" Die "neue Freiheit" der Frauen in der Trümmerzeit 1945–1949', *Journal für Geschichte*, 5(2), 1983, pp. 32–6.

Braun, Christina von, 'Viertes bild: "blut und blutschande"', in Julius H. Schoeps and Joachim Schlör (eds), *Antisemitismus: Vorurteile und Mythen* (Munich: Piper, 1995), pp. 80–95.

Bristow, Edward J., *Prostitution and Prejudice: The Jewish Fight against White Slavery* (Oxford: Oxford University Press, 1982).

Bröckling, Ulrich, *Disziplin: Soziologie und Geschichte militärischer Gehorsamsproduktion* (Munich: Wilhelm Fink, 1997).

Bröckling, Ulrich, 'Schlachtfeldforschung: Die Soziologie im Krieg', in Steffen Martus, Marina Münkler and Werner Röcke (eds), *Schlachtfelder: Codierung von Gewalt im medialen Wandel* (Berlin: De Gruyter, 2003), pp. 189–206.

Browning, Christopher, *Ordinary Men: Reserve Police Battalion 101 and the Final Solution in Poland* (London: Penguin, 2001 [1992]).

Brownmiller, Susan, *Against Our Will: Men, Women and Rape* (New York: Bantam Books 1981 [1975]).

Bruns, Claudia, *Politik des Eros: Der Männerbund in Wissenschaft, Politik und Jugendkultur (1880–1934)* (Cologne: Böhlau, 2008).

Buchmann, Bertrand Michael, *Österreicher in der Deutschen Wehrmacht: Soldatenalltag im Zweiten Weltkrieg* (Vienna: Böhlau, 2009).

Buckel, Sonja, 'Feministische Erfolge im Kampf um die Straflosigkeit sexueller Gewalt im Krieg: Das Beispiel der "comfort women"', in Insa Eschebach and Regina Mühlhäuser (eds), *Krieg und Geschlecht* (Berlin: Metropol, 2008), pp. 209–28.

Bulmer, Sarah and David Jackson, '"You Do Not Live in My Skin": embodiment, voice, and the veteran', *Critical Military Studies*, 2(1–2), 2016, pp. 25–40.

Burds, Jeffrey, 'Sexual Violence in Europe in World War II, 1939–1945', *Politics & Society*, 37(1), 1 March 2009, pp. 35–73.

Buske, Sybille, *Fräulein Mutter und ihr Bastard: Eine Geschichte der Unehelichkeit in Deutschland 1900–1970* (Göttingen: Wallstein, 2004).

Buss, Doris, 'Making Sense of Genocide, Making Sense of Law: International Criminal Prosecutions of Large-Scale Sexual Violence', in Amy E. Randall (ed.), *Genocide and Gender in the Twentieth Century: A Comparative Survey* (London: Bloomsbury Academic, 2015), pp. 277–97.

Buss, Doris, 'Rethinking "Rape as a Weapon of War"', *Feminist Legal Studies*, 17, 2009, pp. 145–63.

Buss, Doris, 'Seeing Sexual Violence in Conflict and Post-Conflict Societies', in Doris Buss, Joanne Lebert, Blair Rutherford, Donna Sharkey and Obijiofor Aginam (eds), *Sexual Violence in Conflict and Post-Conflict Societies* (New York: Routledge, 2014), pp. 3–27.

Büttner, Maren, '"Der ganze Krieg ist ja Wahnsinn": Erinnerungen an Frauen im Kontext von Wehrmachtsdesertionen', in Maren Büttner and Magnus Koch (eds), *Zwischen Gehorsam und Desertion* (Cologne: PapyRossa, 2003), pp. 161–99.

Büttner, Maren and Magnus Koch (eds), *Zwischen Gehorsam und Desertion: Handeln, Erinnern, Deuten im Kontext des Zweiten Weltkrieges* (Cologne: PapyRossa, 2003).

Cahill, Ann J., *Rethinking Rape* (Ithaca, NY: Cornell University Press, 2001).

Campbell, Kirsten, 'The Gender of Justice? Current Problems and Directions in the Field of Sexual Violence in Armed Conflict', in Gaby Zipfel, Regina Mühlhäuser and Kirsten Campbell (eds), *In Plain Sight* (New Delhi: Zubaan, 2019), pp. 230–56.

Campbell, Kirsten, 'The Gender of Transitional Justice: Law, Sexual Violence and the International Criminal Tribunal for the Former Yugoslavia', *The International Journal of Transitional Justice*, 1, 2007, pp. 411–32.

Card, Claudia, 'Rape as a weapon of war', *Hypatia: A Journal of Feminist Philosophy*, 11(4), 1996, pp. 5–18.

Carpenter, Charli R., 'Gender-Based Violence Against Men in Complex Emergencies: An Agenda for the Protection Community', paper presented at the annual meeting of the International Studies Association, Montreal, 17 March 2004, <http://citation.allacademic.com/meta/p_mla_apa_research_citation/0/7/2/9/4/pages72944/p72944-1.php> (last accessed 15 February 2019).

Carpenter, Charli R., 'Gender, Ethnicity and Children's Human Rights: Theorizing Babies Born of Wartime Rape and Sexual Exploitation', in Joakim Ophaug (ed.), *The War Children of the World* (Bergen: War and Children Identity Project, 2003), pp. 24–35.

Cerovic, Masha, 'Fighters Like No Others: The Soviet Partisans in the Wake of War', in Stefan-Ludwig Hoffmann, Sandrine Kott, Peter Romijn and Olivier Wieviorka (eds), *Seeking Peace in the Wake of War: Europe, 1943–1947* (Amsterdam: Amsterdam University Press, 2016), pp. 203–16.

Chiari, Bernhard, *Alltag hinter der Front: Besatzung, Kollaboration und Widerstand in Weissrussland 1941–1944* (Düsseldorf: Droste Verlag, 1998).

Chiari, Bernhard, 'Die Büchse der Pandora: Ein Dorf in Weissrussland 1939–1944', in Rolf-Dieter Müller and Hans-Erich Volkmann (eds), *Die Wehrmacht* (Munich: Oldenbourg, 1999), pp. 879–900.

Chiwengo, Ngwarsungu, 'Bestialisation, Dehumanisation and Counter-Interstitial Voices: Representations of Congo (DRC) conflicts and rape', in Gaby Zipfel, Regina Mühlhäuser and Kirsten Campbell (eds), *In Plain Sight* (New Delhi: Zubaan, 2019), pp. 355–78.

Chiwengo, Ngwarsungu, 'When Wounds and Corpses Fail to Speak: Narratives of Violence and Rape in Congo (DRC)', *Comparative Studies of South Asia, Africa and the Middle East*, 28(1), 2008, pp. 78–92.

Chung, Chin-Sung, 'Discourses of the Japanese Right Wing Groups and the Japanese Government's Approach to the "Comfort Women"', in Barbara Drinck and Chung-noh Gross (eds), *Forced Prostitution in Times of War and Peace: Sexual Violence against Women and Girls*, translated by Katy Derbyshire, Linda Turner, David Andersen and Tony Crawford (Bielefeld: Kleine Verlag, 2007), pp. 181–200. [*Erzwungene Prostitution in Kriegs- und Friedenszeiten*, 2006]

Combs, Nancy Amoury, *Fact-Finding without Facts: The Uncertain Evidentiary Foundations of International Criminal Convictions* (Cambridge: Cambridge University Press, 2010).

Connell, Raewyn W., *Masculinities*, 2nd edition (Cambridge, UK: Polity, 2005 [1995]).

Connell, Raewyn W., 'Masculinity and Nazism', in Anette Dietrich and Ljiljana Heise (eds), *Männlichkeitskonstruktionen im Nationalsozialismus: Formen, Funktionen und Wirkungsmacht von Geschlechterkonstruktionen im Nationalsozialismus und ihre Reflexion in der pädagogischen Praxis* (Frankfurt: Peter Lang, 2013), pp. 37–42.

Conze, Susanne and Beate Fieseler, 'Soviet Women as Comrades-in-Arms: A Blind Spot in the History of War', in Robert W. Thurston and Bernd Bonwetsch (eds), *The People's War: Responses to World War II in the Soviet Union* (Urbana: University of Illinois Press, 2000), pp. 211–34.

Copelon, Rhinda, 'Gendered War Crimes: Reconceptualizing Rape in Times of War', in Julie Peter and Andrea Wolper (eds), *Women's Rights, Human Rights: International Feminist Perspectives* (New York: Routledge, 1995), pp. 197–214.

Copelon, Rhonda, 'Surfacing Gender: Re-Engraving Crimes Against Women in Humanitarian Law', *Hastings Women's Law Journal*, 5(2), 1994, pp. 243–66.

Cottebrune, Anne, 'Blut und "Rasse": Serologische Forschung im Umfeld des Robert Koch-Instituts', in Marion Hulverscheidt and Anja Laukötter (eds), *Infektion und Institution: Zur Wissenschaftsgeschichte des Robert Koch-Instituts im Nationalsozialismus* (Göttingen: Wallstein, 2009), pp. 106–27.

Crenshaw, Kimberlé, 'Demarginalizing the Intersection of Race and Sex: A Black Feminist Critique of Antidiscrimination Doctrine, Feminist Theory and Antiracist Politics', *The University of Chicago Legal Forum*, 1, 1989, pp. 139–67.

Crouthamel, Jason, *An Intimate History of the Front: Masculinity, Sexuality, and German Soldiers in the First World War* (Basingstoke: Palgrave Macmillan, 2014).

Crouthamel, Jason, 'Male Sexuality and Psychological Trauma: Soldiers and Sexual Disorder in World War I and Weimar Germany', *Journal of the History of Sexuality*, 17(1), 2008, pp. 60–84.

Curilla, Wolfgang, *Die deutsche Ordnungspolizei und der Holocaust im Baltikum und in Weissrussland 1941–1944* (Paderborn: Schöningh, 2006).

Czarnowski, Gabriele, 'Frauen als Mütter der "Rasse": Abtreibungsverfolgung und Zwangseingriff im Nationalsozialismus', in Gisela Staupe and Lisa Vieth (eds), *Unter anderen Umständen: Zur Geschichte der Abtreibung. Ausstellungskatalog des Deutschen Hygiene-Museums Dresden* (Berlin: Argon, 1993), pp. 58–72.

Czarnowski, Gabriele, *Das kontrollierte Paar: Ehe- und Sexualpolitik im Nationalsozialismus* (Weinheim: Deutscher Studien Verlag, 1991).

Czarnowski, Gabriele, 'Zwischen Germanisierung und Vernichtung: Verbotene polnisch-deutsche Liebesbeziehungen und die Re-Konstruktion des Volkskörpers im Zweiten Weltkrieg', in Helgard Kramer (ed.), *Die Gegenwart der NS-Vergangenheit* (Berlin: Philo, 2000), pp. 295–303.

Dahlke, Birgit, '"Frau, komm!" Vergewaltigungen 1945 – zur Geschichte eines Diskurses', in Birgit Dahlke, Martina Langermann and Thomas Taterka (eds), *Literaturgesellschaft DDR: Kanonkämpfe und ihre Geschichte(n)* (Stuttgart: Metzler, 2000), pp. 275–311.

Dallin, Alexander, *German Rule in Russia 1941–1945: A Study of Occupation Policies* (Boulder: Westview Press, 1981 [1957]).

De Brouwer, Anne-Marie L. M., *Supranational Criminal Prosecution of Sexual Violence: The ICC and the Practice of the ICTY and the ICTR* (Antwerp: Intersentia, 2005).

De Certeau, Michel, *The Practice of Everyday Life*, translated by Steven F. Rendall (Berkeley: University of California Press, 1984). [*L'invention du quotidien, tome 1: Arts de faire*, 1980]

Dean, Martin, *Collaboration in the Holocaust: Crimes of the Local Police in Belorussia and Ukraine, 1941–44* (New York: St. Martin's Press, 2000).

Delage, Christian, *Nuremberg: The Nazis Facing Their Crimes* (*Nuremberg – Les nazis face à leurs crimes*), documentary film, Arte France, 2006.

Demandt, Philipp, *Luisenkult: Die Unsterblichkeit der Königin von Preussen* (Cologne: Böhlau, 2003).

Diederichs, Monika, 'Stigma and Silence: Dutch Women, German Soldiers and their

Children', in Kjersti Ericsson and Eva Simonsen (eds), *Children of World War II* (Oxford: Berg, 2005), pp. 151–66.

Diehl, Paula, *Macht – Mythos – Utopie: Die Körperbilder der SS-Männer* (Berlin: Akademie Verlag, 2005).

Dienel, Christiane, *Kinderzahl und Staatsräson: Empfängnisverhütung und Bevölkerungspolitik in Deutschland und Frankreich bis 1918* (Münster: Westfälisches Dampfboot, 1995).

Diken, Bülent and Carsten Bagge Laustsen, 'Becoming Abject: Rape as a Weapon of War', *Body & Society*, 11(1), 2005, pp. 111–28.

Donat, Helmut and Arn Strohmeyer (eds), *Befreiung von der Wehrmacht?* (Bremen: Donat, 1997).

Dörner, Bernward, 'Heimtückische Nachrede: Zur Strafverfolgung von Gerüchten über die Homosexualität führender Politiker in der NS-Zeit', in Susanne zur Nieden (ed.), *Homosexualität und Staatsräson: Männlichkeit, Homophobie und Politik in Deutschland 1900–1945* (Frankfurt: Campus, 2005), pp. 294–305.

Dostal, Nikolai (dir.), *Penal Battalion (Štrafbat)*, television series, 2 DVDs, Moscow 2004.

Drolshagen, Ebba, *Nicht ungeschoren davonkommen: Die Geliebten der Wehrmachtssoldaten im besetzten Europa* (Munich: Econ, 2000).

Drolshagen, Ebba, *Wehrmachtskinder: Auf der Suche nach dem nie gekannten Vater* (Munich: Droemer Knaur, 2005).

Duchen, Claire, 'Crime and Punishment in Liberated France: The Case of Les Femmes Tondues', in Claire Duchen and Irene Bandhauer-Schoeffmann (eds), *When the War Was Over: Women, War and Peace, 1940–1956* (London: Leicester University Press, 2000), pp. 233–50.

Dücker, Elisabeth von and Museum der Arbeit (eds), *Sexarbeit: Prostitution – Lebenswelten und Mythen* (Bremen: Edition Temmen, 2005).

Dudden, Alexis, '"We Came to Tell the Truth": Reflections on the Tokyo Women's Tribunal', *Critical Asian Studies*, 33(4), 2006, pp. 591–602.

Du Toit, Louise and Elisabet Le Roux, 'A Feminist Reflection on Male Victims of Conflict-Related Sexual Violence', *European Journal of Women's Studies*, February 2020, pp. 1–14.

Eboe-Osuji, Chile, 'Rape as Genocide: Some Questions Arising', *Journal of Genocide Research*, 9(2), 2007, pp. 251–73.

Edwards, Alison, *Rape, Racism, and the White Women's Movement: An Answer to Susan Brownmiller* (Chicago: Sojourner Truth Organization, 1979).

Eifler, Christine, 'Nachkrieg und weibliche Verletzbarkeit: Zur Rolle von Kriegen für die Konstruktion von Geschlecht', in Christine Eifler and Ruth Seifert (eds), *Soziale Konstruktionen* (Münster: Westfälisches Dampfboot, 1999), pp. 155–86.

Eifler, Christine and Ruth Seifert (eds), *Soziale Konstruktionen – Militär und Geschlechterverhältnis* (Münster: Westfälisches Dampfboot, 1999).

Eisen Bergman, Arlene, *Women of Viet Nam* (San Francisco: Peoples Press, 1974).

Eliach, Yaffa, 'Women of Valor: Partisans and Resistance Fighters', *Journal of the*

Center for Holocaust Studies, 6(4), 1990, <http://www.theverylongview.com/WATH/valor/history.htm> (last accessed 14 March 2019).

Ellenbrand, Petra, *Die Volksbewegung und Volksaufklärung gegen Geschlechtskrankheiten in Kaiserreich und Weimarer Republik* (Marburg: Görich und Weiershäuser, 1999).

Engelen, Beate, *Soldatenfrauen in Preussen: Eine Strukturgeschichte der Garnisonsgesellschaft im späten 17. und 18. Jahrhundert* (Münster: LIT, 2005).

Engert, Jürgen (ed.), *Soldaten für Hitler* (Berlin: Rohwolt, 1998).

Engle Merry, Sally, *The Seductions of Quantification: Measuring Human Rights, Gender Violence, and Sex Trafficking* (Chicago: The University of Chicago Press, 2016).

Enloe, Cynthia, *Maneuvers: The International Politics of Militarizing Women's Lives* (Berkeley, CA: University of California Press, 2000).

Ericsson, Kjersti and Dag Ellingsen, 'Life Stories of Norwegian War Children', in Kjersti Ericsson and Eva Simonsen (eds), *Children of World War II* (Oxford: Berg, 2005), pp. 93–111.

Ericsson, Kjersti and Eva Simonsen (eds), *Children of World War II: The Hidden Enemy Legacy* (Oxford: Berg, 2005).

Eriksson Baaz, Maria and Maria Stern, 'Curious Erasures: The Sexual in Wartime Sexual Violence', *International Feminist Journal of Politics*, 20(3), 2018, pp. 295–314.

Eriksson Baaz, Maria and Maria Stern, *Sexual Violence as a Weapon of War? Perceptions, Prescriptions, Problems in the Congo and Beyond* (London: Zed Books, 2013).

Eriksson Baaz, Maria and Maria Stern, 'Why Do Soldiers Rape? Masculinity, Violence, and Sexuality in the Armed Forces in the Congo (DRC)', *International Studies Quarterly*, 53(2), 2009, pp. 495–518.

Eschebach, Insa, '"Ich bin unschuldig." Vernehmungsprotokolle als historische Quellen: Der Rostocker Ravensbrück-Prozess 1966', *WerkstattGeschichte*, 4(12), 1995, pp. 65–70.

Eschebach, Insa and Regina Mühlhäuser (eds), *Krieg und Geschlecht: Sexuelle Gewalt im Krieg und Sex-Zwangsarbeit in NS-Konzentrationslagern* (Berlin: Metropol, 2008).

Eschebach, Insa and Regina Mühlhäuser, 'Sexuelle Gewalt im Krieg und Sex-Zwangsarbeit in NS-Konzentrationslagern: Deutungen, Darstellungen, Begriffe', in Insa Eschebach and Regina Mühlhäuser (eds), *Krieg und Geschlecht* (Berlin: Metropol, 2008), pp. 11–32.

Eschebach, Insa, Sigrid Jacobeit and Silke Wenk (eds), *Gedächtnis und Geschlecht: Deutungsmuster in Darstellungen des nationalsozialistischen Genozids* (Frankfurt: Campus, 2002).

Essner, Cornelia, *Die 'Nürnberger Gesetze' oder Die Verwaltung des Rassenwahns 1933–1945* (Paderborn: Schöningh, 2002).

Fauroux, Camille, 'Shared Intimacies: Women's Sexuality in Foreign Worker's Camps 1940–1945', *German History*, 38(3), 2020.

Fehrenbach, Heide, '"Ami-Liebchen" und "Mischlingskinder": Rasse, Geschlecht und Kultur in der deutsch-amerikanischen Begegnung', in Klaus Naumann (ed.), *Nachkrieg in Deutschland* (Hamburg: Hamburger Edition, 2001), pp. 178–205.

Fehrenbach, Heide, *Race after Hitler: Black Occupation Children in Postwar Germany and America* (Princeton: Princeton University Press, 2005).
Feimster, Crystal, 'Rape and Justice in the Civil War', *New York Times*, 25 April 2013.
Felder, Björn M., *Lettland im Zweiten Weltkrieg: Zwischen sowjetischen und deutschen Besatzern 1940–1946* (Paderborn: Schöningh, 2009).
Ferguson, Niall, *The Pity of War: Explaining World War I* (New York: Basic Books, 1999).
Fieseler, Beate, 'Der Krieg der Frauen: Die ungeschriebene Geschichte', in Peter Jahn (ed.), *Mascha, Nina, Katjuscha* (Berlin: Christoph Links Verlag, 2002), pp. 11–20.
Fieseler, Beate, 'Rotarmistinnen im Zweiten Weltkrieg: Motivationen, Einsatzbereiche und Erfahrungen von Frauen an der Front', in Klaus Latzel, Franka Maubach and Silke Satjukow (eds), *Soldatinnen: Gewalt und Geschlecht im Krieg vom Mittelalter bis heute* (Paderborn: Schöningh, 2011), pp. 301–30.
Fieseler, Beate, '"Stell dich doch auf den Nevskij!" Prostitution im Russland des 19. Jahrhunderts', *Osteuropa*, 56(6), 2006, pp. 285–301.
Finzsch, Norbert, 'Geschichte der Sexualität in den USA und in Deutschland: Stand der Forschung, Probleme und Methoden zwischen Foucaultscher Diskursanalyse und Oral History', in Ansgar Nünning and Roy Sommer (eds), *Kulturwissenschaftliche Literaturwissenschaft: Disziplinäre Ansätze – Theoretische Positionen – Transdisziplinäre Perspektiven* (Tübingen: Gunter Narr, 2004), pp. 197–214.
Flaschka, Monika J., '"Only Pretty Women Were Raped": The Effect of Sexual Violence on Gender Identities in Concentration Camps', in Sonja M. Hedgepeth and Rochelle G. Saidel (eds), *Sexual Violence against Jewish Women during the Holocaust*, (Waltham, MA: Brandeis University Press, 2010), pp. 77–93.
Förster, Jürgen, 'Das Unternehmen "Barbarossa" als Eroberungs- und Vernichtungskrieg', in Militärgeschichtliches Forschungsamt (ed.), *Das Deutsche Reich und der Zweite Weltkrieg*, vol. 4: *Der Angriff auf die Sowjetunion* (Stuttgart: Deutsche Verlags-Anstalt 1983), pp. 435–40.
Foucault, Michel, *The History of Sexuality, Volume 1: An Introduction*, translated by Robert Hurley (New York: Pantheon Books, 1978). [*Histoire de la sexualité: La Volonté de savoir*, 1976]
Foucault, Michel, *'Society Must Be Defended': Lectures at the Collège de France, 1975–76*, edited by Mauro Bertani and Alessandro Fontana, translated by David Macey (New York: Picador, 2003). [*Il fait défendre la société*, 1997]
Foucault, Michel, 'Technologies of the Self', in Luther H. Martin, Huck Gutman and Patrick H. Hutton (eds), *Technologies of the Self: A Seminar with Michel Foucault* (London: Tavistock Publications, 1988), pp. 16–49.
Fout, John, 'Homosexuelle in der NS-Zeit: Neue Forschungsansätze über Alltagsleben und Verfolgung', in Burkhard Jellonek and Rüdiger Lautmann (eds), *Nationalsozialistischer Terror gegen Homosexuelle* (Paderborn: Schöningh, 2002), pp. 163–72.
Freund-Widder, Michaela, *Frauen unter Kontrolle: Prostitution und ihre staatliche Bekämpfung in Hamburg vom Ende des Kaiserreichs bis zu den Anfängen der Bundesrepublik* (Münster: Lit, 2003).

Frevert, Ute, 'Militär als Schule der Männlichkeiten', in Ulrike Brunotte and Rainer Herrn (eds), *Männlichkeiten und Moderne: Geschlecht in den Wissenskulturen um 1900* (Bielefeld: Transcript, 2008), pp. 57–76.

Freytag, Claudia, 'Kriegsbeute "Flintenweib": Rotarmistinnen in deutscher Gefangenschaft', in Peter Jahn (ed.), *Mascha, Nina, Katjuscha* (Berlin: Christoph Links Verlag, 2002), pp. 32–6.

Friedman, Jonathan C., *Speaking the Unspeakable: Essays on Sexuality, Gender, and Holocaust Survivor Memory* (Lanham, MD: University Press of America, 2002).

Friedrich, Jörg, *Das Gesetz des Krieges. Das deutsche Heer in Russland 1941 bis 1945: Der Prozess gegen das Oberkommando der Wehrmacht* (Munich: Piper, 1993).

Frischauer, Willi, 'The Brothel Brigade', *The Times Literary Supplement*, 30 August 1972.

Fritz, Stephen G., *Frontsoldaten: The German Soldier in World War II* (Lexington: The University Press of Kentucky, 1995).

Gaevert, Thomas and Martin Hilbert, *Women as Booty: The Wehrmacht and Prostitution (Frauen als Beute: Wehrmacht und Prostitution)*, documentary film, Aquino Film, 2005.

Gabriel, Lisa, 'The Literature Database www.warandgender.net: An ongoing project', in Gaby Zipfel, Regina Mühlhäuser and Kirsten Campbell, *In Plain Sight* (New Delhi: Zubaan, 2019), pp. 450–458.

Garraio, Júlia, 'Hordes of Rapists: The Instrumentalization of Sexual Violence in German Cold War Anti-Communist Discourses', translated by João Paulo Moreira, *Revista Crítica de Ciências Sociais Annual Review*, 5, 2013, <https://journals.openedition.org/rccsar/476> (last accessed 7 August 2019).

Gebhardt, Miriam, *Als die Soldaten kamen: Die Vergewaltigung deutscher Frauen am Ende des Zweiten Weltkrieges* (Munich: DVA, 2015).

Geissbühler, Simon, 'The Rape of Jewish Women and Girls during the First Phase of the Romanian Offensive in the East, July 1941: A Research Agenda and Preliminary Findings', *Holocaust Studies: A Journal of Culture and History*, 19(1), 2013, pp. 59–80.

Geliebter Feind! Liebe zu deutschen Besatzungssoldaten in Frankreich, documentary film, broadast on Phoenix, 2 January 2001 [BBC production 1999].

Gellately, Robert and Nathan Stoltzfus (eds), *Social Outsiders in Nazi Germany* (Princeton: Princeton University Press, 2001).

Gerlach, Christian, *Kalkulierte Morde: Die deutsche Wirtschafts- und Vernichtungspolitik in Weissrussland 1941 bis 1944* (Hamburg: Hamburger Edition, 1999).

Gertjejanssen, Wendy Jo, *Victims, Heroes, Survivors: Sexual Violence on the Eastern Front during World War II*, unpublished dissertation, University of Minnesota, 2004 <http://www.victimsheroessurvivors.info/VictimsHeroesSurvivors.pdf> (last accessed 21 January 2019).

Giles, Geoffrey, 'The Denial of Homosexuality: Same-Sex Incidents in Himmler's SS and Police', *Journal of the History of Sexuality*, 11(1/2), 2002, pp. 256–90.

Giles, Geoffrey, 'The Institutionalization of Homosexual Panic in the Third Reich', in Robert Gellately and Nathan Stoltzfus (eds), *Social Outsiders in Nazi Germany*, pp. 233–55.

Gilman, Sander L., *Freud, Race, and Gender* (Princeton: Princeton University Press, 1993).

Glowacka, Dorota, 'Sexual Violence Against Men and Boys During the Holocaust: A Genealogy of (Not-So-Silent) Silence', *German History*, 38, 2020.

Goff, Stan, 'The Tactics of Everyday Life', in Andrew Boyd and Dave Oswald Mitchell (eds), *Beautiful Trouble: A Toolbox for Revolution* (New York: OR Books, 2012).

Goldberg, David Theo, *Racist Culture: Philosophy and the Politics of Meaning* (Malden, MA: Blackwell, 1993).

Goldenberg, Myrna, 'Lessons Learned from Gentle Heroism: Women's Holocaust Narratives', in *The Annals of the American Academy of Political and Social Science* 548, 1996, pp. 78–93; <http://www.theverylongview.com/WATH/essays/lessons.htm> (last accessed 13 March 2019).

Goldenberg, Myrna, 'Memoirs of Auschwitz Survivors: The Burden of Gender', in Dalia Ofer and Lenore J. Weitzman (eds), *Women and the Holocaust* (New Haven: Yale University Press, 1998), pp. 327–39.

Goldenberg, Myrna, 'Sex, Rape, and Survival: Jewish Women and the Holocaust', 2005 <http://www.theverylongview.com/WATH/essays/sexrapesurvival.htm> (last accessed January 28, 2019).

Goldenberg, Myrna, 'Sex-Based Violence and the Politics and Ethics of Survival', in Myrna Goldenberg and Amy H. Shapiro (eds), *Different Horrors, Same Hell: Gender and the Holocaust* (Seattle: University of Washington Press, 2013), pp. 99–127.

Goldstein, Joshua, *War and Gender: How Gender Shapes the War System and Vice Versa* (Cambridge: Cambridge University Press, 2001).

Goltermann, Svenja, 'Die Beherrschung der Männlichkeit: Zur Deutung psychischer Leiden bei den Heimkehrern des Zweiten Weltkriegs 1945–1956', *Feministische Studien*, 18(2), 2000, pp. 7–19.

Graml, Hermann, 'Die Wehrmacht im Dritten Reich', *Vierteljahrshefte für Zeitgeschichte*, 45(2), 1997, pp. 365–84.

Gray, Colin S., *Modern Strategy* (Oxford: Oxford University Press, 1999).

Greer, Germaine, *The Female Eunuch* (London: MacGibbon & Kee, 1970).

Greiner, Bernd, *War Without Fronts: The USA in Vietnam*, translated by Anne Wyburd with Victoria Fern (London: Vintage Books, 2010). [*Krieg ohne Fronten: Die USA in Vietnam*, 2007]

Greku, Elena, 'Die Deutschen in den sowjetischen Lehrbüchern für Literatur nach dem Zweiten Weltkrieg', in Olga Kurilo (ed.), *Der zweite Weltkrieg im deutschen und russischen Gedächtnis* (Berlin: Avinus, 2006), pp. 133–42.

Griese, Karin, 'Einleitung', in medica mondiale e.V. and Karin Griese (ed.), *Sexualisierte Kriegsgewalt und ihre Folgen* (Frankfurt: Mabuse-Verlag GmbH, 2004), pp. 9–16.

Grenz, Sabine, 'Prostitution, eine Verhinderung oder Ermöglichung sexueller Gewalt? Spannungen in kulturellen Konstruktionen von männlicher und weiblicher

Sexualität', in Sabine Grenz and Martin Lücke (eds), *Verhandlungen im Zwielicht: Momente der Prostitution in Geschichte und Gegenwart* (Bielefeld: Transcript, 2006), pp. 319–442.

Grenz, Sabine, *(Un)heimliche Lust: Über den Konsum sexueller Dienstleistungen* (Wiesbaden: VS Verlag für Sozialwissenschaften, 2005).

Griffin, Susan, 'Rape: the all-American crime', *Ramparts Magazine*, 10(3), 1971, pp. 26–35.

Gross, Jan T., 'The Jewish Community in the Soviet Annexed Territories on the Eve of the Holocaust: A Social Scientist's View', in Lucjan Dobroszycki and Jeffrey S. Gurock (eds), *The Holocaust in the Soviet Union: Studies and Sources on the Destruction of the Jews in the Nazi-Occupied Territories of the USSR, 1941–1945* (Armonk, NY: M. E. Sharpe, 1993), pp. 155–71.

Gross, Jan T., 'A Tangled Web: Confronting Stereotypes Concerning Relations Between Poles, Germans, Jews, and Communists' in István Deák, Jan T. Gross and Tony Judt (eds), *The Politics of Retribution in Europe: World War II and Its Aftermath* (Princeton: Princeton University Press, 2000), pp. 74–129.

Grossmann, Atina, 'The Difficulty of Historicizing Rape and Sexual Violence: Victims, Resisters, and Liberators in World War II', lecture at the *Women's Bodies as Battlefields* conference, in unpublished *Reader* (Hamburg: Hamburger Institut für Sozialforschung, 2001).

Grossmann, Atina, *Jews, Germans, and Allies: Close Encounters in Occupied Germany* (Princeton: Princeton University Press, 2007).

Grossmann, Atina, 'A Question of Silence: The Rape of German Women by Occupation Soldiers', *October*, 72, 1995, pp. 43–63.

Grossmann, Atina, 'Women and the Holocaust: Four Recent Titles', *Holocaust and Genocide Studies*, 16(1), 2002, pp. 94–108.

Gullace, Nicoletta F., 'Sexual Violence and Family Honor: British Propaganda and International Law During the First World War', *American Historical Review*, 102(3), 1997, pp. 714–49.

Gusarov, Katya, 'Sexual Barter and Jewish Women's Efforts to Save Their Lives: Accounts from the Righteous Among the Nations Archives', *German History*, 38(3), 2020.

Haase, Norbert, '". . . eine Sportveranstaltung, wenn auch etwas besonderer Art . . ." Der Mord an den Litauer Juden im Sommer 1941: Aus dem Tagebuch eines Augenzeugen', *Tribüne: Zeitschrift zum Verständnis des Judentums*, 30(120), 1991, pp. 200–8.

Haase, Norbert, *'Gefahr für die Manneszucht': Verweigerung und Widerstand im Spiegel der Spruchtätigkeit von Marinegerichten in Wilhelmshaven (1939–1945)* (Hanover: Verlag Hahnsche Buchhandlung, 1996).

Haberling, Wilhelm, 'Army Prostitution and its Control: An Historical Study', in Victor Robinson (ed.), *Morals in Wartime* (New York: Publishers Foundation, 1943), pp. 3–90.

Hagemann, Karen, 'German Heroes: The Cult of the Death for the Fatherland in Nineteenth-Century Germany', in Stefan Dudink, Karen Hagemann and John

Tosh (eds), *Masculinities in Politics and War: Gendering Modern History* (Manchester: Manchester University Press, 2004), pp. 116–34.

Hagemann, Karen and Stefanie Schüler-Springorum (eds), *Home/Front: The Military, War and Gender in Twentieth-Century Germany* (Oxford: Berg, 2002). [*Heimat – Front: Militär und Geschlechterverhältnisse im Zeitalter der Weltkriege*, 2002]

Hájková, Anna, 'Between Love and Coercion: Queer Desire, Sexual Barter and the Holocaust', *German History*, 38(3), 2020.

Hájková, Anna, 'Sexual Barter in Times of Genocide: Negotiating the Sexual Economy of the Theresienstadt Ghetto,' *Signs: Journal of Women in Culture and Society*, 38(3), 2013, pp. 503–33.

Halbmayr, Brigitte, 'Sexualized Violence Against Women During Nazi "Racial" Persecution', in Sonja M. Hedgepeth and Rochelle G. Saidel (eds), *Sexual Violence against Jewish Women during the Holocaust* (Waltham, MA: Brandeis University Press, 2010), pp. 29–44.

Hamburger Institut für Sozialforschung (ed.), *Eine Ausstellung und ihre Folgen: Zur Rezeption der Ausstellung 'Vernichtungskrieg: Verbrechen der Wehrmacht 1941 bis 1944'* (Hamburg: Hamburger Edition, 1999).

Harnischmacher, Robert and Josef Muether, 'Das Stockholm-Syndrom: Zur psychischen Reaktion von Geiseln und Geiselnehmern', *Archiv für Kriminologie*, 1/2, 1987, pp. 1–12.

Hartmann, Christian, 'Verbrecherischer Krieg – verbrecherische Wehrmacht? Überlegungen zur Struktur des deutschen Ostheers', *Vierteljahrshefte für Zeitgeschichte*, 52, 2004, pp. 1–75.

Harvey, Elizabeth, *Women and the Nazi East: Agents and Witnesses of Germanization* (New Haven: Yale University Press, 2003).

Haury, Thomas, *Antisemitismus von links: Kommunistische Ideologie, Nationalismus und Antizionismus in der frühen DDR* (Hamburg: Hamburger Edition, 2002).

Heberle, Renee, 'Deconstructive Strategies and the Movement Against Sexual Violence', *Hypatia: A Journal of Feminist Philosophy*, 11(4), 1996, pp. 63–76.

Hedgepeth, Sonja M. and Rochelle G. Saidel (eds), *Sexual Violence against Jewish Women during the Holocaust* (Waltham, MA: Brandeis University Press, 2010).

Heer, Hannes, 'Einübung in den Holocaust: Lemberg Juni/Juli 1941', *Zeitschrift für Geschichtswissenschaft*, 49(5), 2001, pp. 409–27.

Heer, Hannes, 'Killing Fields: Die Wehrmacht und der Holocaust', in Hannes Heer and Klaus Naumann (eds), *Vernichtungskrieg: Verbrechen der Wehrmacht 1941 bis 1944* (Hamburg: Hamburger Edition, 1995), pp. 57–77.

Heer, Hannes, 'Killing Fields: The Wehrmacht and the Holocaust in Belorussia, 1941–42,' in Hannes Heer and Klaus Naumann (eds), *War of Extermination* (London: Berghahn, 2004), pp. 55–79.

Heer, Hannes, 'The Logic of the War of Extermination: The Wehrmacht and the Anti-Partisan War', in Hannes Heer and Klaus Naumann (eds), *War of Extermination* (London: Berghahn, 2004), pp. 92–126.

Heer, Hannes, *Tote Zonen: Die deutsche Wehrmacht an der Ostfront* (Hamburg: Hamburger Edition, 1999).

Heer, Hannes and Klaus Naumann (eds), *Vernichtungskrieg: Verbrechen der Wehrmacht 1941 bis 1944* (Hamburg: Hamburger Edition, 1995).

Heer, Hannes and Klaus Naumann (eds), *War of Extermination: The German Military in World War II, 1941–1944*, translated by Roy Shelton (London: Berghahn, 2004 [2000]).

Heer, Hannes and Klaus Naumann, 'Introduction', in Hannes Heer and Klaus Naumann (eds), *War of Extermination* (London: Berghahn, 2004), pp. 1–12.

Heim, Susanne and Götz Aly, 'Die Ökonomie der "Endlösung": Menschenvernichtung und wirtschaftliche Neuordnung', *Beiträge zur nationalsozialistischen Gesundheits- und Sozialpolitik*, 5, 1987, pp. 11–90.

Hein, Bastian, *Die SS: Geschichte und Verbrechen* (Munich: C. H. Beck, 2015).

Heineman, Elizabeth D., 'The Hour of the Woman: Memories of Germany's "Crisis Years" and West German National Identity', *The American Historical Review*, 101(2), April 1996, pp. 354–95.

Heineman, Elizabeth D., 'Introduction: The History of Sexual Violence in Conflict Zones', in Elizabeth D. Heineman (ed.), *Sexual Violence in Conflict Zones* (Philadelphia: University of Pennsylvania Press, 2011), pp. 1–21.

Heineman, Elizabeth D. (ed), *Sexual Violence in Conflict Zones: From the Ancient World to the Era of Human Rights* (Philadelphia: University of Pennsylvania Press, 2011).

Heineman, Elizabeth D., 'Sexuality and Nazism: The Doubly Unspeakable?', *Journal of the History of Sexuality*, 11(1/2), January–April 2002, pp. 22–66.

Heineman, Elizabeth D., *What Difference Does a Husband Make? Women and Marital Status in Nazi and Postwar Germany* (Berkeley: University of California Press, 1999).

Heinemann, Isabel, *'Rasse, Siedlung, deutsches Blut': Das Rasse- und Siedlungshauptamt der SS und die rassenpolitische Neuordnung Europas* (Göttingen: Wallstein, 2003).

Heinemann, Marlene E., *Gender and Destiny: Women Writers and the Holocaust* (Westport, CT: Greenwood Press, 1986).

Henke, Josef, *Persönlicher Stab Reichsführer-SS: Bestand NS 19 (Findbücher zu den Beständen des Bundesarchivs, Band 57)*, (Koblenz: Bundesarchiv, 1997).

Henry, Nicola, *War and Rape: Law, Memory, and Justice* (London: Routledge, 2011).

Henschel, Gerhard, *Neidgeschrei: Antisemitismus und Sexualität* (Hamburg: Hoffmann und Campe, 2008).

Herbert, Ulrich, *Hitler's Foreign Workers: Enforced Foreign Labor in Germany under the Third Reich*, translated by William Templer (Cambridge, UK: Cambridge University Press, 1997). [*Fremdarbeiter: Politik und Praxis des 'Ausländereinsatzes' in der Kriegswirtschaft des Dritten Reiches*, 1985]

Herzog, Dagmar (ed.), *Brutality and Desire: War and Sexuality in Europe's Twentieth Century* (Basingstoke: Palgrave Macmillan, 2009).

Herzog, Dagmar (ed.), *Lessons and Legacies VII: The Holocaust in International Perspective* (Evanston, IL: Northwester University Press, 2006).

Herzog, Dagmar, *Sex After Fascism: Memory and Morality in Twentieth-Century Germany* (Princeton: Princeton University Press, 2005).

Herzog, Dagmar, 'Sexual Violence Against Men: Torture at Flossenbürg', in Carol Rittner and John K. Roth (eds), *Rape: Weapon of War and Genocide* (St. Paul: Paragon House, 2012), pp. 29–44.

Herzog, Dagmar, *Sexuality in Europe: A Twentieth-Century History* (Cambridge, UK: Cambridge University Press, 2011).

Hiden, John and Patrick Salmon, *The Baltic Nations and Europe: Estonia, Latvia and Lithuania in the Twentieth Century* (London: Routledge, 1991).

Higate, Paul, '"Switching On" for Cash: The Private Militarised Security Contractor as Geo-Corporeal Actor', in Kevin McSorley, *War and the Body* (London/New York: Routledge, 2015), pp. 106–127.

Hilberg, Raul, *The Destruction of the European Jews*, 3 volumes (New Haven: Yale University Press, 2003 [1961]).

Hill, Alexander, *The War Behind the Eastern Front: The Soviet Partisan Movement in North-West Russia 1941–1944* (London: Frank Cass, 2005).

Hockey, John, 'No More Heroes: Masculinity in the Infantry', in Paul Higate (ed.), *Military Masculinities* (Westport, CT: Praeger, 2013), pp. 15–25.

Hockey, John, '"Switch On": Sensory Work in the Infantry', *Work, Employment and Society*, 23(3), 2009, pp. 477–93.

Höhn, Maria, *GIs and Fräuleins: The German-American Encounter in 1950s West Germany* (Chapel Hill: University of North Carolina Press, 2002).

Hoover Green, Amelia, *The Commander's Dilemma: Violence and Restraint in Wartime* (Ithaca, NY: Cornell University Press, 2018).

Horne, John, and Alan Kramer, *German Atrocities 1914: A History of Denial* (New Haven: Yale University Press, 2001).

Hornung, Ela, 'Das Schweigen zum Sprechen bringen: Erzählformen österreichischer Soldaten in der Deutschen Wehrmacht', in Walter Manoschek (ed.), *Die Wehrmacht im Rassenkrieg: Der Vernichtungskrieg hinter der Front* (Vienna: Picus, 1996), pp. 182–205.

Horowitz, Sara R. 'The Gender of Good and Evil: Women and Holocaust Memory', in Jonathan Petropoulos and John K. Roth (eds): *Gray Zones: Ambiguity and Compromise in the Holocaust and its Aftermath* (New York: Berghahn Books, 2005), pp. 165–178.

Hrabar, Roman, Zofia Tokarz and Jacek E. Wilczur, *Kinder im Krieg – Krieg gegen Kinder: Die Geschichte der polnischen Kinder 1939–1945* (Reinbek bei Hamburg: Rowohlt, 1981).

Huber, Christian Thomas, *Die Rechtsprechung der deutschen Feldkriegsgerichte bei Straftaten von Wehrmachtssoldaten gegen Angehörige der Zivilbevölkerung in den besetzten Gebieten* (Marburg: Tectum, 2007).

Hügel-Marshall, Ika, *Invisible Woman: Growing up Black in Germany, New Edition*, translated by Elizabeth Gaffney (New York: Peter Lang, 2008). [*Daheim unterwegs*, 1998]

Humburg, Martin, *Das Gesicht des Krieges: Feldpostbriefe von Wehrmachtssoldaten aus der Sowjetunion 1941–1944* (Opladen: Westdeutscher Verlag, 1998).

Hüppauf, Bernd, 'Emptying the Gaze: Framing Violence Through the Viewfinder', *New German Critique*, 72, 1997, pp. 3–44.

Hürter, Johannes, *Hitlers Heerführer: Die deutschen Oberbefehlshaber im Krieg gegen die Sowjetunion 1941/42* (Munich: Oldenbourg, 2006).
Inal, Tuba, *Looting and Rape in Wartime: Law and Change in International Relations* (Philadelphia: University of Pennsylvania Press, 2013).
Ingrao, Christian, *The SS Dirlewanger Brigade: The History of the Black Hunters*, translated by Phoebe Green (New York: Skyhorse Publishing, 2013). [*Les chasseurs noirs: Essai sur la Sondereinheit Dirlewanger*, 2006]
International Criminal Tribunal for Rwanda (ICTR), *Amended Indictment Against Pauline Nyiramasuhuko*, Case No. ICTR-97-21-I, 10 August 1999, <http://unictr.irmct.org/sites/unictr.org/files/case-documents/ictr-98-42/indictments/en/010301.pdf> (last accessed 13 February 2019).
Jahn, Peter (ed.), *Mascha, Nina, Katjuscha: Frauen in der Roten Armee 1941–1945* (Berlin: Christoph Links Verlag, 2002).
Jahn, Peter, 'Vorwort', in Peter Jahn and Ulrike Schmiegelt (eds), *Foto-Feldpost*, p. 7.
Jahn, Peter and Ulrike Schmiegelt (eds), *Foto-Feldpost: Geknipste Kriegserlebnisse 1939–1945* (Berlin: Elefanten Press, 2000).
Janssen, Karl-Heinz, '"Vorwärts mit Gott für Deutschland!"', in Theo Sommer (ed.), *Gehorsam bis zum Mord? Der verschwiegene Krieg der deutschen Wehrmacht – Fakten, Analysen, Debatte* (Hamburg: Zeitverlag Bucerius, 1995), pp. 7–12.
Jarvis, Michelle and Kate Vigneswaran, 'Challenges to Successful Outcomes in Sexual Violence Cases', in Michelle Jarvis and Serge Brammertz (eds), *Prosecuting Conflict-Related Sexual Violence at the ICTY* (Oxford: Oxford University Press, 2016), pp. 33–72.
Joachim, Ingeborg, 'Sexualisierte Kriegsgewalt und ihre Folgen', in medica mondiale e.V. and Karin Griese (eds), *Sexualisierte Kriegsgewalt und ihre Folgen* (Frankfurt: Mabuse-Verlag GmbH, 2004), pp. 57–94.
Joeden-Forgey, Elisa von, 'The Devil in the Details: "Life Force Atrocities" and the Assault on the Family in Times of Crisis', *Genocide Studies and Prevention*, 5(1), 2010, pp. 1–19.
Johr, Barbara and Helke Sander, *BeFreier und Befreite: Krieg, Vergewaltigungen, Kinder* (Frankfurt: Fischer, 1995).
Jureit, Ulrike, *Erinnerungsmuster: Zur Methodik lebensgeschichtlicher Interviews mit Überlebenden der Konzentrations- und Vernichtungslager* (Hamburg: Ergebnisse, 1999).
Jureit, Ulrike, 'Zwischen Ehe und Männerbund: Emotionale und sexuelle Beziehungsmuster im Zweiten Weltkrieg', *WerkstattGeschichte*, 22(10), 1999, pp. 61–73.
Jütte, Robert, *Contraception: A History*, translated by Vicky Russell (Cambridge, UK: Polity, 2008). [*Lust ohne Last: Geschichte der Empfängnisverhütung von der Antike bis zur Gegenwart*, 2003]
Kalikov, Jury, *Prostitution in Estonia, Latvia and Lithuania* (Budapest: Central European University – Center for Policy Studies/Open Society Institute, 2004) <http://pdc.ceu.hu/archive/00002057/01/kalikov.pdf> (last accessed 1 April 2019).
Kaminski, Hartmut (dir.), *Liebe im Vernichtungskrieg: Die Frauen im Osten und die deutschen Besatzungssoldaten*, documentary film, broadcast on SWR II, 7 July 2001.

Kaplan, Marion, *The Making of the Jewish Middle Class: Women, Family, and Identity in Imperial Germany* (Oxford: Oxford University Press, 1991).

Kappeler, Andrea, *The Russian Empire: A Multiethnic History*, translated by Alfred Clayton (London: Routledge, 2013). [*Russland als Vielvölkerreich: Entstehung, Geschichte, Zerfall*, 2008]

Katz, Steven T., 'Thoughts on the Intersection of Rape and "Rassenschande" During the Holocaust', in *Modern Judaism*, 32(3), 2012, pp. 293–322.

Keller, Jörg, 'Küss' die Hand gnäd'ge Frau ... – oder: Ist die Soldatin möglich?', in Ruth Seifert and Christine Eifler (eds), *Gender und Militär: Internationale Erfahrungen mit Frauen und Männern in den Streitkräften* (Königstein: Ulrike Helmer, 2003), pp. 248–66.

Kieler, Marita, *Tatbestandsprobleme der sexuellen Nötigung, Vergewaltigung sowie des sexuellen Mißbrauchs widerstandsunfähiger Personen* (Berlin: Tanea, 2003).

Kienitz, Sabine, *Beschädigte Helden: Kriegsinvalidität und Körperbilder 1914–1923* (Paderborn: Schönigh, 2008).

Kim, Myung-Hye, 'Narrative Darstellung und Produktion von Wissen: Erzählungen koreanischer Frauen, die das System sexueller Versklavung durch die japanische Armee überlebt haben', in Insa Eschebach and Regina Mühlhäuser (eds) *Krieg und Geschlecht* (Berlin: Metropol, 2008), pp. 187–205.

Klausch, Hans-Peter, *Antifaschisten in SS-Uniform: Schicksal und Widerstand der deutschen politischen KZ-Häftlinge, Zuchthaus- und Wehrmachtstrafgefangenen in der SS-Sonderformation Dirlewanger* (Bremen: Edition Temmen, 1993).

Klein, Peter, *Die 'Gettoverwaltung Litzmannstadt' 1940–1944: Eine Dienststelle im Spannungsfeld von Kommunalbürokratie und staatlicher Verfolgungspolitik* (Hamburg: Hamburger Edition, 2009).

Knoch, Habbo, *Die Tat als Bild: Fotografien des Holocaust in der deutschen Erinnerungskultur* (Hamburg: Hamburger Edition, 2001).

Knoch, Peter (ed.), *Kriegsalltag: Die Rekonstruktion des Kriegsalltages als Aufgabe der historischen Forschung und der Friedenserziehung* (Stuttgart: J.B. Metzler, 1989).

Knoch, Peter, 'Kriegsalltag', in Peter Knoch (ed.), *Kriegsalltag* (Stuttgart: J.B. Metzler, 1989), pp. 222–51.

Koch, Magnus, *Fahnenfluchten: Deserteure der Wehrmacht im Zweiten Weltkrieg – Lebenswege und Entscheidungen* (Paderborn: Schönigh, 2008).

Koch, Magnus, '"Nichts als Fliegen ...": Männlichkeit und "Eigensinn" in den Erinnerungen des Luftwaffensoldaten Eugen Bosch', in Maren Büttner and Magnus Koch (eds), *Zwischen Gehorsam und Desertion* (Cologne: PapyRossa, 2003), pp. 78–107.

Koller, Christian, *'Von Wilden aller Rassen niedergemetzelt': Die Diskussion um die Verwendung von Kolonialtruppen in Europa zwischen Rassismus, Kolonial- und Militärpolitik (1914–1930)* (Stuttgart: Franz Steiner, 2001).

Koller, Christian, 'Die "Schwarze Schmach" – afrikanische Besatzungssoldaten und Rassismus in den zwanziger Jahren', in Marianne Bechhaus-Gerst and Reinhard Klein-Arendt (eds), *AfrikanerInnen in Deutschland und schwarze Deutsche: Geschichte und Gegenwart* (Münster: LIT, 2004), pp. 155–69.

Kormina, Zanna and Sergej Styrkov, 'Niemand und nichts ist vergessen: Die Okkupation in mündlichen Zeugnissen' in *Osteuropa*, 55(4–6), 2005, pp. 444–61.
Krausnick, Helmut, 'Die Einsatzgruppen vom Anschluss Österreichs bis zum Feldzug gegen die Sowjetunion: Entwicklung und Verhältnis zur Wehrmacht', in Helmut Krausnick and Hans-Heinrich Wilhelm (eds), *Die Truppe des Weltanschauungskrieges* (Stuttgart: Deutsche Verlags-Anstalt, 1981), pp. 13–278.
Krausnick, Helmut and Hans-Heinrich Wilhelm (eds), *Die Truppe des Weltanschauungskrieges: Die Einsatzgruppen der Sicherheitspolizei und des SD 1938–1942* (Stuttgart: Deutsche Verlags-Anstalt, 1981).
Kreindler, Isabelle, 'The Soviet Deportation of Nationalities: A Summary and Update', *Soviet Studies*, 38(3), 1986, pp. 388–91.
Krog, Antjie, *Country of My Skull: Guilt, Sorrow, and the Limits of Forgiveness in the New South Africa* (London: Vintage, 1999).
Kruse, Kuno, 'Major Kurt Werner: Retter des jüdischen Flamencotänzers Rubinstein', in Wolfram Wette (ed.), *Zivilcourage: Empörte, Helfer und Retter aus Wehrmacht, Polizei und SS* (Frankfurt: Fischer, 2004), pp. 274–86.
Kuber, Johannes, '"Frivolous Broads" and the "Black Menace": The Catholic Clergy's Perception of Victims and Perpetrators of Sexual Violence in Occupied Germany, 1945', in Sara K. Danielsson (ed.), *War and Sexual Violence: New Perspectives in a New Era* (Paderborn: Schöningh, 2019), pp. 183–208.
Kühne, Thomas, *Belonging and Genocide: Hitler's Community, 1918–1945* (New Haven, CT: Yale University Press, 2010).
Kühne, Thomas, *Kameradschaft: Die Soldaten des nationalsozialistischen Krieges und das 20. Jahrhundert* (Göttingen: Vandenhoeck & Ruprecht, 2006).
Kühne, Thomas, 'The Pleasure of Terror: Belonging through Genocide', in Pamela E. Swett, Corey Ross and Fabrice d'Almeida (eds), *Pleasure and Power in Nazi Germany* (London: Palgrave Macmillan, 2011), pp. 234–55.
Kühne, Thomas, *The Rise and Fall of Comradeship: Hitler's Soldiers, Male Bonding and Mass Violence in the Twentieth Century* (Cambridge, UK: Cambridge University Press, 2017).
Kundrus, Birthe, 'Forbidden Company: Romantic Relationships Between Germans and Foreigners, 1939–1945', *Journal of the History of Sexuality*, 11(1/2), 2002, pp. 201–22.
Kundrus, Birthe, *Kriegerfrauen: Familienpolitik und Geschlechterverhältnisse im Ersten und Zweiten Weltkrieg* (Hamburg: Christians, 1995).
Kundrus, Birthe, *Moderne Imperialisten: Das Kaiserreich im Spiegel seiner Kolonien* (Cologne: Böhlau, 2003).
Kundrus, Birthe, 'Nur die halbe Geschichte: Frauen im Umfeld der Wehrmacht zwischen 1939 und 1945 – Ein Forschungsbericht', in Rolf-Dieter Müller and Hans-Erich Volkmann (eds), *Die Wehrmacht* (Munich: Oldenbourg, 1999), pp. 719–38.
Kundrus, Birthe, 'Regime der Differenz: Volkstumspolitische Inklusionen und Exklusionen im Warthegau und im Generalgouvernement 1939–1944', in Frank Bajohr and Michael Wildt (eds), *Volksgemeinschaft: Neue Forschungen zur Gesellschaft des Nationalsozialismus* (Frankfurt: Fischer, 2009), pp. 105–23.

Kurilo, Olga (ed.), *Der zweite Weltkrieg im deutschen und russischen Gedächtnis* (Berlin: Avinus, 2006).
La resistenza: Beiträge zu Faschismus, deutscher Besatzung und dem Widerstand in Italien (Erlangen: Verein zur Förderung alternativer Medien, 2008).
Lacey, Kate, 'Driving the Message Home: Nazi Propaganda in the Private Sphere', in Lynn Abrams and Elizabeth Harvey (eds), *Gender Relations in German History: Power, Agency and Experience from the Sixteenth to the Twentieth Century* (Durham, NC: Duke University Press, 1996), pp. 189–210.
Langhamer, Claire, 'Love and Courtship in Mid-Twentieth-Century England', *The Historical Journal*, 50(1), 2007, pp. 173–96.
Laqueur, Thomas Walter, *Solitary Sex: A Cultural History of Masturbation* (Brooklyn: Zone Books, 2003).
Latzel, Klaus, *Deutsche Soldaten – nationalsozialistischer Krieg? Kriegserlebnis – Kriegserfahrung 1939–1945* (Paderborn: Schöningh, 1998).
Latzel, Klaus, 'Die Zumutungen des Krieges und der Liebe – zwei Annäherungen an Feldpostbriefe', in Habbo Knoch (ed.), *Kriegsalltag* (Stuttgart: J. B. Metzler, 1989), pp. 204–21.
Latzel, Klaus, 'Kollektive Identität und Gewalt', in: Peter Jahn and Ulrike Schmiegelt (eds), *Foto-Feldpost* (Berlin: Elefanten Press, 2000), pp. 13–22.
Lauretis, Theresa de, 'The Violence of Rhetoric: Considerations on Representation and Gender', in *Technologies of Gender: Essays on Theory, Film, and Fiction* (Bloomington: Indiana University Press, [1985] 1987), pp. 31–50.
Lazreg, Marnia, *Torture and the Twilight of Empire: From Algiers to Baghdad* (Princeton: Princeton University Press, 2008).
Lebzelter, Gisela, 'Die "Schwarze Schmach": Vorurteile – Propaganda – Mythos', *Geschichte und Gesellschaft*, 11(1), 1985, pp. 37–58.
Leiby, Michele, 'Digging in the Archives: The Promise and Perils of Primary Documents', *Politics and Society*, 37(1), 1 March 2009, pp. 75–99.
Lejeune, Philippe, 'How Do Diaries End?', *Biography*, 24(1), 2001, pp. 99–112.
Lemke Muniz de Faria, Yara-Colette, *Zwischen Fürsorge und Ausgrenzung: Afrodeutsche 'Besatzungskinder' im Nachkriegsdeutschland* (Berlin: Metropol, 2002).
Lenin, Vladimir Ilyich, 'Capitalism and Female Labour', in Robert C. Tucker (ed.), *The Lenin Anthology* (New York: W. W. Norton & Company, 1975), pp. 682–3.
Lentin, Ronit, 'Introduction: (En)Gendering Genocides', in Ronit Lentin (ed.), *Gender & Catastrophe* (London: Zed Books, 1997), pp. 2–17.
Lenz, Claudia, *Haushaltspflicht und Widerstand: Erzählungen norwegischer Frauen über die deutsche Besatzung 1940–1945 im Lichte nationaler Vergangenheitskonstruktionen* (Tübingen: Edition Diskord, 2003).
Lenz, Hans-Joachim, Willi Walter and Ludger Jungnitz, 'Gewalt gegen Männer im Kontext von Krieg und von Wehr- und Zivildienst', in Ludger Jungnitz, Hans-Joachim Lenz, Ralf Puchert, Henry Puhe and Willi Walter (eds), *Gewalt gegen Männer in Deutschland: Personale Gewaltwiderfahrnisse von Männern in Deutschland* (Opladen: Barbara Budrich, 2007), pp. 113–37.
Lieb, Peter, 'Täter aus Überzeugung? Oberst Carl von Andrian und die Judenmorde der

707. Infanteriedivision 1941/42. Das Tagebuch eines Regimentskommandeurs: Ein neuer Zugang zu einer berüchtigten Wehrmachtsdivision', *Vierteljahrshefte für Zeitgeschichte*, 50(4), 2002, pp. 523–57.

Lilienthal, Georg, *Der 'Lebensborn e.V.': Ein Instrument nationalsozialistischer Rassenpolitik*, 2nd edition (Frankfurt: Fischer, 2003).

Lilienthal, Georg, '"Rheinlandbastarde", Rassenhygiene und das Problem der rassenideologischen Kontinuität: Zur Untersuchung von Reiner Pommerin: "Sterilisierung der Rheinlandbastarde"', *Medizinhistorisches Journal*, 15(4), 1980, pp. 426–36.

Lilly, Robert J., *Taken by Force: Rape and American GIs in Europe during World War II* (Basingstoke: Palgrave Macmillan, 2007).

Liulevicius, Vejas Gabriel, *War Land on the Eastern Front: Culture, National Identity and German Occupation in World War I* (Cambridge, UK: Cambridge University Press, 2000).

Longerich, Peter, *Heinrich Himmler*, translated by Jeremy Noakes and Lesley Sharpe (Oxford: Oxford University Press, 2012). [*Heinrich Himmler: Biographie*, 2008]

Loth, Wilfried, *Der Weg nach Europa: Geschichte der europäischen Integration 1939–1957*, 2nd edition (Göttingen: Vandenhoeck & Ruprecht, 1991).

Lower, Wendy, *Nazi Empire-Building and the Holocaust in Ukraine* (Chapel Hill: University of North Carolina Press, 2005).

Lüdtke, Alf, *Eigen-Sinn: Fabrikalltag, Arbeitererfahrungen und Politik vom Kaiserreich bis in den Faschismus* (Hamburg: Ergebnisse, 1993).

Lüdtke, Alf, *The History of Everday Life: Reconstructing Historical Experiences and Ways of Life*, translated by William Templer (Princeton: Princeton University Press, 1995). [*Alltagsgeschichte: Zur Rekonstruktion historischer Erfahrungen und Lebensweisen*, 1989]

Mai, Alexander, *Geschlechtskrankheiten als Gegenstand präventiven und therapeutischen Wirkens im Wehrmachtssanitätswesen von 1934 bis 1945*, unpublished dissertation, Leipzig University Faculty of Medicine, 2000.

Mailänder, Elissa, 'Making Sense of a Rape Photograph: Sexual Violence as Social Performance on the Eastern Front, 1939–1944', *Journal of the History of Sexuality*, 26(3), 2017, pp. 489–520.

Mailänder Koslov, Elissa, *Gewalt im Dienstalltag: Die SS-Aufseherinnen des Konzentrations- und Vernichtungslagers Majdanek 1942–1944* (Hamburg: Hamburger Edition, 2009).

Mallmann, Klaus-Michael, '"Mensch, ich feiere heut' den tausendsten Genickschuss": Die Sicherheitspolizei und die Shoah in Westgalizien', in Gerhard Paul (ed.), *Die Täter der Shoah* (Göttingen: Wallstein, 2002), pp. 109–36.

Mallmann, Klaus-Michael, Volker Riess and Wolfram Pyta (eds), *Deutscher Osten 1939–1945: Der Weltanschauungskrieg in Photos und Texten* (Darmstadt: Wissenschaftliche Buchgesellschaft, 2003).

Margolis, Rachel, 'Einführung', in Rachel Margolis and Jim Tobias (eds), *Die geheimen Notizen* (Frankfurt: Fischer, 2005), p. 11–18.

Mark, James, 'Remembering Rape: Divided Social Memory and the Red Army in Hungary 1944-1945', *Past & Present*, 188(1), 2005, pp. 133-61.
Markovna, Nina, *Nina's Journey: A Memoir of Stalin's Russia and the Second World War* (Washington, DC: Regnery Gateway, 1989).
Marlowe, David H., 'The Manning of the Force and the Structure of Battle. Part 2: Men and Women', in Robert K. Fullinwider (ed.), *Conscripts and Volunteers: Military Requirements, Social Values, and the All-Volunteer Force* (Totowa, NJ: Rowman & Allanheld, 1983), pp. 185-230.
Marszolek, Inge, '"Ich möchte Dich zu gerne mal in Uniform sehen": Geschlechterkonstruktionen in Feldpostbriefen', *WerkstattGeschichte*, 22(1), 1999, pp. 41-59.
Martschukat, Jürgen and Olaf Stieglitz, *'Es ist ein Junge!' Einführung in die Geschichte der Männlichkeiten in der Neuzeit* (Tübingen: edition diskord, 2005).
Mass, Sandra, *Weisse Helden, schwarze Krieger: Zur Geschichte kolonialer Männlichkeit in Deutschland 1918-1964* (Cologne: Böhlau, 2006).
Matthäus, Jürgen, 'Das Ghetto Kaunas und die "Endlösung" in Litauen', in Wolfgang Benz and Marion Neiss (eds), *Judenmord in Litauen: Studien und Dokumente* (Berlin: Metropol, 1999), pp. 97-112.
Maubach, Franka, *Die Stellung halten: Kriegserfahrungen und Lebensgeschichten von Wehrmachtshelferinnen* (Göttingen: Vandenhoeck & Ruprecht, 2009).
Maubach, Franka, 'Expansionen weiblicher Hilfe: Zur Erfahrungsgeschichte von Frauen im Kriegsdienst', in Sybille Steinbacher (ed.), *Volksgenossinnen: Frauen in der NS-Volksgemeinschaft* (Göttingen: Wallstein, 2007), pp. 93-111.
Mazower, Mark, 'Military Violence and the National Socialist Consensus: The Wehrmacht and Greece, 1941-1944', in Hannes Heer and Klaus Naumann (eds), *War of Extermination* (London: Berghahn, 2004), pp. 146-74.
McLaren, Angus, *Impotence: A Cultural History* (Chicago: University of Chicago Press, 2007).
McSorley, Kevin (ed.), *War and the Body: Militarisation, Practice and Experience* (London/New York: Routledge, 2015).
McSorley, Kevin, 'War and the Body', in Kevin McSorley (ed.), *War and the Body* (London/New York: Routledge, 2015), pp. 1-31.
Meinen, Insa, *Wehrmacht und Prostitution im besetzten Frankreich* (Bremen: Edition Temmen, 2002).
Meyer, Beate, 'Grenzüberschreitungen: Eine Liebe zu Zeiten des Rassenwahns', *Zeitschrift für Geschichtswissenschaft*, 55(11), 1997, pp. 916-36.
Meyer, Beate, *'Jüdische Mischlinge': Rassenpolitik und Verfolgungserfahrung 1933-1945* (Hamburg: Dölling und Galitz, 1999).
Meyer, Sybille and Eva Schulze, *Von Liebe sprach damals keiner: Familienalltag in der Nachkriegszeit* (Munich: C. H. Beck, 1985).
Mibenge, Chiseche, *Sex and International Tribunals: The Erasure of Gender from the War Narrative* (Philadelphia: University of Pennsylvania Press, 2013).
Millett, Kate, *Sexual Politics* (New York: Doubleday, 1970).
Milton, Sybil, 'Women and the Holocaust: The Case of German and German-Jewish

Women', in Carol Rittner and John K. Roth (eds), *Different Voices: Women and the Holocaust* (New York: Paragon House, 1993), pp. 213–49.

Mischkowski, Gabriela and Gorana Mlinarevic, '... *and that it does not happen to anyone anywhere in the world*': *The Trouble with Rape Trials – Views of Witnesses, Prosecutors and Judges on Prosecuting Sexualised Violence during the War in the former Yogoslavia* (Cologne: medica mondiale e.V., 2009), <https://www.medica mondiale.org/fileadmin/redaktion/5_Service/Mediathek/Dokumente/English/ Documentations_studies/medica_mondiale_and_that_it_does_not_happen_to_ anyone_anywhere_in_the_world_english_complete_version_dec_2009.pdf> (last accessed 9 March 2020).

Mischkowski, Gabriela, *'Damit die Welt es erfährt': Sexualisierte Gewalt im Krieg vor Gericht – Der Foca Prozess vor dem Internationalen Kriegsverbrechertribunal zum ehemaligen Jugoslawien* (Cologne: Bundesministerium für Familie, Senioren, Frauen und Jugend and medica mondiale e.V., 2003), <https://www.medic-amondiale.org/fileadmin/redaktion/5_Service/Mediathek/Dokumente/ Deutsch/Dokumentationen_Studien/medica_mondiale_Damit_die_Welt_es_ erfaehrt-2002.pdf> (last accessed 13 February 2019).

Mischkowski, Gabriela, '"Ob es den Frauen selbst irgendetwas bringt, bleibt eine offene Frage": Gabriela Mischkowski, Referentin für Gender Justice bei medica mondiale e.V., im Gespräch über Probleme und Zwickmühlen der internationalen Strafgerichtsbarkeit', in Insa Eschebach and Regina Mühlhäuser (eds), *Krieg und Geschlecht* (Berlin: Metropol, 2008), pp. 229–48.

Mitscherlich, Alexander, 'Zwei Arten der Grausamkeit', in Alexander Mitscherlich, *Gesammelte Schriften*, vol. 5 (Sozialpsychologie 3), Helga Haase (ed.) (Frankfurt am Main: Suhrkamp, 1983), pp. 322–42.

Möller, Christina, 'Sexuelle Gewalt im Krieg', in Jana Hasse, Erwin Müller and Patricia Schneider (eds), *Humanitäres Völkerrecht: Politische, rechtliche und strafgerichtliche Dimensionen* (Baden-Baden: Nomos, 2001), pp. 280–303.

Möller, Christina, *Völkerstrafrecht und Internationaler Strafgerichtshof – kriminologische, straftheoretische und rechtspolitische Aspekte* (Münster: LIT, 2003).

Moodrick-Even Khen, Hilly B. and Alona Hagay-Frey, 'Silence at the Nuremberg Trials: The International Military Tribunal at Nuremberg and Sexual Crimes Against Women in the Holocaust', *Women's Rights Law Reporter*, 35, 2013, pp. 43–66.

Moon, Katherine H. S., *Sex Among Allies: Military Prostitution in U.S.-Korea Relations* (New York: Columbia University Press, 1997).

Mosse, George L., *The Image of Man: The Creation of Modern Masculinity* (Oxford: Oxford University Press, 1996).

Mühlenberg, Jutta, *Das SS-Helferinnenkorps: Ausbildung, Einsatz und Entnazifizierung der weiblichen Angehörigen der Waffen-SS 1942–1949* (Hamburg: Hamburger Edition, 2011).

Mühlhäuser, Regina, 'Between "Racial Awareness" and Fantasies of Potency: Nazi Sexual Politics in the Occupied Territories of the Soviet Union, 1941–1945', in Dagmer Herzog (ed.), *Brutality and Desire* (Basingstoke: Palgrave Macmillan, 2009), pp. 197–220.

Mühlhäuser, Regina, 'Rasse, Blut und Männlichkeit: Politiken sexueller Regulierung in den besetzten Gebieten der Sowjetunion (1941–1945)', *Feministische Studien*, 25(1), 2007, pp. 55–69.

Mühlhäuser, Regina, 'Reframing Sexual Violence as a Weapon and Strategy of War: The Case of the German Wehrmacht During the War and Genocide in the Soviet Union, 1941–1944', in *Journal of the History of Sexuality*, 26(3), 2017, pp. 366–401.

Mühlhäuser, Regina, 'Sex, Race, Violence, "Volksgemeinschaft": German Soldiers' Sexual Encounters with Local Women and Men During the War and the Occupation in the Soviet Union, 1941–1945', in Devin O. Pendas, Mark Roseman and Richard F. Wetzell (eds), *Beyond the Racial State* (Cambridge, UK: Cambridge University Press, 2017), pp. 455–81.

Mühlhäuser, Regina, 'Sexual Violence and the Holocaust', in Andrea Pető (ed.), *Gender: War* (Farmington Hills: Macmillan Reference USA, 2017), pp. 101–16.

Mühlhäuser, Regina, 'Sexuelle Gewalt als Kriegsverbrechen: Eine Herausforderung für die Internationale Strafgerichtsbarkeit', *Mittelweg 36*, 13(2), 2004, pp. 33–48.

Mühlhäuser, Regina, 'Understanding Sexual Violence During the Holocaust: A Reconsideration of Research and Sources', *German History*, 38(3), 2020.

Mühlhäuser, Regina, 'Vergewaltigungen in Deutschland 1945: Nationaler Opferdiskurs und individuelles Erinnern betroffener Frauen', in Klaus Naumann (ed.), *Nachkrieg in Deutschland* (Hamburg: Hamburger Edition, 2001), pp. 384–408.

Mühlhäuser, Regina, 'Vergewaltigung', in Christian Gudehus and Michaela Christ (eds), *Gewalt: Ein interdisziplinäres Handbuch* (Stuttgart: Metzler, 2013), pp. 164–69.

Mühlhäuser, Regina, '"You Have to Anticipate What Eludes Calculation": Reconceptualizing Sexual Violence as Weapon and Strategy of War', in Gaby Zipfel, Regina Mühlhäuser and Kirsten Campbell (eds.), *In Plain Sight* (New Delhi: Zubaan, 2019), pp. 3–29.

Mühlhäuser, Regina and Ingwer Schwensen, 'Sexuelle Gewalt in Kriegen: Auswahlbibliographie', *Mittelweg 36*, 10/5, 2001, pp. 21–32.

Müller, Rolf-Dieter, 'Liebe im Vernichtungskrieg: Geschlechtergeschichtliche Aspekte des Einsatzes deutscher Soldaten im Rußlandkrieg 1941–1944', in: Frank Becker et al. (eds), *Politische Gewalt in der Moderne: Festschrift für Hans-Ulrich Thamer* (Münster: Aschendorff, 2003), pp. 239–67.

Müller, Rolf-Dieter, *The Unknown Eastern Front: The Wehrmacht and Hitler's Foreign Soldiers*, translated by David Burnett (London: I. B. Taurus, 2012). [*An der Seite der Wehrmacht: Hitlers ausländische Helfer beim 'Kreuzzug gegen den Bolschewismus' 1941–1945*, 2007]

Müller, Rolf-Dieter and Hans-Erich Volkmann (eds), *Die Wehrmacht: Mythos und Realität* (Munich: Oldenbourg, 1999).

Müller, Sven Oliver, *Deutsche Soldaten und ihre Feinde: Nationalismus an Front und Heimatfront im Zweiten Weltkrieg* (Frankfurt: Fischer, 2007).

Musial, Bogdan, *Sowjetische Partisanen 1941–1944: Mythos und Wirklichkeit* (Paderborn: Schöningh, 2009).

Muth, Kerstin, *Die Wehrmacht in Griechenland – und ihre Kinder* (Leipzig: Eudora, 2008).
Naimark, Norman M., 'The Russians and Germans: Rape During the War and Post-Soviet Memories', in Raphaëlle Branche and Fabrice Virgili (eds.), *Rape in Wartime: A History to be Written* (Basingstoke: Palgrave Macmillan, 2012), pp. 201–19.
Naimark, Norman M., *The Russians in Germany: A History of the Soviet Zone of Occupation, 1945–1949* (Cambridge, MA: Harvard University Press, 1995).
Nakahara, Michiko, 'Righting History: Herstory from Taiwan', lecture at the *Women's Bodies as Battlefields* conference, in unpublished *Reader* (Hamburg: Hamburger Institut für Sozialforschung, 2001).
Naumann, Klaus (ed.), *Nachkrieg in Deutschland* (Hamburg: Hamburger Edition, 2001).
Naumann, Klaus, 'Die "saubere" Wehrmacht: Gesellschaftsgeschichte einer Legende', *Mittelweg 36*, 7(4), 1998, pp. 8–18.
Neitzel, Sönke and Harald Welzer, *Soldaten – On Fighting, Killing and Dying: The Secret World War II Tapes of German POWs*, translated from the German by Jefferson Chase (London: Simon and Schuster, 2012). [*Soldaten: Protokolle vom Kämpfen, Töten und Sterben*, 2011.]
Nelson, Robert L., 'German Comrades – Slavic Whores: Gender Images in the German Soldier Newspapers of the First World War', in Karin Hagemann and Stefanie Schüler-Springorum (eds), *Home/Front* (Oxford: Berg Publishers, 2002), pp. 69–85.
Nesaule, Agate, *A Woman in Amber: Healing the Trauma of War and Exile* (New York: Penguin Books, 1995).
Neumann, Alexander, *'Arzttum ist immer Kämpfertum': Die Heeressanitätsinspektion und das Amt 'Chef des Wehrmachtsanitätswesens' im Zweiten Weltkrieg (1939–1945)* (Düsseldorf: Droste, 2005).
Ní Aoláin, Fionnuala, 'The Gender Politics of Fact-Finding in the Context of the Women, Peace and Security Agenda', in Philip Alston and Sarah Knuckey (eds), *The Transformation of Human Rights Fact-Finding* (New York: Oxford University Press, 2015), pp. 89–106.
Ní Aoláin, Fionnuala, 'Sex-Based Violence and the Holocaust: A Reevaluation of Harms and Rights in International Law', *Yale Journal of Law and Feminism*, 12, 2000, pp. 43–85.
Niethammer, Lutz, 'Heimat und Front: Versuche, zehn Kriegserinnerungen aus der Arbeiterklasse des Ruhrgebiets zu verstehen', in Lutz Niethammer (ed.), *'Die Jahre weiss man nicht, wo man die heute hinsetzen soll.' Faschismuserfahrungen im Ruhrgebiet: Lebensgeschichte und Sozialkultur im Ruhrgebiet 1930 bis 1960*, vol. 1 (Berlin: Dietz, 1983), pp. 163–232.
Nikolić-Ristanović, Vesna, *Women, Violence and War: Wartime Victimization of Refugees in the Balkans*, translated by Borislav Radović (Budapest: Central European University Press, 2000). [*Žene, nasilje i rat*, 1995]
Niven, Bill (ed.), *Germans as Victims: Remembering the Past in Contemporary Germany* (Houndmills: Palgrave Macmillan, 2006).

Nolte, Hans-Heinrich, 'Vergewaltigungen durch Deutsche im Russlandfeldzug', *Zeitschrift für Weltgeschichte: Interdisziplinäre Perspektiven*, 10(1), 2009, pp. 113-34.

Nutkiewicz, Michael, 'Shame, Guilt, and Anguish in Holocaust Survivor Testimony', *The Oral History Review*, 30(1), 2003, pp. 1-22.

Ofer, Dalia, and Leonore J. Weitzman (eds), *Women in the Holocaust* (New Haven: Yale University Press, 1998).

Ofer, Dalia and Leonore J. Weitzman, 'Introduction: The Role of Gender in the Holocaust', in Dalia Ofer and Lenore J. Weitzman (eds), *Women in the Holocaust* (New Haven: Yale University Press, 1998), pp. 1-18.

Oldenburg, Manfred, *Ideologie und militärisches Kalkül: Die Besatzungspolitik der Wehrmacht in der Sowjetunion 1942* (Cologne: Böhlau, 2004).

Olsen, Kåre, *Vater: Deutscher. Das Schicksal der norwegischen Lebensbornkinder und ihrer Mütter von 1940 bis heute*, translated by Ebba Drohlshagen (Frankfurt: Campus, 2000). [*Krigens barn: De norske krigsbarna og deres mødre*, 1998]

Oosterhoff, Pauline, Prisca Zwanikken and Evert Ketting, 'Sexual Torture of Men in Croatia and Other Conflict Situations: An Open Secret', *Reproductive Health Matters*, 23(12), 2004, pp. 68-77.

Ophaug, Joakim (ed.), *The War Children of the World, Report 3* (Bergen: War and Children Identity Project, 2003).

Paul, Christa, *Zwangsprostitution: Staatlich errichtete Bordelle im Nationalsozialismus* (Berlin: Edition Hentrich, 1994).

Paul, Gerhard, '"Bloodlands" 41: Gewalt in Bildern – Bilder als Gewalt – Gewalt an Bildern', in Gerhard Paul (ed.), *BilderMACHT: Studien zur Visual History des 20. und 21. Jahrhunderts* (Göttingen: Wallstein, 2013), pp. 155-98.

Paul, Gerhard (ed.), *Die Täter der Shoah: Fanatische Nationalsozialisten oder ganz normale Deutsche?* (Göttingen: Wallstein, 2002).

Paul, Gerhard, 'Von Psychopathen, Technokraten des Terrors und "ganz gewöhnlichen" Deutschen: Die Täter der Shoah im Spiegel der Forschung', in Gerhard Paul (ed.), *Die Täter der Shoah* (Göttingen: Wallstein-Verlag, 2002), pp. 13-90.

Paul, Wolfgang, *Die Truppengeschichte der 18. Panzer-Division 1940-1943* (Reutlingen: Preussischer Militär-Verlag, 1989).

Paulick, Jane, 'Occupation Children: Sleeping with the Enemy', *Deutsche Welle*, 25 June 2005, <https://web.archive.org/web/20050507150013/http://www6.dw-world.de/en/2099.php> (last accessed 11 February 2019).

Pendas, Devin O., Mark Roseman and Richard F. Wetzell (eds), *Beyond the Racial State: Rethinking Nazi Germany* (Cambridge, UK: Cambridge University Press, 2017).

Pennington, Reina, 'Offensive Women: Women in Combat in the Red Army', in Paul Addison and Angus Calder (eds), *Time to Kill: The Soldier's Experience of War in The West* (London: Pimlico, 1997), pp. 249-62.

Pető, Andrea, 'Stimmen des Schweigens: Erinnerungen an Vergewaltigungen in den Hauptstädten des "ersten Opfers" (Wien) und des "letzten Verbündeten" Hitlers (Budapest) 1945', *Zeitschrift für Geschichtswissenschaft*, 47(10), 1999, pp. 892-913.

Petter, Wolfgang, 'Militärische Massengesellschaft und Entprofessionalisierung des

Offiziers', in Rolf-Dieter Müller and Hans-Erich Volkmann (eds), *Die Wehrmacht*, pp. 359–70.

Picaper, Jean-Paul and Ludwig Norz, *Die Kinder der Schande: Das tragische Schicksal deutscher Besatzungskinder in Frankreich*, translated from the French by Michael Bayer (Munich: Piper, 2005). [*Enfants maudits*, 2004]

Plassmann, Max, 'Wehrmachtsbordelle: Anmerkungen zu einem Quellenfund im Universitätsarchiv Düsseldorf', *Militärgeschichtliche Zeitschrift*, 62(1), 2003, pp. 157–73.

Podolsky, Anatoly, 'The Tragic Fate of Ukrainian Jewish Women under Nazi Occupation, 1941–1944', in Sonja M. Hedgepeth and Rochelle G. Saidel (eds), *Sexual Violence against Jewish Women during the Holocaust* (Waltham, MA: Brandeis University Press, 2010), pp. 94–107.

Pohl, Dieter, 'Die Einsatzgruppe C 1941/1942', in Peter Klein (ed.), *Die Einsatzgruppen in der besetzten Sowjetunion 1941/42* (Berlin: Edition Hentrich, 1997), pp. 71–87.

Pohl, Dieter, *Die Herrschaft der Wehrmacht: Deutsche Militärbesatzung und einheimische Bevölkerung in der Sowjetunion 1941–1944* (Munich: Oldenbourg, 2008).

Pohl, Rolf, *Feindbild Frau: Männliche Sexualität, Gewalt und die Abwehr des Weiblichen* (Hanover: Offizin, 2004).

Pohl, Rolf, 'Massenvergewaltigung: Zum Verhältnis von Krieg und männlicher Sexualität', *Mittelweg 36*, 11(2), 2002, pp. 53–75.

'The Politics of Generating Knowledge: A Conversation with Members of the SVAC-Network', in Gaby Zipfel, Regina Mühlhäuser and Kirsten Campbell (eds), *In Plain Sight* (New Delhi: Zubaan Books, 2019), pp. xix–xlix.

Pommerin, Reiner, *Sterilisierung der Rheinlandbastarde: Das Schicksal einer farbigen deutschen Minderheit, 1918–1937* (Düsseldorf: Droste, 1979).

Prantl, Heribert (ed.), *Wehrmachtsverbrechen: Eine deutsche Kontroverse* (Hamburg: Hoffmann und Campe, 1997).

Przyrembel, Alexandra, *'Rassenschande': Reinheitsmythos und Vernichtungslegitimation im Nationalsozialismus* (Göttingen: Vandenhoeck & Ruprecht, 2003).

Quine, Maria Sophia, *Population Politics in Twentieth Century Europe: Fascist Dictatorships and Liberal Democracies* (London: Routledge, 1996).

Quinkert, Babette, *Propaganda und Terror in Weissrussland 1941–1944: Die deutsche 'geistige' Kriegführung gegen Zivilbevölkerung und Partisanen* (Paderborn: Schöningh, 2008).

Rass, Christoph, *'Menschenmaterial': Deutsche Soldaten an der Ostfront. Innenansichten einer Infanteriedivision 1939–1945* (Paderborn: Schöningh, 2003).

Reemtsma, Jan Philipp, 'Die Natur der Gewalt als Problem der Soziologie', *Mittelweg 36*, 15(5), 2006, pp. 2–25.

Reemtsma, Jan Philipp, 'Die Wiederkehr der Hobbesschen Frage: Dialektik der Zivilisation', *Mittelweg 36*, 3(6), 1995, pp. 47–56.

Reemtsma, Jan Philipp, 'Über den Begriff "Handlungsspielräume"', *Mittelweg 36*, 11(6), 2002, pp. 5–23.

Reemtsma, Jan Philipp, *Trust and Violence: An Essay on a Modern Relationship*, translated by Dominic Bonfiglio (Princeton: Princeton University Press, 2012). [*Vertrauen und Gewalt: Versuch über eine besondere Konstellation der Moderne*, 2008]

Rees, Laurence, *Their Darkest Hour: People Tested to the Extreme in WWII* (London: Ebury Press, 2007).
Reichelt, Katrin, 'Profit and Loss: The Economic Exploitation of the Riga Ghetto (1941-1943)', in Andris Caune, Aivars Stranga and Margers Vestermanis (eds), *The Issues of the Holocaust Research in Latvia: Reports of an International Conference on the Holocaust Studies in Latvia, 16-17 October 2000, Riga* (Riga: Latvian History Institute Press, 2001), pp. 169-84.
Reifarth, Dieter and Viktoria Schmidt-Linsenhoff, 'Die Kamera der Täter', in Hannes Heer and Klaus Naumann (eds.), *Vernichtungskrieg*, pp. 475-502.
Reulecke, Jürgen and Thomas Kohut, '"Sterben wie eine Ratte, die der Bauer ertappt": Letzte Briefe aus Stalingrad', in Jürgen Reulecke (ed.), *'Ich möchte einer werden so wie die . . .': Männerbünde im 20. Jahrhundert* (Frankfurt: Campus, 2001), pp. 177-93.
Rhodes, Belina, 'Amerasians in the Philippines', in Joakim Ophaug (ed.), *The War Children of the World* (Bergen: War and Children Identity Project, 2003), pp. 79-83.
Richter, Timm C., 'Die Wehrmacht und der Partisanenkrieg in den besetzten Gebieten der Sowjetunion', in Rolf-Dieter Müller and Hans-Erich Volkmann (eds), *Die Wehrmacht* (Munich: Oldenbourg, 1999), pp. 837-57.
Riddle, John M., *Contraception and Abortion from the Ancient World to the Renaissance* (Cambridge, MA: Harvard University Press, 1992).
Ringelheim, Joan, 'The Split Between Gender and the Holocaust', in Dalia Ofer and Lenore J. Weitzman (eds), *Women in the Holocaust* (New Haven: Yale University Press, 1998), pp. 340-50.
Ringelheim, Joan, 'Women and the Holocaust: A Reconsideration of Research', in Carol Rittner and John K. Roth (eds), *Different Voices: Women and the Holocaust* (New York: Paragon House, 1993), pp. 373-405.
Roberts, Mary Louise, *What Soldiers Do: Sex and the American GI in World War II France* (Chicago: University of Chicago Press, 2013).
Röger, Maren, *Kriegsbeziehungen: Intimität, Gewalt und Prostitution im besetzten Polen 1939 bis 1945* (Frankfurt: S. Fischer, 2015).
Römer, Felix, *Der Kommissarbefehl: Wehrmacht und NS-Verbrechen an der Ostfront 1941/42* (Paderborn: Schöningh, 2008).
Römer, Felix, '"Im alten Deutschland wäre solcher Befehl nicht möglich gewesen": Rezeption, Adaption und Umsetzung des Kriegsgerichtsbarkeitserlasses im Ostheer 1941/42', *Vierteljahrshefte für Zeitgeschichte*, 56(1), 2008, pp. 53-99.
Römer, Felix, *Kameraden: Die Wehrmacht von innen* (Munich: Piper, 2012).
Roos, Julia, 'Backlash Against Prostitutes' Rights: Origins and Dynamics of Nazi Prostitution Policies', *Journal of the History of Sexuality*, 11(1/2), 2002, pp. 67-94.
Rosenthal, Gabriele, 'Sexuelle Gewalt in Kriegs- und Verfolgungszeiten: Biographische und transgenerationelle Spätfolgen bei Überlebenden der Shoah, ihren Kindern und EnkelInnen', in medica mondiale e.V., Marlies W. Fröse and Ina Volpp-Teuscher (eds), *Krieg, Geschlecht und Traumatisierung: Erfahrungen und Reflexionen*

in der Arbeit mit traumatisierten Frauen in Kriegs- und Krisengebieten (Frankfurt: IKO, 1999), pp. 25-56.

Rossino, Alexander B., 'Destructive Impulses: German Soldiers and the Conquest of Poland', *Holocaust and Genocide Studies* 11(3), 1997, pp. 351-65.

Roth, John K., 'Equality, Neutrality, Particularity: Perspectives on Women and the Holocaust', in Elizabeth R. Baer and Myrna Goldenberg (eds), *Experience and Expression* (Detroit: Wayne State University Press, 2003), pp. 5-22.

Rother, Rainer (ed.), *Der Weltkrieg 1914-1918: Ereignis und Erinnerung*, exhibition catalogue (Berlin: Deutsches Historisches Museum, 2004).

Rüggeberg, Stefanie, 'Besatzerkinder: Die Suche nach den eigenen Wurzeln', *Hamburger Abendblatt*, April 4, 2006, p. 9.

Rutsch, Hans-Dieter, *Mein Vater der Feind: Russenkinder*, television documentary broadcast on Arte, May 18, 2007.

Rutz, Rainer, *Signal: Eine deutsche Auslandsillustrierte als Propagandainstrument im Zweiten Weltkrieg* (Essen: Klartext, 2007).

Sauerteig, Lutz, 'Militär, Medizin und Moral: Sexualität im Ersten Weltkrieg', in Wolfgang U. Eckart and Christoph Gradmann (eds), *Die Medizin und der Erste Weltkrieg* (Pfaffenweiler: Centaurus-Verlagsgesellschaft, 1996), pp. 197-226.

Scarry, Elaine, *The Body in Pain: The Making and Unmaking of the World* (Oxford: Oxford University Press, 1985).

Schäfer, Torsten, *'Jedenfalls habe ich auch mitgeschossen'. Das NSG-Verfahren gegen Johann Josef Kuhr und andere ehemalige Angehörige des Polizeibataillons 306, der Polizeireiterabteilung 2 und der SD-Dienststelle von Pinsk beim Landgericht Frankfurt am Main 1962-1973: Eine textanalytische Fallstudie zur Mentalitätsgeschichte* (Hamburg: LIT, 2007).

Scheffler, Wolfgang, 'The Fate of the German, Austrian and Czech Jews Deported to the Baltic States 1941-1945: A Historical Overview', translated by Caroline Gay, in *Buch der Erinnerung. Die ins Baltikum deportierten deutschen, österreichischen und tschechoslowakischen Juden*, compiled by Wolfgang Scheffler and Diana Schulle, vol. 1 (Munich: K. G. Saur, 2003), pp. 44-78.

Scherr, Rebecca, 'The Uses of Memory and the Abuses of Fiction: Sexuality in Holocaust Fiction and Memoir', *Other Voices: The (e)Journal of Cultural Criticism*, 2(1), February 2000, <http://www.othervoices.org/2.1/scherr/sexuality.php> (last accessed 16 January 2019).

Scherstjanoi, Elke, 'Das Bild vom feindlichen Fremden: Zur Rekonstruktion von Deutschen- und Deutschlandbildern bei Bürgern der Sowjetunion im Grossen Vaterländischen Krieg', in Olga Kurilo (ed.), *Der zweite Weltkrieg im deutschen und russischen Gedächtnis* (Berlin: Avinus, 2006), pp. 95-105.

Schikorra, Christa, 'Forced Prostitution in the Nazi Concentration Camps', translated by Patricia Szobar, in Dagmar Herzog (ed.), *Lessons and Legacies VII: The Holocaust in International Perspective* (Evanston, IL: Northwestern University Press, 2006), pp. 169-78.

Schikorra, Christa, 'Prostitution of Female Concentration Camp Prisoners as Slave Labor: On the Situation of "Asocial" Prisoners in the Ravensbrück Women's

Concentration Camp', in Wolfgang Benz and Barbara Distel (eds), *Dachau and the Nazi Terror 1933–1945*, vol. II: *Studies and Reports* (Dachau: Verlag Dachauer Hefte, 2002), pp. 246–58. ['Prostitution weiblicher KZ-Häftlinge als Zwangsarbeit', 2000]

Schmiegelt, Ulrike, '"Macht Euch um mich keine Sorgen . . ."', in Peter Jahn and Ulrike Schmiegelt (eds), *Foto-Feldpost* (Berlin: Elefanten Press, 2000), pp. 23–31.

Schmitt, Britta, 'Regulieren, tabuisieren, kriminalisieren: Ethisch-religiöse Wurzeln der Prostitutionspolitik in Europa', *Osteuropa*, 56(6), 2006, pp. 33–54.

Schmuhl, Hans-Walter, *Grenzüberschreitungen: Das Kaiser-Wilhelm-Institut für Anthropologie, menschliche Erblehre und Eugenik, 1927–1945* (Göttingen: Wallstein, 2005).

Schneider, Christoph, 'Täter ohne Eigenschaften: Über die Tragweite sozialpsychologischer Modelle in der Holocaust-Forschung', *Mittelweg 36*, 20(5), 2011, pp. 3–23.

Schneider, Franka, '"Einigkeit im Unglück"? Berliner Eheberatungsstellen zwischen Ehekrise und Wiederaufbau', in Klaus Naumann (ed.), *Nachkrieg in Deutschland* (Hamburg: Hamburger Edition, 2001), pp. 206–26.

Schulte, Jan Erik, Peter Lieb and Bernd Wegner (eds), *Die Waffen-SS: Neue Forschungen* (Paderborn: Schöningh, 2014).

Schwan, Heribert and Helgard Heindrichs, *Der SS-Mann: Josef Blösche – Leben und Sterben eines Mörders* (Munich: Droemer, 2003).

Schwarz, Gudrun, *Eine Frau an seiner Seite: Ehefrauen in der 'SS-Sippengemeinschaft'* (Hamburg: Hamburger Edition, 1997).

Schwarz, Gudrun and Gaby Zipfel, 'Die halbierte Gesellschaft: Anmerkungen zu einem soziologischen Problem', *Mittelweg 36*, 7(1), 1998, pp. 78–88.

Schwendinger, Julia R. and Herman Schwendinger, *Rape and Inequality* (Beverly Hills: Sage, 1983).

Schwensen, Ingwer, 'Sexuelle Gewalt in kriegerischen Konflikten: Auswahlbibliographie für die Erscheinungsjahre 2002 bis 2008', *Mittelweg 36*, 18/1, 2009, pp. 67–90.

Seidler, Franz W., *Prostitution, Homosexualität, Selbstverstümmelung: Probleme der deutschen Sanitätsführung 1939–1945* (Neckargemünd: Vowinckel, 1977).

Seidler, Victor, 'Bodies, Masculinities and Complex Inheritances', in Kevin McSorley (ed.), *War and the Body* (London/New York: Routledge, 2015), pp. 225–30.

Seidman, Naomi, 'The Last Will and Testament of the Ninety-Three Bais Yaakov Girls of Krakow (1942)', unpublished manuscript, n.d., n.p., <https://thebaisyaakovproject.com/wp-content/uploads/2019/03/Beautiful_Martyrs_The_Ninety-Three_Bais.pdf> (accessed 3 Jan. 2020).

Seifert, Ruth, 'Im Tod und Schmerz sind nicht alle gleich: Männliche und weibliche Körper in den kulturellen Anordnungen von Krieg und Nation', in Steffen Martus, Marina Münkler and Werner Röcke (eds), *Schlachtfelder: Codierung von Gewalt im medialen Wandel* (Berlin: Akademie, 2003), pp. 235–46.

Seifert, Ruth, *Militär – Kultur – Identität: Individualisierung, Geschlechterverhältnisse und die soziale Konstruktion des Soldaten* (Bremen: Edition Temmen, 1996).

Seifert, Ruth, 'Vicissitudes of Gender as an Analytical Category: Sexual Violence in Armed Conflict Revisited', in Gaby Zipfel, Regina Mühlhäuser and Kirsten Campbell (eds.), *In Plain Sight* (New Delhi: Zubaan, 2019), pp. 257–77. [*Massenvergewaltigungen: Krieg gegen die Frauen*, 1993]

Seifert, Ruth, 'War and Rape: A Preliminary Analysis', in Alexandra Stiglmayer (ed.), *Mass Rape: The War Against Women in Bosnia-Herzegovina*, translated by Marion Faber (Lincoln: University of Nebraska Press, 1994), pp. 54–72.

Seifert, Ruth, 'Weibliche Soldaten: Die Grenzen des Geschlechts und die Grenzen der Nation', in Jens-Rainer Ahrens, Maja Apelt and Christiane Bender (eds), *Frauen im Militär: Empirische Befunde und Perspektiven zur Integration von Frauen in die Streitkräfte* (Wiesbaden: VS Verlag für Sozialwissenschaften, 2005), pp. 230–41.

Shik, Na'ama, 'Sexual Abuse of Jewish Women in Auschwitz-Birkenau', in Dagmar Herzog (ed.), *Brutality and Desire* (Basingstoke: Palgrave Macmillan, 2009), pp. 221–46.

Siebold, Guy L. 'The Essence of Military Group Cohesion', *Armed Forces and Society*, 33(2), 2007, pp. 286–95.

Sigusch, Volkmar, *Geschichte der Sexualwissenschaft* (Frankfurt: Campus, 2008).

Sinnreich, Helene, '"And It Was Something We Didn't Talk About": Rape of Jewish Women During the Holocaust', *Holocaust Studies: A Journal of Culture and History*, 14(2), 2008, pp. 1–22.

Sivakumaran, Sandesh, 'Sexual Violence Against Men in Armed Conflict', *The European Journal of International Law*, 18(2), 2007, pp. 253–76.

Sjoberg, Laura, *Women as Wartime Rapists: Beyond Sensation and Stereotyping* (New York: New York University Press, 2016).

Skvorcova, Dar'ja, 'Das Bild der deutschen Armee im postsowjetischen Film (1995–2004)', in Olga Kurilo (ed.), *Der zweite Weltkrieg im deutschen und russischen Gedächtnis* (Berlin: Avinus, 2006), pp. 169–74.

Smith, Richard, 'Loss and Longing: Emotional Responses to West Indian Soldiers During the First World War', in Ashley Jackson (ed.), *The British Empire and The First World War* (London: Routledge, 2017), pp. 419–28.

Snyder, David Raub, *Sex Crimes Under the Wehrmacht* (Lincoln: University of Nebraska Press, 2007).

Snyder, Timothy, *Bloodlands: Europe between Hitler and Stalin* (London: The Bodley Head, 2011).

Sommer, Robert, 'Camp Brothels: Forced Sex Labour in Nazi Concentration Camps', in Dagmar Herzog (ed.), *Brutality and Desire* (Basingstoke: Palgrave Macmillan, 2009), pp. 168–96.

Sommer, Robert, *Das KZ-Bordell: Sexuelle Zwangsarbeit in nationalsozialistischen Konzentrationslagern* (Paderborn: Schöningh, 2009).

Sommer, Robert, 'Warum das Schweigen? Berichte von ehemaligen Häftlingen über Sex-Zwangsarbeit in nationalsozialistischen Konzentrationslagern', in Insa Eschebach and Regina Mühlhäuser (eds), *Krieg und Geschlecht* (Berlin: Metropol, 2008), pp. 147–66.

Steinkamp, Peter, 'Ungewöhnliche Todesfälle bei der Wehrmacht: Autoerotische

Unfälle von Soldaten', in Wolfgang U. Eckart and Alexander Neumann (eds), *Medizin im Zweiten Weltkrieg: Militärmedizinische Praxis und medizinische Wissenschaft im 'Totalen Krieg'* (Paderborn: Schöningh, 2006), pp. 195–206.

Steinkamp, Peter, *Zur Devianz-Problematik in der Wehrmacht: Alkohol- und Rauschmittelmissbrauch bei der Truppe*, dissertation, Albert-Ludwigs-Universität Freiburg im Breisgau, 2008, <http://www.freidok.uni freiburg.de/volltexte/5681/> (last accessed 15 January 2019).

Stelzl-Marx, Barbara, '"Russenkinder" und "Sowjetbräute": Besatzungserfahrungen in Österreich 1945–1955', in Andreas Hilger, Mike Schmeitzner and Clemens Vollnhals (eds), *Sowjetisierung oder Neutralität? Optionen sowjetischer Besatzungspolitik in Deutschland und Österreich 1945–1955* (Göttingen: Vandenhoeck und Ruprecht, 2006), pp. 479–508.

Stoler, Ann Laura, 'Racial Histories and Their Regimes Of Truth', in Philomena Essed and David Theo Goldberg (eds), *Race Critical Theories: Text and Context* (Malden, MA: Blackwell, 2002), pp. 369–91.

Szobar, Patricia, 'Sexual Stories in the Nazi Courts of Law: Race Defilement in Germany, 1933 to 1945', *Journal of the History of Sexuality*, 11(1&2), 2002 (Special Issue: Sexuality and German Fascism), pp. 131–63.

Szobar, Patricia, 'The Prosecution of Jewish-Gentile Sex in the Race Defilement Trials', in Peter Hayes and Dagmar Herzog (eds), *Lessons and Legacies VII: The Holocaust in International Perspective* (Evanston, IL: Northwestern University Press, 2006), pp. 159–68.

Tanaka, Yuki, *Japan's Comfort Women: Sexual Slavery and Prostitution during World War II and the US Occupation* (London: Routledge, 2002).

Tanaka, Yuki, 'Rape and War: The Japanese Experience', in Indai Lourdes Sajor (ed.), *Common Grounds: Violence Against Women in War and Armed Conflict Situations* (Quezon City: Asian Center for Women's Human Rights, 1998), pp. 148–86.

Tanaka, Yuki, 'War, Rape and Patriarchy: The Japanese Experience', in Gaby Zipfel, Regina Mühlhäuser and Kirsten Campbell (eds.), *In Plain Sight* (New Delhi: Zubaan, 2019), pp. 30–51.

Tec, Nechama, *Defiance: The Bielski Partisans* (Oxford: Oxford University Press, 1993).

Tec, Nechama, *Resilience and Courage: Women, Men, and the Holocaust* (New Haven: Yale University Press, 2003).

Tec, Nechama, 'Women Among the Forest Partisans', in Dalia Ofer and Lenore J. Weitzman (eds), *Women in the Holocaust* (New Haven: Yale University Press, 1998), pp. 223–33.

Timm, Annette F., *Politics of Fertility in Twentieth-Century Berlin* (Cambridge: Cambridge University Press, 2010).

Timm, Annette F., 'Sex with a Purpose: Prostitution, Venereal Disease, and Militarized Masculinity in the Third Reich', in Dagmar Herzog (ed.), *Sexuality and German Fascism* (New York: Berghahn Books, 2005), pp. 223–55.

Tobias, Jim G., 'Die Massenexekutionsstätte Ponary bei Wilna 1941–1944', in Rachel

Margolis and Jim Tobias (eds), *Die geheimen Notizen* (Frankfurt: Fischer, 2005), pp. 21–46.
Tombs, David, 'Honor, Shame, and Conquest: Male Identity, Sexual Violence, and the Body Politic', *Journal of Hispanic-Latino Theology*, 9(4), 2002, pp. 21–40.
Ueberschär, Gerd R. and Wolfgang Wette (eds), *'Unternehmen Barbarossa': Der deutsche Überfall auf die Sowjetunion 1941* (Paderborn: Schöningh, 1984).
Usborne, Cornelie, 'Female Sexual Desire and Male Honor: German Women's Illicit Love Affairs with Prisoners of War During the Second World War', *Journal of the History of Sexuality*, 26(3), 2017, pp. 454–88.
Utas, Mats, 'Victimcy, Girlfriending, Soldiering: Tactic Agency in a Young Woman's Social Navigation of the Liberian War Zone', *Anthropological Quarterly*, 78(2), 2005, pp. 403–30.
Vestermanis, Margers, 'Local Headquarters Liepaja: Two Months of German Occupation in the Summer of 1941', in Hannes Heer and Klaus Naumann (eds), *War of Extermination* (London: Berghahn, 2004), pp. 219–36.
Virgili, Fabrice, 'Enfants de Boches: the war children of France', in Kjersti Ericsson and Eva Simonsen (eds), *Children of World War II* (Oxford: Berg, 2005), pp. 138–50.
Virgili, Fabrice, 'Le Sexe Blessé', in François Rouquet, Fabrice Virgili and Danièle Voldman (eds), *Amours, Guerres et Sexualité 1914–1945*, exhibition catalogue, BDIC/Musée de l'armée (Paris: Gallimard, 2007), pp. 138–46.
Virgili, Fabrice, *Naître ennemi: Les enfants de couples franco-allemands nés pendant la Seconde Guerre mondiale* (Paris: Payot, 2009).
Virgili, Fabrice, *Shorn Women: Gender and Punishment in Liberation France*, translated by John Flower (Oxford: Berg, 2002). [*La France 'virile': des femmes tondues à la Libération*, 2000]
Vossler, Frank, *Propaganda in die eigene Truppe: Die Truppenbetreuung in der Wehrmacht 1939–1945* (Paderborn: Schöningh, 2005).
Walke, Anika, 'Biographien jüdischer Überlebender in der Sowjetunion – Flucht, Widerstand und (Nicht-)Anerkennung', in David Gaunt, Paul A. Levine and Laura Palosuo (eds), *Collaboration and Resistance During the Holocaust: Belarus, Estonia, Latvia, Lithuania* (Bern: Peter Lang, 2004), pp. 479–506.
Warburg, Jens, 'Paradoxe Anforderungen an soldatische Subjekte avancierter Streitkräfte im (Kriegs-)Einsatz', in Maja Apelt (ed.), *Forschungsthema: Militär: Militärische Organisationen im Spannungsfeld von Krieg, Gesellschaft und soldatischen Subjekten* (Wiesbaden: Verlag für Sozialwissenschaften), pp. 245–70.
Warring, Anette, 'War, Cultural Loyalty and Gender: Danish Women's Intimate Fraternization', in Kjersti Ericsson and Eva Simonsen (eds), *Children of World War II* (Oxford: Berg, 2005), pp. 35–52.
Watanabe, Mina, 'Passing on the History of "Comfort Women": The Experiences of a Women's Museum in Japan', *Journal of Peace Education*, 12(3), 2015, pp. 236–46.
Waxman, Zoe, 'An Exceptional Genocide? Sexual Violence in the Holocaust', in Amy E. Randall (ed.), *Genocide and Gender in the Twentieth Century: A Comparative Survey* (London: Bloomsbury, 2015), pp. 107–120.

Waxman, Zoe, *Women in the Holocaust: A Feminist History* (Oxford: Oxford University Press, 2017).
Weber, Jürgen (ed.), *PartisanInnen im Piemont: Antifaschistischer Widerstand in Nordwestitalien* (Constance: Querblick, 1996).
Weitzman, Lenore J., 'Living on the Aryan Side in Poland: Gender, Passing, and the Nature of Resistance', in Dalia Ofer and Lenore J. Weitzman (eds), *Women in the Holocaust* (New Haven: Yale University Press, 1998), pp. 187–222.
Welzer, Harald, *Täter: Wie aus ganz normalen Menschen Massenmörder werden* (Frankfurt: Fischer, 2005).
Wenk, Silke, 'Rhetoriken der Pornographisierung: Rahmungen des Blicks auf die NS-Verbrechen', in Insa Eschebach, Sigrid Jacobeit and Silke Wenk (eds), *Gedächtnis und Geschlecht* (Frankfurt: Campus, 2002), pp. 269–94.
Werner, Frank, '"Noch härter, noch kälter, noch mitleidloser": Soldatische Männlichkeit im deutschen Vernichtungskrieg', in Anette Dietrich and Ljiljana Heise (eds), *Männlichkeitskonstruktionen im Nationalsozialismus: Formen, Funktionen und Wirkungsmacht von Geschlechterkonstruktionen im Nationalsozialismus und ihre Reflexion in der pädagogischen Praxis* (Frankfurt: Peter Lang, 2013), pp. 45–63.
Werth, Alexander, *Russia at War 1941–1945* (New York: Carroll & Graf, 1984 [1964]).
Wette, Wolfram, 'Militärgeschichte von unten: Die Perspektive des "kleinen Mannes"', in Wolfram Wette (ed.), *Der Krieg des kleinen Mannes: Eine Militärgeschichte von unten* (Munich: Piper, 1995).
Wiedemann, Charlotte, 'Der Zwischenmensch', *Frankfurter Rundschau online*, 31 October 2003 (last accessed 31 January 2007).
Wiesinger, Barbara N., *Partisaninnen: Widerstand in Jugoslawien (1941–1945)* (Vienna: Böhlau, 2008).
Wildt, Michael, 'Sind die Nazis Barbaren? Betrachtungen zu einer geklärten Frage', *Mittelweg 36*, 15(2), 2006, pp. 8–26.
Wildt, Michael, *An Uncompromising Generation: The Nazi Leadership of the Reich Security Main Office*, translated by Tom Lampert (Madison: University of Wisconsin Press, 2010). [*Generation des Unbedingten: Das Führungskorps des Reichssicherheitshauptamtes*, 2002]
Wildt, Michael, 'Volksgemeinschaft: A Controversy', translated by Andrew F. Erwin, in Devin O. Pendas, Mark Roseman and Richard F. Wetzell (eds), *Beyond the Racial State* (Cambridge, UK: Cambridge University Press, 2017), pp. 317–34.
Wilhelm, Hans-Heinrich, 'Die Einsatzgruppe A der Sicherheitspolizei des SD 1941/42: Eine exemplarische Studie', in Helmut Krausnick and Hans-Heinrich Wilhelm (eds.), *Die Truppe des Weltanschauungskrieges* (Stuttgart: Deutsche Verlags-Anstalt, 1981), pp. 281–636.
Wiltenburg, Mary and Marc Widmann, 'WWII G. I. Babies: Children of the Enemy', *Spiegel online*, 2 January 2007, <http://www.spiegel.de/international/spiegel/wwii-g-i-babies-children-of-the-enemy-a-456835.html> (last accessed 11 February 2019).
Winter, Johannes, 'Hauptmann Willi Schulz: Judenretter und Deserteur', in Wolfram

Wette (ed.), *Retter in Uniform: Handlungsspielräume im Vernichtungskrieg der Wehrmacht* (Frankfurt: Fischer, 2002), pp. 123–41.

Withuis, Jolande, 'Die verlorene Unschuld des Gedächtnisses: Soziale Amnesie in Holland und sexuelle Gewalt im Zweiten Weltkrieg', in Insa Eschebach, Sigrid Jacobeit and Silke Wenk (eds), *Gedächtnis und Geschlecht* (Frankfurt: Campus, 2002), pp. 77–96.

Wood, Elisabeth Jean, 'Armed Groups and Sexual Violence: When is Wartime Rape Rare?', *Politics & Society*, 37(1), 2009, pp. 131–61.

Wood, Elisabeth Jean, 'Conflict-Related Sexual Violence and the Policy Implications of Recent Research', *International Review of the Red Cross*, 96(894), 2014 (Special Issue: Sexual Violence in Armed Conflict), pp. 457–78.

Wood, Elizabeth A., 'Prostitution Unbound: Representations of Sexual and Political Anxieties in Postrevolutionary Russia', in Jane T. Costlow, Stephanie Sandler and Judith Vowles (eds), *Sexuality and the Body in Russian Culture* (Stanford: Stanford University Press, 1993), pp. 124–35.

Wood, Elisabeth Jean, 'Sexual Violence During War: Toward an Understanding of Variation', in Stathis N. Kalyvas, Ian Shapiro and Tarek Masoud (eds), *Order, Conflict, and Violence* (Cambridge, UK: Cambridge University Press, 2008), pp. 321–51.

Wood, Elisabeth Jean, 'Variation in Sexual Violence During War', *Politics & Society*, 34(3), 2006, pp. 307–42.

Wolf, Gerhard, *Ideologie und Herrschaftsrationalität: Die nationalsozialistische Germanisierungspolitik in Polen* (Hamburg: Hamburger Edition, 2012).

Women's Caucus for Gender Justice, *Definitions of Crimes of Sexual Violence in the ICC*, <http://iccwomen.org/resources/crimesdefinition.html> (last accessed 13 February 2019).

Wrochem, Oliver von, *Erich von Manstein: Vernichtungskrieg und Geschichtspolitik* (Paderborn: Schöningh, 2006).

Wurzer, Georg, 'Die Erfahrung der Extreme: Kriegsgefangene in Russland 1914–1918', in Jochen Oltmer (ed.), *Kriegsgefangene im Europa des Ersten Weltkriegs* (Paderborn: Schöningh, 2006), pp. 97–125.

Yahil, Leni, *The Holocaust: The Fate of European Jewry, 1932–1945*, translated by Ina Friedman and Haya Galai (Oxford: Oxford University Press, 1990). [*ha-Sho'ah*, 1987]

Yang, Hyunah, 'Korean "Military Comfort Women" in Their Own Voices: Experiences of the "Testimony Team"', lecture at the *Women's Bodies as Battlefields* conference, in unpublished *Reader* (Hamburg: Hamburger Institut für Sozialforschung, 2001).

Yang, Hyunah, 'Revisiting the Issue of Korean "Military Comfort Women": The Question of Truth and Positionality', *positions: east asia cultures critique*, 5(1), 1997, pp. 51–71.

Yarborough, Trin, *Surviving Twice: Amerasian Children of the Vietnam War* (Dulles: Potomac Books, 2005).

Yoshimi, Yoshiaki, *Comfort Women: Sexual Slavery in the Japanese Military During*

World War II, translated by Suzanne O'Brien (New York: Columbia University Press, 2000). [*Jugun Ianfu*, 1995]

Yuval-Davis, Nira, *Gender and Nation* (London: Sage Publications, 1997).

Yuval-Davis, Nira, 'Militär, Krieg und Geschlechterverhältnisse', in Christine Eifler and Ruth Seifert (eds), *Soziale Konstruktionen* (Münster: Westfälisches Dampfboot, 1999), pp. 18–43.

Zalewski, Marysia, Paula Drumond, Elisabeth Prügl and Maria Stern (eds), *Sexual Violence against Men in Global Politics* (London: Routledge, 2018).

Zantop, Susanne, *Colonial Fantasies: Conquest, Family, and Nation in Precolonial Germany, 1770–1870* (Durham, NC: Duke University Press, 1997).

Zayas, Alfred de, 'Die Wehrmacht und die Nürnberger Prozesse', in Hans Poeppel, Wilhelm-Karl Prinz von Preussen and Karl Günther von Hase (eds), *Die Soldaten der Wehrmacht*, 3rd edition (Munich: Herbig, 1999).

Zeck, Mario, *Das Schwarze Korps: Geschichte und Gestalt des Organs der Reichsführung SS* (Tübingen: Niemeyer, 2002).

Zeitschrift zur Bekämpfung von Geschlechtskrankheiten, volumes 15 (1914), 16 (1915/16) and 19 (1919/20).

Zipfel, Gaby, 'Ausnahmezustand Krieg? Anmerkungen zu soldatischer Männlichkeit, sexueller Gewalt und militärischer Einhegung', in Insa Eschebach and Regina Mühlhäuser (eds), *Krieg und Geschlecht* (Berlin: Metropol, 2008), pp. 55–74.

Zipfel, Gaby, '"Blood, Sperm, and Tears": Sexual Violence in War', translated by Paula Bradish, *Eurozine*, 29 November 2001, <https://www.eurozine.com/blood-sperm-and-tears-2/> (last accessed 16 January 2019). ['"Blood, sperm, and tears': Sexuelle Gewalt in Kriegen', 2001]

Zipfel, Gaby, '"Let Us Have a Little Fun": The Relationship Between Gender, Violence and Sexuality in Armed Conflict Situations', translated by Karen Bennett, *Revista Crítica de Ciências Sociais Annual Review*, 5, 2013, <https://journals.openedition.org/rccsar/469> (last accessed 7 August 2019).

Zipfel, Gaby, 'Liberté, Egalité, Sexualité', *Mittelweg 36*, (27)4, 2018, pp. 87–108.

Zipfel, Gaby, 'What do bodies tell?', in Zipfel, Mühlhäuser and Campbell (eds), *In Plain Sight* (New Delhi: Zubaan, 2019), pp. 190–202.

Zipfel, Gaby, 'What is Sexual About Sexual Violence?' in Gaby Zipfel, Regina Mühlhäuser and Kirsten Campbell (eds), *In Plain Sight* (New Delhi: Zubaan, 2019), pp. 203–220.

Zipfel, Gaby, Regina Mühlhäuser and Kirsten Campbell (eds), *In Plain Sight: Sexual Violence in Armed Conflict* (New Delhi: Zubaan, 2019).

INDEX

abortion, 8, 228, 255, 258–9, 264
alcohol
　communal drinking in the Wehrmacht, 4, 27–9, 78, 207–8
　intoxication and visits to brothels, 89, 122, 134
　offences of excessive consumption of, 87, 88
　sexual violence whilst drunk, 27–9, 55, 93–4
Allied Forces, 31, 63, 311, 317, 322, 329; see also British soldiers; Soviet soldiers; U.S. soldiers
antisemitism
　clichés of Jewish prostitution, 78–9
　the 'Final Solution' in the Soviet Union, 69–70
　Race Laws and, 35, 70–3, 78, 79–80
　rape and the Nazi idea of 'race defilement', 36–41
　during the Soviet invasion, 35–6, 71
　syphilis as a Jewish disease, 131
　see also Jews
Army High Command (OKH)
　anti-partisan operations, 60–1, 67–8
　dangers of consensual relations with local women, 206–7, 209, 224–5, 308
　dangers of sexual bartering and prostitution, 130–1, 132, 133–4, 135–6, 306
　establishment of military-controlled brothels, 150–2, 156, 160, 163–4, 306

guidelines for soldierly conduct, 36, 91–2
knowledge of their men's sexual encounters, 7–8
see also military command
bodies
　affects and emotions, 3, 5, 11, 40, 49, 54, 62–3, 74, 87, 111, 321–2, 326, 328, 330
　soldiers' bodily reactions, 49, 87, 326, 328
　soldiers' sensory and corporeal experiences, 3, 328–30
　vulnerability, 5, 61, 75, 76, 325, 328, 330
Bormann, Martin, 260–1, 282
Borodyanskaya-Knysh, Elena Efimovna, 83
Brauchitsch, Walther von, 129–30, 209
British soldiers, 3, 70, 317, 328
brothels
　military-run brothels, 119, 150
　use of by soldiers, 118–19
　see also prostitution; Wehrmacht brothels
Buch, Wolfgang von, 136
Burmeister, Wilhelm, 222, 267, 274–5
bystanders, 8, 65, 69, 74, 319, 322

children, 134, 210; see also occupation children (*Besatzungskinder*)
collaboration
　community consequences of, 203, 268

fraternisation with German officers, 13, 204–6
of German women with Allied soldiers, 311
unwanted pregnancies, 268
consensual relations
after cabaret performances, 211
alcohol consumption and, 207–8
community consequences of, 8
between deserters and local women, 200
as an escape from wartime experiences, 195–6, 197–9
flirtatious encounters, 196–7, 207
with German civilian employees, 215–17
German occupation strategies and, 215–16, 218–20
grey zones, 5, 193
protective relationships, 123, 199–200, 202
public vs private relationships, 202–6
the Race Laws and, 199, 211–13, 214, 215, 308
regional variations in, 200–1, 213–15
scholarship on, 194
soldiers billeted with local families, 208–9
SS regulation of, 211–15
tensions with military policy, 206–7
tensions with relations back home, 198, 209–10
viewed as fraternising relationships, 204–6
Wehrmacht's regulation of, 206–11
women's motives for, 200–6
see also marriages
Conti, Leonardo, 134

Demianova, Genia, 42–3
Democratic Republic of Congo (DRC), 5–6, 7, 10
discipline
and attitudes towards local women, 93–4
inciting resistance recruitment, 53, 91
instruction on sexual discipline, 132–4
military, 305
Military Jurisdiction Decree, 84, 85, 87, 90, 95

penalties for crimes of sexual violence, 29–30, 52, 89–90, 95, 130
perceptions of the sexual honour of 'Soviet women', 90–1
of personnel with sexually transmitted diseases, 142–4
of rape and military strategy, 323–5
sexual violence and the Nazi Race Laws, 36–41, 70–3, 78, 79–80, 90, 91, 92–3, 94
sexual violence as an honour crime, 29–31, 51–2, 57–9, 64
sexual violence within anti-partisan strategies, 91–2
sexual violence's impact on the military community, 86–8, 94–5, 129–30, 305–6
Special Wartime Penal Code, 89
for SS members in consensual relations, 211–12, 215
see also Manneszucht (masculine discipline and restraint)

Eastern campaign
antisemitism, 35–6, 73
civilian food shortages, 117–18, 120–1, 305
Commissar Order, 84, 88
defeat of, 230–1
economic plundering strategy, 50–1, 120
execution of enemy combatants, 85
invasion of 1941, 35
and the mass murder of Jews, 69, 70–3, 80
Military Jurisdiction Decree, 84, 85, 87, 90, 95
sexual violence as part of, 33–4
Soviet evacuations, 49–50
Epelfeld, Naum, 35–6
Erren, Gerhard, 78

female soldiers
female partisans, 61, 63, 64, 65–7
female SS guards, 320
Red Army female personnel, 13, 44, 61–3, 66, 195
Wehrmacht and SS auxiliaries, 63, 158, 314

genital inspections
of Jewish boys and men, 61, 76

genital inspections (*cont.*)
  of soldiers, 138, 147, 329
  of women in Wehrmacht brothels, 156–7
  of women 'suspected of prostitution', 126, 127–9
genital mutilation, 5, 55
  of men, 47, 76
  of soldiers, 144, 329
  of women, 29, 47
Germany
  birth rate, 257–8, 260–1
  Eastern workers in, 123, 208, 220
  women's wartime sexual experiences, 311
Goebbels, Joseph, 230
Göring, Hermann, 29–30

Hartelt, Helmut, 70–3
Heydrich, Reinhard, 151
Hilgenfeldt, Erich, 256, 282
Hilger, Otto, 121
Himmler, Heinrich
  approach to prostitution, 147–8, 156
  concerns over birth rate, 257–8
  model of biological fatherhood, 310
  Nazi Race Laws and consensual relationships, 36, 211–13, 214, 215
  occupation children policies, 256, 263, 268, 269, 270, 272, 274, 275–6, 278, 284–5
  population policy, 258–9
  racial selection programme, 144–5
  registration of occupation children, 265–6, 267
Hitler, Adolf, 255–6, 258, 262–3
homosexual encounters, 5, 129, 130
humiliation
  communal voyeurism of executions, 77
  of forced nudity, 41, 305
  public humiliation of Jews, 73–4, 75, 81–2

impotence, 86, 311, 328
international law, 28–31, 32–3, 316, 324–5
International Military Tribunal for the Far East (IMTFE), 30–1
International Military Tribunal (IMT) *see* Nuremberg trials
Ivanovna, Antonina, 154

Jews
  communal voyeurism of executions, 77
  effeminisation of Jewish men, 76–7, 81
  enforced sexual violence amongst prisoners, 77
  the 'Final Solution' in the Soviet Union, 69–70, 73
  genital inspections of, 61, 76
  German soldiers' relationships with Jewish women, 77–8, 79–80, 202
  mandatory identification of, 273
  performance of sexual acts to ensure survival, 78, 80–1
  pogroms in the Soviet Union, 73–5
  rapes of women and the Nazi Race Laws, 36–41, 70–3, 78, 79–80, 92–3, 94, 318–20
  removal of clothing prior to execution, 81–2
  sexual violence in the ghettos, 74–5
  sexual violence prior to executions, 80–1, 82–4
  see also antisemitism

Katzmann, Fritz, 74
Kaufmann, Hinda, 37
Keitel, Wilhelm, 143, 150, 209
Kinkelin, Dr, 276–7, 280
Klemm, Hildegard, 159
Kohzina, Elena, 51
Kosmodemyanskaya, Zoya, 46

Lebensborn, 257, 259
looting
  of houses, 37, 45, 50–1, 155
  legal definition of, 324–5

Maeger, Herbert, 121
Manneszucht (masculine discipline and restraint)
  sexual self-control under, 87–8, 133, 305
  and the Special Wartime Penal Code, 89
  term, 87
Manstein, Field Marshal Erich von, 29, 122–3
marriages
  ban between Germans and foreigners, 223–5, 308

doctors examinations for marriage
  eligibility certificates, 226–9
kinship questionnaires, 275
marriage permit applications, 5, 194,
  199, 217
  between non-Germans, 217, 220
  policies on Baltic women, 214,
    217–25, 253
  racial evaluation criteria for marriage
    applications, 221–3
masculinity
  collective perpetration of gang rapes,
    42–3
  effeminisation of Jewish men, 76–7,
    81
  equation of virility with vitality, 3–4,
    325
  hegemony of military masculinity,
    65, 305
  impact of violence on sexual urges,
    86–7, 130, 328
  leisure-time activities, 78
  'lust rapes' vs 'evil rapes', 5–6
  male bonding via sexual violence,
    48–9
  male honour/dishonour, 30, 43, 52,
    135, 147, 219
  military perceptions of, 2–4, 328–9
  misogyny, 49
  model of biological fatherhood,
    310
  post-war crisis in, 311, 312
  responses to armed women, 61–3
  rituals of, 4, 7–8
  sexual violence's impact on military
    discipline, 86–8, 94–5, 129–30
  sexually transmitted diseases as proof
    of, 135
  see also *Manneszucht* (masculine
    discipline and restraint); men
Medalje, Ella, 41–2
Medem, Walther-Eberhard Freiherr von,
  219–20, 253–4, 255
medical services
  care of soldiers' sex lives, 209–10
  confidentiality for patients with
    sexually transmitted diseases,
    138–9
  examination of women as sources of
    infection, 126, 127–9, 140–2
  issue of marriage eligibility
    certificates, 226–9
  lectures to the troops, 133–4, 136

questionnaires on the origins of
  a sexually transmitted disease,
  139–41
sanitation stations, 135–7, 143
SS medical service guidance on sexual
  encounters, 146–8
supervision of Wehrmacht brothels,
  154, 156–8, 307–8
Wehrmacht-issue condoms, 134,
  135
see also sexually transmitted diseases
Meiser, Anton, 51–2
men
  castration of, 76
  genital inspections of, 61, 76
  genital mutilation of, 47, 76, 81
  man-on-man sexual violence, 5, 76–7
  as victims of sexual violence, 41, 316
military command
  concerns over the sex life of soldiers
    in the field, 129–32, 163–4
  concerns over the spread of sexually
    transmitted diseases, 130–1
  creation of norms banning sexual
    violence, 317–18
  disciplinary measures for sexually
    transmitted disease sufferers, 143
  involvement in genocide, 70
  Military Jurisdiction Decree, 84,
    85–6
  military tactics as environmental
    adaptation, 331–3
  prohibition against distribution of
    troop rations, 122–3
  regulation of consensual
    relationships, 206–11
  sexual policies of, 308–9, 322–3,
    330–1
  toleration of rape, 7, 323–5, 331
  see also Army High Command
    (OKH); Reichsführer-SS (RF-SS);
    Wehrmacht High Command
    (OKW)
Minnieur, Horst, 70–3
Molotov, Vyacheslav M., 28–9
mutilation; see also genital mutilation

Norway
  Nazi plans for the Nordicisation of
    the German *Volk*, 258–9
  occupation children
    (*Besatzungskinder*), 254, 258–9,
    265, 266, 276, 278, 280, 283

nudity
　in front of an armed enemy, 60–1
　humiliation of forced undressing, 40, 41, 55, 59, 61, 74, 75, 77, 81–2, 305
　public displays of half-naked female corpses, 46, 47
　rape prior to execution, 83–4
　removal of clothing prior to execution, 81–2
Nuremberg trials, 28–9, 30

Oberg, Carl, 150
occupation
　protective measures against sexual assaults, 55–6
　sexual violence during domestic work, 53–4, 93–4
　sexual violence in private houses where soldiers were quartered, 51–2
　women workers in Germany, 57
　see also partisans
occupation children (*Besatzungskinder*)
　categories of German blood, 268–71, 272, 277
　citizenship status of, 281
　of consensual liaisons, 205
　control measures for occupation children, 261–3
　in Eastern Europe and Russia, 259–60
　estimated numbers of, 8–9, 255–7, 268, 273–4
　evaluation of the mothers, 264–5, 267, 272, 276, 277–8, 283–4
　'Führer Decree on Supporting the Illegitimate Children of Reich Germans from the Occupied Eastern Territories', 262–3, 266, 274–5, 276, 280, 282, 284
　Germanisation strategies for, 254–5, 269, 271–3, 282–3
　Himmler's policy for, 256, 263, 268, 269, 270, 272, 274, 275–6, 278, 284–5
　of Latvian women, 253–4, 255, 273
　maternal guardianship of, 281, 282–4
　non-marital classification, 281–2
　of Norwegian or Dutch women, 254, 258–9, 265, 266, 276, 278, 280, 283

　overview of policy on, 309–10
　perspectives on their parents' relationship, 205–6
　proclamation of German interest in children in the occupied Eastern regions, 262–3
　proof of paternity, 264, 265, 267–8, 277–80, 310
　racial evaluation of, 268–9, 271–4, 275, 282–3
　racial selection processes for, 271–3, 274–7
　registration process for, 263–8
　stigma of, 268–9, 282
　term, 8
　threat from occupation children, 260–1

partisans
　anti-partisan operations, 60–1, 67–8, 91–2
　body searches and sexual violence, 66–7
　consensual liaisons with German soldiers, 203–4
　deployment of female agents, 66
　emergence of the Soviet partisan movement, 59–60
　incitement to join, 53, 91
　treatment of female partisans, 63–6
　use of reports of rape for propaganda, 91–2
　women fighters, 63
Pawlowicz, Sala, 39–41, 49
Payr zu Enn und Caldiff, Major Hans von, 255–6, 273
photographic sources
　distancing frame, 46
　of female corpses, 45–6
　Foto-Feldpost exhibition, 195
　groups of German men with women's bodies, 47–9
　of the pogroms in the Soviet Union, 73–4
　pornographic elements, 46
　private photos by Wehrmacht soldiers, 19–26, 245–52
　public display of half-naked bodies, 46–7
　role of the photographer, 46, 48
　Vernichtungskrieg exhibition, 117
　Wehrmacht brothels, 312–13

power
  institutional knowledge and, 332
  power relations and sexual violence, 47, 54, 55
  powerlessness of women survivors, 13–14, 42, 56
  women in consensual relationships and, 202–3
pregnancy, 8, 28, 56, 80, 223, 254, 264–6, 283
propaganda
  devious female Bolshevist narratives, 195, 207
  sexual violence as part of, 42–3, 91–2, 304
prostitution
  black markets in, 124–5, 306
  boundaries of, 123
  civilian food shortages and, 117–18
  community consequences of, 8
  forced examinations of women, 126, 127–9
  Jewish women and, 78–9
  within Nazi ideology, 119
  perceptions of the sexual honour of 'Soviet women', 90–1, 119
  and the prevention of sexual deviancy, 130
  under the Soviet regime, 123–4, 152
  and the spread of sexually transmitted diseases, 126–9, 130–1
  as a threat to the military community, 130–2
  Wehrmacht regulation of, 150–1
  women suspected of, 125–6
  see also brothels; sexual bartering; Wehrmacht brothels
protective relationships, 123, 199–200; see also consensual relations

'race defilement'
  Nazi laws and policies, 36–7, 93, 318–20
  post-war interpretations of, 9, 318
  soldiers' views of, 37–41, 70–75, 78, 79–82, 92–3
racial policies
  categories of German blood, 268–71, 272, 277
  consensual relations and, 199, 211–15, 308
  flexibility of in practice, 309

  lack of racial awareness and offspring/children born, 231
  marriages between non-Germans, 217, 220
  marriages to Estonian, Latvian and Lithuanian women, 214, 217–19, 221, 222, 223
  pollution taboos, 318
  power of Nazi ideologies of, 318
  racial evaluation criteria for marriage applications, 221–3
  racial evaluation of occupation children, 268–9, 271–4, 275, 282–3
  racial hygiene goals, 133
  racially related peoples category, 270
  sexual violence and the Race Laws, 9, 13, 36–41, 70–3, 78, 79–80, 90, 91, 92–3, 94, 318–20
  SS 'race defilement' prohibition, 36, 70–3, 211–13
  threat of race-mixing to the Reich, 270–1
  Wehrmacht and, 36, 37, 70–3
  Wehrmacht brothels and, 156, 307–8
rape
  commanders' toleration of, 7, 323–5, 331
  coverage in post-war trials, 30–1, 32
  definitions of, 39
  gang rapes, 42–3, 54–5
  and ideological beliefs, 9, 309, 321–2
  implications for military discipline, 86–8, 94–5
  of Jewish men, 76–7
  of Jewish women prior to executions, 82–4
  limited sexual abuse of Jewish women in concentration camps, 318–20
  by local collaborators, 41–2
  'lust rapes' vs 'evil rapes', 5–6
  murder of the victims of, 54
  within the occupied territories, 320–1
  in private vs public settings, 54–5
  and the Race Laws, 9, 13, 36–41, 70–3, 78, 79–80, 92–3, 94, 318–20
  shame and suspicion of the victim, 13–14
  source material on, 13
  use for Soviet propaganda, 91–2
  virginity narratives, 43

Red Army *see* Soviet soldiers
Reese, Willi Peter, 27, 28, 78
Reichenau, Field Marshal Walter von, 122
Reichsführer-SS (RF-SS)
  knowledge of his men's sexual encounters, 7–8, 212, 306
  sexual encounters with local women, 213, 215
  support for military supervised brothels, 163–4
  see also Himmler, Heinrich; military command
Reimbold, Franz, 64–5
Remarque, Erich Maria, 312
Rosenberg, Alfred, 214, 256, 262, 266, 268–9, 273, 275–6, 282
Rothe, Frank, 37–8

Sajer, Guy, 312
Schmidt, Ilse, 158
Schmidt, Rudolf, 255, 268
sexual bartering
  authorities monitoring of, 125
  boundaries of, 123, 193
  for food rations, 120–1, 122, 305
  threat to military community, 130
  in the workplace, 121–2
sexual commerce *see* prostitution
sexual encounters
  appeal of foreign men in uniform, 54
  during armed conflicts, 1–2, 4–5
  conquest narratives, 1
  gendered and sexual behaviour, 11
  with rear-echelon soldiers, 192–4
  term, 5
sexual enslavement
  'comfort stations' of the Japanese Army, 30–1
  during domestic work, 53–4, 93–4
  fictional depictions, 14–15, 312
  in Wehrmacht brothels, 155–6
sexual torture, 5, 29, 40–1, 65, 320, 323
sexual violence
  alleged complicity of victim, 14, 327
  during armed conflicts, 4–7
  body searches and, 66, 75, 321
  in concentration camps, 318–20
  damage to the social subjectivity, 8, 47, 327
  definitions of, 28
  demonstrative sexual violence, 55, 68–9

feminist scholarship on, 12, 31–2
following alcohol consumption, 27–9, 55, 93–4
genocidal sexual violence, 73–84, 320
harm of sexual violence, 8
as an honour crime, 29–31, 51–2, 57–9, 64
implications for military discipline, 86–8, 94–5, 129–30, 305–6
in the Jewish ghettos, 74–5
language for, 72
life force atrocities, 320
little awareness of criminal nature of, 14, 31, 32, 321, 324–7
man-on-man, 5, 76–7
and the mass murder of Soviet Jews, 70–3
officers' punishment of, 29–30
penalties for crimes of sexual violence, 89–90, 95, 130
planned attacks, 57–9
post-war narratives of, 311–12
prevention of by military commanders, 317–18
in propaganda, 42–3, 91–2, 304
laws and policies against 'race defilement', 36–41, 70–3, 78, 79–80, 90, 91, 92–3, 94
sexuality and, 325–8
as a weapon, 7, 32–3, 86, 306, 330–4
Western interpretations of, 10–11, 316
women as loot perceptions, 35–6, 43–5, 51
women's suppression of, 13–14, 326–8
sexually transmitted diseases
  concealment of, 138
  control of in Wehrmacht brothels, 150, 157–8, 160, 162–3, 306–7
  disciplinary measures, 142–4
  group instruction by medical officers, 133–4, 136
  'Guide to racial hygiene instruction', 133
  instruction on sexual discipline, 132–4
  military command's concerns over, 130–1
  punishments for SS personnel with, 148–9
  sanitation stations, 135–7, 143

as sign of masculinity, 135
syphilis as a Jewish disease, 131
as threat to the German people, 133
through prostitution, 126–9, 130–1
tracing the source of the infection, 139–42
treatments for, 137–9
Wehrmacht-issue condoms, 134, 135
sources
documentation of sexual encounters, 312–13
ego sources, 12–13
gendered and sexual behaviour of the time, 11
gender-specific narrative aspects, 34
interpretation of data on sexual encounters, 10–12
post-war narratives, 13–15
women's accounts of rape, 13
see also photographic sources
Soviet soldiers, 27, 28, 73, 118, 148, 207, 285, 311, 314
conscription, 50
execution of as prisoners of war, 84–5
female Red Army soldiers, 61–3, 65–7, 195
partisan support for the Red Army, 59, 61–3, 65–7
treatment of female victims of sexual violence, 13–14
treatment of women suspected of collaboration, 201–5
women associated with the Red Army, 44
Soviet Union (USSR)
Babi Yar massacre, 69, 83
birth rate, 260–1
Nazi economic plundering, 50–1, 120
perceptions of the sexual honour of 'Soviet women', 90–1, 119
pre-invasion evacuations, 49–50
prostitution under, 123–4, 152
rear-echelon soldiers in, 192–4
regional variations in relationships with the Germans, 200–1
soldiers' descriptions of Russian women, 195–6
see also Eastern campaign
spectatorship
demonstrative sexual violence, 41–2, 55, 68–9, 74, 77

exclusion of spectators, 43, 54–5, 319
photographic sources, 45–6
SS (*Schutzstaffel*)
Einsatzgruppen (death squads), 69
executions of Jewish women after sexual acts, 80–1
figure of the ideal SS man, 2, 144–6, 150
guidance on sexually transmitted diseases, 146–8
instructional lectures and genital inspections, 147
involvement in genocide, 70
Lebensborn organisation, 257, 259
punishments for SS personnel with sexually transmitted diseases, 148–9
'race defilement' laws and, 36, 70–3
regulation of consensual relationships, 211–15
'Sanitary Regulation for the General SS', 145
sexual policies of, 119–20
treatment of female partisans, 63–6
volunteers to, 2
see also Reichsführer-SS (RF-SS)
Stachow, Hasso G., 312
Stimler, Barbara, 38–9

torture, 40–1, 65
Trampedach, Friedrich, 150, 215, 218–19, 222, 262, 283

United Nations (UN), 32
Unold, General Georg von, 274
U.S. soldiers, 285, 317, 323, 328, 329

Vegesack, Siegfried von, 155
Volksgemeinschaft (people's community)
belonging to, 132–3, 218–20, 319
exclusion from, 88, 132, 145, 216–20, 222–3, 225
Manneszucht concept and, 87–8
occupation children's value for, 9, 271–3, 274–7
'race' and 'ethnicity' Nazi conceptions of, 213, 221–9
racial selection processes for, 145

Wehrmacht
conscripts to, 2
distribution of condoms, 134, 135
foreign volunteers to, 159–60

Wehrmacht (cont.)
  moral code, 29–30
  myth of the sexually abstinent
    German man, 9
  laws and policies against 'race
    defilement', 36, 37, 70–3
  regulation of consensual
    relationships, 206–11
  rituals of masculinity, 4, 7–8
  sexual conquest norms, 43–5, 51
  sexual policies of, 119–20
  sexual violence's impact on the
    military community, 45, 88–9
  treatment of female partisans, 63–6
  volunteers to, 41
  women auxiliaries in, 63
  see also Army High Command
    (OKH)
Wehrmacht brothels
  administration of, 154–5
  concerns over, 152, 160–2
  and the control of sexually
    transmitted disease, 150, 157–8,
    160, 162–3, 306–7
  establishment of, 8–9, 149–51,
    152–4, 306–7
  medical services' supervision of, 154,
    156–8, 307–8
  military hierarchies and, 158–9
  in the occupied territories, 151–2

photographic sources, 312–13
the Race Laws and, 156, 307–8
sexual enslavement in, 155–6
soldiers of different nationalities,
  159–60
in the Soviet territories, 152, 153–4,
  306–7
Wehrmacht High Command (OKW)
  anti-partisan strategies, 60–1, 67–8,
    91–2
  dangers of consensual relations with
    local women, 206–7, 208, 209,
    223, 224, 308
  dangers of sexual bartering and
    prostitution, 130–1, 132, 306
  knowledge of their men's sexual
    encounters, 7–8
  occupation children, 254, 256, 257,
    263, 273
  sanitation regulations, 136–7, 143
  support for supervised brothels,
    150–2, 163–4
  treatment of female partisans, 92,
    207
  treatment of political prisoners, 66,
    84–5, 92
  see also military command
Wetzel, Dr Erhard, 223

Zvychaina, Olena, 120, 194

EU representative:
Easy Access System Europe
Mustamäe tee 50, 10621 Tallinn, Estonia
Gpsr.requests@easproject.com

www.ingramcontent.com/pod-product-compliance
Lightning Source LLC
Chambersburg PA
CBHW051555230426
43668CB00013B/1856